How to access your on-line resources

Kaplan Financial students will have a MyKaplan account and these extra resources will be available to you online. You do not need to register again, as this process was completed when you enrolled. If you are having problems accessing online materials, please ask your course administrator.

If you are not studying with Kaplan and did not purchase your book via a Kaplan website, to unlock your extra online resources please go to www.en-gage.co.uk (even if you have set up an account and registered books previously). You will then need to enter the ISBN number (on the title page and back cover) and the unique pass key number contained in the scratch panel below to gain access.

You will also be required to enter additional information during this process to set up or confirm your account details.

If you purchased through Kaplan Flexible Learning or via the Kaplan Publishing website you will automatically receive an e-mail invitation to register your details and gain access to your content. If you do not receive the e-mail or book content, please contact Kaplan Publishing.

Your code and information

This code can only be used once for the registration of one book online. This registration and your online content will expire when the final sittings for the examinations covered by this book have taken place. Please allow one hour from the time you submit your book details for us to process your request.

Please scratch the film to access your unique code.

Please be aware that this code is case-sensitive and you will need to include the dashes within the passcode, but not when entering the ISBN.

CIMA

Subject E3

Strategic Management

Study Text

Published by: Kaplan Publishing UK

Unit 2 The Business Centre, Molly Millars Lane, Wokingham, Berkshire RG41 2QZ

Copyright © 2017 Kaplan Financial Limited. All rights reserved.

No part of this publication may be reproduced, stored in a retrieval system or transmitted in any form or by any means electronic, mechanical, photocopying, recording or otherwise without the prior written permission of the publisher.

Acknowledgements

We are grateful to the CIMA for permission to reproduce past examination questions. The answers to CIMA Exams have been prepared by Kaplan Publishing, except in the case of the CIMA November 2010 and subsequent CIMA Exam answers where the official CIMA answers have been reproduced.

Notice

The text in this material and any others made available by any Kaplan Group company does not amount to advice on a particular matter and should not be taken as such. No reliance should be placed on the content as the basis for any investment or other decision or in connection with any advice given to third parties. Please consult your appropriate professional adviser as necessary. Kaplan Publishing Limited and all other Kaplan group companies expressly disclaim all liability to any person in respect of any losses or other claims, whether direct, indirect, incidental, consequential or otherwise arising in relation to the use of such materials.

Kaplan is not responsible for the content of external websites. The inclusion of a link to a third party website in this text should not be taken as an endorsement.

British Library Cataloguing in Publication Data

A catalogue record for this book is available from the British Library.

ISBN: 978-1-78415-922-1

Printed and bound in Great Britain.

Contents

		Page
Chapter 1	The process of strategy formulation	1
Chapter 2	Strategic analysis: Mission, vision and stakeholders	41
Chapter 3	Strategic analysis: Ethics and corporate social responsibility	83
Chapter 4	Strategic analysis: External environmental analysis	119
Chapter 5	Strategic analysis: Internal environmental analysis	157
Chapter 6	Position and gap analysis	199
Chapter 7	Strategic options and choice	239
Chapter 8	The performance measurement mix	309
Chapter 9	Information technology and e-business	365
Chapter 10	Information for advantage and knowledge management	427
Chapter 11	Customers, suppliers and supply chain management	459
Chapter 12	Change management – understanding the context of change	509
Chapter 13	Change management – change leadership	537

	Contents	Page
Chapter 1	The process of strategy formulation	1
Chapter 2	Stakeholders, Mission, Vision and statement	19
Chapter 3	Ethical analysis, Risks and corporate social responsibility	59
Chapter 4	Strategic analysis: External environment analysis	95
Chapter 5	Strategic analysis: Internal environment analysis	151
Chapter 6	Position and Gap analysis	205
Chapter 7	Strategic options and choice	231
Chapter 8	The performance measurement mix	289
Chapter 9	Information technology and e-business	339
Chapter 10	Information technology services and knowledge management	377
Chapter 11	Customers, suppliers and supply chain management	419
Chapter 12	Change management – being aware the context of change	465
Chapter 13	Change management – change leadership	491

chapter Intro

Introduction

How to use the materials

These official CIMA learning materials have been carefully designed to make your learning experience as easy as possible and to give you the best chances of success in your Objective Test Examination.

The product range contains a number of features to help you in the study process. They include:

- a detailed explanation of all syllabus areas;
- extensive 'practical' materials;
- generous question practice, together with full solutions.

This Study Text has been designed with the needs of home study and distance learning candidates in mind. Such students require very full coverage of the syllabus topics, and also the facility to undertake extensive question practice. However, the Study Text is also ideal for fully taught courses.

The main body of the text is divided into a number of chapters, each of which is organised on the following pattern:

- **Detailed learning outcomes.** These describe the knowledge expected after your studies of the chapter are complete. You should assimilate these before beginning detailed work on the chapter, so that you can appreciate where your studies are leading.
- **Step-by-step topic coverage.** This is the heart of each chapter, containing detailed explanatory text supported where appropriate by worked examples and exercises. You should work carefully through this section, ensuring that you understand the material being explained and can tackle the examples and exercises successfully. Remember that in many cases knowledge is cumulative: if you fail to digest earlier material thoroughly, you may struggle to understand later chapters.
- **Activities.** Some chapters are illustrated by more practical elements, such as comments and questions designed to stimulate discussion.
- **Question practice.** The text contains three styles of question:
    - Exam-style objective test questions (OTQs)
    - 'Integration' questions – these test your ability to understand topics within a wider context. This is particularly important with calculations where OTQs may focus on just one element but an integration question tackles the full calculation, just as you would be expected to do in the workplace.

- 'Case' style questions – these test your ability to analyse and discuss issues in greater depth, particularly focusing on scenarios that are less clear cut than in the Objective Test Examination, and thus provide excellent practice for developing the skills needed for success in the Strategic Level Case Study Examination.

- **Solutions.** Avoid the temptation merely to 'audit' the solutions provided. It is an illusion to think that this provides the same benefits as you would gain from a serious attempt of your own. However, if you are struggling to get started on a question you should read the introductory guidance provided at the beginning of the solution, where provided, and then make your own attempt before referring back to the full solution.

If you work conscientiously through this Official CIMA Study Text according to the guidelines above you will be giving yourself an excellent chance of success in your Objective Test Examination. Good luck with your studies!

Quality and accuracy are of the utmost importance to us so if you spot an error in any of our products, please send an email to mykaplanreporting@kaplan.com with full details, or follow the link to the feedback form in MyKaplan.

Our Quality Co-ordinator will work with our technical team to verify the error and take action to ensure it is corrected in future editions.

Icon Explanations

Definition – These sections explain important areas of knowledge which must be understood and reproduced in an assessment environment.

Key point – Identifies topics which are key to success and are often examined.

Supplementary reading – These sections will help to provide a deeper understanding of core areas. The supplementary reading is **NOT** optional reading. It is vital to provide you with the breadth of knowledge you will need to address the wide range of topics within your syllabus that could feature in an assessment question. **Reference to this text is vital when self studying**.

Test your understanding – Following key points and definitions are exercises which give the opportunity to assess the understanding of these core areas.

Illustration – To help develop an understanding of particular topics. The illustrative examples are useful in preparing for the Test your understanding exercises.

Study technique

Passing exams is partly a matter of intellectual ability, but however accomplished you are in that respect you can improve your chances significantly by the use of appropriate study and revision techniques. In this section we briefly outline some tips for effective study during the earlier stages of your approach to the Objective Test Examination. We also mention some techniques that you will find useful at the revision stage.

Planning

To begin with, formal planning is essential to get the best return from the time you spend studying. Estimate how much time in total you are going to need for each subject you are studying. Remember that you need to allow time for revision as well as for initial study of the material.

With your study material before you, decide which chapters you are going to study in each week, and which weeks you will devote to revision and final question practice.

Prepare a written schedule summarising the above and stick to it!

It is essential to know your syllabus. As your studies progress you will become more familiar with how long it takes to cover topics in sufficient depth. Your timetable may need to be adapted to allocate enough time for the whole syllabus.

Students are advised to refer to the notice of examinable legislation published regularly in CIMA's magazine (Financial Management), the students e-newsletter (Velocity) and on the CIMA website, to ensure they are up-to-date.

The amount of space allocated to a topic in the Study Text is not a very good guide as to how long it will take you. The syllabus weighting is the better guide as to how long you should spend on a syllabus topic.

Tips for effective studying

(1) Aim to find a quiet and undisturbed location for your study, and plan as far as possible to use the same period of time each day. Getting into a routine helps to avoid wasting time. Make sure that you have all the materials you need before you begin so as to minimise interruptions.

(2) Store all your materials in one place, so that you do not waste time searching for items every time you want to begin studying. If you have to pack everything away after each study period, keep your study materials in a box, or even a suitcase, which will not be disturbed until the next time.

(3) Limit distractions. To make the most effective use of your study periods you should be able to apply total concentration, so turn off all entertainment equipment, set your phones to message mode, and put up your 'do not disturb' sign.

(4) Your timetable will tell you which topic to study. However, before diving in and becoming engrossed in the finer points, make sure you have an overall picture of all the areas that need to be covered by the end of that session. After an hour, allow yourself a short break and move away from your Study Text. With experience, you will learn to assess the pace you need to work at. Each study session should focus on component learning outcomes – the basis for all questions.

(5) Work carefully through a chapter, making notes as you go. When you have covered a suitable amount of material, vary the pattern by attempting a practice question. When you have finished your attempt, make notes of any mistakes you made, or any areas that you failed to cover or covered more briefly. Be aware that all component learning outcomes will be tested in each examination.

(6) Make notes as you study, and discover the techniques that work best for you. Your notes may be in the form of lists, bullet points, diagrams, summaries, 'mind maps', or the written word, but remember that you will need to refer back to them at a later date, so they must be intelligible. If you are on a taught course, make sure you highlight any issues you would like to follow up with your lecturer.

(7) Organise your notes. Make sure that all your notes, calculations etc. can be effectively filed and easily retrieved later.

Objective Test

Objective Test questions require you to choose or provide a response to a question whose correct answer is predetermined.

The most common types of Objective Test question you will see are:

- Multiple choice, where you have to choose the correct answer(s) from a list of possible answers. This could either be numbers or text.

- Multiple choice with more choices and answers, for example, choosing two correct answers from a list of eight possible answers. This could either be numbers or text.

- Single numeric entry, where you give your numeric answer, for example, profit is $10,000.

- Multiple entry, where you give several numeric answers.

- True/false questions, where you state whether a statement is true or false.

- Matching pairs of text, for example, matching a technical term with the correct definition.

- Other types could be matching text with graphs and labelling graphs/diagrams.

In every chapter of this Study Text we have introduced these types of questions, but obviously we have had to label answers A, B, C etc rather than using click boxes. For convenience we have retained quite a few questions where an initial scenario leads to a number of sub-questions. There will be questions of this type in the Objective Test Examination but they will rarely have more than three sub-questions.

Guidance re CIMA on-screen calculator

As part of the CIMA Objective Test software, candidates are now provided with a calculator. This calculator is on-screen and is available for the duration of the assessment. The calculator is available in each of the Objective Test Examinations and is accessed by clicking the calculator button in the top left hand corner of the screen at any time during the assessment.

All candidates must complete a 15-minute tutorial before the assessment begins and will have the opportunity to familiarise themselves with the calculator and practise using it.

Candidates may practise using the calculator by downloading and installing the practice exam at http://www.vue.com/athena/. The calculator can be accessed from the fourth sample question (of 12).

Please note that the practice exam and tutorial provided by Pearson VUE at http://www.vue.com/athena/ is not specific to CIMA and includes the full range of question types the Pearson VUE software supports, some of which CIMA does not currently use.

Fundamentals of Objective Tests

The Objective Tests are 90-minute assessments comprising 60 compulsory questions, with one or more parts. There will be no choice and all questions should be attempted.

Structure of subjects and learning outcomes

Each subject within the syllabus is divided into a number of broad syllabus topics. The topics contain one or more lead learning outcomes, related component learning outcomes and indicative knowledge content.

A learning outcome has two main purposes:

(a) To define the skill or ability that a well prepared candidate should be able to exhibit in the examination.

(b) To demonstrate the approach likely to be taken in examination questions.

The learning outcomes are part of a hierarchy of learning objectives. The verbs used at the beginning of each learning outcome relate to a specific learning objective, e.g.

Calculate the break-even point, profit target, margin of safety and profit/volume ratio for a single product or service.

The verb '**calculate**' indicates a level three learning objective. The following tables list the verbs that appear in the syllabus learning outcomes and examination questions.

CIMA VERB HIERARCHY

CIMA place great importance on the definition of verbs in structuring Objective Test Examinations. It is therefore crucial that you understand the verbs in order to appreciate the depth and breadth of a topic and the level of skill required. The Objective Tests will focus on levels one, two and three of the CIMA hierarchy of verbs. However they will also test levels four and five, especially at the management and strategic levels. You can therefore expect to be tested on knowledge, comprehension, application, analysis and evaluation in these examinations.

Level 1: KNOWLEDGE

What you are expected to know.

VERBS USED	DEFINITION
List	Make a list of.
State	Express, fully or clearly, the details of/facts of.
Define	Give the exact meaning of.

For example you could be asked to make a list of the advantages of a particular information system by selecting all options that apply from a given set of possibilities. Or you could be required to define relationship marketing by selecting the most appropriate option from a list.

xi

Level 2: COMPREHENSION

What you are expected to understand.

VERBS USED	DEFINITION
Describe	Communicate the key features of.
Distinguish	Highlight the differences between.
Explain	Make clear or intelligible/state the meaning or purpose of.
Identify	Recognise, establish or select after consideration.
Illustrate	Use an example to describe or explain something.

For example you may be asked to distinguish between different aspects of the global business environment by dragging external factors and dropping into a PEST analysis.

Level 3: APPLICATION

How you are expected to apply your knowledge.

VERBS USED	DEFINITION
Apply	Put to practical use.
Calculate	Ascertain or reckon mathematically.
Demonstrate	Prove with certainty or exhibit by practical means.
Prepare	Make or get ready for use.
Reconcile	Make or prove consistent/compatible.
Solve	Find an answer to.
Tabulate	Arrange in a table.

For example you may need to calculate the projected revenue or costs for a given set of circumstances.

Level 4: ANALYSIS

How you are expected to analyse the detail of what you have learned.

VERBS USED	DEFINITION
Analyse	Examine in detail the structure of.
Categorise	Place into a defined class or division.
Compare/contrast	Show the similarities and/or differences between.
Construct	Build up or compile.
Discuss	Examine in detail by argument.
Interpret	Translate into intelligible or familiar terms.
Prioritise	Place in order of priority or sequence for action.
Produce	Create or bring into existence.

For example you may be required to interpret an inventory ratio by selecting the most appropriate statement for a given set of circumstances and data.

Level 5: EVALUATION

How you are expected to use your learning to evaluate, make decisions or recommendations.

VERBS USED	DEFINITION
Advise	Counsel, inform or notify.
Evaluate	Appraise or assess the value of.
Recommend	Propose a course of action.

For example you may be asked to recommend and select an appropriate course of action based on a short scenario.

Information concerning formulae and tables will be provided via the CIMA website, www.cimaglobal.com, and your EN-gage login.

E3
STRATEGIC MANAGEMENT

Syllabus overview

E3 builds on the insights gained from E1 and E2 about how organisations effectively implement their strategies by aligning their structures, people, process, projects and relationships. E3 aims to develop the skills and abilities of the strategic leaders of organisations, enabling them to create the vision and direction for the growth and long-term sustainable success of the organisation. This involves successfully managing and leading change within the process of strategy formulation and implementation.

Summary of syllabus

Weight	Syllabus topic
20%	A. Interacting with the organisation's environment
30%	B. Evaluating strategic position and strategic options
20%	C. Leading change
15%	D. Implementing strategy
15%	E. The role of information systems in organisational strategy

E3 – A. INTERACTING WITH THE ORGANISATION'S ENVIRONMENT (20%)

Learning outcomes
On completion of their studies, students should be able to:

Lead	Component		Indicative syllabus content
1 evaluate the influence of key external factors on an organisation's strategy.	(a)	evaluate the influence and impact of the external environment on an organisation and its strategy	<ul><li>Different organisation environments (including profit and not-for-profit organisations).</li><li>The key environmental drivers of organisational change and their prioritisation.</li><li>**Note:** The emphasis should be on the evaluation and prioritisation of the environmental drivers specific to the organisation and not upon the production of a generic PEST analysis.</li></ul>
	(b)	recommend approaches to business/government relations and to relations with society	<ul><li>Non-market strategy and forms of corporate political activity.</li></ul>
	(c)	discuss the drivers of external demands for environmental sustainability and corporate social responsibility and the organisation's response	<ul><li>External demands for sustainability and responsible business practices and ways to respond to these.</li></ul>
	(d)	recommend how to build and manage strategic relationships with stakeholders (including suppliers, customers, owners, government and the wider society).	<ul><li>Stakeholder management (stakeholders to include internal stakeholders, government and regulatory agencies, non-governmental organisations and civil society, industry associations, customers and suppliers).</li><li>Building strategic alliances with stakeholders.</li><li>The customer portfolio: customer analysis and behaviour, including the marketing audit and customer profitability analysis as well as customer retention, relationship management and loyalty.</li><li>Strategic supply chain management.</li><li>Implications of interactions with the external environment for Chartered Management Accountants.</li></ul>
2 evaluate ethical issues arising from the organisation's interaction with its environment.	(a)	evaluate ethical issues and their resolution within a range of organisational contexts.	<ul><li>Business ethics and the CIMA Code of Ethics for Professional Accountants (Parts A and B) in the context of the implementation of strategic plans.</li></ul>

E3 – B. EVALUATING STRATEGIC POSITION AND STRATEGIC OPTIONS (30%)

Learning outcomes
On completion of their studies, students should be able to:

Lead	Component	Indicative syllabus content
1 evaluate the process of strategy formulation.	(a) evaluate the processes of strategic analysis and strategic options generation	<ul><li>Vision and mission statements and their use in orientating the organisation's strategy.</li><li>The process of strategy formulation.</li><li>Strategic options generation (e.g. using Ansoff's product/market matrix and Porter's generic strategies).</li><li>Scenario planning and long-range planning as tools in strategic decision making.</li><li>Value drivers (including intangibles) of business and the data needed to describe and measure them.</li><li>Game theory approaches to strategic planning and decision making. **Note**: Complex numerical questions will not be set.</li><li>Real Options as a tool for strategic analysis. **Note**: Complex numerical questions will not be set.</li><li>Acquisition, divestment, rationalisation and relocation strategies in the context of strategic planning.</li></ul>
	(b) recommend strategic options	<ul><li>The identification and evaluation of strategic options, including the application of the suitability, acceptability and feasibility framework.</li></ul>
	(c) discuss the role and responsibilities of directors in the strategy formulation and implementation process.	<ul><li>The role and responsibilities of the board of directors and senior managers in making strategic decisions (including issues of due diligence, fiduciary responsibilities and corporate social responsibility).</li><li>The role of the Chartered Management Accountant in the strategy development process.</li></ul>

Learning outcomes
On completion of their studies, students should be able to:

Lead		
2 evaluate **tools and techniques used in strategy formulation.**		**Indicative syllabus content**
	Component	
	(a) evaluate strategic analysis tools	- Audit of key resources and capabilities needed for strategy implementation. - Forecasting and the various techniques used: trend analysis, system modelling, in-depth consultation with experts (e.g. the Delphi method).
	(b) recommend how to manage the product portfolio of an organisation to support the organisation's strategic goals	- Management of the product portfolio.
	(c) produce an organisation's Value Chain.	- Value Chain Analysis.

E3 – C. LEADING CHANGE (20%)

Learning outcomes
On completion of their studies, students should be able to:

Lead	Component	Indicative syllabus content
1 advise on the important aspects of organisational change.	(a) evaluate the key impacts of organisational change on organisations	• The impact of change on organisational culture (including the cultural web and McKinsey's 7s model).
	(b) evaluate the role of leadership in managing the change process and building and managing effective teams.	• Team building, collaboration, group formation and shared knowledge and accountability.
2 evaluate tools and methods for successfully implementing a change programme.	(a) evaluate tools, techniques and strategies for managing and leading the change process.	• The importance of managing critical periods of adaptive, evolutionary, reconstructive and revolutionary change. • Tools, techniques and models associated with organisational change. • Approaches, styles and strategies of change management.
3 recommend change leadership processes in support of strategy implementation.	(a) evaluate the role of the change leader in supporting strategy implementation	• Change leadership and its role in the successful implementation of strategy. • The role of the change leader in effective strategic communication.
	(b) recommend appropriate leadership styles within a range of organisational change contexts.	• The advantages and disadvantages of management styles on the successful implementation of strategy. • Executive mentoring and coaching to promote effective change leadership.

E3 – D. IMPLEMENTING STRATEGY (15%)

Learning outcomes
On completion of their studies, students should be able to:

Lead		
1 evaluate the tools and techniques of strategy implementation.	**Component**	**Indicative syllabus content**
	(a) evaluate alternative models of strategic performance measurement in a range of business contexts	<ul><li>Alternative strategic business unit (SBU) performance measures, including shareholder value added (SVA) and economic value added (EVA).</li><li>Alternative models of measuring strategic performance (e.g. the Balanced Scorecard (BSC) and the performance pyramid as strategic evaluation tools).</li></ul>
	(b) recommend solutions to problems in strategic performance measurement.	<ul><li>Setting appropriate strategic targets through the use of a range of non-financial measures of strategic performance and their interaction with financial ones.</li><li>Evaluation of strategic targets through the development of critical success factors (CSFs).</li><li>Linking CSFs to Key Performance Indicators (KPIs) and corporate strategy, and their use as a basis for defining an organisation's information needs.</li><li>Effective communication of strategic performance targets, including the need to drive strategic performance through stretch targets and promotion of exceptional performance.</li><li>The role of the Chartered Management Accountant in the process of strategic performance evaluation.</li></ul>

E3 – E. THE ROLE OF INFORMATION SYSTEMS IN ORGANISATIONAL STRATEGY (15%)

Learning outcomes
On completion of their studies, students should be able to:

Lead	Component	Indicative syllabus content
1 evaluate the information systems requirements for successful strategic implementation.	(a) evaluate the information systems required to sustain the organisation	<ul><li>The purpose and contents of information systems strategies.</li><li>The classifications of knowledge.</li><li>Learning organisations.</li></ul>
	(b) advise managers on the development of strategies for knowledge management.	<ul><li>Knowledge management systems and knowledge-based organisations.</li><li>The need for information systems strategy to be complementary to the corporate and individual business unit strategies.</li></ul>
2 evaluate the opportunities for the use of IT and IS for the organisation, including Big Data.	(a) evaluate the impact of IT/IS on an organisation and its strategy	<ul><li>The impact of IT, including the internet, on an organisation (utilising frameworks such as Porter's Five Forces and the Value Chain).</li></ul>
	(b) evaluate the strategic and competitive impact of information systems, including the potential contribution of Big Data.	<ul><li>Competing through exploiting information, rather than technology (e.g. use of databases to identify potential customers or market segments, and the collection, analysis, storage and management of data).</li><li>Aligning information systems with business strategy (e.g. strategic importance of information systems; information systems for competitive advantage; information systems for competitive necessity).</li><li>Contemporary developments in the commercial use of the internet (e.g. e-business, virtual organisations and Web 2.0, Big Data, social and other forms of digital marketing).</li><li>The role of Big Data and Digitisation in knowledge-based organisations.</li></ul>

chapter 1

The process of strategy formulation

Chapter learning objectives

Lead	Component
B1. Evaluate the process of strategy formulation	(a) Evaluate the processes of strategic analysis and strategic options generation. (c) Discuss the role and responsibilities of directors in the strategy formulation and implementation process.

Indicative syllabus content

- The process of strategy formulation.
- The role and responsibility of the board of directors and senior managers in making strategic decisions (including issues of due diligence, fiduciary responsibilities and corporate social responsibility).
- The role of the Chartered Management Accountant in the strategy formulation process.

The process of strategy formulation

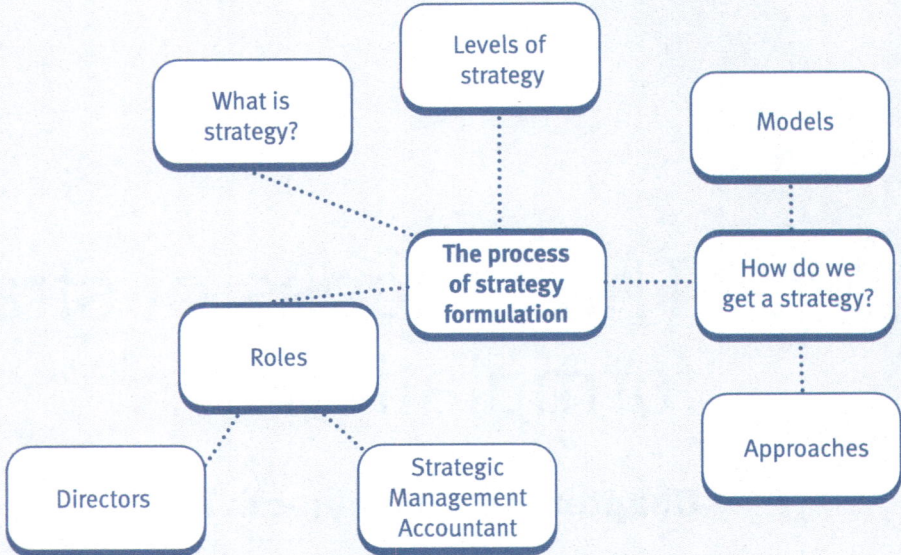

1 Introduction

In this chapter we look at the process of strategy formulation and the role of directors within that process. This is fundamental to your understanding of the E3 syllabus as a whole. However, before we look at how strategies are created, we will first look at what we mean by the word 'strategy'.

2 What is strategy?

Strategy can be defined in a number of different ways, including:

'A course of action, including the specification of resources required, to achieve a specific objective.'

CIMA official terminology

'Strategy is the direction and scope of an organisation over the long term: which achieves advantage for the organisation through its configuration of resources within a changing environment, to meet the needs of markets and to fulfil stakeholder expectations.'

Johnson, Scholes and Whittington (Exploring corporate strategy)

Essentially strategy involves setting the future plans of the organisation, but it requires a comprehensive understanding of the organisation's:

- resources (such as cash, assets and employees)
- environment (such as markets, political and economic issues, customers and competitors)

- stakeholders (anyone with an interest in the business, such as shareholders, staff, customers, government, etc) and what they expect of the organisation.

This will allow organisations to decide how they are going to achieve a sustainable competitive advantage in the market(s) they operate within.

The characteristics of strategic decisions

In their book 'Exploring Corporate Strategy', Johnson, Scholes and Whittington outline the characteristics of strategic decisions. They discuss the following areas:

- Strategic decisions are likely to be affected by the scope of an organisation's activities, because the scope concerns the way the management conceives the organisation's boundaries. It is to do with what they want the organisation to be like and be about.
- Strategy involves the matching of the activities of an organisation to its environment.
- Strategy must also match the activities of an organisation to its resource capability. It is not just about being aware of the environmental threats and opportunities but about matching the organisational resources to these threats and opportunities.
- Strategies need to be considered in terms of the extent to which resources can be obtained, allocated and controlled to develop a strategy for the future.
- Operational decisions will be affected by strategic decisions because they will set off waves of lesser decisions.
- As well as the environmental forces and the resource availability, the strategy of an organisation will be affected by the expectations and values of those who have power within and around the organisation.
- Strategic decisions are apt to affect the long-term direction of the organisation.

In his book 'Competitive Strategy', Michael Porter put it this way:

'The essence of formulating competitive strategy is relating a company to its environment.'

3 Levels of strategy

Strategy can be broken down into three different levels.

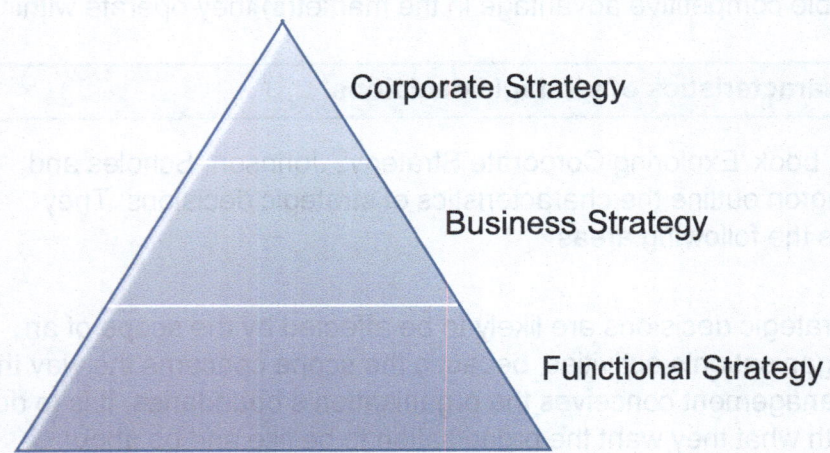

Corporate (or strategic) level

This is the highest level of strategy within the organisation and examines the strategies **for the organisation as a whole**. In particular it focuses on which businesses and markets the organisation should operate within.

Corporate strategy is therefore often concerned with issues such as:

- acquisitions, disposals and diversification
- entering new industries
- leaving existing industries.

Business (or management) level

Having selected a market, the organisation must develop a plan to be successful in that market. Business strategy therefore looks at **how the organisation can compete successfully in the individual markets** that it chooses to operate within.

Business strategy is concerned with issues such as:

- achieve advantage over competitors
- meet the needs of key customers
- avoid competitive disadvantage.

Corporate strategy affects the organisation as a whole, but business strategy will focus upon **strategic business units (SBUs)**. An SBU is a unit within an organisation for which there is an external market for products distinct from other units.

Functional (or operational) level

This level of strategy is concerned with how the component parts of the organisation in terms of resources, people and processes are pulled together to form a strategic architecture which will effectively deliver the overall strategic direction. It looks at the **day to day management strategies of the organisation**.

Operational strategy is concerned with:

- human resource strategy
- marketing strategy
- information systems and technology strategy
- operations strategy.

These could be unique to the SBU and benefit from being individually focused or the corporate unit may seek to centralise them and so benefit from synergy.

Strategy Types

```
                    Corporate centre
              ┌───────────┼───────────┐
            Div 1       Div 2       Div 3
           ┌─┼─┐       ┌─┼─┐       ┌─┼─┐
          F1 F2 F3    F1 F2 F3    F1 F2 F3
```

- ✓ One corporate strategy
- ✓ Three business strategies
- ✓ A choice for functional strategies

Remember that all three levels are linked. A corporate or business level strategy is only going to succeed if it is supported by appropriate operational strategies.

For instance, a hotel chain may have a high level strategy of 'excellence in customer care', but the success or failure of this will depend on the staff who clean the rooms and cook the meals, etc. Therefore the day to day activities **must** be focused on achieving the corporate level strategy.

It is worth mentioning that *formulating* the strategy is the easy part. Actually *implementing* it is the difficult part. Premiership football clubs in the UK will all have strategies in place to win their league. Only one will actually do so!

The process of strategy formulation

> **Illustration 1 – Levels of planning**
>
> Gap is an international clothing retailer. Classification of different levels of planning could be as follows.
>
> **Strategic**
>
> - Should another range of shops be established to target a different segment of the market? (Gap opened Banana Republic, a more up-market chain to do just that.)
> - Should the company raise more share capital to enable the expansion?
>
> **Business**
>
> - Which geographical markets should the new range of shops open in?
> - How often should inventories be changed to ensure the business keeps up with changing fashions?
> - What prices should be charged in the new stores relative to rivals?
>
> **Operational**
>
> - How will suitable premises be found and fitted out for the new range of shops?
> - Which staff should be hired for the new stores?
> - Which IT systems need to be installed in the stores?
>
> Gap's strategic decision to create the Banana Republic chain had to be supported by new business and operational level strategies. For example, poor business strategies for Banana Republic (such as pricing goods too high relative to rivals) would have led to the failure of the new stores. Likewise, poor operational strategies (such as poor training for employees in the new stores) would have damaged Banana Republic's brand and ruined Gap's overall strategic level strategy.

Whichever approach is chosen, remember that many different types of organisation will need a strategy. This will include companies (large and small), unincorporated businesses, multinational organisations, not-for-profit organisations such as charities, schools and hospitals, etc.

Anywhere that is likely to have a management accountant is likely to need a strategy. Remember that the exam itself will be based on any of these types of organisation. Be prepared for a wide range of scenarios!

chapter 1

4 The strategic planning process

Having an appropriate strategy is seen as vital to the future success of most organisations. So how does an organisation create a strategy?

There are a number of different models that can be adopted. None can be considered to be the 'best' approach – it simply depends on which one each organisation feels is the most appropriate for their needs.

4.1 The rational model

The rational model is a logical, step-by-step approach. It requires the organisation to analyse its existing circumstances, generate possible strategies, select the best one(s) and then implement them.

The rational model follows a series of set stages as shown in the diagram below:

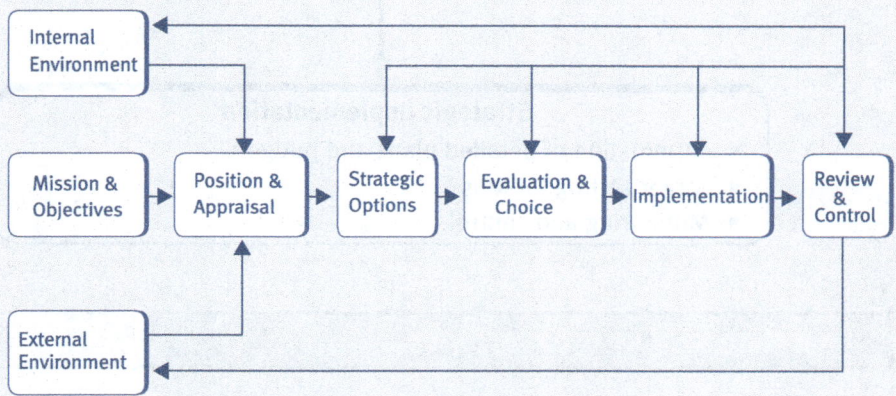

Johnson, Scholes and Whittington took the stages from the rational model and grouped them into three main stages:

The process of strategy formulation

Strategic analysis
- External analysis to identify opportunities and threats
- Internal analysis to identify strengths and weaknesses
- Stakeholder analysis to identify key objectives and to assess power and interest of different groups
- Gap analysis to identify the difference between desired and expected performance.

Strategic choice
- Strategies are required to 'close the gap'
- Competitive strategy – for each business unit
- Directions for growth – which markets/products should be invested in
- Whether expansion should be achieved by organic growth, acquisition or some form of joint arrangement.

Strategic implementation
- Formulation of detailed plans and budgets
- Target setting for KPIs
- Monitoring and control.

Illustration 2 – The rational model

H plc is a company with a chain of high-street stores selling CDs and DVDs across country V. It has posted significant losses in the last three financial years and wishes to create a strategy using the rational model.

Mission and objectives

In this stage, H will decide on what it needs to accomplish. For this business, it may consider its mission to be a 'turnaround' of the organisation's fortunes.

While this gives an overall direction to the organisation, it will also need to convert this into specific objectives, or targets. These may include (for example) a return to profitability, a reduction of costs by fifteen percent and a rise in sales by three percent over the next five years.

H can use these objectives to assess when it has achieved its mission of turning the business around.

Position and appraisal

This stage will require H to undertake a detailed analysis of its situation. It needs to understand its operations and external environment before it can suggest how to achieve its mission.

H will examine its internal environment – for example the quality and number of its stores, the ability and motivation of its staff and its cash balances. It will also examine its external environment – noting the shift in the market towards online downloading of music and films, rather than the purchase of DVDs and CDs.

H will also examine its stakeholders at this point to try and understand what they expect from the company. For example, what do H's shareholders want? Are they willing to invest more money into the company? What do H's customers expect from H and how powerful are they in determining H's overall strategic direction?

Strategic options

Once H has gained an understanding of its position (and why it is making significant losses), it can suggest possible strategic options that would help it achieve its mission.

For example, it could consider offering online downloads to customers as well as selling through its traditional stores. Alternatively it could continue selling via its stores, but dispose of any that are unprofitable. There are likely to be a number of different options that H could consider.

Evaluation and choice

Based on H's position analysis, H will pick the strategic option that best fits its circumstances. For example, it may lack the cash and skills to create a new online download site, meaning that it simply chooses to dispose of any unprofitable stores.

Implementation

H undertakes the chosen strategy. This involves choosing and closing any stores identified as underperforming as well as dealing with any unexpected problems (such as the reaction of staff unions).

Review and control

Once H's new strategy has been implemented it can go back to its initial mission and objectives. Has the store closure led to a return to profits, a reduction in costs by fifteen percent and a rise in sales by three percent? If not, H will need to decide on a new strategy to accomplish these goals.

The process of strategy formulation

Illustration 3 – The JSW approach

A full-price airline in considering setting up a 'no-frills', low-fare subsidiary. The strategic planning process, according to JSW, would include the following elements:

Strategic analysis: Competitor action, oil price forecasts, passenger volume forecasts, availability of cheap landing rights, public concern for environmental damage, effect on the main brand.

Strategic choices: Which routes to launch? Set up a subsidiary from scratch or buy an existing low-cost airline? Which planes to use? Which on-board services to offer?

Strategic implementation: Setup of new subsidiary. Staff recruitment and training. Acquisition of aircraft and obtaining of landing slots.

Test your understanding 1

Which THREE of the following are stages in the rational model of strategic development?

- A   Implementation
- B   Strategic analysis
- C   Mission and objectives
- D   Review and control
- E   Strategic planning
- F   Operational strategy

Advantages and disadvantages of deliberate long-term planning

Advantages of adopting a long-term planning approach (such as the rational model discussed above) include:

- **Forces managers to look ahead** – formal planning methodologies require managers to identify changes in the organisation's circumstances and look at ways to deal with them. This will help to ensure that the organisation stays relevant in its market and survives in the long term.

- **Improved control** – the organisation is forced to identify a mission and objectives. This will be communicated to management, meaning that they know what targets they are working towards/being assessed against. This will also improve goal congruence.

- **Identifies key risks** – by undertaking detailed analysis, management can identify key external and internal risks and create contingency plans to deal with these.

- **Encourages creativity** – management will have to generate ideas for the organisation, meaning that it can benefit from their experience and ability to innovate.

Disadvantages of formal, long-term planning include:

- **Setting corporate objectives** – it may be difficult for the organisation to create an overall mission and objectives. This is often due to the contradictory needs of key stakeholders. For example, maximising profit for shareholders may require restructuring to the organisation that causes employee redundancy. Dealing with stakeholder conflict will be dealt with in chapter 2.

- **Short-term pressures** – The pressures on management are often for short-term results. It can therefore be difficult to motivate managers by setting long-term strategies when short-term problems can consume their entire working day.

- **Difficulties in forecasting accurately** – it may be hard to identify long-term trends in the market - especially in fast-moving industries such as computing. This may make it difficult to create a strategy that is effective for the organisation over several years.

- **Bounded rationality** – the internal and external analysis undertaken as part of long-term strategic planning is often incomplete. This means that any strategies developed by the organisation based on this incomplete analysis may be ineffective.

- **Rigidity** – Once a long-term plan is created, managers often believe it should be followed at all costs – even if it is clearly no longer in the best interests of the organisation. This can also lead to the long-term strategy stifling initiative as managers refuse to act 'outside the plan'.

- **Cost** – the strategic planning process can be costly, involving the use of specialists, sometimes a specialist department, and taking up management time.

- **Management distrust** – the strategic planning process involves the use of management accounting techniques, including forecasting, modelling, cost analysis and operational research. This may be unfamiliar to some managers, leading to resistance. It is worth noting that many academics mistrust these models – not just managers!

4.2 The emergent approach – Mintzberg

Strategies are not always formally planned. In reality, strategies may evolve in response to unexpected events that impact on the organisation. **Mintzberg referred to these as emergent strategies**.

Mintzberg argued that in a changing environment, the rational model is often too slow and quickly becomes outdated. As an alternative, Mintzberg suggested that in reality, an emergent approach to strategy development occurs, whereby strategy tends to evolve rather than result from a logical, formal process. An emergent approach is evolving, continuous and incremental.

A strategy may be tried and developed as it is implemented. If it fails a different approach will be taken. It is likely to be more short term than the traditional process. To attempt to rely on emergent strategies in the longer term requires a culture of innovation where new ideas are readily forthcoming.

In effect the timing, order and distinctions between analysis, choice and implementation become blurred in emergent approaches. For this reason the analysis/choice/implementation identified earlier approach is sometimes shown as a triangle rather than a straight line in the emergent approach.

Note that the emergent approach does not necessarily mean that the organisation does not have a formal plan for the future. However to be successful it will need to be able to amend this strategy for unexpected events.

Illustration 4 – The emergent model

The emergent model

Pfizer, a multinational pharmaceutical company, developed a drug known as Sildenafil in an attempt to deal with high blood pressure in patients.

The drug was ultimately unsuccessful, but patients in the test groups reported an interesting side-effect. Pfizer sold the drug as Viagra and started a new multi-billion dollar market.

4.3 Logical incrementalism

This approach suggests that strategy tends to be a small-scale extension of past policy, rather than radical change.

Incrementalism (initially developed by **Lindblom**) does not believe that the rational model of decision-making is sensible and suggests that, in the real world, it is rarely used. This is because:

- Strategy is not usually decided by autonomous strategic planning teams that have time to impartially sift all the information and possible options before deciding on the optimal solution.

- Instead, managers have to sift through the options themselves. Due to time and knowledge constraints (also known as **bounded rationality**), this means that they usually only choose between relatively few options.

- This typically leads to strategy being small scale extensions of past policy – in other words, managers try to make small changes to what they know has worked well in the past.

This approach to strategy has a number of advantages over the traditional rational model. In particular it is often more acceptable to stakeholders as consultation, compromise and accommodation are built into the process. In addition, it is less of a cultural shift for the organisation to adopt an incremental approach to strategy as the organsation will not be trying to implement major shifts in its activities.

However, incrementalism may mean that the organisation has no overall long-term plan, causing it to suffer from strategic drift, eventually leading to it being unable to meet the needs of its customers. In addition, it could mean that the organisation fails to make major changes if needed.

> **Test your understanding 2**
>
> Which of the following statements are consistent with incrementalism?
>
> A Strategy tends to be small-scale extensions of past policies
> B No formal planning should be undertaken – the business should simply react to events as they occur
> C Strategy development should follow a series of logical stages
> D Detailed internal and external analysis should be undertaken before deciding on the future strategy of the organisation

4.4 Freewheeling opportunism

Freewheeling opportunism suggests that organisations should avoid formal planning and instead simply take advantage of opportunities as they arise.

The main justification for this is that formal planning takes too long and is too constraining – especially for organisations in fast-changing industries, such as pharmaceuticals and technology development. It may also suit any experienced managers who happen to dislike planning.

Problems with a lack of formal planning

Freewheeling opportunists dislike formal planning. However, there are a number of practical risks involved with this approach.

- **Failure to identify risks** – the business is not being forced to look ahead. This means that it may fail to identify key risks, which means that it will not have contingency plans in place to deal with these, should they arise.

- **Strategic drift** – the organisation does not have an overall plan for the future, meaning that it may be difficult for it to effectively compete in its market in the long term.

- **Difficulty in raising finance** – investors typically like to know what plans the organisation has for the future. If the company does not have a formal plan, it may be difficult to convince shareholders and banks (amongst others) that the company is a worthwhile investment.

- **Management skill** – freewheeling opportunists require managers that are highly skilled at understanding and reacting to the changing market. Less able or experienced managers will find this a difficult approach to use.

Test your understanding 3

T plc is an electronics manufacturer, which has recently created a detailed strategic review of its operations, as well as its external environment. T identified that it had significant skills with regards to the manufacture of electronic displays and launched a range of flat screen televisions. Unfortunately, its new product range, while praised by reviewers, failed to sell well to the public. T therefore abandoned its original strategy and took advantage of an offer by HHH, another electronics manufacturer, to make screens for HHH's popular mobile smartphones.

> Which approach to strategy is closest to that adopted by T when accepting HHH's offer?
>
> A   Emergent
> B   Rational
> C   Incrementalist
> D   Opportunism

4.5 Which approach to strategy should we adopt?

We have identified four different approaches to developing a strategy. While we have already mentioned that there is no 'correct' approach, it is important that you can justify which one would be the most appropriate for a particular organisation to adopt.

We can consider the four approaches as a spectrum:

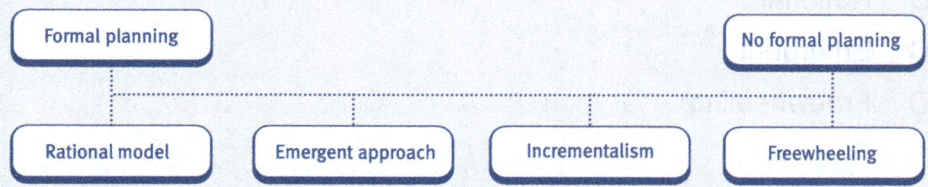

More formal planning approaches, such as the rational model (and to a degree the emergent model) tend to suit organisations which:

- exist in relatively stable industries, meaning there is sufficient time to undertake detailed strategic analysis
- have relatively inexperienced managers, as the formal planning approach helps to ensure they are familiar with the organisation as well as providing a series of guidelines they can follow to help them develop a strategy.

More informal approaches, such as freewheeling opportunism (and to a degree incrementalism) tend to suit organisations which:

- are in dynamic, fast changing industries where there is little time to undertake formal strategic analysis
- have experienced, innovative managers who are able to quickly identify and react to changes in the organisation and its environment
- do not need to raise significant external finance (external investors typically prefer a formal planning approach).

The process of strategy formulation

Note that incrementalism is unlikely to be suitable for new organisations as they have no past strategies upon which they can base their future policy.

Test your understanding 4

K is a small organisation which makes plastic toys. The company was very recently formed by Mr V. Mr V is a skilled entrepreneur with many years of experience in the industry.

The toy industry is incredibly fast-changing, with new innovations being developed regularly. In addition, tastes and trends change regularly, meaning that sales of toys can drop quickly as they fall out of fashion.

Mr V is aware that K will often require radically new strategies in order to keep up with these changes.

Which ONE of the following approaches to strategic development would be most appropriate for K to adopt?

A   Incrementalism

B   Rational

C   Emergent

D   Freewheeling

Test your understanding 5 – HAA – (Case Style)

You are Ali, a management accountant working for HAA plc – a computer games company that operates in country F. You have just found the following note from your manager on your desk:

NOTE

Hi Ali,

As I'm sure you're aware, HAA is planning to expand abroad, into the European market. To support this, we have undertaken a detailed review of our existing operations and the European market. This has been used to produce a three-year budget and operational plan for our proposed European operations.

The European electronics market has always been seen as a difficult market for new entrants. This is due to the fast-moving, innovative nature of the companies currently operating there. HAA has a high spend on research and development and our directors feel that the company is well placed to compete with European games manufacturers.

I'm meeting with the directors in fifteen minutes so I need you to make some brief notes for me evaluating our current approach to strategic planning. Can you suggest any more appropriate approaches we should consider?

Thanks

Required:

Draft a response to your manager, as requested.

(15 minutes)

Strategic planning for not-for-profit organisations (NFPs)

Strategic planning

Many of the organisations in exam questions will be profit-seeking businesses. However, some may involve charities, councils, schools, hospitals and other organisations where profit is not the main objective. With such an 'NFP' a discussion of objectives is likely to be problematic for the following reasons:

- It is more likely to have multiple objectives. A large teaching hospital may want to give the best quality care and treat as many patients as possible and train new doctors and research new techniques. Conflict is inevitable.

  This is not just an issue for NFPs, profit-seeking organisations also have multiple stakeholders with conflicting demands.

- It will be more difficult to measure objectives. How can one measure whether a school is educating pupils well? Performance in exams? Percentage going on to university? Percentage getting jobs? Percentage staying out of prison once they leave?

- There may be a more equal balance of power between stakeholders. In a company, the shareholders hold ultimate power. If they do not use it, the directors generally get their way. In a school, the balance of power may be more even (or even undefined) between parents, governors, the headmaster and the local education authority.

- The people receiving the service are not necessarily those paying for it. The Government and local NHS trusts determine a hospital's funding, not the patients. Consequently there may be pressure to perform well in national league tables at the expense of other objectives.

The process of strategy formulation

In spite of these problems, NFPs are still likely to need strategies. In the UK, for example, many public sector organisations have to produce strategic plans for between one and five years ahead as this is a Government requirement.

One of the reasons for this is that the public sector is required to hit certain targets and key performance indicators (KPIs), which are set by central government. In a company these targets and KPIs are used to ensure that the business is competitive. For a public sector organisation, they are used by the government to exert control over the activities of the organisation and to ensure that the government's funding is being used appropriately.

The 3Es

Public sector organisations and charities often have difficulty in using traditional private-sector-based approaches to objective setting since they do not make a profit by which their success or failure can be measured. One way to address this problem is to use the following approach.

The 'three **Es** approach' of the Audit Commission:

- **Economy** looks solely at the level of inputs, e.g. did the hospital spend more or less on drugs this year? Or on nurses' wages?
- **Efficiency** looks at the link between outputs and inputs (the internal processes approach). The 'internal processes approach' looks at how well inputs have been used to achieve outputs – it is a measure of efficiency. For example, what was the average cost per patient treated? What was the average spend per bed over the period? What was the bed occupancy rate that this achieved?
- **Effectiveness** looks at the outputs (the goal approach). The 'goal approach' looks at the ultimate objectives of the organisation, i.e. it looks at output measures. For example, for an NHS hospital, have the waiting lists been reduced? Have mortality rates gone down? How many patients have been treated?

The best picture of the success of an organisation is obtained by using all of the above approaches and by examining both financial and non-financial issues. Think about effectiveness meaning 'doing the right things' and efficiency 'about doing things right'.

Illustration 5 – The 3Es

Consider O – a large teaching hospital based in a major city which is funded by the Central Government. O may want to analyse its value for money using the 3Es in the following ways:

Economy:

O is given an annual budget by the Central Government. Economy is likely to look at whether this budget has been met. Has O spent more overall than expected? Has more or less been spent on drugs or wages than predicted? These would help O measure if it has been economical with the use of its funds.

Efficiency:

How well have O's inputs been used to generate its desired outputs? This looks at O's internal processes and could include measures such as the average cost per patient, average spend per hospital bed, or the spend per student in the period.

Effectiveness:

This looks solely at the outputs of O's operations. For example, has O had a higher or lower mortality rate than expected? What percentage of students have qualified or passed exams? How long is the patient waiting list at O?

Test your understanding 6

H College is a government funded provider of education to several thousand students in country G. It aims to ensure that at least 75% of all exams sat by its students are passed.

In the last year, it achieved a pass rate of 75% on its exams (the same as the previous year). The head of the college claimed that this was in spite of the government limiting H College's budget rise to 3%, which meant that H College was unable to provide the level of service it had in previous years. Inflation in the economy of country G is 2%.

The government's official auditor has discovered that the cost per student has risen by 5% in H College over the last year, due to internal problems in operations.

H College is expected to offer value for money (VFM). Which aspect of VFM has H College managed to achieve over the last year?

A   Efficiency

B   Economy

C   Effectiveness

D   Ethical behaviour

The process of strategy formulation

5 Approaches to strategic planning

While each aspect of strategic planning is important, firms may prioritise the perspectives in different ways:

5.1 A traditional approach – stakeholders

The traditional approach starts by looking at stakeholders and their objectives (e.g. increase EPS by 5% per annum). The emphasis is then on formulating plans to achieve these objectives.

Objectives are very important but this approach is often flawed in so far as objectives are often set in isolation from market considerations and are thus unrealistic.

However, this approach can be particularly useful for not-for-profit organisations where a discussion of mission and objectives is often key.

5.2 A 'market-led' or 'positioning' approach

The more modern 'positioning' approach starts with an analysis of markets and competitors' actions before objectives are set and strategies developed.

The essence of strategic planning is then to ensure that the firm has a good 'fit' with its environment. If markets are expected to change, then the firm needs to change too. The idea is to be able to predict changes sufficiently far in advance to control change rather than always having to react to it.

The main problem with the positioning approach lies in predicting the future. Some markets are so volatile that it is impossible to estimate further ahead than the immediate short term.

5.3 A 'resource-based' or 'competence-led' approach

Many firms who have found anticipating the environment to be difficult have switched to a competence or resource-based approach, where the emphasis of strategy is to look at what the firm is good at – its core competences.

Ideally these correlate to the areas that the firm has to be good at in order to succeed in its chosen markets (critical success factors or CSFs – see chapter 6 for more detail on this area) and are also difficult for competitors to copy.

Test your understanding 7

J Ltd is a company which offers home television repairs to customers. It has an excellent reputation for customer service and good quality workmanship. J feels that this has given it a competitive advantage in the market.

J is considering launching a car maintenance and repair service. It feels that its excellent reputation is likely to make such a move successful.

Which of the following approaches to strategic planning is J adopting?

A   A positioning approach

B   A traditional stakeholder approach

C   A resource-led approach

D   A corporate approach

Test your understanding 8 – GYU – (Case Style)

You have just received an email from your manager.

To: A

From: A. B Jones

Date: 17/05/XX

Subject: GYU

Hi A,

You may not have heard of GYU – they are a new client of ours. GYU is a large company which manufactures mobile phone handsets. This is an extremely competitive market and GYU has recently been struggling to keep up with other companies in its sector. This is due to the fast-paced nature of the market. New handsets with increasingly complex features are constantly being launched by competitors and the directors of GYU are concerned that the range of handsets manufactured by the company are beginning to look dated.

This has caused a sharp fall in GYU's cash balances and in response, for the first time in its history, GYU has had to cut its dividend. The fall, which was around 10%, was met with an angry response by shareholders and GYU's share price has fallen significantly since the announcement.

The process of strategy formulation

> While GYU's position appears weak, it is still seen as a market leader in the production of mobile handset software. While the reviews of its handsets are no longer entirely favourable, most customers agree that the software on the mobile phones is significantly superior to that produced by any of GYU's competitors.
>
> I'm about to have a meeting with GYU's directors for the first time and I think they will ask me to advise them about the three different approaches to strategy that GYU could use and which is the most appropriate for their business. I'd like you to email me back in the next fifteen minutes and tell me your thoughts on these matters.
>
> **Required:**
>
> Reply to the manager as requested.
>
> **(15 minutes)**

6 The role and responsibilities of directors

The responsibilities of directors and senior managers

Directors have a fiduciary duty to shareholders. This means they have been placed in a position of trust and must act in good faith to further the interests of their company, rather than their own interests. They also have a duty to exercise care and skill.

In most discussions the interests of the company and those of the shareholders are seen as one and the same. Thus directors should put shareholders' interests first in any and all strategic planning decisions.

This raises a number of key issues that are developed throughout the E3 syllabus:

- How can we ensure that **shareholders'** interests are prioritised? In some respects this is the main theme of corporate governance, discussed later in this chapter.

- What about the interests of other **stakeholder** groups? Stakeholder analysis and the related issues of ethics and corporate social responsibility (CSR) are covered in chapter 3.

- How should the performance of companies, divisions and managers be **measured** to ensure congruence with the objective of maximising shareholder value? Performance measurement is developed in chapter 8.

Directors' duties in the UK

The complete range of directors' duties and responsibilities varies from one country to another and are usually derived from a mixture of common law, stock exchange regulations, statute and governance regulations.

In the UK, for example, the Companies Act 2006 codifies seven duties:

- the duty to act within powers
- the duty to promote the success of the company
- the duty to exercise independent judgment
- the duty to exercise reasonable care, skill and diligence
- the duty to avoid conflicts of interest and of duties
- the duty not to accept benefits from third parties
- the duty to declare interest in proposed transactions or arrangements.

Company or shareholders?

Directors' duties under company law (as opposed to specific duties under other statutes such as those relating to health and safety or the environment) are owed to the company, rather than directly to an individual shareholder or group of shareholders.

Breaches of those duties can (subject to certain exceptions) be enforced only by the company, not by its shareholders. However, while in most cases shareholders will have the same interests as the company, there can be conflicts if the company, through its directors, is proposing to act in a way which benefits some shareholders to the detriment of others or, indeed, which is seen to benefit the directors. In such circumstances the affected shareholders may be able to take action themselves.

As a general rule, directors should ensure they act fairly towards all shareholders although this will not necessarily mean exact equality of treatment.

> **Wider stakeholder concerns – corporate social responsibility**
>
> Within the second duty listed above – "to promote the success of the company", the Act highlights that directors must have regard (among other things) to certain specific matters, i.e.:
>
> - the likely consequence of any decision in the long term
> - the interests of the company's employees
> - the need to foster the company's business relationships with suppliers, customers and others
> - the impact of the company's operations on the community and the environment
> - the desirability of the company maintaining a reputation for high standards of business conduct
> - the need to act fairly as between the members of the company.
>
> This is not intended to be an exhaustive list of factors (so matters such as financial profitability and value to shareholders clearly continue to be relevant), but does highlight the need to consider wider stakeholder concerns.

7 Corporate governance

In the Cadbury Report (1992) governance is defined as "the system by which companies are directed and controlled".

This definition has subsequently been expanded to "the system by which companies are directed and controlled in the interests of shareholders and other stakeholders". This expanded definition highlights the agency issues involved and wider concerns over social responsibility.

Purpose and objectives of corporate governance

When talking about governance we make a distinction between purposes and objectives:

- The main purpose of governance is to monitor those parties within the company who control the resources owned by investors.
- The main objective of governance is to contribute to improved performance and accountability in creating long-term shareholder value.

CORPORATE GOVERNANCE

PURPOSES

Primary:
Monitor those parties within a company who control the resources owned by investors.

Supporting:
- Ensure there is a suitable balance of power on the board of directors.
- Ensure executive directors are remunerated fairly.
- Make the board of directors responsible for monitoring and managing risk.
- Ensure the external auditors remain independent and free from the influence of the company.
- Address other issues, e.g. business ethics, corporate social responsibility (CSR), and protection of 'whistleblowers'.

OBJECTIVES

Primary:
Contribute to improved corporate performance and accountability in creating long-term shareholder value.

Supporting:
- Control the controllers by increasing the amount of reporting and disclosure to all stakeholders.
- Increase level of confidence and transparency in company activities for all investors (existing and potential) and thus promote growth.
- Ensure that the company is run in a legal and ethical manner.
- Build in control at the top that will 'cascade' down the organisation.

Further detail on governance

The Board of Directors is responsible for the governance of their companies. This is where strategy is set.

Relevant aims of corporate governance (for E3):

- to increase the **disclosure** to stakeholders in general
- to ensure that companies are **run on ethical grounds** and do not operate illegally
- to provide **increased confidence** in the company for existing and potential investors and thus promote investment in companies and subsequent economic growth
- to increase **transparency** at the board level of operations.

Corporate governance seeks to improve the confidence of stakeholders in the companies that operate within an environment. Better confidence sees improved investment by stakeholder groups.

The process of strategy formulation

Key ideas

The latest edition of the code of corporate governance came into force for accounting periods starting on or after 29 June 2010. This guidance was further updated 28 September 2012.

The principles of the UK Corporate Governance Code relate to the following areas:

- leadership
- effectiveness
- accountability
- remuneration
- relations with shareholders.

Leadership

- Every company should be **headed by an effective board** which is collectively responsible for the long-term success of the company.
- There should be a **clear division of responsibility** between running the board (the role of the chairman) and running the company's business (the role of the CEO). These two roles should not be held by one individual.
- **Boards should include non-executive directors**, who should constructively challenge and help develop proposals on strategies.
- The Chairman of the Board has the responsibility of achieving a **culture of openness and debate** and ensuring that adequate time is given to discussions.

Effectiveness

- The board and its committees should have an **appropriate balance of skills**, **experience**, independence and knowledge.
- Companies are to explain, and report on progress with, their **policies on boardroom diversity**.
- There should be a **formal, rigorous and transparent procedure for the appointment of new directors** to the board.

Accountability

- The board should **present a balanced and understandable assessment** of the company's position and prospects.
- Directors must **publish a statement of their responsibility** for preparing the accounts, as well as reporting that the report and accounts are **fair, balanced, understandable and provide all necessary information for shareholders.**
- The board should **conduct a review of the effectiveness of the risk management and internal controls** in the organisation at least annually.

Remuneration

- There should be a **formal and transparent procedure for developing policy on executive remuneration** and for fixing the remuneration packages of individual directors. No director should be involved in deciding his or her own remuneration.
- Executive rewards are to be subject to the recommendations of a **remuneration committee.**

Relations with shareholders

- The board as a whole has a responsibility for ensuring that a satisfactory dialogue with shareholders takes place.
- The board should use the AGM to communicate with investors and to **encourage their participation.**
- Companies are encouraged to **recognise the contribution of other providers of capital** (rather than simply shareholders) and confirm the board's interest in listening to their views on the company's overall approach to governance.

The implications of governance for strategy

The results of the increasing focus on governance issues are as follows:

- Increasing power of governance bodies.
- Increasing shareholder power, ensuring that companies are run with shareholders' interests prioritised.
- Greater pressure on boards to formulate strategy and be seen to control the businesses concerned.
- Greater scrutiny of quoted businesses, resulting in more short-termism.

The process of strategy formulation

- Greater emphasis on risk assessments, so directors may feel pressured to undertake lower-risk (and hence lower-return) projects.
- Greater scrutiny of mergers and acquisitions in particular.

How does corporate governance impact organisational strategy?

Corporate governance is very important to help maximise the effectiveness of an organisation's strategy. This is for a number of reasons.

- Corporate governance works to ensure that no individual can dominate the board of directors (by ensuring the CEO and Chairman roles are separated as well as the presence of independent non-executive directors). This helps to ensure that no-one is powerful enough to force through inappropriate or ineffective strategy. The non-executive directors should be able to impartially assess whether a proposed strategy is in the best interests of the organisation.

- Corporate governance should help to improve the diversity of the board of directors. This allows the board to identify a wide range of possible strategies, as well as analyse them from a variety of different viewpoints.

- Adequate internal audit and control systems should ensure that the board has accurate information about the current operations of the company. This will enable them to develop more effective strategies for the organisation. In addition, strong internal control increases the chance that the organisation will be able to implement its strategies successfully.

- Having good corporate governance is attractive to investors. This will make it easier for the organisation to raise the funding necessary to invest in the new strategies that they have identified.

It is therefore extremely important that companies consider corporate governance principles if they wish to develop and implement successful strategies.

chapter 1

Test your understanding 9

Which of the following is NOT a strategic aim of corporate governance?

A   To reduce costs within the organisation

B   To increase the organisation's transparency to stakeholders

C   To improve investor confidence in the organisation

D   To ensure that the organisation abides by relevant laws and acts ethically

Test your understanding 10 – ADF – (Case Study)

You are the Finance Director of ADF – a large national firm that retails clothes direct to the public through a chain of 250 high-street stores in country F. You have just received the following email from the Managing Director (MD), Carlos Smith:

To: Anne Accountant

From: Carlos Smith

Date: 1/5/20XX

Subject: Review of corporate governance arrangements

Hi Anne,

As you may be aware, we are currently reviewing our corporate governance arrangements within the company after some of our investors expressed concerns. I felt that you would be the right person to ask about this as I'm aware you've studied this topic.

You're probably aware that ADF's executive directors are all employees who have worked their way up through the company. Half of the board is made up of non–executive directors.

If you remember, the Chairman of the board is a retired director of a major electrical retailer. All of the other non–executive directors are personal friends of his and were appointed on his recommendation.

As you know, only one member of the board is female. All the directors are from country F and between the ages of 45 and 55.

> The company does have a small internal audit department but this is understaffed. The Head of Internal Audit has stated several times that the work undertaken on ADF's stores is minimal and that a number of stores have never been visited by internal audit.
>
> As we discussed at the Board meeting last week, the company is concerned that its current market is saturated and is looking to expand abroad into neighbouring countries, though the Chairman has expressed concern over this as he feels it is too risky.
>
> I'd be grateful if you could identify any weaknesses in our corporate governance. Please could you explain how each weakness will effect the company strategically. I'm meeting a few other Board members to discuss this in 20 minutes, so I be grateful if you could give this some urgent attention.
>
> Thanks
>
> Carlos
>
> **Required:**
>
> Draft a reply to Carlos, as requested.
>
> **(20 minutes)**

8 The role of the management accountant

It is important to appreciate the role of management accountants within the process of developing strategy. Normally this will involve providing information to aid in strategic planning and decision–making.

Strategic management accounting

Strategic management accounting is a 'form of management accounting in which emphasis is placed on information which relates to factors **external** to the entity, as well as non-financial information and internally generated information'.

CIMA Official Terminology

This indicates some key differences between **strategic** and **traditional** management accountants.

External focus

Traditional management accountants tend to focus on internal company issues. This is because their role is, amongst other things, to:

- aid in the creation of operational strategies for the business
- safeguard company assets – both tangible and intangible
- measure and report both financial and non–financial performance to managers
- ensure efficient use of assets and resources.

Strategic management accountants must provide information to help managers make key strategic decisions. This requires a stronger external focus – especially regarding the behaviour of competitors, customers and suppliers. This information will be vital to allow the business to understand the market it is operating in, which is a fundamental part of strategic planning.

Forward-looking

A large part of a traditional management accountant's role is to do with the measurement of historic performance of a business and its divisions.

Strategic management accountants need to be more forward-looking. This is because they will be analysing strategies that the business will employ in the future, rather than looking back at past performance.

Information provided by strategic management accountants

The information provided by strategic management accountants (SMAs) will include:

- **competitor analysis** – identification of competitors and detailed analysis of their activities
- **customer profitability** – which customers are the most important?
- **pricing decision** – forecasting of customer behaviour as well as competitor responses may help the business to decide on product pricing
- **portfolio analysis** – identification of key products and the strategies that should be adopted for each
- **corporate decision support** – this could include helping managers to decide whether or not to launch new products or enter/leave new markets.

- **customer profitability analysis** – the SMA can help the business to identify which of its customers are most profitable and which may be costing the business money. This will be examined in more detail in chapter 11.
- **evaluation of brand value** – SMAs can help assess the value of an organisation's brand name, which may be useful when considering acquisitions and disposals of businesses or strategic business units.
- **strategic information for acquisitions, disposals and mergers** – the SMA can help to assess what value such actions could have for an organisation.
- **investment in strategic management systems** – SMAs can help management assess the need for and value of investment in new information technology and systems.

A comparison of the information produced by strategic and traditional management accountants may be useful:

Traditional management accountants:	Strategic management accountants:
Cost structure	Competitor cost structure
Product costs	Competitor product costs
Market share	Relative market share
Profitability	Relative profitability
Price margins	Competitor price margins

Value of strategic management information

The information produced by strategic management accountants will help the business in a number of ways, including:

- more effective strategic planning
- increased awareness of the business and its environment
- increased control over business performance
- better decision–making

Test your understanding 11

Which ONE of the following statements is consistent with the role of a typical strategic management accountant?

A They focus primarily on the provision of information about internal company issues to management.

B The information they provide to management is typically forward-looking.

C Their primary focus is on the provision of financial information to management.

D They typically focus on the production of the organisation's financial statements

The process of strategy formulation

9 Summary

By the end of this chapter, you should be able to discuss:

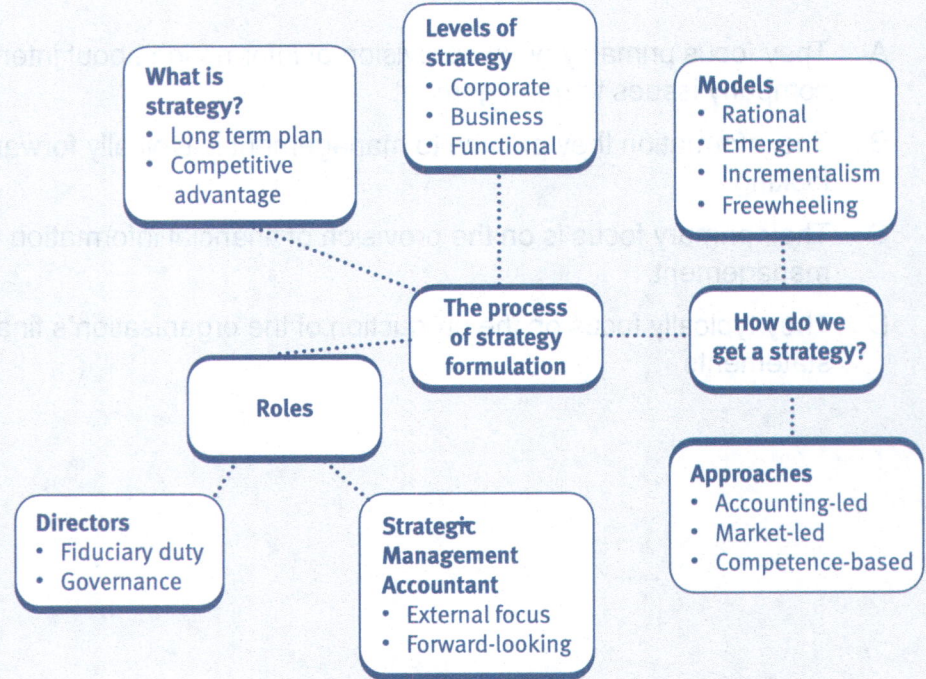

Test your understanding answers

Test your understanding 1

The correct answers are A, C and D.

Test your understanding 2

The correct answer is A

B relates to freewheeling opportunism.

C and D relate to the rational model.

Test your understanding 3

The correct answer is A

T has created a formal strategy after extensive analysis of its position. While this is consistent with the rational model, T has subsequently abandoned this and reacted to unforeseen events – i.e. the failure of its product to sell well.

This willingness to adapt to events as they occur is consistent with the emergent approach.

Note that incrementalism would involve small scale extensions to past strategies. HHH's proposal is significantly different to its original strategy, so this does not appear to be the case.

HHH is still basing its actions, at least in part, on a formally designed original strategy. This would indicate that it is not following an opportunistic approach.

The process of strategy formulation

Test your understanding 4

The correct answer is D

The pace of change in the market would tend to indicate that formal planning is not viable. This would suggest that the rational and emergent models are less useful. Incrementalism suggests that future strategies are small scale extensions of what has worked in the past. Again, this is clearly not appropriate given the need for radically new strategies highlighted in the scenario.

Test your understanding 5 – HAA – (Case Style)

Meeting notes

Current approach to strategy

HAA is currently using the rational model to develop its strategies. This involves taking a logical, step-by-step approach. HAA has clearly done this by undertaking such detailed planning, including strategic analysis of the market and the production of detailed operating plans.

The key advantage of such an approach to HAA is the level of understanding it will give them in the new market. They are currently not used to operating in the European market, so the initial strategic analysis they have performed will be invaluable. It will give them a picture of the their own capabilities as well as the European market they will be entering.

However, the European market is fast-moving, both due to its nature (high-tech) and the level of innovation by competitors. HAA will have to be prepared to quickly change its approach to deal with unexpected developments in the market. If the company produces a detailed operational plan, this may stifle the innovation that is required.

In addition, given the lack of experience that HAA has in the European market, any detailed forecasts it produces may prove to be unreliable. This may cause it to make inaccurate decisions based on flawed market predictions.

Alternative approaches to strategy for HAA

HAA could adopt the **emergent model.** While this would still involve some initial formal planning, these plans would merely be a starting point for the European operations. They will be continuously reviewed and updated as the games market changes, improving HAA's chances of success in the fast–moving market.

Alternatively HAA could choose the **freewheeling opportunism** approach to strategy. This would involve not producing a formal strategy – instead merely taking advantage of opportunities as they arise. The more rapidly the market evolves, the more applicable this approach may be, although it is considered too high risk for many managers.

Test your understanding 6

The correct answer is C

Effectiveness looks at the outputs of the organisation. As H has achieved its goal of a 75% pass rate, it has been effective.

Economy looks at the level of inputs – in this case, inputs have risen by 3% in the year (above inflation), but the efficiency with which H has used these inputs has fallen significantly. These factors would indicate a lack of efficiency and economy.

Test your understanding 7

The correct answer is C

J has identified a key resource or capability – its strong reputation. It is now looking for new ways to capitalise on this.

The process of strategy formulation

Test your understanding 8 – GYU – (Case Style)

There are three main approaches to strategic planning that GYU could take.

Traditional

This would involve GYU examining its key stakeholders and developing objectives that will meet their needs. The two key stakeholders in the scenario are GYU's customers and shareholders. The shareholders are clearly upset with the reduction in their dividend and will expect GYU to reverse this in coming years. The customers will be looking for handsets with more features and that are less 'dated'.

Unfortunately, while these are important objectives, they may be difficult for GYU to accomplish in the short term. Given the poor level of its finances, it may struggle to either increase dividends or invest enough in research and development to update its product line.

Market-led

This will involve the examination of GYU's competitors and market. Doing so should help GYU to ensure that it is competitive in what is a very fast-paced market.

While this appears to have been a weakness of GYU's to date (given the fact that it seems to have fallen so far behind many of its competitors), it may be inherently difficult in the mobile phone handset market. As the market is changing so rapidly, it may be difficult for GYU to accurately predict future trends and create appropriate strategies.

Resource-based

This involves GYU focusing its business strategies on areas that it is good at. For GYU its key area of skill is in the production of mobile handset software. It is acknowledged to be the market leader in this area and it appears to be very important to customers. Any future strategies should therefore be based around leveraging this area of skill.

For example, if it feels unable to produce handsets that are competitive, GYU could consider focusing on producing software which could then be licensed on other manufacturer's handsets. If this is a big enough market, this could help GYU to turn its business around.

Conclusion

Based on the information provided, the resource–based approach is likely to be best for GYU.

Test your understanding 9

The correct answer is A

Corporate governance is not designed to reduce organisational costs. It may, in fact, have the opposite effect due to the management time and additional staff required by corporate governance codes.

Test your understanding 10 – ADF – (Case Study)

To: Carlos Smith

From: Anne Accountant

Date: 1/5/20XX

Subject: Review of corporate governance arrangements

Dear Mr Smith,

Thank you for your email. I have looked through the information you provided and have identified the following weaknesses:

Lack of diversity of the board of directors

Most of the directors in ADF are older men from country F. There is only one woman on the board.

Having a diverse board can ensure that the company has a wide range of experience to draw on when making decisions.

For example, ADF wants to expand abroad. By having directors from other countries or with experience of these foreign markets, the company would be far better placed to achieve this growth.

The process of strategy formulation

Lack of independence of non–executive directors

All the non–executive directors are linked to the Chairman. This makes it unlikely that they will act impartially. They are likely to vote along with the Chairman.

This could lead them to reject acceptable projects, such as the proposed foreign expansion, merely because the Chairman disapproves.

Weak internal audit

The fact that the directors allow ADF to have such an inadequate internal audit function indicates an alarming lack of control. If they are unable to rely fully on the accounts produced, they may find it difficult to implement sensible strategies in the future.

Overall

The ultimate goal of corporate governance is to provide investors with increased confidence in the company and increase the transparency of the board's decisions.

Should investors feel that ADF has poor corporate governance, it can damage ADF's reputation with investors. This may harm its share price and make it harder for the company to raise much needed finance in the future – which is likely to be important if it is planning overseas expansion.

I hope this helps. If you need any further information, please let me know.

Kind regards

Anne

Test your understanding 11

The correct answer is B

Strategic management accountants tend to focus on information that is both internal and external, financial and non-financial information, and forward-looking. This will help management to make the best strategic decisions possible by having all relevant information to hand. Note that strategic management accountants would not usually focus on the production of the financial statements of the organisation – this role would usually be filled by financial accountants.

chapter 2

Strategic analysis: Mission, vision and stakeholders

Chapter learning objectives

Lead	Component
A1. Evaluate the influence of key external factors on an organisation's strategy	(b) Recommend approaches to business/government relations and to relations with society
	(c) Recommend how to build and manage strategic relationships with stakeholders (including suppliers, customers, owners, government and the wider society)
B1. Evaluate the process of strategy formulation	(a) Evaluate the processes of strategic analysis and strategic options generation

Indicative syllabus content

- Non–market strategy and forms of corporate political activity.
- Stakeholder management (stakeholders to include internal stakeholders, government and regulatory agencies, non–governmental organisations and civil society, industry associations, customers and suppliers).
- Vision and mission statements and their use in orientating the organisation's strategy.
- Building strategic alliances with stakeholders.

Strategic analysis: Mission, vision and stakeholders

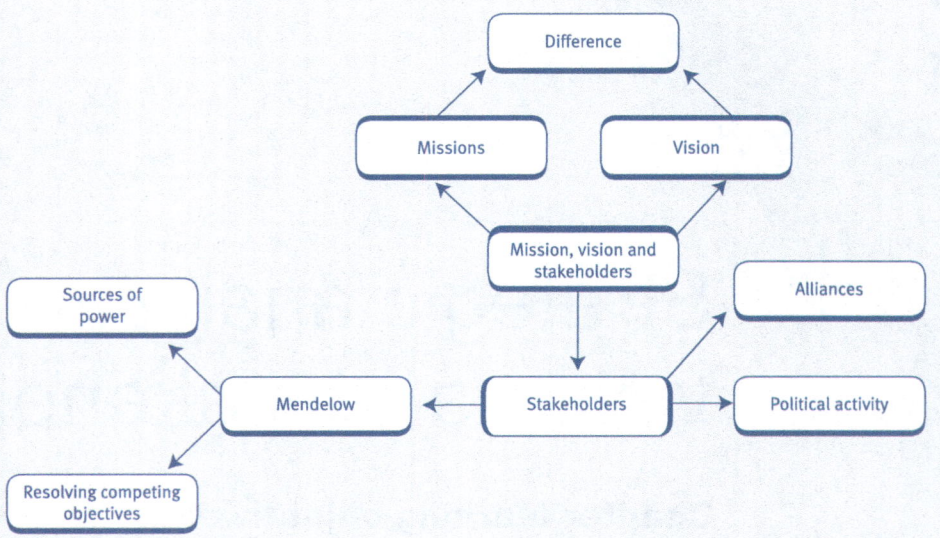

1 Mission

Missions

A mission is:

The 'fundamental objective(s) of an entity expressed in general terms'.

(CIMA Official Terminology)

The mission therefore is the **basic purpose of the organisation** and tries to identify the reason it exists. Ultimately the strategies of the organisation should be designed to support the accomplishment of this mission.

It is important that the organisation is able to communicate its mission both internally and externally, which requires the creation of a mission statement.

'The mission says *why* you do what you do, not the means by which you do it.'

Peter Drucker

Mission statements

A mission statement is:

A 'published statement, apparently of the entity's fundamental objective(s). This may or may not summarise the true mission of the entity'.

(CIMA Official Terminology)

Essentially, the mission statement is a **statement in writing that outlines the organisation's mission and summarises the reasoning and values that underpin its operations**.

There is no 'correct' format for the mission statement and it will vary in style and length for each organisation. However, typically it is a short, punchy (and hopefully memorable) explanation of the reason the organisation exists.

> **Illustration 1 – Examples of missions**
>
> We are a global family with a proud heritage passionately committed to providing personal mobility for people all around the world.
>
> **(Ford Motor Company)**
>
> Our Mission is:
>
> - To refresh the world in mind, body and spirit.
> - To inspire moments of optimism through our brands and actions.
> - To create value and make a difference everywhere we engage.
>
> **(Coca Cola)**
>
> To create lasting solutions to poverty, hunger and social injustice.
>
> **(Oxfam)**
>
> Google's mission is to organise the world's information and make it universally accessible and useful.
>
> **(Google)**

Characteristics of mission statements

There are a number of fundamental questions that an organisation will need to address in its search for its purpose and mission. According to Drucker, these are:

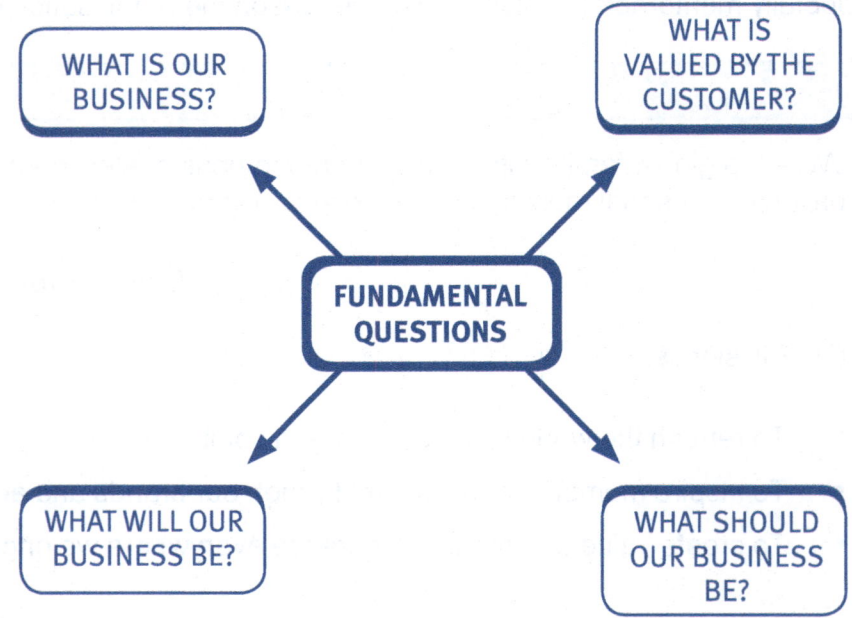

Mission statements will therefore typically have some or all of the following characteristics:

- usually a brief statement of no more than a page in length (often much shorter)
- very general statement of entity culture
- states the aims (or purposes) of the organisation
- states the business areas in which the organisation intends to operate
- open-ended (not stated in quantifiable terms)
- does not include commercial terms, such as profit
- not time-assigned
- forms a basis of communication to the people inside the organisation and to people outside the organisation
- used to formulate goal statements, objectives and short-term targets
- guides the direction of the entity's strategy and as such is part of management information.

Mission statements fulfil a number of purposes:

- **to communicate to all the stakeholder groups** – everyone involved in the organisation will be made aware of its mission and should therefore know what to expect from the organisation.

- **to help develop a desired corporate culture** – by communicating core values, policies and expected standards of behaviour to key groups, such as employees.

- **to assist in strategic planning** – the organisation should ensure that its strategies are consistent with its overall mission and therefore its corporate values. The mission statement can also be used as a way of screening out potentially unsuitable strategies.

However there are a number of criticisms of mission statements, including:

- **they may not represent the actual values of the organisation** – as evidenced by the official CIMA definition of a mission statement.

- **they are often vague** – mission statements tend to be stated in very general terms, using phrases that are difficult to measure (such as Coca-Cola's desire to 'refresh the world').

- **they are often ignored** – mission statements are often seen as a public relations exercise and are not used by employees or managers when developing strategies.

- **they may become quickly outdated** – especially in fast-moving industries.

The process of creating a mission statement

The process of writing a mission statement

Mission statements are normally drafted by the senior managers or directors of the organisation, as they are uniquely positioned to understand the needs and aims of the business at a high level.

Usually the first step in creating a mission statement is to analyse the stakeholders of the organisation – customers, shareholders and employees (amongst others). More detail on this stage can be found later in this chapter.

The directors of the company should identify the needs and aims of these stakeholders. They can then attempt to create a mission statement that reflects these aims and that shows how the organisation wants to relate to the stakeholders.

Strategic analysis: Mission, vision and stakeholders

A draft mission statement can then be written and distributed to key stakeholders for review. Any feedback can be built into the final mission statement, which can then be published and widely distributed to as many interested parties as possible.

The life span of a mission statement

There are no set rules on how long a mission statement will be appropriate for an organisation. It should be reviewed periodically to ensure it still reflects the company's environment.

If the market or key stakeholders have changed since the mission statement was written, then it may no longer be appropriate.

Illustration 2 – Yahoo

Yahoo – an internet search based company – had a mission statement in the early 2000s which identified that it wanted to be 'the most essential global internet service for consumers and businesses'.

However, by 2007 Yahoo was beginning to struggle due to the rise of major competitors such as Google, whose mission statement was 'to organise the world's information and make it universally accessible and useful.' Yahoo felt that its existing mission statement did not show stakeholders how it was different to these rivals.

It therefore made its mission statement more specific, changing it to reflect that it wanted to 'connect people to their passions, their communities and the world's knowledge'.

This attempted to show the difference between the two companies. Yahoo wished to position itself in the entertainment market, rather than merely providing information like Google.

As time moved on, Yahoo identified more about its target markets and the need to connect not only with users and their desire for more personalised service, but also their advertisers and key sources of revenue. By 2012, their mission statement had developed further into:

'Yahoo! is the premier digital media company. Yahoo! creates deeply personal digital experiences that keep more than half a billion people connected to what matters most to them, across devices and around the globe. That's how we deliver your world, your way. And Yahoo!'s unique combination of Science + Art + Scale connects advertisers to the consumers who build their businesses.'

Test your understanding 1

JJJ Ltd's mission statement is 'to offer fantastic service to all customers'. The mission statement has recently been created by senior management but has not been widely circulated to anyone else. The CEO of JJJ has stated that all of the high-level strategies created by the organisation need to be measured against this mission.

Which ONE of the following benefits is JJJ most likely to see from its new mission statement in the short term?

A   Rapid change in JJJ's corporate culture to a focus on quality

B   Improved awareness amongst stakeholders of JJJ's goals

C   Improved strategic decision-making

D   Improved image to customers

Test your understanding 2 – (Integration question)

The mission statement of C plc is "to provide our customers with a top quality product at a fair price".

Required:

Evaluate the usefulness of this mission statement.

(5 minutes)

2 Vision statements

Vision statements are often confused with mission statements, but the two are subtly different.

While a mission statement defines the present purpose and state of an organisation, the vision statement identifies the ideal position that the company wants to reach within the medium to long-term. It is, essentially, the **longer term aspirations** of the organisation.

Strategic analysis: Mission, vision and stakeholders

Illustration 3 – Examples of vision statements

A just world without poverty.

(Oxfam)

Our vision is a world without Alzheimer's.

(Alzheimer's Association)

To make people happy.

(Disney)

To become the world's leading consumer company for automotive products and services.

(Ford Motor Company)

Vision statements help give a longer term direction to the organisation's strategies and are designed to help staff make decisions and behave in a way that helps move the company towards its ideal long-term position.

Unfortunately, they have many of the same drawbacks as mission statements.

Illustration 4 – mission or vision?

The main difference between vision and mission is illustrated by the statements produced by Microsoft:

Mission statement:

To help people and businesses throughout the world realise their full potential.

Vision statement:

A personal computer in every home running Microsoft software.

This shows that the mission statement focuses on the company's present operations. The vision shows the ideal state that the company wishes to achieve in the future.

3 Objectives

A mission is an open-ended statement of the firm's purpose and strategy. Objectives are more specific and seek to translate the mission into a series of mileposts for the organisation to follow.

To be useful for motivation, evaluation and control purposes, objectives should be SMART:

- **S**pecific – clear statement, easy to understand
- **M**easurable – to enable control and communication down the organisation
- **A**ttainable – it is pointless setting unachievable objectives
- **R**elevant – appropriate to the mission and stakeholders
- **T**imed – have a time period for achievement.

Key issues

In the same way that an organisation's overall strategic plans need to be translated into a hierarchy of lower level tactical and operational plans, there will be a hierarchy of objectives where the mission statement is translated into detailed strategic, tactical and operational objectives and targets.

Typical issues this gives rise to are as follows:

- Objectives drive action, so it is important that goal congruence is achieved and the agreed objectives do drive the desired strategy.
- It can be difficult (although necessary) to prioritise multiple, often conflicting objectives.
- This is made more complex when some objectives are hard to quantify (e.g. environmental impact).
- There will be a mixture of financial and non-financial objectives.
- There is always the danger of short-termism.
- Objectives will vary across stakeholder groups and a strategy may satisfy some groups but not others.

Primary and secondary objectives

Organisations will typically set themselves different types of objective, with some being more important than others.

Primary objectives (also known as corporate objectives) are the major, overriding objectives of the organisation. They can be financial or non-financial but relate to the organisation as a whole and, typically, the needs of its stakeholders.

Secondary objectives directly relate to the various strategies that the organisation needs to adopt in order to meet its primary objective.

For instance, a company may set itself a primary objective of growing returns for its shareholders. It will then need to implement a number of strategies to help it achieve this – each strategy having its own 'secondary' objective. These secondary objectives could (for example) be an increase in customer satisfaction, increased sales growth, reduced wastage, or the launch of a number of innovative new products.

If the company can achieve these secondary objectives then it will be closer to meeting its primary objective of growing shareholder returns.

Illustration 5 – primary and secondary objectives

On its website, Tesco plc describes its primary purpose (or objective) as being:

'We make what matters better, together...... to inspire and earn trust and loyalty from all of our stakeholders.'

The primary objective of Tesco is therefore to ensure that its stakeholders are happy with the company's activities. This will ensure that it retains the support of key groups such as customers, suppliers and shareholders.

However, this primary objective is supported by a number of secondary objectives, such as:

- meeting customer needs
- acting responsibly towards local communities
- improving staff teamworking
- showing trust and respect to employees
- reducing levels of food waste

If Tesco is able to meet its secondary objectives, it will be well placed to achieve its primary objective of earning stakeholder trust.

Long and short-term objectives

Objectives can either be long or short-term in nature. Short-term objectives typically focus on what the organisation wishes to accomplish over the coming year or so. Short-term objectives should be designed to help the organisation work towards achieving its longer term goals.

For example, a small retailer may have a long-term objective to grow its turnover by 25% within five years time. This will need to be supported by a number of short-term objectives, such as a need to grow sales by 5% over the next financial year, or move to larger premises within the next six months.

If resources are scarce (or simply badly planned by management), then short-term and long-term objectives may be in conflict. For example, an organisation may set aggressive short-term profit targets for the coming year for its managers. This could lead to managers making decisions that meet the short term profit objectives but which compromise the long-term success of the organisation, such as:

- Reduced research and development investment, thereby reducing the organisation's ability to innovate and continue to meet its customer needs in the future.

- Reducing investment in the organisation's brand (such as cutting advertising costs), which may lead to loss of customers in the longer term.

- Delaying or cancelling capital investment (such as new production facilities or retail space) which may reduce the ability of the organisation to grow in the future.

- Reducing expenditure on staff motivation and training which may lead to higher staff turnover in future, as well as reduction in service quality offered to customers causing a fall in goodwill.

Management therefore must be careful when setting short-term and long-term objectives. In reality, there may have to be a tradeoff between the two, but they should not be in direct conflict with each other.

Strategic analysis: Mission, vision and stakeholders

The role of the strategic management accountant in setting

Strategic management accountants (SMAs) will be vital when an organisation considers the setting of its objectives.

- **Setting objectives** – SMAs will help the managers of the organisation to identify suitable objectives that help support its overall mission and/or vision.

- **Defining objectives** – it is important that objectives are appropriately designed to meet the required SMART criteria. Failure to do this can lead to the objective being ineffective. SMAs can ensure objectives have been appropriately phrased.

- **Seeing the big picture** – it is easy for objectives to be in conflict with each other (such as long-term versus short-term objectives). SMAs can help management ensure that the objectives that they are setting are congruent.

- **Monitoring outcomes** – SMAs will gather information to see whether the organisation is meeting its objectives. If objectives are being missed, they can investigate why in order to help management take action.

- **Updating objectives** – remember that objectives are based on the organisation's mission. They must be realistic and relevant to the organisation's circumstances. If any of these factors change, the objectives may need to be updated to ensure they continue to be useful. As SMAs are typically involved in monitoring the organisation's environment, they are well placed to aid management with updates to objectives.

Test your understanding 3

Which of the following is **NOT** a required feature of an objective?

A   Measurable

B   Strategic

C   Timed

D   Attainable

chapter 2

Test your understanding 4

Q Ltd is owned by three shareholders. They have stated their desire to improve the profitability of the company and thereby increase their dividends.

Q Ltd has created a number of objectives to respond to its shareholders needs. One of these is to 'delight its customers and the world at large with our products by the end of the next financial year'.

One of Q's managers has suggested that this does not meet all of the criteria for an objective.

Which of the following criteria **IS** being met by Q's objective?

A   Measurable
B   Relevant
C   Attainable
D   Timed

Test your understanding 5 – JAA – (Case style)

JAA plc is a publisher of both fiction and non–fiction books, a market in which it faces significant competition.

It has recently published a new mission statement:

'JAA will continue to grow and innovate as an organisation, while acting in a socially responsible way.'

For a future meeting of the Board of Directors, the Marketing Director has been asked to prepare a presentation to discuss this in more detail. She has asked you to help her by suggesting objectives that could be used to help the company achieve its missions of 'growth' and 'innovation'.

The Marketing Director has suggested that the only objective for 'social responsibility' will be the happiness of the workforce.

Strategic analysis: Mission, vision and stakeholders

Required:

Recommend, with reasons, TWO possible objectives each for BOTH growth and innovation for JAA, as requested by the Marketing Director.

Comment on her proposed objective for social responsibility and recommend, with reasons, an alternative.

(10 minutes)

Not-for-profit organisation (NFP) objectives

While we often look at organisations that seek to make a profit, there are many organisations for whom this is not the primary objective. These include:

- government departments and agencies
- trade unions
- schools
- charities (e.g. Oxfam, Red Cross)
- mutual associations (e.g. building societies)

Rather than seeking to make a profit, these organisations will try to satisfy particular needs of their members or the sections of society they have been set up to benefit.

Illustration – the Chartered Institute of Management Accountants

The objectives of the Institute are (amongst other things):

- 'To promote and develop the science of Management Accountancy and to foster and maintain investigations into and research into the best means and methods of developing and applying such science...'
- '...by means of examination and other methods of assessment to test the skill and knowledge of persons desiring to enter the profession.'

The services provided by many NPOs are limited only by the funds they have available. This means they normally aim to:

- raise as much money as possible
- spend this money as effectively as possible on the target group (with the minimum of administration costs).

> Setting formal objectives can be difficult for NPOs. This is often due to the wide range of possible stakeholders as well as the fact the stakeholders who provide the funds may be different to the stakeholders who benefit from the NPO's activities (e.g. a charity). This gives much more power to the providers of finance and their objectives may not be the same as the NPO's.

4 Stakeholders

Mission and objectives need to be developed with two sets of interests in mind:

(1) the interests of those who have to carry them out – typically managers and staff

(2) the interests of those who focus on the outcome – such as shareholders, customers, suppliers, etc.

Together these groups are known as **stakeholders**, 'those persons and organisations that have an interest in the strategy of the organisation.'

(CIMA Official Terminology)

Given the range of differing interests that these stakeholders will have in the organisation, it is not surprising to find that the mission may take several months of negotiation before it is finalised. The key aspect is that the organisation must take its stakeholders into account when formulating its mission and objectives.

The mission-setting process can be a useful basis for getting the stakeholder groups to communicate their ideas and then be able to appreciate other viewpoints.

Stakeholder groups and their differing needs

It is worth noting that stakeholders are not only interested in the organisation's mission statement. In fact, they are far more interested in the strategies which the organisation is undertaking as it is these strategies that are likely to impact upon the different stakeholder groups. It is this influence and interest which organisations need to carefully manage.

In order to consider its stakeholders when developing strategies, the organisation must first identify who its stakeholders are and what they want or expect.

Strategic analysis: Mission, vision and stakeholders

A large company, for example, could have a wide range of stakeholders, including:

Stakeholder:	Objectives:
Internal stakeholders	
Managers and employees	Career development, pay, job security, enjoyable jobs.
External stakeholders	
Government and regulatory agencies	Compliance with relevant laws and regulations, collection of taxation.
Civil society (including NGOs (charities, pressure groups), civic clubs, trade unions, public groups, social and sports clubs, co-operatives, environmental groups, professional associations, consumer organisations and media).	Varied – could include: Pollution controls, health of public, human or member rights.
Industry associations	Member rights, compliance with industry rules and practises.

Connected stakeholders	
Shareholders	Profit, share price and dividends.
Customers	Low prices, good quality products, good service.
Financiers	Interest payments, security, meeting loan agreement terms.
Suppliers	Assured demand, fair prices paid, payments made on time.

As you can identify from the table above, some stakeholder objectives are likely to directly conflict with one another. Examples of conflict include:

- shareholders want higher profits, employees want better pay and working conditions
- customers want may want 24/7 service, while employees want working arrangements which fit into their personal lifestyles and home and family arrangements
- customers want high quality and low prices, shareholders want high profits
- suppliers want prompt payment, lenders want overdraft limits adhered to.

This means that it may be impossible for an organisation to satisfy the needs of all of its stakeholders. It must therefore find a way to prioritise its stakeholders, which is normally done by analysing their level of power and interest in the organisation.

The more power and interest, the greater the involvement in setting the mission and strategy.

Actors (Braithwaite and Drahos)

It is worth mentioning Braithwaite and Drahos to consider the full range of 'actors' who may have an influence on the way an organisation conducts its business.

- **Organisations of states:** Organisations formed by groups of states that meet and employ staff to explore common agendas (e.g. the WTO, the EU).
- **States:** Organised political communities with governments and geographical boundaries recognised by international law (e.g. Sweden).
- **Organisations formed by firms** [Corporations] and/or business organisations with common agendas, such as Chambers of Commerce.
- **Corporations:** Organisations formed by actors who invest in them as commercial vehicles (e.g. Ford, British Telecom).
- **Non-Governmental Organisations (NGOs):** Organisations (excluding business organisations) that explore common agendas. They can be international (e.g. Consumers International) or national (e.g. British Standards Institute).
- **Mass publics:** Large audiences of citizens who express together a common concern about an issue.
- **Knowledge based (epistemic) communities:** These consist of state, business and NGO representatives who meet sporadically and share a common discourse based on shared knowledge – sometimes technical knowledge requiring professional training; CIMA is an example.

[Civil society]

The last three groups may be collectively termed **civil society.** Civil society includes, among others, non-government organisations; people's organisations; civic clubs; trade unions; gender, cultural, and religious groups; charities; social and sports clubs; co-operatives; environmental groups; professional associations; academic and policy institutions; consumers/consumer organisations and the media.

5 Mendelow's power/interest matrix

Mendelow's matrix is a model which can be used to prioritise stakeholders and decide how to deal with each of them. It does this by examining their level of power (how much control they have over the organisation) with their level of interest (how likely the stakeholder is to try and exercise their power over the organisation).

Stakeholder Mapping: The Power Interest Matrix

Sources of stakeholder power

Typically, stakeholder power can come from a number of sources:

- **Positional power:** This arises because of an individual's position in the organisational hierarchy and is reflected in their formal authority and reputation. Directors, for example, will usually be powerful because of their rank in the organisation.

- **Resource power:** This arises because an individual can control, obtain or create resources or other items of value. For instance, a unionised workforce will be powerful as they control the key labour resource in the business.

- **System power:** This arises because a stakeholder has high visibility or political access and relevance to a particular situation. A director who is closely connected to a major shareholder is likely to have significant power within the organisation.

- **Expert power:** This arises where an individual has information, knowledge or expertise that is important to the organisation. Skilled employees, for example, will normally have more power than unskilled employees as they have skills that are important to the business and they are harder to replace.

- **Personal power:** This arises because an individual has good communication skills and reputation and (usually) is well liked within the organisation. A popular director is likely to have more power in an organisation, as staff will be willing to follow his or her instructions.

Applying Mendelow's matrix

- **Minimal effort**

    Their low level of interest and power makes these stakeholders open to influence. They are more likely than others to accept what they are told and follow instructions.

- **Keep informed**

    These stakeholders are likely to have high levels of interest in the strategy but lack sufficient power to influence it. Management needs to convince opponents to the strategy that the plans are justified; otherwise these stakeholders will try to gain power by joining with parties with high power but low interest.

- **Keep satisfied**

    The key here is to keep these stakeholders satisfied to avoid them gaining interest and moving to the "key players" box. This could involve reassuring them of the outcomes of the strategy well in advance.

- **Key players**

    These stakeholders are potentially the most influential stakeholders in the strategic planning process. Their participation in the planning process is vital. Management, therefore, needs to communicate plans to them and then discuss implementation issues.

Managing the relationship with stakeholder groups

Powerful stakeholder groups must have confidence in the management team of the organisation. The organisation should ensure therefore that adequate management systems are in place. Some suggestions:

- Allocate organisational responsibility for the process of stakeholder management along with a budget.
- Use a team to manage stakeholders and decide on appropriate management techniques – ensuring a broad range of opinion and expertise.
- Establish and order the objectives of the organisation. Identify the areas for potential conflict and target resources into those areas.
- Frequent face-to-face meetings with the key player and keep satisfied groups.
- Communication processes for the keep informed and minimal effort groups – possibly via public Q&A sessions.
- Periodic formal reporting to stakeholders including, for example, the use of a website for 'frequently asked questions'.

It is worth remembering that this is complicated by the fact that individuals may be part of more than one stakeholder group at any point in time. For example, factory workers can also be members of the local community or even elected local government officials. This can mean that there are conflicts between their interests and objectives regarding a particular decision that the company is about to make.

Test your understanding 6

According to Mendelow, which ONE of the following methods should be adopted to manage a stakeholder with high power and low interest?

A   Keep informed

B   Key players

C   Keep satisfied

D   Minimal effort

Test your understanding 7

Country N is split into a number of regions, each with their own local government. The local government (LG) is given funding by the central government of country N, though LG officials are elected by local residents every four years. Resident turnout at local elections is high and local elections often result in a number of changes to LG officials.

LG budget is spent on a large number of local issues, such as transport and education for the region – issues that have a significant effect on the lives of local residents. The central government of country N has ultimate control over the amount of money that LG receives. However, central government rarely intervenes in LG affairs unless there is evidence of mismanagement of funds.

One LG has recently undertaken stakeholder analysis using Mendelow's matrix and identified local residents and central government as two of these stakeholder groups.

Which ONE of the following methods would be appropriate for each of these stakeholders?

	Local residents	Central government
A	Keep satisfied	Key players
B	Key players	Keep satisfied
C	Keep informed	Key players
D	Key players	Keep informed

Test your understanding 8 – AYL – (Case style)

You are Joe, a strategic management account at AYL, which operates the only public hospital within a small city in country U. All of its income is provided by the central government. However, due to a recent economic downturn, the central government is urgently looking for ways to save money. It has therefore decided to significantly cut AYL's budget for the coming period.

The management of AYL have therefore been looking at ways of reducing their expenditure while attempting to minimise the impact on the services provided to the public. They are planning to freeze pay for the semi-skilled nurses working at the hospital.

Strategic analysis: Mission, vision and stakeholders

Your manager has left you the following note:

Note

Hi Joe,

Our proposed pay freeze has prompted significant opposition from nurses. Nurses are not heavily unionised, but the remaining staff members in the hospital, such as doctors, are all members of the same union. There are no plans to cut the number of remaining staff jobs in the hospital, or to freeze the wages of anyone other than the nurses.

Can you please write me some briefing notes identify the key stakeholders that the managers will need to consider. Using Mendelow's matrix, recommend what approach the managers of AYL should take in relation to each one. I know what Mendelow's matrix looks like, so please don't draw it in your briefing note.

Required:

Draft the briefing notes as requested by the manager.

(15 minutes)

Resolving competing stakeholder objectives

Cyert and March suggest four ways to resolve conflicting stakeholder objectives.

- **Satisficing** involves negotiations between key stakeholders to arrive at an acceptable compromise.

- **Sequential attention** is when management focus on stakeholder needs in turn. For example, staff may receive a pay rise with the clear implication that it will not be their 'turn' again for a few years and so they should not expect any further increases.

- **Side payments** are where a stakeholder's primary objectives cannot be met so they are compensated in some other way. For example, a local community may object to a new factory being built on a site that will cause pollution, noise and extra traffic. The firm concerned may continue to build the factory but try to appease the community by also building local sports facilities.

- **Exercise of power** is when a deadlock is resolved by a senior figure forcing through a decision simply based on the power they possess.

Test your understanding 9

L runs a small business which sells second hand motor vehicles. She did not offer a pay rise to her staff last year, stating that she had not earned sufficient profits to be able to do so. However, she promised that she would offer a pay rise this year – regardless of whether a significant profit was made or not.

Which ONE of Cyert and March's stakeholder conflict resolution strategies is L adopting?

A   Sequential attention
B   Satisficing
C   Exercise of power
D   Side payments

Stakeholder alliances

As outlined above, organisations do not exist in isolation and can be affected by a wide variety of stakeholders. Some of these stakeholders can become important allies, helping the organisation to achieve its goals.

Stakeholder analysis

Not all stakeholders will make useful allies for the organisation. Using Mendelow's matrix will help the organisation determine the most important stakeholders and the ones that would be sensible to consider as potential allies.

For example, a company may wish to focus on major shareholders, as well as significant customers and suppliers, as these groups are likely to have a high degree of interest and power – making them more useful as allies.

Matching needs

A strategic alliance will only work if it benefits both parties. Once the organisation has located potential partners, it needs to research what their aims are, as well as considering how they could link with its own and support its own aims.

For example, if a manufacturing company knows that a government wishes to attract more jobs to a given region, it may suggest opening a factory in the region in exchange for subsidies.

Creation of the alliance

Once the organisation has identified the benefits of an alliance, it will be in a position to negotiate the terms with the desired partner. The alliance will need to be monitored on an ongoing basis to ensure that both parties are achieving the benefits they wanted.

Illustration 6 – Stakeholder alliances

Alliances can form between any organisations with matching interests.

Microsoft and Dell are an example of this. Dell is one of the world's largest manufacturers of personal computers and Microsoft writes the operating system used by the majority of these computers.

The two companies work together to ensure that the technological development of Dell's computers (i.e. memory and processor speed) keeps pace with Microsoft's software.

This arrangement benefits both organisations as it maximises the functionality of their products and provides their mutual customers with the best possible experience.

Test your understanding 10 – WRL – (Case style)

You are an accountant working in HHH – an accounts consultancy firm. You have received the following email from one of HHH's senior partners:

To: M. Williams

From: A. Scott

Date: 10/05/20XX

Subject: WRL meeting this afternoon

As you are probably aware, we are meeting with the managers of WRL later this afternoon to discuss several key issues, and I need you to do some research for me. I need a report in 45 minutes that covers the following:

(i) Categorise, according to Mendelow's matrix, any three of the stakeholder groups of WRL with respect to the decision about the disposal of the polluted water. You should explain what the power and interests of the three stakeholder groups you have categorised are likely to be.

Note: I don't want you to draw the Mendelow matrix

(ii) Advise the Board of WRL of the actions it should take to resolve the problem of its stakeholders' competing objectives.

(iii) Discuss the extent to which WRL's mission statement is consistent with its plan to put the polluted water in the lake.

To help you with this, I've attached a copy of our background analysis of WRL and its current situation. Please read it carefully and email me back within the next 45 minutes so I have time to prepare before the meeting.

Thanks

A. Scott

Attachment 1 – Background to WRL

WRL is a multi-national gold mining company. Its mission statement explains that 'WRL exists to make the maximum possible profit for its shareholders whilst causing the least damage to the environment. WRL will, at all times, be a good corporate citizen'.

In 2007 WRL was granted a licence to mine for gold by the national government of Stravia, a small country whose economy is mainly based on agriculture. The national government of Stravia was very keen to develop its economy and saw gold mining as an important aspect of this. The area where WRL was granted the licence is very remote and has no towns or cities nearby. There are small villages near the site of the gold mine. One of the conditions of the licence is that WRL would employ local people wherever possible, which it has done. WRL is entitled under the terms of the licence to dispose of the waste from the gold mining wherever is convenient for it.

The terms of the licence granted a payment by WRL to the national government of Stravia, payable in US dollars, which in 2009 totalled $50 million. This is a significant amount of foreign exchange for Stravia's economy. Similar levels of payment by WRL to the national government are likely to continue annually for the foreseeable future. The mine has operated profitably since it began.

Strategic analysis: Mission, vision and stakeholders

WRL's mine is in an area controlled by the Eastern state government. The Eastern state government was not involved in the negotiations to bring WRL to Stravia and is not entitled to any payment from WRL. However, Stravia's national government granted the Eastern state government $1 million in 2009 from the payments which it received from WRL.

The Eastern state government discovered that WRL's proposed mining techniques use a great deal of water which becomes polluted. The cheapest way for WRL to dispose of this polluted water is to dispose of it in a lake near the mine and it intends to do this.

The Eastern state government feared that if the polluted water was disposed of in the lake this would kill all the aquatic life in the lake and have a long-lasting adverse effect on the lake and the surrounding area. Therefore, the Eastern state government took legal action against WRL in the Eastern state courts to prevent the disposal of the polluted water in the lake.

During the court action, WRL argued that if it was not allowed to dispose of the polluted water in the lake its mining operations in Stravia would become uneconomic and the mine would have to close. A small number of WRL's shareholders argued that it was better to close the mine than to pollute the lake.

The state courts granted the Eastern state government's request to prevent WRL disposing of the polluted water in the lake. However, upon appeal to the National Supreme Court, WRL has been granted permission to pump the polluted water into the lake as its licence imposes no restrictions.

Required:

Send the email as requested by the partner.

(45 minutes)

6 Non-market strategy

When businesses consider their stakeholders, they typically focus on the needs of those groups that help them directly gain competitive advantage, such as customers, suppliers and competitors – who collectively form the organisation's 'market environment'. In reality, however, competitive advantage can be built or lost outside of this market environment.

Non-market strategy refers to an organisation's relationship and interactions with it's 'non-market' environment – such as:

- governments
- regulators
- charities
- pressure groups
- the media
- the public at large.

Essentially non-market strategy sees the organisation as having social and political considerations, rather than simply economic concerns.

For example, governments can have a major impact on an organisation through their policies, such as through the setting or removal of subsidies or licenses to operate, employee legislation, environmental regulation and taxation policies.

Energy utility companies are under intense pressure from many governments (and the regulators that they have set up to monitor the energy industry) to not only provide affordable energy for their customers, but also to offer acceptable customer service levels and improve their environmental footprint. Failure on the behalf of the energy companies to meet these targets could lead to fines, other penalties, or even closure in extreme circumstances.

It is therefore vital that an organisation constantly scans its environment to identify these non-market issues in advance and hopefully create appropriate strategies to deal with them. Models such as PEST analysis (which we will examine in more detail in chapter 4) are vital tools to help with this.

However, it is easy for an organisation to feel that they must simply accept and try to manage non-market issues as they arise. In reality, organisations may wish to try and actually influence non-market issues. For instance, rather than simply waiting for governments to pass new laws, organisations may wish to influence political decision making – a process referred to as **corporate political activity**.

Porter's view on the influence of government

The influence of government on an industry

Porter identifies seven ways in which a government can affect the structure of an industry.

- Capacity expansion. The government can take actions to encourage firms or an industry as a whole to increase or cut capacity. Examples include capital allowances to encourage investment in equipment; regional incentives to encourage firms to locate new capacity in a particular area, and incentives to attract investment from overseas firms. The government is also (directly or indirectly) a supplier of infrastructure such as roads and railways, and this may influence expansion in a particular area.

- Demand. The government is a major customer of business in all areas of life and can influence demand by buying more or less. It can also influence demand by legislative measures. The tax system for cars is a good example: a change in the tax relief available for different engine sizes has a direct effect on the car manufacturers' product and the relative numbers of each type produced. Regulations and controls in an industry will affect the growth and profits of the industry, for example minimum product quality standards.

- Divestment and exit. A firm may wish to sell off a business to a foreign competitor or close it down, but the government might prevent this action because it is not in the public interest (there could be examples in health, defence, transport, education, agriculture and so on).

- Emerging industries may be controlled by the government. For instance, governments may control numbers of licences to create networks for next-generation mobile phones.

- Entry barriers. Government policy may restrict investment or competition or make it harder by use of quotas and tariffs for overseas firms. This kind of protectionism is generally frowned upon by the World Trade Organisation, but there may be political and economic circumstances in which it becomes necessary.

- Competition policy. Governments might devise policies which are deliberately intended to keep an industry fragmented, preventing one or two producers from having too much market share.

- New product adoption. Governments regulate the adoption of new products (e.g. new drugs) in some industries. They may go so far as to ban the use of a new product if it is not considered safe (a new form of transport, say). Policies may influence the rate of adoption of new products, e.g. the UK Government 'switched off' the analogue television networks in 2012, effectively forcing users to buy digital, cable or satellite services.

Illustration 7 – non market strategy in action

Toyota Prius

Toyota is the market leader in the production and sale of hybrid cars. In the US it successfully lobbied the California state government to allow drivers of its flagship Prius hybrid model use car lanes which were reserved for vehicles with two or more passengers – even if the Prius contained no passengers. It also convinced the state government to allow Prius owners to park for free in public owned carparks.

This lobbying required little investment from Toyota, but significantly boosted their green credentials, as well as giving their cars a competitive advantage in the market place. However, this was accomplished through their interactions with the government, meaning that this is an example of a non-market strategy.

Novartis

Non-market strategies do not have to only relate to political issues. Non-market strategy also looks at an organisation's interactions with wider society.

Novartis is a leading pharmaceutical company which tried for a number of years to gain a patent for one of its anti-cancer drugs (Glivec) in India. India denied a patent, stating that the drug was not a sufficient improvement over existing anti-cancer drugs to warrant a patent. As well as engaging in a high profile court case over the issue, Novartis also offered its new drug to needy Indian patients at a drastically reduced price, as part of its 'corporate citizenship' programmes. This helped to build its brand, improve its image with the wider public and thereby undermine its critics. As such, this is another example of a non-market strategy.

Corporate political activity

Corporate political activity (CPA) is the involvement by an organisation in the political process, with the aim of obtaining certain policy preferences.

CPA can take many forms, including:

- **Lobbying** – this can involve members of the organisation (or hired professional lobbyists) putting their case to government officials such as ministers, MPs or civil servants, in an attempt to win their support.

- **Directorships** – the business may give MPs or retired senior civil servants non-executive directorships, in the hope that they will take an interest in legislation that affects the business and will exercise their influence.

- **Influencing public opinion** – the business may attempt to change public perception on a key issue through advertising, media or even gathering petitions. The business will hope that public feeling will affect the legislative agenda.

- **Donations** – the business may fund individual candidates or whole political parties as a way of influencing future legislation.

- **Associations** – an organisation may try to act upon the government collectively through the creation of an association with other interested parties. In theory this collective action should have more influence on governmental policy than each company acting alone. In the UK examples of this within the business world include:
    - the Confederation of British Industry (CBI), representing the private business sector
    - the Institute of Directors (IOD)
    - the Federation of Small Businesses (FSB)

- **Legal action** – if an organisation believes that a proposed or enacted law is unfair, they may take direct action through the courts for its repeal.

Corporate political activity and ethics

Several of the methods that organisations can use as part of their corporate political activities (CPA) may raise ethical concerns. For example:

- donations to candidates or political parties could be seen as bribery, which would be highly unethical

- offering directorships to MPs or retired civil servants in order to gain favourable votes on relevant legislation could equally be seen as a form of bribery

- advertising campaigns, petitions or legal action could be seen as a way of large, well-resourced organisations bringing unfair pressure on the public or government on certain issues, simply for their own profit.

It is therefore very important that organisations consider what actions to take as part of their CPA. Organisations therefore need to carefully consider:

- relevant law (i.e. anti-bribery legislation) AND
- professional ethics (such as the CIMA code of ethics discussed in chapter 3)

when deciding on a strategy.

Test your understanding 11

K is a large, multinational manufacturer of food and drink products. It has manufacturing facilities in five countries, but it sells in almost ninety countries around the world – typically through local supermarkets.

Which of the following options are examples of non-market strategy for K? Select ALL that apply.

A   K participates in an annual charity fund-raising day in country H to help meet its corporate social responsibility duties

B   K has centralised its purchasing function, allowing it to improve its ability to get quantity discounts from suppliers

C   K has recently started an online petition in country G against proposed new restrictive health and safety laws

D   K's stores in country B have joined a trade association to help improve planning restrictions for retail stores

E   K has cut the prices of its goods by fifteen percent in country K in order to attract new shoppers

Strategic analysis: Mission, vision and stakeholders

7 Summary

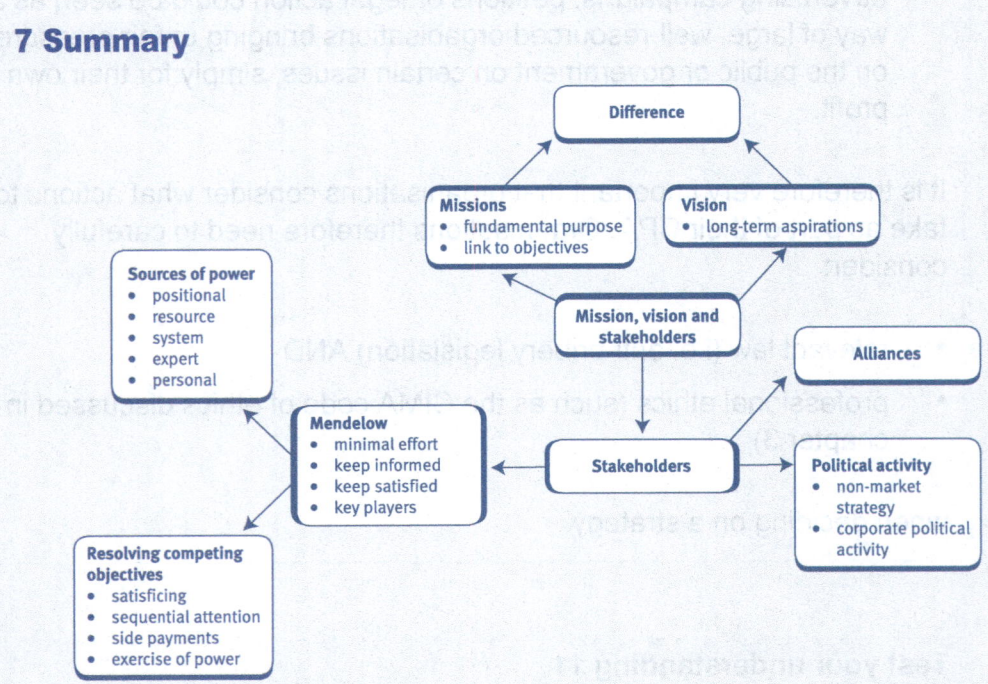

chapter 2

Test your understanding answers

Test your understanding 1

The correct answer is C

Mission statements will be of limited use if they are not widely publicised. If the Board fails to advertise the mission, it will have little immediate effect on other stakeholders, such as staff and customers.

However, it will give the Board a yardstick to measure their strategies against going forward. This should mean that their decisions are more consistent.

Test your understanding 2 – (Integration question)

This can be criticised as a mission statement for a number of reasons.

- It does not state the business areas in which the company intends to operate. As such it would not be useful to assess a strategy of market development, for example.
- It does not give a reason for the company's existence. In particular, the statement fails to give any indication why the company will be better than its competitors in what it does.
- It appears to focus on customer requirements only, and has nothing to say about other stakeholder groups, particularly employees and shareholders. It does not actually define who its customers are or who it wants its customers to be.
- It is dull. Short mission statements should be inspiring.
- It communicates nothing about the firm's values to employees.
- The terms 'top quality' and 'fair price' are unclear in their meaning. It is not clear what is meant by 'quality', nor what 'fair' is in terms of price. Assuming that it will be expensive to achieve top quality, how high might a fair price be? Does it mean fair to the customer or fair to the shareholders? Taken at face value there is a danger the company could make a loss!

In defence of the statement it does highlight the need to meet customer expectations in order to be successful.

On balance, however, the mission statement will fail to inspire employees, determine culture or assist strategic planning.

Strategic analysis: Mission, vision and stakeholders

Test your understanding 3

The correct answer is B

Objectives should be SMART – specific, measurable, attainable, relevant and timed.

Test your understanding 4

The correct answer is D

The objective asks for the company to 'delight' customers – which is not easy to measure. The chances of the company delighting its customers and the rest of the world seem low – especially by the end of the next financial year – suggesting that it is not attainable. It is also not directly relevant to the shareholders needs of raising profits and dividends.

The only aspect of an objective that is present is that there is a time limit built in.

Test your understanding 5 – JAA – (Case style)

Possible objectives for JAA could include:

Growth

JAA could set itself an objective to increase its **sales volume** – either in terms of the additional number of books it wishes to sell, or in terms of the percentage increase it wishes to see compared to its current sales volume.

The company could also consider setting itself an objective relating to its **market share.** As it operates in a highly competitive market, JAA may wish to set itself an objective to achieve a set percentage share of the total market for fiction and non–fiction books.

Innovation

To achieve this objective, JAA could set itself objectives relating to the **number of new books launched** each year. By bringing more new books to market than its competitors, it may be able to increase its market share and put pressure on other publishers.

JAA could also set objectives relating to the **number of new ways of selling its products** that it utilises. This could involve selling its books online, as electronic downloads or through tablet computers and electronic readers.

Marketing director's suggestion

The marketing director has suggested that the happiness of employees could be used as the sole objective for social responsibility. While it is correct that an employer who has good social responsibility should see an increase in staff happiness, this will not make a good objective on its own.

Firstly, social responsibility extends beyond how the company treats its employees. To get a full picture, the company needs to examine how its actions are impacting on other stakeholders and the wider environment.

In addition, employee happiness in itself is not directly measurable, meaning it cannot be a good objective. The marketing director needs to be more specific. For example, she could measure the staff turnover to get an indication of how staff feel about the company.

Test your understanding 6

The correct answer is C

By definition.

Strategic analysis: Mission, vision and stakeholders

Test your understanding 7

The correct answer is B

Local residents are highly affected by the LG's decisions and are willing to exert significant power (as evidenced by the high turnout at elections). This would indicate high power and high interest, making them key players.

Central government also seems to have high power as they control the funding to the LG. However, they rarely get involved in LG operations unless there is evidence of mismanagement. This would suggest they should be kept satisfied.

Test your understanding 8 – AYL – (Case style)

Nurses

Given the proposals to cut or freeze their pay in the coming period, nurses will have **high interest** in the proposals.

However, they are not unionised. This would tend to indicate a **lower level of power** as they lack a clear ability to co-ordinate strike action and could be relatively easy to replace due to their relatively low level of skill.

Under Mendelow's matrix, nurses should therefore be **kept informed**. The management of AYL need to try and convince them of the need for the pay freeze in order for the hospital to continue to function. This may, however, be difficult to do. This may lead to the nurses attempting to gain power by unionising and joining with the other workers in AYL, or alternatively lobbying the government.

Patients

If the proposed pay cuts are implemented, patients are unlikely to see a significant change in their level of care. This will give them a **low level of interest**.

In addition, while patients may collectively have an influence on the elected national government, there is no indication that patients have any kind of organisation, indicating a **low level of power**.

Mendelow's matrix would therefore suggest that the managers of AYL should adopt a **minimal effort** approach with regards to patients in this area. They are likely to accept what the management tell them as long as it does not affect their level of care. Should it do so, they may become more interested.

Other members of hospital staff

As it stands, there is no evidence that any other types of hospital staff will be affected by the pay cuts. Given the fact that the nurses are not part of the main union that represents the other members of staff, it is likely that they will have **low interest**.

However, should they choose to take an interest, the remaining members of staff will probably have **high power**. They are unionised and include key members of staff (skilled doctors). This means that any strike action could be extremely damaging to the hospital.

As such, the managers of AYL should adopt an approach of **keeping them satisfied**. By reassuring other workers that their circumstances are not affected by the cuts, AYL may be able to prevent them taking an active interest in the proposals.

Central government

The government ultimately controls the budget for the hospital. This gives it **high power**.

In addition, it is currently looking for ways to reduce its expenditure, so it has **high interest** in the success of AYL's proposals.

AYL have no choice but to adopt a **key players** approach. They need to fully communicate their plans to the central government and ensure they are happy with the proposals. If the central government recommends changes to the proposed cuts, AYL's managers would be wise to accept them.

Test your understanding 9

The correct answer is A

Last year, L focused on giving herself a sufficient return. This year, she is making other stakeholders (her staff) a priority.

Strategic analysis: Mission, vision and stakeholders

Test your understanding 10 – WRL – (Case style)

To: A. Scott

From: M. Williams

Date: 10/05/20XX

Subject: Re: WRL Meeting this afternoon

Please find below my analysis of the points you wished me to examine for WRL. Please let me know if you wish to discuss any of these points in more detail.

Kind regards

A. Scott

(i) **Categorisation of three stakeholder groups in WRL**

Eastern State Government/Local residents – High Interest, Low power (keep informed)

The Eastern state government, representing the local population of the area around the mine has proven it has high levels of interest in the project.

On a positive note, the mine will provide local employment as well as a payment from the central government of $1m. However, it will also have a significant adverse effect on the local environment, which has caused the state government to take legal action against WRL.

The Eastern state government seems to have low levels of power. It was not part of the negotiations and it appears that after its unsuccessful legal action against WRL it has no further power to prevent the mine from going ahead.

Central Stravian government – Low Interest, High Power (keep satisfied)

The central government seems to have been unconcerned with possible effects on the environment as they have not built any controls into the licence with WRL. After the initial negotiations were concluded, the central government seems to have taken relatively little interest in the problems that have arisen with the project.

Should they decide to take an active interest in the future, however, they would undoubtedly have significant power over the project and could ultimately decide to close it down.

The Central government's interest may increase if the impact on the environment is a concern for local residents – meaning that it is possible they may become key players in the future.

WRL Shareholders – Low Interest, High Power (keep satisfied)

RL's shareholders ultimately own the company and therefore they have significant control over its actions. Should a significant number of shareholders become unhappy with the operations in Stravia, it would put pressure on the company to withdraw.

In addition, as the investors in the company, they will also have a great deal of interest in WRL providing them with sufficient return on their investment. However, only a small number of shareholders have indicated any concern over the potential pollution of the lake in Stravia. The majority seem uninterested in the pollution, as long as their returns are sufficient.

(ii) **Advice on the actions needed to resolve competing stakeholder objectives**

The key conflict here is between the needs of the bulk of WRL's shareholders to make a profit and the concerns of the Eastern state government and a small minority of shareholders over pollution in the surrounding area. Unfortunately, this conflict is not easily resolved.

Reduction of environmental impact – One possible method is to investigate ways of treating the polluted water before it is pumped into the lake. While this may be more expensive, it may allow a compromise position to be found whereby the damage to the lake is minimised but the project is still economically viable for WRL.

Publicity – Failing this, WRL may need to attempt a damage-limitation exercise. This could involve the publicising of the positive effects of the mine on the local economy and residents. The Eastern state government presumably represents the needs of the residents, so highlighting the benefits of the new mine may go a long way towards calming their fears.

Withdrawal – Alternatively, given WRL's insistence on being a good corporate citizen, it could opt to pull out of Stravia completely and look for alternative investments that will not pollute the environment to such a degree.

Strategic analysis: Mission, vision and stakeholders

It is unclear whether many alternatives are available for WRL to pursue. If not, this may not be acceptable to shareholders, who for the most part seem to support the Stravian mine. There may also be financial penalties for WRL withdrawing from its agreement with the central government.

WRL could use the model proposed by Cyert & March, who examined possible ways to deal with stakeholder conflict. These include:

- Satisficing – this would involve keeping the most powerful stakeholders happy – presumably in WRL's case, this would be its shareholders.

- Sequential attention – this involves WRL taking turns prioritising stakeholders needs. This would be unlikely to be useful in this scenario due to the conflicting nature of the stakeholders needs.

- Side payments – if WRL is unable to deal with the Eastern State Government's needs, it could look at other ways of compensating them. Perhaps offering additional payments would appease the local government.

- Exercise of power – ultimately if, as in this case, no agreement can be reached, the most powerful stakeholders can exercise their influence and force a settlement.

Conclusion – It should be noted that ultimately there may be no way to completely resolve this stakeholder conflict. In these cases, stakeholder analysis would indicate the need to side with the most powerful groups – the 'key players' – who in this case would be the shareholders.

(iii) **Discussion of the extent to which WRL's mission statement is consistent with its plan to pollute the lake.**

WRL's mission statement breaks down into three key statements. The proposed strategy in Stravia should be analysed to see whether it conforms to these.

To make the maximum possible profit for its shareholders

WRL obviously feels that this project is profitable for investors. After negotiations with the local government it has decided to proceed and feels it will only become uneconomic if the waste water has to be disposed of in an environmentally friendly way.

Causing the least damage to the environment

WRL would appear to not be meeting this requirement due to the damage about to be done to the lake and local environment. However, given the vague nature of the mission statement, WRL may argue this is the least possible damage to the environment, given the nature of their business. The damage to the lake could be seen as the least damage they can do whilst still meeting their other goal of maximising investor returns.

Be a good corporate citizen

Again, the answer to whether WRL is meeting this part of its mission statement is more complex than it might initially appear.

Certainly the effect on the local environment of the polluted water would not be consistent with good corporate citizenship.

However, it could be argued that WRL is also providing significant investment in the local area – with jobs for local workers as well as the $1m payout that the Eastern state government received.

Contributing to the local economy could be seen as meeting the requirement for good corporate citizenship.

Test your understanding 11

The correct answers are A, C and D

Remember that non-market activities will not relate to stakeholders such as suppliers (option B) and customers (option E). A, C and D all relate to activities that relate to society (option A) or political issues (options C and D), which would form part of a non-market strategy.

Strategic analysis: Mission, vision and stakeholders

chapter 3

Strategic analysis: Ethics and corporate social responsibility

Chapter learning objectives

Lead	Component
A1. Evaluate the influence of key external factors on an organisation's strategy	(c) Discuss the drivers of external demands for environmental sustainability and corporate social responsibility and the organisation's response to these.
A2. Evaluate ethical issues arising from the organisation's interaction with its environment	(a) Evaluate ethical issues and their resolution within a range of organisational contexts

Indicative syllabus content

- External demands for sustainability and responsible business practices and ways to respond to these.
- Business ethics and the CIMA Code of Ethics for Professional Accountants (Parts A and B) in the context of the implementation of strategic plans.

Strategic analysis: Ethics and corporate social responsibility

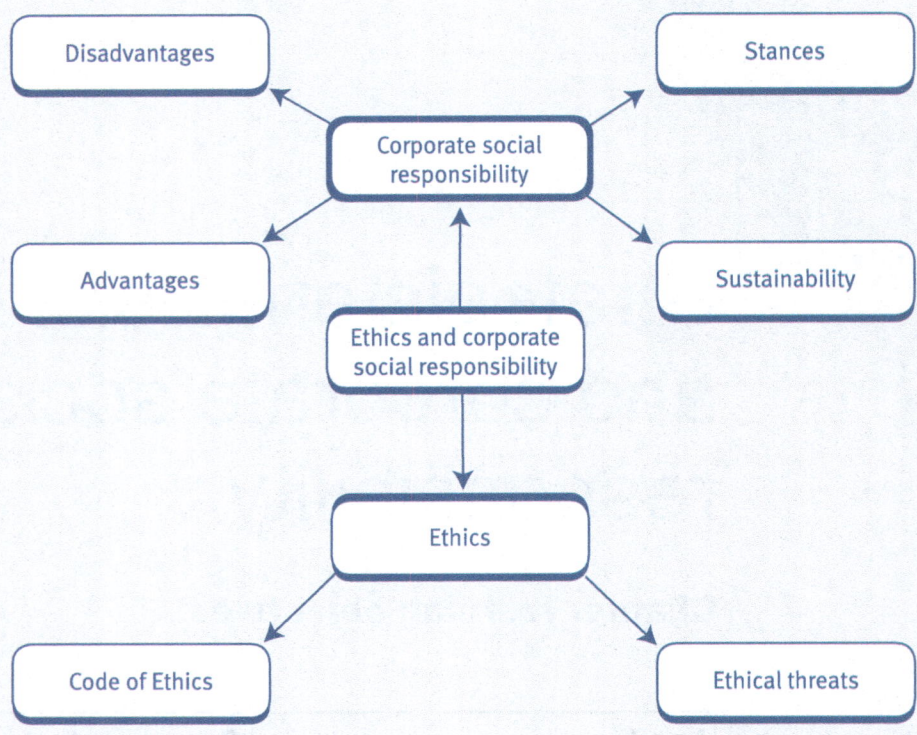

1 What is corporate social responsibility?

In the modern world, it is seen as being increasingly important to consider how organisations manage their business processes to have an overall positive impact on society.

It is worth noting that corporate social responsibility (CSR) is distinct from ethics. Business ethics comprise principles and standards that govern behaviour in the world of business.

 CSR, however, refers to a **firm's obligation to maximise its positive impacts upon stakeholders while minimising the negative effects**.

The extent to which the organisation fulfils the economic, legal, ethical and charitable responsibilities placed on it by its stakeholders will determine to what extent it is seen as having good CSR.

The problem is that there is no one definition or theory of CSR.

Consider the following points. Is it ethical to:

- Experiment on animals?
- Drill for oil?
- Build roads through countryside?
- Pay high salaries to senior executives?

Different individuals will have different views on each of these issues.

As far as possible, managers have to take account of a range of differing viewpoints when deciding on their strategies. In addition, there is always the need to balance a company's responsibility to society with its responsibility to earn financial returns for its investors.

Illustration 1 – corporate social responsibility issues

Nikon is a well-known multinational company that specialises in the manufacture of cameras and other photographic and visual equipment. The company's corporate social responsibility (CSR) statement (extracts of which are shown below) highlights a number of key examples of issues that companies need to consider when thinking about CSR.

Nikon CSR charter (extracts)

Sound corporate activities

The Nikon Group endeavors to comply with international regulations, related laws, and internal rules, exercise sound and fair corporate practices, earn the trust of stakeholders such as customers, shareholders, employees, business partners, and society. The Group will maintain constructive relationships with administrative bodies, remaining politically neutral and complying with laws, and will not engage in relationships with individuals or groups that threaten social order or safety.

Provision of valuable goods and services for society

The Nikon Group will provide valuable products and services with superior quality and safety to society, endeavoring to increase the satisfaction and trust of our customers and contributing to the healthy development of society.

Respect for human beings

The Nikon Group will respect diversity and individual human rights and provide a healthy and safe working environment in which all persons receive fair treatment without discrimination. It will also oppose enforced labor and child labor and respect fundamental human rights as well as workers' rights.

Protection of the natural environment

The Nikon Group will proactively engage in environmental efforts and work to protect the natural environment, as these are common issues for all of mankind.

Responsibility to society as a corporate citizen

The Nikon Group will carry out corporate activities that take into account the cultures and practices of each country and region and proactively engage in activities that contribute to society as a good corporate citizen.

Socially responsible behavior within the supply chain

The Nikon Group will encourage socially responsible behavior within its supply chain.

Transparent operating activities

The Nikon Group will communicate extensively with customers, shareholders, employees, business partners, and society and disclose business information in a timely and fair manner. It will also conduct reliable financial reporting through accurate accounting processes.

Responsibility of top management

Top management and employees in managerial positions within each department must understand that they play an essential role in fulfilling the spirit of this Charter and thus, in addition to leading by example, they must ensure that this information is disseminated to everyone in the Group and all related parties.

Arguments against CSR

It can be argued that companies should not pursue corporate social responsibility. Milton Friedman argues that:

'The business of business is business.'

This means that the primary purpose of a business is to try and earn a profit. In a company, for instance, the managers have been employed in order to earn the owners of the business a return on their investment.

As such, it is a manager's duty to act in a way that maximises shareholder wealth, while conforming to all relevant laws and customs. If a manager does anything that is not directly related to wealth maximisation, he is failing in his responsibilities to the owners and therefore acting unethically.

For example, it can be argued that it is not right for a manager to donate any company funds to charity. The manager should instead work to maximise the return to the owner. If the owner wishes to make donations to charity, he can do so out of his earnings from the business.

In addition, it can be argued that maximising the wealth of business owners is, in itself, socially responsible. This is because:

- Increased returns will lead to increased tax payments made to the state. These can then be passed on to 'worthy causes'.
- A high proportion of company shares are owned by pension funds. This means that any gains will go to help provide pensions to individuals who may well be disadvantaged.

Don't forget that there may also be practical reasons why a business chooses not to pursue CSR. These can include:

- Increased cost of sourcing materials from ethical sources (e.g. Fairtrade products or free-range eggs).
- Having to turn away business from customers considered to be unethical (e.g. an 'ethical' bank may choose not to invest in a company that manufactures weapons).
- The management time that can be taken up by CSR planning and implementation.

Arguments for CSR

Not everyone agrees with Friedman's statements. There are a number of reasons why many businesses feel that CSR is a vital part of their strategy. These include:

- A key part of running a successful business is the ability to offer customers and consumers what they need. One of those needs is often a requirement for socially responsible behaviour from the organisation.

  Basically, **having good CSR can attract customers**! This can be because good CSR tends to enhance a company's reputation and therefore its brand. It can also be used a basis for differentiation in the market place – given the choice, many customers will prefer to trade with a company they feel is ethical.

- Good CSR is likely to involve good working conditions for employees, allowing the business to **attract a higher calibre of staff**.
- Avoiding discrimination against workers is likely to give the company **access to a wider human resource base**.
- Avoiding pollution will tend to save companies in the long run – many governments are now **fining or increasing taxes of more polluting businesses**.
- Sponsorship and charitable donations are tax deductible, improve staff morale and can be seen as a **form of advertising**.

Ultimately, having good CSR can **increase the financial value of the business**. Remember that the value of the business will be the present value of its perceived future cash flows discounted at its risk-adjusted cost of capital.

- Good CSR will reduce the risk of adverse environmental reactions against the company. Anything that reduces risk should lower the risk adjusted cost of capital, increasing the value of the company.
- A socially responsible business will be allowed to operate for longer in society. This will mean that there will be more years of cash flows in the future. This would also increase the value of the company.

2 Approaches to corporate social responsibility

If an organisation wishes to consider how it should approach corporate social responsibility, there are a number of models that it can use to help it.

Carroll's corporate social responsibility model

Carroll (The Pyramid of Corporate Social Responsibility: Toward the Moral Management of Organizational Stakeholders), devised a four-part model of CSR:

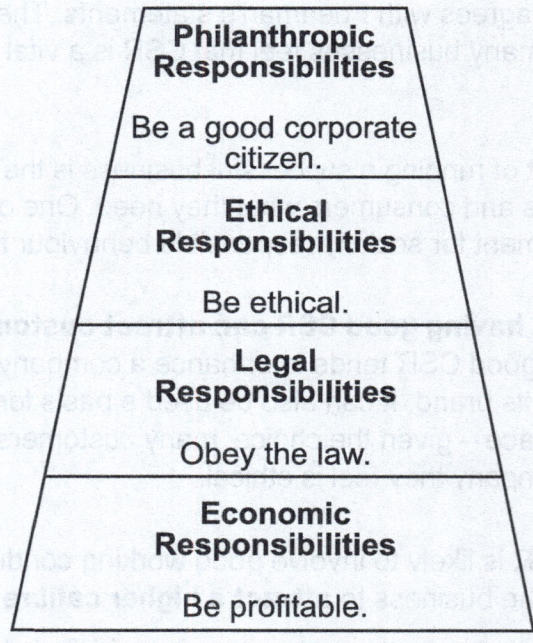

True CSR requires satisfying all four parts consecutively.

Economic responsibility – be profitable

- This is the fundamental level – all other levels rest on this.
- Shareholders demand a reasonable return.
- Employees want safe and fairly paid jobs.
- Customers demand quality at a fair price.

Legal responsibility – obey the law

- The law is a baseline for operating within society.
- It is an accepted rule book for company operations.

Ethical responsibility – do what is right and fair

- This relates to doing what is right, just and fair.
- Actions taken in this area provide a reaffirmation of social legitimacy.
- This is naturally beyond the previous two levels.

Philanthropic responsibility – be a good corporate citizen

- Relates to discretionary behaviour to improve the lives of others.
- Charitable donations and recreational facilities.
- Sponsoring the arts and sports events.

The different parts will help the management of an organisation to understand the various obligations that society expects from them.

Carroll suggests four possible strategies (or philosophies) that the organisation can adopt with regard to corporate social responsibility.

Reaction

The corporation denies any responsibility for social issues, arguing that it is not to blame or required to act.

Defence

The corporation admits responsibility but fights it, doing the very least that seems to be required. Typically this is only done as an attempt to defend the organisation's current position.

Strategic analysis: Ethics and corporate social responsibility

Accommodation

The corporation accepts responsibility and does what is demanded of it by relevant groups.

Proaction

The corporation seeks to go beyond industry norms and anticipates future expectations by doing more than is currently expected. The organisation attempts to improve society.

> **Illustration 2 – Carroll's philosophies in action**
>
> Q is a large, multinational company which manufactures a popular carbonated soft drink – Yu. Yu is one of the leading soft drinks in country H and accounts for around 75% of Q's profits. In recent months it has been reported in the international press that one of the flavourings in Yu has been linked to an increased risk of cancer, though at much higher levels than those found in Yu. This has led to Yu being criticised by pressure groups, who have already complained about Yu's high sugar content which they claim is not healthy for Q's customers (though Yu's sales continue to rise). The Government of country H has not stated that they will ban the ingredient, though it has indicated concern over rising levels of obesity in the local population.
>
> Q's management could consider adopting any of Carroll's four corporate social responsibility philosophies with regards to Yu.
>
> **Reaction**
>
> Q denies that there is any problem with Yu whatsoever. Its managers release a statement arguing that there is clearly no health risk associated with consumption of Yu by customers as the government has not made the product illegal. Q then ignores the issue and makes no changes to Yu's recipe.
>
> **Defence**
>
> Q's management accepts that there is a potential risk from the high sugar content and the flavouring identified by the international press. It therefore places additional health information on the bottle about the calorie content of the drink, along with a 'suggested amount' that should be consumed each day. It argues that this suggested consumption level would also reduce any risk to the consumer of the flavouring identified in the international press.
>
> The pressure groups claim this is insufficient as most consumers do not read the label on soft drinks they consume.

Accommodation

Q's managers form a focus group made up of consumers, government health officials and pressure group representatives to discuss their concerns. After lengthy discussions to ensure it fully understands their needs, Q lowers the sugar content of Yu and replaces it with natural low-calorie sweeteners to reduce the calorie content but without altering the taste of the product. It also changes the recipe to eliminate the need for the flavouring in question to ensure the government and consumer confidence is maintained.

Proaction

Q undertakes detailed analysis of its product and the impact of all the ingredients it uses on consumer health. Unlike its competitors, Q significantly reduces the level of sugar in Yu, as well as eliminating all artificial additives in an attempt to reduce any negative health impact of consuming Yu.

Test your understanding 1

L operates a popular chain of gyms. As well as standard exercise equipment, L's gyms also have personal trainers that work with clients for an extra monthly fee (the personal trainer earns 25% of this, with L keeping the remainder). L also has cafes in each of its gyms, which serve food and drink to gym members.

L is aware that some customers feel that they are not seeing any benefit from attending its gyms or seeing a personal trainer. One customer recently complained that 'L's cafes offer food that is high in fat and salt, meaning customers that eat there will get little benefit from their earlier workout. L's personal trainers also have an incentive to ensure that clients make slow process so that they can continue to earn revenue from the client for as long as possible.'

L has decided to use Carroll's corporate social philosophies model to decide how to react to these issues.

Strategic analysis: Ethics and corporate social responsibility

> Which of the following approaches are most consistent with an accommodation strategy? Select all that apply.
>
> A   If the service offered to customers does not breach any local laws, no further action needs to be taken by L
>
> B   Admit that the service being offered to customers is not appropriate or socially responsible
>
> C   Add nutritional information to the menu in the cafe to provide more information to customers
>
> D   Redesign personal trainer pay in order to remove any incentive to ensure clients make slow progress
>
> E   Introduce a healthier menu for customers in the cafe

Ethical stances (Johnson, Scholes and Whittington)

Johnson, Scholes and Whittington (Exploring corporate strategy) define an ethical stance as:

'The extent to which an organisation will exceed its minimum obligations to stakeholders.'

There are four possible ethical stances:

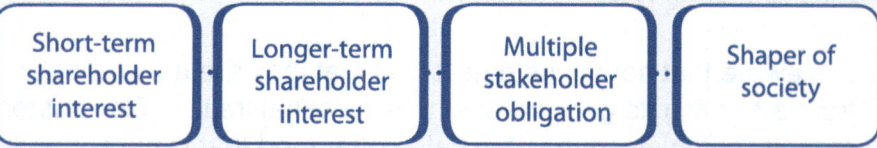

Short-term shareholder interest (STSI)

This ethical stance has a short-term focus in that it aims to maximise profits in the financial year. Organisations with this ethical stance believe that it is the role of governments to set the legal minimum standard, and anything delivered above this would be to the detriment of their taxpayers.

Longer-term shareholder interest (LTSI)

This ethical stance takes broadly the same approach as the short-term shareholder interest except that it takes a longer-term view. Hence it may be appropriate to incur additional cost now so as to achieve higher returns in the future. An example could be a public service donating some funds to a charity in the belief that it will save the taxpayer the costs associated with providing the entire service should the charity cease to work. Hence this ethical stance is aware of other stakeholders and their impact on long-term profit or cost.

Multiple stakeholder obligation (MSO)

This ethical stance accepts that the organisation exists for more than simply making a profit, or providing services at a minimal cost to taxpayers. It takes the view that all organisations have a role to play in society and so they must take account of all the stakeholders' interests. Hence they explicitly involve other stakeholders, and believe that they have a purpose beyond the financial.

Shaper of society

This ethical stance is ideologically driven and sees its vision as being the focus for all its actions. Financial and other stakeholders' interests are secondary to the overriding purpose of the organisation.

> **Test your understanding 2**
>
> J runs a business which sells flowers from a small shop. He ensures that all of his flowers are sourced from ethically responsible suppliers, even though this is not legally required. While these flowers are more expensive to purchase, he feels that his ethical approach differentiates him from his rivals and allows him to charge a premium price.
>
> Which ONE of Johnson, Scholes and Whittington's ethical stances is J adopting?
>
> A   Shaper of society
>
> B   Multiple stakeholder obligation
>
> C   Longer-term shareholder interest
>
> D   Short-term shareholder interest

3 Sustainability

One aspect of CSR that is also becoming increasingly important is sustainability.

Sustainability is the use of resources in such a way that they do not compromise the needs of future generations. It also involves not polluting the environment at a rate faster than they can be absorbed.

There are many examples of this. For example, some logging companies plant a tree for every one they fell.

Other companies try to make their products easy to recycle, helping to ensure that materials are reused rather than wasted. The computer manufacturer Apple has used this as part of its marketing approach for some years.(http://www.apple.com/recycling/)

The reason that sustainability is so important for many businesses is that acting in a sustainable manner not only helps look after the environment and the wider community, but it strengthens the business and helps ensure its long-term survival.

It is worth noting that sustainability is increasingly being seen as important within the public sector. Ensuring that goods and services procured by the public sector are sustainable can help meet environmental goals across government, save considerable amounts of public money; and help support innovation and economic growth. This will involve taking account of a wide range of costs, such as pollution impacts, carbon emissions and waste disposal.

The difficulty for many businesses is that many companies focus on short term gains, rather than the long-term sustainability of the business and its environment. This is often evident in businesses that offer senior managers bonuses based on short-term or annual performance.

However, it should be noted that sustainability can lead to cost savings for an organisation in the short term. For example, an organisation that reduces packaging on its products may have a positive impact on the environment by generating less waste, but it will also reduce its costs, thereby improving profits.

4 Incorporating sustainability and CSR into strategy

CIMA itself has been heavily involved in identifying and discussing the implications of sustainability for the business. To this end, in 2010 they published a research article discussing this.

The article came to six key conclusions:

- Strong ethical principles that go beyond upholding the law can add great value to a brand, whereas failure to do the right thing can cause social, economic and environmental damage, undermining a company's long–term prospects in the process.

- Once they have adopted an ethical approach, companies will often find there are bottom-line benefits from demonstrating high ethical standards.

- The ethical tone comes from the top.

- High-quality management information on social, environmental and ethical performance is vital for monitoring the environmental and social impacts of a company and for compiling connected reports showing how effective its governance arrangements are.

- Corporate communications and reporting on sustainability need to do more than just pay lip service to the green agenda. They need to provide hard evidence of the positive impact on society, the environment and the strategic returns for the business, and how any negative effects are being addressed.

- Management accountants have a particular ethical responsibility to promote an ethics-based culture that doesn't permit practises such as bribery.

The full report can be found here:

http://www.cimaglobal.com/Thought-leadership/Research-topics/Sustainability/incorporating-ethics-into-strategy.

Illustration 3 – Corporate social responsibility in action

Corporate social responsibility is seen as vital for many organisations. One company that is often hailed as a leader in this area is Ben & Jerry's – a US based manufacturer of ice-cream, frozen yoghurt and sorbet. The company has stated that 'business has a responsibility to the community and the environment'.

Ben & Jerry's CSR has included the following:

- Fair Trade ingredients – this ensures that suppliers of many of the company's raw materials enjoy safe working conditions, reasonable work hours and are paid fairly.

- Ethically sourced supplies – as well as a commitment to Fair Trade, the company also ensures, where possible, that it sources ingredients from suppliers who share its values. For example, Ben & Jerry's has historically sourced free-range eggs and sustainably produced dairy for its products.

- Community work – the company has engaged with communities to improve sustainability. Ben & Jerry's Vermont Dairy Farm Sustainability Project was launched in 1999 and sought to develop practical methods for dairy farms to reduce nitrogen and phosphorous run-off in order to prove water quality and overall sustainability.

- Corporate philanthropy – the company donates a portion of its pre-tax profits to corporate philanthropy via, in part, the Ben & Jerry's Foundation.

Further CIMA information on sustainability

In December 2010, CIMA collaborated with the AICPA and CICA in a report entitled 'Evolution of corporate sustainability practices'.

Some key issues that this report raised include:

General

Business sustainability is about ensuring that organisations implement strategies that contribute to long–term success. Organisations that act in a sustainable manner not only help to maintain the well–being of the planet and people, they also create businesses that will survive and thrive in the long run.

The accounting profession can play an important role in this. Accountants can serve as leading agents for change by applying their skills and competencies to develop sustainability strategies, facilitate effective implementation, accurate measurement and credible business reporting.

Why do businesses have sustainability plans?

According to research conducted by CIMA, the key reasons include:

- **Compliance** – the need to comply with laws and regulations.
- **Reputational risk** – companies are concerned with how stakeholders will view them if they fail to act in a sustainable manner.
- **Cost-cutting and efficiency** – acting in a sustainable manner (for example becoming more energy-efficient) can help to reduce business expenditure. This is especially valuable for smaller companies.

Ten elements of organisational sustainability

The following areas are considered crucial to the successful embedding of sustainability within an organisation. It is worth noting that the accounting function will be useful in a number of these areas.

Strategy and oversight

- Board and senior management commitment.
- Understanding and analysing the key sustainability drivers for the organisation.
- Integrating the key sustainability drivers into the organisation's strategy.

Execution and alignment

- Ensuring that sustainability is the responsibility of everyone within the organisation (not just a specific department).
- Breaking down the sustainability targets and objectives for the organisation as a whole into targets and objectives which are meaningful for individual subsidiaries, divisions and departments.
- Processes that enable sustainability issues to be taken into account clearly and consistently in day-to-day decision-making.
- Extensive and effective sustainability training.

Performance and reporting

- Including sustainability targets and objectives in performance appraisal.
- Champions to promote sustainability and celebrate success.
- Monitoring and reporting sustainability performance.

The full report can be found here:

http://www.cimaglobal.com/Documents/
Thought_leadership_docs/CIMA_AICPA_CICA sustainability_report.pdf

Test your understanding 3 – Router – (Case style)

You are A. North – and you have recently been provided with the following letter from one of your company's major clients, Router plc (a major mining company).

Letter from Router plc

H. West
21 Epp Way
Helway
Helland
HDH 67TY

Dear Mr North,

Router plc has an opportunity to mine for gold in a remote and sparsely populated area. The mining process proposed in this instance would remove all vegetation from the land concerned. After mining has finished, there will remain substantial lakes of poisonous water which will remain toxic for a hundred years.

The mining process is profitable, given the current high world value of gold. However, if the company were to reinstate the mined land, the process would be extremely unprofitable. The company has received permission from the government to carry out the mining. The few local residents are opposed to the mining.

As you know, our mission statement says that we will 'endeavour to make the maximum possible profit for our shareholders while recognising our wider responsibility to society'.

Several investors have raised concerns regarding our mission statement, suggesting that it is 'contradictory'. I would appreciate your thoughts on this.

We are aware that our decision relating to the above gold mining opportunity could potentially cause a conflict between our objectives. We would be grateful for your advice on how we can deal with strategies that cause such a conflict.

Finally, could you please outline the ethical issues surrounding the proposed gold mining operations for our consideration.

Thank you for your help and we look forward to your urgent response.

Kind regards

H. West

Required:

Draft a response to the above letter.

(45 minutes)

5 CIMA's code of ethics

Introduction

CIMA's code of ethics is an 81-page document that offers guidance on how to recognise and respond to tricky ethical situations. You are only expected to be aware of the main concepts in the code in the exam. The code is structured as follows:

- Part A: fundamental principles and general application of the code
- Part B: professional accountants in business
- Part C: professional accountants in public practice.

The full content of the code can be found at:

http://www.cimaglobal.com/Professional-ethics/

However, the E3 syllabus only examines parts A and B of the code.

Section 100.1 of part A states that professional accountants should "act in the public interest" and therefore "responsibility is not exclusively to satisfy the needs of an individual client or employer".

Strategic analysis: Ethics and corporate social responsibility

The code provides a conceptual framework with guidance on fundamental ethical principles:

- Integrity
- Objectivity
- Professional competence and due care
- Confidentiality
- Professional behaviour

> **Fundamental ethical principles**
>
> ### Integrity
>
> Integrity implies fair dealing and truthfulness.
>
> Members are also required not to be associated with any form of communication or report where the information is considered to be:
>
> - materially false or to contain misleading statements
> - provided recklessly
> - incomplete such that the report or communication becomes misleading by this omission.
>
> ### Objectivity
>
> Accountants need to ensure that their business/professional judgement is not compromised because of bias or conflict of interest.
>
> However, there are many situations where objectivity can be compromised, so a full list cannot be provided. Accountants are warned to always ensure that their objectivity is intact in any business/professional relationship.
>
> ### Professional competence and due care
>
> There are two main considerations under this heading:
>
> (1) Accountants are required to have the necessary professional knowledge and skill to carry out work for clients.
>
> (2) Accountants must follow applicable technical and professional standards when providing professional services.

Appropriate levels of professional competence must first be attained and then maintained. Maintenance implies keeping up to date with business and professional developments, and in many institutes completion of an annual return confirming that continued professional development (CPD) requirements have been met.

Where provision of a professional service has inherent limitations (e.g. reliance on client information) then the client must be made aware of this.

Confidentiality

The principle of confidentiality implies two key considerations for accountants:

(1) Information obtained in a business relationship is not disclosed outside the firm unless there is a proper and specific authority or unless there is a professional right or duty to disclose.

(2) Confidential information acquired during the provision of professional services is not used to personal advantage.

The need to maintain confidentiality is normally extended to cover the accountants' social environment, information about prospective clients and employers, and where business relationships have terminated. Basically there must always be a reason for disclosure before confidential information is provided to a third party.

The main reasons for disclosure are when:

(1) it is permitted by law and authorised by the client

(2) it is required by law, e.g. during legal proceedings or disclosing information regarding infringements of law

(3) there is professional duty or right to disclose (when not barred by law), e.g. provision of information to the professional institute or compliance with ethical requirements.

Ethical considerations on disclosure

The accountant needs to consider the extent to which third parties may be adversely affected by any disclosure.

The amount of uncertainty inherent in the situation may affect the extent of disclosure – more uncertainty may mean disclosure is limited or not made at all.

The accountant needs to ensure that disclosure is made to the correct person or persons.

Professional behaviour

Accountants must comply with all relevant laws and regulations.

There is also a test whereby actions suggested by a third party which would bring discredit to the profession should also be avoided.

An accountant is required to treat all people contacted in a professional capacity with courtesy and consideration. Similarly, any marketing activities should not bring the profession into disrepute.

Test your understanding 4

Under the CIMA Code of Ethics, members are not allowed to be associated with any 'materially false or misleading statements'.

Which ONE of the fundamental ethical principles does this statement relate to?

A   Integrity
B   Professional competence
C   Objectivity
D   Professional behaviour

Test your understanding 5 – (Integration question)

Explain why each of the following actions appears to be in conflict with fundamental ethical principles.

(1) An advertisement for a firm of accountants states that their audit services are cheaper and more comprehensive than a rival firm.

(2) An accountant prepares a set of accounts prior to undertaking the audit of those accounts.

(3) A director discusses an impending share issue with colleagues at a golf club dinner.

(4) The finance director attempts to complete the company's taxation computation following the acquisition of some foreign subsidiaries.

(5) A financial accountant confirms that a report on his company is correct, even though the report omits to mention some important liabilities.

(6) You believe your colleague has asked you to include what you believe to be misleading information in your forecast

(7) Your analysis of a strategic proposal suggests that profitability will be improved by making 30 people redundant.

(8) You can outsource your manufacturing to a country where labour costs are much lower.

(9) Your country is allowed, legally, to dump its waste into a river. This will kill all aquatic life along a 50-mile stretch.

Resolving ethical conflicts

The code is clear that the professional accountant should respond to an ethical conflict. Inaction or silence may well be a further breach of the code.

Ethical conflicts can be resolved as follows:

(1) Gather all relevant facts.

(2) Establish ethical issues involved.

(3) Refer to relevant fundamental principles.

(4) Follow established internal procedures.

(5) Investigate alternative courses of action.

(6) Consult with appropriate persons within the firm.

(7) Obtain advice from professional institutes.

(8) If the matter is still unresolved, consider withdrawing from the engagement team/assignment/role.

Additional resources

For more examples of real-life ethical dilemmas and their recommended solutions, see the CIMA website.

http://www.cimaglobal.com/Professional-ethics/Ethics/Responsible-business/Ethical-dilemma/Case-studies/

Strategic analysis: Ethics and corporate social responsibility

Test your understanding 6 – (Integration question)

Explain your response to the following ethical threats.

(1) Your employer asks you to suggest to a junior manager that they will receive a large bonus for working overtime on a project to hide liabilities from the financial statements.

(2) In selecting employees for a new division, you are advised to unfairly discriminate against one section of the workforce.

(3) You have been asked to prepare the management accounts for a subsidiary located in South America in accordance with specific requirements of that jurisdiction. In response to your comment that you do not understand the accounting requirements of that jurisdiction, your supervisor states 'no problem, no one will notice a few thousand dollars' error anyway'.

Test your understanding 7 – ABC – (Case style)

One of your colleagues, a junior accountant at ABC Ltd has sent you the following email:

Email
To: J. Bank
From: A. Halifax
Date: 15/06/XX
Subject: Professional ethics

Hi J,

I was hoping you could give me some advice!

The IT Director of ABC Ltd asked me undertake a cost-benefit analysis of a proposed new IT system. The IT Director will use this analysis to try and convince the Board of Directors of ABC that they should invest in the new system.

As part of my analysis, I found that the new system will not run properly on ABC's existing computers. This means that ABC would have to replace the majority of their desktop computers and servers, leading to an excess of costs over benefits.

The IT Director has suggested that I downplay the costs of replacing the IT infrastructure as he was sure that he 'could find a work-around' that would allow the existing computers to use the new software, though he was currently uncertain how this would be accomplished.

chapter 3

> The IT Director has told me that he 'expects' the cost-benefit analysis to show a favourable result for the new system and has indicated that my future promotion prospects may depend on this being the case.
>
> Could you email me back right away and explain the CIMA fundamental ethical principles that I would be breaching if I agree to the IT Director's request. I need to know before I decide on the appropriate course of action.
>
> Thanks for your help!
>
> A
>
> **Required:**
>
> Reply to the email as requested.
>
> **(15 minutes)**

Ethical threats and safeguards

Ethical threat	Safeguard
Conflict between requirements of the employer and the fundamental principles For example, acting contrary to laws or regulations or against professional or technical standards.	• Obtaining advice from the employer, professional organisation or professional advisor • The employer providing a formal dispute resolution process • Legal advice
Preparation and reporting on information Accountants need to prepare/report on information fairly, objectively and honestly. However, the accountant may be pressurised to provide misleading information.	• Consultation with superiors in the employing company • Consultation with those charged with governance • Consultation with the relevant professional body

105

Having sufficient expertise Accountants need to be honest in stating their level of expertise – and not mislead employers by implying they have more expertise than they actually possess. Threats that may result in lack of expertise include time pressure to carry out duties, being provided with inadequate information or having insufficient experience.	• Obtaining additional advice/training • Negotiating more time for duties • Obtaining assistance from someone with relevant expertise
Financial interests Situations where an accountant or close family member has financial interests in the employing company. Examples include the accountant being paid a bonus based on the financial statement results which he is preparing, or holding share options in the company.	• Remuneration being determined by other members of management • Disclosure of relevant interests to those charged with governance • Consultation with superiors or relevant professional body
Inducements – receiving offers Refers to incentives being offered to encourage unethical behaviour. Inducements may include gifts, hospitality, preferential treatment or inappropriate appeals to loyalty. Objectivity and/or confidentiality may be threatened by such inducements.	• Do not accept the inducement! • Inform relevant third parties such as senior management and professional association (normally after taking legal advice)
Inducements – giving offers Refers to accountants being pressurised to provide inducements to junior members of staff to influence a decision or obtain confidential information.	• Do not offer the inducement! If necessary, follow the conflict resolution process outlined in the next section

Confidential information Accountants should keep information about their employing company confidential unless there is a right or obligation to disclose, or they have received authorisation from the client. However, the accountant may be under pressure to disclose this information as a result of compliance with legal processes such as anti-money laundering/terrorism – in this situation there is a conflict between confidentiality and the need for disclosure.	• Disclose information in compliance with relevant statutory requirements, e.g. money laundering regulations
Whistleblowing Situations where the accountant needs to consider disclosing information, where ethical rules have been broken by the client.	Follow the disclosure provisions of the employer, e.g. report to those responsible for governance. Otherwise disclosure should be based on assessment of: legal obligations, whether members of the public will be adversely affected, gravity of the matter, likelihood of repetition, reliability of the information, reasons why employer does not want to disclose.

Strategic analysis: Ethics and corporate social responsibility

Test your understanding 8

The management accountant of L plc has recently discovered that the company is about to launch a major new product which is expected to cause a huge increase in company profits. He has therefore purchased a number of shares in L plc, as he expects the share price to rise significantly when the new product is launched.

Which TWO of the CIMA fundamental ethical principles is the management accountant likely to be in breach of?

A   Objectivity

B   Integrity

C   Professional behaviour

D   Confidentiality

E   Professional competence

F   Honesty

Test your understanding 9

The CEO of G Ltd has stated at a recent board meeting that 'the company has a responsibility to consider the needs of a wide range of stakeholders and ensure that we minimise any negative impacts that G Ltd has upon them.'

Which ONE of the following best describes the concept referred to by the CEO of G Ltd?

A   Ethics

B   Stakeholder management

C   Non-market strategy

D   Corporate social responsibility

6 Summary

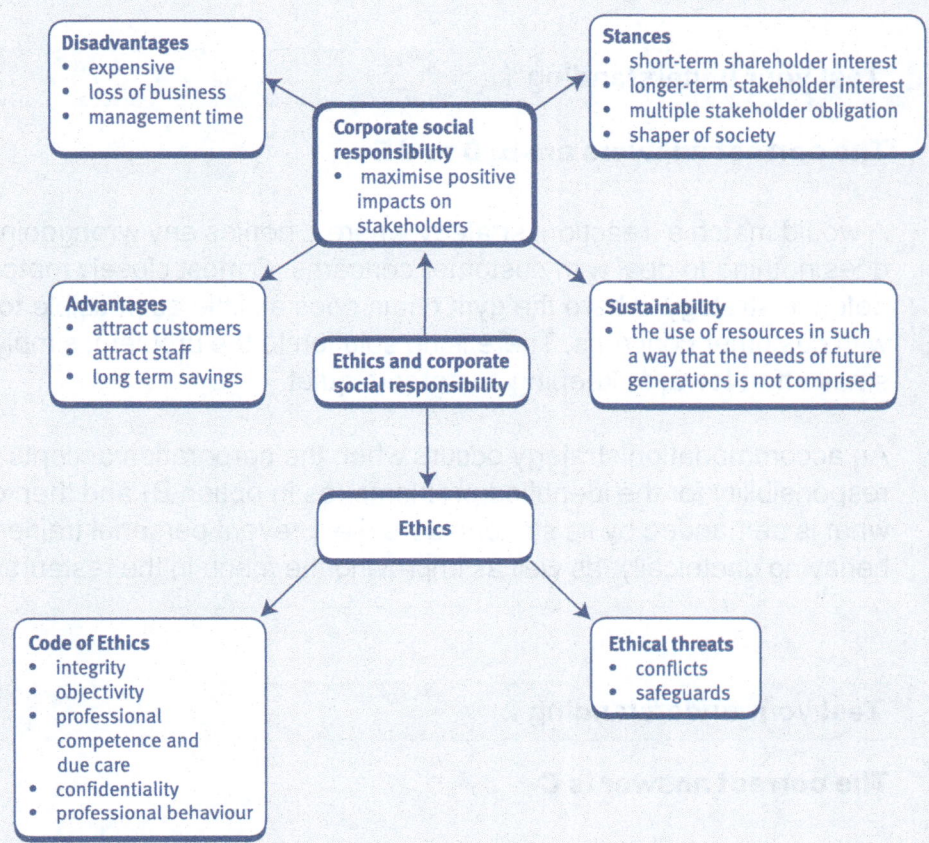

Test your understanding answers

Test your understanding 1

The correct answers are B, D and E

A would match a 'reaction' strategy where L denies any wrongdoing and does nothing to deal with customer concerns. C most closely matches a defence strategy, where the gym chain does as little as possible to deal with customer concerns. There is no solution to the problem, simply a small effort towards keeping customers quiet.

An accommodation strategy occurs when the corporation accepts responsibility for the identified problems (as in option B) and then does what is demanded by its stakeholders (i.e. prevent personal trainers from behaving unethically, as well as improving the menu in the restaurant).

Test your understanding 2

The correct answer is C

This approach is also known as 'enlightened self-interest'. J is going beyond regulations in an attempt to win customers in the longer term and stand out in his market.

J is showing no signs of considering the role he plays in society or his responsibility to wider stakeholders, suggesting that he is not operating as a shaper of society or under the multiple stakeholder objectives level.

Test your understanding 3 – Router – (Case style)

A. North
Business Advice Ltd
122 Left Way
Helland
HYY GT65

Dear Mr West,

Thank you for your recent letter. I have pleasure in enclosing our thoughts on each of your queries below.

Conflicting mission statement

The mission statement that Router plc has published states that the firm aims to make the 'maximum possible profit'. It is quite common for objectives of this kind to be included in mission statements.

In addition, the 'wider responsibilities to society' are recognised. This company objective is difficult to measure and there will be instances where this conflicts with the maximisation of profit. The gold-mining project provides a perfect example of this. It is expected to be profitable, but also result in the loss of vegetation and the creation of poisonous lakes for the one hundred years.

While the business could attempt to repair the local environment, doing so would make the mine unprofitable, leading to a loss of value to Router's shareholders.

However, it could be argued that in the long run, being socially responsible could increase the wealth of Router's shareholders. Router needs the government to grant it licences in order to mine for gold and shareholders to continue investing in it. If it develops a reputation as a 'dirty' firm, both stakeholders may change their minds. This would cause a loss of profits and a drop in the share price. This would of course mean a fall in shareholder wealth.

Strategic analysis: Ethics and corporate social responsibility

Dealing with conflicting objectives

As identified above, Router's objectives may conflict with each other. Methods of dealing with this include:

(1) **Establish a hierarchy of objectives:** Prioritise objectives and score alternative projects against them. For Router, it may need to decide which is more important – its wider social responsibilities or its desire to maximise profits.

(2) **Satisficing:** Router could try to give each stakeholder group something of what it wants. In this case, it could proceed with the mine and then provide some small amount of environmental restitution so that some of the damage is repaired.

(3) **Sequential attention:** This involves giving each stakeholder group's interests consideration over time, though not necessarily for every project. The effect is to keep them on board. In this case the mine could be abandoned because the environmental costs are too great. However, the next project, with less environmental damage, will be adopted. Shareholders and environmentalists will both feel that something has been achieved.

(4) **Side payments:** These are compensatory payments to keep stakeholders content. Perhaps good quality housing could be provided for the labour force which could be left after the works had finished. This could be pointed to as some compensation for the environmental damage and population displacement.

The principal ethical issues in mining are:

(1) **The use of non-renewable resources:** The mining operation results in non-replaceable resources being extracted from the mine. This deprives both the present owners and future generations of the resources. Adequate compensation should be provided to the current owners and the resources extracted should not be wasted out of consideration for future generations.

(2) **The use of power in negotiations:** In the negotiations it is important that the profit motive does not lead to Router acting improperly and exploiting the present owner of the mining rights. Where the country is poor this is a particular concern.

(3) **The environmental damage:** Poisoning the land for a hundred years is clearly not a socially acceptable outcome. Router has an ethical duty to minimise the effect of this pollution by developing a plan to deal with the problem. This should be seen as the minimum the company should do.

(4) **Impacts on the life of local residents:** While they may benefit from the economic boost the mine provides to the region, it is likely that the pollution will also affect them. While there may only be a small number of local residents, this does not give Router the right to ignore their needs. They should explain the steps the company is going to take to minimise the effect on their local environment.

(5) **Safety of procedures:** Mining is an industry noted for its poor safety record. Router must ensure that strict safety guidelines are in place and that they are followed by the workforce. It should ensure these conform to best practises in its industry – even if this is more than the legal requirements in the country of operation.

I hope this answers your queries. If you wish to discuss these issues further, please do not hesitate to contact us.

Kind regards

A. North

Test your understanding 4

The correct answer is A

By definition.

Test your understanding 5 – (Integration question)

(1) Potential conflict with professional behaviour – audit services observe the same standards, therefore implying that a rival has lower standards suggests that a firm is not complying with professional standards.

(2) The accountant is likely to lose objectivity because errors in the accounts made during preparation may not be identified when those accounts are reviewed.

(3) As the information is likely to be confidential, discussing it in a public place is inappropriate.

(4) The accountant needs to ensure that knowledge of the foreign country's taxation regime is understood prior to completing the return, otherwise there is the possibility that the appropriate professional skill will not be available.

(5) There is an issue of integrity. The accountant should not allow the report to be released because it is known that the report is incorrect.

(6) This is an issue of integrity. Accountants must not be associated with any form of communication or report that they know to be either materially false or misleading.

(7) The reduction of the number of staff in an organisation in order to increase profit is not necessarily unethical. For example, if the business has an unnecessarily high number of employees, reducing this number may be appropriate. However, the accountant would need to ensure that the analysis was accurate, as it will impact on individual's livelihoods. If there is any uncertainty in the results, they may need to consider whether it should be disclosed. In addition, the accountant will need to be aware of the implications and should ensure that the decision-makers are made aware of the potential ethical considerations.

(8) Again, this is an operational decision. There are ethical concerns over the loss of current staff which the accountant should make the decision-maker aware of along with the potential adverse impact on the reputation of the company.

(9) Ethics involves avoiding negative impacts on the environment that the company operates in. Even though legal, the decision to dump pollution into a river is unethical due to the impact on marine life. Should an accountant be complicit in such an action, it is likely to bring the profession into disrepute.

chapter 3

Test your understanding 6 – (Integration question)

Threat 1

- Do not offer the inducement!
- If necessary, follow the conflict resolution process of the employer.
- Consider the impact of the financial statements being misrepresented.

Threat 2

- Obtaining advice from the employer, professional organisation or professional advisor.
- The employer providing a formal dispute resolution process.
- Legal advice.

Threat 3

- Obtaining additional advice/training.
- Negotiating more time for duties.
- Obtaining assistance from someone with relevant expertise.

Test your understanding 7 – ABC – (Case style)

Email
To: A. Halifax
From: J. Bank
Date: 15/06/XX
Subject: Re: Professional ethics

Hi A,

If you agree to the IT Director's demands, you will be in breach of several parts of the CIMA Code of Ethics.

Integrity

This requires members not to be associated with any form of communication or report where the information is materially false, provided recklessly or incomplete.

You have identified a potential problem with the proposed new system that would involve a large outflow of cash to upgrade ABC's infrastructure.

Following the IT Director's suggestion would involve you ignoring the issue without a firm idea of how it will be resolved (the IT Director is simply suggesting a vague 'work-around'). This means that the report will be incomplete and misleading to its users.

Objectivity

This requires accountants to ensure that their judgement is not compromised because of bias or conflict of interest.

You are only likely to agree to the IT Director's demands because failing to do so could jeopardise your career. This would clearly be acting in your own self-interest.

Professional competence and due care

This requires accountants to follow all applicable technical and professional standards when providing services.

You are aware that the cost-benefit analysis, when undertaken properly, shows an unfavourable result for the new IT system. Failing to use the correctly obtained result could be seen as a failure to meet professional and technical standards.

Professional behaviour

This principle requires accountants to avoid any activities that might bring the profession into disrepute.

If you are found to have knowingly misled the Board of Directors into buying a system that is not cost effective, it would clearly damage confidence in the accountancy profession as a whole.

I hope that helps! Let me know if you need any more information and I'll try to help.

A.

Test your understanding 8

The correct answers are C and D

The accountant is in breach of confidentiality as he is using information for his own personal gain (regardless of whether he communicates this information to others). He also risks bringing the profession into disrepute (and could be in breach of insider dealing laws), which breaches professional behaviour.

There is no evidence that he is producing any reports or providing information relating to the new product, which would tend to suggest that integrity, objectivity and professional competence are not being breached.

Note that honesty (while being preferable!) is not a fundamental ethical principle.

Test your understanding 9

The correct answer is D

Note that sustainability is part of CSR – however the CEO appears to be referring to the wider concept of how the organisation looks after its social responsibility.

Strategic analysis: Ethics and corporate social responsibility

118

chapter 4

Strategic analysis: External environmental analysis

Chapter learning objectives

Lead	Component
A1. Evaluate the influence of key external factors on an organisation's strategy	(a) Evaluate the influence and impact of the external environment on an organisation and its strategy
B1. Evaluate the process of strategic formulation	(b) Evaluate the processes of strategic analysis and strategic options generation
B2. Evaluate tools and techniques used in strategy formulation	(a) Evaluate strategic analysis tools

Indicative syllabus content

- Different organisation environments (including profit and not-for-profit organisations)
- The key environmental drivers of organisational change and their prioritisation.

Strategic analysis: External environmental analysis

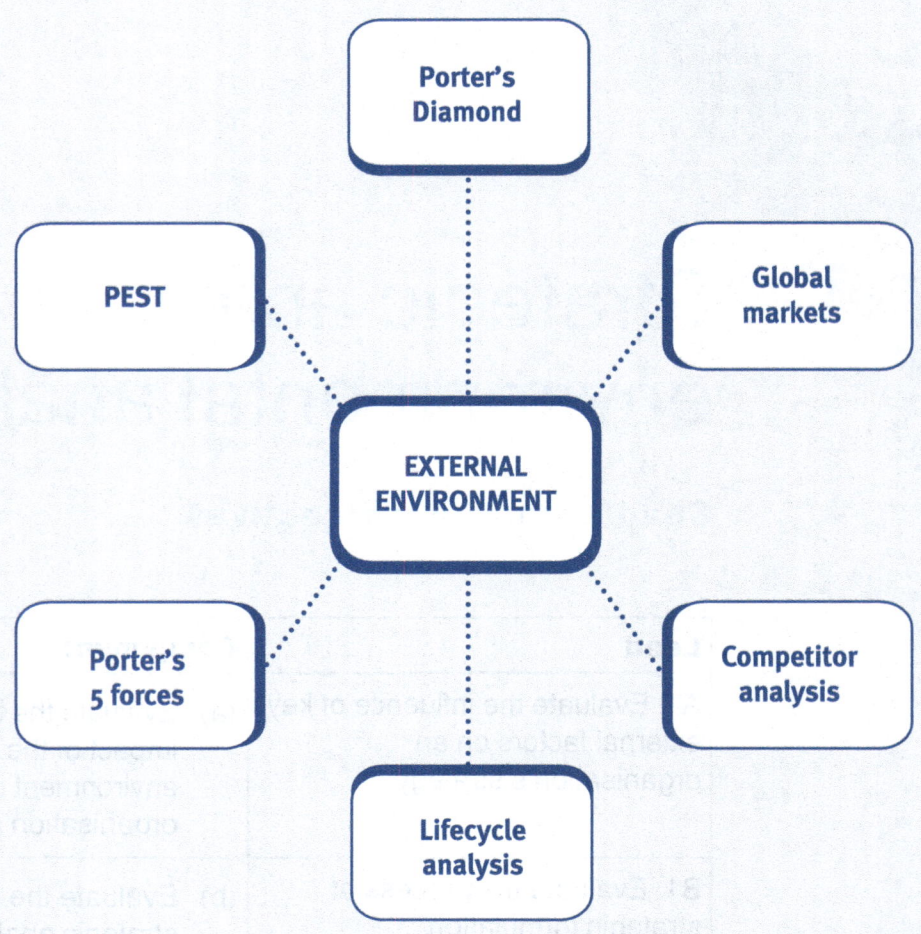

1 Introduction

The first part of undertaking analysis of an organisation's overall position is a detailed appraisal of its external environment. The organisation must understand what is happening in the outside world that could impact on its future strategies.

There are a number of different models that can be used to help organisations undertake this analysis, each of which focus on a different part of its environment.

Purpose of environmental analysis

Why should an organisation bother to spend the time (and money) needed to undertake a complete environmental analysis? There are several key purposes, including:

- **Identification of threats and opportunities**

    Analysing its environment can help an organisation to identify potential problems it may have to face (such as future changes in legislation that will affect its operations) as well as possible areas for growth and development that it may wish to take advantage of.

- **Assessment of competition**

    Environmental analysis involves, in part, the examination of the organisation's competitors. Understanding how rivals are acting in the market may help the organisation stay more competitive in the market.

- **Identification of strengths and weaknesses**

    Understanding its strengths and weaknesses will help the organisation to decide on appropriate strategies. These strategies may be to deal with its weaknesses or build on its strengths.

- **Meeting stakeholder needs**

    Environmental analysis will help the organisation gain a clear understanding of what its key stakeholders require from it. While shareholders are likely to want a high return on their investment, other stakeholders may have different demands on the organisation. These were explored in more detail in chapter 2.

Problems with environmental analysis

While environmental analysis is extremely useful for organisations, it is becoming increasing difficult to undertake. The reason for this is the increasing volatility and rate of change in the global market.

The business environment has become more volatile for a number of reasons, including:

- Changing technology is leading to the development of new products and services and/or altering how existing ones are delivered. For instance, the rise of online gaming has had a serious impact on companies such as Game and HMV in the UK, who both sell computer games on physical discs.

- Continuing weakness in the global economy has led to unpredictable demand in the market and made it more difficult for many organisations to access credit.

- Increasing globalisation of many markets means that organisations may be affected by issues in many different countries. A company like Ford, which trades globally, may be affected by issues in any of the countries it operates within.

Strategic analysis: External environmental analysis

- The development of high-growth, emerging economies – such as the 'BRIC' economies (Brazil, Russia, India and China) – means that organisations looking to expand may need to consider ways of tapping into these new markets.

All of these issues mean that an organisation's environment will be changing all the time. This may lead to environmental analysis quickly becoming outdated.

It is therefore important that companies consider undertaking environmental analysis on a regular basis.

2 PEST analysis

Exam focus

- PEST analyses the **general macro-environment**, identifying key drivers of change and hence sources of risk.
- Particularly good at identifying whether a market is growing/declining and why.
- Can also be used to generate ideas for a position analysis (SWOT) – identifying opportunities and threats.

Model

P	Political (including legal)
E	Economic
S	Social
T	Technological

Also known as SLEPT (with **legal** issues added) and PESTLE (with **environmental** issues added).

Look for factors on local, industry, national and global levels, both now and in the future.

Political	**Social**
• Change of government • New laws • Political union • War • Tax • Global political moves	• Demography • Culture & lifestyle • Education • Income • Consumerism
Economic	**Technological**
• Interest rates • Exchange rates • Inflation • Unemployment • Balance of payments • Business cycle	• Rate of development & transfer • Innovation • Obsolescence • Changing cost base
Legal	**Environmental**
• Health and safety legislation • Consumer laws • Data protection laws • Accounting regulations	• Pollution • Wastage • Climate and climate change

Criticisms of PEST analysis

PEST analysis is an excellent way of gaining an understanding of the main environmental issues that may affect the organisation, but it does have a number of drawbacks, including:

- The issues identified by a formal PEST analysis may quickly become irrelevant. This is particularly a problem in fast-moving industries, such as computing or mobile phones.

- The PEST analysis process is prone to bias. Different managers may have different ideas on what the important issues are that need to be included in the analysis.

- The PEST may be incomplete. It can be difficult (or impossible) for managers to correctly identify and understand every environmental issue that might affect the organisation in the future. This problem is sometimes referred to as 'bounded rationality'.

Strategic analysis: External environmental analysis

Test your understanding 1

Y is a retailer of clothes in country H.

Which THREE of the following issues would most likely be identified under the 'social' heading of PEST analysis carried out for Y?

A   Unemployment levels in country H

B   Change of government

C   Education levels

D   Changing fashions

E   Changing tax regimes

F   Increased use of automation in production

G   Shift in customer attitudes towards ethical consumerism

Test your understanding 2

H is a company that manufactures toys. Its core business has stayed constant for many years, allowing H to make reasonable profits. H's managers have an excellent knowledge of the market and wider industry, having worked in H for many years, though the company has not undertaken formal external analysis for many years. One of H's managers has been asked to undertake a PEST analysis for the business. Before he started, he has stated that he feels that the only possible threat to the organisation is changes to the national and international economy.

Which ONE of the following problems with PEST analysis is most likely to arise for H?

A   Issues becoming outdated before the analysis can used

B   Bounded rationality

C   Bias in the issues chosen to be included in the analysis

D   Failure to identify all environmental issues for the organisation

chapter 4

3 Porter's Five Forces analysis

Exam focus

- Five forces examines an organisation's **industry**.
- Just because an industry is large and/or growing, high profits do not necessarily follow. The five forces determine profit potential, both for the industry as a whole and for individual firms/SBUs.
- Strong collective forces give low profitability overall.
- An individual firm can earn better margins than competitors if it can deal more effectively with key forces.
- The model can also be useful to generate ideas for a position analysis – especially threats.

Model

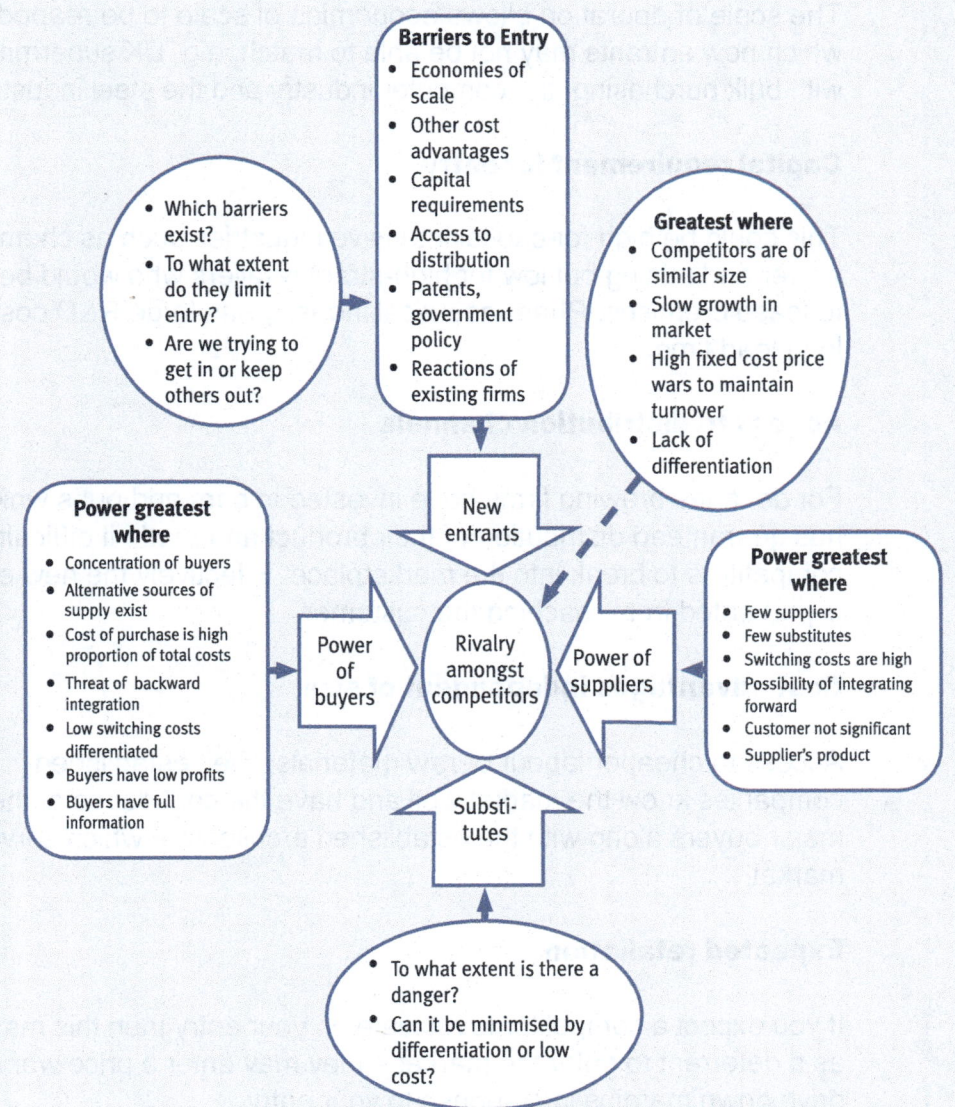

Strategic analysis: External environmental analysis

Explanation of Porter's 5 Forces

(1) **Threat of new entrants**

This will depend upon the extent to which there are **barriers to entry**.

Establish:

- which barriers exist
- the extent to which they are likely to prevent entry
- the organisation's position – is it trying to prevent or attempt entry?

Barriers may include:

Economies of scale

The scale of operation allows economies of scale to be reaped which new entrants may not be able to match, e.g. UK supermarkets with bulk purchasing, the computer industry and the steel industry.

Capital requirement for entry

This could be high for capital intensive industries such as chemicals, power and mining but low for high-street retailers who would be able to lease premises. Pharmaceutical industry has large R&D costs and long lead times.

Access to distribution channels

For decades brewing firms have invested in bars and pubs which has guaranteed distribution of their product and made it difficult for competitors to break into the marketplace. Effectively the new entrant is prevented from reaching the customer.

Cost advantages independent of size

Access to cheaper labour or raw materials. Well-established companies know the market well and have the confidence of the major buyers along with the established architecture which serves the market.

Expected retaliation

If you expect a competitor to retaliate on your entry then this may act as a deterrent to enter the market – they may enter a price war and drive down margins in response to your entry.

Legislation

Legal conditions may exist for entry, e.g. licences and personal guarantees, telecommunications and financial services.

Differentiation

Branding and/or high quality may create customer loyalty and inelastic demand for their product, which may take longer to break down for the new entrant.

Switching costs

Customers may have to invest in the trading relationship via contractual arrangements or an investment in IT. To switch supplier would entail substantial costs and therefore the new entrant would have a challenge on their hands.

(2) Bargaining power of buyers

This is likely to be high when there is a concentration of buyers, particularly if the volume purchases of the buyers are high, e.g. grocery retailing.

This is likely to be further accentuated when the selling industry comprises a large number of small firms and the product is standard with little or no switching costs involved.

(3) Bargaining power of suppliers

Close linkages to the preceding section. Supplier power is likely to be high when:

- the input is important to the buying company
- the supplier industry is dominated by a few suppliers who have secure market positions and are not subject to competitive pressure
- supplier products are branded or involve switching costs
- supplier customers are highly fragmented with little buying power.

(4) Threat of substitutes

Substitutes can render products obsolete and can be direct or indirect. They can be based on actual products or uses, e.g. a Ferrari or a Fiat Punto; a car or a bicycle.

There can also be substitution based on income or even doing without, e.g. new furniture or a holiday; giving up smoking.

The availability of substitutes can place a limit on price and change the basis of the product. Consideration must be given to the ease with which consumers can switch to substitutes along with the perceived value that consumer groups would place on the products. At the same time, evaluation of potential actions to build customer loyalty should be undertaken. For example, advertising to build brand image.

(5) Competitive rivalry

Some markets are more competitive than others. In highly competitive markets companies regularly monitor competitors. It can be intense or remote and tends to depend upon historical development.

Factors affecting level of rivalry:

- The extent to which competitors are in balance – roughly equal-sized firms in terms of market share or finances – often leads to highly competitive marketplaces.
- Stage of the life cycle. During market growth stages all companies grow naturally, whilst in mature markets growth can only be obtained at the expense of someone else.
- High storage costs may lead to cost-cutting to improve turnover which in turn increases the rivalry.
- Extra capacity comes in large increments which means price cutting may follow to fill capacity.
- Difficulty in differentiating products leaves the basis for competition on price or augmented product.
- High exit barriers mean that some companies must stay in the market.

Conclusion

A desirable circumstance would be a situation where there are weak suppliers and buyers, few substitutes with high barriers to entry and little rivalry.

Criticisms of Porter's 5 Forces model

Over the last three decades business has focused on one fundamental idea – the pursuit of sustainable competitive advantage. While the idea of competition is not new, Michael Porter expanded the concept from competing with rivals to incorporating the struggle for power between the firm and five competitive forces. Porter argued that each of these forces can reduce overall industry profitability and the individual firm's share of that profit – their 'profit potential' – because they can influence prices, costs and the level of investment required.

Not everyone agrees with Porter – some would argue that the idea of satisfying customer needs should not be abandoned in favour of a view that sees customers either as direct competitors or as means to the firm's end. Customers are not objects whose reason for being is to be fought over by competitors seeking 'sustainable competitive advantage'. Porter's model might thus distract managers from seeing customers as potential partners.

Other limitations include the following:

Limitations in the use of the 5 Forces model

Dynamic industries
- May find little benefit from industry analysis
- By the time the analysis has been done, the industry has moved on
- Focus more on risk management and competences

Outside-in vs. inside-out
- 5 Forces is of great help to strategic planning but is difficult to apply for competence based businesses (strategic management) – e.g. hi-tech/innovative companies.

Role of government
- Some analysts add this as a 6th force (e.g. Ryanair have sued the EU for allowing airlines such as Air France and Lufthansa to receive government subsidies allowing them to cut the price of European flights).

Collaboration
- Model assumes businesses operate independently against each other and ignores **collaborative** benefits (e.g. joint ventures, alliances etc)

NFP
- 5 Forces focuses on industry profitability → not a main objective of NFPs.
- Also any business not pursuing a profit objective may not find it useful.

Strategic analysis: External environmental analysis

Test your understanding 3

WWW Ltd is a large company that sells paint and wallpaper through homeware retailers in Country X. WWW has several major competitors, each of whom is a similar size to WWW and offers a similar range of products. Due to the generic nature of the products they produce, WWW is unable to secure patents on any of their products.

WWW sells its goods via several retailers, including BBB, which has a 52% share of the paint and wallpaper retail market in Country X. WWW has a one-year rolling contract with BBB to stock their products, though BBB is considering launching its own brand range of paint and wallpaper in the near future. WWW is uncertain of how this will affect their sales agreement with BBB.

Which ONE of the following statements relating to Porter's five forces model is correct in relation to WWW's industry?

A   It has high barriers to entry

B   It has high supplier bargaining power

C   It has high buyer bargaining power

D   It has a high threat of substitutes

Test your understanding 4

Under Porter's five forces model, which ONE of the following would be evidence of HIGH supplier power?

A   Customers are relatively small compared to the supplier

B   Low probability of forward integration by suppliers

C   Large numbers of suppliers

D   Supplier's product is not differentiated

Test your understanding 5 – Hawk – (Case style)

Hawk Leathers Ltd ("Hawk") is a company based in the UK that employs around 60 people in the manufacture and sale of leather jackets, jeans, one- and two-piece suits and gloves. These are aimed primarily at motorcyclists, although a few items are sold as fashion garments.

Hawk sells 65% of its output to large retail chains such as Motorcycle City and Carnells, exports 25% to the USA and Japan, and sells the remaining 10% to individuals who contact the company directly. The latter group of customers specify their requirements for a made-to-measure suit (they are often professional racers whose suits must be approved by the authorities, such as the Auto Cycle Union). The large retailers insist on low margins and are very slow to settle their debts.

There are around a dozen companies in the UK who make similar products to Hawk, plus very many other companies who compete with much lower prices and inferior quality. Hawk's typical selling price for a one-piece suit is £1,000, whereas the low quality rivals' suits retail at around £400. As Hawk say in their literature "if you hit the tarmac, there's no substitute for a second skin from Hawk". Synthetic materials are waterproof, unlike leather, but do not currently offer sufficient protection in an accident.

Sales of leathers in the UK are growing rapidly, mainly due to a resurgence of biking from more mature riders of large, powerful machines. Such riders are often wealthy and have family and financial commitments. Currently Hawk, and its rivals for quality leathers are finding it hard to keep up with demand. However, government policy and EU emissions controls are likely to limit motorcycle performance, and some experts predict that these regulations will cause sales of large motorcycles to level off.

Whilst supplies of leather from Asia, Scandinavia and the UK are plentiful, a key problem is recruiting and training machinists to stitch and line the garments. Hawk has been able to invest in modern machinery to help production but the process is still labour intensive. Hawk has found that the expertise, reputation and skilled labour needed to succeed in the industry takes years to build up.

Although the industry is fairly traditional, there are some new developments such as a website for individual customers to browse and specify requirements, and new colours such as metallics for leathers, and a small but growing demand from non-bikers who are interested in 'recreational' and 'club wear' items.

The Managing Director of Hawk has sent you the following note:

Note

Hi N,

I'm currently heading up an internal strategy group who are looking into Hawk's external position. Could you please analyse the issues facing Hawk's industry using a PEST analysis for me. I also need you to evaluate the strength of each competitive pressure facing Hawk, using Porter's five forces model.

If you could draw on your knowledge of the company and its situation, that would be great. I only need a couple of points under each heading.

If you could send me a copy of your analysis in about forty-five minutes that would be fantastic.

Thanks

MD

Required:

Undertake the analysis requested by the MD.

(45 minutes)

4 Industry life cycle analysis

The life-cycle model suggests that both individual products and services, as well as entire industries, move through a number of different stages in their lives. Understanding this for our organisation can be a useful analysis tool and can help to suggest which strategies the organisation needs to adopt in order to compete successfully.

This model can therefore be used to look at the **industry as a whole** that the organisation operates in, or can be used to assess **individual products or divisions** within the organisation.

Product life cycle

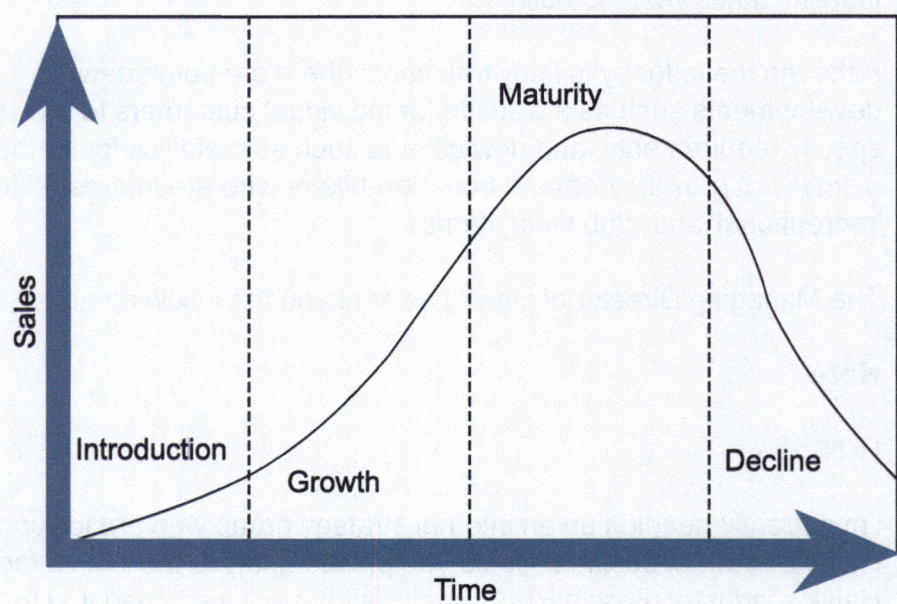

The model can be used to predict competitive conditions and identify key issues for management in corporate appraisals and strategic choices.

Introduction stage

The product is new to the market at this stage. Key points are:

- it will be purchased by 'innovators'
- high launch and marketing costs are likely
- production volumes will be low and product cost will be high
- buyers are unsophisticated
- competition is little if any.

Price elasticity of demand will influence the pricing strategy.

- **Price skimming** is appropriate when the product is known to have a price-inelastic demand.
- **Penetration pricing** is appropriate where the demand is thought to be price-elastic and when gaining market share is seen as more important than fast recovery of development costs.

'Pioneer companies', who are the first to the market with a particular product, are usually forced to sell the concept. These early promotions will help competitor companies who enter later with 'me too' versions of the product concept.

Early entry is risky as heavy requirement for cash and product idea may fail BUT early entry allows the prospect of establishing market share and developing first mover advantage.

Growth stage

During this stage the market grows rapidly. Key points are:

- sales for the market as a whole increase
- new competitors, attracted by the prospects, enter to challenge the 'pioneer'
- new segments may be developed
- demand becomes more sophisticated
- competition levels increase.

The market becomes profitable and cash flows increase to recover the initial investment in development and launch costs.

There are many new consumers with no preference who they buy from.

It will become more difficult in later stages to persuade people to switch from their existing brand. It is important to build a brand during this stage if possible to ease the traumas at the later stages via defensive strategy.

Prices often fall due to economies of scale and increasing competitive pressure, and evidence of differentiation will become apparent, e.g. branding develops.

Maturity stage

During this stage market growth slows or even halts. Key points are:

- fully sophisticated demand
- high levels of competition
- price becomes more sensitive
- demand reaches saturation. The only way to increase market share is to gain business from competitors or from 'late adopters' or 'laggards'
- it would be desirable to have a high market share at this stage or to have successfully developed a niche
- large market share changes can be difficult to achieve at this stage and most companies would concentrate on defensive strategies to protect their current position and compete hard for the new customers coming into the marketplace
- over time the company must be vigilant to detect and anticipate changes in the market and be ready to undertake product or market modifications with a view to lengthening the life.

Decline

During this stage the number of customers falls. Key points are:

- competition reduces as players leave
- price falls to attract business as sophisticated customers expect cheap prices
- slow 'harvesting' must be balanced with straight divestment
- investment kept to a minimum to take up any market share that may be left by departing competitors
- there may be profitable niches remaining after industrial death.

Considerations

- Offer a range of products at various stages of the life cycle – mature products will fund the development of new products
- competencies need to change – at the early stages, creativity and innovation are key whilst at later stages efficiencies and low costs become important
- life cycles are difficult to predict, can change quickly and will vary from one product to another. Turning points are very hard to predict
- management anticipation of decline can cause decline! Reduction in investment and advertising can cause the appropriate market response
- SWOT varies across the life cycle
- strategies will need to change as the organisation progresses through the life cycle.

For example, the market for calculators started with scientists and engineers and then moved to business before moving to higher education students. Finally the market moved to include schoolchildren, which proved to be the largest segment of all. A pioneer wishing to stay the course would experience radical change as they move from the organisational markets to the mass consumer version.

Summary of industry life cycle

	Intro	**Growth**	**Maturity**	**Decline**
Sales	Low	Rapidly rising	Peak	Declining
Costs per customer	High cost	Average	Low	Low
Profits	Negative	Rising	High	Falling
Customers	Innovators	Early adopters	Middle majority	Laggards
Competitors	Few	Growing number	Stable number beginning to decline	Declining number
Objectives	Create product awareness & trial	Maximise market share	Maximise profit whilst defending market share	Reduce expenditure & 'milk the brand'

Strategies

	Intro	**Growth**	**Maturity**	**Decline**
Product	Offer basic product	Offer product extensions, service & warranty	Diversify brands & models	Phase out weak items
Price	Cost plus	Price penetration	Price matching	Price cutting
Promotion	Build product awareness amongst early adopters & dealers	Build awareness & interest in mass market	Stress brand differences & benefits	Reduce to level to maintain hard core loyalty
Place	Limited	Growing	Maximum	Limited

Usefulness of the life cycle model

Management within the organisation can benefit from the use of the life cycle model in a number of ways, including:

- **Improved strategic planning**

  Using the product life cycle helps organisations with their strategic planning. For example, the organisation will realise that the demand for a product typically does not last forever. It can therefore put in place contingency plans to deal with this – for example ensuring the development and launch of new products on a periodic basis. Knowing that it will need to replace even successful products at some point in the future can therefore lead to a more innovative organisational focus.

- **Improved budgeting**

  The life cycle model indicates when products should generate or use cash throughout their lives. Understanding which stage each product in the organisation's portfolio has reached (and will reach in the future) can help the organisation to estimate its future cash flow needs.

- **Proactive Approach**

  Rather than sitting waiting for the decline of a product to begin, the life cycle model allows companies to take a more proactive approach to boosting sales and profits during each stage. For example, if the organisation identifies that a product is moving into decline, it can look at ways of maximising returns by, for example, cutting prices or redesigning the product.

Test your understanding 6

F plc sells a product known as the YYU500. The YYU500 has seen sales growth of around 1% for the last two years, after strong growth in the previous five years. This is due to new products entering the market in competition with the YYU500.

F is therefore considering cutting its prices to be in line with its major rivals. It hopes that this will help it to maintain its market share. Market research indicates that this will now cause a significant increase in the level of sales, even though in previous years price cuts have had little effect on demand.

F is also planning to launch a promotional campaign to highlight the benefits of the YYU500 against its rival products.

Which stage of the product life cycle does the YYU500 appear to have reached?

A   Growth
B   Decline
C   Maturity
D   Introduction

Test your understanding 7

AJJ Ltd has identified that all three of its main products are at the maturity phase of the product life cycle. Which of the following is AJJ likely to be experiencing due to this?

A   High, but declining sales
B   Growing numbers of competitors
C   Product diversification and differentiation strategies
D   Adoption of price skimming strategies

Strategic analysis: External environmental analysis

Test your understanding 8 – (Case style)

You have recently been appointed to the European strategy steering group at PTP Electronics, the holding company for a number of subsidiary companies making household name consumer electronic products. Four products were discussed at the recent meeting. All appear to be profitable, and some large retail outlets sell the whole range of PTP products in their stores.

- Recordable DVD players – the market has been expanding very quickly since its launch four years ago and PTP has a very small share compared to Sony and Panasonic.

- Traditional DVD players – sales are levelling off as people switch to Blu-Ray players and downloading movies over the Internet. PTP's brands have been a market leader since the late 1990s.

- Conventional CRT colour television monitors – demand for CRT TVs is declining as customers and manufacturers turn to newer technologies. PTP has recently built a new factory in Holland to produce plasma and LCD televisions (see below). Consequently it has not pushed sales of conventional TVs, but has a small share of the CCTV market.

- Plasma and LCD televisions – although expensive, PTP sees these as a huge future market with the increase in digital broadcasting. It is the market leader in this field although sales in volume terms are not rising as fast as had been hoped. Launch was five years ago.

You have been asked by the Chairman of the steering group to make a presentation to the rest of the steering group. She has asked that you use the product lifecycle model to identify and comment on the lifecycle position of each product type, with reasons. She also wishes you to evaluate the balance of PTP's product portfolio as a whole. The presentation should advise PTP's directors of one idea that you feel may help improve the portfolio balance.

Required:

Draft notes that you will use to help you make your presentation to the rest of the group as outlined by the Chairman.

(30 minutes)

5 Competitor analysis (competitor intelligence)

This can be defined as a set of activities which examines the comparative position of competing enterprises within a given strategic sector. It seeks to:

- provide an understanding of the company's competitive advantage/disadvantage relative to its competitor's positions
- help generate insights into competitors strategies – past, present and potential
- give an informed basis for developing future strategies to sustain/establish advantages over competitors.

Grant highlights three purposes:

- to forecast competitors' future strategies and decisions
- to predict competitors' likely reactions to a firm's strategic initiatives
- to determine how competitor **behaviour** can be influenced to make it more favourable for the organisation.

A framework for competitor analysis

Step 1: identify competitors

- **Brand competitors** sell similar products to the same customers we serve, e.g. Coke and Pepsi.
- **Industry competitors** sell similar products but in different segments, e.g. BA and Singapore Airlines.
- **Form competitors** sell products that satisfy the same need as ours though technically very different, e.g. speedboat and sports car.
- **Generic competitors** compete for the same income, e.g. home improvements and golf clubs.

Step 2: analyse competitors

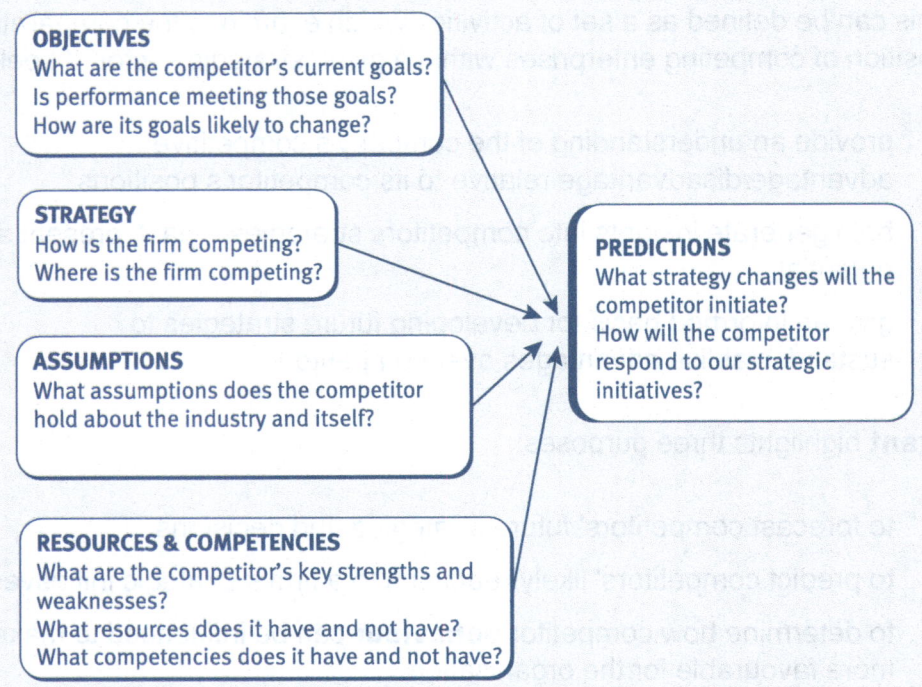

Step 3: develop competitor response profiles

- **Laid back:** Does not respond;
- **Selective:** Reacts to attack in only selected markets;
- **Tiger:** Always responds aggressively;
- **Stochastic:** No predictable pattern exists.

6 The nature of global competition

Why enter foreign markets?

- **Pressure** from shareholders to increase their return on capital employed
- **saturated** domestic markets making home expansion difficult
- **opportunities** as emerging markets arise with increases in economic income and spending power
- **trade barriers coming down** enabling competitors to compete in our domestic markets as well as increasing the opportunities for our company overseas.

Risks arising from entering global markets

- **Marketing mix adaptations** are needed and questions must be addressed as to how these modifications should be made and when. Consideration must be given to the cultural implications and the potential costs involved.
- **Cultures vary** more dramatically when national boundaries are traversed and cultural environment needs full evaluation.
- **Varying cost structures** will exist from one country to another as will the quality of production factors – there may not be sufficient skilled labour and management to enable a global strategy.
- **Different competitive levels** will exist in different markets and the level of competition will need to be determined.
- **Exchange rate volatility** requires the deployment of control systems to protect the company.
- **Different economic situations** will alter the demand for the product and the availability of factors of production.
- **Political involvement** as governments will seek to be involved in decisions. Careful planning will be needed to ensure that no conflict arises or, if likely, the allocation of responsibility to a suitably qualified individual.
- **Political situation** should be considered with regard to war, terrorism and government stability. What are the risks to our personnel and our organisation?
- **Entry requirements?** What do we have to do to get in? Is it legal and ethical?

Benefits of entering global markets

- **Economies of scale** are possible as research and development can now be spread over wider production volumes. Bulk-buying discounts may be available as the volume of our purchases and our reputation increases.
- **Management opportunity** is increased and this may prove motivational to certain types of managers whilst at the same time allowing those managers to experience a wider range of cultural situations.
- This in turn allows the **challenge to the traditional home cultural** perspective. Items can be viewed from a different perspective with cultural benchmarks being developed.
- **Cheaper sources of raw materials** and labour may allow the development of a competitive advantage which could be sustainable for a period of time.
- **Market development** as the emerging markets bring a whole new range of consumers who will be embarking on their 'first buy' and so may not be as 'fussy' as consumers in a saturated market.

- **Risk reduction** via portfolio spread will arise when different markets are combined into a portfolio.
- **Political sponsorship** will be possible as national governments, keen to boost or maintain home employment, offer attractive packages to global companies to invest in that country.
- **Political power** becomes possible as the company grows in size and is seen to be contributing to wealth creation as opposed to exploitation of the nation concerned.

7 Competitive advantage of nations – Porter's Diamond

This model suggests reasons why some nations are more competitive than others and why some industries within nations are more competitive than others. This can be used in a number of different ways:

- The organisation can understand what, if any, factors have caused it to be successful in its current country or countries of operation.
- The model can be used by the organisation to assess whether a particular country is suitable for expansion into.
- Governments can identify how to adjust their policies in order to attract or strengthen certain industries.

Porter identified four key factors (or dimensions) that determine the relative attractiveness of different countries to a particular industry.

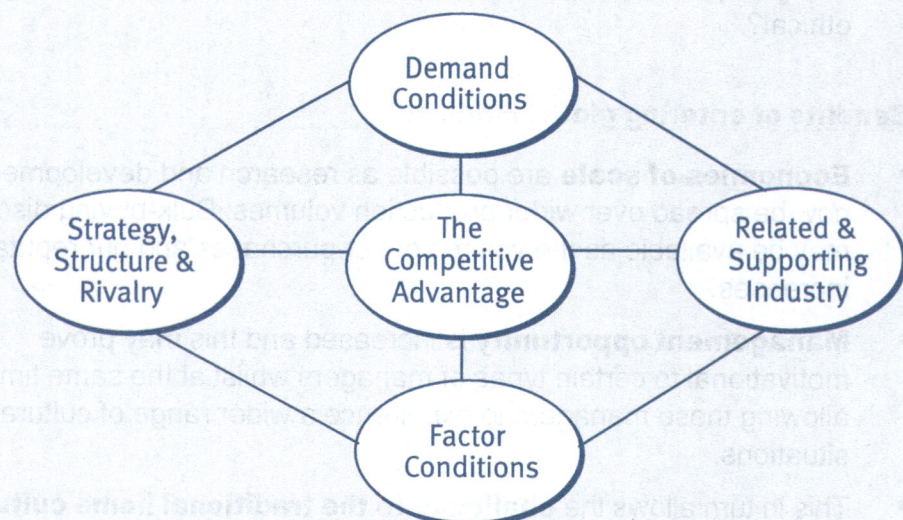

Factor conditions – supply side

A supply of production factors that convey advantage. They provide initial advantage which is then subsequently built upon to develop more advanced factors. Basic factors are unsustainable as they are easily copied (unskilled labour) whilst advanced factors can convey the advantage as they are less easy to emulate (scientific expertise).

They include human, physical, knowledge, capital and infrastructure, for example:

- linguistic ability of the Swiss has provided advantage in the banking industry
- financial expertise within the UK.

You can use the national identity as the basis for a brand, e.g. New Zealand lamb.

Demand conditions – demand side

Sophisticated home demand can lead to the company developing significant advantages in the global marketplace. Fussy consumers set high standards for products whilst past experience of the product's progress through the life cycle in the home market can provide valuable input to new strategic initiatives.

- Japanese customers have high expectations of their electrical products, which forces producers to provide a technically superior product for the global marketplace. They are so used to dealing with sophisticated customers that when they come across unsophisticated markets, they excel way beyond the competition.
- Nokia – a Finnish Telecoms company.

Related and supporting industry – the value chain and system

Advantage conveyed by the availability of superior supplier industries, e.g. Italy has a substantial leatherwear industry which is supported by leather-working plants and top fashion and design companies.

Strategy, structure and rivalry – the competition element

Different nations have different approaches to business in terms of structure and the intensity of rivalry that can take place. If a company is used to dealing with strong competition then it will have experience of rivals' attacks and so will be better able to fight them off.

Domestic rivalry can keep the organisations 'lean and mean' so that when they go out into the global marketplace they can compete more successfully with the less capable foreign competition, e.g. Nokia and Finland's approach to the regulation of telecoms.

Governments can promote this rivalry via policy.

Other events

Porter points out that countries can produce world-class firms due to two further factors:

- **The role of government** – subsidies, legislation and education can all impact on the other four elements of the diamond to the benefit of the industrial base of the country.

- **The role of chance events** – wars, civil unrest, chance discoveries and others can also change the four elements of the diamond unpredictably.

A business will initially choose to enter markets in those countries where the above conditions are most favourable. This involves considering the attractiveness of the markets and the barriers to entry that may exist. Strong position audit is needed to assess our company's strategic capability in these new segments.

Research is critical before entering a foreign market. Then on a regular basis, more research is needed as well as the setting up of systems to ensure that it is continually updated and monitored.

> **Criticisms of Porter's Diamond model**
>
> The following criticisms are made of Porter's Diamond model:
>
> - Porter developed the model by looking at ten developed countries. The model thus only really applies to developed economies.
>
> - Porter argues that inbound foreign direct investment does not increase domestic competition significantly because domestic firms lack the capability to defend their own markets and face a process of market-share erosion and decline. However, there seems to be little empirical evidence to support that claim.
>
> - The Porter model does not adequately address the role of multi-national corporations. There seems to be ample evidence that the diamond is influenced by factors outside the home country.
>
> - Porter's analysis focused on manufacturers, banks and management consultancy firms. Some have questioned its relevance to service-based companies such as McDonalds.

- Porter's focus is on the domestic country rather than which foreign markets have been targeted. A careful choice of target is essential to ensure that the firm has the competences required for success.
- Not all firms from a given country are successful, suggesting that corporate management is more important than geographical location.

Test your understanding 9

B is an airline, which operates in a number of different countries around the world. It is currently considering entry into country G, but is concerned that there are not enough skilled workers in country G for their needs.

Insert the missing TWO words into the sentence below:

According to Porter's Diamond model, country G lacks a key _____ and therefore may not be an appropriate expansion target for B.

Test your understanding 10

AHH is a supermarket chain which is considering expansion into country L. It has decided to analyse the decision using Porter's Diamond.

Consider the following lists of issues relating to the AHH's expansion as well as the dimensions of Porter's Diamond.

Issue	Dimension
A Lack of farmers required for fresh produce	1 Demand conditions
B A range of existing supermarkets serving a large number of customers	2 Strategy, structure and rivalry
C Lack of available land to build supermarkets	3 Factor conditions
D AHH currently operates in highly competitive markets	4 Related and supporting industry

Show which issue relates to each dimension by pairing the appropriate letter and number (e.g. A1, B4, etc).

Test your understanding 11 – (Integration question)

Australia has a long-established wine industry, but in the 1970s it decided to expand exports to Europe and the USA, since growth was becoming limited in domestic markets.

Australian producers had benefitted from strong domestic demand, and had produced excellent results by cultivating grape varieties imported from Europe, combined with innovative techniques such as cool fermentation in stainless steel containers. Producers had achieved success in a wide range of wines including red, white, sparkling, dry and sweet.

Although many producers started out as independent small businesses, major listed groups such as Penfolds had consolidated many of these small producers into well-known labels.

Required:

(a) Discuss two reasons why Australian wine producers decided to enter foreign markets, and two risks arising.

(b) By giving one example of each element, use Porter's Diamond to evaluate the degree of competitive advantage achieved by the Australian wine industry.

8 Summary

EXTERNAL ENVIRONMENT

- **Porter's Diamond**
  - Factor conditions
  - Demand conditions
  - Related and supporting industry
  - Strategy, structure and rivalry

- **PEST**
  - Political
  - Economic
  - Social
  - Technological

- **Global markets**
  - Why enter foreign markets?
  - Risks
  - Benefits

- **Porter's 5 forces**
  - Competitive rivalry
  - Threat of substitutes
  - Threat of new entrants
  - Power of customers
  - Power of suppliers

- **Lifecycle analysis**
  - Stages
  - Strategies
  - Balanced portfolio?

- **Competitor analysis**
  - Identify competitors
  - Analyse competitors
  - Develop response profiles

Test your understanding answers

Test your understanding 1

The correct answers are C, D and G

A is economic, B and E are political, while F is technological.

Test your understanding 2

The correct answer is C

The company seems to be in a stable, fairly slow-moving industry, so A is less likely to be an issue. B and D are the same issue (just stated differently) – the scenario mentioned that management had a deep knowledge of the market, reducing the risk of bounded rationality.

However, as can be seen from the scenario, the manager in charge of undertaking the PEST analysis already has definite ideas about what is important, which could lead to bias creeping into his work.

Test your understanding 3

The correct answer is C

Barriers to entry appear to be low. Given the lack of patents and its distributor's plans to enter the market, WWW should be worried about the threat of new entrants.

Supplier power is unknown. No information is provided about WWW's suppliers – it's retail partner is a customer.

Customer power seems to be high – BBB has alternative wallpaper and paint suppliers it could choose to stock and seems keen to, potentially, replace WWW's products with its own in the short to mid-term.

Substitutes are not mentioned in the scenario. BBB will turn into a rival to WWW if it enters the market.

Test your understanding 4

The correct answer is A

If the customer is relatively small, the supplier is likely to have more power in their relationship as it does not rely on the customer for a large proportion of its sales.

The other three options would all suggest low supplier power – if suppliers are unlikely to take over the business (low chance of forward integration), there are many of them for the business to choose from, or it easy to switch to other suppliers due to a lack of differentiation in their products, the customer enjoy higher power over the supplier.

Test your understanding 5 – Hawk – (Case style)

PEST analysis

Political factors

Approval from the ACU is vital for Hawk's racing suits. Whilst this will require regular inspections, it is important for credibility amongst customers. It may be seen as an endorsement of quality for the entire range (the so-called "halo effect").

Government/EU regulation that could damage motorcycle sales is an issue for the whole industry. If there is a clamp down it might seriously threaten sales. Hawk might consider setting up a lobby group with other manufacturers.

Economic factors

The recession in the UK economy (and foreign markets) is likely to result in lower disposable incomes for what is often a luxury purchase. Hawk may well find a major dip in sales as the recession continues.

The weakening pound is making exports to the USA and Europe easier, but is increasing the import costs of leather. There is little Hawk can do about that, so it is likely to seek new global markets such as the BRIC economies (Brazil, Russia, India and China).

Strategic analysis: External environmental analysis

Social factors

There has been a growth in demand from mature riders ("born-again bikers"). Have companies such as Hawk done any research to assess the life of this trend? How effective is Hawk's marketing at reaching this potentially important market segment?

More emphasis on safety of riders who often have family; this is a boost for the industry and Hawk's customers are likely to be responsible bikers.

Technological factors

Relevant issues include website ordering and metallic paints but neither of these is especially important. However, Hawk and others should be aware of new ideas that could help with their processes.

Porter's five forces

Threat of new entrants

The threat of new entrants is reasonably high from overseas rivals but is limited by existing entry barriers. These include recruiting skilled staff, close associations with racing teams, established relationships with major retailers and brand reputation.

Bargaining power of customers

The power of customers depends on which customers are being considered. For individual customers it is low because they will be loyal to the brand and are not buying in bulk.

However, for the large retailers there is higher power that arises from the volumes purchased. Retail chains will exercise this power in terms of designs, lead times, prices paid and credit period taken. Hawk need to meet these needs or risk losing major customers to existing/new competition.

It will also be high for the professional racing teams. Having Hawk's products associated with top class racing teams is imperative to maintain the quality of its brand in the marketplace. Suits must be made to a high quality and exactly to customer specification/compliance with the Auto Cycle Union's requirements.

Bargaining power of suppliers

The power of suppliers is generally low, because leather and machinery are readily available. (Note: It may be that supply of leather of the required quality for professional suits is limited, in which case the power would be higher.)

However, supplies of skilled labour are limited and Hawk may find it has to pay high wages.

Threat of substitutes

Hawk believes that the threat from substitutes is low and states that only leather can offer the required degree of abrasion resistance. Clearly this must be kept under review as newer fabrics and technologies may change this perception.

The threat of substitute products/fabrics may be higher in the fashion lines, although this does not yet constitute a major proportion of Hawk's turnover.

Competitive rivalry

Rivalry is considered to be low. Those "rivals" that offer cheap leathers are not really rivals at all, because serious bikers will not contemplate such offerings.

Furthermore, sales are rising so quickly that all players are working at near capacity without the need to take customers from one another.

Summary

The key risk areas for Hawk do not come from within the industry as, with the exception of the power of larger retailers, competitive forces are low. However, there are major issues that impact the industry as a whole in respect of the current economic climate and government policy.

(**Tutorial note:** each point within the models has been explained and assessed for its importance. Finally key points must be highlighted in order to then formulate or appraise strategy.)

Test your understanding 6

The correct answer is C

The seeming saturation of the market and the increase in competition would suggest the product is at the maturity stage. This stage typically sees the volume of product sales become more sensitive to selling price changes.

Test your understanding 7

The correct answer is C

A would indicate products that are in decline. B would tend to occur during growth, while D would usually be part of the introduction/growth phase of the product life cycle.

Test your understanding 8 – (Case style)

Presentation notes:

(**Tutorial note:** it is relatively straightforward to classify the individual products/SBUs but make sure you justify your choice. The higher skills element is in looking at the bigger picture to evaluate the overall portfolio balance.)

The market for recordable DVD recorders is still expanding and hence is in the growth phase. PTP really must try to boost its presence in this crucial market area (see below), or risk being left behind by rivals.

Sales of conventional DVD players are static, indicating a market that is mature and possibly saturated. This is a problem given PTP's historical dependence on this product stream. The risk is that profits will soon decline or disappear if retailers lose interest in this product group.

The market for conventional CRT televisions is in decline, suggesting that PTP should focus instead on LCD and plasma televisions – the growth area. However, the niche in CCTV products may have a longer-term future, depending on the degree of competition.

Despite being a market leader, PTP's sales of LCD and plasma televisions are only rising modestly suggesting that the industry (or at least PTP's products) are still in late introduction or early growth stages. PTP believes that this segment is going to be huge, so will need to invest heavily in marketing and product development to ensure it can capitalise on the high growth when it arises.

Overall portfolio evaluation

The balance of a portfolio can be assessed against a range of criteria including cash flow, growth, risk and investment required. This can be achieved to some extent by having products at different stages throughout the lifecycle. While PTP has products at different stages within the lifecycle, the main problems with its portfolio are:

- CRT TVs are facing decline but PTP does not have any new products in the development stage to replace them.
- The overall portfolio may require a net investment of cash in the future. Conventional DVD players may be strong cash generators but both recordable DVD players and LCD and Plasma TVs require investment to benefit from future growth.

Suggestions for re-balancing the portfolio include:

- Invest to develop Blu-Ray players and recorders. PTP might offer a guaranteed trade-in value for old units if customers purchase a new Blu-Ray DVD.
- Switch production away from the old factory to the new one in Holland, perhaps selling the old site and using the proceeds for an acquisition of a home entertainment-focused business.

Test your understanding 9

The correct answer is FACTOR CONDITIONS

The business is missing a key factor that would enable it to operate in the target country.

Strategic analysis: External environmental analysis

Test your understanding 10

The correct answers are: A4, B1, C3, D2

A4 – Lack of farming indicates a missing related industry for a supermarket.

B1 – Large numbers of existing supermarkets could indicate that there is insufficient spare demand for AHH to win if it wishes to expand into country L.

C3 – The lack of land is a specific missing factor that AHH also needs in order to successfully expand into country L.

D2 – AHH's success in other competitive markets may indicate that it has the necessary strategy and structure to deal with the competition in country L.

Test your understanding 11 – (Integration question)

Why enter export markets?

Australian producers would have been under pressure to increase profits since some are effectively listed companies. Furthermore, it is likely that domestic markets had become saturated. There must be a limited consumption in Australia, therefore producers' attention would turn to export volumes. They would have spotted an opportunity to target growth markets in the UK and Europe.

Likely risks

One risk would have been culture and tradition. For example, wine drinking in the UK was far less common than it is today, and the risk would have been non-acceptance by a UK market.

Equally, the French are very protective of their own wines and reluctant to stock those from other countries. National bias would be a major barrier to overcome in some wine-drinking countries.

Another risk would be financial – namely exchange rate fluctuations and costs involved in transporting a product that is over 85% water for thousands of miles.

Porter's Diamond

Factor conditions would include the availability of land, the favourable climate, and the skill of Australian winemakers (so impressive that they have exported their talents back to European producers – the so-called "flying winemakers"). These would combine to give a strong advantage to Australia, because few rival countries possess such a favourable mix.

Demand conditions are also strong; Australia has an alcohol tolerant culture, and domestic consumers would have set high standards. However, this would also apply to countries such as France, so this factor may have given Australia a medium-level advantage overall.

Related and supporting industries will be strong since Australia is a modern, developed industrial nation. This will confer a medium-level advantage compared to Western-European countries and the USA, but a strong one compared to, say, Chile. Australian firms may also have had an advantage as they could have invested in newer technologies while rivals in France would have been committed to traditional methods.

Strategy structure and rivalry would be favourable, since there is a properly developed stock market, and reasonably intense local rivalry. This would give a strong advantage compared to developing economies such as Argentina and Bulgaria. It would also give a strong advantage compared to countries with old-fashioned rules about wine, such as France (these rules often prevent true competition).

Strategic analysis: External environmental analysis

chapter 5

Strategic analysis: Internal environmental analysis

Chapter learning objectives

Lead	Component
B1. Evaluate the process of strategy formulation	(a) evaluate the process of strategic analysis and strategic options generation
B2. Evaluate tools and techniques used in strategy formulation	(a) Evaluate strategic analysis tools (c) Produce an organisation's Value Chain

Indicative syllabus content

- Audit of key resources and capabilities needed for strategy implementation.
- Value-chain analysis.
- Value drivers (including intangibles) of business and the data needed to describe and measure them.

Strategic analysis: Internal environmental analysis

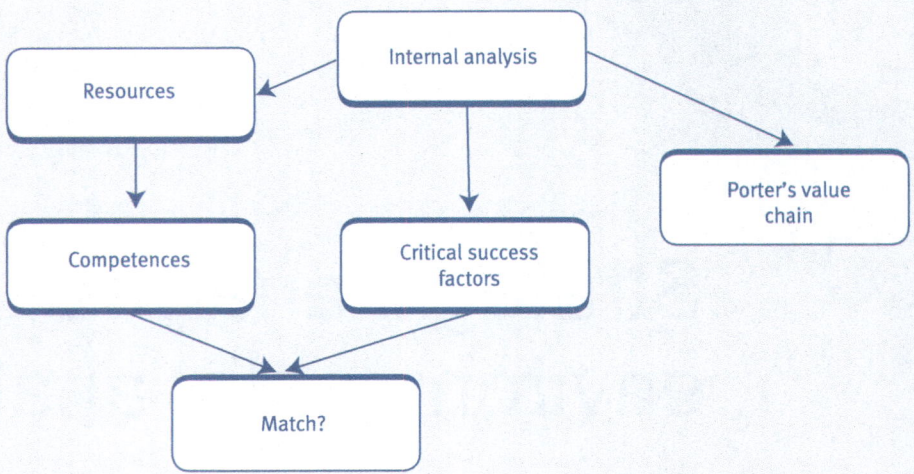

1 Introduction

The last chapter identified the key external issues that an organisation would need to consider when deciding upon an appropriate strategy.

In this chapter we will look at how an organisation examines its internal environment – the key issues within its own operations that it needs to consider as part of its overall strategic analysis.

The process of internal analysis typically involves the following stages:

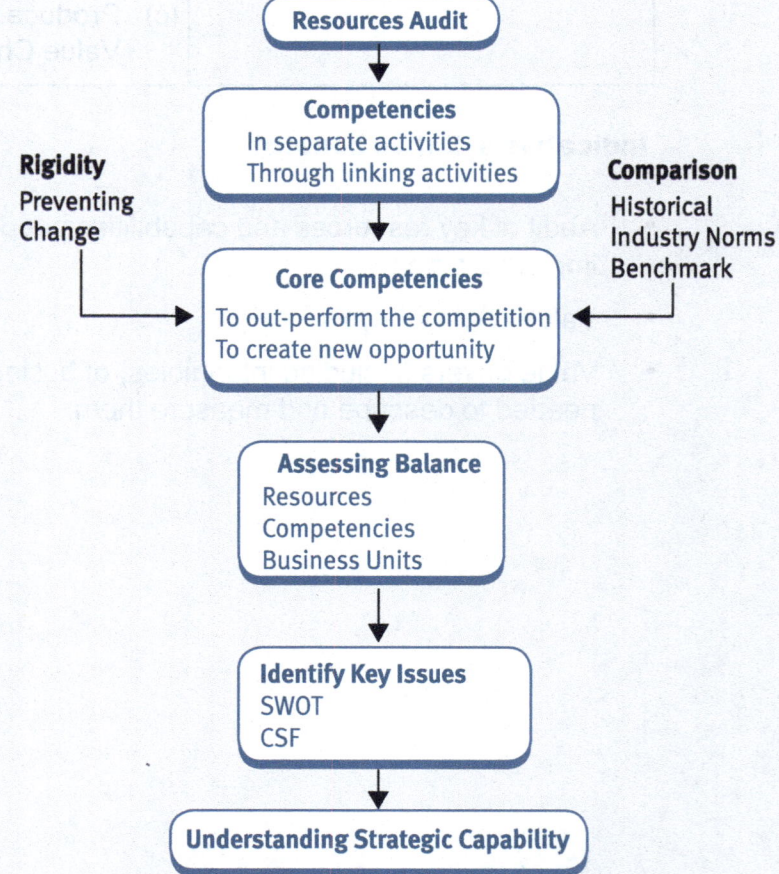

We will now look at these stages in more detail.

Internal analysis is a crucial part of developing a strategy. It helps the organisation to identify what it is capable of – what skills and assets it possesses. Understanding this will help the organisation identify which strategies it is capable of implementing.

2 Resource audit

The resources audit identifies the resources that are available to an organisation and seeks to start the process of identifying competencies.

It attempts to assess the relative strength of the resource base – the quantity of resources available, the nature of those resources and the extent to which those resources are unique and difficult to imitate.

One model in particular may help managers undertaking a resource audit locate these key factors.

M's model

This model suggests that the items in a position audit can be categorised into factors beginning with 'M':

- **Manpower (human resources):** The human assets of the firm, their skills and morale.
- **Money:** The company's cash position, gearing, investment plans, short and long term finance, etc.
- **Management:** The quality, expertise and experience of the top team. Is the firm well managed and does is have the skills and vision needed to progress?
- **Machinery:** The physical assets of the business, their flexibility, relative costs and the quality of what they produce.
- **Markets:** The products and the markets the company currently operates in. The quality and position of the products.
- **Materials:** The relationship between the company and its suppliers. Cost, quality and future availability of materials.
- **Methods:** The processes adopted by the business – outsourcing, JIT, etc.
- **Management information:** Quality and timeliness of information provided to managers. Will impact on quality of decisions made.
- **Make-up:** The culture and structure of the organisation. Also, branding and other intangibles.

Strategic analysis: Internal environmental analysis

This is not an exhaustive list to memorise. Instead it is a memory aid to help the resource auditor to identify all the key resources that are central to a business' success.

Resources can alternatively be grouped under four headings:

- **physical or operational resources**
- **human resources**
- **financial resources**
- **intangibles.**

The key is to know what you have available to you and how this will help you in any strategic initiative. At the same time the organisation needs to know what it is lacking and how things may change in the future. Shortage of resources will often constrain strategic initiative.

Note that the audit should also include resources that can be accessed by the organisation, not just legally owned. Some strategically important resources may exist, such as a network of contacts or customers or maybe via a strategic alliance or joint venture.

Resources are needed to undertake a strategy. They will not ensure its ultimate success. For that, the resources will need to be combined together into competencies.

Test your understanding 1

H Ltd has a strong brand name. Which of the following resource classifications would this be included within?

A   Markets

B   Make-up

C   Methods

D   MIS

3 Competences

Resources are combined together to achieve a competence.

A competence is a group of abilities, resources or skills that enable the organisation to act effectively.

There are two key types of competence that you need to be aware of:

- **Core competences** – these are things that you are able to do that are difficult for your competitors to emulate. They form the basis of competitive advantage and are referred to by Johnson and Scholes as '**the order winners**'.

- **Threshold competences** – these are things that you do well that simply enable you to compete in the market. They do not give competitive advantage – if they are not satisfied, you will not even be considered by the customer. They are referred to as '**the order qualifiers**'.

Illustration 1 – Coca–Cola

The Coca-Cola Corporation has, for many years, maintained a very strong position in the soft drinks market. Consider its flagship product, Coca-Cola. This has largely survived competition from supermarkets' own-brand colas. There is no great secret in how to make a reasonable imitation (though purists would argue that the imitations are not as good) and the resources needed are not demanding. The own-label colas sell at much lower prices, so how has Coca-Cola managed to keep its dominant position?

It has been argued that physical resources are often less important. These are likely to form the **threshold competences**. Coca-Cola has bottling plants, access to suitable water, and a formulation for its drink. However, its competitors also have these things. They do not give Coca-Cola a competitive edge.

The reason Coca-Cola has managed to maintain its dominant position mainly lies in the non-physical or intangible resources, such as a very powerful brand. The **core competences** lie in managing the brand by producing memorable global advertising, global recognition, careful sponsorship and responding to customer requirements (diet/caffeine-free products).

Over time the core competence will become threshold as:

- cultures adjust and expectations develop
- customers and consumers become more sophisticated in terms of their needs and expectations
- competitors imitate our core competences

Organisations need to ensure that they are continually monitoring their marketplace to ensure that their core competencies are still valid and that all thresholds are duly satisfied.

Remember, what is good today is not necessarily good tomorrow!

Illustration 2 – Changing competences

When Apple launched its iPhone in 2007, it had a number of features that gave it competitive advantage, including:

- full colour touch-screen interface
- use of premium materials
- aesthetically pleasing design
- user-friendly software interface
- linked to the strong Apple brand

Today, rival mobile phone manufacturers have made many of these features standard in their products, meaning that they would no longer be considered 'order winners'. For example, most modern smartphones include touch-screen interfaces, strong design standards and premium materials. These 'core' features have thus become 'threshold' over time.

Competence audit

As well as the resource audit mentioned earlier in the chapter, the organisation may well undertake a **competence audit**. This will typically involve:

- analysis of what competences the organisation has, as well as how well resources are being deployed to create them.
- categorisation of competences as core or threshold. This will be done by looking at historic data, industry norms and benchmarking exercises (which will usually be undertaken by specialist teams).

Test your understanding 2

Insert the missing word into the following statement:

_____ competences are those that help an organisation to achieve competitive advantage over its rivals.

4 Critical success factors

Critical success factors (CSFs) are the limited number of areas in which results, if they are satisfactory, will ensure successful competitive performance for the business.

They are the vital areas where 'things must go right' and where the business must outperform its competitors.

It is important, therefore, that any assessment of resources, competences, strengths and weaknesses is done by reference to what we have to be good at.

For example, having the highest quality in the industry may be admirable but it misses the point if the market is driven by price wars and customers are only willing to pay low prices.

Examples of CSFs for major industries include:

- in the automobile industry – styling, an efficient dealer network, vehicle performance and fuel efficiency
- in the food manufacturing industry – new product development, good distribution channels, health aspects (e.g. low fat)
- in the supermarket industry – having the right product mix, competitive pricing.

The organisation's critical success factors should tie into their corporate objectives. For example, if a supermarket's objective is to grow its market share, it will need to ensure that understands what it must do in order to successfully implement this strategy (i.e. what its CSFs will be).

The problem with CSFs is that they are often vague. As mentioned above, a supermarket may have a CSF of having 'competitive pricing', but how would the company know whether its pricing is 'competitive' or not?

In order to deal with this, organisations will need to create ways of measuring whether their CSFs are being met. These measures are known as key performance indicators, or KPIs.

Strategic analysis: Internal environmental analysis

> **Test your understanding 3 – (Integration question)**
>
> What might a parcel delivery service such as DHL identify as two of its main critical success factors?

> **Illustration 3 – Mission, CSF and KPI**
>
> A, a major supermarket chain in the country O, has a **corporate mission to be 'the best value retailer in country O.'**
>
> One of A's **critical success factors (CSFs) is that it needs to sell its goods for a lower price than its major rivals.** This will attract customers in the fiercely competitive country O supermarket industry, where many customers choose their supermarket based on price.
>
> In order to measure this CSF, A has set itself a **key performance indicator (KPI) to keep its average selling price ten percent below that of its rivals**. It monitors its rivals' selling prices and amends its own prices on a daily basis to ensure that it achieves this KPI.
>
> A can therefore be confident that if it meets its KPI, its major CSF will have been achieved. This will help it meet its overall mission.

> **Illustration 4 – Critical success factors**
>
> The following is an example of CSFs developed for a shipping terminal.
>
> | Critical success factor | Indicator | Mechanism for measurement |
> |---|---|---|
> | Customer satisfaction | • Complaints
 • Insurance claims
 • Losses of stock | • Complaints register
 • Correspondence
 • Internal audit |
> | Maintenance of premises | • Repair costs | • Inspection |
> | Efficient use of staff | • Time standards for loading and unloading | • Training schedules
 • Direct inspection |

164

Test your understanding 4 – (Integration question)

Using the CSFs previously identified for a parcel delivery company such as DHL, explain how the company might measure their performance.

Sources of CSFs

Rockart claims that there are four sources for CSFs:

(1) The industry that the business is in – each has CSFs that are relevant to any company within it.

   For example, the car industry must have as one of its CSFs 'compliance with pollution requirements regarding exhaust gases'.

(2) The company itself and its situation within the industry – e.g. its competitive strategy and its geographic location.

   For example, a firm that has decided to compete on the basis of quality could have CSFs relating to identifying and delivering key product features that are valued by customers.

(3) The wider environment – e.g. the economy, the political factors and consumer trends in the country or countries that the organisation operates in.

   For example, in a time of oil shortages 'energy supply availability' could be a critical success factor.

(4) Temporal organisational factors – these are areas of company activity that are unusually causing concern because they are unacceptable and need attention.

   For example, a company with liquidity problems may place "short term cash management" as a CSF to ensure survival.

Strategic analysis: Internal environmental analysis

Test your understanding 5

H is a retailer of garden furniture. It has recently been told by its major shareholders that they wish to see a one-off increase in dividends from the company next year, meaning that H needs to improve its cash flow quickly.

According to Rockart, which of the following sources of critical success factors (CSFs) is being described above?

A   The industry that H is in

B   Temporal organisational factors

C   The wider environment

D   The company and its position in the industry

Test your understanding 6 – GGG – (Case style)

You have recently been provided with the following document giving you some background to GGG – a company that you have applied to work for as a strategic management accountant.

Background document – GGG Trains

GGG operates trains across Country H. The train infrastructure (stations and tracks) are owned by the Government of Country H. GGG has a fifteen year franchising agreement with the Government which allows it to exclusively operate the trains across the entire national railway network. GGG is now seven years through its current franchise agreement.

While the franchise agreement is for fifteen years, it is reviewed annually by the Government. The Government wishes to maximise the number of residents of Country H that use the trains (as opposed to motor vehicles), as this will help Country H meet its international environmental targets for carbon emission reductions.

The road network in Country H is old and is often significantly congested. However, train passenger numbers are only growing slowly. A recent Government survey has suggested that this is because passengers still feel that GGG tickets are too expensive and that the services offered are usually overcrowded and often late. GGG's staff are felt to lack knowledge and are 'unhelpful' to customers.

The Government of Country H is threatening to strip GGG of its franchise unless it shows substantial improvement. GGG's managers have several initiatives planned to improve the issues highlighted by the survey, and are currently considering how they can measure whether these initiatives are being successful.

Required:

As part of your job application, you have been asked to suggest FOUR of the critical success factors that GGG's management might identify. For each critical success factor identify ONE key performance indicator that GGG could use to see if its initiatives are being effective. Justify your choices.

(20 minutes)

The link between CSFs and competences

Note that CSFs and competences are slightly different concepts.

- CSFs are what the organisation **needs** to be good at in order to compete in the market.
- Competences are what the organisation **is** good at.

It should, however, be clear that in order for an organisation to be successful, its competences and CSFs should be as closely aligned as possible – which is why regular analysis of both is so important. The organisation's strategy must look at ways of maximising the correlation between the two.

Test your understanding 7

HHH has stated that it wishes to ensure that it delivers 95% of goods to customers within 15 days of them placing an order.

Is this an example of:

A   A mission

B   A key performance indicator

C   A critical success factor

D   A vision

Strategic analysis: Internal environmental analysis

Test your understanding 8

B Ltd has identified a critical success factor (CSF):

Have the best complaints handling department in the industry.

Which ONE of the following would be the most suitable key performance indicator for this CSF?

A   Increase customer happiness by 15%

B   Reduce the number of complaints received by 20%

C   Improve the effectiveness of training for complaints staff

D   Reduce the average time taken to deal with complaints by 15%

Test your understanding 9 – RCH – (Case style)

RCH, an international hotel group with a very strong brand image has recently taken over TDM, an educational institution based in Western Europe. RCH has a very good reputation for improving the profitability of its business units and prides itself on its customer focus. The CEO of RCH was recently quoted as saying 'Our success is built on happy customers: we give them what they want'. RCH continually conducts market and customer research and uses the results of these researches to inform both its operational and longer term strategies.

TDM is well-established and has always traded profitably. It offers a variety of courses including degrees both at Bachelor and Masters levels and courses aimed at professional qualifications. TDM has always concentrated on the quality of its courses and learning materials. TDM has never seen the need for market and customer research as it has always achieved its sales targets. Its students consistently achieve passes on a par with the national average. TDM has always had the largest market share in its sector even though new entrants continually enter the market. TDM has a good reputation and has not felt the need to invest significantly in marketing activities. In recent years, TDM has experienced an increasing rate of employee turnover.

RCH has developed a sophisticated set of Critical Success Factors which is integrated into its real-time information system. RCH's rationale for the take-over of TDM was the belief that it could export its customer focus and control system, based on Critical Success Factors, to TDM. RCH believed that this would transform TDM's performance and increase the wealth of RCH's shareholders.

chapter 5

> **Required:**
>
> (i) Identify four Critical Success Factors which would be appropriate to use for TDM.
>
> (ii) Recommend, with reasons, two Key Performance Indicators to support each of the four Critical Success Factors you have identified.
>
> (30 minutes)

5 Value drivers

Value drivers are activities or features that enhance the perceived value of a product or service by customers and which therefore create value for the producer. Value drivers can be tangible or intangible.

For example, a high-street electronics retailer could have several value drivers, including:

- Product mix
- Convenient store locations
- Knowledgeable, friendly staff

If these value drivers are present, it will attract customers to the retailer's stores and may help it achieve a competitive advantage over rivals.

One of the main models that can be used to identify the value drivers of an organisation is Porter's Value Chain.

6 Porter's Value Chain

Porter's Value Chain

Support Activities					
Firm Infrastructure					Margin
Human Resource Management					
Technology Development					
Procurement					
Inbound Logistics	Operations	Outbound Logistics	Marketing & Sales	Service	Margin

Primary Activities

169

Strategic analysis: Internal environmental analysis

This is a means by which the activities within and around the organisation are identified and then related to the assessment of competitive strength.

Resources are of no value unless they are deployed into activities that are organised into routines and systems. These should then ensure that products are produced which are valued by customers and consumers. Porter argued that an understanding of strategic capability must start with an identification of the separate value-adding activities.

Primary activities

These activities are involved in the physical creation of the product, its transfer to the buyer and any after-sales service. Porter divided them into five categories:

(1) **Inbound logistics** are activities concerned with receiving, storing and distributing the inputs to the product. They include materials handling, stock control and transport.

(2) **Operations** transform these various inputs into the final product – machining, packing, assembling, testing and control equipment.

(3) **Outbound logistics** relate to collecting, storing and distributing the product to buyers.

(4) **Marketing and sales** provide the means whereby consumers and customers are made aware of the product and transfer is facilitated. This would include sales administration, advertising, selling and so on.

(5) **Service** relates to those activities which enhance or maintain the value of a product such as installation, repair, training and after-sales service.

Support activities

Each of the primary activities are linked to support activities and these can be divided into four areas:

(1) **Procurement** refers to the processes for acquiring the various resource inputs to the primary activities – not the resources themselves. As such it occurs throughout the organisation.

(2) **Technology development** – all value activities have a technological content, even if it is just 'know how'. IT can affect product design or process and the way that materials and labour are dealt with.

(3) **Human resource management,** which involves all areas of the business and is involved in recruiting, managing, training, developing and rewarding people within the organisation.

(4) **Infrastructure** refers to the systems of planning, finance, quality control, information management, etc. All are crucially important to an organisation's performance in primary activities. It also consists of the structures and routines that sustain the culture of the organisation.

Generally

The primary and secondary activities are designed to help create the organisation's margin by taking inputs and using them to produce outputs with greater value.

The value chain can be used to:

- give managers a deeper understanding of precisely what their organisation does
- identify the key processes within the business that add value to the end customer – strategies can then be created to enhance and protect these, and
- identify the processes that do not add value to the customer. These could then be eliminated, saving the organisation time and money.

The value system

Looks at linking the value chains of suppliers and customers to that of the organisation.

Can add value by:

- Enhancing the supply – e.g. organic food for ready meals.
- Controlling of the retail process – e.g. car dealerships.
- Linking it all together to give advantage – Porter's diamond.

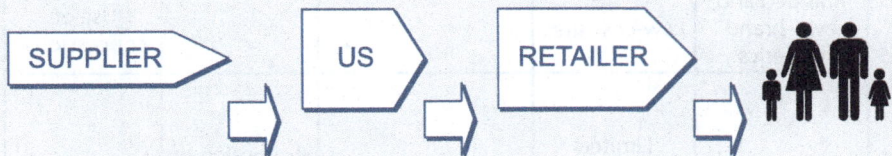

Strategic analysis: Internal environmental analysis

Illustration 5 – The Value Chain

Marks and Spencer plc compete in, amongst other areas, the food and grocery market. They have configured their value chain in order to offer customers a differentiated service.

FI	Central control of operations & credit services				
TD		Recipe research	Electronic point of sale	Customer research and testing	Itemised billing
HRD	Recruitment of mature staff	Client care training	Flexible staff to help with enquiries and packing		
P	Own label products	Prime retail positions		Adverts in quality press and poster sites	
	Dedicated refrigerated transport	In-store food halls Modern store design Dairy cabinets	Collect by car service	No price discounts	No quibble refunds
	IL	O	OL	M/S	S

Lidl also operates in the food and grocery market, but their value chain supports a cost–leadership approach.

Minimum head office costs				
Use of casual staff	De-skilled store ops	Dismissal for check-out error		
Branded and own-brand generics	Low-cost sites			Use of concessions
Bulk warehousing	Limited product range Price points Basic store design	Customers encouraged to use boxes Packing benches	Promotion of low prices Store manager decides stock	Nil

Test your understanding 10

Which THREE of the following are **primary** activities in Porter's value chain?

A   Service
B   Infrastructure
C   Procurement
D   Marketing and sales
E   Technology development
F   Procurement
G   Operations

Test your understanding 11

A manager at HG plc (which manufactures plasma televisions) has developed a new computerised system which will help the inventory control of finished units at HG's warehouse. She believes that this will reduce the time taken to ship these goods by around 25%.

Which ONE of the following primary activities with HG's value chain will the new system be directly improving?

A   Inbound logistics
B   Operations
C   Outbound logistics
D   Infrastructure

Strategic analysis: Internal environmental analysis

Test your understanding 12

H is an accountancy firm. It gathers data from its clients' systems and uses this to create a set of year end accounts. A recent internal analysis exercise has allowed H to create a list of its key internal activities. It now wishes to classify these activities using Porter's value chain.

H's internal activities	Value chain activity
A Creation of clients' year end accounts	1 Inbound logistics
B Meeting with client to deliver and discuss year end accounts	2 Infrastructure
C Central quality control systems to ensure accuracy of accounts	3 Outbound logistics
D Receiving and storing data from client systems	4 Operations

Show which of H's internal activities relates to each value chain activity by pairing the appropriate letter and number (e.g. A1, B4, etc).

Test your understanding 13 – Reggs – (Case style)

Background

Reggs is a long established bakers, based in country G. It specialises in selling pastries, cakes, sandwiches and basic tea and coffee, through a chain of high-street stores. It has grown rapidly over the last ten years and now operates more than 1,500 stores across the country.

Reggs marketing strategy is to focus on the low prices of its food, with heavy advertising in the free press and tabloids. It sells the majority of its products for less than its competitors – a strategy which has paid dividends as country G is suffering an extended period of poor economic growth.

To achieve these low prices, Reggs uses its purchasing power to source large amounts of good quality raw materials at low prices. These goods are transferred to a central warehouse. Reggs uses a sophisticated stock management system to track all materials and ensure that they are used before they perish.

The raw materials are then sent (using Reggs own fleet of delivery vans) to several regional bakeries, where G's products are part-baked. The part-baked products are then sent to the individual high-street stores, where they are completed. Much of this process is automated, enabling Reggs' to hire low-skilled workers. This automation has meant that Reggs feel that quality control is no longer necessary. The company does not keep track of customer complaints as these are normally dealt with by the in-store staff. No formal policies have been produced to guide employees when dealing with complaints.

The high-street stores are of a very basic design, with a large counter and racks of produce. There is no seating and, due to Reggs' popularity, there are often long queues filling the stores. Reggs' management is concerned that this may be putting off some potential customers from patronising the company. However, Reggs has not undertaken any significant customer research in some years as its managers have felt that its rapid growth indicates that there are no significant problems.

Reggs management are keen to expand the business further and are looking at their strategic options. One suggestion is to alter Reggs' traditional product range. Some lower priced items would be removed to make way for more expensive, luxury foods which will have a higher margin attached to them. These items would not travel well and would therefore need to be produced in the high-street stores. This would require moderately skilled workers.

Reggs feels that this may help to attract customers away from its competitors – such as coffee shops. These are significantly more expensive than Reggs, but have a much higher perceived quality of food and drink. Typically these competitors have well-designed, comfortable seating areas, enabling them to charge higher prices.

You are a management accountant working for Reggs. You report to the Operations Director, who has sent you the following email:

To: L. Ray
From: O. Flow
Date: 12/05/XX
Subject: Value chain

Hi L,

As you are aware, we have been considering making some changes to our operations (as we discussed the other day). I need you to undertake some analysis for me. Specifically, I would like you to analyse our primary activities of the value chain, identifying any weaknesses. Please identify how each activity enables our business to sell its goods at low prices. (I don't need a diagram of the value chain).

Could you also discuss the drawbacks of the strategy we are currently considering – relating to more expensive, luxury products. How far would the proposals impact on the existing value chain?

I am attending a meeting about this in forty-five minutes, so please email back by then with your thoughts.

Kind regards

O.Flow

Required:

Email the Operations Director as requested.

Benefits and criticisms of Porter's Value Chain

Proponents suggest that the value chain model has many benefits, including:

- It provides a generic framework to analyse both the behaviour of costs as well as the existing and potential sources of differentiation.

- Activities that are not adding value can be identified and addressed – for example, improved so they do add value or outsourced if this is not possible.

- It emphasises the importance of (re)grouping functions into activities to produce, market, deliver and support products, to think about relationships between activities and to link the value chain to the understanding of an organisation's competitive position.

- It makes it clear that an organisation is multifaceted and that its underlying activities need to be analysed to understand its overall competitive position.

- It is an attempt to overcome the limitations of portfolio planning in multidivisional organisations. Rather than assuming that SBUs should act independently, Porter used his Value Chain analysis to identify synergies or shared activities between them and to provide a tool to focus on the whole rather than on the parts.

The main criticisms of Porter's Value Chain model are as follows:

- It is more suited to a manufacturing environment and can be difficult to apply to a service provider

- The Value Chain model was intended as a quantitative analysis. However, this is time consuming since it often requires recalibrating the accounting system to allocate costs to individual activities.

The value shop

The value shop is an alternative representation of a value chain for a professional services firm which was developed in 1998 by Stabell and Fjelstad.

A value shop is considered to be a workshop which mobilises resources to solve specific problems. This may involve repeating a generic set of activities until a satisfactory solution is reached. The shop model applies to many organisations, particularly those whose main purpose is to identify and exploit specific opportunities like designing a bespoke product.

The model has the same support activities as Porter's Value Chain but the primary activities are described differently. In the value shop they are:

- problem finding and acquisition
- problem solving
- choosing among solutions
- execution and control/evaluation.

The management in the value shop organisation therefore focuses on areas such as the assessment of problems and opportunities, the mobilisation of resources, project management, the delivery of solutions, the measurement of outcomes and also learning.

The value shop primary activities are arranged in a circle showing that they are cyclical, with an organisation often moving back and forth to develop or reject theories before reaching a conclusion.

Test your understanding 14

J wishes to link her inbound logistics activities to the outbound logistics operations of her suppliers in order to maximise efficiency.

Which of the following concepts is this referring to?

A   Value Shop
B   Value Driver
C   Value System
D   Value Linkage

Strategic analysis: Internal environmental analysis

Test your understanding 15 – Bowland – (Case style)

Bowland Carpets Ltd is a major producer of carpets within the UK. The company was taken over by its present parent company, Universal Carpet Inc., in 20X3. Universal Carpet is a giant, vertically-integrated carpet manufacturing and retailing business, based within the USA but with interests all over the world.

Bowland Carpets operates within the UK in various market segments, including the high-value contract and industrial carpeting area – hotels and office blocks, etc. – and in the domestic (household) market. Within the latter the choice is reasonably wide, ranging from luxury carpets down to the cheaper products. Industrial and contract carpets contribute 25% of Bowland Carpets' total annual turnover, which is currently $80 million. Up until 15 years ago the turnover of the company was growing at 8% per annum, but since 20X2 sales revenue has dropped by 5% per annum in real terms.

Bowland Carpets has traditionally been known as a producer of high-quality carpets, but at competitive prices. It has a powerful brand name, and it has been able to protect this by producing the cheaper, lower-quality products under a secondary brand name. It has also maintained a good relationship with the many carpet distributors throughout the UK, particularly the mainstream retail organisations.

The recent decline in carpet sales revenue, partly recession induced, has worried the US parent company. It has recognised that the increasing concentration within the European carpet manufacturing sector has led to aggressive competition within a low-growth industry. It does not believe that overseas sales growth by Bowland Carpets is an attractive proposition as this would compete with other Universal Carpet companies. It does, however, consider that vertical integration into retailing (as already practised within the USA) is a serious option. This would give the UK company increased control over its sales and reduce its exposure to competition. The president of the parent company has asked Jeremy Smiles, managing director of Bowland Carpets, to address this issue and provide guidance to the US board of directors. Funding does not appear to be a major issue at this time as the parent company has large cash reserves on its balance sheet.

You have been contacted by Jeremy Smiles, who has asked for briefing notes covering the following key issues:

(a) To what extent do the distinctive competences of Bowland Carpets conform with the key success factors required for the proposed strategy change?

(b) In an external environmental analysis concerning the proposed strategy shift what are likely to be the key external influences which could impact upon the Bowland Carpets decision?

Required:

Draft the briefing notes as requested.

(45 minutes)

Test your understanding 16 – (Integration question)

A university which derives most of its funds from the government provides undergraduate courses (leading to bachelor's degrees) and post-graduate courses (leading to master's degrees). Some of its funds come from contributions from student fees, consultancy work and research. In recent years the university has placed emphasis on recruiting lecturers who have achieved success in delivering good academic research. This has led to the university improving its reputation within its national academic community, and applications from prospective students for its courses have increased.

The university has good student support facilities in respect of a library which is well stocked with books and journals and up-to-date IT equipment. It also has a gymnasium and comprehensive sports facilities. Courses at the university are administered by well-qualified and trained non-teaching staff who provide non-academic (that is, not learning-related) support to the lecturers and students.

The university has had no difficulty in filling its courses to the level permitted by the government, but has experienced an increase in the number of students who have withdrawn from the first year of their courses after only a few months. An increasing number of students are also transferring from their three-year undergraduate courses to other courses within the university but many have left and gone to different universities. This increasing trend of student withdrawal is having a detrimental effect on the university's income as the government pays only for students who complete a full year of study.

Strategic analysis: Internal environmental analysis

You are the university's management accountant and have been asked by the Vice-Chancellor (who is the Chief Executive of the university) to review the withdrawal rate of students from the university's courses.

Required:

Apply Value Chain analysis to the university's activities, and advise the Vice-Chancellor how this analysis will help to determine why the rate of student withdrawal is increasing.

(30 minutes)

7 Summary

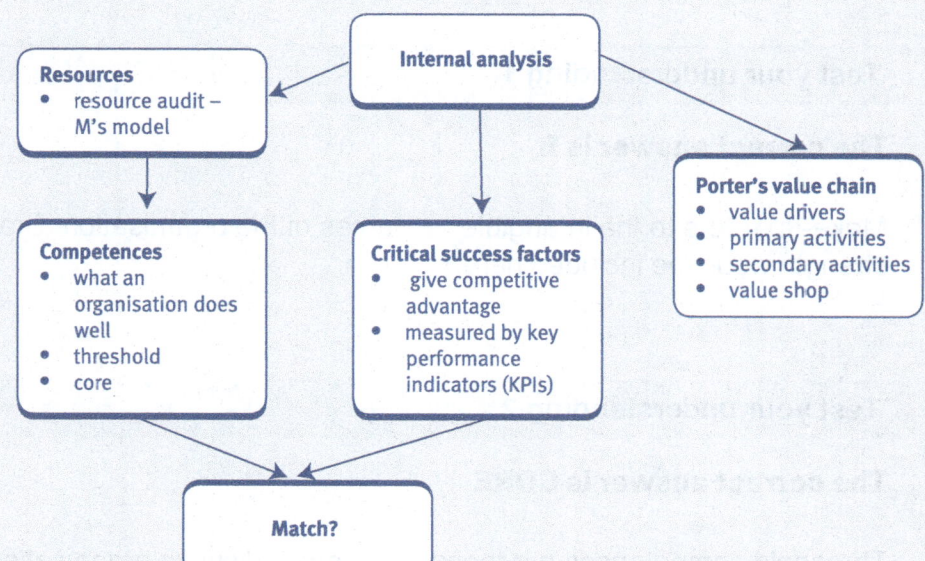

Test your understanding answers

Test your understanding 1

The correct answer is B

Make-up refers to the intangible resources of the organisation. Brand strength would be included here.

Test your understanding 2

The correct answer is CORE

Threshold competences are those that simply allow an organisation to compete with its rivals, but which do not give competitive advantage.

Test your understanding 3 – (Integration question)

The two main critical success factors would probably be:

- speedy collection from customers after their request for a parcel to be delivered
- rapid and reliable delivery.

Test your understanding 4 – (Integration question)

Their performance can be measured by establishing key performance indicators for each CSF and measuring actual achievements against them. For example:

- Collection from customers within three hours of receiving the order for orders received before 2.30p.m. on a working day.
- Next-day delivery for 100% of parcels to destinations within the UK.
- Delivery within two days for 100% of parcels to destinations within Europe.

chapter 5

Test your understanding 5

The correct answer is B

There is a short-term need for the organisation to improve cash flow, indicating a temporal organisational issue.

Test your understanding 6 – GGG – (Case style)

There are a number of issues that the Government's survey has highlighted as areas of concern, which GGG should view as its critical success factors/objectives.

Growth in use of the railways

The Government wishes to **maximise the use of the railways in Country H**.

This would appear to be a key objective as it will help them to meet their international environmental targets and will reduce pressure on the road network.

A key performance measure here could be the annual percentage growth in passenger numbers. This will be a simple thing for GGG to measure and an area they can agree targets on with the Government.

Note that dealing with the other objectives (below) is likely to improve this area as well.

Value for money

The Government survey has indicated that the public views GGG's ticket prices as too high, which is putting them off travelling by train.

GGG therefore needs to find a way of **improving its perceived value for money if it wishes to grow passenger numbers.**

A key performance measure could be to ensure that the average ticket price is no more that the equivalent cost of travel by car or bus. This is likely to ensure that passengers see the train as a viable financial option.

Strategic analysis: Internal environmental analysis

Reduce overcrowding

The frequent overcrowding of the trains is a serious issue which causes discomfort for passengers and is limiting uptake of train travel.

GGG needs to **increase its capacity and reduce overcrowding if it wishes to attract customers**.

A key performance measure could be the average number of passengers having to stand per km of track. If GGG is able to put on more services (especially at peak times) this should fall, indicating reduced overcrowding.

Improve punctuality

Delays to the trains mean that passengers do not wish to travel as they cannot reliably guarantee that they will arrive at their destination on time.

Again, in order to attract customers, **GGG will need to improve the punctuality of its trains.**

The performance here could be measured by setting targets for the percentage of trains that arrive more than, say, five minutes after their stated arrival time. If this figure falls, GGG will be accomplishing its objective in this area.

Unhelpful staff

This is another area in which the Government survey has indicated problems – **GGG needs to improve on the level of service provided by its staff.**

Again this seems to be putting off potential customers (or at least reducing the likelihood of repeat business) and needs to be dealt with.

To measure whether this is being improved, GGG could set itself targets in areas such as a reduction in the number of complaints received about staff each year.

Alternatively, it could set targets on the average number of days of staff training per year, as improvements in this area are likely to improve the problem of unhelpful staff with poor knowledge of GGG's operations.

Note: The requirement only asks for FOUR critical success factors and ONE performance measure for each. Additional points have been added to this answer for completeness.

Test your understanding 7

The correct answer is B

This is an example of a measured target set by the organisation, suggesting that it is a KPI.

A mission, vision or CSF would be at a higher, more general level and would likely lack the specific measures set out in option B.

Test your understanding 8

The correct answer is D

A and C cannot easily be measured and therefore would not make suitable KPIs. B is not linked to the handling of complaints and therefore is not relevant to B's CSF.

D is measurable and, if achieved, would indicate that the CSF is being accomplished successfully.

Test your understanding 9 – RCH – (Case style)

(i) Identification of four CSFs appropriate for TDM

Critical success factors for TDM may include:

- **Employee satisfaction** – given that TDM is in a service industry, staff are likely to be key to its products and high levels of staff turnover are a concern.

- **Course quality** – given the competitive nature of the market, it is vital that TDM continues to offer appropriate courses that will attract students.

- **Student satisfaction** – in order to be successful, TDM must ensure students are pleased with their courses. If not, they may move to alternative suppliers and may dissuade other students from using TDM.

- **Strong financial results** – after the takeover, TDM will need to make sufficient profits to maximise the wealth of RCH shareholders.

(ii) **Recommended key performance indicators**

TDM's performance can be measured by establishing key performance indicators for each CSF and measuring actual achievements against them.

Employee satisfaction

Number of staff leaving each period

This is the most direct measure of whether staff members are satisfied with their roles within the business. TDM is experiencing increasingly high staff turnover, which may mean they are losing valuable, skilled members of staff.

Sickness/absence per staff member per month

De-motivated or unhappy staff can tend to take more time off work due to sickness. TDM should monitor this as an indirect measure of staff satisfaction, especially as it is likely to cause disruption to courses.

Course quality

Pass rates compared to national average

TDM currently achieve exam pass rates that are comparable to the national average. Given the competitive nature of the market they operate in, this is likely to be something prospective students use as a way of choosing a tuition provider.

Number of students choosing not to complete the course compared to average

If a course is of poor quality (either poor materials or tuition), students may choose not to complete the course – either ceasing to study with TDM or moving onto an alternative course. If the number of students doing this is above average, it should be investigated and targets put in place to bring it down to average.

Student satisfaction

Percentage student approval rating

TDM could give students a questionnaire at the end of each course. This could ask them about how they rate the course, the tutor and the course material. This could be invaluable for identifying problem areas that the business needs to resolve. This would be likely to please RCH given their focus on customer research.

Percentage of students going on to further studies with TDM

TDM offers a range of courses, including degrees at both Bachelor and Masters level. If students feel that TDM have provided a good service, they will be more likely to take their studies further with the organisation.

Strong financial results

Market share

While TDM currently has the largest market share in its segment, large numbers of competitors are continually entering the market. If market share begins to fall, it will have a damaging effect on the profitability of the business.

Profit targets

Given that RCH has purchased TDM with the specific intention of increasing profitability, it is likely that they will have specific targets in mind for the business that TDM will need to work to achieve. For example, TDM may need to measure profit margins to ensure they meet the targets set by RCH.

Test your understanding 10

The correct answers are A, D and G

The other options are all secondary.

Test your understanding 11

The correct answer is C

Outbound logistics looks at management of finished goods as well as delivery to the customer.

Strategic analysis: Internal environmental analysis

Test your understanding 12

The correct answers are A4, B3, C2, D1

Remember that the value chain can be applied to service industries as well. In this case, the chain may show the acquisition and handling of data/information rather than raw materials.

In this case, the firm will receive information from its clients relating to their financial statements. This is inbound logistics (D1)

The firm will then use this information to create the clients' financial statements – the main operation of H. This gives us A4.

The prepared accounts will centrally quality checked prior to a client meeting. This is relates to the way the firm is organised and its systems, giving C2.

Finally, the accounts will be given to the client and discussed with them, forming H's outbound logistics – B3.

Test your understanding 13 – Reggs – (Case style)

Email

To: O.Flow
From: L. Ray
Date: 12/05/XX
Subject: Re: Value Chain

Dear O,

Porter's value chain helps to identify the activities within and around the organisation. These can then be used to help assess the organisation's competitive strength.

Primary activities

Inbound logistics

This relates to the receiving, storing and distributing the inputs to the product.

For Reggs, this involves the storage of raw materials in its central warehouse, followed by the transfer of these materials to the regional bakeries. This is particularly important for Reggs due to the perishable nature of its goods.

Reggs source "good quality" raw materials that are satisfying customer demand.

It is vital that materials are used promptly to ensure wastage is minimised in order to keep costs low and a sophisticated IT system helps to ensure this.

Operations

This examines the transformation of raw materials into the final product.

In Reggs, this occurs in two stages – firstly when the product is initially part-baked in the regional bakeries and secondly (after transport) when the baking is completed in the high-street stores. In both cases, the company automates as much as possible to keep costs low. This also ensures that employees do not need any specialised skills, keeping wage costs low.

A weakness here seems to be a lack of quality control. The assumption that automation means that there will not be any mistakes made seems worrying and there is a risk that problems may not be picked up, potentially damaging Reggs' reputation and overall brand.

Outbound logistics

This relates to the storing and distributing of products to customers. For Reggs, customers visit their 1,500 stores to buy food, meaning that outbound logistics is minimal. This stage of the value chain simply relates to making sales to customers in store.

This appears to be a major weakness for Reggs, who appear to be overwhelmed by the numbers of customers demanding their products, leading to long queues. While the level of demand is encouraging, long queues may be losing custom for Reggs, who may wish to look at ways of improving the efficiency with which customers are dealt with – although some research should be undertaken first to see whether this is a sufficient problem to warrant investment.

Marketing and sales

Reggs appears to be targeting the lower-end of the market by sourcing advertising in the free press and tabloids. This is consistent with its approach of stressing the low-cost aspect of its food. Given the economic conditions in country G, this appears to be a sensible approach.

The basic store design also reinforces the image that Reggs is a low-cost business, strengthening its market image.

Service

This looks at after-sales care for customers.

At present, this does not appear to be a significant area of concern for Reggs. Complaints are not monitored by the company, instead being left to low-skilled employees in store.

Again, this is consistent with the low-cost approach of the business, but does risk damaging Reggs' reputation in the event of any serious problems occurring and does not enable Reggs to use customer feedback in an effective way.

Overall

Reggs has a well-designed supply chain that allows for minimal wastage and maximum efficiency. It allows the business to gain competitive advantage by operating as a cost leader within its market. However, it lacks a positive approach to customer feedback.

Proposed strategy

If Reggs begins offering luxury items, it will have a significant impact on the value chain of the organisation.

- Reggs will need to procure higher quality materials – potentially requiring new suppliers. The luxury items will replace existing products, meaning that Reggs will be ordering less of its existing raw materials, which may undermine its economies of scale.

- Materials will have to be transported directly from the warehouse to the stores, where the luxury items will be made. This will increase the complexity and cost of Reggs' internal transport system.

- The manufacturing of the luxury goods will require moderately skilled workers. Reggs currently employs workers who have low levels of skills, as this keeps wages low. It will incur significant additional costs to hire new workers.

- The new luxury items do not match the current brand image of the company. Reggs has basic stores, little service and advertising that focuses on the low cost of the items. Offering luxury, high priced items does not match this cost leadership strategy. It may fail to attract customers and lead to Reggs becoming "stuck in the middle".

- Should the new luxury goods take off and allow Reggs to grow its customer base, it may cause additional pressure on the queuing systems of the stores. The staff already seem unable to cope with the volume of custom they have at peak periods. Reggs may wish to deal with this problem first, before trying to capture more customers.

There are also a number of other reasons why the Reggs proposals may not be a success.

- Reggs has failed to carry out any significant market research into either proposal. This means that the company risks proceeding with investments that may not be what customers want. At best this could waste money – at worst, Reggs could alienate its customer base.

- Reggs is also eliminating existing, presumably profitable, products to make way for the new luxury items. If these are unsuccessful, it may fail to increase its profits overall. Higher priced items may struggle due to the weaker economy in the country.

- It should also be noted that Reggs is assuming that they can compete with coffee shop chains by simply offering higher quality goods. In reality, there are likely to be other factors, such as the comfortable surroundings and atmosphere, as well as the coffee shop brand names, which may make it hard for Reggs to successfully attract their customers.

Overall, the business needs to undertake significant additional research in order to ensure that the proposal is worth both the disruption to the value chain and the potential brand image confusion that it may cause.

I hope this helps – if you need any further information, please let me know.

Kind regards

L.Ray

Test your understanding 14

The correct answer is C

By definition.

Strategic analysis: Internal environmental analysis

Test your understanding 15 – Bowland – (Case style)

Key answer tips

Part (a) of the question can be split into three parts – what are Bowland's existing competencies, what are the key success factors needed in retailing, and do these two things match up. So a good approach would be to split your time evenly between all three elements

For part (b) an external analysis is normally a combination of both the PESTEL and 5 Forces models, but with only 15 marks available (and working on the basis of two marks per well-explained point) you do not have to cover every element. So if, for example, you can't determine any relevant 'Technical' issues then just leave this factor out.

Briefing notes

Bowland's competences

An organisation's **distinctive competences** are those things which an organisation does particularly well. They include the organisation's unique resources and capabilities as well as its strengths and its ability to overcome weaknesses. These competences can include aspects such as budgetary control, a strong technology base, a culture conducive to change and marketing skills.

Key success factors are those requirements which it is essential to have if one is to survive and prosper in a chosen industry/environment. These can include areas such as good service networks, up-to-date marketing intelligence and tight cost controls where margins are small.

It is not guaranteed that the distinctive competences and the key success factors are always in alignment. A company moving into the retail sector may have an excellent product research and development capability, but this alone will not help if it has no concept of service, or poorly sited retail outlets. It is critical to ensure that what the company excels at is what is needed to be successful in that particular area.

The **strengths of Bowland Carpets** include **strong brand names** which maintain integrity within the different market segments where the company operates. The company has a **balanced portfolio of customers** and the **range of products is equally balanced**, ensuring that any sectoral decline can be compensated for by growth in other markets. Other strengths which the company currently has include a **good relationship with distributors and strong support from a powerful parent company.** Some of its distinctive competences, such as a strong brand and a reasonable range of products, are critical in the proposed new environment, as will be the financial support of the parent company. However, there are some aspects which are cause for concern in the proposed new business environment.

The strength in the contract and industrial carpet segment will not be affected by the proposed vertical integration – sales tend to be through a direct sales force. The strong **relationship with distributors** will however be **jeopardised by the opening up of retail outlets**. Other retail chains will be unwilling to permit a rival to operate so freely, and therefore there will be a reluctance to stock Bowland's carpets. Unless Bowland Carpets can obtain wide retail market coverage to compensate for this potential problem, sales revenue will be adversely affected.

The **cost of developing extensive market coverage** will be enormous and whether it is in high-street outlets or specialist out-of-town centres the investment may be greater than the parent company has budgeted for. The company also has **no expertise in site appraisal and selection.** Although the newly structured value chain will generate greater control there is an associated **lack of flexibility** along with an **increase in the fixed cost base** of the business.

Another key success factor is the **need for expertise in retailing**. It may be that the UK company can import this from the USA but the culture of marketing household durables may not be transferable internationally. Bowland Carpets as the domestic company has no experience in this field.

A critical factor in successful retailing is the ability to provide a **comprehensive range of products**. Does Bowland Carpets have one? It is unlikely that the competitive carpet manufacturers will provide such a supply to one of their rivals.

It would, therefore, appear that there is no close conformity between the distinctive competences of Bowland Carpets and the key success factors required in the carpet retailing sector.

External environment

The **external environment** scan is an essential prerequisite prior to selecting a strategic option. It enables the company to identify and understand the key external and uncontrollable influences which will have an impact upon the company's strategy. The environment is increasingly turbulent and often hostile. Without this knowledge and appreciation the strategist will be operating in a minefield. The acquisition of the external information is obtained by scanning the environment continuously and monitoring key indicators, which should enable the company to position itself appropriately with respect to the external environment and the competition. The external scan should be structured around a SLEPT framework covering the following environments – social, legal, economic, political and technological. In addition it is also important to assess potential competitive reactions as part of the scanning process.

Strategic analysis: Internal environmental analysis

The environmental scan will influence the decision as to whether Bowland Carpets should concentrate on the UK or seek diversification elsewhere, either in products or markets. Possible factors are as follows:

- **Social issues:** Trends towards increasing car-centred shopping (superstores and out-of-town sites) or movements back to city-centre shopping: trends in fashion and furnishing – will carpets become a fashion item and result in greater replacement sales? Other factors of importance to Bowland include the rate of growth or decline in populations and changes in the age distribution of the population. In the UK there will be an increasing proportion of the national population over retirement age. In developing countries there are very large numbers of young people. Rising standards of living lead to increased demand for certain types of goods. This is why developing countries are attractive to markets.

- **Legal issues:** Laws in the UK differ from the US. They come from common law, parliamentary legislation and government regulations derived from it, and obligations under EU membership and other treaties. Legal factors that can influence decisions include aspects of employment law, e.g. minimum wage, laws to protect consumers and tax legislation. The monopoly/competition issues in this case are likely to be insignificant.

- **Economic issues:** An increased concentration for Bowland Carpets within the UK economy will depend upon future economic prospects, taxation policy (sales tax) and interest rates, income distribution and unemployment (influencing site location), trade barriers (cheap imports from Third World suppliers, or even low-cost tufted carpets from countries such as Belgium).

- **Political issues:** Government policy affects the whole economy and governments are responsible for enforcing and creating a stable framework in which business can be done. The quality of government policy is important in providing physical infrastructure, (e.g. transport), social infrastructure, (e.g. education) and market infrastructure, (e.g. planning and site development – town centre or out-of-town developments).

- **Technological issues:** Is retailing technology evolutionary or revolutionary? Will it be costly or labour saving? Will inventory control be facilitated – so saving costs? Technology contributes to overall economic growth. It can increase total output with gains in productivity, reduced costs and new types of product. It influences the way in which markets are identified – database systems make it much easier to analyse the marketplace. Information technology encourages de-layering of organisational hierarchies and better communications.

- **Competitive issues:** It will be necessary to assess the likely responses of both carpet distributors and carpet manufacturers to the proposed incursion by Bowland Carpets. Will the reactions be benign or will they be aggressive?

Test your understanding 16 – (Integration question)

Application of the value chain to university process

Approach

A specialist value chain question that would warrant a brief introduction and possibly a diagram. Don't go mad with the diagrams that do not 'add value' that much. Value chain analysis (VCA) is a method of reviewing all the activities of an organisation and how they interact with each other. Key linkages are identified and areas that create value are focused upon. VCA is not restricted to just the organisation but also the suppliers and customers.

In this question we will have to address the issue of university suppliers of resources:

- students
- staff
- premises
- facilities

And customers/consumers:

- degree holders
- employers
- society.

The starting point is to identify the objectives for the university in this context. There appear to be three particular issues.

- Students dropping out in the first year.
- Students transferring to another university or just leaving.
- Students swapping courses within the university.

The idea is to look at the primary and support activities to establish why these problems may be arising.

Strategic analysis: Internal environmental analysis

Primary activities

Inbound logistics	Operations	Outbound logistics	Marketing & sales	Service
• Student supply • Staff supply • Facilities supply • Course selections	• Course • Lecturing • Research • Library • IT access • Premises	• Skills base • Employer view • Graduate view	• Marketing mix structure • USP/CA? • Promotions • Research? • Price elasticity	• Support functions • Admin. functions • Social aspects • Post-qualification career assistance

Secondary activities

Procurement	Technology	HRM	Infrastructure
• Food & drink • Accommodation • Building work • Support staff • Books • Students & staff	• Availability • Content • Training • Change	• Staff selection processes • Staff turnover rates • Appraisal processes • Admin. staff processes	• Culture • Layout • Org. Structure • Faculties • Planning systems • Control systems (FFWD & FBK)

These are some of the things that should be looked at within this context. Processes need to be viewed at first hand and discussed to see how the 'chain' links up. All that needs to happen for the chain to fail is for one link to break.

How will it help?

This model is twenty years' old and designed for application in the private sector but it does have its uses here. The model acts as a **simple starting point** to focus management attention onto the issues. It is not designed to provide an answer, rather to get the 'ball rolling' for management in trying to identify where the problems lie. Managers will have seen it before and be vaguely familiar with it so there will be less resistance. Solutions to these kinds of problems come from reasoned debate from informed people.

VCA will start management thinking where they can add value. They will consider how they differ from the competition and on what basis they will attract staff and students in the future. It will force them to identify the order winners or **'core competencies'**.

At the same time, the process will identify the **threshold competencies,** or order qualifiers, that are needed. Failure to satisfy threshold competencies will lead to consumer dissatisfaction. This would lead to the student problems evident in this case so it looks like VCA would be useful here in spotting those threshold competencies that are not being satisfied. Universities are age-old organisations and are not well known for embracing change. It is possible that this university may be suffering from competence slip – that is the situation that arises when a past core competence becomes threshold as a result of increasing consumer sophistication. That means, as the consumer gains more experience of the product, they become more expectant of the service offered. The VCA will force management to consider the issues of **competitive advantage and disadvantage.**

The analysis will see research into student, employer and staff perceptions whilst at the same time may see the application of benchmarking techniques. This would compare a similar institution with ours to see where any issues may exist. So VCA:

- Is the starting point for discussion.
- Gets people from all areas of the business talking – team perspective so a range of opinion and expertise.
- Starts or improves communication, and feedback and forward are encouraged.
- Step-by-step analysis allows the competencies to be analysed.

Strategic analysis: Internal environmental analysis

chapter 6

Position and gap analysis

Chapter learning objectives

Lead	Component
B1. Evaluate the process of strategy formulation	(a) Evaluate the processes of strategic analysis and strategic options generation
B2. Evaluate tools and techniques used in strategy formulation	(a) Evaluate strategic analysis tools

Indicative syllabus content

- Forecasting and the various techniques used: trend analysis, system modelling, in-depth consultation with experts (e.g. Delphi method).

- Scenario planning and long-range planning as tools in strategic decision-making.

- Game theory approaches to strategic planning and decision-making. *Note: complex numerical questions will not be set.*

- Real options as a tool for strategic analysis. *Note: complex numerical questions will not be set.*

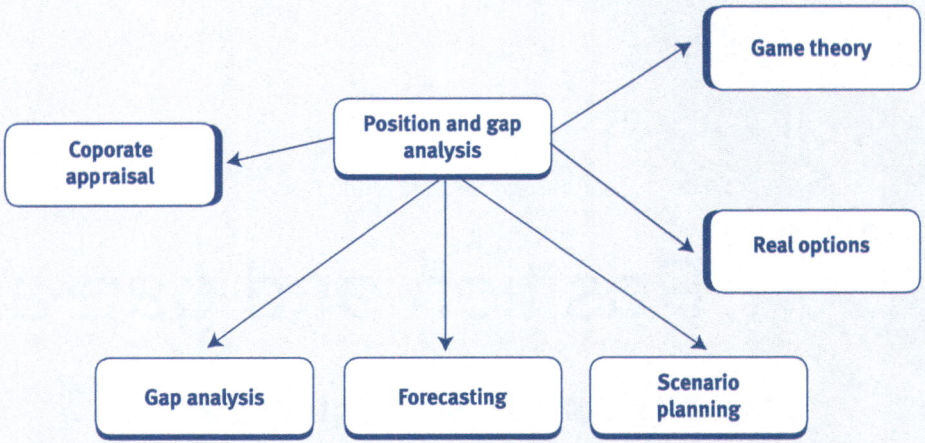

1 Position auditing (SWOT)

In the previous four chapters we have examined the methods that can be used to analyse the current situation of an organisation – internally, externally and with specific reference to its stakeholders, mission and objectives.

This analysis can be summarised in a formal corporate appraisal, which is typically referred to as a SWOT analysis (strengths, weaknesses, opportunities and threats).

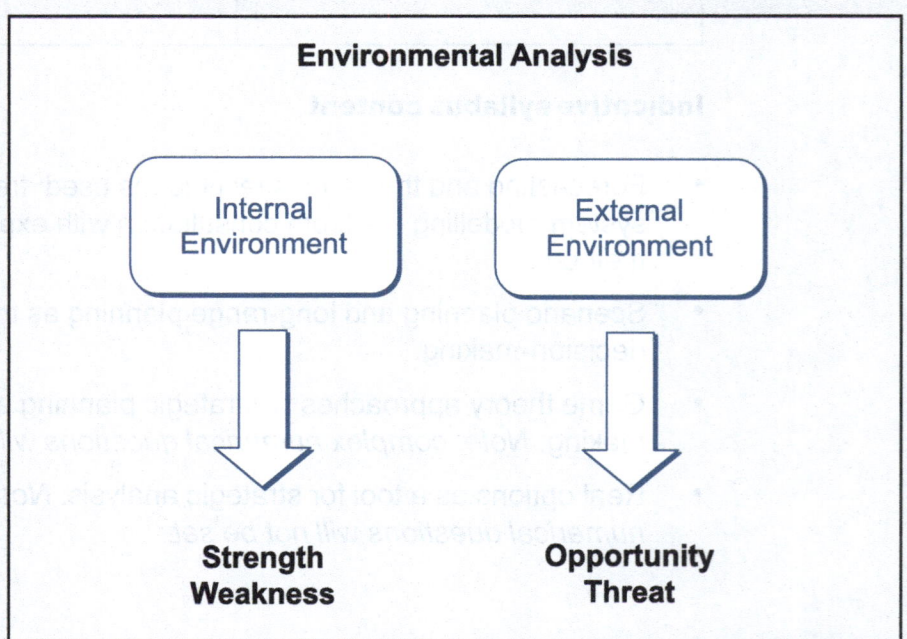

Internal environmental analysis will look for the **strengths and weaknesses** of the organisation.

External environmental analysis will look for the **opportunities and threats** that the organisation needs to be aware of.

Resource Based (Internal)

S	W
• The things we are doing well • The things we are doing that the competition are not • Major successes	• The things we are doing badly (need to correct or improve) • The things we are not doing but should be • Major failures
O	T
• Events or changes in the external environment that can be exploited • Things likely to go well in the future	• Events or changes in the external environment we need to protect ourselves from or defend ourselves against • Things likely to go badly in the future

Position Based (External)

The internal and external appraisals of SWOT analysis will be brought together and it is likely that alternative strategies will emerge.

This is an essential part of the strategic management process as it helps the organisation answer the question – **'Where are we now?'**.

If an organisation is unsure of its current position then it will be very difficult to plot a successful strategy. It establishes the starting point for the process of strategic choice.

Key points

- SWOT analysis is a tool to assist the position audit process. It is not the only tool: e.g. the competitor analysis framework works well in this context and can provide a useful framework to analyse a company.

- Position auditing asks the question 'Where are we now?' and is viewed by many as being the starting point for the process of strategic choice.

- The audit will usually be undertaken by a team with a preset budget, objectives listing and support functions.

- The management accountant will be involved with delivering and monitoring the information flows into the process.

Position and gap analysis

The position audit would seek to identify:

- **Threats focusing on weakness:** This would usually have top priority and the company should seek to identify and consider possible solutions. This requires a defensive response of some kind and may well necessitate rapid change.

- **Threats focusing on strength:** this requires a review of the supposed strength to ensure that it is still as strong as previously thought. Remember what is good today, may not be so tomorrow.

- **Opportunity focusing on strength:** this gives the organisation the chance to develop strategic advantage in the marketplace. Check the research and assess the strengths again.

- **Opportunity focusing on weakness:** this will require management to make a decision as to whether to change and pursue the opportunity or, alternatively, ignore the prospect and ensure resources are not wasted in this area in future. Usually substantial change will be required if the company is going to pursue the opportunity. Check that the company's internal competencies will allow them to exploit the opportunity.

The review should initially seek to identify what would happen if the organisation chose to do nothing. Remember this is always a strategic option!

The exercise is designed to allow the following:

- identification of the **current issues** relating to the organisation concerned

- analysis and identification of the relevant **problems** facing the organisation

- consideration of the **strategic capability** of the company and its history.

Test your understanding 1

C Ltd is a large company and is a market leader in a highly competitive industry. has recently undertaken a corporate appraisal and identified that it has a significant amount of cash available for future investment. It is considering using this to purchase one of its smaller rivals.

Within the corporate analysis, which ONE of the following categories would C's cash surplus be included within?

A   Weakness

B   Strength

C   Opportunity

D   Threat

Test your understanding 2

VVV plc is an organisation that manufactures stationery. It has used various analysis tools in order to identify key issues surrounding the business. It has identified four major issues – one from each of the four major analysis tools that it used.

VVV's issues	Analysis tool
A Increased government subsidies for recycled paper	**1** SWOT
B Low levels of staff morale within VVV	**2** Five forces
C Customers do not see VVV's after sales care as important	**3** PEST
D Customers have relatively low levels of influence over VVV's strategy	**4** Value chain

Identify which analysis tool was used to identify each of VVV's issues by pairing the appropriate letter and number (e.g. A1, B4, etc).

Test your understanding 3 – (Integration question)

Qualispecs has a reputation for quality, traditional products. It has a group of optician shops, both rented and owned, from which it sells its spectacles. Recently it has suffered intense competition and eroding customer loyalty, but a new chief executive has joined from one of its major rivals, Fastglass.

Position and gap analysis

Fastglass is capturing Qualispecs' market through a partnership with a high-street shopping group. These shops install mini-labs in which prescriptions for spectacles are dispensed within an hour. Some competitors have successfully experimented with designer frames and sunglasses. Others have reduced costs through new computer-aided production methods.

Qualispecs has continued to operate as it always has, letting the product 'speak for itself' and failing to utilise advances in technology. Although production costs remain high, Qualispecs is financially secure and has large cash reserves. Fortunately the country's most popular sports star recently received a prestigious international award wearing a pair of Qualispecs' spectacles.

The new Chief Executive has established as a priority the need for improved financial performance. Following a review she discovers that:

(a) targets are set centrally and shops report monthly. Site profitability varies enormously, and fixed costs are high in shopping malls

(b) shops exercise no control over job roles, working conditions, and pay rates

(c) individual staff pay is increased annually according to a predetermined pay scale. Everyone also receives a small one-off payment based on group financial performance.

Market analysts predict a slowdown in the national economy but feel that consumer spending will continue to increase, particularly among 18- to 30-year-olds.

Required:

Produce a corporate appraisal of Qualispecs, taking account of internal and external factors, and discuss the key strategic challenges facing the company.

(30 minutes)

2 Gap analysis

Once an organisation has undertaken a detailed corporate appraisal, it may wish to check whether it is on course to meet its longer term strategic objectives.

For example, a large company may have announced that it aims to double its profits within the next five years. The question is, given the current state of the company, is this really likely to happen?

To answer that question, many organisations undertake gap analysis. This involves forecasting the organisation's future position (if it continues with its current strategies) and examining whether this future position will meet the organisation's goals.

Gap analysis is the comparison between an entity's ultimate objective and the expected performance from projects, both planned and under way, identifying means by which any identified difference or gap might be filled.

CIMA official terminology

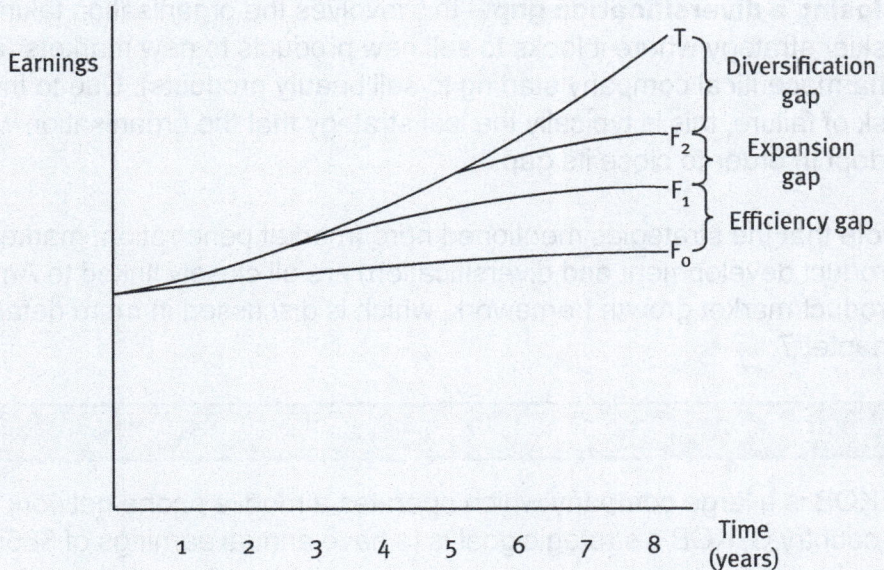

(1) The firm sets its key strategic objective for some time in the future (T), such as achieving a certain level of sales in five years time.

(2) The firm then forecasts its likely performance from current operations (F_0), after efficiency savings have been made (F_1) and after new strategic initiatives (F_2). (Note: These are often separated out as there is a greater degree of uncertainty associated with new initiatives.)

(3) Identify any remaining 'gap'. New strategies will be needed to close this gap. This gap is referred to as the 'diversification' gap.

Closing the gap

There are a number of possible ways of closing the gaps identified by the company:

Closing an efficiency gap – this typically involves undertaking an 'efficiency drive'. The organisation looks to make cost savings and any other actions that will improve the output for a given set of inputs. This is usually the easiest way of closing a gap and is therefore normally undertaken first.

Position and gap analysis

It can also involve looking at market penetration strategies, which involve considering how to sell more of the organisation's current products in their current markets (such as through price cuts, advertising or new packaging, for example).

Closing an expansion gap – this involves looking at ways that the organisation can expand its sales. It could either adopt a market development approach, where it looks to sell its existing products to new markets, or alternatively it could choose a product development strategy where it tries to sell new products to its existing customer base.

Closing a diversification gap – this involves the organisation taking a riskier strategy where it looks to sell new products to new markets (e.g. a pharmaceutical company starting to sell beauty products). Due to the higher risk of failure, this is typically the last strategy that the organisation would adopt in order to close its gap.

Note that the strategies mentioned here (market penetration, market and product development and diversification) are all closely linked to Ansoff's product/market growth framework, which is discussed in more detail in chapter 7.

Illustration 1 – gap analysis

KOB is a large company which operates a mobile phone network in country C. KOB's strategic goal is to have annual earnings of $85m in ten years time.

KOB's strategic management accountant has undertaken detailed forecasts of KOB's expected performance over the next ten years and discovered that, if the company continues with its current strategies, it will only have earnings of $78m in ten years time, giving an overall strategic gap of $7m.

KOB's managers have therefore identified a number of strategies to close this gap.

- **Closing the efficiency gap** – KOB have identified a number of telephone masts that are currently not required. By decommissioning these, as well as outsourcing customer service to overseas call centres, KOB estimates that earnings will rise by $4m after ten years.

- **Closing the expansion gap** – the mobile phone market is highly competitive within country C. However, KOB is considering rolling out its mobile phone services into nearby country G. The market here is less developed and KOB estimates that it will be earning around $1m of earning each year from country G in ten years time.

> The previous strategies should close $5m of the overall strategic gap. As they have not covered the entire gap, KOB may consider undertaking a riskier diversification strategy in order to close the remaining gap.
>
> - **Closing the diversification gap** – KOB is considering selling fixed line internet access to customers in country C. KOB has no experience of this product and believes that it will be mainly selling to consumers who are not its current customers. However, KOB predicts that, due to its well known brand name, it will be able to earn over $1m each year within ten years.
>
> The various strategies adopted by KOB have therefore closed the strategic gap and KOB should be able to meet (or exceed) its target of $85m in annual earnings within the ten year window.

It is worth noting that a plan is what you want to happen whilst a forecast is what you predict will happen given the current context and assumptions. The whole approach of gap analysis is based upon the feed forward control concept, i.e. the comparison of plan with forecast.

The aim is to identify deviance before the problems of missed targets arise so enabling corrective action to take place in advance. The strategy is too important to leave to reactive control systems. A proactive approach is needed and this will see the need for a significant spend on the forecasting systems. Spending will normally include:

- the team
- IT
- data sourcing and audit
- scenario planning
- time to facilitate the action
- uncertainty evaluation techniques such as 'what if' analysis, high-low forecasting and simulation exercises.

The problems with gap analysis

The whole concept revolves around dealing with uncertainty in the environment. Recent times have seen the business environment becoming increasingly uncertain. This increasing amount of uncertainty makes the predictive capabilities of systems less effective. The predictive process works to an extent if the environmental context can be identified. The uncertainty that exists brings with it new unexpected parameters that can render the whole process a costly waste of time. This has been held as a reason for the abandonment of gap analysis.

Position and gap analysis

The other issue is that in recent years there has been an increasing number of powerful stakeholder groups emerging with the knock-on effect being that there is a greater range of often conflicting objectives. Gap analysis does not entertain the multiplicity of objectives with conflict and compromise running through the whole system.

The benefits of gap analysis

(1) The approach acts as a simple starting point to initiate further debate and consideration.

(2) It is easy to understand and as such acts as an effective communication device.

(3) It highlights the need to keep an eye on the long-term time horizon and draws attention away from the short-term focus.

(4) It provides some basic options that may be considered for closing the gap.

(5) If it is held as a tool to assist and not as the solution provider, the approach still has a place in most planning systems within organisations.

(6) It allows the questioning of the realism of the objective – if there is a gap, it may be that the objective is unrealistic given the strategic capability of the organisation. This may lead to a reappraisal of the objectives and the generation of more realistic versions.

(7) Stable environments will still provide a basis for effective gap analysis

Test your understanding 4

F's strategic management accountants have recently undertaken gap analysis. They have forecasted the likely position of the company after taking account of planned efficiency savings as well as after all planned strategic initiatives. They have identified that there is still a gap between F's forecast position and it's ideal position.

This remaining gap is referred to as the _____ gap.

Required:

Insert the missing word in the above sentence.

3 Forecasting

A key part of gap analysis is forecasting.

A forecast is a prediction of future events and their quantification for planning purposes.

CIMA official terminology

Clearly gap analysis relies on accurate forecasts of future performance. The strategies developed as a result of gap analysis are only as good as the quality of the forecast that they rely on. So how do we forecast company or market performance – in some cases looking ahead over a number of years?

Statistical models

An organisation could adopt one of several statistical models to try and quantify key forecast figures.

Regression analysis

This looks at how a particular variable correlates (or varies) with another variable.

For example, an airline may wish to investigate the link between passenger numbers and average ticket prices (usually the number of passengers falls as the ticket price rises). Regression will allow the airline to calculate an estimate of the relationship between the two factors, based on past results. This can then be used in its forecasts for coming years. For example, if it intends to raise ticket prices to increase earnings, it can predict what effect this will have on passenger numbers, giving it an accurate forecast of expected earnings.

Time series analysis

Time series analysis involves the identification of short- and long-term trends in previous data and the application of these patterns for projections. In other words, it looks at how a particular factor varies over time.

For example, a jewellery firm may find that its results are strongly affected by the price of gold. Time series analysis will help the firm look at the past gold price movements and use them to predict what the future price of gold will be. This can then be used in forecasting to help the firm estimate its cost of goods sold, or to decide on a pricing strategy (amongst other things).

Trend analysis is a particularly useful tool for companies who have to forecast demand that is influenced by seasonal fluctuations, or where demand is strongly influenced by the business cycle.

Drawbacks of statistical models

While the above models can be useful in helping quantify key forecast figures, they have a number of inherent limitations, including:

- they assume that past results are a good indication of the future. For instance, our jewellery firm may find that the price of gold has risen sharply in past years. This is not conclusive proof that it will continue to do so.
- regression analysis assumes that the two factors are strongly correlated (i.e. linked to each other). The airline firm mentioned above could plot passenger numbers in past years against the average cost of a newspaper on its flights. Regression analysis would calculate the relationship – but there is not likely to be a causal link between the two, giving rise to misleading forecasts.
- regression analysis is only likely to be accurate within the range of the past data collected.
- it can be very difficult to accurately build in seasonal and other fluctuations into time series analysis, meaning that forecast results using this method can be inaccurate.

Other forecasting models

System modelling

Many large firms seek to develop sophisticated programmes to model economic systems, market competition and so on.

The difficulty lies in identifying all the variables and defining how they relate to each other.

A number of software products are available to help with this. Most large accounting packages will include forecasting facilities, and Enterprise Resource Management (ERM) software generally includes facilities to model business processes.

Intuitive forecasting methods

What distinguishes intuitive techniques is the relative emphasis they place on judgement, and the value of such techniques lies not in their statistical sophistication but in the method of systematising expert knowledge.

Intuitive forecasting techniques include the use of think tanks, Delphi methods, scenario planning, brainstorming and derived demand analysis.

Intuitive forecasting methods

Think tank

A think tank comprises a group of experts who are encouraged, in a relatively unstructured atmosphere, to speculate about future developments in particular areas and to identify possible courses of action. The essential features of a think tank are:

- the relative independence of its members, enabling unpopular, unacceptable or novel ideas to be broached
- the relative absence of positional authority in the group, which enables free discussion and argument to take place
- the group nature of the activity that not only makes possible the sharing of knowledge and views, but also encourages a consensus view or preferred scenario.

Think tanks are used by large organisations, including government, and may cross the line between forecasting and planning. However, the organisations that directly employ, or fund, them, are careful to emphasise that their think-tank proposals do not necessarily constitute company or government policy.

Think tanks are useful for generating ideas and assessing their feasibility, as well as providing an opportunity to test out reactions to ideas prior to organisational commitment.

The Delphi technique

Delphi seeks to avoid the group pressures to conformity that are inherent in the think tank method. It does this by individually, systematically and sequentially interrogating a panel of experts.

- Members do not meet, and questioning is conducted by formal questionnaires.
- Where the experts are speculating about the future, they are asked for subjective probabilities about their predictions.
- A central authority evaluates the responses and feeds these back to the experts who are then interrogated in a new round of questions

The system is based on the premise that knowledge and ideas possessed by some but not all of the experts can be identified and shared and this forms the basis for subsequent interrogations.

Brainstorming

This is a method of generating ideas. There are different approaches but a popular one is for a number of people (no fewer than six, no more than fifteen) drawn from all levels of management and expertise to meet and propose answers to an initial single question posed by the session leader.

- Each person proposes something, no matter how absurd.
- No one is allowed to criticise or ridicule another person's idea.
- One idea provokes another, and so on.
- All ideas are listed and none rejected at this initial stage.
- Rationality is not particularly important, but what is essential is that a wide range of ideas emerges and in the ensuing discussion that these ideas are picked up, developed, combined and reshaped.
- Only after the session are ideas evaluated and screened against rational criteria for practicality.

Brainstorming provides a forum for the interchange of ideas without erecting the normal cultural, behavioural and psychological barriers that so often inhibit the expression of ideas.

Derived demand

Derived demand exists for a commodity, component or good because of its contribution to the manufacture of another product.

For example, the demands for the chromium, copper and rubber used in the manufacture of many different products, including cars, are derived demands.

The forecasting technique involves analysing some aspects of economic activity so that the level of other aspects can be deduced and projected. The principle is simple, but the practice is complex and costly.

Take the example of chrome matched with car manufacture. In order to forecast the demand for cars (thus chrome) the forecaster will be faced with the mammoth task of analysing an enormous number of influences and correlated factors.

Due to its cost and complexity the technique has a very restricted use.

4 Foresight

Foresight goes beyond simple forecasting and tries to identify possible ways that the future of the organisation could develop.

The value of strong brands, loyal customers, etc has diminished over time as the business environment has become more dynamic. Whereas once a company could rely on these things to bring them future success, they are increasingly unable to do so. Organisations must therefore develop vision and foresight.

For organisations, foresight means not only predicting the future but developing an understanding of all the potential changes, which if managed properly could produce many new opportunities.

By carrying out techniques to develop foresight, management try to shape the future, rather than 'wait' for it to happen and become a victim of changes they are unable to adapt to. The concept is crucial in the global commercial environment, where technological changes for example, or non-traditional competition can erode a company's dominant position overnight.

Advantages of foresight

In their book 'Research Foresight: Creating the future', John Irvine and Ben Martin give the advantages of foresight as the 5Cs:

- **Communication** – bringing together groups of people and providing a structure in which they can communicate.
- **Concentration** – on the longer term.
- **Coordination** – enabling different groups to harmonise their future R&D activities.
- **Consensus** – creating a measure of agreement on future directions and research priorities.
- **Commitment** – to the results among those who will be responsible for translating them into research advances, technological developments and innovations for the benefit of society.

Position and gap analysis

Techniques to improve an organisation's foresight include:

- **Scenario planning** – see below.
- **Visioning** – involves management developing a 'mental image' of the organisation in the future. This should be realistic, attractive and better than the company's current state. Management can then devise ways to reach this future ideal.
- **The Delphi method** – see above.
- **Morphological analysis** – the systematic investigation of all the components of large-scale problems. A matrix is used to identify new, reasonable combinations of these components that could result in plausible new outcomes.
- **Relevance trees** – start with a clear goal, which is traced back through the trends and events on which it depends so that the organisation can determine what needs to change or be developed for the desired outcome to be achieved.
- **Issues analysis** – issues arise through the convergence of trends and events. Potentially significant issues should be analysed in terms of probability and impact (i.e. risk).
- **Opportunity mapping** – identifying gaps in the current environment in order to reveal new business opportunities.
- **Cross impact analysis** – involves recording events on a matrix and at each matrix intersection analysing how the event in the row could affect the likelihood of occurrence of the event in the column.
- **Role-playing** – a group of people are given a description of a hypothetical future situation and are told to behave as they believe they would if that situation were true.

Test your understanding 5

Y plc is attempting to forecast future events in its market. It has therefore hired a number of industry experts to identify possible developments over the next ten years. Y plc wishes to avoid any risk of the experts it has hired simply conforming with each other's opinions, so it has decided to interrogate them by questionnaire, meaning that they will never meet in person.

Which ONE of the following approaches to forecasting is Y adopting?

A Think tank

B Brainstorming

C Derived demand

D Delphi method

5 Scenario planning

Competence slip and organisational failure have been linked to the notion that management have failed to grasp the way that society is moving and have not conceptualised a possible future marketplace. It has been suggested that managers need a picture or scenario of where the world may be in a few years' time.

For example, how would an accountancy training college meet its objectives under the following circumstances:

(1) a merger between three accountancy bodies
(2) wide demand for computer-based training
(3) changes to immigration laws leading to a reduction in the number of overseas students.

The steps involved in scenario planning

Scenario planning involves the following steps:

(1) Identify high-impact, high-uncertainty factors in the environment.

Relevant factors and driving forces could be identified through a strategic analysis framework such as a PEST analysis. Once identified, factors need to be ranked according to importance and uncertainty.

For example, in the oil industry there may be a need to form a view of the business environment up to twenty-five years ahead and issues such as crude oil availability, price and economic conditions are critical.

(2) For each factor, identify different possible futures.

For example, oil companies would consider possible political uncertainty in oil-producing countries and the attitudes of future governments to climate change, pollution and energy policy.

Precision is not possible but developing a view of the future against which to evaluate and evolve strategies is important.

At 3M, for example, the general manager of each business unit is required annually to describe what his or her industry will look like in fifteen years.

(3) Cluster together different factors to identify various consistent future scenarios.

For example, two key factors may have been identified as:

(a) the threat of new entrants

(b) new legislation that may reduce the potential for profit.

Clearly, if new legislation is passed that reduces industry profit potential, then the likelihood of new entrants will fall.

This process usually results in between seven and nine mini-scenarios.

(4) 'Writing the scenario' – for the most important scenarios (usually limited to three), build a detailed analysis to identify and assess future implications.

As part of this, planners typically develop a set of optimistic, pessimistic and most likely assumptions about the impact of key variables on the company's future strategy.

The result of this detailed scenario construction should include:

- financial implications – anticipated net profits, cash flow and net working capital for each of three versions of the future
- strategic implications – possible opportunities and risks
- the probability of occurrence, usually based on past experience.

(5) For each scenario, identify and assess possible courses of action for the firm.

For example, Shell was the only major oil company to have prepared for the shock of the 1970s oil crisis through scenario planning and was able to respond faster than its competitors.

Some strategies make sense whatever the outcome, usually because they capitalise on or develop key strengths of the firm. For example, the firm concerned may have a global brand name and could seek to strengthen it by increasing its advertising spend in the short term.

However, in many cases, new resources and competences may be required for existing strategies to succeed. Alternatively, entirely new strategies may be required.

(6) Monitor reality to see which scenario is unfolding.

(7) Revise ("redeploy") scenarios and strategic options as appropriate.

Construction of scenarios

These need to be well thought out if they are to be effective. Hence the following should be considered:

- use a team for a range of opinions and expertise
- identify time-frame, markets, products and budget
- stakeholder analysis – who will be the most influential in the future?
- trend analysis and uncertainty identification
- building of initial scenarios
- consider organisational learning implications
- identify research needs and develop quantitative models.

As mentioned above, Shell makes use of scenario planning extensively in order to predict future changes in the energy industry so that it can attempt to prepare for them.

How useful is scenario planning?

The downside

- Costly and inaccurate – uses up substantial resources and time
- tendency for cultural distortion and for people to get carried away
- the risk of the self-fulfilling prophecy, i.e. thinking about the scenario may be the cause of it
- many scenarios considered will not actually occur.

The upside

- Focuses management attention on the future and possibilities
- encourages creative thinking
- can be used to justify a decision
- encourages communication via the participation process
- can identify the sources of uncertainty
- encourages companies to consider fundamental changes in the external environment.

Position and gap analysis

Test your understanding 6

Which THREE of the following are disadvantages of scenario planning?

A   Bounded rationality

B   Reduced communication within the organisation

C   High cost

D   Risk of self-fulfilling prophecy

E   Wastes management time

F   Discourages creative thinking

Test your understanding 7 – UHJ – (Case style)

UHJ is a multinational company, based in Europe, which manufactures aircraft components. This is a fast–moving, dynamic market with a large number of innovative competitors attempting to take UHJ's market share.

UHJ recently expanded into the North American market and set up a new division with two factories on the west coast. Since this expansion, however, the North American market has been hit by a significant economic downturn. This downturn has continued for the last year and analysts are uncertain of how far and when it will recover.

This has led to a large reduction in orders for aircraft components and has meant that the North American division of UHJ is now barely breaking even. Its future profitability for the next few years depends on a large order from a North American airline, VTH. VTH will announce a decision on this order next month.

UHJ has recently been approached with an offer by one of its rivals to buy the factories for what UHJ considers to be a fair price. UHJ wishes to avoid closing the factories as it feels that the closure costs and redundancy payouts that would be required would be extremely high.

Your manager has recently attended a seminar on scenario planning, but is concerned that he did not fully understand what is involved.

He has asked you to prepare him some briefing notes, explaining what scenario planning is and how it would benefit UHJ.

Required:

Prepare the briefing notes as requested by your manager.

(10 minutes)

Test your understanding 8 – NSF – (Case style)

The National Sports Foundation (NSF) for Country Z is a public body which operates within the central government department for Sport and Culture. NSF's role is to support and develop a sporting environment across all communities in Country Z and to increase the number of people participating in sport.

NSF is mainly funded by the Government of Country Z. Up until 2010, it employed several hundred staff and also relied upon thousands of volunteers throughout Country Z to run the various sporting clubs and associations, such as amateur football clubs and children's out of school sports activities. Following cuts in Government funding in 2010, NSF's level of staffing was considerably reduced. This resulted in NSF relying more on private sector partnerships and volunteers.

Until three years ago, the economic, social and technological environment in Country Z had been relatively stable, with NSF receiving guaranteed funding from the Government and the numbers of sports participants and volunteers being reasonably predictable. Therefore, the Board of NSF has not considered frequent and regular environmental analysis to be necessary.

NSF's Board has been taken by surprise by the changes that have occurred in the environment in the last three years. In addition to Government funding cuts, local administrative government bodies have been forced to sell off local community sports grounds and facilities to raise finance. Furthermore, the level of financial and operational support provided by private sector organisations has also declined due to similar economic challenges. Increasingly stricter regulations and rules have resulted in fewer volunteers throughout the country. The rapid growth in technology-based entertainment products has been blamed for the reduction in the number of young people participating in sports. In addition, NSF has failed to consider the changing demographics and ageing population of Country Z and the impact that this will have on sports participation in future years.

Position and gap analysis

The Chairman of the Board of NSF has recently attended several conferences where the value of undertaking thorough 'environmental analysis' has been discussed. The Chairman now realises that there is a serious gap in NSF's knowledge about the environment in which it operates. He considers that if NSF is to continue successfully in the future then it must improve its foresight to actively plan for the future.

The Chairman has therefore contacted you and asked you to produce some briefing notes to help him apply this knowledge to NSF. His email is shown below:

To: A. Waterman
From: C. H. Airman
Date: 15/08/XX
Subject: Scenario planning for NSF

Hi A,

Hope you are well. As you know I have recently attended a number of conferences on foresight and scenario planning and I want to try and decide how they could be applied to NSF. I know this is a topic you have studied recently and I would like you to outline a few things to me.

To start, please explain the concept of foresight and TWO techniques (other than scenario planning) which could be used by NSF in the development of foresight.

I also need you to analyse each of the key stages that would be included in a scenario planning process which could be used by NSF.

I'm going into a meeting with the other board members about this in about thirty minutes, so please email back by then.

Kind regards

C.H.

Required:

Draft the email requested by the Chairman.

(30 minutes)

chapter 6

6 Game theoretic approaches to strategic planning

A key aspect of strategic planning is anticipating the actions of competitors and acting accordingly. Game theory has been used to great effect in this matter.

Game theoretic approaches to strategic planning

Game theory

In many markets it is important to anticipate the actions of competitors as there is a high interdependency between firms – i.e. the results of my choice depend to some extent on your choices as well.

Game theory is concerned with the interrelationships between the competitive moves of a set of competitors and, as such, can be a useful tool to analyse and understand different scenarios.

Game theory has two key principles:

(1) Strategists can take a rational, informed view of what competitors are likely to do and formulate a suitable response.
(2) If a strategy exists that allows a competitor to dominate us, then the priority is to eliminate that strategy.

Despite the simplicity of these principles, game theory has become very complex.

Many of the bidders for third-generation mobile phone licences in the early 2000s and the governments auctioning those licences used game theory principles. In the UK this resulted in over a hundred rounds of bidding and revenue raised of £22 billion.

Example

The most famous example of game theory is the "Prisoner's dilemma" game. This can be applied to companies as follows:

Suppose there are two companies, A and B, who between them dominate a market. Both are considering whether to increase their marketing spend from its current low level.

- If just one firm decides to increase their spend, then it will see their returns increase.
- However, if both increase the spend then both end up with lower returns than at present.

Position and gap analysis

These could be shown by the following pay-off table (figures = net profit).

		Competitor A	
		High spend	Low spend
Competitor B	High spend	A = 5 B = 5	A = 3 B = 10
	Low Spend	A = 10 B = 3	A = 7 B = 7

Viewed individually the dominant strategy for both firms is to invest heavily. Taking A's perspective:

- If B does not increase spending, then the best plan of action for A would have been to invest heavily.
- If B does increase spending, then the best plan of action for A would have been to invest heavily.

However, the end result ("equilibrium") is likely to be that both firms increase spending and thus end up worse off than if they had both kept their marketing spend at its current low level. Some degree of collusion to keep the spend low would benefit both parties.

Note: The original version of the prisoners' dilemma.

Suppose two men perpetrate a crime together and are later arrested by the police.

Unfortunately the police have insufficient evidence for a conviction, and, having separated both suspects, visit each of them to offer the chance of betraying their accomplice. Suppose the possible outcomes are as follows:

- If one testifies (defects from the other) for the prosecution against the other and the other remains silent (cooperates with the other), the betrayer goes free and the silent accomplice receives the full 10-year sentence.
- If both remain silent, both prisoners are sentenced to only six months in jail for a minor charge.
- If each betrays the other, each receives a five-year sentence.

Each prisoner must choose to betray the other or to remain silent. Each one is assured that the other would not know about the betrayal before the end of the investigation.

How should the prisoners act?

The unique equilibrium for this game is that rational choice leads the two players to both play defect, even though each player's individual reward would be greater if they both played cooperatively.

Application

A common application of this is to price wars. Price wars between two evenly matched competitors usually results in lower profits for all concerned and no change in market share. No one wins, except the customer.

Test your understanding 9

TRT is a large company that manufactures light bulbs. The light bulb market has been mature for many years, with little innovation and TRT has only three other rivals in the market – all of roughly equal size to TRT. The markets that TRT operate in have strict legislation restricting collusion between competing companies.

A new type of lightbulb has recently been developed by an entrepreneur, Mr B, which provides the same light as a current lightbulb, but which uses a fraction of the electricity of traditional bulbs and which (in theory) will never need to be replaced. Mr B has stated that he is absolutely unwilling to sell this patented new product exclusively to just one supplier. Instead, he wishes to license the technology to any company who is willing to pay a fixed annual fee for a pre-set 15 year period.

TRT's strategic management accountant has calculated that if TRT is the only company that decides to license the new lightbulb, it will earn around $5m each year for the foreseeable future. It will make a loss of around $2m each year if one of its rivals also licenses the product and this loss will widen the more of its rivals decide to enter the market.

Which of the following options is the most appropriate for TRT to take in order to deal with this situation?

A   Attempt to copy the technology behind the new lightbulbs, avoiding having to pay a license fee to Mr B

B   Negotiate with rival companies and agree a mutually beneficial strategy when negotiating with Mr B

C   Attempt to negotiate an exclusive deal with Mr B

D   Invest in the new lightbulbs as quickly as possible in the hope that rival companies will avoid investing

7 Real options

When deciding on a strategic project, there are three possible 'real options' that a manager may wish to take into account.

- **Option to follow on**

    When choosing a project, many managers will make their choice on the basis of Net Present Value (NPV). Projects with a positive NPV will be accepted as they increase shareholder wealth. Negative NPV projects will be rejected.

    However, under options theory this may not always be the case. This is because a project with a negative NPV could provide the business with the opportunity to invest in other, more profitable projects in the future.

    For example, an electronics company may find that designing, manufacturing and selling printers has a negative NPV due to the low prices that can be charged in this market. However, the investment will allow the company to sell a range of ink cartridges that have much higher profit margins and a larger positive NPV.

- **Option to abandon**

    If a project requires a large capital investment and has an uncertain outcome, the option to abandon may be valuable.

    For example, if a civil engineering company enters a fixed price contract to build a stadium, having an option to abandon the project will significantly reduce its risk. Should the costs spiral above the value of the contract, the company will be able to abandon the project and limit its losses.

- **Option to delay**

    The option to delay the beginning of a project can also be valuable to a business.

    A UK house-building company, for example, may have an option to build on a plot of land at any point over the next several years. Unfortunately, due to the current economic downturn, house prices have fallen sharply. The company can therefore delay the building of the homes until the market has recovered and house prices rise to a more acceptable level.

Generally these options will become more valuable as their duration increases and as the level of uncertainty in the project rises. Remember that you will not be asked for complex calculations in this area of the syllabus.

Test your understanding 10

UPP is an organisation that sells custom-made accountancy software to large or complex organisations. It has recently been approached by the government of country L, which wishes to employ UPP to create an accountancy software solution for country L's national health service, which runs the hospitals and doctors surgeries throughout the country.

UPP is concerned that the government demands a fixed fee contract. It is aware that costs on software development are often hard to accurately estimate and this could lead to UPP making significant losses if the contract becomes more complex than originally anticipated. It is therefore negotiating with the government a clause in the contract that will allow UPP to exit the contract if costs rise above a certain level.

Under real option theory, the clause UPP is negotiating is referred to an option to _____.

Required:

Insert the missing word in the above sentence.

Test your understanding 11

Which of the following changes would BOTH lead to a rise in the value of a real option?

	Option duration	Project uncertainty
A.	Increases	Increases
B.	Increases	Decreases
C.	Decreases	Increases
D.	Decreases	Decreases

8 Summary

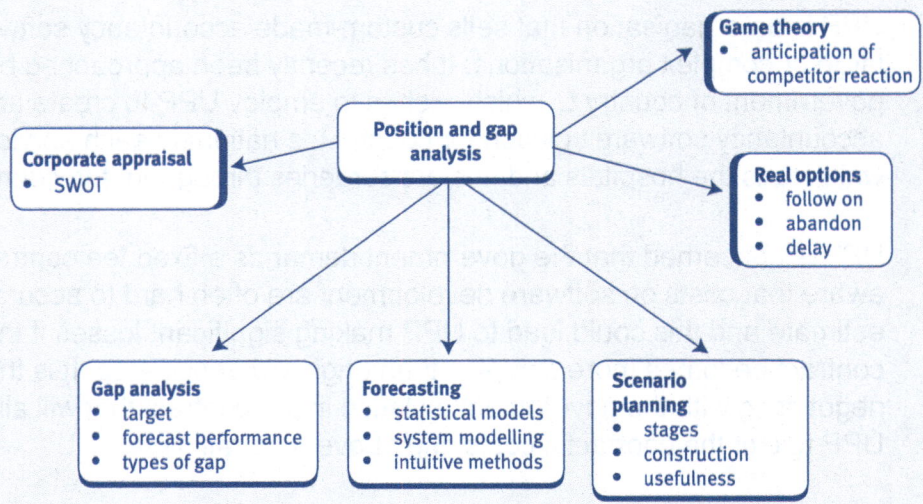

Test your understanding answers

Test your understanding 1

The correct answer is B

Strengths are internal to the organisation. Note that the opportunity to purchase C's rival would likely be classified as an opportunity.

Test your understanding 2

The correct answers are: A3, B1, C4, D2

Increased government subsidies is likely to be identified within a PEST analysis, under the 'economic' heading.

Low levels of staff morale is an internal weakness within VVV and would be identified within a SWOT analysis.

Note that it could be argued that increased subsidies could also be identified by a SWOT analysis as an opportunity/threat. However, as staff morale would only be identified within a SWOT, these subsidies must have been found by VVV's PEST analysis (as we must pair each point to one analysis tool).

After sales care (or service) is part of Porter's value chain, while customer power and its influence over strategy is a key part of the five forces model.

Position and gap analysis

Test your understanding 3 – (Integration question)

Corporate appraisal

A corporate appraisal is an overview of an organisation's current position. It leads on from the internal and external analysis undertaken as part of the business planning process.

As the company works towards achieving its objectives, the corporate appraisal is a summary of the company's:

- strengths within the organisation relative to competitors
- weaknesses within the organisation relative to competitors
- opportunities available from the external environment
- threats from the external environment.

The company must develop a strategy which:

- capitalises on the strengths
- overcomes or mitigates the impact of weaknesses
- takes suitable opportunities
- overcomes or mitigates the threats.

In the case of Qualispecs:

Strengths

- Reputation for quality.

    Quality is a major reason why people buy products, and continuing to build on this reputation will ensure customers continue to buy Qualispecs's products.

- Financially secure/large cash reserves.

    Qualispecs does not need to rush into the implementation of new strategies. It can take its time to ensure strategies chosen are appropriate for the business and implemented effectively. They also have funds to invest in new ventures without having to raise external funds.

- Backing of a famous sports star.

    This helps to improve the image of Qualispecs's products which in turn should result in higher sales, particularly amongst the younger market that might be influenced by the sports star.

- New chief executive.

    The group has a new chief executive who has joined from a rival, Fastglass. Fastglass has been a successful and innovative company and the chief executive may be able to bring new ideas and provide a fresh approach.

- Established group with many stores.

    The group has a good basic infrastructure including many stores and experienced staff. This allows them to implement new strategies quickly and easily.

Weaknesses

- Slower dispensing of spectacles.

    Customer service is worse than competitors in this respect and may be a reason for the reducing customer loyalty.

- Less trendy products than competitors.

    Some competitors have successfully sold designer frames. These are likely to be stylish and trendy compared to Qualispecs' traditional products. Qualispecs may need to update products more often with the latest designs.

- Smaller product range than competitors.

    Some competitors have a wider product range than Qualispecs. This provides more choice, which may attract customers, and also gives competitors the opportunity to on-sell products, i.e. selling prescription sunglasses at the same time as standard spectacles.

- Older production methods causing higher costs.

    This will either cause prices to be higher than competitors or margins to be less. In either case competitors have a distinct advantage.

- Varying performance around the group.

  Little action is being taken to improve performance of poorly performing stores causing varying performance around the group. This indicates a weakness in internal control systems and perhaps also in development and training programmes.

- Little autonomy for shops.

  Without autonomy there is little a shop manager can do to improve local operations. In London, for instance, pay may need to be higher to attract the right staff. With no local control over pay levels, shop managers may find it hard to employ good staff and hence improve their business.

  This lack of autonomy may also be demotivating to managers. Responsibility was one of the major factors outlined by Hertzberg in his motivation theory as a way to motivate staff.

- No incentive to improve for staff.

  The use of group-based bonuses means that people cannot be rewarded for good individual performance. Individuals have little incentive to improve therefore.

Opportunities

Note: Opportunities should be in relation to the market as a whole. They therefore need to be available to all competitors in the market.

- To adopt new technologies to reduce costs (see earlier)
- to stock a wide range of up-to-date products (see earlier)
- consumer spending will continue to increase.

Despite a slowdown in the economy, consumer spending is likely to increase, suggesting an increasing market size in the future. There is therefore further opportunity for all competitors to increase sales.

- Targeting 18- to 30-year-olds.

  The 18- to 30-year-old age group offers a particular opportunity since its spending is likely to increase especially quickly. There is therefore an opportunity to understand this group's needs and to target it specifically.

- Develop a partnership with a high-street shopping group.

    Fastglass has already done this successfully and Qualispecs could follow suit. There are likely to be limited suitable partners so Qualispecs must act quickly before other firms make arrangements with the best partners.

Threats

- Intense competition/eroding customer loyalty.

    Existing competitors are adopting new strategies with great success (e.g. Fastglass developed joint ventures). This has resulted in Qualispecs' customers moving to competitors, thus reducing profits. This is likely to be a continued threat to Qualispecs, who needs to respond.

Test your understanding 4

The correct answer is DIVERSIFICATION

By definition.

Test your understanding 5

The correct answer is D

By definition.

Test your understanding 6

The correct answers are: A, C and D

Test your understanding 7 – UHJ – (Case style)

UHJ is faced with a dynamic and rapidly changing environment in the North American market. Scenario planning is the detailed and credible analysis of how the business environment might develop in the future, based on various environmental influences and drivers for change. The target for this analysis should be areas where the organisation considers there to be a high degree of uncertainty or opportunity.

Scenario planning would therefore enable UHJ to calculate and examine various possible strategic outcomes.

For example, UHJ would be able to examine the possible impact of the economic downturn lasting for several years, or alternatively beginning to reverse immediately. It could also compare combinations of events, such as:

- the sale of the division, followed by an economic recovery, but the loss of the VTH order
- the retention of the division, followed by a continuation of the economic downturn, along with the acquisition of the VTH order

and so on.

This approach will have two key benefits:

(1) It will help the directors of UHJ to see 'worst-case' scenarios. Should the North American economy suffer a prolonged downturn and the division lose the VTH order, there could be a significant impact on the division, along with the rest of the company. This may help the directors to decide how much of a risk maintaining the North American division is and whether it would be best to sell immediately.

(2) Scenario planning will also help the directors to anticipate potential problems with, or opportunities from, the North American division. For example, if UHJ wants to sell the division and the VTH order is lost, the price it achieves from the sale may well be much lower than is currently on offer. Alternatively, the market may recover in the near future and the sale of the division now may compromise UHJ's future growth prospects.

Test your understanding 8 – NSF – (Case style)

To: C.H. Airman
From: A. Waterman
Date: 15/08/XX
Subject: Re: Foresight

Dear C.H.

Thank you for your email. I've outlined the issues below as requested.

Foresight has been described as the 'art and science of anticipating the future'. For organisations such as NSF, foresight not only means predicting the future, but also developing an understanding of all potential changes which, if managed properly, could produce many new opportunities. There are a number of techniques which can be used to improve the foresight of an organisation. These include:

Visioning

A possible or desirable future state of the organisation is developed as a mental image by the management of the organisation. This vision may start off vaguely as a dream but should be firmed up into a concrete statement of where the organisation wants to be. The critical point is that the vision articulates a view of a realistic, credible and attractive future for the organisation, which is viewed as being an improvement on the current state of affairs.

Issues analysis

Issues arise through the convergence of trends and events. A trend is a trajectory that an issue takes because of the attention it receives and the socio-political forces that affect it. This convergence usually manifests itself because there are unfavourable events, which are sudden and unanticipated, public interest develops and becomes more important or there is increased political pressure. The issues should be analysed in terms of their impact on the organisation and their probability of occurrence.

Role Playing

This is where a group of people are given a description of a hypothetical future situation and are asked to behave as though they believe that the situation is true and happening.

Delphi Technique

This seeks to avoid the group pressures of conformity that are inherent in other group based forecasting methods. It does this by interrogating a panel of experts individually and sequentially and is based on the premise that knowledge and ideas possessed by some, but not all, of the experts can be identified and shared and this forms the basis of future interrogations.

Others which could be discussed are:

- Opportunity mapping
- Cross impact analysis
- Relevance trees

Note: Your answer only needs to explain two of the above techniques

Scenario planning, as a tool, will provide NSF with a better understanding of what could happen in the environment in which it operates and help to minimise surprises.

The stages could be as follows:

(1) **Define the scope of the scenario**

NSF will need to decide what knowledge is most important to it. Consideration of its most important market segments and customers and the time frame it wishes to consider (i.e. how far into the future) should be paramount. It will need to decide whether the scenario is to be focussed on a specific issue e.g. the impact of the technology on the participation of children or a more blue sky approach where it asks a question such as; 'what is the future of community participation in sport in Country Z?'

(2) **Identify and map the major stakeholders**

A consideration of who the main stakeholders are in the sporting environment should be undertaken and how they are likely to drive change over the period under consideration. For NSF this would most probably include the Government of Country Z (as the main funder), its volunteers and its customers. All of these stakeholders would need to be evaluated in terms of their impact and power to influence the future activities of NSF.

(3) Identify the basic trends and uncertainties affecting the business

In assessing the trends and factors that would be identified in an environmental analysis and considering how they may change in the future, NSF would most probably want to focus upon the technological advances and the increasing use of the internet by children and young adults and its effect upon sport participation. Since it is very dependent upon the Government for its revenue it would also consider the trends in the economy which would affect its income. Also the changing demographics would be a major consideration for NSF.

(4) Identify the key trends and uncertainties

Of the basic trends that have been identified NSF would need to decide which are the key uncertainties. These trends and uncertainties will be the 'drivers for change' which will require contingency planning activities and will shape the future of the industry. In the case of NSF this would certainly include the declining Government funding and societal and demographic changes. These will be the main drivers forcing change in NSF.

(5) Construct initial scenario themes, or skeleton outlines

Possible future scenarios should then be created by forming the key trends and uncertainties into coherent themes. Usually two alternative scenarios are produced but more can be identified if necessary. NSF might develop one scenario where the economy continues to be depressed and funding continues to decline with sport becoming less important to society. This would be the 'negative' scenario. The alternative 'positive' scenario might feature a booming economy with many members of society both volunteering and actively participating in sport activities.

(6) Check for plausibility and internal consistency

Effective scenarios are both internally consistent and plausible. This means that different directions that the trends have taken in the scenario could logically happen together and the events described could happen within the timescale chosen.

(7) **Develop learning scenarios**

The next stage would be to 'flesh out' the scenarios so that they become full descriptions of the sector and conditions that are expected to prevail in the future timeframe. This is often done by writing a detailed piece of narrative. The managers of NSF would need to consider the detailed aspects of each scenario in terms of impact upon NSF's staff, possible plans for re-training, more detailed financial analysis and an overall view of the sporting environment in Country Z.

Note: There is no one perfect method of producing scenario plans and the following answer is one of a number of ways in which scenarios can be developed. Candidates will be rewarded for appropriate stages which are applied to the NSF.

I hope this helps you for your meeting – if you need any more information, please let me know.

Kind regards

A.

Test your understanding 9

The correct answer is D

The technology is patented, meaning that it cannot be copied. This means that A cannot be the correct option.

B would involve TRT colluding with its rivals, which would likely breach the strict anti-trust regulation in its markets.

C is unlikely to be a success as Mr B has stated that he will not offer an exclusive contract to any one company.

D may be the best approach. If TRT can gain a license from Mr B first, it may reduce the chances of a rival company attempting to also obtain a license as doing so would incur significant losses.

Test your understanding 10

The correct answer is ABANDON

By definition.

Test your understanding 11

The correct answer is A

The value of a real option will rise as the project becomes more uncertain and as the duration of the option rises.

Position and gap analysis

chapter 7

Strategic options and choice

Chapter learning objectives

Lead	Component
B1. Evaluate the process of strategy formulation	(a) Evaluate the process of strategic analysis and strategic options generation (b) Recommend strategic options
B2. Evaluate tools and techniques used in strategy formulation	(a) Evaluate strategic analysis tools (b) Recommend how to manage the product portfolio of an organisation to support the organisation's strategic goals

Indicative syllabus content

- The identification and evaluation of strategic options, including the application of the suitability, acceptability and feasibility framework.
- Strategic options generation (e.g. using Ansoff's product/market matrix and Porter's generic strategies)
- Acquisition, divestment, rationalisation and relocation strategies and their place in the strategic plan
- Management of the product portfolio

Strategic options and choice

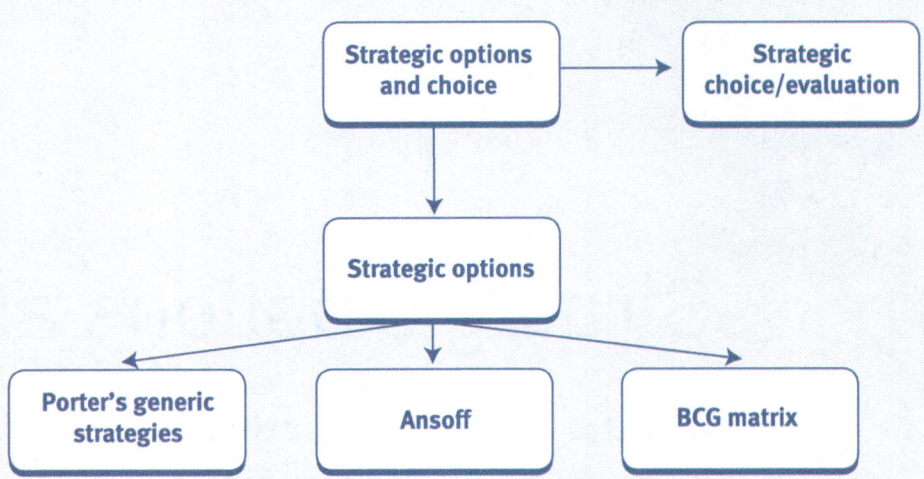

1 Strategic analysis and choice

Once the position has been identified, the organisation will be aware of the environments and the current strategic capability of the organisation. So the questions is "What should we do now to enable us to have the best chance of achieving our objectives?" In other words, which strategy should we follow?

There are many ways to achieve the end result! There is no one strategy that should be deployed in any given circumstance, rather a range of possible strategies that could be used singly or jointly.

2 Key decisions to make

As part of strategic choice there are three key levels of strategy to consider:

(1) **Where to compete?**

Which markets/products/SBUs should be part of our portfolio?

(2) **How to compete?**

For each SBU, what should be the basis of our competitive advantage?

(3) **Which investment vehicle to use?**

Suppose an attractive new market has been identified. Should the organisation enter the market via organic growth, acquisition or some form of joint expansion method, such as franchising?

3 Strategic options – the strategic models

There are several models that you must be familiar with.

- Porter – generic strategies – looks at competitive strategy
- Ansoff – product/market matrix – directions for growth
- BCG – growth/share matrix.

Each of these models suggests several possible strategies that the organisation could adopt. The organisation can then pick the one that best fits its circumstances, which it will have identified from the internal and external analysis that it has undertaken.

You need to understand the basics of each model. However, the key to examination success will be to successfully demonstrate your ability to apply them in a scenario.

Benefits

- These models provide a useful starting point for the discursive process as they initiate discussion amongst the management teams.
- They are well-known and as such have credibility. This results in their easy application with minimal resistance.
- They generate options that can be used in the debate and allow comparison.
- They can in some instances be linked to each other to enhance the analysis.
- They can be used simply or be developed into more complicated applications.

Limitations

- They are simplistic – most are two-by-two models.
- Given their prominence in management education, undue emphasis tends to be placed upon them and there is a tendency at times to think that the models will provide a solution.
- They are dated and were produced when environments were very different. They tend to suggest that strategic choice is a straightforward process.
- They serve as a good basis for analysis, but are not perfect and do not apply to every situation.

4 Porter's Generic Strategies

Porter suggests that competitive advantage arises from the selection of a generic strategy which best fits the organisation's environment and then organising value-adding activities to support the chosen strategy.

		Competitive stance	
Strategic scope	*Broad scope. Targets whole market.*	Cost leadership	Differentiation
	Narrow scope. Targets one segment	Focus	

Cost leadership – being the lowest-cost producer.

Differentiation – creating a customer perception that the product is superior to that of competitors so that a premium can be charged, i.e. that it is different and that customers are willing to pay more for this difference.

Focus – utilising either of the above in a narrow profile of market segments, sometimes called niching.

Porter argues that organisations need to address two key questions:

- Should the strategy be one of differentiation or cost leadership?
- Should the scope be wide or narrow?

He argues that organisations can run the risk of trying to satisfy all three and end up being 'stuck in the middle'. This seems to suggest that Porter was advocating that organisations need to make a basic competitive decision early on in the strategic determination process.

Cost leadership strategy

This approach is based upon a business organising itself to be the lowest-cost producer.

Note that this does not mean producing an inferior product – cost leadership means that the organisation's product is comparable to those of its rivals, but is made more efficiently.

Potential benefits are:

- business can earn higher profits by charging the same price as competitors or even moving to undercut where demand is elastic
- lets company build defence against price wars
- allows price penetration entry strategy into new markets
- enhances barriers to entry
- develops new market segments.

Care needs to be taken when deciding on a pricing strategy as a cost leader. Cutting prices to below those of rivals can trigger a damaging price war, as well as potentially suggesting to customers that the product is inferior to those produced by more expensive competitors. Cost leaders may therefore choose to sell their products at a comparable price to those charged by rivals, but earn more profit which can be reinvested (such as in advertising, expansion or research and development) to gain competitive advantage.

Value chain analysis is central to identifying where cost savings can be made at various stages in the value chain. Attainment depends upon arranging value chain activities so as to:

- reduce costs by copying rather than originating designs, using cheaper materials and other cheaper resources, producing products with 'no frills', reducing labour costs and increasing labour productivity
- achieving economies of scale by high-volume sales allowing fixed costs to be spread over a wider production base
- use high-volume purchasing to obtain discounts for bulk purchase
- locating in areas where cost advantage exists or government aid is possible
- obtaining learning and experience curve benefits.

Differentiation strategy

This strategy is based upon the idea of persuading customers that a product is superior to that offered by the competition. Differentiation can be based on product features or creating/altering consumer perception (i.e. through superior brand development to rivals). Differentiation can also be based upon **process as well as product**. It is usually used to justify a higher price.

Benefits:

- Products command a premium price so higher margins.
- Demand becomes less price elastic and so avoids costly competitor price wars.

- Life cycle extends as branding becomes possible – hence strengthening the barriers to entry.

Value chain analysis can identify the points at which these can be achieved by:

- creating products which are superior to competitors by virtue of design, technology, performance, etc. Marketing spend becomes important
- offering superior after-sales service by superior distribution, perhaps in prime locations
- creating brand strength
- augmenting the product, i.e. adding to it.
- packaging the product
- ensuring an innovative culture exists within the company.

Focus strategy

This strategy is aimed at a segment of the market rather than the whole market. A particular group of consumers are identified with similar needs, possibly based upon age, sex, lifestyle, income or geography and then the company will either differentiate or cost focus in that area.

Benefits:

- smaller segment and so smaller investment in marketing operations
- allows specialisation
- less competition
- entry is cheaper and easier.

Requires:

- reliable segment identification
- consumer/customer needs to be reliably identified – research becomes even more crucial
- segment to be sufficiently large to enable a return to be earned in the long run
- competition analysis – given the small market, the competition, if any, needs to be fully understood
- direct focus of product to consumer needs.

Niching can be done via specialisation by:

- location
- type of end user
- product or product line
- quality
- price
- size of customer
- product feature.

If done properly it can avoid confrontation and competition yet still be profitable. The attractiveness of the market niche is influenced by the following:

- the niche must be large enough in terms of potential buyers
- the niche must have growth potential and predictability
- the niche must be of negligible interest to major competitors
- the firm must have strategic capability to enable effective service of the niche.

Illustration 1 – Cost leadership

Casio Electronics Co. Ltd – Casio has sold over 1 billion pocket calculators. It follows an industry-wide cost leadership approach. Its calculators are certainly not inferior products, being able to perform over two hundred basic scientific functions. How does it do it? Consider its value chain:

- Operations – mass manufactured in China, which has cheaper labour and economies of scale.
- Operations – 'buttons', display and instructions manuals are multi–lingual – reducing the need to make calculators specific to one target country.
- Procurement – mass purchase/production of components.
- Outbound logistics – packaging is robust, yet allows a considerable number of calculators to be shipped at any time.

Strategic options and choice

Illustration 2 – Differentiation

British Airways (BA) is a multinational passenger airline. It has adopted a differentiation approach by offering passengers a higher-quality experience than many of its rivals. This allows it to charge a premium for its flights compared to many other airlines. Again – examination of its value chain may help to explain how it achieves this:

- Procurement – prime landing slots are obtained at major airports around the world.
- Procurement – high-quality food and drink is sourced from suppliers.
- Operations – well-maintained, clean and comfortable aircraft are sourced.
- Operations – high numbers of attendants on each flight.
- Marketing – advertising based on quality of service provided.
- Human resources – training in customer care and the recruitment of high-quality staff.

Illustration 3 – Focus

Ferrari is an example of a company that focuses on a niche market in the automobile industry. It produces extremely high quality cars which command a high premium price. However, this means that Ferrari only has a very small percentage of the global car market, as the majority of consumers will be unable to afford its high sales prices.

This is a risk of the focus approach. The niche targeted may be small and fail to justify the company's attention. In addition the niche may shrink or disappear altogether over time as consumer tastes and fashions change.

Limitations of Porter's generic strategies

In spite of its popularity, there are a number of problems with Porter's generic strategies model, including:

- Porter argues that any business that attempts to adopt more than one of the generic strategies will become 'stuck in the middle'. He suggested that this is because a business will be unable to successfully implement more than one at the same time, leading to strategic drift. In reality this may be too simplistic.

    A number of companies do not fit into one of the classic generic strategies and adopt a 'hybrid' approach. Successful UK supermarket chain Sainsbury's uses a slogan 'Live well for less', suggesting to its potential customers that its products are both lower price than rivals and good quality – both differentiation and cost leadership.

- Cost leadership in itself may not give competitive advantage. Failure to pass on cost savings to customers through lower prices may mean that the business fails to gain an edge over rivals. Passing on the cost savings may trigger a price war with rivals, meaning that the company fails to benefit from the strategy.

- Differentiation may not always lead to a business being able to command a high price for its goods. It may be used to generate increased sales volume – which Porter argued was typically the purpose of a cost leadership approach.

Test your understanding 1

Company W makes motor vehicles. Several years ago, W restructured its value chain to significantly reduce production costs and improve quality. This was in response to similar activities by its W's major rivals.

Because of this, W has been able to maintain its prices at a similar level to those of its competitors, while continuing to produce a wide range of cars that are tailored to a variety of market segments.

W has recently decided to undertake a significant investment in advertising, as it feels that its brand is one of the most recognised in the market. W wishes to further increase the desirability of its brand, which it feels could allow it to raise its prices slightly in the coming year, while still maintaining its overall sales volume.

Strategic options and choice

According to Porter's generic strategies model, W's current approach to its market is an example of:

A   Cost leadership

B   Focus

C   Stuck in the middle

D   Differentiation

Test your understanding 2

Y is a small business that sells furniture in country H. It is considering its future corporate strategy.

The furniture market is dominated by large manufacturers, who have large factories as well as close relationships with key suppliers of raw materials. Y is currently the twentieth largest manufacturer of furniture in country H.

Y's market analysis has identified that there are a moderate number of self-employed individuals in country H who work from home and who desire standard office furniture that is also fashionable. However, there are several companies who have built up established brand names in this sector of the market.

Y currently makes furniture for small to medium sized businesses (such as desks and office chairs). Products in this segment of the market are fairly generic as businesses typically choose a furniture supplier based on price. There are a large number of other suppliers of this style of furniture in country H – including several of the larger manufacturers.

Y is concerned that it lacks the appropriate skills to make other types of furniture.

Which of the following strategies is the most appropriate for Y to adopt?

A   Focus

B   Differentiation

C   Cost leadership

D   Y is stuck in the middle

Test your understanding 3 – AVA – (Case style)

You work as a strategic management accountant for AVA, an airline company that offers regular passenger flights from several countries in country L to destinations all over the world.

AVA is a long-established company which has historically offered a low-cost service with few passenger comforts or luxuries. Customers have to book seats online, with no chance for interaction with an AVA staff member. Seats (which are renowned by customers for their lack of leg room) cannot be pre-booked and AVA has a poor record for delays and cancellations.

In spite of this, AVA has managed to achieve reasonable profits by being able to offer its flights at extremely low prices. In recent years, however, the company's profits have fallen as the economy of country L has started to recover from a long recession. This has led the company to start looking at ways of improving profitability.

You have been contacted by the Finance Director (FD) of AVA. His email is shown below:

To: H. Pimm
From: FD
Date: 16/09/XX
Subject: AVA Strategic direction

Hi H,

As you know, last year the directors felt that the company was missing out on the lucrative first class service market – currently dominated by several major international airlines which are significantly larger than AVA. While first class travellers require more services and better facilities, we would be able to charge them a relatively high ticket price.

The company therefore converted the front section of several of its aircraft into 'first class' with fewer seats and more leg room. Passengers book these seats through a separate system which enables them to speak to an adviser if they had any problems. AVA also offers free food and drink on the flight to first class passengers. This service is not be available to standard class customers.

The airplanes AVA upgraded were all based on one of its major routes. Unfortunately, uptake was disappointing and AVA wishes to try and understand why.

The directors would like you to evaluate our first class offering. They feel that examining our existing and first class strategies using Porter's generic strategies would be a good place to start.

Strategic options and choice

> Please have the report on my desk in thirty minutes, so I have time to consider it before speaking to the other directors.
>
> Thanks
>
> FD
>
> **Required:**
>
> Draft the report as requested in the FD's email.
>
> (30 minutes)

5 Ansoff

The product/market growth framework

A commonly used model for analysing the possible strategic directions that an organisation can follow. Hence useful in areas of strategic choice:

		Products	
		Existing	*New*
Markets	Existing	Market penetration	Product development
	New	Market development	Diversification

Market penetration

The main aim is to increase market share using existing products within existing markets.

Approach

First attempt to stimulate **usage by existing customers:**

- new uses of advertising
- promotions, sponsorships
- quantity discounts.

Then attempt to attract **non-users** and **competitor customers** via:

- pricing
- promotion and advertising
- process redesign, e.g. Internet/e-commerce

Key notes:

Considered when:

- overall market is growing
- market not saturated
- competitors leaving or weak
- strong brand presence by your company with established reputation
- strong marketing capabilities exist within your company.

Market development

Aims to increase sales by taking the present product to new markets (or new segments). Entering new markets or segments may require the development of new competencies which serve the particular needs of customers in those segments, e.g. cultural awareness/linguistic skills.

Movement into overseas markets is often quoted as a good example as the organisation will need to build new competencies when entering international markets.

Approach

- Add **geographical** areas – regional and national
- add **demographic** areas – age and sex
- new **distribution** channels.

Key notes

- **Slight** product modifications may be needed
- advertising in different media and in different ways
- research – primary research at this point given significance of the investment
- company is structured to produce one product and high switching costs exist for transfer to other product types
- strong marketing ability is needed, usually coupled with established brand backing, e.g. Coca-Cola

Strategic options and choice

Product development

Focuses on the development of new products for existing markets.

Offers the advantage of dealing with known customer/consumer bases.

Approach:

- develop product features of a significant nature
- create different quality versions.

Key notes:

Company needs to be innovative and strong in the area of R&D and have an established, reliable marketing database.

Constant innovation allows for the developing sophistication of consumers and customers and ensures that any product-related competitive advantage is maintained.

Diversification

The risky option?

Approach:

New products to new markets.

Key notes:

Appropriate when existing markets are saturated or when products are reaching the end of their life cycle. It can spread risk by broadening the portfolio and lead to 'synergy-based benefits', allegedly.

This goes through periods of being in and out of favour and the debate is always continuing as to whether this is a good strategic option. Critics argue that it is madness to take resources away from known markets and products only to allocate them to businesses that the company essentially knows nothing about. This risk has to be compensated for by higher rewards, which may or may not exist.

Brand stretching ability is often seen as being the critical success factor for successful diversification – this is a possible discussion point. The new business and its strategy may well have 'teething problems' with its implementation and this may damage brand reputation.

Reasons suggested:

- Objectives can no longer be met in known markets – possibly due to a change in the external environment.
- Company has excess cash and powerful shareholders;
- Possible to 'brand stretch' and benefit from past advertising and promotion in other SBUs.
- Diversification promises greater returns and can spread risk by removing the dependency on one product.
- Greater use of distribution systems and corporate resources such as research and development, market research, finance and HR leading to synergies.

Overall

It is worth noting that, unlike Porter's generic strategies model, Ansoff does not argue that a business should only adopt **one** of the four possible strategies. It is possible for an organisation to adopt multiple strategies simultaneously. For example, UK retailer Marks and Spencer has launched a number of new advertising campaigns designed to boost sales of its products (market penetration), while also offering its existing food ranges in motorway service stations (market development).

Illustration 4 – Ansoff

- Kellogg's have repositioned their products through various advertising campaigns **(market penetration)**. For example, the 'have you forgotten how good they taste?' campaign was to remind adults, who buy cereals for their children, of the virtues of their product.

- Kwik Fit, a motor repair company, took the opportunity to cross sell insurance to customers on their database who had visited their outlets to have equipment fitted **(product development – 'piggybacking')**.

- Kaplan now sell their ACCA courses in Eastern Europe and Asia, amongst other countries, rather than just their traditional UK markets **(market development)**.

- Virgin, a multinational conglomerate, has expanded into a wide range of different activities, including airlines, trains, cosmetics, wedding wear and so on **(diversification)**.

Strategic options and choice

Limitations of Ansoff's matrix

Limitations of Ansoff's matrix include:

- The matrix is seen as being too simplistic as it fails to take account of the external environment, such as competitor strategies. For a complete picture it is essential that the organisation undertakes detailed external analysis with, for example, SWOT, PEST and Five Forces.
- The matrix focuses on ways that the organisation can grow. In reality, not all companies want to grow their business. They may wish to simply defend their current position or may be focused on survival.
- Any decision made by management using Ansoff's matrix is subjective – the model does not show the company which strategy is optimal. As such, ineffective strategies can still easily be selected.

Test your understanding 4

Consider the following diagram of Ansoff's matrix:

		Market	
		New	Existing
Product	New	A	C
	Existing	B	D

Which of the following strategies is located in quadrant B on the above diagram?

A Market penetration
B Product development
C Diversification
D Market development

Test your understanding 5

HUF is a business that retails wine, beer and other alcoholic beverages through a large number of stores. It has recently launched a new radio advertising campaign (HUF's normal advertising medium) offering discounts to all customers if they spend more than a certain amount of money in one of HUF's stores.

254

According to Ansoff, which type of strategy is HUF adopting in the above scenario?

A   Diversification

B   Market development

C   Market penetration

D   Product development

Test your understanding 6 – (Integration question)

Esso is a successful oil company. It has run a 'pricewatch' campaign to ensure its fuels are priced at a similar level to supermarkets and other competitors. It has expanded its range of products available at Esso minimarkets to include groceries and household goods. It has signed agreements with China to sell fuels there and is contemplating acquisitions of engineering and textiles companies.

Required:

Categorise these actions using Ansoff's matrix. Explain your choices.

(5 minutes)

As outlined in Ansoff's model (see previous section), diversification refers to a business entering a new market or industry which it is not currently, while also developing new a new product or products for this new market.

Diversification is usually seen as the riskiest of the growth strategies suggested by Ansoff as the business has no experience of the market **or** the product that it is planning to sell.

6 Diversification

Diversification can take **two** main forms:

6.1 Related diversification (concentric diversification)

- Growth into similar industries.
- Growth forward into the customer marketplace.
- Growth backward into the existing supply chain:
    - **Vertical backward** – a company seeks to operate in markets in which it currently obtains its resources, e.g. a supermarket producing some of the products it buys – the benefit would arise from greater control over resource supply.

- **Vertical forward** – a company seeks to move into its customer base, e.g. a brewery establishing its own chain of pubs and off-licences.
- **Horizontal** – involves a company entering into complementary or competing markets, e.g. Honda motorcycles and cars. (Not to be confused with horizontal integration, which refers to the acquisition of a competitor.)

Vertical integration

Taking over a supplier (backwards vertical integration) or customer (forwards vertical integration). Key issues relate to

- Cost.

  Is it cheaper to make a product in-house and avoid paying towards a supplier's profit margin or might the supplier have sufficient economies of scale for them to sell it cheaper than you can make it?

- Quality.

  Making a component in-house means you can tailor it to your own needs and use proprietary expertise... if you have the necessary resources and competences.

- Risk/flexibility.

  Outsourcing gives a firm the flexibility to switch suppliers and so exercise buyer power to drive down prices.

> **Vertical integration**
>
> Backward integration refers to developments into activities which are concerned with inputs to the company's present business, for example a company becoming a supplier of its own raw materials. Sometimes this form of integration is called "upstream" integration.
>
> Forward integration refers to development into activities which are concerned with the company's outputs. For example, a company could set up its own distribution channels rather than relying on outside retailers. Sometimes this form of integration is called "downstream" integration.
>
> Vertical integration can have important benefits and costs which need to be considered in any decision.

Benefits of integration

- Economies of combined operations, e.g. proximity, reduced handling.

- Economies of internal control and coordination, e.g. scheduling and coordinating operations should be better. Information about the market can be fed back to the production companies.

- Economies of avoiding the market, e.g. negotiation, packing, advertising costs are avoided.

- Tap into technology. Close knowledge of the upstream or downstream operations can give a company valuable strategic advantages. For example, computer manufacturers have instituted backwards integration into semi-conductor design and manufacturing to gain a better understanding of the technology and its potential.

- Safeguarding proprietary knowledge. If a firm makes components itself, it does not have to supply specifications to its suppliers; this information therefore stays confidential.

- Assured supply and demand. The firm will have first call on supplies in scarce periods and the greatest chance of having an outlet in periods of low demand. Fluctuations in supply and demand are not eliminated but can, perhaps, be better planned.

- Reduction in bargaining power of suppliers and customers. Two of Porter's forces on a firm are customer and supplier bargaining power. So if your suppliers are giving you a rough time, take them over or set up your own supply company. Similarly with distribution channels.

- Enhanced ability to differentiate. More of the product comes under your control so you have a greater ability to differentiate it. For example, a specialist chain of shops could be established with a distinctive brand image.

- Defend against "lock out". It may be necessary to defend against being cut off from access to suppliers or distributors. For example, if a competitor were buying up your suppliers you would have to acquire your own supplier to ensure continued supply of components.

Costs of integration

- Increased operating gearing. Vertical integration increases the proportion of the firm's costs which are fixed. For example, if the firm were to purchase from an outside source, all those costs would be variable. If the input is produced internally the firm has to bear all the fixed costs of production. Vertical integration increases business risk from this source.

- Reduced flexibility to change partners. If the in-house supplier or customer does not do well, then it is not easy to switch to outsiders. You will probably have to get rid of the in-house company first.

- Capital investment needs. Vertical integration will consume capital resources and must yield a return greater than, or equal to, the firm's opportunity cost of capital, adjusting for strategic considerations, for integration to be a good choice.

- Cut off from suppliers and customers. By integrating a firm may cut itself off from the flow of technology from its suppliers or market research information from its customers. For example, a firm will have to take responsibility for developing its own technology. Other potential suppliers may be reluctant to share their technology as they would be supplying it not only to a customer, but a customer who is also a competitor.

- Dulled incentives. The captive relationship between buyer and seller can quickly lead to inefficiencies. These can quickly spread through the group as too high cost products are passed through.

- Differing managerial requirements. Different businesses need different management skills. Because a company is a successful manufacturer, this does not mean that it can turn its hand to retailing with a reasonable chance of success. Many companies have found that they do best doing what they do best.

Horizontal diversification

Horizontal diversification refers to development into activities that are competitive with, or directly complementary to, a company's present activities. There are three cases.

(a) Competitive products. Taking over a competitor can have obvious benefits, leading eventually towards achieving a monopoly. Apart from active competition, a competitor may offer advantages such as completing geographical coverage.

(b) Complementary products. For example, a manufacturer of household vacuum cleaners could make commercial cleaners. A full product range can be presented to the market and there may well be benefits to be reaped from having many of the components common between the different ranges.

(c) By-products. For example, a butter manufacturer discovering increased demand for skimmed milk. Generally, income from by-products is a windfall: any you get is counted, at least initially, as a bonus.

6.2 Unrelated diversification (conglomerate diversification)

This type of diversification occurs when a business expands into completely new markets or industries with which the business currently shares no common ground.

Advantages

Conglomerate diversification tends to occur when there are limited opportunities for expansion in the organisation's current markets. The only way for such a business to grow may be through unrelated diversification. It provides an opportunity for return if there is nothing else to do with the resources. The company may need to be seen as an 'aggressive' organisation and may embark on this course of action in order to appease powerful stakeholder groups.

The fact that the organisation is operating in a range of different markets reduces the organisation's overall risk. It is unlikely that all of the markets that the organisation operates within will enter decline at the same time, reducing variability of returns.

Even unrelated markets may have some synergies with each other, which could reduce the overall costs of the organisation.

Disadvantages

There is significantly more risk for the organisation if they adopt this strategy as they are launching an new, unproven product into a market that they have little experience or knowledge of. This significantly increases the chances of failure. This can be eliminated to a degree by acquiring an existing business in the new target market (thereby acquiring the industry knowledge required).

For many larger organisations, there will be little gain to shareholders. Shareholders are already likely to hold a diverse portfolio of investments, meaning that they have already diversified away much of their risk. Diversification by one of the companies that they own shares in will therefore do little to help them.

Attempting to operate in new industries may mean that management lose focus on the core markets that the company currently operates within. This could lead to reduced returns for the organisation as a whole.

Strategic options and choice

Test your understanding 7

Which THREE of the following would be likely reasons for an organisation to adopt an unrelated diversification strategy?

A Reduced risk for diversified institutional shareholders

B Increased synergies

C Reduced variability in returns for the organisation

D Possibility of 'brand stretch'

E Increased management focus on core activities

F Existing markets are saturated

G Improved employee morale

Test your understanding 8 – C – (Case style)

C operates several hundred coffee shops across country U. Its stores offer a wide variety of coffee and tea-based drinks that customers can either drink on the premises or take away. In addition to drinks, C also offers a range of sandwiches and cakes.

C has a large number of rivals in the intensely competitive coffee shop market in country U, all of which offer a similar range of products to C and at a slightly lower price.

C has built a reputation for high quality service and is currently the market leader, allowing it to achieve high margins on its products – even in the current economic downturn in country U.

This has allowed C to build a significant cash surplus and it is considering how to further grow its business. At the most recent meeting of the Board of Directors, three directors made suggestions for how to expand the business.

The Finance Director (FD) suggested that C should consider offering a range of other products in its shops. These would include wine and soft drinks as well as hot food. The cash surplus could be used to re-fit the kitchens of C's shops and launch a large advertising campaign across the country. The FD suggested that the margins on these items were even higher than those currently achieved on coffee, leading to higher profits for C in the future.

The Marketing Director (MD) disagreed as she felt that C's coffee shops were currently successful and should not be changed. She recommended investing the cash into opening up branches in neighbouring countries. She stated that C's current branding and product range would be suitable for neighbouring countries with few, if any changes. Many of C's competitors have already entered the countries surrounding country U.

The Operations Director (OD), however, stated that he felt that the coffee and food market in the region was simply too saturated to make further investment worthwhile. Instead, he feels that C should look to invest in a totally new area.

A successful online music store has recently posted significant growth in profits in country U. The OD has identified this as a high-growth market and feels the cash surplus should be used to purchase this business.

Required:

(i) Explain and justify where each of the director's proposals would be placed on Ansoff's matrix

   (**Note:** A diagram is NOT required)

(ii) Identify the strategy suggested by Ansoff that the directors have failed to consider and suggest how this could be applied to C.

(iii) Discuss the advantages and disadvantages of the CEO's proposal to purchase the online music store.

(45 minutes)

Strategic options and choice

7 Product Portfolio Theory – Boston Consulting Group (BCG)

Boston Consulting Group Growth / Share Matrix

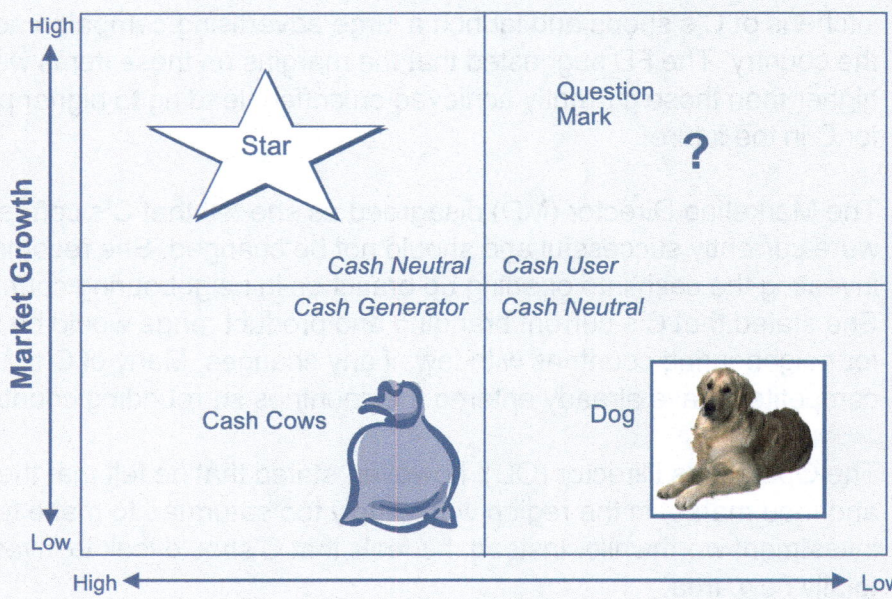

Developed originally to assist managers in identifying cash flow requirements of different businesses or products within their organisation's portfolio and to help to decide whether change in the mix of businesses is required. A broad portfolio indicates that a business has a presence in a wide range of products and market sectors – this may or may not be a good thing!

Using the BCG matrix typically requires four main steps:

(1) divide the company into SBUs
(2) allocate into the matrix
(3) assess the prospects of each SBU and compare against others in the matrix
(4) develop strategic objectives for each SBU.

Relative market share – the ratio of SBU market share to that of largest rival in the market sector. BCG suggests that market share gives a company cost advantages from economies of scale and learning effects. The dividing line is set at 1 – i.e. a high market share suggests that the product is a market leader. A figure of 4 suggests that SBU share is four times greater than the nearest rival. A figure of 0.1 suggests that the SBU is 10% of the sector leader.

Market growth rate – represents the growth rate of the market sector concerned. High-growth industries offer a more favourable competitive environment and better long-term prospects than slow-growth industries. The dividing line is set at 10%.

SBUs are entered onto the matrix as dots with circles around the dots denoting the revenue relative to total corporate turnover. The bigger the circle, the more significant the unit.

Using the matrix

The model suggests that appropriate strategies would be:

- **hold** – adopt strategies to keep the product in its current quadrant – i.e. invest heavily in advertising or promotion for a star product in order to maintain its current high market share.
- **build** – increase investment in the product in an attempt to boost its market share.
- **harvest** – reduce investment in the product in order to maximise the net cash return from the product to the business.
- **divest** – disposal/closure of the product in order to release any cash currently tied up within it.

Cash cows – hold or harvest

These products or SBUs have a high market share in a low-growth market. They have usually reached the 'maturity' stage of their life cycle (see chapter 4 for more information on the product/industry life cycle).

Cash cows, as the name suggests, are usually strongly profit and cash generating. This is because they are market leaders with relatively high sales and this has often allowed them to create significant economies of scale.

The fact that the market is low growth indicates that it is no longer attractive for new entrants, or for heavy investment by any participating company. This means that capital requirements are low for the cash cow and that the cost of defensive strategies (such as advertising) are also likely to be fairly low.

A company will often adopt a harvesting strategy towards its cash cows, maximising cash flows by keeping investment to a minimum where possible, while trying to maintain the product and prevent it from entering decline for as long as possible.

Note that profits from cash cows can be used to support other products in their development stage. Therefore for a company to have a balanced portfolio, it needs some of these cash cow products.

Strategic options and choice

Stars – hold or build

Stars have high market share in an attractive, high-growth market. They are most likely in the 'growth' stage of their life cycle.

As they are likely to be the market leader, they offer attractive long-term prospects and, if maintained could one day become a cash cow when the rate of market growth finally slows.

Stars rarely generate significant amount of cash or profits for the company. While they generate high levels of sales, they operate in an attractive, high-growth market meaning that they are likely to be facing significant levels of competition. This requires the company to spend large amounts of money to beat off competitor attack strategies, through marketing and research and development (amongst other things), as well as having to aggressively try and win new customers in the expanding market.

In addition, in order to sustain the level of growth in the market, stars require high levels of capital investment.

The company therefore usually adopts a 'build' strategy, involving heavy investment to keep attracting new customers (as well as defending those it already has).

Question marks (also known as problem children) – build or divest

Questions marks have low market share in an attractive, rapidly growing market. They may be at the 'growth' or 'introduction' stage of their life cycle.

Given the rapid growth in the market, there is opportunity for significant development of question marks. However, given the currently low market share, there is high risk of failure – the product may fail to grow its market share and will not therefore become a star.

As such, management typically adopts a 'double or quits' approach to question marks. If they feel that the product stands a good chance of success, they will adopt a build strategy and try to grow market share through heavy investment in expansion, marketing and promotion. If they are not confident in the future success of the product, they may choose to divest, exiting the market.

Ultimately, question marks are risky – they will usually absorb substantial management time and cash and may not be successfully developed.

Dogs – harvest or divest

Dogs have a low market share of a slow growing (or even contracting) market. It may be a product which has entered the 'decline' stage of its life cycle, or could even be a question mark that never successfully grew. It is likely to be making small profits or losses and will be fairly cash neutral.

There is usually seen as being little point for the business to try and grow market share. The market is no longer attractive and it is dominated by other, rival products. To invest in the dog would require significant cost and risk, with relatively little chance of a reasonable return. This most commonly leads to the BCG matrix suggesting that the product is divested.

However, it is important not to divest the product without further analysis. Some dog products support other, more valuable products sold by the business. For example, a computer printer manufacturer may accept a 'dog' printer model as it allows them to sell more valuable ink cartridges, which enjoy very high profit margins. Alternatively a 'dog' product may be used as a retailer as a loss leader to attract customers.

The dog may also still be profitable. There is little point divesting a product which is still making acceptable returns and may still be helping to earn shareholders money.

Be aware that sometimes dogs cannot be divested – particularly in the public sector where failing schools for example will need to be reinvested in and possibly restructured but certainly not divested.

Whatever the reason for keeping the dog, a harvest strategy would be adopted, keeping costs low and maximising what little profit or cash flow can be made from the product.

BCG recommendations

Once the company has completed its portfolio analysis, it can identify a number of overall portfolio issues:

- Is the portfolio in balance? While the business does not necessarily need any dog products, it would expect to have products in the other three quadrants of the grid. It needs cash cows to support stars and develop question marks, but if it only has cash cows it may find that they all enter decline at the same time – stars and question marks may be the successful products of the future.

- Some less attractive parts of the portfolio may be divested – in particular dog products (if not profitable or support for other products) and question marks that the management lacks confidence in.

Strategic options and choice

Limitations of the BCG

Limitations

- Simplistic – only considers two variables

- connection between market share and cost savings is not strong – low-market share companies use low-share technology and can have lower production costs

- cash cows do not always generate cash – cash cows may still require substantial cash investment just to remain competitive and defend their market share.

- fail to consider value creation – the management of a diverse portfolio can create value by sharing competencies across SBUs, sharing resources to reap economies of scale or by achieving superior governance. BCG would divert investment away from the cash cows and dogs and fails to consider the benefit of offering the full range and the concept of 'loss leaders'.

- over-emphasis on being the market leader – many companies have products that are not market leaders, but which are highly profitable.

Test your understanding 9

You have been given the following data regarding four products currently sold by company YX:

Product	Revenue – total market ($m)	Revenue – YX ($m)	Market share of largest competitor	Market growth rate
Whizz	400	40	45%	1%
Bang	60	20	10%	4%
Wallop	100	5	1%	15%
Pop	96	4.8	30%	–5%

Show where each product would be categorised using the BCG matrix below. You can place more than one product in each category.

Stars	Question marks
Cash cows	Dogs

Test your understanding 10

O sells four products.

Product H1 is a type of protective shoe. It has recently lost its market leader position as the market for protective clothing continues to shrink. Financially, H1 is breaking even.

Product E2 is a vented umbrella. It has only recently been launched and has yet to see strong sales growth in the market. O feels that the umbrella market is likely to grow strongly over the next few years due to global warming.

Product Y4 is a waterproof coat. It is the top selling coat in O's market and, as with product E2, O expects ongoing growth due to the changing climate.

Finally, product B3 is a waterproof boot. B3 is far superior to the market leaders, but is struggling to gain acceptance in the popular, rapidly growing footwear market.

According to the BCG matrix model, which ONE of the above four products would O be most likely to adopt a holding strategy for?

A   H1
B   E2
C   Y4
D   B3

Strategic options and choice

Test your understanding 11 – GC – (Case style)

GC is a conglomerate that comprises five strategic business units (SBUs), all operating as subsidiary companies. Your manager has sent you an email attachment which gives information relating to each SBU (and the market leader or nearest competitor):

Current market share

	GC %	Market leader %	Nearest competitor %	Market growth expected by GC
Building brick manufacturer (Declining profitability)	3	25		Small
Parcel carriage service (Long established, faces strong competition. Turnover and profitability over last three years have been stable but are expected to decline as competition strengthens)	1	6		Nil
Food manufacturer producing exclusively for household consumption (Long established with little new investment. High levels of turnover and profitability, which are being sustained)	25		5	Slowly declining
Painting and decorating contracting company (Established three years ago. Continuous capital injections from group over that period. Currently not making any profit)	0.025	0.5		Historically high but now forecast to slow down

| Software development and supply company

(Acquired two years ago. Market share expected to increase over next two years. Sustained investment from the group but profitability so far low) | 10 | | 8 | Rapid |

Your manager has left a note on your desk asking you to prepare briefing notes for him covering the following issues:

(a) Comment on GC's overall competitive position by applying the Boston Consulting Group growth/share matrix analysis to its portfolio of SBUs.

(b) Discuss how GC should pursue the strategic development of its SBUs in order to add value to the overall conglomerate group.

Required:

Prepare the briefing notes as requested by your manager.

(45 minutes)

8 Acquisition

Businesses may choose to grow in one of several main ways, including acquisitions, mergers or organic growth.

Acquisition refers to a corporate action in which a company buys most, if not all, of the target company's ownership stakes in order to assume control of the target firm.

Mergers are business combinations that result from the creation of a new reporting entity formed from the combining parties.

Note that, for our purposes in the E3 examination, there is little or no strategic difference between an acquisition and a merger.

Organic growth is growth through internally generated projects, such as increased output, customer base expansion, or new product development.

Acquisition may be more expensive than organic growth because the owners of the acquired company will need to be paid for the risks they have already taken. On the other hand, if the company goes for organic growth it must take the risks itself so there is a trade-off between cost and risk.

Strategic options and choice

A company can gain synergy by bringing together complementary resources in their own business and that being acquired. Synergy is defined as **'the advantage to a firm gained by having existing resources which are compatible with new products or markets that the company is developing'**.

For example, sales synergy may be obtained through the use of common marketing facilities such as distribution channels. Investment synergy may result from the joint use of plant and machinery or raw materials.

An acquisition must add value in a way the shareholder cannot replicate in order to avoid the risks associated with diversified companies (see Ansoff).

Acquisition v organic growth

Advantages of acquisitions over organic growth

Acquisition has some significant advantages over internal growth.

- High-speed access to resources – this is particularly true of brands; an acquisition can provide a powerful brand name that could take years to establish through internal growth.

- Avoids barriers to entry – acquisition may be the only way to enter a market where the competitive structure would not admit a new member or the barriers to entry were too high.

- Less reaction from competitors – there is less likelihood of retaliation because an acquisition does not alter the capacity of the competitive arena.

- It can block a competitor – if Kingfisher's bid for Asda had been successful it would have denied Walmart its easy access to the UK.

- It can help restructure the operating environment – some mergers of car companies were used to reduce overcapacity.

- Relative price/earnings ratio – if the P/E ratio is significantly higher in the new industry than the present one, acquisition may not be possible because it would cause a dilution in earnings per share to the existing shareholders. But if the present company has a high P/E ratio it can boost earnings per share by issuing its own equity in settlement of the purchase price.

- Asset valuation – if the acquiring company believes the potential acquisition's assets are undervalued, it might undertake an asset-stripping operation.

Disadvantages of acquisitions growth

There are some disadvantages associated with this method of growth.

- Acquisition may be more costly than internal growth because the owners of the acquired company will have to be paid for the risk already taken. On the other hand, if the company decides on internal growth, it will have to bear the costs of the risk itself.
- There is bound to be a cultural mismatch between the organisations – a lack of 'fit' can be significant in knowledge-based companies, where the value of the business resides in individuals.
- Differences in managers' salaries – another example of cultural mismatch that illustrates how managers are valued in different countries.
- Disposal of assets – companies may be forced to dispose of assets they had before the acquisition. The alliance between British Airways and American Airlines was called off because the pair would have had to free up around 224 take-off and landing slots to other operators.
- Risk – of not knowing all there is to know about the business it seeks to buy.
- Reduction in return on capital employed – quite often an acquisition adds to sales and profit volume without adding to value creation.

9 Joint methods of expansion

Joint development methods

These include:

- Joint venture
- strategic alliances
- franchising
- licenses
- outsourcing.

In any joint arrangement key considerations are

- sharing of costs
- sharing of benefits
- sharing of risks
- ownership of resources
- control/decision making.

Joint development methods

Joint venture

A separate business entity whose shares are owned by two or more business entities. Assets are formally integrated and jointly owned.

A very useful approach for:

- sharing cost
- sharing risk
- sharing expertise.

In the UK, an example of a joint venture is Virgin Trains – a company whose share capital is 51% owned by the Virgin Group and 49% owned by Stagecoach. The joint venture allowed the two companies to work together to take advantage of the privatisation of the nationalised British Rail.

Strategic alliance

A strategic alliance can be defined as a cooperative business activity, formed by two or more separate organisations for strategic purposes, that allocates ownership, operational responsibilities, financial risks, and rewards to each member, while preserving their separate identity/autonomy.

Alliances can allow participants to achieve critical mass, benefit from other participants' skills and can allow skill transfer between participants.

The technical difference between a strategic alliance and a joint venture is whether or not a new, independent business entity is formed.

A strategic alliance is often a preliminary step to a joint venture or an acquisition. A strategic alliance can take many forms, from a loose informal agreement to a formal joint venture.

Alliances include partnerships, joint ventures and contracting out services to outside suppliers.

Seven characteristics of a well-structured alliance have been identified.

- **Strategic synergy** – more strength when combined than they have independently.
- **Positioning opportunity** – at least one of the companies should be able to gain a leadership position (i.e. to sell a new product or service; to secure access to raw materials or technology).
- **Limited resource availability** – a potentially good partner will have strengths that complement weaknesses of the other partner. One of the partners could not do this alone.
- **Less risk** – forming the alliance reduces the risk of the venture.
- **Co-operative spirit** – both companies must want to do this and be willing to co-operate fully.
- **Clarity of purpose** – results, milestones, methods and resource commitments must be clearly understood.
- **Win-win** – the structure, risks, operations and rewards must be fairly apportioned among members.

Some organisations are trying to retain some of the innovation and flexibility that is characteristic of small companies by forming strategic alliances (closer working relationships) with other organisations. They also play an important role in global strategies, where the organisation lacks a key success factor for some markets.

An example of a strategic alliance is that pursued by Starbucks in 2012, in an attempt to break into the Indian coffee shop market. It formed an alliance with Tata Global Beverages – a large Indian drinks company – with both parties investing $80m in order to open a number of Starbucks stores across India. Starbucks had significant experience of running coffee shops, while Tata had strong local knowledge of the growing Indian drinks market.

Franchising

The purchase of the right to exploit a business brand in return for a capital sum and a share of profits or turnover.

- The franchisee pays the franchisor an initial capital sum and thereafter the franchisee pays the franchisor a share of profits or royalties.
- The franchisor provides marketing, research and development, advice and support.
- The franchisor normally provides the goods for resale.

Strategic options and choice

- The franchisor imposes strict rules and control to protect its brand and reputation.
- The franchisee buys into a successful formula, so risk is much lower.
- The franchisor gains capital as the number of franchisees grows.
- The franchisor's head office can stay small as there is considerable delegation/decentralisation to the franchisees.

A classic example of franchising is McDonalds. Within the UK, for example, around half of all McDonalds restaurants are franchises.

Licensing

The right to exploit an invention or resource in return for a share of proceeds. Licensing differs from a franchise because there will be little central support.

In the UK, many beers such as Heineken and Fosters were 'brewed under licence' in the UK for many years, with the original companies that developed the beers simply taking a share of the proceeds from the local brewers.

Outsourcing

Outsourcing means contracting out aspects of the work of the organisation, previously done in-house, to specialist providers. Almost any activity can be outsourced – examples include information technology or payroll.

Mobile telecommunications company O2 has recently announced plans to outsource its customer contact centres in the UK.

The public sector may also undertake outsourcing. For example, in 2013 Barnet Council in London announced plans to outsourced much of its corporate procurement, IT and HR services to Capita – a private sector company.

Test your understanding 12

H Ltd wishes to rapidly expand its popular chain of retail stores, but does not have the capital needed to do so. It has decided to consider joint development methods in order to aid its growth, but H Ltd's owner T is uncertain about which method to use.

T is unwilling to allow any other individual or organisation to have significant influence over H's strategic operations as he is used to having the final say over all major decisions within the company.

T wishes to avoid any damage to H's brand name. As such, he wants staff to continue to be trained centrally, as well as all fixtures, fittings and inventory to be purchased from authorised suppliers only.

Which of the following methods of joint development would be most appropriate for H Ltd?

A   Licensing

B   Franchising

C   Joint venture

D   Strategic alliance

Test your understanding 13 – (integration question)

Which of licensing, joint venture, strategic alliance and franchising might be the most suitable for the following circumstances?

(1) A company has invented a uniquely good ice cream and wants to set up an international chain of strongly branded outlets.

(2) Oil companies are under political pressure to develop alternative, renewable energy sources.

(3) A beer manufacturer wants to move from their existing domestic market into international sales.

10 Divestment

May occur because:

- The SBU no longer fits with the existing group. The company may wish to focus on core competences.

- The SBU may be too small and not warrant the management attention given to it.

- Selling the SBU as a going concern may be a cheaper alternative to putting it into liquidation if redundancy and wind-up costs are considered.

- The parent company may need to improve its liquidity position.

- There may be a belief that the individual parts of the business are worth more than the whole when shares are selling at less than their potential value, e.g. ICI's demerger of its bio-sciences business, later called Zeneca.

- An MBO (management buy out) is one way a divestment can occur.

11 International growth

When deciding whether to expand abroad, a business has several possible strategies that it can adopt:

- **Exporting strategy** – the firm sells products made in its home country to buyers abroad. This often starts with the receipt of a chance order or perhaps poor sales at home force the business to export or collapse.

- **Overseas manufacture** – the firm may either manufacture its products in a foreign country and then either import them back to its home country or sell them abroad. Either way, the firm is involved in direct foreign investment because it is purchasing capital assets in another country. For example, Nissan Motors is a Japanese company, but operates plants to build its motor vehicles across the world, including North-East England.

- **Multinational** – these firms co-ordinate their value-adding activities across national boundaries. For example, a multinational car manufacturer will have engine plants in one country, car body plants in another and electrics in a third. Production capacity is often duplicated around the world.

- **Transnational** – these are 'nation-less' firms that have no 'home' country. Employees and facilities are treated identically, regardless of where they are in the world. The company may be listed on several national stock exchanges. This is often considered to be (currently) largely theoretical.

When deciding between which approach to take if expanding abroad, consideration should be given to the following points:

- **Exposure to risk** – both foreign exchange risk and political risk.

- **Need for capital investment** – this will be lower if an exporting strategy is used.

- **Customer relationships** – given the distance between the manufacturer and its foreign consumers, this can be hard to maintain in an exporting strategy.

- **Transportation costs** – manufacturing at a distance from your target market will increase the cost of getting the units to them.

- **Ethical issues** – if operating in countries with less developed labour laws, should the company take advantage of this to keep costs low?

- **Cultural issues** – managing operations in foreign countries can be difficult due to differences in language and customs. This can also make advertising and operational control difficult.

chapter 7

> **Test your understanding 14**
>
> YH operates a large number of food production facilities, based in country N. In particular, YH's operations focus on the growing and harvesting of soft fruit. YH then sorts and grades the fruit, before shipping it to retailers, such as large supermarkets.
>
> YH has struggled to find the amount of farmland it needs in order to expand its production in its home country. In recent years, therefore, YH has been buying farmland and facilities in several new countries around the world. This has allowed it to expand its sales into a number of new geographical markets and grow its business.
>
> This business model has been so successful that a significant majority of YH's fruit is now grown abroad, with some of it even being brought back into country N to meet demand from YH's customers.
>
> Which of the following options is the best match to the international growth strategy being adopted by YH?
>
> A   Transnational
>
> B   Exporting
>
> C   Multinational
>
> D   Overseas manufacture

12 Evaluating strategies – making a strategic choice

So far in this chapter we have looked at a number of models which provide the company with different options for strategies. Management can then select the strategy that they believe is most appropriate for the organisation – for example if following Porter's generic strategies, managers may decide that a cost leadership approach would be the best strategy to adopt.

This raises a very important question – **how do managers know whether a particular strategy should be adopted by the organisation?**

Strategies need to have 'strategic fit' with their environment if they are to be effective. This 'fit' will be with both their internal and external environments and so the ability to assess viability relies very much on the reliability of the position audit.

Strategic options will be generated by various stakeholder groups (and by use of the various models discussed earlier in this chapter) and debate/discussion will need to follow to assess the viability of each option and make a final selection.

Strategic options and choice

The final selection will be a function of the following:

(1) Relative stakeholder power and their personal characteristics
(2) information available and perceived reliability
(3) historical experience
(4) presentation of options – manner
(5) other corporate experiences
(6) expectations for the future
(7) objectives ordering and perceived ordering – there will be a significant political involvement at this stage.

Viability – a basic approach

According to Johnson and Scholes, potential strategies can be evaluated against the following three criteria:

- **Suitability** is concerned with whether the strategy addresses the circumstances in which an organisation is operating – its strategic position.
- **Feasibility** is concerned with whether the strategy could be made to work in practice and as such looks at more detailed practicalities of strategic capability.
- **Acceptability** is concerned with the expected performance outcomes (such as return or risk) of a strategy and the extent to which these would be in line with the expectations of stakeholders.

For a strategy to be accepted, it must meet all three of these criteria.

Suitability

Is the proposed strategy a suitable response to environmental events and trends. Do we have **strategic fit**? You should consider whether the proposed course of action fits with the existing position. Will it cause any problems elsewhere in the company?

(1) Will it take advantage of **opportunities?**
(2) Will it build on our **strengths?**
(3) Will it help us meet our **mission and objectives**?
(4) How will new products fit with existing ones? Is the new **portfolio** balanced?

Use within Ansoff's matrix

A market development strategy would 'fit' where:

- Channels of distribution are available
- a business has a strong marketing presence
- products are superior to competitors
- an unsaturated markets exist
- spare production capacity exists
- economies of scale are possible.

A product development strategy would 'fit' where:

- brand reputation is high
- the brand is transportable
- strong research capabilities exist.

A market penetration strategy would 'fit' where:

- current markets are not saturated
- present customers will rebuy
- competitors are weak
- spare production capacity exists.

A consolidation strategy would 'fit' where:

- there is a lack of funding
- owners do not want to grow
- human resources not available
- any kind of restraining factor exists.

A diversification strategy would 'fit' where:

- there is a strong brand presence
- significant resources are available to enable the development of new competencies
- market research base is reliable and competent.

Strategic options and choice

Example

Gucci sought growth in sales and so expanded into lower-priced goods and stretched its brand. It also pushed its products in department stores and duty-free channels. It let its name appear on many licensed products such as watches and perfumes.

Sales soared – the company was very happy!

But it soon found that sales in its traditional high-priced, high-margin segment were plummeting as its traditional buyers became disillusioned by the fact that Gucci was now worn by many people thus removing the exclusivity of the product.

Gucci's strategy was not suitable.

Feasibility

Can the necessary resources and competencies be obtained and the required changes be implemented? Any new strategy will require change of some kind and this is likely to meet resistance from some quarters. We will need to question whether the company concerned has the strategic capability to pursue the course of action concerned.

So the key questions revolve around:

(1) Resources – basic and unique.
(2) Competencies – threshold and core.
(3) Implementation issues with regard to dealing with **strategic change**.

Considerations should cover:

- Cultural change required and realism of change
- timescales
- potential resistance
- raw materials availability
- human resources availability
- distribution channel access
- marketing requirements
- IT requirements and skills

- finance:
    - How much is needed?
    - Where will it come from?
    - What options exist?
    - What will the impact be on our financial position and performance?

Don't forget the basic analysis relating to identifying the threshold and core competencies. Are there any sources of competitive advantage or disadvantage?

Acceptability

Any proposed strategy will need to be acceptable to the stakeholders of the organisation, both in terms of "returns" and risk.

All stakeholders will need to be considered relative to their power – the more powerful the stakeholder group, the greater the influence they will have and the more the strategist will have to consider their views.

Some areas for consideration:

- A new strategy usually involves some internal changes and due consideration will need to be given to the **staff** who may have to confront different work practices. Resistance is likely.
- **Financiers** often have required rates of return and liquidity positions.
- **Owners** may well have non-financial requirements of their investment. They may prefer to have less risk and accept a lower reward as the inevitable cost. They could require that all actions conform to their cultural expectations, e.g. Anita Roddick at the Body Shop.
- **Customers, consumers and suppliers** may also have required standards that must be met by the company.
- Local and national **governments** may have some concerns about any strategic proposals with regard to legality and political implications.
- Don't forget the **public** and their ability to form into 'pressure groups'. Ethical considerations may need to be included in the evaluation.

Evaluating "acceptability" will often involve quantitative analysis such as NPV calculations. However, it must be noted that conventional NPV analysis tends to undervalue projects with significant future flexibility. Real option theory, covered in more detail in the F3 paper, is an attempt to incorporate such flexibility into a "strategic NPV".

Strategic options and choice

Tests of a winning strategy

The SAF (suitability, acceptability, feasibility) approach is very useful but other considerations have been added which are worthy of note.

The first is referred to as the **competitive advantage test** and raises the questions:

- What is it?
- How long can it last?

The second question highlights that competitive advantage may not be sustainable, in other words does the **performance measurement** system show predicted improvement?

Thompson poses this strategic management principle:

'The more a strategy fits the enterprise's external and internal situation, builds sustainable competitive advantage and improves company performance, the more it qualifies as a winner.'

Strategy evaluation – the role of the management accountant

Making strategic decisions

Strategic options can be evaluated using the suitability, feasibility, acceptability framework.

The strategic management accountant will contribute to the acceptability and feasibility aspects in particular:

Aspect	Key concerns	Typical financial analysis
Acceptability	Returns to stakeholders	• Cash flow forecasts to ensure dividend growth requirements can be met • NPV analysis • ROCE • Valuation of real options • Shareholder value analysis • Economic value added • Cost/benefit analysis • Ratio analysis (e.g. dividend yield, growth)

	Risk	• Sensitivity • Break-even • Ratio analysis (e.g. gearing, dividend cover) • Expected values
Feasibility	Resources	• Cash flow forecast to identify funding needs • Budgeting resource requirements • Ability to raise finance needed • Working capital implications • Foreign exchange implications

Test your understanding 15

LL is a company that makes and sells clothing made out of wool. It has been having problems manufacturing sufficient garments for its customers for several years as demand has increased significantly. LL's current wool spinning process has been identified as a bottleneck process.

It is considering the purchase of an automated spinning machine that it believes will significantly improve the speed of its manufacturing process. In addition it will allow LL to lay off around fifty members of staff (who are heavily unionised).

The machine will cost around $5m. LL does not have this cash available, but believes that it will be able to raise these funds from its investors.

LL will only purchase the machine if it is:

(i) suitable

(ii) acceptable; AND

(iii) feasible

From the information given above, which of these three criteria does the acquisition of the machine meet?

A   Suitable and acceptable only
B   Suitable only
C   Acceptable and feasible only
D   Suitable and feasible only

Test your understanding 16

When evaluating the acceptability of a new strategy, which of the following analysis tools would be the most useful?

A   BCG matrix
B   Porter's five forces
C   Mendelow's matrix
D   Porter's value chain

Test your understanding 17 – (Integration question)

You work for Blueberry – a quoted resort hotel chain based in Europe.

The industry

The hotel industry is a truly global business characterised by the following:

- Increasing competition.
- An increasing emphasis on customer service with higher standards being demanded.
- In particular the range of facilities, especially spas, is becoming more important as a differentiating factor.

Performance

- Blueberry offers services at the luxury end of the market only, based on a strong brand and prestigious hotels – although its reputation has become tarnished over the last five years due to variable customer satisfaction levels.

- Despite a reputation for having the most prestigious coastal resort hotels along the Mediterranean in 20X0, Blueberry was loss-making in the financial years 20X4/5 and 20X5/6.

- To some extent this situation has been turned around in 20X6/7 with an operating profit of €11 million. However, shareholders are putting the board under pressure to increase profits and dividends further.

- Management have responded to this by setting out an ambitious plan to upgrade hotel facilities throughout the company and move more upmarket. The bulk of the finance is planned to come from retained profits as Blueberry has historically kept its financial gearing low.

Acquisition opportunity

Your manager has arrived in the office and has said the following:

'I've just been told that the Board of Blueberry have been approached by the owner of 'The Villa d'Oeste', a luxury hotel on the shores of Lake Como in Italy, who is considering selling it. The hotel has an international reputation with world-class spa facilities and generates revenue throughout most of the year due to Lake Como's mild micro-climate. The asking price will be approximately €50m. Please spend the next 15 minutes writing some brief notes of issues we should take into account when evaluating the purchase.'

Required:

Draft the notes for your manager.

(15 minutes)

Strategic options and choice

Test your understanding 18 – GGG – (Case style)

You are L. Carter, a strategic management account working for HF&H – a large accountancy practise. One of HF&H's clients is GGG. A partner in HF&H has left the following note on your desk:

Note

Hi L,

I'm going to be meeting several key managers from GGG shortly and I need you to prepare some briefing notes for me. I've left you a briefing document giving you some background information about the company.

Once you've familiarised yourself with the briefing document, please prepare some notes, which need to include the following:

- Analyse the opportunities available to GGG, using Ansoff's strategic directional growth vector matrix.

- Evaluate the opportunities available to GGG in each of the four areas of the Ansoff strategic directional growth vector matrix using Johnson, Scholes and Whittington's Suitability, Acceptability and Feasibility framework.

- Recommend, with your justifications, which strategic directions, as set out in Ansoff's strategic directional growth vector matrix, would be most appropriate for GGG to follow.

I'm meeting the clients in 45 minutes, so please have the notes ready by then.

Thanks

P.

Briefing document – GGG

GGG is a privately owned unlisted company which runs 20 residential care homes for the elderly. A residential care home for the elderly is a building where a number of older people live and receive care (that is, their physical needs are provided for), normally on a full-time basis. The elderly residents may pay the care home fees themselves or they may be paid by their relatives or by the local government authority.

The elderly residents of GGG's care homes are all capable of making decisions for themselves. All of GGG's care homes are located in and around two cities both located in the south of country X. GGG employs around 400 staff in the care homes, some of whom work part-time, and a small team of highly experienced administrators. GGG's care homes all have modern facilities and their staff are highly trained and dedicated. GGG has always been a profitable business, even though its care homes normally have a small amount of spare capacity. GGG has approximately 25% market share in the south of country X. The remainder of the market is shared by a small number of local government funded and operated care homes and some other small private businesses.

Due to the rising costs of operating care homes as a result of increased regulation and the general economic environment, a number of small privately owned care homes in the region have recently closed. The owners of some other privately owned care homes are considering closing or selling them. GGG is also aware that this trend is occurring nationally across country X.

A national shift in the demographics of the population in the last 30 years has resulted in a significant rise in the proportion of elderly members of society. Added to this, the increased social movement of families has resulted in an increasing demand for care home places for the elderly. GGG undertakes limited advertising, relying more on word-of-mouth recommendations and referrals from local hospitals and doctors to obtain its customers.

The prices charged to care home residents by the local government authority run care homes are lower than those charged by GGG, due to central government subsidies. However, the Managing Director of GGG is confident that the services and facilities provided by GGG are superior to those offered by the local government funded care homes.

Although GGG currently offers only full-time care for its elderly residents, there is a growing need for the market to offer 'relief care' packages. This is where elderly people, who do not normally live in residential care homes, could use any of the 20 care homes' facilities for short periods of time (normally 1 week), in order to enable their normal carers (usually family members) to take holidays or rest periods.

Strategic options and choice

A number of GGG's elderly residents are often referred to local hospitals by their doctors for treatments and therapies. Many of GGG's staff are fully qualified nurses and these treatments and therapies could be undertaken by the staff of GGG in each of its care homes. These hospital visits for treatments and therapies can be disruptive and upsetting for residents who often prefer to remain in GGG's care homes and be cared for by staff with whom they are familiar. However, if GGG were to offer these additional facilities within its care homes it will need investment in training and new facilities.

Required:

Prepare the notes as requested in the note from P.

chapter 7

13 Summary

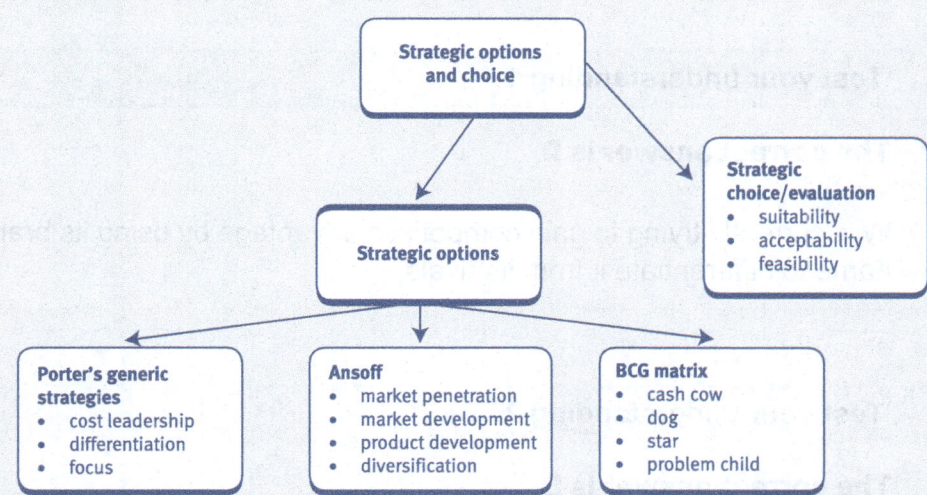

Test your understanding answers

Test your understanding 1

The correct answer is D

W is currently trying to gain competitive advantage by using its brand name to differentiate it from its rivals.

Test your understanding 2

The correct answer is D

Y appears to be stuck in the middle.

Its size prevents it from achieving the economies of scale of its larger rivals, meaning that cost-leadership appears unlikely.

The product that Y currently produces seems to be fairly generic and Y seems to lack the skills to do anything different. Note that Y's current customers seem to mainly be interested in price, so a differentiation strategy would be difficult to undertake here.

Finally, there seems to only be one niche market that Y has identified – that of home workers. However this is a relatively small part of the market and it appears to be well served by the several existing companies.

Overall, this is a very difficult market for Y as it will find it difficult to find a way to out-compete its rivals.

Test your understanding 3 – AVA – (Case style)

Report
To: FD
From: H. Pimm
Date: 16/09/XX
Title: Evaluation of AVA first class offering

Introduction

Porter argued that organisations could adopt one of three main strategies in order to gain competitive advantage – focus, differentiation and cost leadership. This report will use Porter's model to analyse the first class strategy at AVA.

Current strategy in AVA

AVA has adopted a classic cost leadership approach. It has removed a number of 'extras' from the service it provides to customers – such as excess leg room, direct customer service and seat reservations.
AVA has done this in order to keep its costs low. These savings can then be passed onto the customer in the form of low ticket prices, driving demand and enabling AVA to outcompete its rivals.

Cost leadership requires the price elasticity of the market to be high – in other words if AVA offers a low price for its product it needs to be able to generate a high volume of sales. This will allow it to cover its high fixed costs in spite of the relatively low contribution made by each ticket sale.

As the economy in country L has returned to growth, it is likely that customers will have more disposable income and therefore be willing to spend more money on flights with additional features – such as increased leg room. AVA has started to see the effect of this as its passenger numbers start to fall.

First class strategy in AVA

AVA's new approach is to offer a section of 'first class' seats to customers at the front of each airplane which provide more leg room and free food and drink, as well as better customer service.

This seems to be an attempt to move into a differentiation approach, where AVA will be starting to charge a premium for some of its flights due to additional features that wealthier clients may value.

For this to work, AVA must be able to offer a real alternative to the existing first class airline services – either through the actual services offered to its customers or through its brand name and image.

Strategic options and choice

Evaluation of the proposal

Expansion into the first class market could provide a limited amount of diversification for AVA. Its low cost approach would seem to be struggling as customers are able to afford better quality flights and this problem is likely to continue as the economy grows.

In addition, the move into first class flights would help to improve AVA's profitability as first class tickets command higher margins than AVA's standard tickets.

However, there are a number of practical problems with the proposals.

Firstly, AVA may be struggling to attract more affluent customers as the new first class model is inconsistent with its brand image. AVA has a poor reputation in the market for comfort and reliability – things that are likely to strongly appeal to first class customers.

In addition, the first class market is already dominated by several major airlines that have experience of catering to the needs of this market segment. Unless AVA is able to find some way of truly differentiating its product from these rivals, it is unlikely that it will ever outperform them in the market.

It is worth noting that attempting to operate both differentiated and cost leadership approaches is likely to cause the organisation considerable cultural problems – staff may find it difficult to offer an excellent service to some customers but not others.

Conclusion

Overall by proceeding with its first class strategy, AVA risks becoming 'stuck in the middle' and failing to compete effectively within the market. It may therefore wish to consider an alternative plan which is more in keeping with its current strategy.

Test your understanding 4

The correct answer is D

By definition.

Test your understanding 5

The correct answer is C

HUF is trying to sell more of its existing product lines (and is therefore not adopting a product development strategy) to its existing customers. Note that HUF is continuing to use radio advertising, indicating that it is not trying to attract new market segments (and is therefore not adopting a market development strategy).

If HUF was diversifying, it would be offering new products to new markets, which is clearly not happening in the scenario.

Test your understanding 6 – (Integration question)

- **Pricewatch** – market penetration – building sales from existing customer base via lower prices (cost leadership).

- **Esso minimarkets** – product development – addressing customer bases who already use Esso outlets. Could also be categorised as market development if minimarkets are effectively acting as local ('corner') shops.

- **Distribution to China** – market development – taking existing products/technologies and selling them to a new market.

- **Acquisitions** – diversification – this involves Esso moving into completely new markets/industries.

Test your understanding 7

The correct answers are C, D and F

Operating in several unrelated markets diversifies the risk of the organisation, reducing the variability in its returns. Note that this is unlikely to be of benefit to institutional investors, who will likely already hold a diversified portfolio of shares.

If the company believes that its existing brand name will also be recognised in its new venture (or it can 'stretch' its brand), this may increase the likelihood of a diversification strategy being adopted.

Finally, a diversification strategy is useful if the organisation's existing markets are saturated. Diversification may be the only way for the organisation to continue to grow.

Strategic options and choice

Test your understanding 8 – C – (Case style)

(i) **Ansoff's matrix**

Ansoff identified four main growth strategies in his matrix, depending on whether new or existing products were being offered to new or existing markets.

New products in C's coffee shops

While the products that the FD is suggesting, such as wine and ice-cream, are food and drink – like C's current products – they represent a significant departure from C's current image of a 'coffee-shop'. They should therefore be classed as new products.

The FD seems to feel that C will manage to grow its profits due to the higher margins achieved on these new items, rather than due to any significant increase in volume. This would seem to indicate that C will be relying on its existing customers.

C would therefore be attempting to sell new products to our existing customers. In Ansoff's matrix, this would be called product development.

Expansion into new countries

Expansion abroad will clearly help C to break into new markets and attract a whole new set off customers. Given the success of the current product range, the MD is suggesting that no changes are made when opening up foreign stores.

Overall, C would be attempting to sell its existing products to a new market – an approach that Ansoff called market development.

Online music

This is a completely new business area for C. It would involve selling music – a completely different range of products to its current offering.

In addition, it is likely to appeal to a totally new range of customers – especially as it will involve trading online, which does not appear to be something that C currently does.

C will therefore be selling new products to new markets – which Ansoff termed diversification. In this case, it would appear to be unrelated or conglomerate diversification.

(ii) **Alternative strategy**

The only strategy suggested by Ansoff that has not been suggested by the directors would involve C attempting to sell more of its existing products to its current market.

This is referred to by Ansoff as market penetration.

Application to C

C will need to look for ways to increase its market share. This may be difficult given the competitive nature of the market it operates in and the fact that its rivals offer similar products to it at a similar price.

C does achieve high margins on its products. This could give it scope to consider lowering its prices – especially as it is currently more expensive than its competitors. This may be attractive to customers in the current economic downturn and could encourage customers to 'defect' from rival coffee chains.

It should be noted that if C does lower its prices, this could have a detrimental effect on the perceived quality of its products and services by customers.

Alternatively, C could attempt to make use of its unique selling point – good quality service. This has made it a market leader in country U and stressing this in its advertising could also grow its market share further.

(iii) **Proposed acquisition of online music store**

As mentioned earlier, this is an example of unrelated or conglomerate diversification. This could have several advantages and disadvantages for C.

Advantages:

Saturated current market – the coffee market appears to be saturated in country U. In addition, many of U's competitors have already expanded into the countries around country U, indicating they may also be highly competitive already. C may find it difficult to achieve future growth if it stays within its current market.

Spreading of risk – by operating in two unrelated markets, C will be spreading its risk. Online music sales have performed well over the last year in country U – in spite of the poor economic climate which has seen a fall in the amount spent on coffee. By operating in both markets, C may be able to enjoy more stable returns.

Surplus cash – the acquisition of the music store would allow C to get a return on the surplus cash it currently holds. This may be seen favourably by investors.

Disadvantages:

Increased risk

C is planning to enter a new market that is has no experience of. It currently does not appear to have an online presence, meaning that it may well not know how to best run the online music store once it has been purchased.

No economies of scale

By expanding into the online music industry, C is unlikely to enjoy significant synergies.

In fact, the opposite may well be true. C's managers may find that operating such an unfamiliar business takes up a significant proportion of their time. This may have a negative effect on C's core coffee shop business.

Brand Damage

An unsuccessful venture into the online music industry could affect the brand of "C" which in should a highly competitive industry could have severe consequences.

Lack of a clear generic strategy

Using Porters understanding of strategic thinking C is clearly a differentiator – Entering into new industries such as online music could negatively affect this clear generic strategy.

Shareholder reaction

Shareholders often dislike unrelated diversification as it often has few benefits to them. If C's shareholders had wished to spread their risk, they could simply invest some of their money in the shares of a company in a different industry to C.

Test your understanding 9

Stars	Question marks
Wallop	

Cash cows	Dogs
Bang	Whizz
	Pop

Test your understanding 10

The correct answer is C

H1 appears to be a dog, suggesting a divestment strategy would be appropriate.

E2 and B3 are question marks. These need to be divested or built on. Given the attractive nature of the market for these products, O may wish to consider investing heavily to try and increase its market share.

Y4 is a star. It is a market leader in a growing market. O needs to adopt a holding strategy, defending its market share and maintaining its position as a star until the market slows and Y4 becomes a cash cow.

Strategic options and choice

Test your understanding 11 – GC – (Case style)

Part (a)

- **Brick manufacturer** – dog
- **Parcel service** – dog
- **Food manufacturer** – cash cow, maybe dropping from star. Largely depends upon the current growth rate
- **Painting and decorating** – problem child. High growth at present but forecast to decline. Opportunity to turn this into a star
- **Software development company** – star

(May consider a diagram with SBUs located on the matrix.)

Representations in all sectors of the matrix with two dogs present. May need to question what to do with the problem child and the dogs. Dogs may need to be divested or harvested. Problem child needs management attention to stop it becoming a dog.

Food manufacturer (cash cow) will generate cash flows that can be used to fund the development of the star software company. Little need for strategic investment will see the cash surpluses rising.

Star will need investing in and penetration strategies will be appropriate. Branding strategies may be initiated with a view to future defence when star becomes the cash cow. Current cash cow will need defending.

SBUs will each need different business strategies as positions vary. Levels of competition and demand sophistication will vary across the SBU marketplaces and the research and information systems will become ever more important.

Part (b)

Considerations

Divest dogs – gets rid of the poor products quickly. But may not be poor performers! May be better to Harvest instead – slow decline leads to less damage elsewhere within the group in terms of bad publicity.

Niche dogs – a deliberate strategy to take the SBU into a specialist marketplace by aiming at a specific market segment and seek to earn high return from this focused approach.

Market development for dogs and problem children – aiming to expand market share and improve value via improved profitability.

Product development for the cash cow as a form of defensive strategy to extend the life cycle and the subsequent cash flows – but will the cash cow really be cash generative? Will it not need to reinvest to maintain threshold competence in the market place?

Market penetration for the star – the market is expanding with many new users and strategies should be aimed at building market share.

Aim to develop **synergy*** within the group:

- Possible **brand stretching** – taking the good reputation and respect from one brand name and attach it to other products in the form of either aggressive or defensive strategy, e.g. use a link from the food manufacturing to painting and decorating and/or software development.

- Possible sharing of **distribution channels** – there seems to be little scope for this given the diverse nature of the product portfolio.

- Possible use of **central resources** – scope here for central marketing function if a common linkage could be found (such as a brand). HR and IT functions offer scope for value added via cost savings on the functions.

McKinsey approach

- Manage investor relations
- turnaround strategies at SBU level
- outsourcing
- benchmarking
- cost reduction programmes
- manage structure of portfolio via acquisition, divestment and demerger
- consider and deploy value adding "group" activities such as brand stretching.

* The idea that combining certain operations/functions will produce a benefit in numerical terms that will be greater than the sum of the individual parts. The creation of 'excess value' from combination – what some refer to as '2 + 2 = 5'.

Strategic options and choice

Test your understanding 12

The correct answer is B

T has two major requirements – consistency with the existing H stores and the need to retain control of H and its operations.

Licensing another organisation to trade as H would not allow T to maintain control over the day to day operations of the new stores.

Strategic alliances and joint ventures, by their nature, would require T to form partnerships with third party organisations who would work together (or set up a jointly owned company) to operate the new H stores. Again, this would lead to H losing control and being forced to compromise with the other organisation(s) he had entered an alliance with.

Franchising would allow H to control many of the day to day operations of the new stores and would also enable him to still make the key strategic decisions for the organisation. The franchisee would have to work within the pre-set guidelines in the franchise agreement, which may include central training of staff and supplier selection.

Test your understanding 13 – (integration question)

(1) A franchise arrangement would work well here. There is more than just manufacturing involved – there is the whole retail offering, and entering into franchise agreements would be a quick, effective way of expanding.

(2) Unless the oil companies felt that, because of their size, there was no need for joint research, development, marketing and lobbying, a strategic alliance of some sort could be useful. Research costs and findings could be shared. Together they could bring powerful pressure to bear on governments to, for example, allow more generous time scales for implementation of the new technology. Alternatively, the new energy technology could be developed within a joint venture organisation.

(3) Almost certainly, this company would expand by licensing local brewing companies to make and distribute its product.

Test your understanding 14

The correct answer is D

YH is currently manufacturing (or growing) the bulk of its products overseas to meet demand, with some of this produce even finding its way back to country N. This would suggest an overseas manufacture strategy.

YH does grow some of its fruit in its home country, but given that this is a minority of its goods, it cannot be convincingly matched to an exporting strategy.

As YH does not obviously co-ordinate value adding activities between its overseas facilities (they are all similar growing and processing facilities in each country) it is not a multinational. The fact that it still has a home country in which it is based would indicate that it is not a transnational.

Test your understanding 15

The correct answer is D

The purchase appears to be suitable as it will help the company deal with the problems it is facing with supplying its customers by removing a major bottleneck.

It will also be feasible as the company has the ability to raise the cash needed to complete the purchase.

However, it is unlikely to be acceptable to employees due to the reduction in staff numbers it will cause. This is likely to be a problem for LL as employees are heavily unionised and could act collectively to resist the layoffs.

Test your understanding 16

The correct answer is C

Acceptability looks at the reaction of key stakeholders to the proposed strategy. Mendelow's matrix would be the most appropriate way of identifying these stakeholders as well as their relative interest and power.

Test your understanding 17 – (Integration question)

Suitability

- The hotel market is becoming increasingly more competitive, so it might make more sense for Blueberry to try to diversify its activities more.
- Furthermore, the acquisition does not address Blueberry's underlying problems of inconsistent customer service levels.
- On the other hand, the Villa d'Oeste already has a world class spa facility and would fit well into Blueberry's current strategy of moving more 'upscale'.
- Also the goodwill attached to the Villa's reputation could enhance Blueberry's image, depending on branding decisions.

Feasibility

- Financing the acquisition could prove problematic:
- Debt finance: Historically the Board have chosen to keep Blueberry's financial gearing level relatively low. Blueberry's existing clientele of shareholders may thus resist any major increase in gearing.
- Equity finance: Given losses in two out of the last three years, Blueberry may struggle to raise the purchase price via a rights issue.

Acceptability

- Growth by acquisition is generally quicker than organic growth, thus satisfying institutional shareholders' desire to see growth in revenues and dividends.
- Further work is needed to assess whether the €50m asking price is acceptable.
- Buying another hotel should enable Blueberry to gain additional economies of scale with respect to insurance, staff costs such as pensions and purchasing economies on drinks. This should boost margins and profitability further.
- The new hotel would fit well into Blueberry's existing portfolio of hotels, for example, by having significant cash inflows throughout the year in contrast to Blueberry's highly seasonal business, thus reducing the overall level of risk.

> **Preliminary recommendations**
>
> - The opportunity to acquire the Villa d'Oeste should be rejected on the grounds that financing the acquisition would be problematic at present.
> - Blueberry should instead focus on improving facilities and quality in existing hotels before looking to expand through acquisition.

> **Test your understanding 18 – GGG – (Case style)**
>
> **Briefing notes**
>
> **Ansoff**
>
> GGG could utilise the Ansoff growth vector matrix to analyse the possible future strategic directions it could follow.
>
> *Market penetration*
>
> GGG could attempt to increase its market share with its existing services to its current market or region. The market is a growing one; with the change in demographics, therefore, market penetration is a real option for GGG. As it currently has 25% of its region's market with the rest fragmented between local government run and privately owned care homes, there is potential for GGG to undertake promotional activities in order to obtain business from these competitors. In particular, the sale and closure of a number of the privately run care homes could be an opportunity to obtain a greater share of the market through targeting these care homes customers. GGG may have to consider its pricing strategies however, as its prices may well be higher than its competitors. It may need to consider a reduction of prices or some form of discounted offer to attract customers who are currently paying less than they would be charged in GGG's care homes.

Strategic options and choice

Product Development

GGG could attempt to offer new services to its existing market or region.

Within the scenario, there is mention of a new 'relief package' facility that is becoming popular with customers. GGG could consider offering its facilities for customers within its region for this new service. This would have to be investigated further to ensure that GGG has the capacity and facilities to offer such a service. If there is clearly a growing need for this type of package, then GGG could try to gain early market entry in order to gain early mover advantage. The issue for GGG is likely to be capacity constraints and the need to weigh up the benefits and costs of the option against those of offering continued longer term care to its residents.

In addition, the additional services that could be offered by the qualified staff and nurses of GGG to its patients as an alternative to referral to hospitals could be a form of product development. However, this is likely to involve investment in re-training and facilities.

Market Development

GGG could attempt to increase its revenues by offering its current services to new customers or at a different geographical location. One option would be to consider moving into another geographical region in its own country to offer its services to the elderly. This is a possibility as the national geographic trend suggests increasing demand nationally for elderly care. However, this is a riskier strategy as GGG currently has no experience of its competitive environment outside its own region and the competitive market may be very different. In addition, GGG would require heavy investment in facilities outside of the region. However, the market conditions are likely to be the same as in its own region and, therefore, it could consider buying or merging with another private care home outside of its current region. However, GGG must consider the rising costs of running care homes and the consequent need for it to price its services accordingly.

Diversification

GGG could consider offering new services to new customers. For example, the trained staff and nurses could be used to offer other nursing and rehabilitation services to individual customers, other care homes or to GP surgeries. These could be offered within the facilities of GGG or could be offered on site in customers' homes.

GGG's administrators are also highly experienced and GGG could consider utilising their experience to offer consultancy and management services to other care homes which might consider outsourcing their management and administration function to GGG.

Evaluation of opportunities

According to the Johnson, Scholes and Whittington approach, an organisation's potential strategies can be evaluated against the following criteria:

- Suitability: whether a strategy fits with the organisation's operations and its strategic position.
- Acceptability: whether a strategy fits with the expectations of the stakeholders.
- Feasibility: whether the strategy can be implemented, taking into consideration practical considerations such as time, cost and capabilities.

GGG must consider if the proposed strategy is suitable to respond to environmental events and opportunities and whether it fits with the current strategic position. It would need to consider whether it had the right level of resources and competences. It would also have to consider its key stakeholders in terms of both risk and return. It is important to note that GGG must also consider 'who' their customers are, as customers will include not only the actual residents of the care home but also their families or their current carers. Reviewing each of the strategies identified in the Ansoff matrix, GGG should consider:

Market penetration

Suitability: This strategy would appear suitable as GGG has spare capacity and also this option builds upon GGG's current expertise so there is clear strategic fit.

Acceptability: The key stakeholders such as staff and management are unlikely to be opposed to this strategy as it is a mere development of the current activities of GGG. Existing customers should find it acceptable as long as current standards of operation are not affected if the care homes now take on more customers.

Feasibility: GGG has the resources in terms of capacity and competences to undertake this strategy. However, further growth could mean the need to invest in more facilities if spare capacity limits are exceeded. GGG would also need to consider the costs of advertising.

Strategic options and choice

Product Development

Suitability: This strategy continues to fit with GGG's strategic position and would certainly exploit an obvious market opportunity. It will complement the existing long term care facilities and should help to balance GGG's portfolio. Therefore it is suitable.

Acceptability: Staff may find this strategy unacceptable if it requires additional training or detracts them from the care of GGG's existing long term care customers. Existing customers should be neutral in the decision as long as it does not affect the standard of their care and potential customers are likely to be positive towards the proposal.

Feasibility: Investment in facilities and training may make this option unfeasible but GGG would have to weigh up the long term benefits of building market share through subsequent conversion from short-term care residents into long-term residents and by improving quality of care by providing services in-house rather than necessitating referral to hospital.

Market Development

Suitability: There is certainly a potential for opportunities outside of its current geographical region. The national trend suggests increasing demand nationally for elderly residential care. However, GGG has no experience of its competitive environment outside its own region and the competitive market may be very different. GGG does not know whether its own service would be superior from that offered by competitors.

Acceptability: Staff and managers may not find this strategy acceptable as it might affect their own workloads, location and roles. However, current customers are likely to be neutral to the proposal.

Feasibility: Can GGG find the right facilities or a suitable partner to merge with or acquire? Costs of relocation of some staff or recruitment and training would need to be carefully considered. There might be some resistance from staff and competitors. Also, GGG needs to consider timescales and possible local Government resistance. Therefore, market development may not be feasible.

Diversification

Suitability: GGG has the necessary skills to undertake diversification although additional training may be required. In the present climate it would appear that the opportunities for this development may be limited. It would fit with the current activities of GGG and therefore has strategic fit.

Acceptability: The staff may find this acceptable as it would develop their skills and enhance their job roles. Existing customers are also likely to find this acceptable as it would not mean disruption to them assuming the new services do not detract from their own care. However, GPs and hospitals may not find this acceptable as they may not agree that the same level of care can be offered by GGG's staff.

Feasibility: GGG will have to invest heavily in training and facilities which may make this unfeasible. There may also be resistance to this from local GPs and hospitals. Therefore, GGG may find this strategy unfeasible.

Recommendation

In the current market and competitive environment, where GGG is managing to remain profitable despite other similarly businesses failing, the recommended options for GGG would be to follow a market penetration strategy with product development.

The current geographical market clearly has potential for GGG so there is no need for a market development strategy. A market penetration strategy would allow GGG to exploit the current trends and build upon its own strength and reputation. It is also the least risky option in a time when costs are clearly rising. Product development with the care relief packages should also be considered as it has clear potential for GGG to exploit its current spare capacity and to use its expertise to develop a clearly growing market need.

Strategic options and choice

308

chapter

8

The performance measurement mix

Chapter learning objectives

Lead	Component
D1. Evaluate the tools and techniques of strategy implementation	(a) evaluate alternative models of strategic performance measurement in a range of business contexts (b) recommend solutions to problems in strategic performance measurement

Indicative syllabus content

- Alternative strategic business unit (SBU) performance measures, including shareholder value added (SVA) and economic value added (EVA).

- Alternative models of measuring strategic performance (e.g. the Balanced Scorecard (BSC) and the performance pyramid as strategic evaluation tools).

- Setting appropriate strategic targets through the use of a range of financial and non-financial measures of strategic importance and their interaction with financial ones.

- Evaluation of strategic targets through the development of critical success factors (CSFs).

- Linking CSFs to Key Performance Indicators (KPIs) and corporate strategy and their use as a basis for defining an organisation's information needs.

The performance measurement mix

- Effective communication of strategic performance targets, including the need to drive strategic performance through stretch targets and promotion of exceptional performance.
- The role of the Chartered Management Accountant in the process of strategic performance evaluation.

chapter 8

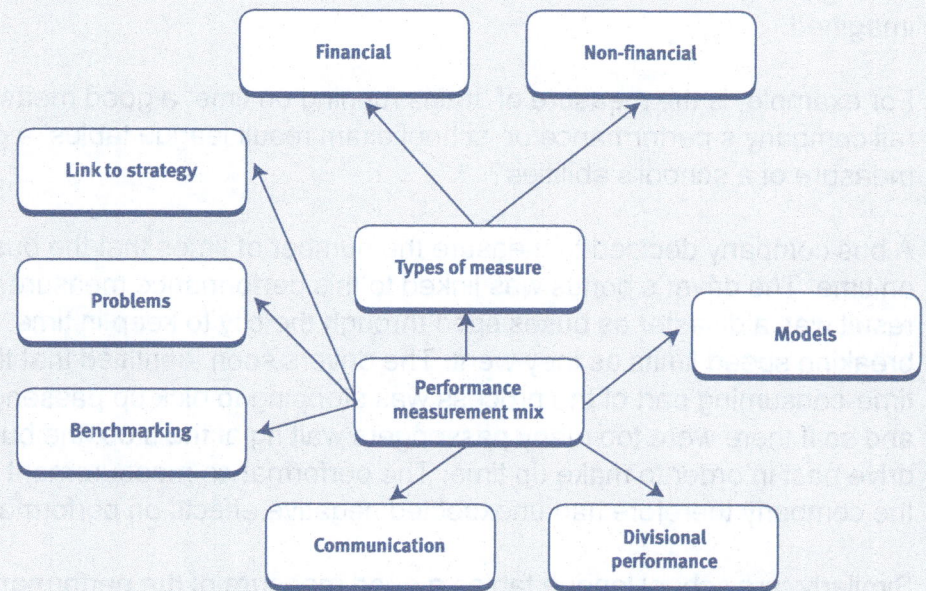

1 The performance measurement mix

Performance measurement is the process of assessing the proficiency with which a reporting entity succeeds, by the economic acquisition of resources and their efficient and effective deployment, in achieving its objectives. Performance measures may be based on non-financial as well as on financial information.

CIMA official terminology

So far we have looked at how an organisation decides on an appropriate strategy to undertake. The strategy then needs to be converted into a range of performance measures that can be monitored by management. This is important for two reasons:

- management must be able to identify whether the strategy is having the desired effect on the organisation's output.

- setting performance measures is a way of communicating targets to staff and other key stakeholders, indicating the organisation's priorities. Rewards can be linked to the achievement of these measures.

For example, an organisation may have decided to implement a new strategy to improve the quality of its output. It will want to create a range of performance measures that support this – such as monitoring the number of defective products produced, or the number of customer complaints. This will allow the organisation to see whether its strategy is having the desired effect and is actually improving quality. Management will also be able to set targets for staff in each of these areas, focusing the attention of workers on the need to improve quality.

The performance measurement mix

Setting performance measures is often more difficult than would first be imagined.

For example, is the measure of 'trains running on time' a good measure of a rail company's performance or 'school exam result league tables' a good measure of a school's abilities?

A bus company decided to measure the number of times that the buses ran on time. The driver's bonus was linked to this performance measure. The result was a disaster as buses sped through the city to keep in time, breaking speed limits as they went. The drivers soon identified that the most time-consuming part of the process was stopping to pick up passengers and so if there were too many passengers waiting at the stop, the bus would drive past in order to make up time. The performance measurement used by the company therefore had unexpected negative effects on performance.

Similarly, are school league tables a good measure of the performance of each school? Critics argue that that they do not take into account the circumstances of each school and the factors such as pupil backgrounds, reducing their usefulness.

The challenge is to be able to design a measurement mix that can be used in the control process and not prove to be a burden and/or misleading.

How do performance measures control what people do?

In *Measuring Business Performance: Why, What, How (1998)*, Neely suggested that there were four ways in which performance measures could act to control the behaviour of people within the organisation. He referred to these reasons as the 'four CPs'.

Imagine that the managers of a manufacturing business have just informed staff that they will be assessed on the quality of the goods that they produce.

- **Confirm priorities** – the fact that management have chosen to measure and report on quality indicates to workers that this is an area that is important and that needs to be prioritised.

- **Compel progress** – workers will want to ensure that they meet quality targets as failure to do so may adversely affect their pay or career prospects. Remember that measures can be the basis for bonus payments (giving rise to an additional CP not identified by Neely – cash prizes!)

- **Check position** – the management of the business (as well as individual staff members) will be able to monitor progress relating to quality and see whether they are on course to meet their targets or not. If not, action can be taken to improve performance.

> • **Communicate position** – measures of production quality can be used by management (and other interested parties, such as quality control organisations, trade associations or even investors) to assess and understand how the organisation is performing.

2 Critical success factors and their link to performance measurement

It is clear that the organisation needs to ensure that its performance measurement mix ties into its overall strategy. How can this be accomplished? If our overall strategy is to, for example, become a cost leader in our market in order to outperform our rivals, what do we measure to help us ensure that we are doing this successfully?

One useful way of generating a performance measurement mix for the organisation is to identify the critical success factors (CSFs) that are determined by our strategy. CSFs were discussed in detail in chapter 5.

Critical success factors are the limited number of areas in which results, if they are satisfactory, will ensure successful competitive performance for the organisation.

CSFs tie in to the organisation's overall strategy. For example, if our strategy is cost leadership, our CSFs could include:

- lower labour costs than rivals
- efficient production

These CSFs would then be translated into key performance indicators (KPIs) – which are specific, measured targets that can be used to assess whether the CSF has been achieved.

For example, KPIs for 'efficient production' could include:

- maximum kg of materials wasted
- average time taken to produce one unit of the product, etc.

A strong performance measurement mix is likely to reflect the CSFs and KPIs identified by the organisation, as these are areas that the organisation needs to do well at in order to outperform its rivals – a key issue for most businesses.

Remember that whatever the organisation chooses as its performance measurement mix will need to be monitored going forward. Management will need to ensure that information systems are put in place to collect data to allow performance in these areas to be measured on an ongoing basis.

The performance measurement mix

If our cost leader (above) wishes to target its staff performance based on the average time they take to produce units, it will need to create systems to keep track of how long each employee works for and how many units they individually produce.

Note that, as with the organisation's KPIs, the performance measurement mix is likely to cover a wide range of criteria – both financial and non-financial.

Changes to the performance measurement mix

The changing environment presents new risks and opportunities and these must be monitored and identified as early as possible. It is therefore likely that new measures will be added to the mix over time. However, consideration must also be given to keeping the mix as uncomplicated as possible and as such old unnecessary measures should be dropped.

When changing the performance measurement mix, management need to be aware of the following points:

- too many changes may lead to 'indicator overload', confusing employees about what the company wants them to do.
- if something is included as part of the performance measurement mix, the importance of this item is being highlighted to staff. If you change the mix, what are you telling people?
- if a measure is dropped from the mix, you are telling your staff that this item is no longer important. Is this what you want to achieve?

3 Financial and non-financial measures

Financial performance measures

These indicators concentrate on the revenue, profits, cash and capital position of the business.

Typical indicators may include (but are not limited to):

Sales margin (gross profit margin):

$$\frac{\text{Revenue} - \text{cost of sales}}{\text{Revenue}} \times 100\%$$

- this indicator focuses on the profitability of the business' trading account.

Operating profit margin:

$$\frac{\text{Profit (before interest and tax)}}{\text{Revenue}} \times 100\%$$

- this indicator focuses on the profitability of the business in both its trading and its net operating expenses.

Return on capital employed:

$$\frac{\text{Profit (before interest and tax)}}{\text{Capital employed}} \times 100\%$$

- ROCE measures the profitability of a business or division against the assets utilised in that business. (Capital employed is normally measured as shareholders funds + long–term debt).

Remember the principle of **controllability** when using these measures to assess divisional performance. The costs used in both cases should only be those that the division can directly control. Expenses such as head office costs would normally be excluded as it would be unfair to assess divisional managers on spending that they cannot alter.

Advantages of financial measures of performance

- Culturally expected
- focus on financial objectives
- comparable across companies
- cheap
- established framework for preparation in many cases
- tend to focus onto resource generation and so survival in the long term.

Disadvantages of financial measures of performance

- Inflation distortion
- leads to suboptimal and short-termist behaviour
- lack of comparability
- understood by the 'select few' – i.e. trained accountants and managers
- subjectivity can exist in calculation, e.g. depreciation.

Non-financial performance measures

Non-financial performance indicators are measures of performance based on non-financial information that may originate in and be used by operating departments to monitor and control their activities without any accounting input.

CIMA official terminology

Put simply, businesses also need to focus on factors that actually cause profits to be earned – the non-financial measures.

For instance in an accountancy training business, sales and market share (financial issues) are caused by student pass rates, student satisfaction, class sizes, tutor quality, etc (non-financial issues). These non-financial issues will also need to be measured. If performance in these areas begins to fall, it will not be long before the financial measures deteriorate as well.

Advantages of non-financial measures

- Wider view
- easier to calculate
- easy to understand (sometimes)
- not distorted by inflation
- can emphasise broad spectrum of management
- positive motivational implications.

Disadvantages of non-financial measures

- Some can be difficult to calculate
- subjectivity exists in design, interpretation and calculation
- can lead to indicator overload
- costly
- culture clash implications
- constant change requires constant monitoring.

Test your understanding 1

Which THREE of the following are advantages to an organisation of using non-financial performance measures, rather than traditional financial measures?

A Culturally expected
B Gives a wider view of business performance
C Less subjective measurement
D Allows earlier problem identification
E Not distorted by inflation
F Cheaper to measure

Test your understanding 2

Y plc has noticed that its return on capital employed (ROCE) has fallen significantly over the last twelve months. One of the junior management accountants has made the following statements regarding this:

(i)   Y's gearing must have risen in the year

(ii) Y may find it hard to raise additional finance in the coming year

(iii) The ROCE may have fallen due to reductions in Y's gross profit margins

(iv) The ROCE may have fallen due to large dividends paid out during the last year

Which of the above statements is/are correct?

A (i) and (ii) only
B (i) and (iii) only
C (ii) and (iii) only
D (ii) and (v) only

4 The balanced scorecard

Presented by **Kaplan & Norton** in 1992 – 'Kaplan's cockpit'

'An approach to the provision of information to management to assist strategic policy formulation and achievement. It emphasises the need to provide the user with a set of information which addresses all relevant issues of performance in an objective and unbiased fashion. The information provided may include both financial and non-financial elements and cover areas such as profitability, customer satisfaction, internal efficiency and innovation'.

Its aim is to provide a broad range of both financial and non-financial measures designed to reflect the complexity and diversity of business circumstance.

It was a response to traditional performance measurement which had tended to focus on a narrow range of performance measures and caused management to adopt a short-term focus.

Kaplan likened running a business to flying a plane – airspeed, altitude, heading and fuel level are just a few of the pieces of information needed. Yet, in many businesses, managers have to rely on a narrow set of financial indicators to support their decision making – and this in an environment with many more complexities than a plane.

The balanced scorecard approach brings together a wide range of measures to give managers a broader perspective of their business performance.

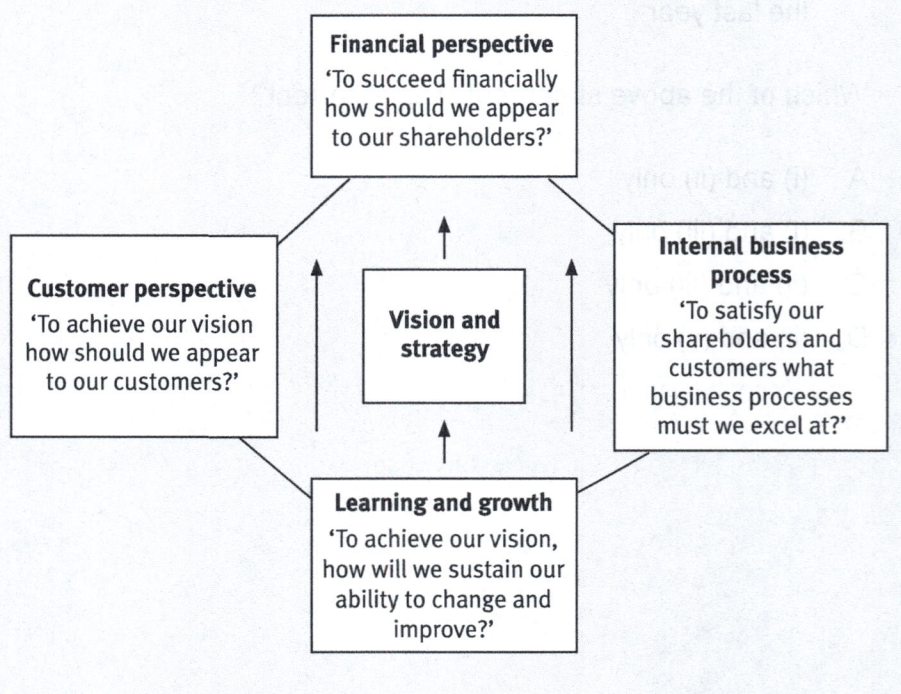

This is a powerful tool that assists in the running of an organisation. Gains in one area need to be considered with the losses that may arise in other areas and vice versa. Thus the manager's view is broadened and the tendency to concentrate on one measure is reduced, hopefully removed.

Possible measures for the balanced scorecard

The measures used within the balanced scorecard will vary between organisations, but some typical examples are shown below for each of the four perspectives:

Financial perspective

- increased revenue
- improvements to key ratios, such as gross margin, net margin or ROCE
- rising market share
- increased cash flow
- reduction or increase in gearing

Internal business perspective

- reduction in production time
- reduction in number of errors/defects
- reduced wastage
- reduction in time taken to supply customers/deal with customer queries

Customer perspective

- increase in number of new customers attracted
- increase in number of customers returning (repeat business)
- reduction in number of customer complaints
- rise in positive feedback from customers
- reduction in returns from customers
- number of orders delivered on time to customers

Innovation and learning (learning and growth)

- number of days of staff training
- number of new products or services launched
- increase in number of sales made through new channels – such as online

The performance measurement mix

- increase in proportion of sales of new products
- reduction in staff turnover (increased staff satisfaction)
- number of new business ideas generated by staff

Remember that this list is not exhaustive. In your exam you will need to select the performance measures that best fit the organisation in question.

Illustration 1 – The balanced scorecard

For a train company, a balanced scorecard could include indicators such as:

Customer perspective

- Percentage of trains running on time/cancelled
- percentage of trains running per hour between destinations
- cleanliness levels
- seat availability.

Internal business process

- Staff attendance rates
- number of training days per annum per staff member
- average time taken to process ticket enquiries
- percentage of trains in full working order.

Learning and growth

- Investment in new rolling inventory
- investment in new passenger facilities (e.g. internet access on-board).

Financial perspective

- Profit levels
- revenue growth
- revenue by activity
- cost control versus budget.

Strategy mapping

Strategy mapping – implementing the balanced scorecard more effectively

Strategy mapping was developed by Kaplan and Norton as an extension to the balanced scorecard and to make implementations of the scorecard more successful.

The steps involved are:

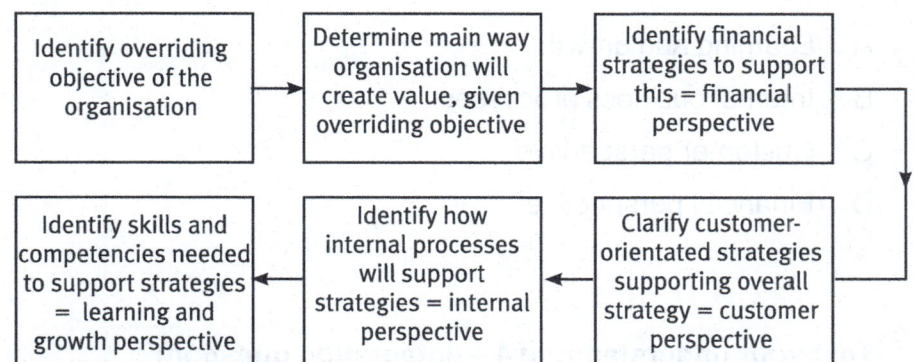

- At the head of the strategy map is the overriding objective of the organisation which describes how it creates value. This is then connected to the organisation's other objectives, categorised in terms of the four perspectives of the balanced scorecard, showing the cause-and-effect relationships between them.

- The strategy map helps organisations to clarify, describe and communicate the strategy and objectives, both within the organisation and to external stakeholders, by presenting the key relationships between the overall objective and the supporting strategy and objectives in one diagram.

Problems:

- Organisations have often found it difficult to translate the corporate vision into behaviour and actions which achieve the key corporate objectives.

- In practice many employees do not understand the organisation's strategy, and systems such as performance management and budgeting are not linked to the strategy.

The performance measurement mix

Test your understanding 3

A bus company uses Kaplan and Norton's balanced scorecard as a way of developing its performance measurement mix.

One of the measures it has chosen to use is the number of days of driver training each year. The company feels that this will reduce the number of accidents and casualties due to more skilled and motivated drivers.

Which ONE of the balanced scorecard perspectives would this measure relate to?

A   Learning and growth

B   Internal business processes

C   Customer perspective

D   Financial perspective

Test your understanding 4 – (Integration question)

Suggest some critical success factors (CSFs) and key performance indicators (KPIs) for each perspective of the balanced scorecard for an electronics manufacturer.

Benefits and drawbacks of the balanced scorecard

The main benefits are:

- It avoids management reliance on short-termist or incomplete financial measures.

- By identifying the non-financial measures, managers may be able to identify problems earlier. For example, managers may be measuring customer satisfaction directly as part of the balanced scorecard. If this changes, steps can be taken to improve it again before customers leave and it starts to impact on the company's finances.

- It can ensure that divisions develop success measures for their division that are related to the overall corporate goals of the organisation

- It can assist stakeholders in evaluating the firm if measures are communicated externally.

The drawbacks are:

- It does not provide a single overall view of performance. Measures like ROCE are popular because they conveniently summarise 'how things are going' into one convenient measure.

- There is no clear relation between the balanced scorecard and shareholder analysis.

- Measures may give conflicting signals and confuse management. For instance, if customer satisfaction is falling along with one of the financial indicators, which should management sacrifice?

- It often involves a substantial shift in corporate culture in order to implement it.

Test your understanding 5 – CCC – (Case style)

T is the Chief Executive Officer of a motor car insurance company, CCC. T, together with the Board of Directors, developed a mission statement in 2013 following a detailed analysis of the company's operations and market place. The mission statement states that 'CCC wants to continually grow through its commitment to quality and delivering value to its customers'. CCC has developed a complementary vision statement which aspires to:

- Provide superior returns to our shareholders
- Continually improve our business processes
- Delight our customers
- Learn from our mistakes and work smarter in the future

CCC's overriding objective, also developed in 2013, is to double the size of its revenue by the end of 2017.

T has identified the following areas of concern:

- Poor customer service has led to CCC losing 15% of its customers in 2013/2014. The customer sales manager had sponsored an initiative to reward customers with a discount if they renewed their motor insurance. However, most of the sales executives were not familiar with the details of this scheme and did not mention it to customers considering renewing their insurance. The discount scheme had not affected the rate of loss of customers.

- The average age of CCC's personal computers (PCs) was five years. There have been many complaints from CCC's staff that their PC's are not adequate for the demands of 2014. The last time an initiative had been undertaken to bring PCs up to date was in 2011.

The performance measurement mix

- CCC's internal auditors had conducted performance reviews in three departments during 2013. They found a common pattern in all three departments: many of the staff had only minimal educational qualifications which were inadequate for the jobs they were doing. This resulted in an unacceptable level of errors being made. No initiatives had been undertaken to address this problem.

- Investors have been critical of the low dividend yield on their CCC shares.

T is worried because, despite the time and effort put into the development of the mission and vision statements and the overriding objective, CCC is not making sufficient progress towards achieving its revenue target. Its revenue growth rate in 2013 was 10%.

CCC's shortfall against its revenue target was discussed at a recent Board meeting. The Corporate Affairs Director stated that "the Board is 100% behind our strategy and vision but it's just not happening. I have experience in my previous company of working with an integrated model, the Balanced Scorecard. Could the Balanced Scorecard help CCC?"

T has asked you, a strategic management accountant working in CCC, for a report covering the following areas:

(i) Advice on how a Balanced Scorecard could assist in delivering CCC's vision and strategy.

(ii) Assume that CCC has adopted a Balanced Scorecard approach to help it achieve its vision. Recommend FOUR perspectives and for each perspective show:
   - An objective
   - A measure
   - A target
   - An initiative

(iii) Discuss briefly TWO drawbacks of the Balanced Scorecard.

Required:

Draft the report as requested by T.

(45 minutes)

5 The performance pyramid

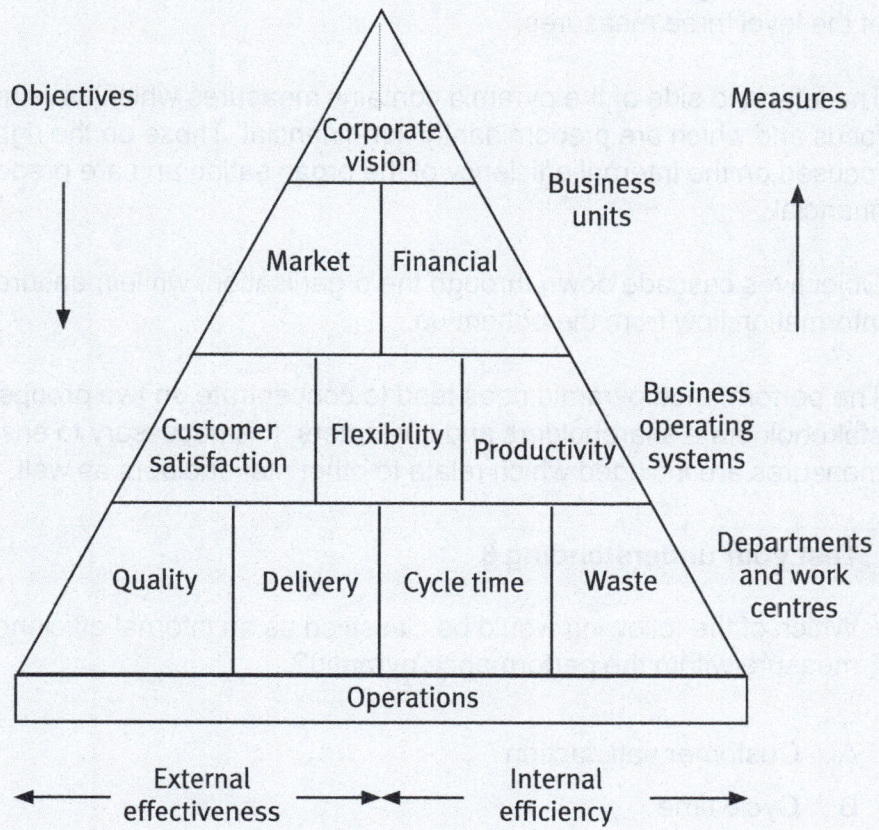

The performance pyramid framework

The performance pyramid was developed by Lynch and Cross as a model to understand and define the links between objectives and performance measures **at different levels** in the organisation.

The performance pyramid is designed to ensure that the activities of every department, system and business unit support the overall vision of the organisation.

At the top of the pyramid is the vision through which the organisation describes how it will achieve long-term success and competitive advantage.

The second level, **the business unit**, includes the critical success factors (CFSs) in terms of market-related measures and financial measures that need to be achieved to meet the organisation's overall vision.

The third level, the **business operating systems**, includes measures which relate to the internal systems and processes which are needed to meet the needs of customers. For example, measures of flexibility which relate to how responsive the system is to customer demands. They will link to the market and financial measures identified at level two.

The performance measurement mix

The lowest level of the pyramid, **departments and work centres**, contains the day-to-day operational measures that can be used to monitor the status of the level three measures.

The left-hand side of the pyramid contains measures which have an external focus and which are predominantly non-financial. Those on the right are focused on the internal efficiency of the organisation and are predominantly financial.

Objectives cascade down through the organisation, while measures and information flow from the bottom up.

The performance pyramid does tend to concentrate on two groups of stakeholders – shareholders and customers. It is necessary to ensure that measures are included which relate to other stakeholders as well.

Test your understanding 6

Which of the following would be classified as an internal efficiency measure within the performance pyramid?

A   Customer satisfaction

B   Cycle time

C   Delivery

D   Quality

Test your understanding 7

G plc has set its staff targets relating to improvements in the number of customer complaints received.

Which level of the performance pyramid is G measuring?

A   Corporate vision

B   Departments and work centres

C   Business units

D   Business operating systems

chapter 8

Test your understanding 8 – Ochil – (Case style)

Ochil is an engineering manufacturing company specialising in the production of mobile machinery for the construction industry. The company has identified and defined a market in which it wishes to operate. This will provide a new focus for an existing product range. Ochil has identified a number of key competitors and intends to focus on close co-operation with its customers in providing products to meet their specific design and quality requirements. Efforts will be made to improve the effectiveness of all aspects of the cycle, from product design to after-sales service to customers. This will require inputs from a number of departments in the achievement of the specific goals of the new proposal. Efforts will be made to improve productivity in conjunction with increased flexibility of methods.

An analysis of forecast financial and non-financial data relating to the new proposal is shown in Schedule 1 below.

Schedule 1

	2015	2016	2017
Total market size ($m)	120	125	130
Ochil sales ($m)	15	18	20
Ochil total costs ($m)	14.1	12.72	12.55
Ochil sundry statistics			
Production achieving design quality standards	95%	97%	98%
Returns from customers (% of deliveries)	3.0%	1.5%	0.5%
Cost of after-sales service ($m)	1.5	1.25	1.0
Sales meeting planned delivery dates	90%	95%	99%
Average cycle time (customer enquiry to delivery) (weeks)	6	5.5	5
Components scrapped in production (%)	7.5%	5.0%	2.5%
Idle machine capacity (%)	10%	6%	2%

The company is considering the implementation of a new performance measurement system in an attempt to make a clear link between performance and strategy and to be flexible and adapt to an ever changing business environment. The directors are therefore considering implementing the performance pyramid.

The managing director of Ochil has asked you to prepare an analysis of the new proposal for the period 2015 to 2017. The analysis should use the information provided in the question, together with the data in Schedule 1.

The performance measurement mix

The analysis should contain the following:

(i) Discussion of the external effectiveness of the proposal in the context of ways in which (1) Quality and (2) Delivery are expected to affect customer satisfaction and hence the marketing of the product.

(ii) Discussion of the internal efficiency of the proposal in the context of ways in which the management of (1) Cycle time and (2) Waste are expected to affect productivity and hence the financial aspects of the proposal.

(iii) Discussion of the potential benefits to Ochil of implementing the performance pyramid.

Required:

Prepare an analysis as requested by the managing director.

(30 minutes)

Fitzgerald and Moon

The building block model

Dimensions
Profit
Competitiveness
Quality

Resource Utilisation

Flexibility
Innovation

Standards
Ownership
Achievability
Equity

Rewards
Clarity
Motivation
Controllabilitiy

Fitzgerald and Moon adopted a framework for the design and analysis of performance management systems. The model was first devised as a solution to performance measurement problems in service industries. But it can be applied successfully to other manufacturing and retail businesses to evaluate business performance.

Fitzgerald and Moon based their analysis on three building blocks:

- **Dimensions**

    Dimensions are the goals for the business and suitable measures must be developed to measure each performance dimension. Below are six dimensions in the building block model, along with examples of measures that could be used under each.

    – **Profit**

        Measures: successful financial performance and growth, increased sales or margins.

    – **Competitiveness**

        Measure: number of new customers, repeat business, market share.

    – **Resource utilisation**

        Measure: optimum use of scarce resources, wastage, idle time.

    – **Quality issues**

        Measure: minimising defects and errors, reliability of service/delivery to the customer, response times

    – **Innovation**

        Measure: product/service development – including time taken to develop new products and services, as well as the number of new products or services launched.

    – **Flexibility**

        Measure: the ability to respond to changing needs, customer waiting times, overtime worked by staff.

The performance measurement mix

- **Standards**

    These are the measures used. To ensure success it is vital that employees view standards as achievable and fair and take ownership of them.

- **Rewards**

    To ensure that employees are motivated to meet standards, targets need to be clear and linked to controllable factors.

Financial performance and competitiveness were seen as the "results" and the others as "determinants" of success.

Fiztgerald and Moon suggested that these six dimensions could be used to generate the key performance measures that the business would need to monitor.

Test your understanding 9

JKJ is a small company that sells office stationery, such as paper and pens. It has set targets in the following areas as performance measures for its employees:

- number of new product lines offered to customers
- increased revenue and margins
- number of defective products returned by customers

Which of the following dimensions from the Fitzgerald and Moon building block model have **not** been considered by JKJ as part of the above measures? Select all that apply.

A   Resource utilisation

B   Innovation

C   Flexibility

D   Profit

E   Quality issues

6 Benchmarking schemes

Benchmarking is 'the establishment, through data gathering, of targets and comparators, through whose use relative levels of performance (and particularly areas of underperformance) can be identified. By the adoption of identified best practices it is hoped that performance will improve.'

CIMA Official Terminology

Most organisations have systems in place to help management monitor key factors such as profits and sales. However, if the financial results or market share of the firm start to deteriorate, management needs to know the reasons why.

The purpose of benchmarking is to help management understand how well the firm is carrying out its key activities and how its performance compares with other, successful, organisations who carry out similar operations (often those considered **best in class**).

A famous example of this is the Rank Xerox company. In the 1970s, such was the dominance of the firm that the word 'Xerox' meant 'photocopier'. A decade later and they had serious competition, most notably from Canon. Something had gone wrong...but what?

Rank Xerox found that clients were switching to other providers because Rank Xerox machines were perceived to always be out of order. It used benchmarking to restore its fortunes.

Types of benchmarking

Seber identifies **three** basic types:

Internal

- This is where another branch or department of the organisation is used as the benchmark
- used where conformity of service is the critical issue – either threshold or core competence
- easily arranged, cheaper and culturally relevant
- but, culturally distorted and unlikely to provide innovative solutions.

Competitor

- Uses a direct competitor with the same or similar process
- essentially aims to render the competition core competence as threshold
- relevant for the industry and market
- but, will the competitor really be keen to hand over their basis for success?

Process or activity

- Focus upon a similar process in another company which is not a direct competitor, e.g. an airline and a health service
- looks for new, innovative ways to create advantage as well as solving threshold problems
- takes time and is expensive
- but, resistance likely to be less and can provide the new basis for advantage.

Implementing a benchmarking scheme

This will involve:

(1) identifying what is wrong within the current organisation
(2) identifying best practice elsewhere
(3) contacting, preparing for a site visit
(4) gathering, evaluating and communicating the results.

It will need:

- key executive commitment from the outset
- establishment of teams for those ranges of opinions and expertise
- a team to manage the project
- a team for the site visit
- budget allocations and training to be given
- a formalised process.

Problems

- Best practice companies unwilling to share data
- what is 'best practice'?
- costly in terms of time and money – opportunity cost
- provides a retrospective view in a turbulent environment – what is best today may not be so tomorrow. As one writer put it: 'Benchmarking is the refuge of the manager who's afraid of the future.'
- successful benchmarking firms can find themselves inundated with requests for information from much less able firms from whom they can learn little
- managers may become demotivated if they are compared against a better-resourced rival.

Test your understanding 10

J plc is a medium-sized training organisation based in country V. It operates fifteen centres in major towns and cities across V. Each centre offers IT training accredited by the ITTO (International Technology Training Organisation). Staff are required to follow centrally produced teaching plans which have been approved by J's head office and the ITTO when delivering these courses. J believes that ITTO accreditation is a vital part of its operations.

J has one major competitor, IHG Ltd, within country V. IHG Ltd also offers IT training, but their courses are not ITTO accredited and course content and style varies significantly between IHG centres.

J is aware that a number of universities offer ITTO accredited courses within country V. However J does not see these as competitors as they typically attract school-leavers, rather than the corporations that are J's main customers. The average university pass rate for ITTO courses is currently higher than J's.

J wishes to undertake a benchmarking exercise. Which of the following types of benchmarking would be most appropriate to J?

A   Competitor
B   Process
C   Internal
D   Strategic

The performance measurement mix

Test your understanding 11 – K and L – (Case style)

A company which manufactures and distributes industrial oils employs a team of salespeople who work directly from home and travel around different regions in the country. Each member of the sales team has his or her own geographical area to cover and they visit clients on a regular basis.

The sales team staff are each paid a basic monthly salary. Each member of the team is set an identical target for sales to be achieved in the month. A bonus payment, in addition to the basic salary, is made to any member of the team who exceeds his or her monthly sales target.

Generally, experience has been that the members of the sales team succeed in improving on their sales targets each month sufficiently to earn a small bonus. However, the managers are unclear whether all the team members are achieving their maximum potential level of sales.

Consequently they are considering introducing a system of benchmarking to measure the performance of the sales team as a whole and its individual members.

The Human Resources Director (HRD) is uncertain how best to accomplish this and has sent you the following text:

Hi K, could you please send me a quick email setting out how a system of benchmarking could be introduced in the company to measure the performance of the sales team, both as a team and as individuals who will be compared with each other. I'm going into a meeting about this in fifteen minutes, so please make this a priority. Thanks. L.

Required:

Prepare the email as requested by the HRD.

(15 minutes)

chapter 8

7 Divisional performance

While the Balanced Scorecard and performance pyramid both identify the need for a wide range of performance measures, financial performance is still extremely important – especially when monitoring the performance of divisions or other strategic business units (SBUs) within the organisation.

There are a wide number of measures that can be used to examine divisional performance, including:

- Economic value added (EVA)
- Shareholder value analysis (SVA)
- Triple bottom line

8 EVA and SVA

EVA™ (Economic Value Added)

EVA (developed by Stern Stewart & Co) is an estimate of true economic profit after making corrective adjustments to GAAP accounting.

EVA refers to the profit less a charge for capital employed in the period. Accounting profit may be adjusted, for example, for the treatment of goodwill and research and development expenditure, before economic value is calculated.

CIMA official terminology

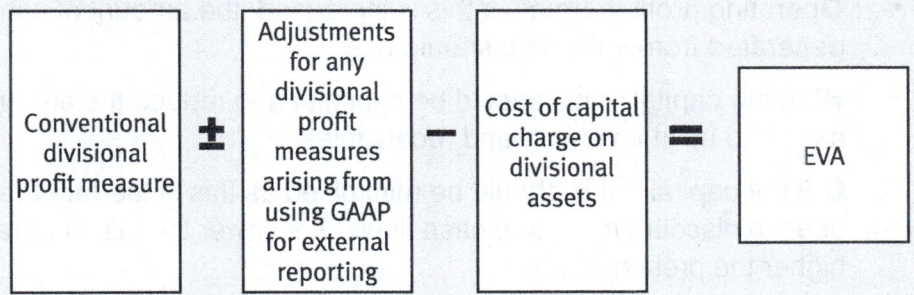

- Adjustments are made to avoid the immediate write-off of value-building expenditure such as research and development expenditure, advertising expenditure or the purchase of goodwill.
- Adjustments are intended to produce a figure for capital employed which is a more accurate reflection of the base upon which shareholders expect their returns to accrue and to provide a profit after tax figure which is a more realistic measure of the actual cash yield generated for shareholders from recurring business activities.

SVA (Shareholder Value Analysis)

A variation along the same theme as EVA. The main aim of the organisation is to add value to shareholder wealth. This can be defined in a variety of ways and usually results in a form of balanced scorecard being used.

Shareholder value is the total return to the shareholders in terms of both dividends and share price growth, calculated as the present value of the future free cash flows of the business discounted at the weighted average cost of the capital of the business less the market value of its debt.

CIMA official terminology

Essentially this means that management need to ensure that their strategies maximise the wealth of the shareholders of the company, by ensuring that they increase the present value of the returns that they will receive from their shares.

Rappaport has a model that is frequently mentioned. He suggested that future cash flows should be discounted at a suitable cost of capital and that shareholder value would be increased if this measure were to increase.

In order to maximise future cash flows and reduce the cost of capital, he identified seven value drivers:

- **S**ales growth rate – assuming sales are profitable, this should increase cash flow.
- **L**ife of the project – if the firm can forecast growth over a longer period, there will be more cash flows to discount.
- **O**perating profit margin – if this is increased, the amount of cash generated from each sale should rise.
- **W**orking capital – this should be minimised to reduce the amount of cash tied up in inventory and receivables.
- **C**ost of capital – this should be minimised as this is the rate that will be used to discount the future cash flows. The lower the discount rate, the higher the present value.
- **A**sset investment – if growth demands high levels of capital investment, this will represent a large outflow of cash.
- **T**axation – clearly, any reduction in this rate will reduce cash outflow.

An easy way of remembering these drivers is using the acronym **SLOW CAT**.

Managers should set targets in each of these seven areas in order to ensure they are maximising shareholder wealth.

It is important to remember that value is not just a financial concept. Shareholders can attach non-financial value, e.g. social responsibility of the company – not testing on animals, positive human rights record or even football club membership.

Later work has developed to include other stakeholders and also non-financial perspectives such as social responsibility. Remember, look after the environment in which you operate and you will get a longer life – the implications for increasing future cash flows as a result are substantial.

Advantages of EVA/SVA approaches

- Adjustments made to profit effectively mean we are looking at cash-flow based measures
- consistent with NPV so should ensure better goal congruence between divisional performance and maximising shareholder value. (Note: You can show that the present value of future EVA figures equates to the increase in shareholder value measured by discounted cashflows)
- cost of financing emphasised.

Drawbacks of the EVA/SVA Systems

- Uses accounting data which has been prepared for other purposes and involves subjective provisions and estimates
- it ignores items that don't appear on balance sheets such as brands, staff and inherent goodwill
- confuses management as they are seldom trained fully in its operation and it varies from one company to another
- costly to maintain and resistance is usually high when first deployed
- assumes value can be measured in money terms
- judgement involved by users in evaluation and selection of cost of capital rate to be used.

The performance measurement mix

Test your understanding 12

YU Ltd is a multinational company that makes and sells one major product, the TRT. The company is aware that the TRT is starting to show signs of decline. YU wishes to undertake one or more of the following strategies to deal with this:

(i) Rebranding TRT. YU believes that this will extend the life of the TRT by five years.

(ii) Replacing the current computerised inventory management system which is coming to the end of its useful life.

(iii) Altering YU's internal transfer pricing to reduce its overall tax liability.

(iv) Adjusting YU's reported profit figures to remove the effect of GAAP for external reporting.

Which of the above strategies will be consistent with a shareholder value analysis (SVA) approach?

A   (ii) and (iv)
B   (i) and (iii)
C   (ii) and (iii)
D   (i) and (iv)

9 Triple Bottom Line

As outlined in chapter 3, many organisations are concerned about their impact on the environment and wish to monitor whether they are sustainable.

Triple Bottom Line (TBL) expands traditional accountancy reporting systems, looking at social and environmental performance, rather than simply financial performance. This can be used to help encourage each division and manager within the organisation to act in a socially responsible manner.

The model suggest measuring three areas:

- **profit** (or economic prosperity) – the economic value created by the company, or the economic benefit to the surrounding community and society
- **people** (social justice) – the fair and favourable business practices regarding labour and the wider community in which the company conducts its business
- **planet** (environmental quality) – the use of sustainable environmental practices and the reduction of the environmental impact of the organisation.

TBL has a number of advantages, most of which relate to its improvement of the organisation's corporate social responsibility position:

- attracting ethically aware customers
- attracting better quality staff
- cost reductions (i.e. savings in energy, reduced pollution clean-up costs)
- reduced chance of government legislation

However, there are a number of drawbacks, including:

- **Difficult to Quantify**

    It is often difficult to quantify appropriate social and environmental measures. When a business makes a commitment to protecting the environment by recycling, for example, its impact is not always easily discernible.

- **Management Conflict**

    The organisation's management usually aims to maximise shareholder return. TBL reporting might create conflict as the benefits of any social and environmental actions that a business engages in are likely to emerge over the long term. However, they could have a short-term negative impact on profits, leading to conflict with shareholders.

The performance measurement mix

Test your understanding 13

Which of the following benefits is consistent with the use of triple bottom line (TBL) reporting?

A   Cost savings through reduced wastage

B   Measures are all based on objective cash-flows, rather than subjective accounting profits

C   Decisions made ensure shareholder wealth is maximised

D   Cheap and easy measurement of targets

10 Transfer pricing

(1) In larger multidivisional organisations, it is common to find SBUs trading with each other. This will involve the setting of transfer prices (TP). These prices are often set by the corporate unit and can prove to be problem areas when coming to asses SBU performance.

(2) TPs that are set at marginal cost do not offer the SBU manager an incentive to supply and they may choose to sell resources to outside parties who pay a higher margin. This can have quality implications for the group product who then take second place in terms of supply.

(3) Buying at marginal cost can also give a misrepresented position as performance appears to be better.

(4) In assessing managerial performance, it is usual to exclude the TPs from the performance measurement systems on the grounds that they are not controllable. This has the problem of suggesting that trading between group partners is not important ('what gets measured...').

(5) TPs can be used to assist entry into the international arena and can cause considerable controversy in the countries targeted as well as the divisional managers whose performance is being evaluated. TP can also be used as a basis to avoid taxation. By increasing or decreasing TP, profits can be relocated from high tax economies to low tax economies. As a result, tax authorities allocate substantial time and effort in attempting to identify these practices. One way that has been used in the past is to see whether the organisation concerned is excluding the TP items from the performance measurement mix. If they are doing so, this suggests that the TP is being centrally controlled and tax evasion is suspected.

(6) **The dilemma** – inclusion of the TP items in the measurement mix leads to problems in performance evaluation as uncontrollable items are included in the assessment. However, in so doing you could save millions in tax. To remove the TP items from the measurement system can lead to vastly increased taxation liabilities.

chapter 8

Test your understanding 14 – I.Port – (Case style)

You work for HHF a large company as a strategic management accountant.

You have been sent the following urgent email by the Finance Director (FD)

To: M. Port
From: I. Storm
Date: 16/08/XX
Subject: Divisional performance – STRICTLY CONFIDENTIAL

Hi M,

As you may or may not be aware, divisional managers are paid a bonus which can represent a large proportion of their annual earnings. The bonus is paid when the budgeted divisional profit for the financial year is achieved or exceeded.

Meetings of divisional boards are held monthly and attended by the senior management of the division, and senior members of group management.

With the end of the financial year approaching, there had been discussions in all divisional board meetings of forecast profit for the year, and whether budgeted profit would be achieved. In three board meetings, for divisions that were having difficulty in achieving budgeted profits, the following divisional actions had been discussed. In each case, the amounts involved would have been material in determining whether the division would achieve its budget.

Division A had severely cut spending on training, and postponed routine repainting of premises.

Division B had renegotiated a contract for consultancy services. It was in the process of installing total quality management (TQM) systems, and had originally agreed to pay progress payments to the consultants, and had budgeted to make these payments. It had renegotiated that the consultancy would invoice the division with the total cost only when the work was completed in the next financial year.

Division C had persuaded some major customers to take early delivery, in the current financial year, of products originally ordered for delivery early in the next financial year. This would ensure virtually nil stock at year end.

I'm concerned about these issues and I would like you to send me some briefing notes which discuss the financial accounting, budgeting, ethical and motivational issues which arise from these divisional actions.

> Please also comment on whether any group management action is necessary.
>
> Thanks
>
> I. Port
>
> **Required:**
>
> Draft the briefing notes as requested by the FD.
>
> (30 minutes)

11 Communication

Whatever an organisation's chosen performance measurement mix, it is essential that the targets set for employees and divisions are appropriately communicated by senior management.

This will involve:

- communicating the targets being set and how they will be measured
- identification of why the targets have been selected – why they are important and how they feed into the organisation's overall strategy
- explaining to employees how they will personally be affected by achieving (or failing to achieve) the targets set
- getting feedback from employees about the appropriateness of the targets being set.

Why is effective communication of the performance measurement mix important?

Benefits include:

- if employees understand the reason for the performance targets that they are being set, they are more likely to 'buy in' to the performance measurement mix and see it as important
- an explanation of how the employee's performance is going to be measured will increase the likelihood that they will understand how to meet the targets they are being set
- explaining the impact of hitting or missing their targets (i.e. impact on pay rises or bonuses) will ensure that the employee is aware of the advantages to them personally of conforming to the performance measurement mix, improving their motivation to meet the targets set

- getting feedback from employees can ensure that targets set are achievable. If employees feel that targets are unattainable, they will not be motivated to work to achieve them.

Stretch targets

Communication with employees is particularly important if an organisation sets stretch targets.

Stretch targets are where the organisation sets goals for its employees that are possible, but very difficult for them to meet. The employee is 'stretched' in that they have to perform extremely well in order to achieve the target.

For example, many accountancy firms pay for their junior employees to sit professional accountancy exams. Instead of simply requiring these students to pass their exams, a firm may require a mark of, say, 75% or higher.

In theory, this requirement will stretch the student, making them work hard to achieve the target.

While stretch goals can work well to motivate staff to work hard, care has to be taken when setting them:

- if employees see the stretch target as unachievable it will be demotivating.
- a stretch target may encourage unethical or risk-taking behaviour – our student may be more likely to cheat on their exam in order to achieve the required grade!

As such, setting the right goal is crucial to avoiding behavioural problems.

It is also worth noting that if the employee has performed exceptionally well and met their stretch targets, the organisation will need to offer them sufficient rewards to maintain their motivation. These could include:

- pay rises
- bonuses
- promotions
- more responsibility

Excellent performance by an employee should be communicated throughout the organisation as this can motivate other employees to work harder, as well as proving that the stretch targets are achievable.

The high-achieving employee could also be asked to share their approach to meeting their targets, so that others are able to imitate their example throughout the organisation.

12 Problems with performance measurement

Problems in performance measurement and control in complex business structures

As stated above, a main feature in modern business management is the practice of splitting an enterprise into semi-autonomous units with devolved authority and responsibility.

Such units could be described as 'divisions', subsidiaries or SBUs, but the principles are the same.

This raises the following potential problems.

- How to co-ordinate different business units to achieve overall corporate objectives.
- Goal congruence – managers will be motivated to improve the performance of their local business unit, possibly at the expense of the larger organisation.
- The performance of one unit may depend to some extent on others, making it difficult to implement responsibility accounting effectively.
- Whether/how head office costs should be reapportioned.
- How transfer prices should be set as these effectively move profit from one division to another.

Controllability

Managers should be made accountable for those factors that they can control. This would see a focus onto divisional contribution. This issue of controllability and design poses a few problems:

- What exactly is controllable? Consider shared assets.
- Does controllability change when the long run is considered?
- Transfer pricing issues – should the sales and purchases be included?
- Managerial performance and divisional economic performance are not necessarily the same thing – uncontrollable factors would need to be included when considering economic performance.
- Where does the data originate from? The financial accounting system may not be suitable for performance evaluation of SBUs and may need to be adapted by the management accountant. Reporting or accuracy – which is most important? The faster you go the less reliable the information may become.
- The cultural situation and factors that are likely to motivate the divisional management team.

Test your understanding 15

H runs a small manufacturing company. She is concerned that production levels and production quality have been declining in the last several months. H is therefore planning to set stretch targets for her staff relating to the number of units they produce. Typical production levels require staff to make 25 units per hour. After careful analysis and discussion with staff, H feels that this can be increased to 28 per hour, though this will be difficult for staff to achieve. Any employees who manage to hit the new target will be given a significant bonus at the end of the month.

Which of the following problems is H most likely to face with the stretch targets she has set?

A   Staff will see the target as unachievable and are demotivated

B   The stretch target may lead to staff producing poor quality work

C   Staff will feel no motivation to work towards the stretch target

D   The stretch target will be ignored by staff due to lack of communication

Cost centres, profit centres and investment centres

Key considerations

When assessing divisional performance it is vital that the measures used match the degree of decentralisation in the division:

Type of division	Description	Typical measures
Cost centre	• Division incurs costs but has no revenue stream	• Total cost • Cost variances • Cost per unit and other cost ratios • NFPIs (non-financial performance indicators) related to quality, productivity, efficiency, etc.

345

The performance measurement mix

Profit centre	• Division has both costs and revenue • Manager does not have the authority to alter the level of investment in the division	All of the above PLUS • Sales • Profit • Sales variances • Margins • Market share • Working capital ratios (depending on the division concerned) • NFPIs related to customer satisfaction
Investment centre	• Division has both costs and revenue • Manager does have the authority to invest in new assets or dispose of existing ones	All of the above PLUS • ROI • RI • SVA/EVA These are discussed in more detail above. ROI and RI should be familiar to you from your earlier studies.

In most exam questions you will meet SBUs that are investment centres.

Sub-optimisation

Sub-optimisation refers to actions taken to improve the divisional situation at the expense of the company as a whole. This can arise for a number of reasons:

- **Short-termism**

    Short-termism refers to actions taken to improve the short-run performance at the expense of the long run. For example, cutting discretionary costs such as advertising and training budgets to hit a profit target.

- **Problems intrinsic to the targets used**

    Most measures are linked to profit, which does not have a high correlation with shareholder value.

- **Wrong signals**

    Excessive pressure to hit targets may result in a culture where it is felt to be acceptable to use 'creative accounting' to achieve results.

Wrong signals and inappropriate action

There are many ways in which poorly designed performance management systems can send managers the wrong signals, resulting in dysfunctional behaviour. Berry, Broadbent and Otley identified the following problem areas:

- Misrepresentation – 'creative' reporting to suggest that a result is acceptable.
- Gaming – deliberate distortion of a measure to secure some strategic advantage.
- Misinterpretation – failure to recognise the complexity of the environment in which the organisation operates.
- Short-termism – leading to the neglect of longer-term objectives.
- Measure fixation – measures and behaviour in order to achieve specific performance indicators which may not be effective.
- Tunnel vision – undue focus on stated performance measures to the detriment of other areas.
- Sub-optimisation – focus on some objectives so that others are not achieved.
- Ossification – an unwillingness to change the performance measure scheme once it has been set up.

Test your understanding 16 – (Integration question)

HIH is a large, multinational chain of high-quality hotels. Recently they have expanded rapidly, with growth of over a hundred hotels in the last two years.

Each new hotel is fitted to a high standard by HIH. The head office of HIH is responsible for all advertising and special offers, the setting of prices and any branding changes.

The performance measurement mix

The local hotel managers are responsible for operational decisions, such as which staff to hire and employee training.

HIH sets targets for local managers based on total sales and customer satisfaction feedback. The customer feedback is collected by hotel staff from customer questionnaires.

Required:

Comment on the suitability of the targets set for local hotel managers.

(15 minutes)

The role of the management accountant in performance

The Chartered Management Accountant has a crucial role to play within the organisation when considering the performance measurement mix.

They will help management to decide on the performance measurement mix itself. Management accountants can help managers analyse the organisation's strategy and suggest what measures will ensure this strategy is achieved.

Management accountants will also help managers to decide what targets to set staff in each area of the performance measurement mix. This could include work studies to identify what employee roles involve, followed by calculation of what they can reasonably be expected to achieve.

Management accountants will also help the organisation to design systems to capture relevant information relating to the measurement mix. They will then communicate this to management, enabling them to identify whether the organisation's strategy is being successfully implemented.

13 Summary

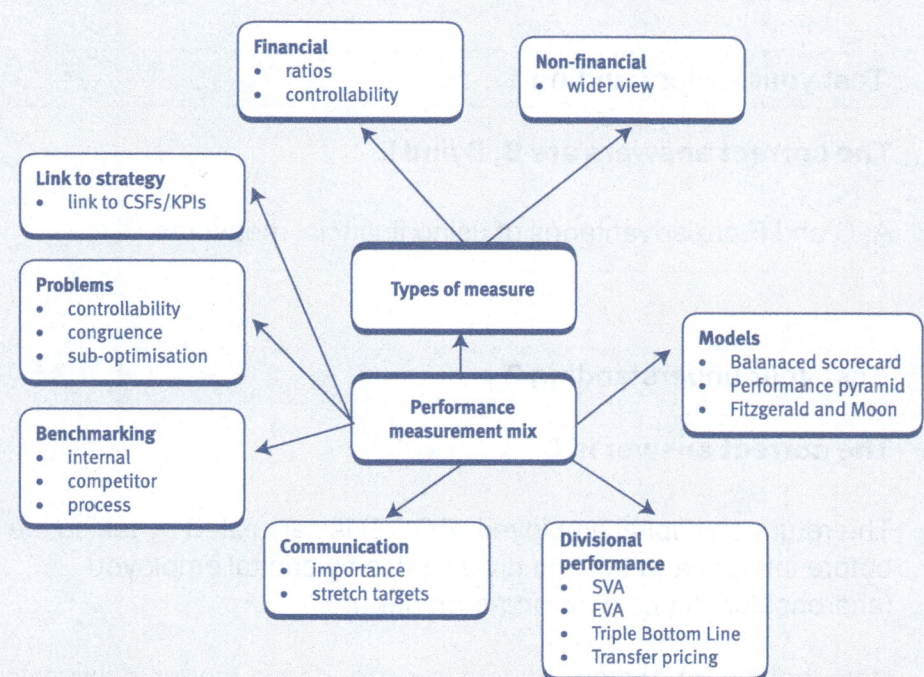

The performance measurement mix

Test your understanding answers

Test your understanding 1

The correct answers are B, D and E

A, C and F are advantages of using financial measures.

Test your understanding 2

The correct answer is C

The return on capital employed (ROCE) is calculated by taking the profit before interest and tax and dividing this by capital employed (shareholders funds plus long-term debt).

Note that the proportions of debt to equity do not matter in this calculation, meaning that a shift in gearing will not necessarily affect the ROCE.

In addition, large dividends would tend to reduce the shareholders funds, which could actually cause an increase in the ROCE, rather than a reduction.

Test your understanding 3

The correct answer is A

Learning and growth relates to both innovation and training for staff though this could also have a positive effect on both customers and service quality.

Test your understanding 4 – (Integration question)

Perspective	Goals/CSFs	Measures/KPIs
Customer	New products	% of sales from new products
	Responsive service	% on-time delivery
	Preferred supplier	Customer ranking
	Partnership ventures	Number of cooperative operations
Internal business	Manufacturing excellence	Production cycle time, unit cost engineering, etc.
	Design productivity	Material efficiency
	New product development	Introduction times, actual versus plan
Learning and growth	Time to market	Introduction times v competition
	Product focus	% of products giving 80% of sales
	Manufacturing	Process time to maturity
	Learning technology	Time to develop next-generation products
Financial	Survival	Cash flow
	Success	Quarterly sales growth
	Prosperity	Increase in market share and return on equity (ROE)

The performance measurement mix

Test your understanding 5 – CCC – (Case style)

Report
To: T
From: A. N. Accountant
Date: 15/01/XX
Subject: Balanced scorecard analysis for CCC

Introduction

The Balanced Scorecard (BS) helps an organisation, like CCC, to identify key issues that it needs to consider in order to maximise the efficiency of its performance measurement mix.

How the Balanced Scorecard could assist CCC

In a widely published model, Johnson and Scholes characterise the strategic management process as consisting of three inter-related elements:

- strategic analysis
- strategic choice
- strategic implementation.

CCC has developed both mission and vision statements and an overriding objective so they have dealt with the first two elements. However, the comments of the Corporate Affairs Director that 'our strategy and vision ..(are)..not happening' indicate that CCC has been unsuccessful in strategic implementation. This is not an unusual situation as firms often experience a disjunction between the three elements. This is one of the reasons that the Balanced Scorecard (BS) was developed by Kaplan and Norton 'to assist strategic policy formation and achievement'.

The BS (See diagram below) comprises four perspectives surrounding the organisation's vision and strategy. Each of these perspectives can be associated with an aspect of CCC's vision statement.

Vision and Strategy

Our vision aspires to:

- provide superior returns to our shareholders
- continually improve our trading methods
- delight our customers
- learn from our mistakes, work smarter in the future

Our strategy is to double the size of our revenue by 2017.

Customer perspective

To achieve our vision how should we appear to our customers?

Delight our customers

Financial perspective

To succeed financially how should we appear to our shareholders?

Provide superior returns to our shareholders

Learning and growth

To achieve our vision, how will we sustain our ability to change and improve?

Learn from our mistakes and work smarter in future

Internal business process

To satisfy our shareholders and customers, what business processes must we excel at?

Continually improve our business processes

Example application of the Balanced Scorecard to CCC

The Balanced Scorecard can be made operational by using:

- Objectives: what CCC wants to achieve
- Measures: these will express the progress made towards an objective
- Targets: these give specific values and timescales for the achievement of the measures
- Initiatives: these are the actions taken to achieve a target

Examples of these four aspects are given below:

Financial perspective

- Objective: Provide increasing dividend returns
- Measure: Dividend yield
- Target: 6% dividend yield by end 2014
- Initiative: Cost cutting exercise to increase profits

The performance measurement mix

Customer perspective

- Objective: Increase customer satisfaction
- Measure: Customer complaints
- Target: Reduce customer complaints to 1% of transactions by mid 2015
- Initiative: Increased training for sales executives

Learning and Growth

- Objective: Raise the educational level of staff
- Measure: Number of graduates
- Target: 50% of staff to be graduates by 2016
- Initiative: Sponsor staff on degree courses

Internal processes

- Objective: Be at the forefront of the use of Information technology
- Measure: Replacement rate for PCs
- Target: All PCs to be no older than 2 yrs by the end of 2014
- Initiative: Seek new PC suppliers

Tutorial note: the examples given above are not exhaustive: candidates were given credit for other appropriate examples.

Potential drawbacks of the Balanced Scorecard

It is possible that the pursuit of one perspective may adversely affect another one. For example, if customer satisfaction was to be increased by increased investment in inventory, the financial perspective could be damaged. In this case, CCC would have to prioritise one of the perspectives even though both of them were helping to deliver the vision and strategy.

As CCC has not used the BS before there may have to be a cultural change for it to work successfully: cultural change can be hard to achieve.

The BS may require substantial investment in dedicated software and training costs.

The BS does not provide a single overall view of performance. Managers and analysts often favour measures which capture overall performance.

Tutorial note: any other appropriate drawbacks identified by candidates would be given credit.

chapter 8

> **Conclusion**
>
> The BS could be used to great effect within CCC. However, before the organisation decides to adopt this approach, it needs to ensure that they have fully understood the drawbacks and prepared strategies to handle these.

> **Test your understanding 6**
>
> **The correct answer is B**
>
> The others are all measures of external effectiveness.

> **Test your understanding 7**
>
> **The correct answer is D**
>
> By definition.

> **Test your understanding 8 – Ochil – (Case style)**
>
> (i) The marketing success of the proposal is linked to the achievement of customer satisfaction. The success will require an efficient business operating system for all aspects of the cycle from product design to after-sales service to customers. Improved quality and delivery should lead to improved customer satisfaction. Schedule 1 shows a number of quantitative measures of the expected measurement of these factors:
>
> Quality is expected to improve. The percentage of production achieving design quality standards is expected to rise from 95% to 98% between 2014 and 2016. In the same period, returns from customers for replacement or rectification should fall from 3% to 0.5% and the cost of after-sales service should fall from $1.5m to $1.0m.
>
> Delivery efficiency improvement that is expected may be measured in terms of the increase in the percentage of goods achieving the planned delivery date. This percentage rises from 90% in 2014 to 99% in 2016.

The performance measurement mix

(ii) The financial success of the proposal is linked to the achievement of high productivity. This should be helped through reduced cycle time and decreased levels of waste. Once again Schedule 1 shows a number of quantitative measures of these factors:

The average total cycle time from customer enquiry to delivery should fall from 6 weeks in 2014 to 5 weeks in 2016. This indicates both internal efficiency and external effectiveness.

Waste in the form of idle machine capacity is expected to fall from 10% to 2% between 2014 and 2016. Also, component production scrap is expected to fall from 7.5% in 2014 to 2.5% in 2016. These are both examples of ways in which improved productivity may be measured.

(iii) Performance pyramid

The performance pyramid should ensure that Ochil's performance measurement system remains dynamic and relevant in a changing business environment. The pyramid measures performance across nine dimensions from corporate vision to individual objectives. The pyramid links the business strategy with the day to day operations ensuring that the different levels support each other.

The measures go far beyond traditional financial measures such as profitability and cash flow. The measures relate to business operating systems and address the driving forces that guide the strategic objectives of Ochil.

Customer satisfaction, flexibility and productivity are the driving forces upon which company objectives are based. The status of these can be monitored using the lower level indicators of waste, delivery, quality and cycle time.

The pyramid views a range of objectives for both external effectiveness and internal efficiency. It makes clear the difference between measures that are of interest to external parties, e.g. customer satisfaction and quality, and measures that are of interest to the business, e.g. productivity and cycle time.

The measures are seen to interact both horizontally at each level and vertically across the levels.

Test your understanding 9

The correct answers are: A and C

The number of new product lines relates to the innovation dimension. Increased revenue and margins is linked to the profit dimension, while the number of defective products is most closely linked to quality issues. The remaining dimensions have not been well covered by the measures set up by JKJ.

Test your understanding 10

The correct answer is B

Competitor benchmarking is not appropriate here as J's rival is not ITTO accredited and is highly inconsistent with its approach to tuition. Neither of these things is likely to make it a suitable candidate for benchmarking.

While J does operate a number of centres, their operations are strictly controlled by central teaching programmes and ITTO requirements. This means it is unlikely that internal benchmarking will identify any major improvements that can be made.

The only group likely to be useful for a benchmarking exercise is universities. These are not rivals to J, so it is likely that this would be a process, or activity, benchmarking exercise. Universities are currently achieving a higher pass rate than J, so benchmarking could be useful for J.

Test your understanding 11 – K and L – (Case style)

Email
To: L
From: K
Date: 19/09/XX
Subject: Re: Benchmarking

Hi L,

As per your text, I've outlined the impact of benchmarking on the department and individuals below.

The areas of the sales department as a whole which will be affected by the introduction of a system of benchmarking are:

Planning: It is important that the company's current practises are reviewed and assessed. If comparisons are made with similar organisations, it is essential that the present processes are understood to allow an objective view to be taken of the firm's current sales management function. An effort will need to be made to identify a firm which is prepared to share information that may be regarded as confidential by many firms.

Research: It will be necessary to identify the activities which can be compared. In a sales department this could include, for example, the number of calls per week, the distances covered by each salesperson, etc. These might be useful starting points for the benchmarking process.

Analysis: The method used and the specification of the variables should be established before comparisons are made with another organisation. It is likely that operating costs, past sales levels and new business generated could all be performance indicators that can be analysed to provide the basis on which benchmarking can be undertaken.

Implementation: The information obtained in the benchmarking exercise will be invaluable in the future in order to monitor the selling activities of the company. In addition it will assist in making better decisions regarding sales in the future.

The impact of benchmarking on individual salespeople would be in the following areas:

Planning: As the activities of each salesperson need to be monitored, it is essential to get their co–operation if the benchmarking process is to be successful. Staff may need to be reassured that it will not affect them adversely.

Research: It is necessary to establish performance measures in a flexible manner as it may be difficult to make direct comparisons. For example, travelling times and the size of purchases by customers are likely to be major performance measures. These targets are currently the same for each sales area, but this may need to be flexed in order to be fair to each salesperson.

Analysis: It will become possible to compare performance within the firm and with other firms operating in the same areas. This could make comparisons more realistic and more effective for determining bonuses.

Implementation: Benchmarking will provide a better appreciation of the factors involved in setting sales targets. By helping to improve the performance of individual salespeople, the performance of the company as a whole can be improved.

I hope that helps – if you need any more information, please let me know.

Kind regards

K

Test your understanding 12

The correct answer is B

(i) will increase the life of the project, while (iii) will reduce the tax liability. Both will specifically improve YU's SVA.

(ii) will not necessarily add to SVA as it will require additional asset investment and there is no evidence that it will reduce YU's overall working capital levels. (iv) relates to EVA, not SVA.

The performance measurement mix

Test your understanding 13

The correct answer is A

Triple bottom line requires measuring the 3Ps - profits, people and planet. This can encourage staff to save money by reducing wastage as they are targeted on their environmental impact. Reducing wastage will help them achieve this and save the company money.

However, measuring the 3Ps can be time consuming and complex. Note that options B and C are benefits of EVA/SVA.

Test your understanding 14 – I.Port – (Case style)

Key answer tips

This question deals with the possibility of management manipulating financial performance measures. To ensure a focused answer (and economic use of time) consider the three suggestions under the four headings in the question. Group management action is required to ensure such proposals being implemented prior to forthcoming bonus calculations.

Briefing notes

Each of the divisions' actions can be discussed as follows:

Division A

In financial accounting terms, the reduction in discretionary expenditure will lead to higher reported divisional profits than would have been the case if the original planned expenditure had taken place. Discretionary expenditure should be charged against profits as it is incurred. No provisions or accruals need to be set up at the year end because the division is not compelled to make the expenditure.

There is some question as to whether the cut in training costs and repainting costs should be separately disclosed in the financial accounts in the overriding objective of giving a true and fair view. This depends on the materiality of the amounts involved, but is unlikely in the context of the group as a whole.

The ethical implications are more serious. The managers of Division A have deliberately manipulated the results in order to achieve the budget and be paid their bonuses. Their duty as managers is to serve the organisation, but they have served their own interests. Perhaps the two decisions can be distinguished from each other. The repainting of the premises is not important to the group; the timing of repainting is just the sort of matter than the group management should be happy to devolve to divisional management. The lack of training is more serious. It will probably lead to higher costs next year, which the group managers would not be happy about.

Division B

In financial accounting terms, the decision to defer payment to the consultants should make no difference to the division's reported profits. If work has been carried out but not yet paid for at the balance sheet date, the division must set up an accrual for the amounts due. This will be charged against profits. So this idea should have no effect on the divisional managers' bonus payable.

The only way that the idea would increase reported profits would be if the division abandoned the accruals concept and tried to defer the charging of the expense until the consultants were paid. This would be contrary to established accounting practices, and would attract criticism from the auditors if the amounts were sufficiently material.

If the divisional managers were familiar with accounting practices, but decided not to accrue for the payments in order to be paid their bonuses, an ethical question arises. These managers have shown themselves to act unethically, and the group managers should warn the divisional managers about their conduct.

If no accruals were made this year, then next year's profits would be lower when the total cost of the contract has to be charged against profits. To avoid this kind of shock, and in the interests of giving a true and fair view, an accrual for the work carried out at the balance sheet date should be set up.

Division C

In financial accounting terms the point of sale is the point when the purchaser starts to take responsibility for the risks and rewards of the goods. This is usually when the purchaser accepts delivery of the goods. So, by delivering goods which are accepted before the balance sheet date, the division has successfully moved the date of sale into the current financial year. The profit on such sales can therefore be included in this year's reported profits, which will help to trigger the bonus payments.

The performance measurement mix

There would only be financial accounting implications to the scheme where it was decided that showing the higher profit this year, with next year's profit being lower than it would otherwise have been, destroys the true and fair view of the accounts. This is unlikely to be the case, particularly in the context of the group as a whole.

The nil stock at the year-end could cause problems at the start of the next financial year. Any large order received early next year could not be satisfied from stock; the purchaser might have to wait some time for the goods to be physically produced before they can be delivered. At best this is only an inconvenience to the purchaser. At the worst the sale may be lost altogether as the purchaser takes his custom elsewhere to a supplier who can deliver from stock. Thus a scheme that was designed to trigger bonus payments to the divisional managers in the current year could end up costing the group sales and consequent profits next year.

As in the other divisions, the divisional management have acted unethically. The possible loss of sales next year, and the pressuring of customers to accept early sales this year, simply so that managers can be paid bonuses this year, is not acceptable.

Group management action

The whole logic of establishing a divisionalised structure within a group is to allow local managements to manage their divisions as they think best, subject to meeting broad group criteria. Normally group management will adopt a hands-off attitude of observing procedures but not interfering. Interference would be resented by the divisional managers with adverse motivational consequences.

None of the proposals in the question is actually illegal, though division B's idea would be contrary to standard accounting practice, if an insufficient accrual were established. So, the group managers may feel unwilling to get involved and criticise the proposals.

However, there is a line to be drawn between legitimate 'income smoothing' (a good thing, since stock markets value highly companies with a smooth profit record) and manipulation of results to earn bonuses this year but which will depress profits next year. The idea of the bonus scheme is to reward good operational performance, not skills at profit manipulation.

So, however unwilling they may be to interfere unnecessarily, the group managers' responsibility to the stakeholders at large means that they must take up each of these issues with the divisional management, if only to prevent these proposals from being put in place every year as the bonus calculations are drawing near.

Test your understanding 15

The correct answer is B

H is worried about production levels AND quality. The targets she is proposing are likely to encourage staff to work quickly – not with more care. This could see H suffering from further declines in quality.

The stretch targets set have been created after discussion with staff - this suggests that they are achievable and that have been fully communicated by H. This means that A and D are incorrect.

The sizeable bonus would indicate that staff will feel motivated to work towards the stretch target, meaning that C is also incorrect.

Test your understanding 16 – (Integration question)

Suitability of targets

Remember that targets set for managers need to be based around areas that they can directly control.

Managers do make the operational decisions in the hotel, meaning that they should have a large degree of control over the customer experience and therefore customer satisfaction.

However, as pricing and special offers are set by head office, they do not have total control over the sales made by the hotel. Should head office set an inappropriate price per room, sales will suffer. It would be unfair to blame the manager for this.

The performance measurement mix

chapter 9

Information technology and e-business

Chapter learning objectives

Lead	Component
E1. Evaluate the information systems requirements for successful strategic implementation	(a) Evaluate the information systems required to sustain the organisation. (b) Advise managers on the development of strategies for knowledge management
E2. Evaluate the opportunities for the use of information technology and information systems for the organisation, including Big Data	(a) Evaluate the impact of IT/IS on an organisation and its strategy (b) evaluate the strategic and competitive impact of information systems, including the potential contribution of Big Data

Indicative syllabus content

- The purpose and content of information systems strategies.
- The need for information systems strategy to be complementary to the corporate and individual business unit strategies.
- The impact of IT, including the internet, on an organisation (utilising frameworks such as Porter's Five Forces & the Value Chain).

- Aligning information systems with business strategy (e.g. strategic importance of information systems, information systems for competitive advantage, information systems for competitive necessity)
- Contemporary developments in the commercial use of the internet (e.g. e-business, virtual organisations and Web 2.0, Big Data, social and other forms of digital marketing).

chapter 9

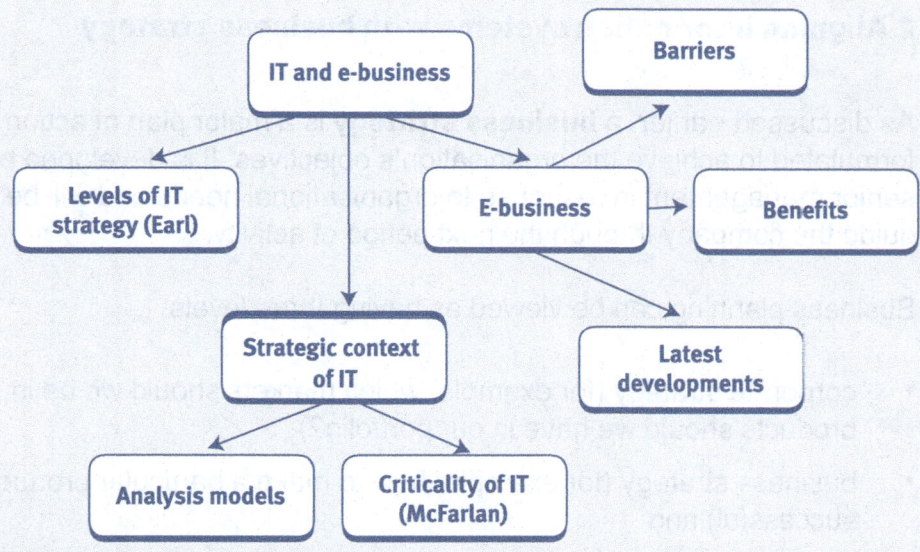

1 What are IT and IS?

In this chapter we will be looking at two related concepts – information technology (IT) and information systems (IS). Many people use these terms interchangeably, but in reality they are different (if linked) ideas.

 'Information systems' is an umbrella term for the systems, people and processes designed to create, store, manipulate, distribute and disseminate information within the organisation.

 'Information technology' falls under the IS umbrella but deals with the technology involved in the systems themselves. It typically includes the hardware, software, databases and networks that the IS runs on.

For example, a business may have a marketing information system that gathers and stores information on customers habits and market research. This information is then interrogated by management to help make decisions on issues such as pricing and advertising.

The term information system refers to the marketing system as a whole – the data gathering process, the hardware and software, as well as the people involved (such as the data input staff and the managers who are responsible for interrogating the system).

Information technology just refers to the hardware and software within the system, such as the computers, networks, hard drives and software that the system runs on.

2 Aligning information systems with business strategy

As discussed earlier, a **business strategy** is a major plan of action formulated to achieve the organisation's objectives. It is developed by senior management in response to organisational needs and will be used to guide the company through the next period of activity.

Business planning can be viewed as having three levels:

- corporate strategy (for example, which markets should we be in, which products should we have in our portfolio?)
- business strategy (for example, how to make a particular product more successful) and
- functional strategy (for example, HR and marketing)

Using this hierarchy, information systems (IS) could be seen as a functional strategy designed to support the overriding corporate and business strategies. IS may act as a core competence and be a source of competitive advantage (i.e. by providing an edge over competitors gained by offering customers greater value, either by means of lower prices or by providing greater benefits and service that justifies higher price).

However, developments in information technology (IT) and IS are triggers for new corporate and business strategy, such as the growth of e-trading, so the relationship is more than simply one of support. The use of IT/IS may be a competitive necessity.

Put simply, IT and IS are a key part of many organisations' internal and external environment, will be a major part of many new strategies adopted by the organisation and may actually provide new opportunities and strategies for the organisation to adopt. It is therefore an absolutely vital part of strategic business planning.

This chapter covers two major themes:

(1) the strategic and competitive impact of information systems (IS)

(2) the impact of the Internet on organisations by looking at e-business.

On a related note, competing through exploiting information is covered in chapter 10.

3 The criticality of IT – the McFarlan grid

While IT and IS may be crucial to many organisations, this is not always the case. Some businesses may find that IT/IS has little strategic impact.

To assess the criticality of IT/IS to the organisation, McFarlan's strategic grid can be used to identify the current and future dependence on information systems (IS). This can help management decide on how much time to devote to strategic analysis of IT/IS in their organisation.

Strategic impact of future systems

	Low	High
Low (Strategic impact of current systems)	**SUPPORT** Applications that improve management and performance but are not critical to the business	**TURNAROUND** (or high potential) Applications that may be of future strategic importance
High	**FACTORY** Applications that are critical to sustaining existing business	**STRATEGIC** Applications that are critical for future success

McFarlan's grid

(a) **Support**

- Information systems (IS) have a support role – a necessity to the working of the organisation. IS have little relevance to the organisation's existing or future success.

- May include accounting operations and payroll but there are no new developments which can contribute significantly to the competitiveness of the organisation.

- There is usually a low level of senior management involvement as the commitment to IS planning is low.

- Such organisations are not characterised by their high investment in IT and it is unlikely that IT plays a significant part in the strategic planning process.

- Earl cites a cement manufacturing company as an example in this sector. Information technology may be used to speed up administration and make occasional improvements to the processes but it is not vital or critical to the manufacture or distribution of cement.

(b) **Factory**

- The organisation depends heavily on IS and IT for operations. However, there is little scope for future development and further IT developments are not likely to add to their competitive edge.

- McFarlan maintains that strategic goal setting and linkage of IS to the corporate plan are not too important if IT has a factory role. IT is critical to the current operation but not to the overall strategic direction.

- Some airlines and retailers would come into this category; Earl mentions a steelworks with an on-line real-time system for controlling production. Even one hour of disruption to these organisations' booking systems or order-processing systems could fundamentally damage their competitive performance.

(c) **Turnaround**

- Existing IT is not too important but future developments are likely to have a significant impact. Companies recognise the growing importance of IT as a means to improve competitive position.

- Possible applications have a high potential to contribute to the organisation's strategic objectives. For example, a professional accounting college.

- The current IT climate has forced firms to reassess their operations and the phrase 'automate or liquidate' can be used to sum up the approach companies need to take in order to stay in business. Significant change is expected.

- Earl identifies that IT budgets are being increased, leadership is coming from the boards and IT directors appear in the governance profile.

- E-commerce has opened up new possibilities for many industries. Consider the selling of books on-line and computer games. Insurance brokers, travel agents – the list goes on.

(d) **Strategic**

- Existing and future IT developments are at the heart of the organisation's success. These firms need significant amounts of planning as the firm would be at a disadvantage if the information processing did not perform well.

- They have applications which they rely on for the smooth running of their day-to-day activities and they have future developments which are vital to their competitive success and are integral to the organisation's strategic objectives. The future is shaped by potential IT activity. A substantial IT budget can be expected.

- Banks and insurance companies are typical of this sector. Earl cites a credit card company and a major bank as examples.

Illustration 1 – Information technology – the strategic context

Many insurance companies used IS/IT in a support role – accounting, sending out premium renewal notices, etc. The industry was very paper-based with customers submitting hand-written claims, accident diagrams and police reports. To save costs and give better customer service, many insurance companies now scan in documents so that they are available to call up on screen. Paper files no longer have to be moved around the office, with the potential of being mislaid. The role of IT in insurance companies went from support, to turnaround to strategic.

Forces that drive an organisation around the grid

Forces that drive an organisation around the strategic grid may be internal or external.

- Internal forces will be concerned with matching the potential of information technology to the organisation's operations and strategy, such as a decision to improve productivity. Porter's value chain is a good model to identify internal forces.

- External forces will be associated with changes in the competitive environment, such as actions of competitors, suppliers or customers. Porter's five forces model can be used to provide a framework to discuss areas where information technology and systems can yield competitive advantage. The advantages may be in defending the organisation against the competitive forces or by attacking and influencing them in its favour.

Test your understanding 1

KKL is a radio station based in one city. It has developed sophisticated IT systems for its broadcasts which allow it to play tracks and advertisements efficiently. This has reduced the need for employees and given KKL a cost advantage over many of its rival stations, which have been struggling financially in recent years. This has allowed KKL to sell advertisements at a lower prices than other radio stations.

KKL's rivals have recently started developing similar systems which will allow them to reduce their own cost base in the coming years. KKL feels that its systems are currently as efficient as they can be made and they believe that there is limited future scope for development of its information systems.

Information technology and e-business

> Where would KKL's IT system be placed on McFarlan's strategic grid?
>
> A   Factory
>
> B   Support
>
> C   Turnaround
>
> D   Strategic

4 IT, IS and IM strategies

If an organisation discovers that information systems are strategically important, they will need to consider what strategies they should adopt in order to make use of them effectively.

Earl's three levels of information strategy

In 1989 **Earl** developed a framework to analyse the linkages between three interrelated types of strategy:

- information systems
- information technology
- information management.

IS (information systems) strategy

IS strategy is concerned with aligning IS development with business needs and with seeking strategic advantage from IT. **It looks at how the organisation can use IS to help meet its strategic objectives**. It is usually formulated at the same level as product/market strategy for the SBU and is long-term in nature.

For example, if an organisation has an overall strategy to expand its sales and market share, the IS strategy looks at what systems could be created to support this long-term goal. This could involve (for example) deciding on whether to develop a website to allow for online sales, or if a new customer management system that helps the company identify customer needs and improve its marketing would be appropriate.

The information strategy is therefore business-led and demand-orientated and is either supporting existing business strategies or developing new strategic choices. An effective IS strategy is typically formed with the key objectives of using the information resource to:

- generate new businesses and/or
- delivering tangible benefits, e.g. increased productivity, enhanced profits and perhaps a reduction in the workforce.

The IS strategy for will involve identifying what information is needed by the organisation to enable it to achieve its business objectives. This includes considering the information needed at strategic, tactical and operational levels and the ways in which those levels of information should interconnect and interact.

Having an IS strategy is a reminder to the organisation that the use of IT/IS should be to support the business and its overall mission. The use of IT/IS is not a goal in itself. The organisation must expect tangible benefits from any investment in IT/IS before it proceeds.

IM (information management) strategy

'Which way, who does it and where is it located?' Essentially, IM strategy relates to the **roles of those involved in the system and their relationship with the system itself**.

Concepts that underpin the formation of the IM strategy include:

- Information and technology need to be managed as efficiently and effectively as other resources.
- The organisational, business and management impact of IT requires these resources to be managed as an integral part of the organisation.

- The information function is too important to be managed without some formalisation when the business strategies are increasingly dependent on or created by IT.

IM strategy is organisation-based, relationships-orientated and management focused. It aims to 'put management into IT' and looks at the people involved with the proposed information system, including:

- the role and structure of the IT activities in the organisation.
- the relationships between the specialists and users and between the centre and SBUs.
- the management controls for IT, management responsibilities, performance measurement and management processes.
- Information management is a highly complex activity, concerned with:
  - identifying the sources of the information that are needed
  - collecting that information in appropriate formats
  - storing information
  - facilitating existing methods of using information
  - identifying new ways of using information
  - ensuring that information can be accessed by all who need it (but **only** by those people).

The initial financial investment in IT provides the impetus for organisations to seek more effective control over the range of IT activities. In this context, IS and IT strategies can only be implemented if they are managed. It is worth noting that Earl outlines the four tasks of information management:

(1) **Planning** – involves the integration of IS and IT strategies with other decision-making processes.

(2) **Organisation** – involves issues of decentralisation and centralisation of the IT function, the formation of steering committees, management education and training, reporting procedures and the responsibilities of IT managers.

(3) **Control** – issues relate to the relationship between IT and finance. Key management activities are performance measurement and investment appraisal of IT.

(4) **Technology** – is related to priorities of the IT strategy, e.g. the design and development of methodologies for IT, security practices and data management techniques.

For example, if a company has decided to create a new marketing information system, the IM strategy would involve deciding which employees will input data into the system. It will consider where that information will be sourced from (i.e. internal or external market research), as well as what controls will be put in place to ensure data is entered correctly. In addition it will look at a management level – who uses the information? Who has access to it? Who has overall responsibility for the system?

IT (information technology) strategy

IT strategy is described as activity-based, supply-orientated and technology-focused. It focuses on the **selection, use and management of the technology itself**.

Information technology (IT) refers to the resources used to manage information:

- hardware and software used within the information system
- communication (such as wi-fi and networks)
- office automation (such as word processing and database software)
- production automation (such as automated assembly lines).

No matter how well designed the information system, it will fail if it uses inappropriate hardware or software.

A company developing a marketing information system would need to consider the software it used to create the system – does it need to be specially written? Will the software being considered allow for the data entry, storage, processing and retrieval required by the organisation? Will the system be able to run on existing computers (hardware) or will new, more powerful ones be needed? Do the computers need to be networked? All of these technical decisions will form the basis of the IT strategy.

It is worth noting that technology changes rapidly over time. IT strategy can be an ongoing strategy within the organisation, as new software and hardware become available that may help the organisation improve its overall information strategy.

The need for information systems strategies

Many organisations have historically viewed their IT and information systems as a necessary resource, but one that was not strategically significant. Nowadays, this attitude has changed as businesses have realised the value of having an IT strategy that fits into the overall corporate strategy.

Information technology and e-business

The reasons for having an IT/IS strategy include:

- The cost of IT/IS is very high in many businesses. Without high-level management, there is a risk of costly mistakes.
- Strong IT/IS systems will help the business to create and maintain a competitive advantage.
- IT is fast-moving. By managing it strategically, a business can take advantage of new opportunities and technology as it becomes available.
- IT/IS systems are often expected by key stakeholders – for instance, many customers will expect a business to have a website. Failure to have reliable IT/IS systems may upset these stakeholders.
- IT/IS can lead to structural changes within the organisation, requiring strategic changes to human resources.
- IT/IS is likely to affect all levels of the business and its management.

Test your understanding 2

Under Earl's model, which of the following would be classified as an information systems strategy?

A Hiring of an IT Director to control the organisation's information systems

B Expansion of the organisation into e-business to meet customer demand

C Design of access controls for IT systems

D Selection of software for a new IT system

Test your understanding 3

P Ltd retails artificial plants. It sells directly to retailers, though it is considering the launch of a new website that will allow it to sell direct to the public. The board (who are also the shareholders) have little experience of IT and are uncertain of whether it is necessary for P.

The Board of P has undertaken detailed analysis and discovered that the cost of developing the website will be relatively low. In addition, P is expecting to only sell relatively modest amounts of goods through the site, as they believe that relatively few consumers will look for their goods online (although they believe the site will still be profitable).

> The chairman has suggested several arguments as to why P needs to hire an IT director, including:
>
> (i) IT changes rapidly and needs someone with appropriate skills to manage it within the business
>
> (ii) The cost of investing in IT will be high – having an IT director could reduce costly mistakes
>
> (iii) IT forms the basis of P's competitive advantage and therefore needs strategic management
>
> (iv) IT is expected by key stakeholders and should therefore have strategic focus.
>
> Which of these arguments are correct when considered in relation to P's website development project?
>
> A   (i) only
> B   (i) and (ii) only
> C   (ii) and (iii) only
> D   (iv) only

5 Information technology – the strategic context

As well as being a key part of internal business strategy, IT and IS can form a significant part of an organisation's internal and external analysis (concepts covered in more detail in chapters 4 to 6). In this section we will explore how IT and IS may feature in some of the major models we saw in these chapters.

Business strategy and information strategy

This section looks at IT/IS strategy in the context of the strategic planning tools discussed in earlier chapters.

Unlike many other resources, IS/IT evolves very quickly and will often play a large part in determining corporate strategy. On a SWOT analysis IS/IT can appear in any of the four quadrants and the appropriate responses have to be made. For example:

- **Strength:** A business has a very advanced IS/IT system that allows it to respond flexibly to orders while maintaining a low cost base.
- **Weakness:** An organisation's system is in disarray and customers are becoming irritated by its inability to deliver the proper goods on time.

- **Opportunity:** Set up new internet site that allows customers to buy over the Web.
- **Threat:** A competitor has spent heavily on IS/IT and can offer very high levels of service as a result.

Illustration 2 – Information technology – the strategic context

MP3 sound compression, the internet and fast broadband connections have forced companies like Sony and EMI to reassess their music-retailing strategies. Technology is a threat to these companies – as well as a significant opportunity!

Illustration 3 – The effect of technology on the business

IT can be a serious threat to organisations if they fail to consider it as part of their strategic analysis.

Two examples of companies affected by this on the UK high street are Jessops and HMV.

Jessops retailed camera and other photographic equipment. While widely recognised as offering strong customer service and having knowledgeable staff, Jessops failed to deal with the rise of online retailing. Online rivals with lower overheads were able to offer similar products to Jessops, but at lower prices. Jessops' inability to alter its strategy to deal with this threat led to its eventual collapse.

HMV also had significant problems due to a failure to keep pace with changing technology. It sells a wide range of DVDs, computer games and music CDs. HMV's core market was slowly eroded by cheaper online retailers – in particular the rise of download sites such as iTunes. HMV failed to effectively move into these growth areas, leading to a sharp decline in its profitability and severe financial distress.

IS/IT and Porter's Five Forces

To analyse the SWOT factors relating to IS/IT, it can be useful to consider how IS/IT can be used to counter Porter's five forces so as to help an organisation have a more comfortable existence than some of its competitors.

- **Rivalry:** Use IT to reduce the effects of tough competition, for example by building strong relationships with customers and lowering costs.

- **Threat of new entrants:** Sophisticated IT applications are expensive, slow to develop and technically challenging. All of these are barriers to entry.
- **Supplier pressure:** Use IT to find new suppliers. Use IT to automatically rotate orders between suppliers. Compare prices on the internet.
- **Customer pressure:** Use IT to improve customer service, for example by allowing on-line ordering.
- **Threat of substitutes:** Use computer-aided design and manufacturing to develop new products first.

IT/IS and Porter's Five Forces

Porter's five forces model may be used to help clarify the overall business strategy. The model provides a framework to discuss areas where information technology and systems can yield competitive advantage. The advantages may be in defending the organisation against the forces or by attacking and influencing them in its favour.

Management should use the model to determine which of the forces poses a threat to the future success of the organisation. By ranking these threats in terms of intensity and immediacy, the most critical can then be considered in terms of how information technology or systems can be used to gain advantage or avoid disadvantage.

Threat of entry – new entrants into a market will bring extra capacity and intensify competition. The strength of the threat from new entrants will depend upon the strength of the barriers to entry and the likely response of existing competition to a new entrant. IT can have two possible roles to counteract the threat.

- *Defensively*, by creating barriers that new entrants to the market find difficult to overcome. IT can increase economies of scale by using computer-controlled production methods, requiring a similar investment in the technology of new entrants. Another defensive move is to colonise the distribution channels by tying customers and suppliers into the supply chain or the distribution chain. The harder the service is to emulate, the higher the barrier is for new entrants.

- *Offensively*, by breaking down the barriers to entry. An example is the use of telephone banking, which reduces the need to establish a branch network. Automated teller machines (ATMs) created new distribution channels enabling 'bank branches' to be set up in airports, out-of-town supermarkets and other areas where there are many potential customers. These machines provided not only expansion of the total market, but also a low-cost method of overcoming the barriers to entry in the areas where the cost of entry was high and space was at a premium.

Intensity of competitive rivalry – this is rivalry between firms making similar products, or offering the same services, and selling them in the same market. The most intense rivalry is where the business is more mature and the growth has slowed down.

IT can be used to compete. Cost leadership can be exploited by IT, for example, where IT is used to support just-in-time (JIT) systems. Alternatively IT can be used as a collaborative venture, changing the basis of competition by setting up new communications networks and forming alliances with complementary organisations for the purpose of information sharing. When Thomson Holidays introduced its on-line reservation system into travel agents' offices, it changed the basis of competition, allowing customers to ask about holiday availability and special deals and book a holiday in one visit to the travel agent.

Threat of substitute products – this threat applies both between industries (e.g. rail travel with bus travel and private car) and within an industry (e.g. long-life milk as substitute for delivered fresh milk). In many cases IS themselves are the substitute product. Word-processing packages are a substitute for typewriters.

IT-based products can be used to imitate existing goods as in electronic keyboards and organs. In the case of computer games, IT has formed the basis of a new leisure industry.

Computer-aided design and computer-aided manufacture (CAD/CAM) have helped competitors to bring innovative products to the market more quickly than in the past.

Interactive information systems add value by providing an extra service to an existing product. An example of this is provided by ICI's 'Counsellor', an expert system that advises farmers on disease control. It analyses data input by the farmer on areas such as crop varieties grown, soil type and previous history of disease and recommends fungicides or other suitable ICI products to solve the farmer's problems.

The threat from substitutes can be minimised by ensuring that an organisation develops a product before its rivals and then protects that product for a number of years by means of patents. This approach is widely used in the pharmaceutical and biotech industries where specialist software is now widely used in the drug discovery process, enabling drugs to be developed that target specific human and animal diseases.

Bargaining power of customers – the bargaining power of customers can be affected by using IT to create switching costs and 'lock' the buyer into products and services. The switching costs may be in both cash terms and operational inconvenience terms. For example, PCs run under Microsoft operating systems are not very efficient when using non-Microsoft application software.

Another form of locking customers in is to develop customer information systems that inform the organisation about the customer's behaviour, purchases and characteristics. This information enables the organisation to target customers in terms of direct marketing and other forms of incentive such as loyalty schemes, where methods of rewarding customer loyalty by giving them 'preferred customer' status are used. If a clothing retailer is launching a new collection it can offer its loyal customers a private viewing. Some airlines have deals such as frequent flyers and air miles as incentives.

The IT techniques at play here include 'data warehousing' – the collection and storage of large volumes of customer information on spending and purchasing patterns, social group, family make-up, etc. This then allows for 'data mining' – the extraction of relevant data from the warehouse as the source for target marketing drives. It was reported recently that Tesco, the UK's largest supermarket group, was mining its customer data to identify customers over the age of 60 who regularly purchased children's clothes, food and toys – possibly leading to a marketing push aimed at grandparents.

Bargaining power of suppliers – the bargaining power of suppliers, and hence their ability to charge higher prices, will be influenced by:

- the degree to which switching costs apply and substitutes are available
- the presence of one or two dominant suppliers controlling prices
- the products offered having a uniqueness of brand, technical performance or design not available elsewhere.

Reducing the suppliers' power to control the supply can erode this power. Where an organisation is dependent on components of a certain standard in a certain time, IT can provide a purchases database that enables easy scanning of prices from a number of suppliers. Suppliers' power can be shared so that the supplier and the organisation both benefit from performance improvements. The Ford Motor Company set up CAD links with its suppliers with the intention of reducing the costs of design specification and change. Both the time taken and the error rate were reduced because specifications did not have to be rekeyed into the suppliers' manufacturing tools.

Test your understanding 4

J is a well-established supermarket chain based in country H. It has recently launched a website that allows customers to shop for their groceries online. The goods purchased will then be delivered to the customer's home by J.

Which ONE of the following effects will the website launch have on J's industry?

A   Increased threat of substitutes

B   Increased threat of new entrants

C   Increased barriers to entry

D   Increased customer power

How IT can play a role in generic strategies

IS/IT and Porter's generic strategies

Porter identified three generic strategies for dealing with the competitive forces (explained in detail in chapter 7). The two basic strategies are overall cost leadership and differentiation. The third strategy – a focus strategy – concentrates on a particular segment of a product line or geographical market – a niche. If it is known which strategy an organisation is currently using to promote their products and/or services, it should be possible to define a role for IS to enhance that strategy.

- **Overall cost leadership** is about competing by offering products or services at low cost and value for money. The emphasis is on cost reduction. For example, driving down inventory levels, with the assistance of IT for supply chain planning and scheduling, can reduce costs. Sales forecasting software that can be fed into manufacturing resources planning applications can be used in shop floor planning and scheduling applications to increase efficiency.

- **Differentiation** is about showing that your product or service is different from those of your competitors through, for example, brand image, customer service or design. A way of differentiating may be to make the ordering process as easy and flexible as possible. This can be done by providing on-line information services to identify the most appropriate product or service, followed up by a simple on-line ordering process. Where the differentiation is by customisation, CAD (computer-aided design) can reduce costs effectively.

- **Focus** – this strategy concentrates on a niche market, e.g. a particular buyer group, market, geographic area, segment or product line. The opportunities for IS/IT include providing access to customer information, trends and competitors so as to maximise competitive thrust and exclude competitors.

Nolan's stage hypothesis

A useful starting point for thinking about the use of information and related technology in organisations is the stage hypothesis developed by Nolan in the 1970s. It was found that data processing (DP) expenditure followed an S-curve of increasing costs, expenditure being gradual at first but increasing dramatically before adopting a more gradual slope again. This curve also represented a path of organisational learning about information technology and its uses within the corporation.

The six stages of IT expenditure according to the hypothesis are:

(1) **Initiation stage** – automation of clerical operations. Typically the more technically-minded employees use technology because they are keen, rather than use it for cost-effectiveness.

This could be seen in a very small start-up business, for example.

(2) **Contagion stage** – rapid growth as users become more familiar with applications and demand more, and where the wider benefits of technology are perceived by more staff.

This could be seen in a start-up business that has begun to show some growth and employ more people.

(3) **Control stage** – planning and methodologies are introduced in order to assert control over developments, and investment in technology is taking place in a planned manner. Controls may be introduced by setting up steering committees and project management teams.

An example would be local government.

(4) **Integration stage** – the integration of the various computing functions within the organisation and there is user involvement in the development stage of information technology.

This would be relevant to most medium to large commercial enterprises.

(5) **Data administration stage** – emphasis is placed on information requirements rather than just processing requirements and there is sufficient information available to support the appointment of staff to manage it.

For example, banks and insurance companies.

(6) **Maturity stage** – the IS/IT planning is brought into line with the business planning and development. The data resources are flexible and the information flows mirror the real-world requirements of the firm. The firm will be using a variety of applications to support its information needs.

For example, airlines, large retailers such as Tesco, internet-based companies such as Amazon.

Despite some criticism over the years (along the lines that the model is too simplistic, or that it inhibits strategic use of information), it is generally accepted that a model of the evolving role of information and communications technology (ICT) in an organisation is of value and that Nolan's model is a good starting point.

Uses for Nolan's stage hypothesis include:

(a) being able to classify organisations into the stage they are presently at, thereby being able to predict their future reactions to technology

(b) being able to identify how the organisation passed through the earlier stages and the problems they specifically encountered

(c) understanding the current status of the organisation in terms of technology and being able to produce strategic plans that are not too ambitious for the stage they have reached

(d) being able to develop plans that will avoid the pitfalls of the later stages in the hypothesis.

IT/IS and the value chain

IT/IS can impact the value chain in a number of different ways:

	Examples
Inbound logistics	- Stock control – MRP, ERP, JIT - Automated warehousing – Bar-coding systems - Virtual warehouses – several outlets, each connected to a system which indicates the total amount of stock available at different sites

Operations	• Robots – automate some of the process
	• CAM – computer aided manufacturing – production control, material and capacity planning
	• CIM – computer integrated manufacturing – machine tools, automated guided vehicles
	• Online tuition delivery in universities and colleges
Outbound logistics	• Automated warehousing – bar-coding systems
	• Order processing
	• Vehicle scheduling
Sales & marketing	• Customer databases – market segmentation, habits, trends
	• Electronic marketing
	• EPOS
	• CRM
Services	• Remote servicing
	• Computer scheduling of repairs
	• Expert systems
	• FAQ
Procurement	• EDI, e-procurement
	• Extranets
HR management	• Workforce planning
	• CBT
Technology development	• CAD – computer aided design
	• Design of extranets/intranets/Web-based products
Infrastructure	• Collaborative workflow
	• Intranets
	• Electronic scheduling
	• Office automation systems
	• ERP – enterprise resource planning – these systems are used for identifying and planning the enterprise-wide resources needed to record, produce, distribute and account for customer orders.

Information technology and e-business

Test your understanding 5

YOU plc has recently decided to invest in an EDI system that will allow it to automatically place orders with its major suppliers. Currently, YOU's purchasing department staff have to place telephone orders to the company's suppliers, which is slow and inefficient.

Which activity within YOU's value chain will the new EDI system improve?

- A   Infrastructure
- B   Inbound logistics
- C   Outbound logistics
- D   Procurement

Test your understanding 6 – (Integration question)

Consider how an estate agent could use IS/IT to improve its competitive position.

6 E-business

The meaning and use of e-business

E-business (electronic business) is the conduct of business processes on the Internet. These processes can include buying and selling products and services, servicing customers, processing payments, collaborating with business partners and sharing information with key stakeholders.

E-commerce is a subset of e-business. It refers more specifically to the buying and selling of goods and services online.

Porter suggested three ways in which IS/IT in general can affect the competitive environment and an organisation's ability to compete. Though these points apply to IS/IT in general, they are particularly important when considering e-business.

- New businesses might become possible. For example, auction sites and photo-album sites.
- The industry structure can be changed. For example, in the music business it can be argued that the large CD publishers have less power because music can be self-published on the internet.

- IS/IT can provide an organisation with competitive advantage by providing new ways of operating. For example, airlines save money by encouraging internet bookings.

Terminology – buy and sell-side e-commerce

Any e-business transaction can be viewed from two perspectives – the organisation's and that of the other party.

- 'Buy-side' e-business focuses on transactions between an organisation and its suppliers.
- 'Sell-side' e-business focuses on transactions between an organisation and its customers.

Stages of e-business

Many businesses tend to develop their approach to e-business over time. Usually this development follows a series of stages.

The stages of e-business can be described as:

Stage		Characteristics
1	Web presence	Static or dynamic web pages but no transactions are carried out. Would show information about the organisation, products, contact details, FAQs (Frequently Asked Questions). Faster updates are possible than with paper-based information and could be cheaper than paper-based catalogues.
2	E-commerce	Buying and selling transactions using e-commerce. Might cut out middlemen, but there is probably no fundamental change in the nature of the business.
3	Integrated e-commerce	For example, information can be gathered about each customer's buying habits. This can allow the organisation to target customers very precisely and to begin to predict demand.
4	E-business	E-business is now fundamental to the business strategy and may well determine the business strategy

This model helps businesses to understand where they are in the process of e-business, and this will help them to decide where to go next with further development.

Information technology and e-business

Test your understanding 7

B retails hair extensions through a small chain of stores. They have recently launched a website for customers to purchase their products. The company does not require customers to create an online account (or profile) when purchasing goods online.

What stage of e-business has B currently reached?

A   E-business

B   E-commerce

C   Web presence

D   Integrated e-commerce

The categories of e-business functions are shown below:

	Delivery by Business	Delivery by Consumer
Business (Exchange initiated by)	B2B Business models, e.g. VerticalNet	B2C Business models, e.g. Amazon.com
Consumer	C2B Business models, e.g. Priceline.com	C2C Business models, e.g. eBay.com

- B2B (business to business). For example, a supermarket IS automatically placing orders into suppliers' IS.

- B2C (business to consumer). Selling over the internet – books, flights, music, etc.

- C2B (consumer to business). Some internet sites display a selection of suppliers' offerings from which the user can choose. A model that largely depends on the internet.

- C2C (consumer to consumer). Auction sites, such as eBay, putting consumers in touch with each other. Amazon does the same by offering second-hand books. This model largely depends on the internet.

Benefits of e-business

Most companies employ e-business to achieve the following:

- **Cost reduction** – trading online can result in lower overheads and cheaper procurement than those incurred by traditional 'bricks and mortar' businesses.

- **increased revenue** – mainly through online sales and the fact that the organisation can appeal to a wider market, rather than just those customers in a small geographical area around its stores. Even small organisations can have access to customers who were not previously available and can gain a global presence via the internet.

- **increased visibility** – having the organisation's website linked to search engines such as Google and Bing will allow customers to easily find the business, leading to increased brand awareness.

- **better information** – e-business allows organisations to gather information about their customers (such as email addresses and buying habits) when they log into an online account. This allows the business to target advertising and special offers to each customer, increasing the effectiveness of marketing activities. Note that advertising online via email is likely to be significantly cheaper than traditional advertising (such as leaflets or letters).

- **enhanced customer service** – offering services online allows an organisation to tailor its services to individual customer's needs, improving the service they receive (e.g. through the use of extranets).

- **employee flexibility** – e-business can allow employees to work from anywhere, enhancing their motivation, as well as improving flexibility for the customer.

The combination of the above should help to enhance the company's competitive advantage.

Illustration 4 – E-business

Many supermarkets now offer a home-delivery service. Over the internet, inventory lists are displayed for customers who fill an electronic 'shopping trolley' and proceed to payment and checkout. A delivery period is chosen (say 4pm–6pm the following day). Supermarket staff pick the goods chosen and pack them for delivery.

Standard shopping lists can be set up by users to speed up the process. The standard lists can be amended each time (for example, extra milk, but no carrots).

Information technology and e-business

The supermarket can also uses the information it gathers from its customers (such as email address, age, gender and buying habits) to advertise to them with direct, targeted marketing (for example emailing them special offers on goods they do not usually buy from the supermarket). This helps to build customer loyalty as well as competitive advantage.

Illustration

Alibaba is the world's largest e-commerce company, which operates predominantly in China. According to the company's website its mission is 'to make it easy to do business anywhere'.

Alibaba was set up in 1999 by Jack Ma, a Chinese English teacher. The initial aim was to help small Chinese businesses trade globally. The company has been described as a combination of eBay and Amazon, in that it is an online company with multiple revenue streams that are more conventional than a social network site. Alibaba.com is a B2B website, which links up businesses around the world looking for suppliers. Wholesalers are linked to distributors around the world, and businesses can trade almost anything, from olive oil to computer components.

Test your understanding 8

Which of the following categories of e-business would an EDI (electronic data interchange) system usually be classified within?

A   B2B

B   C2B

C   B2C

D   C2C

Barriers to e-business

Barriers to e-business can be seen in both the organisation itself and in its suppliers and customers.

- **Technophobia** – senior managers may be distrustful and sceptical about the alleged benefits of e-business.

- **Security concerns** – particularly about hackers, viruses and electronic fraud.

- **Legal issues** – holding customer information online is likely to mean that the organisation has to follow relevant data protection laws.

- **Set-up costs** – simple, static pages are cheap to set up, but dynamic pages, linking to e-commerce systems and databases, with impressive design values are expensive to set up.

- **Running costs** – renting space on a web-server. Also, maintenance of websites is very important as most users are very unforgiving about out-of-date sites. Updating, say with special offers and new product lines, is also needed to encourage return visits, perhaps linked to email campaigns.

- **Limited opportunities to exploit e-business** – some businesses (such as selling books) are more suitable for e-business than others (such as selling carpets).

- **Limited IT resources in-house** – the business may lack relevant skills to set up and maintain e-business systems, so recruitment is needed or all development and maintenance has to be subcontracted.

- **Customer reaction** – customers may not be interested in e-business (for example a pet shop selling animals may not attract many customers online). This means that the business may not recoup its investment in e-business from increased sales revenue.

As mentioned earlier in the chapter, e-business is a strategy that may be used to help rapidly grow sales. If this is not the goal of the organisation it may not be a suitable strategy.

Intranets and extranets

Intranets are internal internets. They exist inside the organisation only, using website and browser technology to display information.

Commonly they contain:

- information about customers
- information about products
- information about competitors
- news/updates
- procedure manuals.

However, there's no reason why accounting information cannot be delivered over intranets.

Extranets are intranets that are connected to external intranets.

For example, a supplier could give customers access to their order processing system so that orders can be placed and tracked. It is when these types of external connection are made that e-business can begin to produce spectacular results.

Other requirements needed to deliver an e-business strategy

Connection to the internet will not, of itself, deliver e-business. Suitable hardware, software and business processes have to be in place. Here are some examples of how e-business could affect various business areas.

Business area	Where e-business could impact	Strategic aim
Research and development	Internet used for research purposes.	To be a leader in innovation.
	Access to research databases.	To develop unique, differentiated products
	Access to patent databases	
Design	Computer-aided design	Fast production of new designs and products. CAD will make designs cheaper (cost leading) and faster (differentiation)
Manufacturing/service provision	Computer-aided manufacturing	Flexible, low cost, but tailored to customers' requirements
	Just-in-time inventories	
	Online delivery of service (such as consultancy or tuition services)	
Communication with customers	Website and email	Improved customer loyalty and increased revenue

Inbound logistics	Organisation of the supply chain	Low cost, low inventory balances, flexible manufacturing
The buy-side e-commerce transactions	Automating the purchases cycle	Low cost as less human intervention
Outbound logistics	Organisation of the distribution chain	Low cost, low inventory balances, fast delivery to customers
The sell-side e-commerce transactions	Automating the sales cycle	Low cost as less human intervention. Greater accuracy

Making websites interactive

One of the most effective things you can do with your website is to give users power over it. Give them choices, tools and features that encourage them to interact with the site and provide them with a sense of control over it.

- Search: Provide users with the ability to search your website for words, phrases and/or provide them with key topics from which to choose. Consider in what format the results are to be presented.

- Online forms: How many, number of fields in each, what needs to be verified before the user submits the form – e.g. have they completed the field for email address?

- 'Members only' section: Is there a section that can only be accessed via a username and password? Where are the usernames and passwords to be stored? How will you handle people who forget their password?

- Interactive questionnaires/surveys/polls: How many, how long, how presented? What will you do with the information provided by the users?

- Animations: How can you (should you) use Flash or other programming devices to bring life into your site and illustrate products and services?

- Subscription email lists: What can users subscribe to by way of email lists, such as e-newsletters?

- Links to other sites: How many and what tools are to be employed during maintenance to check automatically on the veracity of the link?

- Downloadable files: PDFs, images, audio files – how many, in what format, with what restrictions?

- Contact us: What contact details should be on the site – e.g. email, telephone, street address?

- Site map: What is the site map of the website to look like? Just text as links or is a diagram preferred?

- Text-only version of the site: Will you need a text-only version of the website for customers who are visually impaired or with a slow/expensive connection?

- Multilingual requirements: How many languages? How much of the site is to be multilingual? At what point are users to nominate which language they want to view the site in – e.g. home page, a splash page?

- Provision for printing and bookmarking (i.e. allowing users to store the website address in their browser's memory or 'favourites' section). Are users to be able to bookmark specific pages or is the home page sufficient? Do you want any special print function other than the default function supplied by the browser?

7 Latest developments in the commercial use of the internet

Web 2.0

"Web 2.0" refers to a perceived second generation of web development and design that facilitates communication, secure information sharing, interoperability, and collaboration on the World Wide Web.

Although the term Web 2.0 suggests a new version of the World Wide Web, it does not refer to an update to any technical specifications, but rather to cumulative changes in the ways software developers and end-users utilize the Web.

Whereas Web 1.0 was primarily concerned with the web as a source of information, Web 2.0 is seen as the "participatory web" and includes the emergence of web-based communities, hosted services, and applications such as social-networking sites (e.g. Facebook), video-sharing sites (e.g. YouTube), wikis and blogs.

These can offer opportunities to firms in a number of different ways:

- **Advertising**

    For example, viral advertising via popular sites such as Facebook and YouTube.

- **Software as a service (SaaS):** With SaaS customers only pay for software when they need it. The service is provided on-demand via a web browser and is highly attractive to smaller users who cannot justify buying a full version of the software.

    For example, Fortiva offer an e-mail archiving service that complies with US legal requirements.

- **Mashups:** The term "mashup" originated in music where artists would combine parts from different songs to create a new track. The web equivalent is where developers can now mix, match, reuse, and morph web content, data, and services.

    For example, estate agent websites can now include interactive maps where users can see precisely where available properties are and also check local government information on school catchment areas and environmental issues such as flooding.

- **Competence syndication:** Web syndication is where firms make a portion of their website available to other firms, sites or individual subscribers. Competence syndication is where the different parties benefit from each other's competencies

    For example, in 2001 Amazon opened zShops, providing virtual shelf space to online competitors. They could sell their goods through the same system Amazon used, paying a listing fee plus commissions on sales.

- **Using global network effects:** The network effect is the effect that one user of a good or service has on the value of that product to other people. A good example of this is the online auction site eBay – the more people use it the more attractive membership becomes.

    For example, IBM has capitalised on competencies across the world by dramatically changing their business model. Rather than trying to develop their own proprietary operating system to compete with Windows or Linux, IBM chose to get involved in the open-source movement by including open source software, contributing to the open-source community and adapting the open-source philosophy. IBM estimates that this alone has saved the company $1 billion per year.

Strategic benefits of utilising Web 2.0

Web 2.0 allows web users to participate in the web and it encourages collaboration and knowledge sharing. It has a truly significant impact on marketing (especially to those certain demographic groups who use Facebook, Twitter and Myspace to carry out daily social activities).

Organisations need to understand the demographic profile of their customers and the intelligence gathered about customers and their preferences can be critical for a business to achieve competitive advantage.

The ability to get customers to collaborate in the organisation's online marketing also significantly boosts the effectiveness and reach of the organisation's advertising and promotion.

Illustration 5 – Web 2.0 in action

An extremely high proportion of organisations that engage in e-business use at least an element of Web 2.0.

Wikipedia

Wikis are widely used and allow users to add to and edit a bank of knowledge. Wikipedia.org is itself an example of a wiki. Rather than simply being an online encyclopedia that users can access, Wikipedia relies on individual users to update and amend entries to improve their accuracy and reduce the amount of inputting that the website's own central staff has to undertake.

PC Magazine

Media hubs, such as PC Magazine and Digital Spy (amongst many others) link to popular new websites and social networks. This is key to the uptake of many new social networks and websites.

Twitter and Facebook

Large numbers of businesses, such as Royal Mail, McDonalds and Santander, have a presence on social media sites (in particular Twitter and Facebook) as a way of not only advertising (through special offers and electronic word of mouth (eWoM)), but also addressing customer complaints and queries.

These businesses also often have the option on their websites to leave positive reviews on Twitter, or 'like' their page on Facebook in order to increase their brand awareness on these social media sites.

> Small new enterprises may undertake the bulk of their advertising online and through social media sites as it has low cost but can be extremely effective at reaching a large number of potential customers.

Virtual organisations

This occurs where an organisation outsources many of its functions to other organisations and simply exists as a network of contracts with few, if any, functions being kept in-house.

For example, many internet retailers (such as Amazon.co.uk) could be seen as virtual organisations. Their products are bought in from manufacturers, sales are delivered to customers by third-party couriers and even their websites may be maintained and hosted by external IT specialists.

The virtual organisation typically only has a small central core of staff who co-ordinate all of these different third parties and ensure that customer needs are met.

Illustration 6 – Virtual organisations

'Not on the High Street' is an internet based business selling luxury homeware, clothing and gifts. It has enjoyed rapid growth and success since it was launched in 2006.

The company works with over 900 small British businesses. These businesses design, produce and deliver the products to customers. This enables Not on the High Street to sell a wide range of unique products to fulfil the needs of the demanding modern customer, while keeping costs low.

The benefits of adopting a virtual organisation approach include:

- ability to exploit opportunities – a business may not have the time or resources to develop the manufacturing and distribution infrastructure, people competencies and information technology to exploit new opportunities. By forming a virtual organisation it can assemble the components it needs to take advantage of a market opportunity.

- virtual organisations can be made to look much larger than they actually are. This will enable them to compete with large, successful rivals and win lucrative contracts.

- teams of experts can be formed to meet the specific needs of a project. The team can be dissolved and a new team formed for the next project.

- lower costs – investment in assets (e.g. land and buildings, machinery) is minimal. This should help to improve competitive advantage.

The drawbacks of a virtual organisation include:

- difficulty in negotiating a revenue or profit sharing agreement with all the different partner organisations.
- loss of control over the product or service provided to the customer. This could cause a fall in quality.
- Partner organisations may also work for competitors, reducing any competitive advantage that the virtual organisation may achieve.

> **Test your understanding 9 – (Integration question)**
>
> Why is IT important in the development of a virtual organisation?

Social and digital marketing

Digital marketing

This refers to marketing that makes use of electronic devices such as personal computers, smartphones and tablets. It may involve the creation of advertisements on websites, through social media sites (see social media marketing below) and smartphone apps, as well as the use of emails to existing and prospective customers.

There are two main types of digital marketing:

- **push** – the company sends a message to prospective customers without the customer requesting information. Examples would include adverts on web pages and blogs.
- **pull** – the consumer actively seeks out the marketing material. Examples include web searches and websites. Note that businesses often pay major search engines in order for their websites to be displayed prominently in relevant search results.

Digital marketing has a number of advantages over traditional marketing, including:

- lower cost (often)
- easy customisation to individual customers
- wider audience reached
- allows customer interaction

Social media marketing

This refers to the process of advertising through social media sites, such as Twitter and Facebook. As well as the placing of traditional advertisements within the social media sites, social media marketing attempts to create content that attracts attention and encourages readers to share it with their social networks (sometimes referred to as electronic word of mouth (eWoM)).

This approach has several benefits to the organisation, including:

- Improved communication between companies and their customers, with the organisation able to contact individual consumers directly. This may strengthen their relationship, increasing customer loyalty.

- Social network sites typically allow individual followers to repost comments made about the company or its products. This allows information about the company and its products to spread via eWoM, reaching a larger target audience quickly and cheaply.

- Social networking sites contain vast amounts of information on users. This data can be analysed to enable companies to target advertising to those individuals most likely to want their products or services. This will significantly increase the effectiveness of the company's advertising.

- Many companies pay individuals with large numbers of online followers to review or promote their products. This enables positive information about their product to reach the maximum number of prospective customers possible.

Note that organisations have to be careful when using social media for advertising purposes. While positive information about their products and services can be shared online by users, the same can also happen with negative reviews, potentially damaging the company's brand.

Illustration 7 – Social marketing success

In late 2013, Starbucks launched an online initiative through Twitter that allowed users to buy coffee for friends online.

The tweet-a-coffee campaign allowed Twitter users in the US to send a $5 gift card to a friend through the social media site.

Within 2 months, Starbucks had details of over 54,000 Twitter users linked to their Starbucks accounts and had generated over $180,000 in purchases from the campaign.

Information technology and e-business

Illustration 8 – Social marketing failure

In 2012, McDonalds attempted to promote its brand and engage customers on social media by encouraging them to post messages on Twitter including the term #mcdstories.

Unfortunately for McDonalds, many users opted to post bad experiences they had had at McDonalds restaurants, meaning that McDonalds was, essentially, paying to promote a trend that was damaging their brand image.

Illustration - Social marketing failure

Following the 2014 MH370 and MH17 air tragedies which killed over 500 people, Malaysia Airlines launched an ill-conceived social media marketing campaign named 'My Ultimate Bucket List'. The campaign offered Australian and New Zealand contestants the chance to win free flight tickets to attract them to use the airline. The campaign sparked outrage among those families who had lost loved ones, and resulted in the airline changing the name of the competition.

8 Disruptive Technologies

A disruptive technology can be defined as one that displaces an established technology and shakes up the industry, or a ground-breaking product that creates a completely new industry.

The term was first used by Clayton M. Christensen, a professor at Harvard Business School, in 1997 in his book "The Innovator's Dilemma". Christensen wrote of two categories of new technologies: sustaining and disruptive.

Sustaining – a sustaining technology relies on incremental improvements to an already established technology. It helps the organisation to make the product more appealing to the existing market and thus gives a degree of competitive advantage.

For example, in the cosmetics industry standard nail polish was superseded by quick-dry nail polish. In the world of music, the compact disc (CD) quickly became the main format for purchasing music, replacing vinyl and audio cassette.

Disruptive – although the term might sound negative, it is so-called because it can lack refinement, may well have performance problems (because it is new), might appeal only to a limited audience, and may not yet have a proven practical application. It also has the potential to change an industry in a highly significant way.

Historic examples of disruptive technologies include:

- The personal computer, which displaced the typewriter and changed forever the way we work and communicate
- Mobile phones (or cell phones) which disrupted the fixed landline telecoms industry
- Smartphones which, because of the available apps, disrupted not only the cell phone and Personal Digital Assistant (PDA) markets, but also MP3 players, pocket cameras, calculators and GPS devices
- Cloud computing, which has disrupted the market for traditional data storage
- Music sites such as iTunes, which meant that downloading music quickly became the preferred method of purchase as opposed to a hard copy in the form of a CD. This was then superseded by streaming services offered by organisations such as Spotify and Deezer.

Examples of possible future disruptive technologies include:

- The driverless car, a vehicle which will drive itself and not rely on a human being to operate it. Whilst traditional car manufacturers such as BMW and Ford are putting much research effort into making the concept a reality for the mainstream market, it is also bringing new competitors into the industry, such as Google and Apple
- Virgin Galactic, a spaceflight company within Richard Branson's Virgin Group, which is looking to offer suborbital space flights to space tourists. The initial target date for the maiden flight was 2009, but this has been delayed on a number of occasions, most significantly by the loss of one of its aircraft, the *VSS Enterprise*, in October 2014
- High speed travel, such as the Hyperloop One prototype propulsion system being created by Tesla founder Elon Musk. It is claimed that such a system could reduce the time taken to travel from London to Edinburgh to 50 minutes
- Continued development in renewable energy sources, such as concentrated solar power, wind turbines, photovoltaic cells and wave power, all aimed at reducing the Earth's reliance on traditional fossil fuels
- Artificial Intelligence (AI), a term which is used when machines copy the cognitive functions of the human brain in learning and solving problems.

Information technology and e-business

The strategic considerations in such circumstances will be similar for both existing organisations within an industry and those that are looking to diversify or, indeed, develop the industry – there is enormous potential reward, but also considerable risk!

For example, car manufacturers have invested millions of dollars in research and development to create the driverless vehicle, and will also have other barriers to overcome to make the product a reality (such as gaining government approval, getting access to all roads including inner cities and motorways, re-establishing the position with regards to insurance, persuading customers that it is safe, desirable and represents value for money, etc.). The potential reward of making such a concept a reality is enormous, but there is clearly significant risk as well. There may well be the following discussions to manage that risk:

- What are the key risks? For example, if the technology should fail and people are killed?
- How can the risk be shared? For example, entering a Joint Venture with another motor manufacturer
- What if a new competitor emerges with a superior offering that consumers prefer, such as Apple?
- Do we want to take a lead and try to define the market, or is it less risky to be a follower and be a second generation player once the rules of the market have been established?

For organisations that are possibly about to be disrupted by emerging competitors, the same issues will apply, and management will need to make decisions about how their organisation will react. Failure to act appropriately could be disastrous.

Apple v Nokia

In 2007, Nokia was the market leader in the mobile phone market, selling over 435 million units in that year and enjoying a global market share of around 38%, according to the analyst firm Gartner. Its handsets had mass appeal, and the company's focus was on making that hardware better and better, keeping competitors such as Motorola, Sony Ericsson, and Research in Motion (makers of the Blackberry) firmly behind them.

In that same year, Apple launched the iPhone.

By 2013, just 6 years later, Apple was selling 5 times as many units as Nokia, resulting in the latter company leaving the industry altogether when it sold its mobile phone business to Microsoft for $7 billion. The other companies mentioned above also struggled, and popular brands (in addition to iPhone) were being made by companies such as Samsung, LG and HTC.

Commentators suggest that the introduction of the smartphone was a strategic act of genius on the part of Steve Jobs, CEO of Apple. He recognised at an early stage the threat to the company's success story of the new millennium, the iPod, in that phones that could play music would make the need for two devices redundant. He therefore set about making the software of the mobile phone the focus, with its user-friendly touchscreen and App store technology, rather than the hardware as favoured by Nokia. Consumers flocked to it to such an extent that Apple's cumulative revenue from sales of the iPhone is expected to hit $1 trillion at some point in 2018.

Nokia failed to see the threat of the disruptive technology early enough, and decided to exit the industry whilst its business still had value.

Test your understanding 10

H has recently created an online system that allows customers to send very large files to each other by email – a feature that is not present in many standard email systems.

H charges customers a small fee every time they use the system, rather than requiring them to buy and download the software.

Which feature of Web 2.0 is this an example of?

A   Global networking effects
B   Competence syndication
C   Mashups
D   Software as a service

Test your understanding 11

Which THREE of the following are typical features of a virtual organisation?

A   Significant reliance on technology
B   High asset setup costs
C   Relatively low staff levels
D   Low levels of outsourcing to third parties
E   High degree of control over quality
F   Ability to compete with larger, established rivals

Information technology and e-business

Test your understanding 12 – AAP – (Case style)

AAP operates an estate agency business in a northern European country, M. An estate agency business arranges the selling, renting or management of houses and other properties.

AAP has been in business for the last 30 years and has 10 offices located throughout Country M. It specialises in marketing and selling high value, exclusive residential properties in Country M. AAP has seen the number of its property sales decline steadily in the last five years. AAP's Board believes that this is due to the current economic downturn and its impact on residential housing sales rather than as a result of any underlying problems within AAP itself.

AAP uses a standard estate agency software package to manage its buyer enquiries, property viewings and marketing. AAP also uses the estate agency software package to automatically match buyer enquiry details against its database of properties. AAP does not have a customer database to record customer information.

AAP has a website on which it advertises all of its properties located throughout Country M. However, this website only allows customers to view the basic property details such as internal photographs and floor layout. In order to obtain more detailed information on each property, customers must visit one of AAP's offices or telephone one of the agents in order to be sent a printed version of the property details. AAP has an email system which allows customers to contact its offices. The email system is also the main form of internal communication between employees and is often used to transfer files from one office to another. The estate agency software package and the website are not linked. Therefore, if any changes are made to the information held on the estate agency software, this change has to be duplicated on the website. This has, in the past, led to incorrect information being viewed by customers on the website, as the information was not completely up to date.

Until now, investment in information technology has been minimal and the Board of AAP has not considered information technology to be a critical aspect of its business. AAP's Board has never considered developing an e-business strategy as it believes that its main strategic priority is enhancing AAP's reputation of high quality, face to face direct customer service. The Managing Director stated at a recent board meeting that 'we must retain our focus upon keeping our customers happy. Developing our website to sell our properties is merely a distraction from what we do and what our customers want.'

The Marketing Director is concerned that AAP is not keeping up to date with technological developments and that AAP should use its information systems more strategically. Having researched a wide range of websites, the Marketing Director has identified a range of Web 2.0 technologies that AAP could use to improve its own website. He is also aware of a new technology development which enables potential home buyers to receive property details whilst viewing a property, by using location-based applications on their mobile phones.

The Marketing Director intends to write a report to the Board of Directors outlining his research and his belief that AAP could benefit significantly from developing an e-business strategy.

Required:

The Marketing Director has asked you to provide him with a report in which you:

(i) explain the criticality of information systems to AAP, using McFarlan's strategic grid and why the investment in information systems by AAP should be a strategic decision.

(ii) advise on the benefits AND problems of developing an e-business strategy for AAP.

(iii) Recommend, with reasons, TWO different applications of Web 2.0 technology that AAP could adopt.

(45 minutes)

Test your understanding 13 – Good Sports – (Case style)

Good Sports Limited is an independent sports goods retailer owned and operated by two partners, Alan and Bob. The sports retailing business in the UK has undergone a major change over the past ten years. First of all the supply side has been transformed by the emergence of a few global manufacturers of the core sports products, such as training shoes and football shirts. This consolidation has made them increasingly unwilling to provide good service to the independent sportswear retailers too small to buy in sufficiently large quantities. These independent retailers can stock popular global brands, but have to order using the Internet and have no opportunity to meet the manufacturer's sales representatives. Secondly, UK's sportswear retailing has undergone significant structural change with the rapid growth of a small number of national retail chains with the buying power to offset the power of the global manufacturers. These retail chains stock a limited range of high-volume branded products and charge low prices the independent retailer cannot hope to match.

Good Sports has survived by becoming a specialist niche retailer catering for less popular sports such as cricket and hockey. They are able to offer the specialist advice and stock the goods that their customers want. Increasingly since 2000 Good Sports has become aware of the growing impact of e-business in general, and e-retailing in particular. They employed a specialist website designer and created an online purchasing facility for their customers. The results were less than impressive, with the Internet search engines not picking up the company website. The seasonal nature of Good Sports' business, together with the variations in sizes and colours needed to meet an individual customer's needs, meant that the sales volumes were insufficient to justify the costs of running the site.

Bob, however, is convinced that developing an e-business strategy suited to the needs of the independent sports retailer such as Good Sports will be key to business survival. He has been encouraged by the growing interest of customers in other countries to the service and product range they offer. He is also aware of the need to integrate an e-business strategy with their current marketing, which to date has been limited to the sponsorship of local sports teams and advertisements taken in specialist sports magazines. Above all he wants to avoid head-on competition with the national retailers and their emphasis on popular branded sportswear sold at retail prices that are below the cost price at which Good Sports can buy the goods.

Required:

(a) Provide the partners with a short report on the advantages and disadvantages to Good Sports of developing an e-business strategy and the processes most likely to be affected by such a strategy.

(20 minutes)

(b) Good Sports Limited has successfully followed a niche strategy to date. Assess the extent to which an appropriate e-business strategy could help support such a niche strategy.

(15 minutes)

Test your understanding 14 – H plc – (Case style)

H plc is a business that runs a national chain of high-street stores selling a wide range of furniture and household goods. While not a market leader, H has always traded profitably due to targeting the niche market for high-value, designer homewares.

H's revenues and profits have been static for several years and the directors are under pressure from investors to find ways of increasing shareholder returns.

The market for household goods is a saturated one, but the Sales Director (SD) has identified that H could start selling goods online. None of H's competitors have a significant online presence and H itself only has a basic website that lists locations of its stores.

The Managing Director is uncertain about this approach. He is aware that H has had problems implementing information systems in the past. Most recently, the company attempted to implement an online stock system, which would have allowed stores to check stock levels in other, nearby, H stores. This was in response to a number of customer requests.

The system was abandoned due to spiralling costs and problems with the software, which was written in-house by H plc's small IT department.

The SD feels that the problems with the earlier projects were caused by a lack of control. H plc has never employed an IT director and the SD has therefore recommended that if H decides to expand into online retailing, this role will need to be filled.

You have been contacted by the SD and asked to send him an email which can be used at a Board meeting later today.

Information technology and e-business

The email needs to:

- Distinguish between the different levels of information systems strategy, using H plc as an example
- Identify the problems that H plc may encounter when launching its online retail website
- Explain the need for IT to be a strategic decision within H plc

Required:

Draft the email as requested.

(45 minutes)

9 Summary

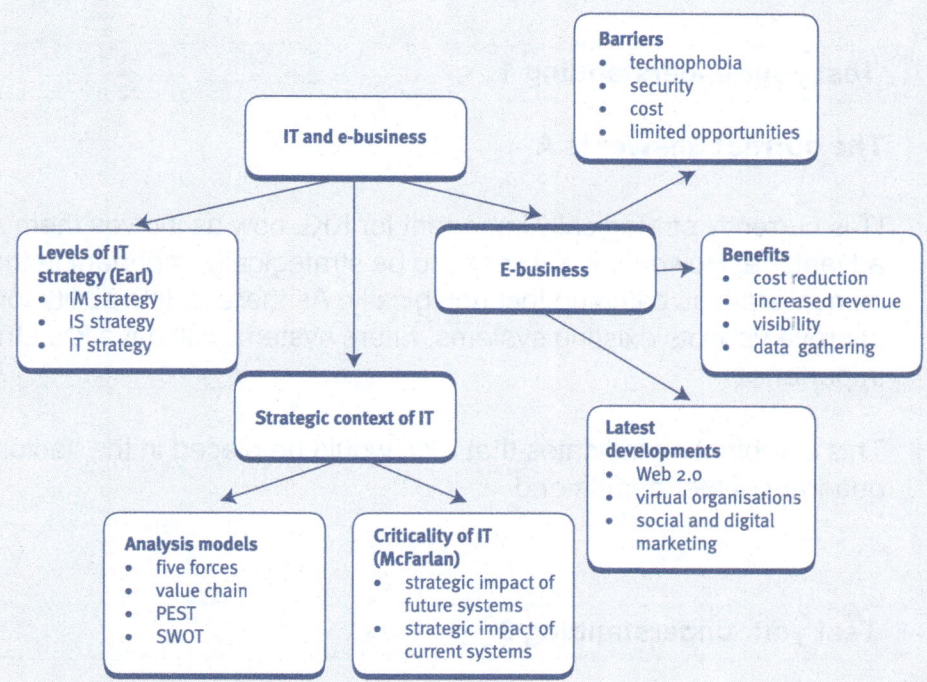

Information technology and e-business

Test your understanding answers

Test your understanding 1

The correct answer is A

IT is currently strategically important for KKL now as it gives them a cost advantage. However it will cease to be strategically important in the future as rival stations catch up technologically. As there is little ability for KKL to improve upon its existing systems, future systems will have low strategic importance.

This combination indicates that KKL would be placed in the 'factory' quadrant of McFarlan's grid

Test your understanding 2

The correct answer is B

A and C are information management strategies, while D is an information technology strategy.

Test your understanding 3

The correct answer is A

The Board has little experience of IT, meaning that hiring someone with appropriate skills will be useful. The website will need constantly updating, needing someone that is skilled and up to date with changing IT.

The cost of developing the website is low and, even though it could over-run, it seems unlikely that this would outweigh the cost of hiring an IT director.

P feels that the sales from its website will be relatively low and will not be used by many consumers. It certainly does not appear to be the basis for P's competition in the market.

Finally, IT is not necessarily expected by key stakeholders in P. P has established that most of its customers will be ambivalent towards the website, and the directors/shareholders are uncertain about its usefulness.

chapter 9

Test your understanding 4

The correct answer is C

Any organisations wishing to break into the market in country H will need to invest in similar online shopping and distribution systems. This will increase the cost of entry into the market (the barriers to entry), reducing the chance of new entrants.

There is no obvious reason why the new system should affect the power of substitutes, or why it would increase the power of J's customers. In fact, offering this additional convenience to customers may actually help to 'tie in' customers and reduce the chance of them moving to J's rivals.

Test your understanding 5

The correct answer is D

The EDI system will improve the system for sourcing and purchasing materials. This is procurement.

Note that inbound logistics refers to inventory management – not the purchasing of inventory itself.

411

Information technology and e-business

Test your understanding 6 – (Integration question)

All of the following technologies could help either to save costs or provide enhanced (and differentiated) service.

- Use of digital cameras to photograph property. The images would then be made available over the web.
- Video of properties that can be downloaded or viewed over the web.
- Graphics programs designed to make floor diagrams easy to produce.
- Standard descriptive phrases ('deceptively large' – or do they mean 'deceptively small'?) that can be used for property write-ups.
- A database of properties, searchable by price, bedrooms, type, area, age, etc.
- Properties linked to an interactive map.
- A database of recent property prices in the area.
- Buyer requirements database.
- Automatic mailing lists to circulate information to buyers.
- Electronic appointments system.
- Computerised accounting system used for property management.

Test your understanding 7

The correct answer is B

B's website allows them to conduct commercial transactions electronically, which indicates that they have moved past the 'web presence' stage. However, their lack of intelligence gathering facilities indicates that they have yet to reach 'integrated e-commerce'.

Test your understanding 8

The correct answer is A

EDI usually involves linking an organisation's systems with those of major suppliers or customers. As these would typically be other businesses, it would most likely be classified as B2B.

chapter 9

Test your understanding 9 – (Integration question)

A key element in supporting the virtual organisation is IT. This is mainly through systems that facilitate co-ordination and communication, decision-making and the sharing of knowledge, skills and resources.

Information systems can reduce the number of levels of management in an organisation by enabling managers to control larger numbers of workers spread over a wider geographical area, and by giving lower-level employees more decision-making authority. It is no longer necessary for these employees to work standard hours each day, nor work in an office or even in the same country as their manager.

With the emergence of global networks, team members can collaborate closely even from distant locations.

Electronic communications systems (such as emails) allow for improved co-ordination and sharing of information between different partner organisations.

IT and IS allows the virtual organisation to monitor the activities of its partner organisations and ensure that they are meeting the needs of customers.

Test your understanding 10

The correct answer is D

By definition.

Test your understanding 11

The correct answers are: A, C and F

Note that virtual organisations typically have relatively low investment costs, as they have little need for machinery or distribution (this is all undertaken by partner organisations). However, to co-ordinate all the various partner organisation requires significant reliance on IT.

Test your understanding 12 – AAP – (Case style)

Report
To: Marketing Director
From: A.N. Accountant
Subject: Web 2.0 and information system issues for AAP

Introduction

This report will examine several issues surrounding IT within AAP and the future effects of issues such as Web 2.0.

(i) McFarlan's strategic grid

McFarlan's strategic grid can be used to identify an organisation's current and future dependence on information systems. The model is based upon two axes which evaluate the strategic impact of the current systems used and the strategic impact of future systems.

Using this model, AAP's current information system is likely to be classified as 'Support'. The existing system used by AAP is not important to the organisation's strategic development and, as it stands, unless there are significant developments in bespoke software or investment in customer databases and mobile applications, then the current information systems are not likely to be a significant strategic impact on AAP. However, AAP is recognising the growing importance of its information systems as a means to improve its competitive position. The use of web technologies and e-commerce is likely to have a high potential to contribute to AAP's strategic objectives.

It could also be argued that the information systems in the estate agency business are 'Strategic' according to McFarlan's grid, as the current information systems are in fact critical to the smooth running of the business and its day to day activities. Future developments are vital to its success and should be a key part of its strategic objectives.

The investment in IS by AAP should be a strategic decision as the effect of not investing could have a significant long-term detrimental effect. Already AAP has experienced a slowdown in the growth of profitability and this decline could continue. Whilst face to face customer contact is important, it should no longer be the sole focus for the company. AAP needs to continue to be innovative and it cannot sit back and wait for customers to telephone its offices.

The cost of IT/IS investment may involve high levels of expenditure for AAP. If this investment is not carefully planned and managed then there is a high risk of costly mistakes. Therefore, a strategic perspective is required to ensure that investment is carefully planned and resources are not wasted on information systems investment.

AAP must find a way to differentiate itself from its competitors. In the current economic climate the need for differentiation in order to win business from its competitors will be crucial for its survival. Strategic investment in information systems could give AAP a competitive advantage. As such, it should be part of AAP's strategic decision making process. This is not a decision that should be taken on an ad-hoc basis. The use of AAP's information systems could be a core driver of its competitive advantage and therefore is a critical part of its strategic decision making process.

Technology in this industry is rapidly developing, with the introduction of mobile applications for home buyers and the various Web 2.0 technologies which can be used. Therefore, AAP must continually monitor and develop its information systems to remain competitive and up to date. Although customers may want a good face to face service it is also likely that they will be increasingly moving towards a greater reliance on information systems to assist them in researching and reviewing properties. Therefore, the speed in the development in technology and the fact that key stakeholders are embracing this technology means that AAP must consider investment in information systems as a strategic decision.

The current developments in the use of systems within the industry are forcing AAP to reassess its operations. Leadership for the current developments is coming from the top of the organisation, via the Marketing Director. Information systems are opening up new possibilities for the estate agency industry. Without investment in new Information Systems, AAP may lose customers and see a further decline in profits. Therefore, investment in IS can be considered to be strategic as the long-term impact of not investing will threaten the future success of the company.

Information systems are likely to be highly complex, requiring the integration of many different forms of technology, such as internal estate agency software, customer and property databases, intranets, external links to other services and websites and website management. Therefore, this will require extremely careful planning and management which must be done at a strategic level otherwise it is likely that technology will become out of control and unmanageable. There are two further considerations for AAP, which are:

(1) Does AAP have the funding to support the necessary expenditure?

(2) Does AAP's management team have the necessary expertise to manage a more sophisticated IT system?

(ii) **Benefits and problems with e-business**

E-business has been defined as 'the transformation of key business processes through the use of internet technologies'. The general estate agency business environment has clearly been affected by the development of e-business, with the recent technological developments identified by the Marketing Director.

Benefits to AAP

An e-business strategy ensures that information systems are considered by the organisation to be a critical and strategic aspect of its business survival. This will focus all staff and management attention on its importance and significance to AAP.

An e-business strategy would allow AAP to be more responsive to its customer needs and improve its customer relationship management through integrating and improving its business processes to focus on its customer needs both face to face and via technological interface. It will enable customers to gain information in a way they prefer, at a time they want, perhaps out of office hours, and this may result in customers recommending AAP to friends. Therefore, the customer experience will be improved.

Using e-business will present AAP with potential new business opportunities – including the advertising and selling of overseas properties. A global presence rather than just a national presence could be achieved if e-business was considered.

By using its website more effectively with the development of an integrated customer database, AAP can use e-business to understand customer buying behaviour more effectively and build up a detailed picture of customer requirements and needs such as popular locations, space requirements and individual customer tastes in types and styles of property required.

AAP would have a greater ability to interact with customers across a range of media – emails, blogs, social media, feedback forms; allowing greater dialogue with more customers via media that they are likely to use regularly.

Other competitors are likely to already be doing this, so AAP will be left behind if it does not follow an e-business strategy.

Sale and purchase of a property is a process that most people undertake infrequently, therefore their experience is vital if customers are to be satisfied. The ability to access AAP's website to get all the required information could result in a positive experience and repeat business at a later date.

Problems

The Board of AAP believes that the key to AAP's continued survival is excellent customer service, as it supplies a specialist service to a niche market. The nature of the business means that face to face contact is crucial in moving customer awareness into action. Therefore, this limits the ability of e-business to replace such personal contact, particularly with older, more traditional buyers.

Cost of investment in e-business may be prohibitive. However, as AAP already has an online presence and uses technology to some extent already with its estate agency software, additional e-business activities are therefore unlikely to be too costly for AAP.

A focus upon technology and not on customers' needs may reduce AAP's personal service which may put some customers off.

Currently, AAP is likely to have a lack of expertise in e-business. This is something which it must get right but currently is not likely to have the expertise to develop an e-business strategy. Lack of current expertise in AAP of e-business may cause resistance amongst AAP's staff who feel that they should be focusing upon the customer and not on e-business and technology.

The ability to effectively increase the customer base as house purchase and sales is an infrequent transaction for most home owners. There may be limited opportunity for repeat business for several years.

Some staff and managers may be sceptical about the benefits that e-business can offer AAP. However, conversely, many younger staff may welcome and embrace the change.

(iii) **Web 2.0**

Web 2.0 refers to the generation of web developments that facilitate communication, information sharing, interoperability and collaboration using the World Wide Web (WWW). It refers to the cumulative changes in the way that technology developers and end-users utilise the WWW.

The two Web 2.0 technologies recommended for AAP in the first instance are:

(1) **'Mash-ups'**

This is where websites can now mix and match their web content and services to suit customer needs. For example, AAP can use interactive maps from geographical information programs from software providers such as Google Earth. These could be used together with links to local government information on school catchment areas or information on local planning application processes. Mash-ups allow individual websites to make use of a range of interactive technologies to enhance the website for optimum customer interaction, without heavy investment. For an estate agency business this is particularly useful as links to external geographical location or information sites are important informational and advice tools for potential customers.

(2) **Blogs – Information Sharing**

An internal blog is a web log that any employee can view. Many blogs are also communal, allowing anyone to post to them. The informal nature of blogs may encourage:

- Employee participation
- Free discussion of issues
- Collective intelligence
- Direct communication between various layers of an organisation
- A sense of community

Internal blogs may be used in lieu of meetings and e-mail discussions, and can be especially useful when the people involved are in different locations, or have conflicting schedules. Blogs may also allow individuals who otherwise would not have been aware of or invited to participate in a discussion to contribute their expertise.

An external blog is a publicly available blog where company employees, teams, or spokespersons share their views. It could be used by AAP to announce new properties on the market or to announce new services or to explain and clarify policies, or to react on public criticism on certain issues. It also allows a window to AAP's culture and is often treated more informally than traditional press releases, though a corporate blog often tries to accomplish similar goals as press releases. In some corporate blogs, all posts go through a review before they are posted. Some corporate blogs, but not all, allow comments to be made to the posts.
In addition, other forms of Web 2.0 technology which could be discussed are:

Social media

By using popular social media network sites such as Facebook, Myspace, Twitter and YouTube, AAP could advertise its services. AAP could set up its own Facebook page where customers could access the latest company adverts and messages and also access message boards where they could contact AAP directly.

Peer to peer networking (P2P)

This is a technique used to share files over the internet or within a closed set of users. As AAP does not make use of an intranet, this could be a very useful form of Web 2.0 technology for AAP to adopt. Currently, email is the main form of communication and file transfer between staff in different locations. P2P would distribute files across many machines meaning that files would be accessible across the network and not just on one user's machine.

Competence syndication

AAP could open up a portion of its website for use by other firms of property related companies such as furniture removal companies, lawyers, interior designers and builders to advertise their services.

Test your understanding 13 – Good Sports – (Case style)

GOOD SPORTS

(a) **To:** Good Sports Limited

From: xxxxx

E-business strategy

Clearly, the markets that Good Sports operates in are being affected by the development of e-business and its experiences to date are mixed to say the least. In many ways the advantages and disadvantages of e-business are best related to the benefit the customer gets from the activity.

- First, through integrating and accelerating business processes, e-business technologies enable response and delivery times to be speeded up.

- Second, there are new business opportunities for information-based products and services.

- Third, websites can be linked with customer databases and provide much greater insights into customer buying behaviour and needs.

- Fourth, there is far greater ability for interaction with the customer, which enables customisation and a dialogue to be developed.

- Finally, customers may themselves form communities able to contact one another.

There is considerable evidence to show how small operators like Good Sports are able to base their whole strategy on e-business and achieve high rates of growth. The key to Good Sports' survival is customer service – in strategic terms they are very much niche marketers supplying specialist service and advice to a small section of the local market. The nature of the business means that face-to-face contact is crucial in moving customers from awareness to action (AIDA – awareness, interest, desire and action). There are therefore limits to the ability of e-business to replace such contact.

Yours, etc.

(b) Good Sports has pursued a conscious niche or focus differentiation strategy, seeking to serve a local market in a way that isolates it from the competition of the large national sports good retailers competing on the basis of supplying famous brands at highly competitive prices. Does it make strategic sense for Good Sports to make the heavy investment necessary to supply goods online? Will this enhance its ability to supply its chosen market?

In terms of price, e-business is bringing much greater price transparency – the problem for companies like Good Sports is that customers may use their expertise to research into a particular type and brand of sports equipment and then simply search the Internet for the cheapest supply. Porter, in an article examining the impact of the Internet, argues that rather than making strategy obsolete it has in fact made it more important. The Internet has tended to weaken industry profitability and made it more difficult to hold onto operational advantages. Choosing which customers you serve and how are even more critical decisions.

However, the personal advice and performance side of the business could be linked to new ways of promoting the product and communicating with the customer. The development of customer communities referred to above could be a real way of increasing customer loyalty. The partners are anxious to avoid head-on competition with the national retailers. One way of increasing the size and strength of the niche they occupy is to use the Internet as a means of targeting their particular customers and providing insights into the use and performance of certain types of equipment by local clubs and users. There is considerable scope for innovation that enhances the service offered to their customers. As always there is a need to balance the costs and benefits of time spent. The Internet can provide a relatively cost-effective way of providing greater service to their customers. There is little in the scenario to suggest they have reached saturation point in their chosen niche market. Overall there is a need for Good Sports to decide what and where its market is and how this can be improved by the use of e-business.

Information technology and e-business

Test your understanding 14 – H plc – (Case style)

To: SD
From: A.N. Other
Date: 15/03/XX
Subject: Information systems in H plc

As requested, please find below my thoughts on the issues you asked about.

(a) **Distinguish between the levels of IS strategy within H plc**

According to Earl, there are three levels of information systems strategy.

Information systems (IS) strategy

In the scenario, H plc is under pressure to grow its returns to investors. This is an over-riding business objective.

IS strategy involves deciding on which systems, broadly, will enable H plc to achieve this objective. The SD's suggestion to expand into online retailing is an example of this.

Information management (IM) strategy

This looks at the roles of management and other members of staff within the overall IS strategy – in other words, who controls and uses the information systems.

For H plc, it will involve deciding on how existing staff will be used in the new IT system, such as who will be responsible for inventory data entry. It will also include the recruitment of an IT director to oversee the process.

Information technology (IT) strategy

This level looks at the practical application of the IS strategy. Given that H plc has decided to expand into online retail, IT strategy will specify the technological requirements of these new systems.

For H plc, this may include new hardware, such as computers and servers. Inventory control and website design software will also be required. This will need to be written internally or purchased externally.

(b) **Identification of problems H plc may encounter when launching online**

As with any major project, there will be problems that H will face with its proposed move into online retailing. These may include:

Setup and running costs

Investors in H are keen to see an increase in their returns. However, the cost of setting up and running an online retailing system may be significant.

H plc will need to determine whether the additional profit it can make by reaching new customers online will exceed these costs. Certainly in the short term the setup costs may well mean that shareholder returns fall.

Any further investment in staff will also increase the IT costs to the company.

Lack of in-house IT resources

The business currently lacks an IT director to take control of the project. While the company may be able to hire someone quickly to fill this role, they will lack experience of H's business by the time the new project is started.

The current IT department is small. They may well lack the time or skills for a project of this magnitude. This indicates further investment will be required to hire additional staff or to buy the new systems from external software houses.

It should also be noted that an online retail system would require H plc to have precise information about its stock levels. It currently does not have an automated inventory control system as this was abandoned.

Lack of customer interest

It is always possible that H's customers will not be interested in purchasing goods online. They may, for example, wish to try out furniture or physically see it for themselves rather than buying it online.

It is unclear from the scenario whether the SD has undertaken any market research. This would be vital before making the decision about beginning online retailing, to avoid launching an expensive website that fails to attract customers.

Technophobia

Given the lack of IT currently in place at H, employees may not see the need for new IT systems and may resist being retrained.

In addition, the MD has expressed concerns about the launch of a new IT system, given the problems H has faced in the past. A project of this scale will require management support in order to be successful.

Security concerns

As H will be processing transactions through its website, it will need to ensure that customers are protected from viruses and that their details are protected from hackers.

(c) **Explanation of the need for IT to be a strategic decision in H plc.**

It is crucial that H has information systems represented at the strategic or board level for several reasons:

Cost of IT/IS

Setting up an online retail store will involve high levels of expenditure for H. There is the risk of costly mistakes if it is not carefully managed. This is evidenced by the failure of its inventory control system.

Failure of such a major project could have a significant impact on the company's financial position.

Competitive advantage

The market H operates in is described as saturated. It will be difficult for H to increase its market share unless it finds a way to differentiate itself.

If the website is a success, it will give H a competitive advantage over its rivals and as such it should be part of H's strategic decision-making process.

Stakeholders

Expansion of H is of great interest to H's shareholders. As such it is crucial that the directors monitor its progress.

In addition, customers are currently unable to check the stock of goods within H plc. They may be very interested in a system that would enable them to save unnecessary journeys into H's stores for goods that are not in stock.

Fast–moving

Technology is a fast-moving area and even if becomes a successful first mover in the market by selling online, competitors are likely to follow H into the online market.

As such, H's IT systems will need to be continually monitored and kept up-to-date to ensure it remains competitive.

I hope this helps, but if you need any further information, please let me know.

Kind regards

A. N. Other

Information technology and e-business

chapter 10

Information for advantage and knowledge management

Chapter learning objectives

Lead	Component
E1. Evaluate the information systems requirements for successful strategic implementation	(a) Evaluate the information systems required to sustain the organisation (b) Advise managers on the development of strategies for knowledge management
E2. Evaluate the opportunities for the use of IT and IS for the organisation, including Big Data	(a) Evaluate the impact of IT/IS on an organisation and its strategy (b) Evaluate the strategic and competitive impact of information systems, including the potential contribution of Big Data.

Information for advantage and knowledge management

Indicative syllabus content

- The classifications of knowledge.
- Learning organisations.
- Knowledge management systems and knowledge-based organisations.
- Competing through exploiting information, rather than technology (e.g. use of databases to identify potential customers or market segments, and the collection, analysis, storage and management of data).
- Contemporary developments in the commercial use of the internet (e.g. e-business, virtual organisations and Web 2.0, Big Data, social and other forms of digital marketing).
- The role of Big Data and digitisation in knowledge-based organisations.

chapter 10

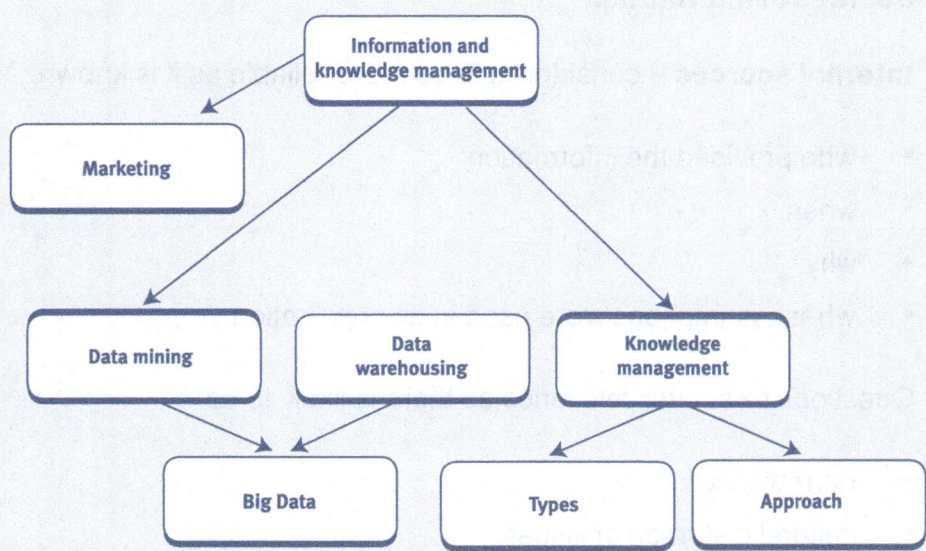

1 Marketing

In order to meet the critical success factors in target segments and develop sustainable competitive advantage over competitors, information is needed.

The systematic gathering, recording and analysing of information about problems relating to the making of goods and services is a crucial early stage in strategic planning.

The gathering of information is therefore an essential activity for a business in order to get to know their market and to remain ahead of the competition. Information is also required to monitor the success of any strategy.

Information issues

The two prime characteristics of information are relevance and reliability. The management accountant is involved in each.

Relevant information assists the decision-making process – the management accountant decides what is relevant.

Reliable information is as accurate as needed – the management accountant decides again and establishes control systems to ensure that accuracy is achieved.

Sources of information

Internal sources – considered to be more reliable as it is known:

- who provided the information
- when
- why
- what assumptions were used in its preparation.

Questions exist over relevance as there is likely to be:

- narrow focus
- cultural distortion of issues.

External sources – considered to be more relevant as a wider range of issues with less cultural distortion. However the 'who, why, when and what' is questionable this time as these are unknown factors.

2 Data warehousing

A data warehouse is a subject-oriented, integrated, time-variant, non-volatile collection of data in support of management's decision-making process.

Put more simply, it is a large relational database that collates a vast amount of data from a variety of sources and makes it available to end-users in an understandable fashion.

A data warehouse supports information processing by providing a solid platform of integrated, historical data from which analysis can be done.

It is:

- a database
- a data extraction tool
- a decision support system
- other analysis tools which extract data from the organisation's production database, reformat and load it into a database designed for querying with an on-line analytical processing systems (OLAP). OLAP allows users to dynamically extract pertinent summary information.

The conventional data warehousing model is a system in which a large centralised store of consolidated business data is maintained by constant updates from the operational systems (branches/stores).

Since operational data are likely to reside in a range of very different systems, e.g. cash register tapes, invoice printing systems and order entry systems, the process of collecting the data needs to be customised and automated. Each store or branch must be responsible for ensuring the timely and accurate delivery of this information. In enterprises where the information is managed centrally, the problem is simpler.

For very large enterprises, the act of centralising all data in a single data warehouse may not be feasible or may even be impossible.

The purpose of data warehousing

Data warehouses traditionally have three primary purposes:

(1) Presentation of standard reports and graphs, consolidating data from a variety of sources into a standard format.
(2) Enabling of comparisons between different factors – for example, how have customer buying habits changed over the last several years?
(3) To allow data mining (see below).

3 Data mining

Data mining is the analysis of data to unearth unsuspected or unknown relationships, patterns and associations.

There are many different definitions of data mining. Almost all of them involve using advanced analytical techniques to discover useful relationships in large databases. Some people's definition of data mining is linked with their definition of data warehousing. **Data warehouses are for storing data, not turning it into information, whereas data mining turns data into information.**

For example, the sales records for a particular brand of tennis racquet might, if sufficiently analysed and related to other market data, reveal a seasonal correlation with the purchase of golf equipment by the same people.

The process uses statistical techniques and technologies to discover relationships and then builds models based on them. Data mining results include:

- **Associations** – when one event can be correlated to another event, e.g. beer purchasers buy peanuts a certain percentage of the time.
- **Sequences** – one event leading to another later event, e.g. a rug purchase followed by a purchase of curtains.

- **Classification** – the recognition of patterns and a resulting new organisation of data, e.g. profiles of customers who make purchases.
- **Clustering** – finding and visualising groups of facts not previously known.
- **Forecasting** – simply discovering patterns in the data that can lead to predictions about the future.

There are two main kinds of models in data mining:

(1) **Predictive models** can be used to forecast explicit values, based on patterns determined from known results. For example, from a database of customers who have already responded to a particular offer, a model can be built that predicts which prospects are likely to respond to the same offer.

(2) **Descriptive models** describe patterns in existing data and are generally used to create meaningful subgroups such as demographic clusters. These could then be used for marketing purposes.

Benefits of data warehousing and data mining

- Faster transaction and query execution can provide competitive advantage. A data warehouse is a large database, regularly updated and organised to permit a high level of query activity. Not all organisations will have a need for this; it will depend on the organisation and what it does.
- With relatively small amounts of data, the specialist data warehouse software and hardware will not be required, as downloading subsets of data from production systems to PCs is a workable solution. However, many organisations need to manage large amounts of data which, when properly analysed, can provide information that leads to competitive advantage.

Disadvantages

- The systems used in different departments will often be incompatible, and that is likely to mean that data is in a wide variety of different formats.
- There are likely to be inconsistencies between different databases where duplicated items of data should, in theory, be identical, but in practice are not.
- The data will need to be analysed and 'cleansed' before it can be integrated into a warehouse. This will not be easy, quick or cheap to achieve.

- Incompatible systems may mean that most of the departments will need to be furnished with new hardware and software before they can use the data warehouse. This is likely to be expensive and disruptive to the day-to-day work of each department.

- Almost all staff who want to use the new system will need training.

- Individual departments may use data in widely different ways and require all manner of different reports. It could be very difficult to create a common interface that is capable of delivering information in every format that may be required. Report formats that are only needed in a single department may not be catered for, and this may cause resentment.

- As the new system proves its worth, more and more demands will be made of it, so ongoing maintenance, adequate network bandwidth, sufficient storage space, and highly flexible upgrade capability are all essential.

- With all data in a single main source, it is vital to ensure that effective back-up arrangements are made and strictly adhered to.

Illustration 1 – Tesco

Tesco is the UK's largest supermarket with a 30% market share. In addition it has global interests and is now the world's second most profitable retailer. One of the reasons for the company's success is its loyalty card, the Clubcard.

The Clubcard is used to gather information about the spending patterns of Tesco's customers. Around five billion pieces of information each week are captured, and this number is constantly growing.

This information is stored in an enormous search engine (a data warehouse) that can be accessed by Tesco and other select partners, such as Coca-Cola and Unilever. The information can be used to assess the success of new product launches as well as which demographics of customer are making the purchases.

The system also allows Tesco to tailor its special offers to particular segments of the market. For example, many families shop at several different supermarkets. Clearly, Tesco would prefer customers to only buy their groceries from its stores. To help it achieve this, it can identify common products that are 'missing' from a customer's shopping. They will then send the customer special offers to encourage the customer to buy these goods at Tesco.

At one Tesco store where this approach was adopted, turnover rose by 12%.

Information for advantage and knowledge management

Test your understanding 1

AY plc runs a supermarket chain with stores across country M. AY wished to understand which products its customers purchase in advance of major storms (which frequently hit country M, damaging homes and businesses).

AY operates a loyalty card scheme for its customers and uses this to track their buying habits. Using this data, AY discovered that, as well as obvious products, such as flashlights and candles, sales of breakfast cereal increased by 400% in the days before a major storm.

AY has recently started stocking breakfast cereal in the front of its stores in the run up to a storm, significantly increasing sales.

Which data mining result is this an example of?

A   Association

B   Classification

C   Clustering

D   Sequences

4 Big Data

Big Data is a term for a collection of data which is so large that it becomes difficult to store and process using traditional databases and data processing applications.

Big Data often also includes more than simply financial information and can involve other organisational data (both internal and external) which is often unstructured.

Examples of data that inputs into Big Data systems can include:

- social network traffic
- web server logs
- traffic flow information
- satellite imagery
- streamed audio content
- banking transactions
- web page histories and content
- government documentation
- GPS tracking

- telemetry from vehicles
- financial market data.

The shift to Big Data

Traditionally, businesses gathered structured information on relevant issues from a variety of sources and placed them into a database, or data warehouse.

As the world has increasingly moved towards digitisation (and especially through the growth of the internet), almost all information relating to the organisation and its environment can be stored electronically. The amount of unstructured data generated by electronic interactions increased significantly – through emails, online shopping, text messages, social media sites as well as various electronic devices (such as smartphones) which gather and transmit data. In fact, it is estimated that around 90% of the information in the world today has been created in the last few years.

The amount of data which businesses have to store and interrogate has therefore increased at an exponential rate, requiring new tools and techniques to make the most of them.

Illustration 2 – Big Data

Ford's modern Hybrid Fusion model of car (which has a hybrid petrol/electric engine) generates up to 25 GB of data per hour and the company is experimenting with vehicles that produce ten times that amount. This data can be used for many purposes, including:

- A computer model has been developed that projects CO_2 emissions generated by the fleet of vehicles on roads worldwide for the next 50 years. This helps Ford to balance fuel economy requirements and environmental considerations.

- Mathematical models have analysed millions of possible vehicle combinations to assist in the construction of a technology roadmap which has resulted in the development of new features such as Ford Auto Start-Stop.

- Ford researchers have developed specific tools such as the Ford Fleet Purchase Planner, which analyses fleet customers' needs and identifies their optimal vehicle choice.

The features of Big Data

According to Gartner, Big Data can be described using the '3Vs':

- **Volume** – this refers to the significant amount of data that the organisation needs to store and process. Match.com (an online dating company) estimates that it has 70 terabytes of data about its customers.

- **Variety** – Big Data can come from numerous sources. For example, Match.com (with user permission) also gathers data on users' browser and search histories, viewing habits and purchase histories to build an accurate view of the sort of person the customer might like to date.

- **Velocity** – data is likely to change on a regular basis and needs to be continually updated. For Match.com, new customers will join the service, or existing customers will find their needs and wants from a partner may change. Match.com needs to continually gather data to ensure that they are able to deal with this.

Another V which is sometimes added by organisations to the above list is:

- **Veracity (truthfulness)** – it is vital that the organisation gathers data that is accurate. Failure to do so will make analysis meaningless. Match.com has found that when gathering customer data, customers may lie to present themselves in the most positive light possible to prospective partners. This will lead to inaccurate matches. Using non-biased sources of information (such as purchasing or web browser histories) rather than relying on customer feedback is therefore important.

Test your understanding 2

U has recently started looking at ways of gathering Big Data for her business. She is concerned that some of the sources of data she has chosen are unreliable and may therefore lead her to inaccurate conclusions.

Which of Gartner's features may be missing from U's Big Data?

A Variety

B Velocity

C Veracity

D Volume

Illustration 3 – Big Data

Netflix has 44 million users worldwide who watch 2 billion hours of programmes a month. The company uses information gathered from the analysis of viewing habits to inform decisions on which shows to invest in. Analysing past viewing figures and understanding viewer populations and the shows they are likely to watch allows the analysts to predict likely viewing figures before a show has even aired. This can help determine if the show is viable.

Illustration 4 – Big Data

Big Data analysis is being used by some organisations to help increase crop yields by providing information to farmers about when to plant, manage and harvest their crops.

The Climate Corporation, a company acquired by agricultural conglomerate Monsanto in 2013, operates an information system that keeps track of weather measurements from 2.5 million locations every day, along with 150 billion soil observations. It processes this data to generate 10 trillion weather simulation data points.

With this information, the company claims it can provide US farmers with temperature, rain and wind forecasts for areas of 200 acres and above for the next 7 day period.

This allows the farmers to decide optimal times to sow, spray and harvest crops to maximise their yields and reduce wastage.

Illustration 5 – Big Data

Cancer Research UK met with leading astronomers to identify how they used algorithms to sift through millions of pictures of the sky to analyse and classify objects. Te aim was to see if similar processes could be used in the fight against cancer; it was found that they could.

Using the astronomy algorithm, Cancer Research can automatically classify hundreds of thousands of cells, look at patterns, and consider how cells are related to each other. This enables precise counting of the cells and to find the average distance between them.

This helps with how breast cancer cells are read, for example. A 3D map is created that links the shape of breast cancer cells to genes turning on and off, matching to real disease outcomes. This enables much earlier diagnosis.

Illustration 6 – Big Data

The Office for National Statistics (ONS) in the UK has committed to investing £17m in a new data science campus at its headquarters in Newport, South Wales. This is after a government-ordered review called for the ONS to be more innovative and for economic statistics to be modernised.

ONS will explore new ways of measuring the economy, including using traffic sensors to gauge activity, mobile phone data to track commuter patterns, and satellite images to estimate populations.

It is hoped that this will result in more timely and broader insights into the economy, following criticisms that official statistics fail to capture the full picture of the modern lifestyle in Britain.

Benefits of Big Data

Big Data has several stated benefits to the organisation, including:

- **Driving innovation** by reducing the time taken to answer key business questions and therefore make decisions.
- **Gaining competitive advantage** by identifying trends or information that has not been identified by rivals.
- **Improving productivity** by identifying waste and inefficiency, or identifying improvements to working procedures.

A recent study by Bain & Co suggested that, of 400 large companies, those that had adopted Big Data analytics have gained a significant market advantage.

Illustration 7 – Big Data benefits

Delivery company UPS equips its delivery vehicles with sensors which monitor data on speed, direction, braking performance and other mechanical aspects of the vehicle.

Using this data to optimise performance and routes has led to significant improvements, including:

- Over 15 million minutes of idling time were eliminated in one year, saving 103,000 gallons of fuel.
- 1.7 million miles of driving were also eliminated in the same year, saving a further 183,000 gallons of fuel.

Big Data problems

As mentioned before, one of the difficulties with Big Data is the ability to convert it to useful information. To help with this, a number of new open-source platforms have emerged to help organisations make sense of Big Data, such as Hadoop and Cassandra, though these may be difficult to integrate with existing data warehouses.

New roles are also emerging in business - such as 'data scientists' whose role is to help the organisation get meaning from the data it stores. However, due to the rapidly changing nature of Big Data analysis, there is a shortage of skills and support for these systems.

It is important to realise that just because something CAN be measured, this does not mean it should be. There is a risk that valuable time and money will be spent measuring relationships and information that has no value for the organisation.

The organisation needs to consider how to keep its data secure from viruses and hackers.

Does the organisation actually own the data it has collected on individuals? There may be legal (Data Protection) and privacy issues if it holds large amounts of data on potential customers.

Illustration 8 – Risks of Big Data

It is widely reported that Walmart tracks data on over 60% of adults in the US, including online and in-store purchasing patterns, Twitter interactions and trends, weather reports and major events. The company argues that this gives them the ability to provide a highly personalised customer experience.

Walmart detractors criticise the company's data collection as a breach of human rights and believe the company uses the data to make judgements on personal information such as political view, sexual orientation and even intelligence levels.

Test your understanding 3

S Ltd is a large business that produces online tax returns for businesses and individuals. It has a large cash surplus and has invested significantly in its IT infrastructure in the last several years. It currently has a large database which stores a wide variety of information about its customers.

Information for advantage and knowledge management

The CEO of S believes that S has failed to fully understand its market. He has proposed that S adopt a Big Data approach. This would involve expanding the current database to enable the storage of information recorded on customer tax returns.

S is confident that it could use this to tailor its products and services to customer needs, as well as identify possible additional services that could be offered to customers. It does not believe that its rivals have adopted this approach to date.

Which of the following concerns should S have about the use of Big Data in this way?

A   High setup costs
B   Lack of IT knowledge
C   Privacy issues
D   Lack of competitive advantage

Test your understanding 4 – (Integration question)

PL is a global firm of accountants and business advisors offering a large range of services to a wide range of clients. The company originally offered just two services (accounting and audit), but has branched out in the last ten years to provide tax, forensic accountancy (in partnership with a large law firm), consulting, insolvency and certain niche advisory services such as environmental reporting.

Evaluate the advantages to PL of adopting a Big Data approach.

(15 minutes)

5 Knowledge management

Knowledge management is the 'systematic process of finding, selecting, organising, distilling and presenting information so as to improve comprehension of a specific area of interest. Specific activities help focus the organisation on acquiring, storing and utilising knowledge for such things as problem solving, dynamic learning, strategic planning and decision making.'

CIMA Official Terminology

Mayo defines knowledge management as the management of the information, knowledge and experience available to an organisation – its creation, capture, storage, availability and utilisation – in order that organisational activities build on what is already known and extend it further.

Knowledge management is a relatively new approach to business in which an organisation consciously and comprehensively gathers, organises, shares and analyses its knowledge to further its aims.

Types of knowledge

There are two main types of knowledge that an organisation needs to be aware of:

- **Explicit** – this is knowledge that has been identified and codified (i.e. written down) in some way. This is relatively easy for an organisation to manage and share.
- **Tacit** – this refers to knowledge that people are often not aware that they possess or that it has value to others. It is therefore very difficult for an organisation to manage.

For example, a training organisation may have an intranet which contains teaching programmes that all tutors can access for guidance on how to teach each course. This would be an example of explicit knowledge. However, individual tutors may have better ways of explaining certain topics. They may not even be aware of this, or that it would be valuable if shared with other tutors. This would be an example of tacit knowledge.

Where the knowledge resides

The intellectual capital can be divided between:

(1) **Human capital,** which comprises: human resources – the knowledge, skills and experience possessed by employees can be easily overlooked in times of crisis, just when it is most needed; this knowledge is vital to all service companies.

(2) **Structural capital,** which is in turn divided into:
    - innovation capital – intellectual property
    - customer capital – address lists and client records
    - organisational capital – e.g. systems for processing policies and claims.

Implementing a knowledge management strategy

There are five main steps in the development and implementation of a knowledge management strategy.

(1) **Gaining top management support.** Like any major strategy, knowledge management will fail unless it has the clear support of the 'top team'.

(2) **Creating the technological infrastructure.** Hardware and software must be acquired and installed in order for the knowledge to be communicated and stored.

(3) **Creating the database structures.** Advanced database management systems may be required. These will need to be specifically designed for the type of knowledge the company is looking to capture.

(4) **Creating a sharing culture.** This involves convincing staff of the benefits, both to the organisation and to themselves, of sharing knowledge for the common good. This is often the most difficult stage.

(5) **Populating the databases and using the knowledge.** The knowledge must be captured and recorded and individuals trained and encouraged to use it.

The benefits of a knowledge management system

These will include:

- higher workforce motivation and reduction in inefficiencies
- increased ability to compete and add value
- a culture where employees are encouraged to innovate and use knowledge to improve efficiency.

Steve Jobs, one of the founders of Apple technology company, is quoted as saying:

'It doesn't make sense to hire smart people and then tell them what to do. We hired smart people so they could tell us what to do.'

Problems in implementing a knowledge-sharing system

- It is not always necessary to invest in expensive technology to address problems in information sharing: often the problem will arise because of organisational matters such as an **inappropriate organisation structure.**

- There may be some **technological barriers** to overcome, such as the need to roll out a suitable modern network across an organisation, if one is not in place already.

- There will be situations in which problems arise because of **incompatible systems** and working methods in different parts of the organisation.

- It is inevitable that some data will have to be **transferred into a new common format** and this can lead to errors, omissions and inconsistencies if not done with great care.

- In certain systems it is possible that **older information will not be held in digital form at all**, or not in a format that can easily be converted into a suitable modern equivalent. Examples include architect's drawings, medical notes written by hand and so on.

- A decision is needed about **how to archive this material**. Will individual older systems be maintained and thoroughly indexed, or will it be accepted that such material has to be recreated from paper records on an ad hoc basis, if it is ever needed? Will archives be held locally or centrally?

- There are **social barriers to information sharing**. For some staff the notion of making their information available to other staff in other offices may be difficult. They will have their own established and familiar methods of organising their information and may even refuse to change their current practices to fall in line with a centrally imposed system.

- There is likely to be some **demotivation amongst staff.** Some may resent having to give up a system that they know and like and learn a new one, especially if they are not given adequate training and adequate time to adapt.

- There may be **political issues and inter office rivalries.** Information is power and some staff may fear that their own status within the organisation will be impaired if they have to share the source of their power with others.

Information for advantage and knowledge management

Appropriate systems

(1) **Networks**

Most organisations connect their PCs and other computers together in local area networks (LANs), enabling them to share data and peripherals such as printers.

LANs may be grouped together into 'work groups' which, in addition to sharing information and software facilities such as email, can run software such as groupware and/or an intranet.

LANs themselves are also being interconnected using sophisticated new hardware to create wide area networks (WANs), sometimes called enterprise networks.

(2) **Groupware**

Groupware is a generic term for software that helps work groups to collaborate on projects. For example a groupware system might have the following features for individual time management.

- a **scheduler** or **calendar** allowing users to timetable their activities for the day and plan meetings with others. It will also be able to generate reminders, for example when a deadline is approaching, or the date of a meeting
- an **address book**
- **to do** lists
- a **journal.** This can automatically record interactions with people involved in a project, such as e-mail messages, and record and time actions such as creating and working on files. The journal will keep track of all of this and is useful both as a record of work done and as a quick way of finding relevant files and messages without having to remember where each one is saved
- a **jotter** for jotting down notes as quick reminders of questions, ideas, and so on.

The advantage is that all this information is available at the touch of a button, rather than relying on Post-it notes, memo pads, hard-copy out-of-date address books, and company telephone directories.

(3) **Intranet**

An intranet is a private network that is contained within an organisation. It may consist of many interlinked local area networks and also use leased lines in the wide area network. Typically, an intranet includes connections through one or more gateway computers to the outside Internet.

The main objective of an intranet is to make information flow more freely by sharing company information and computing resources among employees.

(4) **Extranet**

An extranet is a private, secure extension of the enterprise via the corporate intranet. It allows the organisation to share part of its business information or operations with suppliers, customers, and other business partners using the Internet. For example, an organisation could connect its browser-based purchase order system to the product catalogue database on a supplier's intranet.

Illustration 9 – Knowledge management

Modern IT systems have made sharing and distributing knowledge easier.

The UK government has a massive project in progress to computerise the health records of every UK resident. The aim is that a patient's medical history will be available instantly to any health professional in any hospital or clinic.

Test your understanding 5

Consider the following steps that are required to implement a knowledge management strategy:

(i) Creating database structures

(ii) Gaining top management support

(iii) Creating a sharing culture

(iv) Populating databases and using the knowledge

(v) Creating technological infrastructure

Which order should these steps be placed in?

A   ii, i, v, iv, iii
B   v, ii, i, iv, iii
C   i, iii, ii, v, iv
D   ii, v, i, iii, iv

Test your understanding 6

Consider the following statements relating to knowledge management:

(i)   Tacit knowledge refers to knowledge that has been identified and codified in some way.

(ii) To succeed, knowledge management typically requires buy-in from senior management.

Which of these statements is/are correct?

A   Neither
B   (i) only
C   (ii) only
D   Both

Test your understanding 7

Y has recently created a secure network that provides users with access to a range of sensitive business information. Y has shared access with all its employees, as well as a number of key suppliers and customers.

What type of system has Y implemented?

A   Extranet
B   Groupware
C   Intranet
D   Enterprise network

chapter 10

Learning organisations

A learning organisation (also known as a knowledge-based organisation) is an organisation skilled at creating, acquiring and transferring knowledge and at modifying its behaviour to reflect new knowledge and insights. It is an organisation that facilitates the learning of all its members and continuously transforms itself.

Learning organisations encourage questions and explicitly recognise mistakes as part of the learning process. They encourage testing and experimentation. Because they want to find new answers they recognise that failed answers are as important as successful ones.

Peter Senge outlines five disciplines that individuals and groups should be encouraged to learn to create a learning organisation.

(a) Systems thinking – is the ability to see particular problems as part of a wider whole and to devise appropriate solutions to them.

(b) Personal learning and growth – individuals should be encouraged to acquire skills and knowledge.

(c) Mental models – are deeply ingrained assumptions that determine what people think, e.g. a marketing group may think that price is more important than quality. Learning organisations can use a number of group techniques to make these models explicit and to challenge them.

(d) A shared vision that does not filter knowledge which undermines learning.

(e) Team learning – teams must be trained to learn because there are factors in group dynamics that impede learning.

Test your understanding 8

According to Senge, which THREE of the following are key disciplines of learning organisations?

A   Groupthink
B   Mental models
C   Sharing culture
D   Developing human capital
E   Shared vision
F   Team learning

447

Information for advantage and knowledge management

Test your understanding 9 – (Integration question)

A barrier to knowledge management is that many people believe that keeping knowledge secret gives them unique power. Knowledge management, however, requires that knowledge is uncovered and shared.

What arguments could be used to encourage individuals to freely give up and share information?

Test your understanding 10 – PR – (Case style)

The PR University provides tuition to degree level to 12,000 students, both on campus and by distance-learning courses. The university has 34 different departments, each of which specialises in one specific area, such as economics, geography or astronomy.

Over the past ten years, information systems have been developed in each department to meet the specific needs of that department. However, the systems are incompatible with each other and use a wide range of software applications.

The information systems are becoming expensive to operate, as well as requiring duplication of input where students study in more than one department. Additional duplication occurs when student details have to be entered into the central university database, which is used for monitoring total student numbers.

The Board of Management of the university has decided that the university should develop and implement an integrated database for future information requirements and place all existing data into a single data warehouse.

Moreover, any new system must meet the information requirements of the central database as well as those of the individual departments.

You have been contacted by the Dean of PR University and asked to write a set of briefing notes for him to use at the next Board of Management meeting. Your notes need to cover:

- an evaluation of the use of data within the university
- an explanation of how the Board of Management should use Critical Success Factors (CSFs) in revising the current information system
- a discussion of the disadvantages of data warehousing with specific reference to the situation at PR University.

Required:

Draft the briefing notes as requested by the Dean.

(45 minutes)

Test your understanding 11 – (Integration question)

M-HK provides a passenger ferry service between two large cities separated by the mouth of a major river. The ferries are frequent, well-supported by passengers and cover the distance between the cities in one hour. M-HK also transports passengers and goods by ferry to other cities located on the river mouth. There are other ferry operators besides M-HK providing services between each of these locations.

Required:

(a) Explain what strategic information is required by M-HK's management in respect of customer demand, competition, competitiveness and finance in order to plan its future ferry services.

(20 minutes)

(b) Using the information in your answer to part (a), discuss how M-HK's chartered management accountant should provide reports to M-HK's senior management for operational and strategic planning purposes.

(25 minutes)

6 Summary

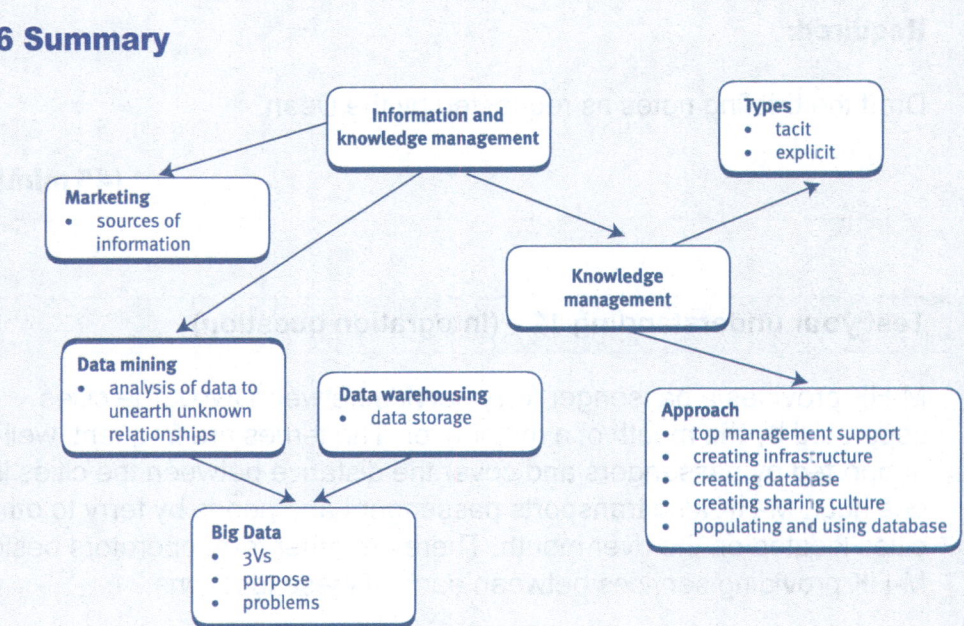

Test your understanding answers

Test your understanding 1

The correct answer is A

Associations occur when one event can be correlated to another. In this case the storm and the purchase of breakfast cereal are clearly correlated with each other.

Test your understanding 2

The correct answer is C

Veracity refers to the accuracy and truthfulness of the data. If this is missing, it can lead to inaccurate conclusions being drawn.

Test your understanding 3

The correct answer is C

S already has a significant amount of IT infrastructure and seems to have the relevant skills to maintain, suggesting that this would not be a problem of adopting Big Data. The fact that the organisation would be the first in its industry to adopt this approach (which it seems confident will improve its service provision) would also seem to suggest that it will gain competitive advantage from such a move.

However, storing such a large amount of personal information opens up the organisation to issues surrounding privacy and data protection. Customers may be unwilling to allow the company to use their personal data in this way and there may be legal implications as well.

Information for advantage and knowledge management

Test your understanding 4 – (Integration question)

Capturing Big Data and having the capability to manage and analyse such data has many business benefits, but also comes with risks.

Companies like PL will gather huge amounts of data about their clients in a wide range of different formats. This data will cover fairly straightforward transactional data, such as the clients' sales history, but will also include less structured data regarding products, services, competitive environment and key personnel.

Traditionally accountancy and advisory firms would have used the data collected to make a very specific conclusion (for example a calculation of tax liability), but wouldn't have harnessed the data gathered to better understand the client and business opportunities for PL. If Big Data management principles were applied, PL could perform analysis on all of this additional information to make decisions regarding cross-selling opportunities, more targeted marketing activity and identify further niche advisory options.

Despite having access to such a wide variety of data, PL needs to take greater care than some companies when using this data. As a professional services firm, they will need to ensure that they are complying with all relevant ethical codes, which may restrict the amount of data shared between departments. PL will also need to observe any relevant data protection legislation as large amounts of data gathered will be sensitive business information about their clients.

Another area that PL can use Big Data management is during the recruitment process. Firms in this industry receive thousands of applications for graduate schemes each year and have traditionally relied on academic qualifications to shortlist candidates.

A wider range of data through networks such as Facebook and LinkedIn can lead to a more meaningful and effective selection process.

Test your understanding 5

The correct answer is D

By definition.

Test your understanding 6

The correct answer is C

The definition in (i) is of explicit knowledge.

Test your understanding 7

The correct answer is A

If the network was only available to employees, it would have been classified as an intranet.

An enterprise network is a system designed to link various company sites (such as offices, manufacturing sites, etc).

Test your understanding 8

The correct answers are B, E and F

The other disciplines are: 'systems thinking' and 'personal learning and growth'.

Test your understanding 9 – (Integration question)

The following arguments could be used:

- If everyone shares their knowledge, each person should gain more than they give up.

- Organisations are often so complex that it is rare that one person can achieve much alone. Teamwork and sharing knowledge is the best way of assuring a safe future.

- Knowledge is perishable. If knowledge is not used quickly then it is wasted. If knowledge cannot be shared the chances are that it will become useless before it can be used.

- Knowledge management is vital to the success of many businesses. If an organisation uses knowledge creatively, the chances are that it will gain a competitive advantage. People within the organisation should not be competing with each other at the expense of the company.

Information for advantage and knowledge management

Test your understanding 10 – PR – (Case style)

Key answer tips

There are some positive points that can be made about current data use within the university, for instance staff appear to be happy with what they have, so beware of suggesting change just for the sake of change. Be sure to link your CSFs to the overall mission of the university or to the performance indicators needed to enable appropriate information systems to be developed. In part (b) some candidates discussed centralised systems in general: however, the question is about data warehousing.

(a) (i) **Data use within the university**

Although the data needs of individual departments are being met there are a number of problems that make information systems in the university as a whole cumbersome and expensive.

Above all the problem is duplication, both of effort and of data. The same data has to be input separately to the system of each department in which a student studies. This is a waste of time and there is a possibility of inconsistency between the records held by different departments.

The various systems are incompatible so information cannot be transferred between them and it will be difficult to develop the proposed integrated database.

Incompatible systems and diversity of applications also mean that it will be difficult for administrative staff to transfer between departments: they will need retraining each time. This may limit career opportunities within the university.

On the other hand staff will be used to their own systems and may resent or resist any centrally imposed change that requires them to abandon a working system and learn new skills.

(ii) **Critical Success Factors for revising the system**

Critical Success Factors (CSFs) are the limited number of areas in which results, if they are satisfactory, will ensure successful performance. They are the vital areas where 'things must go right' for the organisation to flourish.

There is no indication in the scenario of any respect in which the university as a whole is not flourishing or individual departments are performing unsuccessfully. This is not to say that there are no improvements to be made, however, especially as the systems are becoming expensive to operate.

The aims of individual departments are likely to be broadly similar – for instance, to attract sufficient numbers of students, provide X number of teaching hours per week, achieve certain standards in terms of exam results and future employability of graduates. Some departments may also have research interests and goals.

An overriding aim of the university's Board of Management will be to ensure that the entire organisation is on a sound financial footing and its activities are properly funded, and therefore any means of reducing costs (or getting better value from new investment in information systems) will be important.

The Board of Management can establish CSFs in each of these areas and then identify suitable performance indicators that will show whether CSFs are being met. This in turn will help to define what information will be needed in the future to monitor whether CSFs are being achieved.

It is likely that this analysis will reveal a gap between current information provision and required information provision, and appropriate revisions to the current information system, to close the gap, can then be specified.

(b) **Disadvantages of data warehousing**

A data warehouse supports information processing by providing a solid platform of integrated, historical data from which to do analysis. It is a database, data extraction tool, decision support system, or other analysis tool or procedure that extracts data from one or more of the organisation's existing databases, reformats it and loads it into a database designed for querying with an on-line analytical processing system (OLAP). OLAP allows users to dynamically extract pertinent summary information.

Although the concept of data warehousing appears to offer considerable advantages, especially to organisations such as PR University with a large number of disparate legacy systems, there may be considerable problems when trying to implement such a system.

The systems used in different departments of the PR University are incompatible, and that is likely to mean that data is in a wide variety of different formats. As noted earlier there are also likely to be inconsistencies between different databases where duplicated items of data should in theory be identical, but in practice are not.

The data will either need to be analysed and 'cleansed' before it can be integrated into a warehouse, or else some kind of middleware will be required, probably converting all data to a common format such as XML. Whichever option is chosen, with 34 different departments this will not be easy, quick or cheap to achieve.

Incompatible systems will also mean that most of the departments will need to be furnished with new hardware and software before they can use the data warehouse. This is likely to be expensive and disruptive to the day-to-day work of each department.

Moreover, almost all staff who want to use the new system will need training, both in the use of the data warehouse itself, and probably also in the use of new hardware, operating systems and applications software.

Individual departments may use data in widely different ways and require all manner of different reports. It could be very difficult to create a common interface that is capable of delivering information in every format that may be required. Report formats that are only needed in a single department may not be catered for, and this will cause resentment.

Even if the above problems are overcome, scalability is a key issue. As the new system proves its worth, more and more demands will be made of it, so ongoing maintenance, adequate network bandwidth, sufficient storage space, and highly flexible upgrade capability are all essential.

Finally it is worth pointing out that with all the university's data in a single main source it is vital to ensure that effective backup arrangements are made and strictly adhered to. Depending on how the data warehouse is implemented, loss or serious corruption of data could be disastrous.

Test your understanding 11 – (Integration question)

M-HK

Approach

Brief introduction with regard to data sources – internal v. external. Then group answer around the four areas.

Demand

- Segment volumes and prices
- price elasticity
- timing of demand (rush hour?)
- research – forecast growth/decline in numbers by segment.

Competition

- PROSAC
- who are they?
- how do they compete?
- where do they compete?
- customer perceptions of them.

Competitiveness

- Consider their marketing mix and ours
- what are their core competencies and ours?
- any thresholds exposed?
- any chance of exposing?
- customer perceptions of M-HK
- barriers to exit and entry.

Finance

- Funding needs
- sources of finance
- cost of capital
- costings of product
- contribution analysis – actual, forecast and budget.

How to provide reports (Note 'discuss')

Basically, 'how can the management accountant assist' would be a useful planning tool.

- Periodic reporting which would include:
  - narrative
  - numericals with both financial and non-financial (BSC?)
  - comparators provided – past data
  - forecast, budgets, KPIs and variances
  - competitor data
- Face-to-face meeting/discussions with budget centre managers to allow presentation of report and "Q&A" session from centre manager. Can offer advice as necessary and also allows for any corrections or amendments before final publication.
- Benchmarking data can be provided or data from a competitor analysis. Pricing and elasticity of demand.

For operational purposes

- Using predominately internal sources
- on a daily or weekly basis – keep it simple
- focus onto actual v. plan with easy KPIs (easy to understand and prepare) e.g.:
  - revenue by service
  - passenger numbers
  - number of complaints.

For strategic purposes

- Uses more external sources
- on a monthly or quarterly basis
- more elaborate using database of information
- forecasts and budgets with scenario planning
- competitive reviews and competitor analysis.

chapter 11

Customers, suppliers and supply chain management

Chapter learning objectives

Lead	Component
A1. Evaluate the key external factors affecting an organisation's strategy	(d) Recommend how to build and manage strategic relationships with stakeholders (including suppliers, customers, owners, government and wider society)

Indicative syllabus content

- Strategic supply chain management
- Implications of interactions with the external environment for Chartered Management Accountants and the management accounting system
- The customer portfolio: Customer analysis and behaviour, including the marketing audit and customer profitability analysis as well as customer retention and loyalty.
- Building strategic alliances with stakeholders.

Customers, suppliers and supply chain management

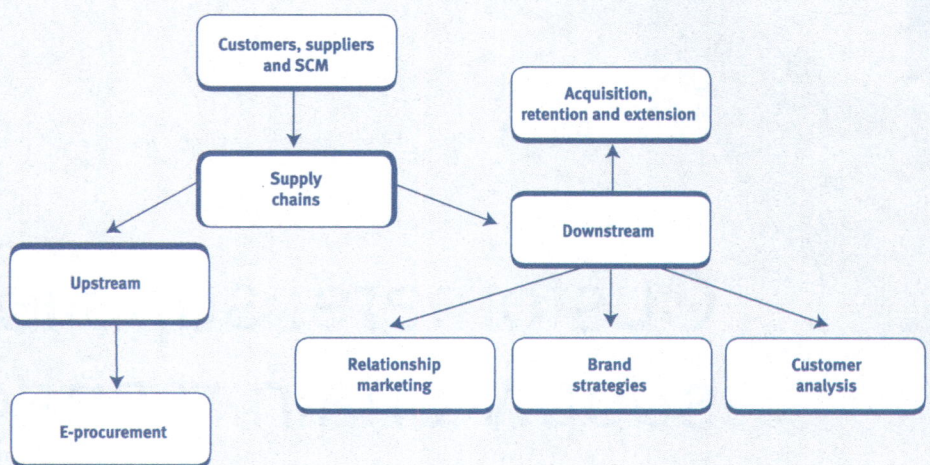

1 Introduction

Customers and suppliers are often key stakeholder groups for an organisation. Two frameworks that we have already met – Mendelow's power/interest matrix and Porter's five forces model – are useful for assessing the power of customers and suppliers and suggesting suitable strategies for dealing with them.

In this chapter the practicalities of managing the relationships with suppliers and customers is considered. In particular the role of e-business in supply chain management is analysed in detail.

2 What is a supply chain?

A supply chain encompasses all activities and information flows necessary for the transformation of goods from the origin of the raw material to when the product is finally consumed or discarded.

This typically involves distribution of the product from the supplier to the manufacturer to the retailer and then on to the final consumer. Each link in the supply chain (i.e. the supplier, or the consumer) is known as a node.

Transactions between the business and its suppliers are referred to as its 'upstream' supply chain. Transactions between the business and its customers are referred to as 'downstream supply chain'.

Businesses are no longer able to just consider their immediate customers and immediate suppliers. This is because problems anywhere in the wider supply chain can have a significant impact on the business.

Illustration 1 – The supply chain

Imagine a (simplified) supply chain for a large, national baker who makes and sells bread through a chain of supermarkets.

The baker makes bread with wheat. This means that the supply chain starts with the farmers who grow the wheat – the original creator of the resource. The farmers then sell this wheat to mills, who convert the wheat into flour. The flour is then purchased by wholesalers who sell the flour in bulk to larger companies, such as our baker. The baker makes the loaves of bread and sells it onto the supermarkets, who sell the bread onto the end consumers (customers).

Management of the supply chain means that the baker needs to be aware of the activities and needs of each part (or node) of the supply chain – from the farmer to the end consumer.

The baker's upstream supply chain includes farmers, mills and wholesalers, while its downstream supply chain is made up of supermarkets and consumers.

Note that problems in any part of the supply chain can affect the baker. For example, if farmers switch from growing wheat to other, more profitable crops then it will lead to a scarcity of flour on the market, pushing the baker's costs up. If the end consumers start to dislike the types of bread that the baker is selling (for example if the market shifts away from white bread to brown or granary breads) then this will affect how many of the baker's products will be stocked by the supermarkets.

As such, even though the baker may not directly transact with the consumer and the farmers, it is still affected by them as they are part of its supply chain.

It is worth noting that managing the supply chain and moving materials and products from node to node includes activities such as:

- production planning
- purchasing
- materials management
- distribution
- customer service
- forecasting.

Customers, suppliers and supply chain management

While each firm can be competitive through improvements to its internal practices, ultimately the ability to do business effectively depends on the efficient functioning of the entire supply chain. This requires the business to seriously consider how to most effectively monitor and control its entire supply chain.

> **Illustration 2 – Supply chain management (SCM)**
>
> A wholesaler's inability to adequately maintain inventory control or respond to sudden changes in demand for stock may mean that a retailer cannot meet final consumer demand. Conversely, poor sales data from retailers may result in inadequate forecasting of manufacturing requirements.

Types of supply chain – push and pull

In the traditional supply chain model, the raw material suppliers are at one end of the supply chain.

- They are connected to manufacturers and distributors, who are in turn connected to a retailer and the end-customer.
- Although customers are the source of the profits, they are at the end of the chain in the 'push' model.

Driven by e-commerce's capabilities to empower clients, many companies are moving from the traditional 'push' business model, where manufacturers, suppliers, distributors and marketers have most of the power, to a customer-driven 'pull' model.

This new business model is less product-centric and more directly focused on the individual consumer – a more marketing-oriented approach.

- In the pull model, customers use electronic connections to pull whatever they need out of the system.
- Electronic supply chain connectivity gives end customers the opportunity to give direction to suppliers, for example about the precise specifications of the products they want.
- Ultimately, customers have a direct voice in the functioning of the supply chain.

E-commerce creates a much more efficient supply chain that benefits both customers and manufacturers. Companies can better serve customer needs, carry fewer inventories, and send products to market more quickly.

chapter 11

Illustration 3 – Supply chain management (SCM)

Several personal computer manufacturers allow users to order over the internet and to customise their machines (for example Lenovo and Dell). PCs are then made to customers' orders.

This is an example of a **pull** supply chain, where the product is not produced until the customer requests it. It is then created to fit their specific needs.

Test your understanding 1

V retails toy cars. He manufactures the product in batches of one thousand and then visits various independent toy shops, trying to convince them to stock them on their shelves.

This is an example of a _____ supply chain.

Required:

Insert the word missing in the above sentence.

Test your understanding 2

When managing a supply chain, a business may wish to ensure that every part of the chain has sufficient cash and/or profits.

Which ONE of the following reasons would best explain this?

- A   To ensure ongoing supply and demand for the business's products
- B   To ensure that the business has sufficient information on all parts of its supply chain
- C   To ensure quality throughout the overall supply chain
- D   To ensure maximum collaboration throughout the chain

3 Upstream supply chain management

As mentioned above, it is crucial for an organisation to monitor and control its entire supply chain. In this section, we will examine some of the methods a company could use to look after its upstream supply chain – i.e. its chain of suppliers.

3.1 Managing supplier relationships

There are a number of general issues that an organisation needs to consider in relation to its suppliers.

Overall supplier strategy

A supply strategy is likely to take account of matters such as the following.

- Sources

    What sources are available and where are they located? Are suppliers' businesses larger or smaller than the buying organisation (this affects bargaining power). Will different suppliers need to be used in different parts of the world?

- Number of suppliers

    If there is only a single source of supply this may bring the advantage of bulk purchase discounts, but the organisation may prefer to have several or multiple suppliers to avoid the risk of failed deliveries and to prevent a single supplier from getting either too powerful or/and complacent.

- Cost, quality and speed of delivery

    These factors are closely interrelated and the strategy will probably need to make compromises to achieve the right balance.3.1

- Make or buy and outsourcing

    The outsourcing decision is effectively the same as the strategy of vertical integration discussed in the chapter "Strategic analysis and choice". The decision will depend on the above factors and whether or not the firm has the required competences and resources to bring the supply in-house.

> **Factors to consider when choosing suppliers**
>
> - What does the company charge?
> - Does it offer discounts or other incentives?
> - Can it deliver the required quality of product or service (for example is it ISO 9001 certified)?
> - Is the supplier willing to customise orders or handle other special needs?
> - How will it ship its products, and how much will that cost?
> - How quickly will orders be delivered?
> - Will delivery quantities be accurate?
> - How will the supplier handle returns or other problems?
> - Is technical support available, if required?
> - How will the supplier manage the account?
> - Do they have adequate technology?
> - Are they financially secure? Credit reports can help here.
> - Are they reliable? Can references be obtained?
> - What credit period is offered?

Antagonism or partnership?

In the past the supply chain was typically defined by **antagonistic** relationships.

- The purchasing function sought out the lowest-price suppliers, often through a process of tendering, the use of 'power' and the constant switching of supply sources to prevent getting too close to any individual source.
- Supplier contracts featured heavy penalty clauses and were drawn up in a spirit of general mistrust of all external providers.
- The knowledge and skills of the supplier could not be exploited effectively: information was deliberately withheld in case the supplier used it to gain power during price negotiations.

Hence no single supplier ever knew enough about the ultimate customer to suggest ways of improving the cost-effectiveness of the trading relationship, for instance buying additional manufacturing capacity or investing in quality improvement activities.

Customers, suppliers and supply chain management

It is now recognised that successful management of suppliers is based upon **partnership** – collaboration and offers benefits to an organisation's suppliers as well as to the organisation itself. By working together organisations can make a much better job of satisfying the requirements of their end market, and thus both can increase their market share.

- Organisations seek to enter into partnerships with key customers and suppliers so as to better understand how to provide value and customer service.
- Organisations' product design processes include discussions that involve both customers and suppliers. By opening up design departments and supply problems to selected suppliers a synergy results, generating new ideas, solutions, and new innovative products.
- To enhance the nature of collaboration the organisation may reward suppliers with long-term sole sourcing agreements in return for a greater level of support to the business and a commitment to ongoing improvements of materials, deliveries and relationships.

> **Service level agreements**
>
> Service level agreements should include the following factors:
>
> - A detailed explanation of exactly what service the supplier is offering to provide.
> - The targets/benchmarks to be used and the consequences of failing to meet them.
> - Expected response time to technical queries.
> - The expected time to recover the operations in the event of a disaster such as a systems crash, terrorist attack, etc.
> - The procedure for dealing with complaints.
> - The information and reporting procedures to be adopted.
> - The procedures for cancelling the contract.

3.2 The use of information technology in upstream supply chain management

The key activities of upstream SCM are procurement and upstream logistics. A good example of how the upstream supply chain can be improved using IT is Tesco:

Illustration 4 – IT in upstream SCM

Tesco

- Largest grocery retailer in the UK
- a typical store stocks 50,000 products
- over 2,000 suppliers, each of which will supply, at most, 200 products.

Date	Objective	Solution	Comments
1980s	Streamline store replenishment	Goods ordered via Electronic Data Interchange (EDI)	
1989	Help suppliers forecast demand	Suppliers sent EDI messages	Suppliers receive messages detailing: • Actual store sales • Depot stockholdings • Tesco's forecasts
1997	Better two-way collaboration Shift responsibility for managing products to suppliers	Tesco Information Exchange (TIE) allowing suppliers to view EPOS data	Suppliers can monitor actual sales in real time (almost!), allowing them to identify changes in demand (by product, store and region) and react accordingly
1999	More effective promotions	Promotions management module added	Suppliers are involved in planning and executing promotions

What is e-procurement?

The term 'procurement' covers all the activities needed to obtain items from a supplier: the whole purchases cycle.

E-procurement is therefore used to describe the electronic methods used in every stage of the procurement process, from the identification of the organisation's requirements through to payment.

Customers, suppliers and supply chain management

E-sourcing, e-purchasing and e-payment

E-procurement is the term used to describe the electronic methods used in every stage of the procurement process, from identification of requirement through to payment. It can be broken down into the stages of e-sourcing, e-purchasing and e-payment.

E-sourcing covers electronic methods for finding new suppliers and establishing contracts.

Not only can e-sourcing save administrative time and money, it can enable companies to discover new suppliers and to source more easily from other countries.

Issuing electronic invitations to tender and requests for quotations reduces:

- administration overheads
- potentially costly errors, as the re-keying of information is minimised
- the time to respond.

E-purchasing covers product selection and ordering.

Buying and selling online streamlines procurement and reduces overheads through spending less on administration time and cutting down on bureaucracy. E-purchasing transfers effort from a central ordering department to those who need the products. Features of an e-purchasing system include:

- electronic catalogues for core/standard items
- recurring requisitions/shopping lists for regularly purchased items. The standard shopping lists form the basis of regular orders and the lists can have items added or deleted for each specific order
- electronic purchase orders despatched automatically through an extranet to suppliers
- detailed management information reporting capabilities.

Improvements in customer service can result from being able to place and track orders at any time of day. An e-catalogue is an electronic version of a supplier's paper catalogue including product name, description, an illustration, balance in hand and so on. User expectations have increased dramatically in recent years as a result of their personal experiences of shopping on the internet. Well-designed websites and web interfaces are essential to offer good functionality so as to maintain user satisfaction.

chapter 11

> **E-payment** includes tools such as electronic invoicing and electronic funds transfers. Again, e-payment can make the payment processes more efficient for both the purchaser and supplier, reducing costs and errors that can occur as a result of information being transferred manually from and into their respective accounting systems. These efficiency savings can result in cost reductions to be shared by both parties.

E-procurement gives rise to a number of specific applications that the organisation can use to manage its upstream supply chain. These include:

- EDI (electronic data interchange) – this involves the organisation linking its systems to those of its suppliers, allowing for faster and more efficient paperless ordering. This can improve the speed and accuracy in the fulfilment of orders.
- Use of the Internet – the organisation can use the Internet to shop around to ensure that they are using the most reliable, cost effective suppliers.
- Disintermediation – the organisation may be able to buy its supplies online directly from an earlier stage in the supply chain (e.g. from a wholesaler rather than a retailer), which could help the business to save money.

Benefits and drawbacks of e-procurement

The benefits of e-procurement

The more of the procurement process that can be automated, the better, as there will be considerable financial benefits.

- Labour costs will be greatly reduced.
- Inventory holding costs will be reduced. Not only should overstocking be less likely, but if orders are cheap to place and process, they can be placed much more frequently, so average inventories can be lower.
- Production and sales should be higher as there will be fewer stock-outs because of more accurate monitoring of demand and greater ordering accuracy.
- The firm may benefit from a much wider choice of suppliers rather than relying on local ones.
- Greater financial transparency and accountability
- Greater control over inventories
- Quicker ordering, making it easier to operate lean or JIT manufacturing systems

- There are also considerable benefits to the suppliers concerned, such as reduced ordering costs, reduced paperwork and improved cash flow, that should strengthen the relationship between the firm and its suppliers.

Potential risks of e-procurement

There are some risks associated with e-procurement. These are:

- technology risks. There is a risk that the system (whether software or hardware) will not function correctly. There are risks that it might not interface properly with the organisation's system. There are very high risks that it will not communicate properly with a wide range of supplier systems
- organisational risks. Staff might be reluctant to accept the new procurement methods
- no cost savings realised. As with all IS/IT projects, it is very difficult to predict all the benefits that can arise. Tangible benefits (such as might arise if fewer staff have to be employed) are relatively easy to forecast. However, intangible benefits (such as better customer service giving rise to an improved reputation) are very difficult to estimate with any accuracy.

Other uses of IT within the upstream supply chain

- Communication – email and other IT-based communication allow for more rapid communication with all parts of the upstream supply chain.
- Information gathering – gathering and processing information on the upstream supply chain that may impact on the organisation is easier thanks to the Internet.
- Extranets – this allows the organisation to grant suppliers access to information that can help enable aid collaboration (such as co-ordination of production and inventory levels) as well as joint development of products.

chapter 11

> **Test your understanding 3 – (Integration question)**
>
> XL Travel are a tour operator based in the capital city of country S. They run weekly trips to the seaside resort of Black Rock (around 140km away) for four–day visits (typically from Friday to Monday).
>
> The tours are very popular, especially with people aged over 65 (who make up over 90% of XL's customers). The company has traded profitably for many years on the back of premium pricing. However, recently profits have started to fall, coinciding with a minority of complaints from regular users. Some users feel that the quality of the trips have fallen and are not up to previous high standards. Other users feel that, whilst XL itself has invested (with attractive new offices, better marketing, more staff and easier booking systems) this investment has gone on the wrong areas.
>
> XL has built up a large cash surplus for further investment. One of the ways it is considering using this cash is to invest in and improve its supply chain.
>
> **Required:**
>
> What are likely to be the elements of XL's upstream supply chain? Give some examples of what areas XL could aim to change?
>
> (20 minutes)

4 Downstream supply chain management

As mentioned earlier in this chapter, downstream supply chain management refers to the need for the organisation to manage its transactions and relationships with the customers and consumers of its products and services.

This can be undertaken in a number of different ways.

4.1 Analysis of customers and their behaviour

In order to be able to effectively manage the organisation's customers, it is vital that their needs and behaviour are analysed and understood. This will help the organisation to improve its service levels (and the product range it offers) in order to better meet customer needs.

Customers, suppliers and supply chain management

Customer analysis and behaviour – industrial markets

Customer behaviour

Here are the main features of industrial buyers:

Motivation

An industrial buyer is motivated to satisfy the needs of the organisation rather than his or her individual needs. Often, purchases are repeat orders when the stock of items has fallen below a certain level and thus the buying motive is clear, i.e. avoiding nil stocks. With significant one-off purchases, the motivation will be the achievement of the organisation's goals or targets. Thus a profit target may mean the buyer placing an emphasis on cost minimisation. A growth target expressed in terms of sales motivates a purchase that will promote that goal.

The influence of the individual or group

An industrial purchase may be made by an individual or group. The individual or group is buying on behalf of the organisation but the buying decision may be influenced by the behavioural complexion of the individual or group responsible. The behavioural complexion will be influenced by the same influences on consumer buyers already discussed.

General organisational influences

Each organisation will have its own procedures and decision-making processes when purchases are made. Large centrally controlled organisations will often have centralised purchasing through a purchasing department. The purchase decisions will tend to be formal with established purchasing procedures. In small organisations there will not be a purchasing department. Purchasing decisions will tend to be made on a personal basis by persons who have other functions as well in the organisation. Personal relationships between the supplier and the buyer will often be very important.

Reciprocal buying

A feature in many industrial markets is the purchase of goods by organisation A from organisation B only on condition that organisation B purchases from organisation A.

Purchasing procedures

An industrial buyer appraises a potential purchase in a more formal way than a consumer buyer. Written quotations, written tenders and legal contracts with performance specifications may be involved. The form of payment may be more involved and may include negotiations on credit terms, leasing or barter arrangements.

Size of purchases

Purchases by an industrial buyer will tend to be on a much larger scale.

Derived demand

Demand for industrial products is generally derived from consumer demands. For example, when consumers demand more motor cars, the demand for steel, glass, components and so on will increase in the industrial sector. Industrial strategists have to know what markets the demand for their products is derived from, and monitor this market as well as their own. This may sound obvious, but when the firm is selling through intermediaries, or in overseas markets, there may be very little contact with users and end-users.

When industrialists predict a downturn in consumer markets, they will often cut back on production in the short run. This, of course, has the effect of lowering demand in the consumer markets through its effect on employment and wages, and is part of the trade cycle process discussed earlier.

Customer analysis – Industrial segmentation

- **Geographic:** The basis for sales-force organisation.
- **Purchasing characteristics:** The classification of customer companies by their average order size, the frequency with which they order, etc.
- **Benefit:** Industrial purchasers have different benefit expectations from consumers. They may be oriented towards reliability, durability, versatility, safety, serviceability, or ease of operation. They are always concerned with value for money.
- **Company type:** Industrial customers can be segmented according to the type of business they are, i.e. what they offer for sale. The range of products and services used in an industry will not vary too much from one company to another. A manufacturer considering marketing to a particular type of company would be well advised to list all potential customers in that area of business.

- **Company size:** It is frequently useful to analyse marketing opportunities in terms of company size. A company supplying canteen foods would investigate size in terms of numbers of employees. Processed parts suppliers are interested in production rate, and cutting lubricants suppliers would segment by numbers of machine tools.

Customer analysis and behaviour – consumer markets

Customer behaviour

It is critical in consumer markets to understand **why** buyers purchase an organisation's goods or services. This will enable an organisation to identify critical success factors (CSFs) in markets.

Critical success factors refer to things that the company needs to do well in order to compete in its market and attract customers. For example, a supermarket may need to be cheaper, or stock a better range of products than its rivals in order to successfully compete.

Customer behaviour analysis will also see if they organisation has the required core competences to meet those CSFs and, hence, to determine an appropriate strategy.

Traditional views of marketing tend to assume that people purchase according to the value-for-money that they obtain. The customer considers the functional efficiency of the alternative products, and arrives at a decision by comparing this with the price. This set of beliefs is demonstrably inadequate in explaining consumer behaviour.

Maslow's hierarchy of needs

Remember that Maslow developed a hierarchy of needs to explain human motivation and behaviour. His 'need hierarchy' is as follows:

- physiological needs
- safety needs
- social needs
- status/ego needs
- self-fulfilment needs.

Products and services could be considered against this hierarchy. For example, insurance and banking are involved with safety needs; cigarettes and alcohol are frequently dependent upon social needs in their promotions; a fast car exploits customers' ego needs.

Cognitive dissonance

Dissonance is said to exist when an individual's attitudes and behaviour are inconsistent. One kind of dissonance is the regret that may be felt when a purchaser has bought a product, but subsequently feels that an alternative would have been preferable. In these circumstances, that customer will not repurchase immediately, but will switch brands. It is the job of the marketing team to persuade the potential customer that the product will satisfy his or her needs, and to ensure that the product itself will not induce dissonant attitudes.

Personality and product choice

Products, and their brand names, tend to acquire attributes in the mind of the potential customer; indeed, this is one of the primary functions of branding. When considering goods or services for a purchase, customers will invariably select those that have an image consistent with their own personality and aspirations.

Influence of other people

When people make purchase decisions, they reflect the values of their social and cultural environment. Often the form of products and services for sale has been determined by that environment. Among the more obvious influences are those of family and of reference groups.

The family is often important in engendering brand purchasing habits in grocery lines, although it also has a far broader influence in forming tastes in its younger members.

Customer analysis – consumer segmentation

Psychological

Consumers can be divided into groups sharing common psychological characteristics. One group may be described as security-oriented, another as ego-centred and so on. These categories are useful in the creation of advertising messages.

A recent trend is to combine psychological and socio-demographic characteristics to give a more complete profile of customer groups. Appropriately called lifestyle segmentation by one of the companies originating the method, this kind of segmentation uses individuals to represent groups that form a significant proportion of the consumer market. These individuals are defined in terms of sex, age, income, job, product preferences, social attitudes and political views.

Purchasing characteristics

Customers may be segmented by the volume they buy (heavy user, medium user, light user, non user). They may be segmented by the outlet type they use, or by the pack size bought. These variables, and many others, are useful in planning production and distribution and in developing promotion policy.

Demographic

Customers are defined in terms of age, sex, socio-economic class, country of origin, or family status. The most widely used forms of demographic segmentation in the UK are the socio-economic classification based on class (A, B, C1, C2, D and E) and the life cycle model (Bachelor, Newly married couple, Full nest 1, Full nest 2, Full nest 3, Empty nest 1, Empty nest 2).

Geographic

Markets are frequently split into regions for sales and distribution purposes. Many consumer goods manufacturers break down sales by television advertising regions.

Benefit

Customers have different expectations of a product. Some people buy detergents for whiteness, others want economy, and yet others stain removal.

It can be seen that, within the same product class, different brands offer different perceived benefits. An understanding of customers' benefits sought enables the manufacturer to create a range of products each aimed precisely at a particular benefit.

4.2 Marketing

A key aspect of managing the downstream supply chain is to ensure effective marketing. This will help to attract customers and improve the image of the organisation with consumers.

There are a number of possible approaches that can be used to help the organisation accomplish this.

The six markets model (Payne)

This model helps the organisation understand **who it needs to market to**. The six markets model advocates that an organisation has six key markets, not just the traditional customer market. Marketing activity should be extended to build and manage relationships in all these areas.

- Customer markets

    The final destination for the product. This ability to reach the customer in a highly competitive environment depends on other parties or relationships.

- Referral markets

    This is the institution or person who refers the customer to the supplier. A bank refers customers to providers of insurance services. The Automobile Association (AA) refers members to a bank or hire purchase company.

- Supplier markets

    Partnerships with suppliers have replaced old adversarial relationships. A supermarket sets up a JIT arrangement with a supplier for short-life articles, such as ready-made salads, in order to retain customer interest in an instant healthy food product.

- Recruitment markets

    A service provider such as PriceWaterhouseCoopers depends on quality staff to deliver quality service. Such an organisation will build up a relationship with careers advisers, professional bodies and others to supply the necessary human resources.

Customers, suppliers and supply chain management

- Influence markets

  Influence marketing used to be called public relations – a new low fat spread depends upon the sponsorship of a body that promotes healthy eating (Weightwatchers).

- Internal markets

  This concept is not dissimilar to the concept of internal quality management. Every department has a customer provider relationship with others. The UK corporate lending market recognises that the supplier of banking services (transaction processing) supports the manager of the client account (the relationship manager).

Relationship marketing

This examines the overall approach to marketing that the organisation can adopt. Should it focus on maximising one-off sales, or focus on long-term customer retention? This is a critical issue for many businesses.

Customers can be lost by a number of factors:

- unhelpful staff
- poor quality of service
- inappropriate prices
- lack of customer care.

The concept of relationship marketing has been defined as the technique of maintaining and exploiting the firm's customer base as a means of developing new business opportunities.

Transaction marketing	Relationship marketing
• concentrates on products	• concentrates on retention and loyalty
• little knowledge of customer	• considerable customer commitment
• product quality a key issue	• considerable customer contact
• little effort on customer retention	• emphasis on quality service
• focus on single sale	• focus on building long-term relationships
• focus on product features	• importance of customer benefits

Branding

Part of an organisation's marketing activity involves decisions on how to manage its brand.

A brand usually has three elements:

- a name and/or logo – e.g. McDonald's
- a colour scheme – e.g. McDonald's has a gold letter M on a red background and the M is shaped like arches.
- associations – attributes, benefits and values associated with the brand – e.g. Volvo cars are associated with safety.

Kotler identified 5 brand strategies:

(1) Line extensions
 - an existing brand is applied to new variants/products within the same product category
 - e.g. Ford Fusion and Ford Focus are both small cars

(2) Brand extensions
 - an existing brand is applied to products in a new product category
 - e.g. Honda cars and motorcycles

(3) Multibrands
 - having many different brands in the same product category
 - e.g. Kellogg's breakfast cereals include Cornflakes, Frosties, Special K, etc

(4) New brands
 - new brands are created for new products and/or markets, usually because existing brands are not deemed suitable.
 - e.g. when the banking arm of the Prudential expanded into internet banking they created a new brand, Egg Banking

(5) Cobrands
 - two brands are combined in an offer so the brands reinforce each other.
 - e.g. Dell Computers with Intel Processors

Customer acquisition

Methods of acquiring customers can be split between traditional off-line techniques (e.g. advertising, direct mail, sponsorship, etc) and rapidly-evolving on-line techniques (e-marketing):

Search engine marketing

- Search engine optimisation – improving the position of a company in search engine listings for key terms or phrases. For example, increasing the number of inbound links to a page through 'link building' can improve the ranking with Google.

- Pay per click (PPC) – an advert is displayed by search engines as a 'sponsored link' when particular phrases are entered. The advertiser typically pays a fee to the search engine each time the advert is clicked.

- Trusted feed – database-driven sites such as travel, shopping and auctions are very difficult to optimise for search engines and consequently haven't enjoyed much visibility in the free listings. Trusted Feed works by allowing a 'trusted' third party, usually a search engine marketing company, to 'feed' a website's entire online inventory directly into the search engine's own database, bypassing the usual submission process.

Online PR

- Media alerting services – using online media and journalists for press releases.

- Portal representation – portals are websites that act as gateways to information and services. They typically contain search engines and directories.

- Businesses blogs (effectively online journals) can be used to showcase the expertise of its employees.

- Community C2C portals (effectively the e-equivalent of a village notice board) – e.g. an oil company could set up a discussion forum on its website to facilitate discussion on issues including pollution.

Online partnerships

- Link-building – reciprocal links can be created by having quality content and linking to other sites with quality content. The objective is that they will then link to your site.

- Affiliate marketing – a commission-based arrangement where an e-retailer pays sites that link to it for sales. For example, hundreds of thousands of sites direct customers to Amazon to buy the books or CDs that they have mentioned on their pages.

- Sponsorship – web surfers are more likely to trust the integrity of a firm sponsoring a website than those who use straight ads.

- Co-branding – a lower cost form of sponsorship where products are labelled with two brand names. For example, as well as including details about their cars, the website Subaru.com also includes immediate co-branded insurance quotes with Liberty Mutual Insurance and pages devoted to outdoor lifestyles developed with LL Bean.

- Aggregators – these are comparison sites allowing customers to compare different product features and prices. For example, moneysupermarket.com allows analysis of financial services products. Clearly a mortgage lender would want their products included in such comparisons.

Interactive adverts

- Banners – banners are simply advertisements on websites with a click through facility so customers can surf to the advertiser's website.

- Rich-media – many web users have become immune to conventional banner ads so firms have tried increasingly to make their ads more noticeable through the use of animation, larger formats, overlays, etc. For example, an animated ad for Barclays banking services will appear on some business start-up sites.

- Some ads are more interactive and will change depending on user mouse movements, for example generating a slide show.

Opt-in e-mail

It is estimated that 80% of all e-mails are spam or viruses. Despite this, e-mail marketing can still deliver good response rates. One survey found only 10% of e-mails were not delivered (e.g. due to spam filters), 30% were opened and 8% resulted in 'clickthroughs'. Options for e-mail include the following.

- Cold, rented lists – here the retailer buys an e-mail list from a provider such as Experian.
- Co-branded e-mail – for example, your bank sends you an e-mail advertising a mobile phone.
- 3rd party newsletters – the retailer advertises itself in a 3rd party's newsletter.
- House list e-mails – lists built up in-house from previous customers, for example.

Viral marketing

- Viral marketing is where e-mail is used to transmit a promotional message from one person to another.
- Ideally the viral ad should be a clever idea, a game or a shocking idea that is compulsive viewing so people send it to their friends.

Test your understanding 4

Which of the following statements are consistent with the concept of transaction marketing?

A   Focus on product quality

B   Emphasis on quality of service

C   Focus on retention and loyalty

D   Investment in customer management

chapter 11

Test your understanding 5

WOT is an organisation based in country F that reviews and recommends electrical and other products to consumers. WOT has around 4 million subscribers in country F, who will typically only buy the products that WOT has highly rated.

JJH is an electronics manufacturer based in country F. According to Payne's six markets model, which of JJH's key markets is WOT classified within?

A Referral

B Customer

C Supplier

D Influence

Test your understanding 6

Which THREE of the following are methods of acquiring customers?

A Electronic data interchange

B Social media marketing

C Search engine optimisation

D Personalisation and customisation

E Extranet access

F Interactive advertisements

4.3 Managing the ongoing relationship with customers

Management of the downstream supply chain for many businesses involves the need to identify their major customers and look for ways to keep them satisfied – ensuring that they do not switch to rival suppliers – as well as trying to identify if more sales can be made to the customer (customer extension).

Customer relationship management

Customer relationship management (CRM) consists of the processes a company uses to track and organize its contacts with its current and prospective customers, with particular emphasis on software-based approaches.

483

CRM is defined as a culture, possibly supported by appropriate information systems, where emphasis is placed on the interfaces between the entity and its customers. Knowledge is shared within the entity to ensure that the customer receives a consistently high service level.

CIMA official terminology

This 'customer focused' approach, which will involve building a strong relationship with the customer as well as gathering, storing and sharing information (often using databases and other specific CRM software) across the organisation, will likely improve customer loyalty.

It is usually argued that retaining existing customers is cheaper that trying to win new customers, so CRM systems may well help the organisation to achieve higher profits.

Customer account profitability (CAP)

Adopting a customer relationship management (CRM) system may not be appropriate for all customers. In reality, businesses are only likely to spend significant time and resources managing their relationship with major customers. But how can the business identify who these major customers are? How much time and effort should be devoted to each of our customers? CAP helps to answer these questions.

CAP is 'analysis of the revenue streams and service costs associated with specific customers or customer groups.'

CIMA Official Terminology

CAP could also be defined as 'the total sales revenue generated from a customer or customer group, less all the costs that are incurred in servicing that customer or customer group'.

The essence of CAP is that it focuses on profits generated by customers and does not automatically equate increases in sales revenues with increases in profitability.

If an analysis of customer profitability is provided then marketing decisions are more easily made on such matters as:

- discounts
- special credit terms
- special after-sales servicing
- whether any efforts are required on a sector given its lack of profitability.

The normal approach to CAP follows five key stages:

(1) **Analyse the customer base and divide it into segments.** This will normally not be into the same segments as used for marketing, but rather based on factors such as order size or annual purchase volume.

(2) **Calculate the annual revenues earned from the customer segments.** Any discounts granted should be taken into account here.

(3) **Calculate the annual costs of serving the segment.** This will require a detailed analysis of the firm's overheads as well as its direct costs.

(4) **Identify and retain the quality customers.** The quality customers are those that provide earnings in excess of costs. They may either be willing to pay a premium price or they may require only a basic level of service.

(5) **Eliminate or re–engineer the unprofitable customer groups.** This may mean ceasing to supply certain customer groups, or alternatively looking at ways of reducing the level of service provided or increasing sales prices.

Illustration 5 – CAP

An insurance company was concerned about the poor profit performance of one of its types of policy. By using CAP analysis, it discovered that the policy was unprofitable when sold to recently retired people. Otherwise, it was profitable.

The reason was discovered to be that recently retired policyholders had more free time with which to ask for information and alter their finances. Dealing with this consumed a higher proportion of the insurance company's time and resources than other customer groups.

The company therefore reduced agents commission on the policies according to the age of the policyholder to deter them from selling to the unprofitable segment.

Advantages and disadvantages of CAP

Advantages

- CAP takes account of non-production costs when determining profitability. Differences between the profitability of different groups of customers are often attributable to the costs of supporting their accounts rather than the production costs of what they buy.

For example, banks often find that pensioners are more likely to be unprofitable customers as they take up a higher proportion of staff time and are less likely to use internet-based services.

- CAP provides a method of identifying customer groups who are of value to the firm, allowing the organisation to decide which customers may be worth additional expenditure to retain – such as through advertising and discounts.

- It provides a technique for assessing the financial value of marketing and product development expenditures. For example, Ferrari invests millions of pounds in supporting its Formula One racing team. CAP analysis would question whether this gives Ferrari additional revenues to justify the costs.

Disadvantages

- CAP can encourage ill-judged product changes. Deciding to remove a product feature based on CAP can have unintended consequences if the customer's behaviour is not fully understood.

    One luxury car company removed the cover of the car's ashtray on the understanding that most customers no longer smoked and those that did preferred to keep the ashtray permanently open. However, customers felt that the cheaper ashtray mechanism indicated that the company was cutting corners on quality. This caused significant damage to the company's reputation.

- Obtaining reliable customer revenue and customer cost figures can be extremely difficult.

    CAP requires a system to accumulate information across all business functions and geographic areas. Most systems used today are unable to perform this necessary function.

- CAP may overlook combinations of products bought.

    For example, although bank accounts lose money when provided to 80 per cent of customers, they are essential if the bank is to sell its credit products, insurance and foreign exchange services.

- CAP can also overlook the life cycle value of the customer. The value of a customer is not restricted to their present revenue and costs.

  For instance, Kotler (1997) cites the example of Taco Bell, an American fast-food restaurant chain. The chain sells tacos for less than $1 each, but estimates that a loyal customer generates up to $11,000 over their lifetime.

  In addition, a customer's value may increase over time. Student accounts may costs banks large amounts of money, but they may become profitable once they enter employment and need credit cards, mortgages and other products from the bank.

Test your understanding 7

Consider the following stages of customer account profitability (CAP) analysis:

(i) identify and retain quality customers
(ii) analyse the customer base and segment
(iii) calculate annual servicing costs for each segment
(iv) calculate annual revenues earned from each segment
(v) eliminate or re-engineer unprofitable segments

Which of the following is the correct order for these five stages?

A   ii, iii, iv, i, v
B   i, iii, ii, v, iv
C   ii, iv, iii, i, v
D   ii, iv, v, iii, i

Customer lifetime value (CLV) analysis

Customer lifetime value (CLV) is the **present value of the future cash flows attributed to the customer relationship**.

Use of customer lifetime value as a marketing metric tends to place greater emphasis on customer service and long-term customer satisfaction, rather than on maximizing short-term sales.

In theory CLV represents exactly how much each customer is worth in monetary terms, and therefore exactly how much a marketing department should be willing to spend to acquire each customer.

In reality, it is difficult to make accurate calculations of CLV due to the complexity of and uncertainty surrounding customer relationships.

Inputs to CLV

Most models to calculate CLV apply to the contractual or customer retention situation. These models make several simplifying assumptions and often involve the following inputs:

- **Churn rate**

    The percentage of customers who end their relationship with a company in a given period. The assumption is that the churn rate is constant across the life of the customer relationship.

- **Discount rate**

    The cost of capital used to discount future revenue from a customer.

- **Retention cost**

    The amount of money a company has to spend in a given period to retain an existing customer. Retention costs include customer support, billing, promotional incentives, etc.

- **Period**

    The unit of time into which a customer relationship is divided for analysis. A year is the most commonly used period. Customer lifetime value is a multi-period calculation, usually stretching 3–7 years into the future. In practice, analysis beyond this point is viewed as too speculative to be reliable. The number of periods used in the calculation is sometimes referred to as the model horizon.

- **Periodic revenue**

    The amount of revenue collected from a customer in the period.

- **Profit Margin (Profit as a percentage of revenue)**

    Depending on circumstances this may be reflected as a percentage of gross or net profit. For incremental marketing that does not incur any incremental overhead that would be allocated against profit, gross profit margins are acceptable.

Test your understanding 8

O3 is a mobile telephone network. It has recently announced that 4% of its customers cancelled their contracts and moved to rival networks in the last year.

Which of the following inputs to customer lifetime value (CLV) analysis is this an example of?

A   Discount rate
B   Churn rate
C   Retention cost
D   Periodic revenue

Marketing audits

The marketing audit is a particular form of position audit which focuses on the products of the firm and the relationship it has with customers.

It helps to not only give the company a deeper understanding of the market it operates in, but also the strategies it will need to implement in order to gain competitive advantage.

The normal stages in a marketing audit include:

(1) **Define the market.** This involves the firm describing the products or services it wishes to offer in the market, as well as the key characteristics of the market itself. These could include size, growth rate and the strategies most likely to succeed in it.

(2) **Determine performance differentials.** The purpose here is to look for segments of the market that are currently not being fulfilled and which may provide an entry-point for the business (or a rival). For example, Subway exploited a niche in the fast-food market by attracting health conscious consumers who were not having their needs met by existing suppliers.

(3) **Profile the strategies of competitors.** This involves 'getting to know your enemy'. Major competitors should be identified, along with a profile of their products, services and style of competitive strategy. The firm's own strategy can then be compared against those of its competitors.

(4) **Determine the strategic planning structure.** This involves deciding how the strategic marketing effort is to be organised, including the assignment of staff and the goals and objectives of the marketing department.

Customer satisfaction and retention

Key to retention is understanding and delivering the drivers of customer satisfaction as satisfaction drives loyalty and loyalty drives profitability.

The 'SERVQUAL' approach to service quality developed by **Parasuraman et al** focuses on the following factors.

Tangibles

- The 'tangibles' heading considers the appearance of physical facilities, equipment, personnel and communications.
- For online quality the key issue is the appearance and appeal of websites – customers will revisit websites that they find appealing.
- This can include factors such as structural and graphic design, quality of content, ease of use, speed to upload and frequency of update.

Reliability

- Reliability is the ability to provide a promised service dependably and accurately and is usually the most important of the different aspects being discussed here.
- For online service quality, reliability is mainly concerned with how easy it is to connect to the website.
- If websites are inaccessible some of the time and/or e-mails are bounced back, then customers will lose confidence in the retailer.

Responsiveness

- Responsiveness looks at the willingness of a firm to help customers and provide prompt service.
- In the context of e-business, excessive delays can cause customers to 'bail-out' of websites and/or transactions and go elsewhere.
- This could relate to how long it takes for e-mails to be answered or even how long it takes for information to be downloaded to a user's browser.

Assurance

- Assurance is the knowledge and courtesy of employees and their ability to inspire trust and confidence.
- For an online retailer, assurance looks at two issues – the quality of responses and the privacy/security of customer information.

- Quality of response includes competence, credibility and courtesy and could involve looking at whether replies to e-mails are automatic or personalised and whether questions have been answered satisfactorily.

Empathy

- Empathy considers the caring, individualised attention a firm gives its customers.
- Most people would assume that empathy can only occur through personal human contact but it can be achieved to some degree through personalising websites and e-mail.
- Key here is whether customers feel understood. For example, being recommended products that they would never dream of buying can erode empathy.

Techniques for retaining customers

Given the above consideration of service quality, firms use the following e-techniques to try to retain customers.

- Personalisation – delivering individualised content through web-pages or e-mail. For example, portals such as Yahoo! enable users to configure their home pages to give them the information they are most interested in.
- Mass customisation – delivering customised content to groups of users through web-pages or e-mail. For example, Amazon may recommend a particular book based on what other customers in a particular segment have been buying.
- Extranets – for example, Dell Computers uses an extranet to provide additional services to its 'Dell Premier' customers.
- Opt-in e-mail – asking customers whether they wish to receive further offers.
- Online communities – firms can set up communities where customers create the content. These could be focussed on purpose (e.g. Autotrader is for people buying/selling cars), positions (e.g. the teenage chat site Doobedo), interest (e.g. Football365) or profession. Despite the potential for criticism of a company's products on a community, firms will understand where service quality can be improved, gain a better understanding of customer needs and be in a position to answer criticism.

> **Customer extension**
>
> Customer extension has the objective of increasing the lifetime value of a customer and typically involves the following.
>
> - 'Re-sell' similar products to previous sales.
> - 'Cross sell' closely related products.
> - 'Up sell' more expensive products.
> - For example, having bought a book from Amazon you could be contacted with offers of other books, DVDs or DVD players.
> - Reactivate customers who have not bought anything for some time.
>
> Key to these is propensity modelling.
>
> **Propensity modelling**
>
> Propensity modelling involves evaluating customer behaviour and then making recommendations to them for future products. For example, if you have bought products from Amazon, then each time you log on there will be a recommendation of other products you may be interested in.
>
> This can involve the following.
>
> - Create automatic product relationships – e.g. through monitoring which products are typically bought together.
> - Using trigger words or phrases – e.g. 'customers who bought …also bought…'.
> - Offering related products at checkout – e.g. batteries for electronic goods

4.4 The use of information technology in downstream supply chain management

IT can be used in a number of ways within the downstream supply chain, including:

- **Electronic Data Interchange (EDI)** – the business can link its sales system to the purchasing system of its major customers, increasing the speed and efficiency of placing orders. This can act as a tie-in/switching cost as it is likely to make it harder for the customer to leave and move to a rival supplier, as this would lead to expense and disruption.

- **E-commerce** – the business may be able to sell online to customers, allowing it to expand its customer base and brand awareness (see chapter 9 for a more detailed discussion of this issue).
- **Intelligence gathering** – online customer transactions can be monitored, helping the business to understand their needs and work to meet them. Online surveys and questionnaires will allow the business to quickly and efficiently ask for customer opinions and feedback. This can all be used to improve the quality of the business's marketing.
- **Communication** – email and other IT systems will allow the organisation to keep in touch with its customers, keeping them informed about order progress, or new products and services they may be interested in.
- **User communities** – the users of some complex products, such as software, set up user communities where members help each other and where pressure on the product supplier can be organised. Strong user communities are valued by their members and the organisation would be wise to look at the comments and queries on the bulletin boards.

The use of intranets and extranets

One key way that an organisation can use IT to improve its downstream supply chain management is through the use of intranets and extranets.

An intranet is a private network within a single company using Internet standards to enable employees to share information using e-mail and web publishing.

An extranet is formed by extending an intranet beyond a company to customers, suppliers and other collaborators.

The benefits of using an extranet are as follows:

- **Information sharing in a secure environment**

    For example, the advertising agency Saatchi allows customers to view draft advertising material during a project.

- **Cost reduction**

    Savings can arise from need fewer people in the ordering process and the elimination of the need to rekey information from paper documents.

- **Order processing and distribution**

    For example, a customer's point of sales terminals can be linked to a supplier's delivery system, ensuring prompt replenishment of goods sold. this results in fewer lost sales due to stock-outs and lower inventory holding.

- **Improved customer service**

    Customer service can be improved through easier / quicker access to information, increased accuracy and consistency of information and quicker response times. Together these build customer confidence and may result in increased revenue.

The effects of IT on the structure of the downstream supply chain

There are three main ways in which e-business can affect an organisation's relationship with its customers:

Disintermediation – in this process intermediate organisations (middlemen) can be taken out of the supply chain. Intermediaries include distributors, wholesalers and agents. The business can therefore sell its product or service direct to the end consumer, rather than selling via a middleman who takes a share of the profits.

For example, musicians can sell their music directly through their own websites rather than being produced and sold through a record company. Games console manufacturers have started selling games that can be downloaded straight to the console, cutting out games retailers and allowing the manufacturer to earn a higher share of the profits from the sale.

The process of **reintermediation** is also found, where the business creates a new intermediary into the downstream supply chain.

Customers, suppliers and supply chain management

In the UK, Confused.com was set up by Admiral (a group of companies that offer various types of insurance) to help users pick between insurance providers for their car and home insurance policies. Admiral therefore introduced a new intermediary into the supply chain as customers now went through the comparison site before purchasing a policy from an insurance company.

Countermediation is where established firms create their own new intermediaries to compete with established intermediaries.

The launch of Confused.com was followed by the creation of several rival comparison sites, including Comparethemarket.com, which was set up by BGL – another UK insurance group.

Illustration 6 – Downstream SCM

An example of disintermediation is seen in the travel industry where travel agents have been cut out of many transactions as the public can book directly with hotels, airlines and rail companies.

The travel industry also gives an example of reintermediation. Companies like lastminute.com and expedia.com are like new travel agents, presenting a wide choice of products and services.

An example of countermediation is Opodo.com, set up by a collaboration of European airlines to encourage customers to book flights directly with them rather than using cost-comparison intermediaries such as lastminute.com.

Test your understanding 9

Z plc offers car insurance to its customers. The car insurance industry is large and made up of hundreds of different rivals, all offering similar insurance products.

One of Z's rivals, M, has recently created a new website that allows consumers to compare quotes quickly and easily from the majority of the car insurance companies in the market.

While not every customer chooses M from the list of quotes they are given, M receives commission from every policy sold through its site.

Z wishes to respond to this change in the market by creating its own comparison website.

Z's planned strategy is an example of:

A   Intermediation

B   Disintermediation

C   Reintermediation

D   Countermediation

Test your understanding 10 – DRB – (Case style)

DRB Electronic Services operates in a high labour cost environment in Western Europe and imports electronic products from the Republic of Korea. It re-brands and re-packages them as DRB products and then sells them to business and domestic customers in the local geographical region. Its only current source of supply is ISAS electronics based in a factory on the outskirts of Seoul, the capital of the Republic of Korea. DRB regularly places orders for ISAS products through the ISAS web-site and pays for them by credit card. As soon as the payment is confirmed ISAS automatically e-mails DRB a confirmation of order, an order reference number and likely shipping date. When the order is actually despatched, ISAS send DRB a notice of despatch e-mail and a container reference number. ISAS currently organises all the shipping of the products. The products are sent in containers and then trans-shipped to EIF, the logistics company used by ISAS to distribute its products. EIF then delivers the products to the DRB factory. Once they arrive, they are quality inspected and products that pass the inspection are re-branded as DRB products (by adding appropriate logos) and packaged in specially fabricated DRB boxes. These products are then stored ready for sale. All customer sales are from stock. Products that fail the inspection are returned to ISAS.

Currently 60% of sales are made to domestic customers and 40% to business customers. Most domestic customers pick up their products from DRB and set them up themselves. In contrast, most business customers ask DRB to set up the electronic equipment at their offices, for which DRB makes a small charge. DRB currently advertises its products in local and regional newspapers. DRB also has a web site which provides product details. Potential customers can enquire about the specification and availability of products through an e-mail facility in the web site. DRB then e-mails an appropriate response directly to the person making the enquiry. Payment for products cannot currently be made through the web site.

Customers, suppliers and supply chain management

Feedback from existing customers suggests that they particularly value the installation and support offered by the company. The company employs specialist technicians who (for a fee) will install equipment in both homes and offices. They will also come out and troubleshoot problems with equipment that is still under warranty. DRB also offer a helpline and a back to base facility for customers whose products are out of warranty. Feedback from current customers suggests that this support is highly valued. One commented that 'it contrasts favourably with your large customers who offer support through impersonal off-shore call centres and a time-consuming returns policy'. Customers can also pay for technicians to come on-site to sort out problems with out-of-warranty equipment.

Dilip Masood, the owner of DRB, has sent you the following email:

To: J. Kooper
From: D. Masood
Date: 17/06/XX
Subject: Supply chain management

Hi J,

I'm sure you're aware that DRB is planning to increase our product range and market share. We plan to grow from our current turnover of £5m per annum to £12m per annum in two years time. I believe that DRB must change its business model if it is to achieve this growth. I believe that these changes will also have to tackle problems associated with:

- Missing, or potentially missing shipments. Shipments can only be tracked through contacting the shipment account holder, ISAS, and on occasions they have been reluctant or unable to help. The trans-shipment to EIF has also caused problems and this has usually been identified as the point where goods have been lost. ISAS does not appear to be able to reliably track the relationship between the container shipment and the Waybills used in the EIF system.

- The likely delivery dates of orders, the progress of orders and the progress of shipments is poorly specified and monitored. Hence deliveries are relatively unpredictable and this can cause congestion problems in the delivery bay.

I also recognise that growth will mean that the company has to sell more products outside its region and the technical installation and support so valued by local customers will be difficult to maintain. I am determined that DRB will continue to import only fully configured products. I am not interested in importing components and assembling them. DRB will also not build or invest in assembly plants overseas or commit to a long-term contract with one supplier.

Bearing this in mind, I would be grateful for your thoughts on a number of key issues.

Firstly, I need you to draw the primary activities of DRB on a value chain. Please comment on the significance of each of these activities and the value that they offer to customers.

Explain how DRB might re-structure its upstream supply chain to achieve the growth required by DRB and to tackle the problems that I have identified.

Also, please explain how DRB might re-structure its downstream supply chain to achieve the growth required.

I need some briefing notes on this in the next 45 minutes as I am about to go into a meeting with our business advisors.

I look forward to your reply.

Kind regards

Dilip

Required:

Draft the briefing notes as requested by Dilip.

(45 minutes)

Customers, suppliers and supply chain management

5 Summary

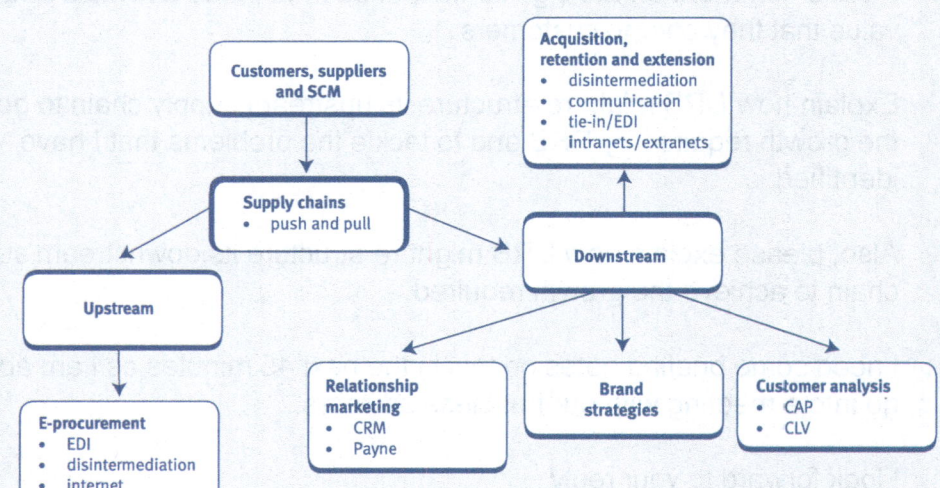

chapter 11

Test your understanding answers

Test your understanding 1

The correct answer is PUSH

V makes his products without reference to customers and then attempts to 'push' them onto his clients.

Test your understanding 2

The correct answer is A

Customers and consumers need to have sufficient cash to buy the product, while suppliers need to have enough cash/profit to want to make the components the business uses to make its products.

Ensuring every link in the supply chain has sufficient cash is therefore an important part of ensuring supply and demand for the business's products.

Test your understanding 3 – (Integration question)

The key elements of XL's upstream supply chain are likely to include:

- travel providers (such as bus, train or airline companies)
- accommodation providers
- local food producers and restaurants
- attractions, activity and excursion providers

While it could also be widened to consider other suppliers, such as local bars and local infrastructure providers (amongst others), supply chain management is likely to focus on the key elements of the supply chain outlined above.

501

Customers, suppliers and supply chain management

A key function of the supply chain is to ensure that the chain contains the correct value system to support XL's competitive advantage. As some customers are beginning to complain, there is growing evidence that it may no longer be doing so.

As such, XL should begin by communicating with a selection of customers (not just those who are complaining) to determine what they would like from their tour and how they feel things could be improved.

XL can then use this information to provide suppliers with areas that they will need to focus on to improve the customer experience.

For example, XL could examine the accommodation it offers. It could consider issues such as location, ease of access, appearance, staffing and facilities.

For travel providers, XL may wish to examine the safety measures, the ease of check-in, luggage facilities and in-journey refreshments and facilities.

Should there be any problem areas for customers that a supplier is either unwilling or unable to change, XL could consider attempting to switch to an alternative supplier.

Test your understanding 4

The correct answer is A

Transaction marketing focuses on the product, rather than the customer or service provided.

Test your understanding 5

The correct answer is D

A referral market occurs when someone refers a consumer to an organisation's products. An insurance broker would be an example of this – the broker is actively referring consumers to certain insurance company products and therefore is part of the insurance company's referral market.

WOT is simply rating and recommending products. This would suggest an influence market, as they are simply endorsing certain products.

chapter 11

Test your understanding 6

The correct answers are B, C and F

The others are methods of retaining or extending existing customers.

Test your understanding 7

The correct answer is C

By definition

Test your understanding 8

The correct answer is B

By definition.

Test your understanding 9

The correct answer is D

M's website is an example of reintermediation. By setting up an equivalent comparison site of its own, Z is countermediating.

Customers, suppliers and supply chain management

Test your understanding 10 – DRB – (Case style)

Briefing notes

(a) A simple value chain of the primary activities of DRB is shown below.

Handling and storing inbound fully configured equipment Quality inspection	Re-branding of products Re-packaging of products	Customer collection Technician delivery and installation	Local advertising Web-based enquiries	On-site technical support Back to base support
Inbound logistics	**Operations**	**Outbound logistics**	**Marketing and sales**	**Service**

Comments about value might include:

Inbound logistics: Excellent quality assurance is required in inbound logistics. This is essential for pre-configured equipment where customers have high expectations of reliability. As well as contributing to customer satisfaction, high quality also reduces service costs.

Operations: This is a relatively small component in the DRB value chain and actually adds little value to the customer. It is also being undertaken in a relatively high cost country. DRB might wish to re-visit the current arrangement.

Outbound logistics: Customer feedback shows that this is greatly valued. Products can be picked up from stock and delivery and installation is provided if required. Most of the company's larger competitors cannot offer this service. However, it is unlikely that this value can be retained when DRB begins to increasingly supply outside the geographical region it is in.

Marketing and sales: This is very low-key at DRB and will have to be developed if the company is to deliver the proposed growth. The limited functionality of the website offers little value to customers.

Service: Customer feedback shows that this is greatly valued. Most of the company's competitors cannot offer this level of service. They offer support from off-shore call centres and a returns policy that is both time consuming to undertake and slow in rectification. However, it is unlikely that this value can be retained when DRB begins to increasingly supply outside the geographical region it is in.

(b) DRB has already gained efficiencies by procuring products through the supplier's website. However, the website has restricted functionality. When DRB places the order it is not informed of the expected delivery date until it receives the confirmation e-mail from ISAS. It is also unable to track the status of their order and so it is only when it receives a despatch email from ISAS that it knows that it is on its way. Because DRB is not the owner of the shipment, it is unable to track the delivery and so the physical arrival of the goods cannot be easily predicted. On occasions where shipments have appeared to have been lost, DRB has had to ask ISAS to track the shipment and report on its status. This has not been very satisfactory and the problem has been exacerbated by having two shippers involved. ISAS has not been able to reliably track the transhipment of goods from their shipper to EIF, the logistics company used to distribute their products in the country. Some shipments have been lost and it is time-consuming to track and follow-up shipments which are causing concern. Finally, because DRB has no long term contract with ISAS, it has to pay when it places the order through a credit card transaction on the ISAS website.

DRB has stated that it wishes to continue importing fully configured products. It is not interested in importing components and assembling them. It also does not wish to build or invest in assembly plants in other countries. However, it may wish to consider the following changes to its upstream supply chain:

- Seek to identify a wider range of suppliers and so trade through other sell-side websites. Clearly there are costs associated with this. Suppliers have to be identified and evaluated and financial and trading arrangements have to be established. However, it removes the risk of single-sourcing and other suppliers may have better systems in place to support order and delivery tracking.

- Seek to identify suppliers who are willing and able to re-brand and package their products with DRB material at the production plant. This should reduce DRB costs as this is currently undertaken in a country where wage rates are high.

- Re-consider the decision not to negotiate long-term contracts with suppliers (including ISAS) and so explore the possibility of more favourable payment terms. DRB has avoided long-term contracts up to now. It may also not be possible to enter into such contracts if DRB begins to trade with a number of suppliers.

- Seek to identify suppliers (including ISAS) who are able to provide information about delivery dates prior to purchase and who are able to provide internet-based order tracking systems to their customers. This should allow much better planning.

- Consider replacing the two supplier shippers with a contracted logistics company which will collect the goods from the supplier and transport the goods directly to DRB. This should reduce physical transhipment problems and allow seamless monitoring of the progress of the order from despatch to arrival. It will also allow DRB to plan for the arrival of goods and to schedule its re-packaging.

DRB might also wish to consider two other procurement models; buy-side and the independent marketplace.

In the buy-side model DRB would use its website to invite potential suppliers to bid for contract requirements posted on the site. This places the onus on suppliers to spend time completing details and making commitments. It should also attract a much wider range of suppliers than would have been possible through DRB searching sell-side sites for potential suppliers. Unfortunately, it is unlikely that DRB is large enough to host such a model. However, it may wish to prototype it to see if it is viable and whether it uncovers potential suppliers who have not been found in sell-side websites searches.

In the independent marketplace model, DRB places its requirements on an intermediary website. These are essentially B2B electronic marketplaces which allow, on the one hand, potential customers to search products being offered by suppliers and, on the other hand, customers to place their requirements and be contacted by potential suppliers. Such marketplaces promise greater supplier choice with reduced costs. They also provide an opportunity for aggregation where smaller organisations (such as DRB) can get together with companies that have the same requirement to place larger orders to gain cheaper prices and better purchasing terms. It is also likely that such marketplaces will increasingly offer algorithms that automatically match customers and suppliers, so reducing the search costs associated with the sell-side model. The independent marketplace model may be a useful approach for DRB. Many of the suppliers participating in these marketplaces are electronics companies.

(c) DRB's downstream supply chain is also very simple at the moment It has a website that shows information about DRB products. Customers can make enquiries about the specification and availability of these products through an e-mail facility. Conventional marketing is undertaken through local advertising and buyers either collect their products or they are delivered and installed by a specialist group of technicians. DRB could tune its downstream supply chain by using many of the approaches mentioned in the previous section.

For example:

- Developing the website so that it not only shows products but also product availability. Customers would be able to place orders and pay for them securely over the website. The site could be integrated with a logistics system so that orders and deliveries can be tracked by the customer. DRB must recognise that most of its competitors already have such systems. However, DRB will have to put a similar system in place to be able to support its growth plans.

- Participating in independent marketplace websites as a supplier. DRB may also be able to exploit aggregation by combining with other suppliers in consortia to bid for large contracts.

- DRB may also consider participating in B2C marketplaces such as eBay. Many organisations use this as their route to market for commodity products.

DRB may also wish to consider replacing its sales from stock approach with sales from order. In the current approach, DRB purchases products in advance and re-packages and stores these products before selling them to customers. This leads to very quick order fulfilment but high storage and financing costs. These costs will become greater if the planned growth occurs. DRB may wish to consider offering products on its website at a discount but with specified delivery terms. This would allow the company to supply to order rather than supply from stock.

Customers, suppliers and supply chain management

Developing the website so that not only shows products but also product availability. Customers would be able to place orders and pay for them securely over the website. The site could be integrated with a logistics system so that orders and deliveries can be tracked by the customer. DRB must recognise that most of its competitors already have such systems. However, DRB will have to put a similar system in place to be able to support its growth plans.

Participating in independent marketplace websites as a supplier. DRB may also be able to exploit aggregation by combining with other suppliers in consortia to bid for larger contracts.

DRB may also consider participating in B2C marketplaces such as eBay. Many organisations use this as their route to market for commodity products.

DRB may also look to consumer-led selling, its sales from stock together with sales from orders. In the current approach, DRB purchases products to order, and the packages and stores those products before selling them on to clients. This leads to very quick or easy fulfilment but high storage and financing costs. Where it sees better margins from these growth sources, DRB may wish to consider offering products via its website at a distance. Chris may specify delivery terms. This would allow the company to surplus its order to the supply chain ...

508

chapter

12

Change management – understanding the context of change

Chapter learning objectives

Lead	Component
C1. Advise on the important elements in the change process	(a) Evaluate the key impacts of organisational change on organisations
C2. Evaluate tools and methods for successfully implementing a change programme	(a) Evaluate tools, techniques and strategies for managing and leading the change process

Indicative syllabus content

- The impact of change on organisational culture (including the cultural web and McKinsey's 7s model)
- The importance of managing critical periods of adaptive, evolutionary, reconstructive and revolutionary change
- Tools, techniques and models associated with organisational change.

Change management – understanding the context of change

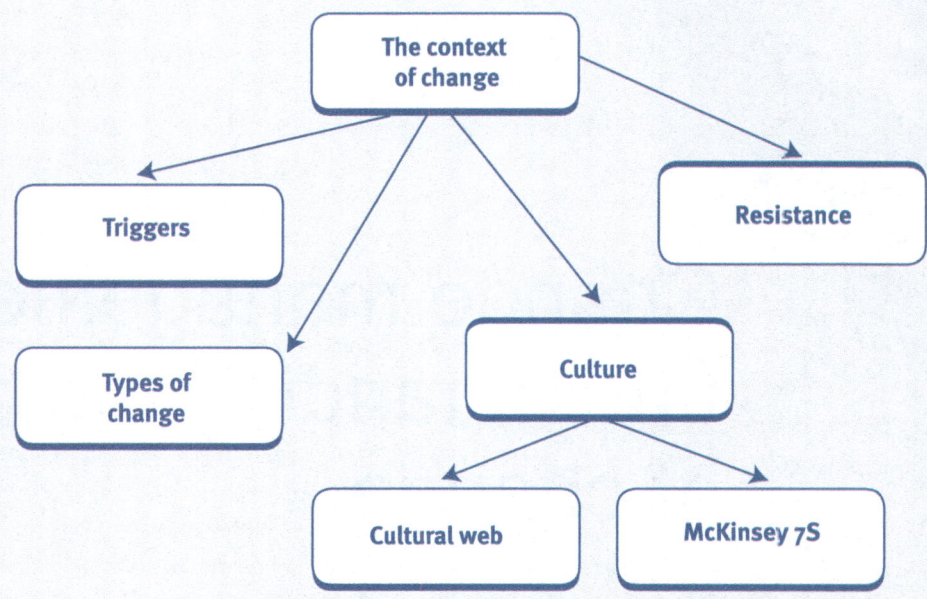

1 Introduction

Internal and external pressures make change inevitable. 'Adapt or die' is the motto of almost every organisation. Some strive to meet the challenge by leading those in the marketplace whilst others hide in niches, snapping at the heels of the major players.

The key questions for all companies are not whether to change or not but rather:

- **What to change?**
- **What to change to?**
- **How to change successfully?**

2 Triggers for change

External triggers

Environmental pressure for change can be divided into two groups.

- General (indirect action) environmental factors – these can be identified using the familiar PEST framework and
- Task (direct action) factors – these can be assessed using Porter's five forces model

Examples of external triggers

Indirect triggers (PEST)

Political/legal	Changes in government
	New environmental protection policies
	New labour laws
	European directives
	Private/public partnerships
Economic	Growth or recession
	Changes in currency and interest rates
	Local labour costs
	Regional prosperity/opportunities
	Disposable income
Social	Attitudes to work and leisure
	Environmentalism
	Attitudes to health/education
	Fashion trends
	Changing national/regional culture
Technological	Growth in Internet
	Public use of IT
	Global sourcing/call centres
	Innovations

Direct triggers (Porter's five forces)

Competitive rivalry	Powerful rivals may force the firm to have to adapt to survive, either through innovation, if a differentiator, or cost cutting if a cost-leader.
Power of customers	Powerful customers could trigger a firm to consider forwards vertical integration
Power of suppliers	Supplier power could encourage a firm to redesign products in order to reduce the reliance on specialist components and thus facilitate multi-sourcing
Threat of new entrants	New entrants may force incumbent firms to improve quality to maintain market share
Threat of substitutes	New technologies may result in substitutes that render existing products obsolete. this could lead to factory closure and reorganisation.

Change management – understanding the context of change

Internal triggers

The reasons for change within the organisation could span any functional area of operation or level of control from strategic to operational.

Philosophy	New ownership
	New CEO
	New initiative/management style
Reorganisation	Takeover/merger
	Divisional restructuring
	Rationalisation/cost reduction
Personnel	Promotions/transfers
	Rules/procedures
	Training/development
Conditions	Location change
	Outsourcing
	Rosters/flexible working
Technology	New procedures/systems
	Changing information demands
	Integration of roles

Problem identification as a precursor to change

The above triggers can be reasons **why** change is considered or even necessary. However, further strategic analysis is needed to determine **what** needs changing.

> **Illustration 1 – Problem identification as a precursor to change**
>
> For example, TGH Textiles is a UK-based clothing manufacturer that has seen falling profits, declining margins and a loss of market share over the last two years. The main reason for this decline is increasing competition from manufacturers in China and India.
>
> The external trigger for change is increased competitive rivalry, but what needs changing?
>
> The first step would involve analysing the firm's cost base and determining customer perceptions regarding relative quality. This should help TGH to see how it's competitive advantage is being eroded. Suppose poor quality is identified as the underlying problem.

> Even then, it is not obvious what needs changing. "Poor quality" could be an underlying problem of customer perception related to brand or design flaws, the quality of raw materials, production problems or an underlying culture where quality is not valued highly enough. Determining the main cause(s) could involve discussions with customers, competitor analysis, Porter's value chain analysis, SWOT and /or benchmarking.
>
> Only then will the directors have a clear idea of what needs changing.

3 Classifying change

Types of organisational change

Change can be classified by the extent (or scope) of the change required, and the speed with which the change is to be achieved:

Types of change

	Extent of change	
Speed of change	**Transformation**	**Realignment**
Incremental	**Evolution:** Transformational change implemented gradually through inter-related initiatives; likely to be proactive change undertaken in participation of the need for future change	**Adaptation:** Change undertaken to realign the way in which the organisation operates; implemented in a series of steps
Big Bang	**Revolution:** Transformational change that occurs via simultaneous initiatives on many fronts: • more likely to be forced and reactive because of the changing competitive conditions that the organisation is facing	**Reconstruction:** Change undertaken to realign the way in which the organisation operates with many initiatives implemented simultaneously: • often forced and reactive because of a changing competitive context

(Exploring strategic change – Balogun, Hope Hailey)

Note that incremental change is also known as "continuous" change while "discontinuous change" refers to the big bang above.

- Transformation entails changing an organisation's culture. It is a fundamental change that cannot be handled within the existing organisational paradigm. This is likely to be a top down process and is normally driven by major external events.

Change management – understanding the context of change

- Realignment does not involve a fundamental reappraisal of the central assumptions and beliefs.

- Evolution can take a long period of time, but results in a fundamentally different organisation once completed. It is normally taken in anticipation of a need for change

- Revolution is likely to be a forced, reactive transformation using simultaneous initiatives on many fronts, and often in a relatively short space of time. It is rapid and likely to affect most, if not all, aspects of what the business does and how it operates – in other words it represents a fundamental change to the organisation's paradigm. It is therefore critical that this type of change is managed effectively.

Change examples

Kaplan think that over the next 5 to 10 years students are going to demand more flexible ways of learning - probably using more technology. Currently a proportion of students want some of this, but a great majority still prefer to be taught in a classroom. Also, Kaplan's existing material and staff can easily be converted to new methods of delivery (for example, paper study texts converted to online materials, tutors teaching online or preparing pre-recorded video rather than in a classroom). Therefore Kaplan does not need major changes, and can change slowly over time. This is **adaptation** – the company needs to adapt to its changing external environment.

Microsoft needs an evolution. The company is still making huge profits each year and the majority of consumers still use Microsoft products (such as Windows) every day. So change isn't needed quickly. But growth has levelled off and many of its previously successful products are in decline (such as the Xbox, Windows software sales, the company's mobile phones, etc.) as it has failed to keep up with the developments of its rivals. So Microsoft needs to transform its business model (this has already begun; the company now gives Windows 10 away for free rather than charging for upgrades) but it can do it gradually over time. This is **evolution.**

Reconstruction happens for organisations that don't need major changes, but who do need to change quickly. Due to UK Government reforms in 2016, UK pension funds have been compelled by law to offer now to pensioners the opportunity to take a lump sum rather than an annuity, and to offer advice to each pensioner on what is best for them. This needs a change in the business model for companies like Aviva. It isn't a massive change and isn't going to cause a lot of disruption, but it needs to happen quickly in order to comply with the law.

The retailer Game went into administration in March 2012, largely due to high fixed costs, an ambitious international expansion programme, and increased competition from online-only retailers. At the time, the company had over 600 stores. The administrators reviewed the portfolio of outlets and decided to close 277 (or almost half!) of them immediately, continuing to trade only the more profitable stores. The company was then sold to private investment company OpCapita, who set about restructuring the business model and developing a new expansion strategy. The financial crisis that had engulfed the company meant that change had to be both quick and transformational - an example of **revolution.**

Strategic change

Strategic change is by definition farreaching. We speak of strategic change when fundamental alterations are made to the business system or the organisational system. Adding a lemonflavoured Coke to the product portfolio is interesting, maybe important, but not a strategic change, while branching out into bottled water was a major departure from CocaCola's traditional business system.

Evolution or revolution?

Another way that evolution can be explained is by conceiving of the organisation as a learning system. However, within incremental change there may be a danger of strategic drift, because change is based on the existing paradigm and routines of the organisation, even when environmental or competitive pressure might suggest the need for more fundamental change.

In selecting an approach to strategic change, most managers struggle with the question of how bold they should be. On the one hand, they usually realise that to fundamentally transform the organisation, a break with the past is needed. To achieve strategic renewal it is essential to turn away from the firm's heritage and to start with a clean slate. On the other hand, they also recognise the value of continuity, building on past experiences, investments and loyalties. To achieve lasting strategic renewal, people in the organisation will need time to learn, adapt and grow into a new organisational reality.

The 'window of opportunity' for achieving a revolutionary strategic change can be small for a number of reasons. Some of the most common triggers are:

Change management – understanding the context of change

- **competitive pressure** – when a firm is under intense competitive pressure and its market position starts to erode quickly, a rapid and dramatic response might be the only approach possible. Especially when the organisation threatens to slip into a downward spiral towards insolvency, a bold turnaround can be the only option left to the firm.

- **regulatory pressure** – firms can also be put under pressure by the government or regulatory agencies to push through major changes within a short period of time. Such externally imposed revolutions can be witnessed among public sector organisations (e.g. hospitals and schools) and highly regulated industries (e.g. utilities and telecommunications), but in other sectors of the economy as well (e.g. public health regulations). Some larger organisations will, however, seek to influence and control regulation.

- **first mover advantage** – a more proactive reason for instigating revolutionary change, is to be the first firm to introduce a new product, service or technology and to build up barriers to entry for late movers.

Test your understanding 1

Strategic change can be classified as evolution, adaptation, reconstruction or revolution. The classification depends on both the scope and speed of the change.

Which ONE of the following combinations of extent and speed of change would be classified as an evolutionary change?

	Extent	Speed
A	Transformation	Big bang
B	Realignment	Big bang
C	Transformation	Incremental
D	Realignment	Incremental

Test your understanding 2

H makes and sells a patented chemical, known as LKL, widely used in cosmetics. LKL has recently been found to increase the risk of cancer of users. This has led to a ban on all cosmetics containing LKL.

H has therefore started urgently looking for alternative uses for LKL. It has identified that LKL can be an effective pesticide and, due to its lack of contact with humans the increased risk of cancer will not be an issue. H has therefore started looking for pesticide manufacturers to sell to.

Which ONE of the following types of organisational change is occurring at H?

A   Reconstruction

B   Evolution

C   Revolution

D   Adaptation

Test your understanding 3 – (Integration question)

Historically the directors of Zed Bank have resisted change, seeking to offer a traditional approach to its customers. However, recent problems within the banking industry and an increasingly competitive market has forced the Board to consider a number of important initiatives, including:

- enhancing its current services to customers by providing them with on-line internet and telephone banking services; and
- reducing costs by closing many of its rural and smaller branches (outlets).

In an attempt to pacify the employee representatives (the Banking Trade Union) and to reduce expected protests by the communities affected by branch closure, a senior bank spokesperson has announced that the changes will be 'incremental' in nature. In particular, she has stressed that:

- the change will be implemented over a lengthy time period
- there will be no compulsory redundancies
- banking staff ready to take on new roles and opportunities in the online operations will be retrained and offered generous relocation expenses.

For customers, the bank has promised that automatic cash dispensing machines will be available in all the localities where branches (outlets) close. Customers will also be provided with the software needed for Internet banking and other assistance necessary to give them quick and easy access to banking services.

The leader of the Banking Trade Union is 'appalled' at the initiatives announced. He has argued that the so-called 'incremental' change is in fact the start of a 'transformational' change that will have serious repercussions, not only for the Union's members but also for many of the bank's customers.

Change management – understanding the context of change

> **Required:**
>
> Distinguish incremental change from transformational change. Explain why the bank spokesperson and the trade union leader disagree over their description of the change.
>
> **(15 minutes)**

4 Organisational culture

Definition

Culture is the set of values, guiding beliefs, understandings and ways of thinking that are shared by the members of an organisation and is taught to new members as correct. It represents the unwritten, feeling part of the organisation.

Culture is 'the way we do things around here' (Charles Handy).

Culture is a set of 'taken-for-granted' assumptions, views of the environment, behaviours and routines (Schein).

Cultural processes of change

The inherent culture of the organisation is important for two reasons:

Firstly the existing culture can become "embedded" and hence resistant to change. Overcoming this resistance can be a major challenge.

Secondly the existing culture can limit the types of strategy development and change that are considered.

- Faced with forces for change, managers will seek to minimise the extent to which they are faced with ambiguity and uncertainty by defining the situation in terms of that which is familiar.

- This can explain why some firms adopt incremental strategies and, worse, why some fail to address the impact of environmental triggers, resulting in strategic drift.

chapter 12

> **Illustration 2 – Cultural process of change**
>
> Faced with a change trigger such as declining performance, management are likely to react as follows:
>
> (1) First managers will try to improve the effectiveness and efficiency of the existing strategy
>
> e.g. through tighter controls
>
> (2) If this is not effective, then a change in strategy may occur but in line with existing strategies
>
> e.g. through market development, selling existing products into markets that are similar to existing ones and managing the process in the same way as they are used to.
>
> (3) Even when managers know intellectually that more radical change is needed, they find themselves constrained by existing routines, assumptions and political processes.

The cultural web

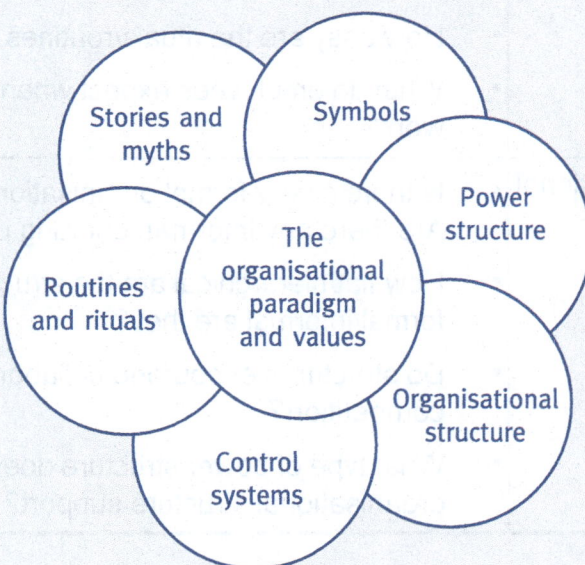

The cultural web was devised by Gerry Johnson as part of his work to attempt to explain why firms often failed to adjust to environmental change as quickly as they needed to. He concluded that firms developed a way of understanding their organisation – called a paradigm – and found it difficult to think and act outside this paradigm if it was particularly strong.

519

Change management – understanding the context of change

Using the cultural web to map change

The concept of the cultural web is a useful device for mapping out change but its real worth is in the fact that we can identify which elements of culture need to change.

Key questions to ask include:

Stories	• What stories do people relate within the organisation and what do they say about the organisation's values? • How pervasive are these beliefs (through the levels of the organisation)? • What do current staff tell new staff when they join? • Do stories relate to: strengths or weaknesses, successes or failures, conformity or mavericks? Who are the heroes and villains? • What norms do the mavericks deviate from?
Routines and rituals	• What behaviour do routines encourage? Which would look odd if changed? • What are the key rituals that staff undertake regularly? What core beliefs do they reflect? • What do training programmes emphasise? • How easy are the rituals/routines to change? • What do employees expect when they come to work?
Organisational structures	• Is there a very formal organisational structure? Are there any informal reporting mechanisms? • How flat/hierarchical are the structures? How formal/informal are they? • Do structures encourage collaboration or competition? • What type of power structure does the overall organisational structure support?

Control systems	• What is most closely monitored/controlled in my organisation? • Is emphasis on reward or punishment? Are there many/few controls? • Are all employees aware of the control mechanisms in place? • Is the organisation well controlled?
Power structures	• What are the core beliefs of the leadership in my organisation? • Who has the power to make decisions? • Is power used effectively and appropriately? • How is power distributed in the organisation? • What are the main blockages to change?
Symbols	• What language and jargon are used in the organisation? • How internal or accessible are they? • What aspects of strategy are highlighted in publicity? • What status symbols are there? • Are there particular symbols that denote the organisation to the outside world/customers?
Overall	• What are the (four) key underlying assumptions that are the paradigm? • What is the dominant culture? • How easy is this to change?

Illustration 3 – The cultural web

Suppose you are acting as a consultant to the technical services department of a local government authority. You have found that departments are not very responsive to the needs of users and that service is inconsistent from one branch to another.

A strategic change workshop with managers resulted in the following cultural web:

Change management – understanding the context of change

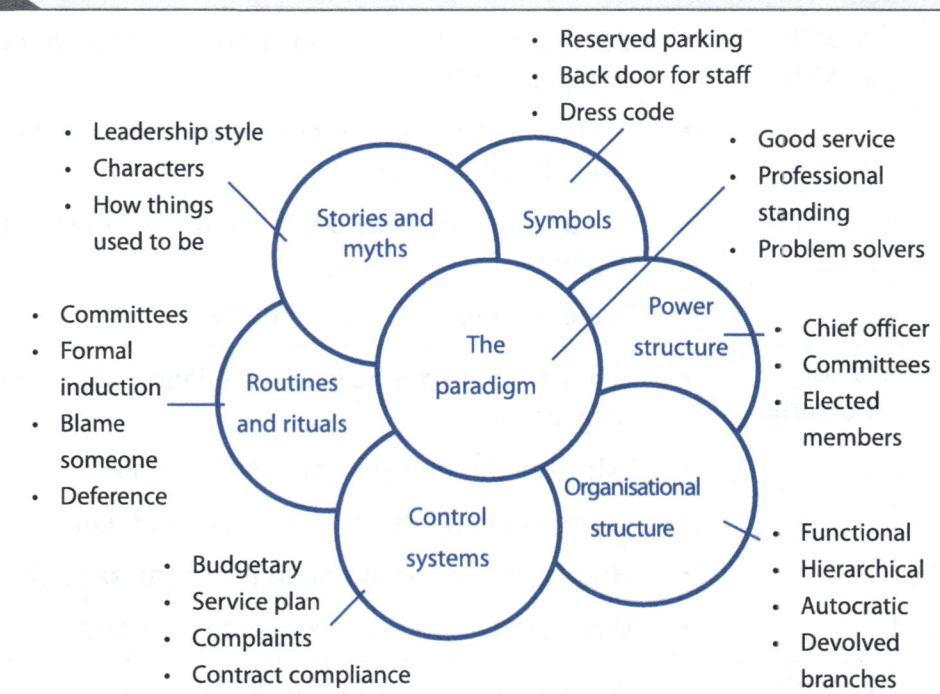

What is notable about the paradigm is that staff believe they are providing a "good service", that they have a high professional standing and see themselves as problem solvers. Unfortunately their problem solving and professional standards do not appear to be customer focused. The fact that stories and myths focus on how things "used to be" indicate staff are out of touch with user needs.

Furthermore, given the degree of local autonomy, an emphasis on status symbols such as parking spaces and a blame culture, it is hardly surprising that co-operation and standardisation across branches is poor.

These are the cultural challenges that must be met if effective change is to be implemented.

Test your understanding 4

D has recently been hired by B Brothers Ltd, a large department store which is owned and run by the Bond family. The family has owned and run the store for 75 years and little has changed in the management approach.

D has been hired in order to make suggestions relating to strategic changes needed within B Brothers, which has seen falling profitability for the last five years.

His first suggestion was to eliminate the private dining room that was set aside for senior managers. D suggested that this room was too expensive to run and damaged management's ability to interact with more junior members of staff.

D's suggestion was met with significant opposition, with senior management suggesting that he had 'failed to understand the culture of B Brothers'.

Which ONE aspect of B Brothers' corporate culture would D's suggestion have directly impacted upon?

A   Power structure

B   Control systems

C   Symbols

D   Stories and myths

Test your understanding 5

G Ltd is a training organisation based in country S. G's mission statement, which is regularly promoted by management is 'to enable students to achieve their long-term goals in the workplace'.

Employees, however, believe that the company's main aim is to simply make a profit and this has caused problems with customer service and student satisfaction at G Ltd.

According to the cultural web model, there appears to be confusion between managers and students over the organisation's _____.

Which ONE of the following words correctly fills the gap in the sentence above?

A   Mission

B   Paradigm

C   Objectives

D   Vision

Test your understanding 6 – HBY – (Case style)

HBY is a manufacturer of children's toys based in country U. It makes scale models of motor vehicles and trains using traditional methods. This means there is a heavy reliance on manual labour with a focus on quality. HBY's sales have declined since their peak around twenty years ago, although they have been static for many years. The company is owned by the founding family (who also occupy most of the senior positions on HBY's Board of Directors) and has always returned acceptable profits, with the family regularly consulting their workers regarding the strategic decisions made by the board – in spite of the organisation's rigid, bureaucratic structure. The many levels of management create a defined career path for staff, and the directors place a strong emphasis on individual growth and development.

Recently, the family have decided to sell the company to a large, multinational toy-maker, WDG, who wishes to add HBY's well-known brand name to its portfolio. WDG is a listed company and is under pressure from its shareholders to increase dividends and profits.

HBY's employees have been informed of many of WDG's plans for the company, including a move to cheaper, more automated production processes. WDG has not spoken with any staff representatives of HBY to date and redundancies have not been confirmed, though staff expect them to be significant.

WDG has announced that it will be replacing several levels of HBY's managers with a single tier of their own senior staff, who will have oversight over all of HBY's employees and remaining managers. Whereas staff at HBY have historically been left to get on with their work, unless there were specific problems, WDG's Board have stated that they will be more hands-on, helping train staff on the 'new, improved manufacturing processes being introduced by WDG'.

WDG has also suggested that the company's pay structure will be altered. Previously, staff were awarded a bonus based on a range of indicators, including sales and customer complaints. WDG wishes to pay staff on a piecework basis and is planning to cut back on the regular social gatherings that HBY has historically provided for its workers.

Finally, WDG has indicated that it no longer wishes to pursue the quality accreditation that HBY has attained for the last ten years, as the 'costs outweigh the benefits'.

The staff of HBY have expressed their concern to the current owners. Staff are unionised and they have stated their intention to strike over the proposals. A number of HBY's senior managers have stated that WDG 'clearly fails to understand the culture of HBY and should not be allowed to destroy the organisation that HBY's staff have worked so hard to build.'

chapter 12

> **Required:**
>
> Draft a report to the management of WDG, which identifies the various aspects of the existing culture of HBY, using an appropriate model to structure your report.
>
> You should also use your report to explain the reasons for HBY's staff resisting the proposed takeover by WDG.
>
> **(25 minutes)**

5 McKinsey 7S Model

Like the cultural web, McKinsey's 7S model looks at corporate culture and the various components that it is made up of. McKinsey saw culture as seven interconnected elements, each beginning with the letter S.

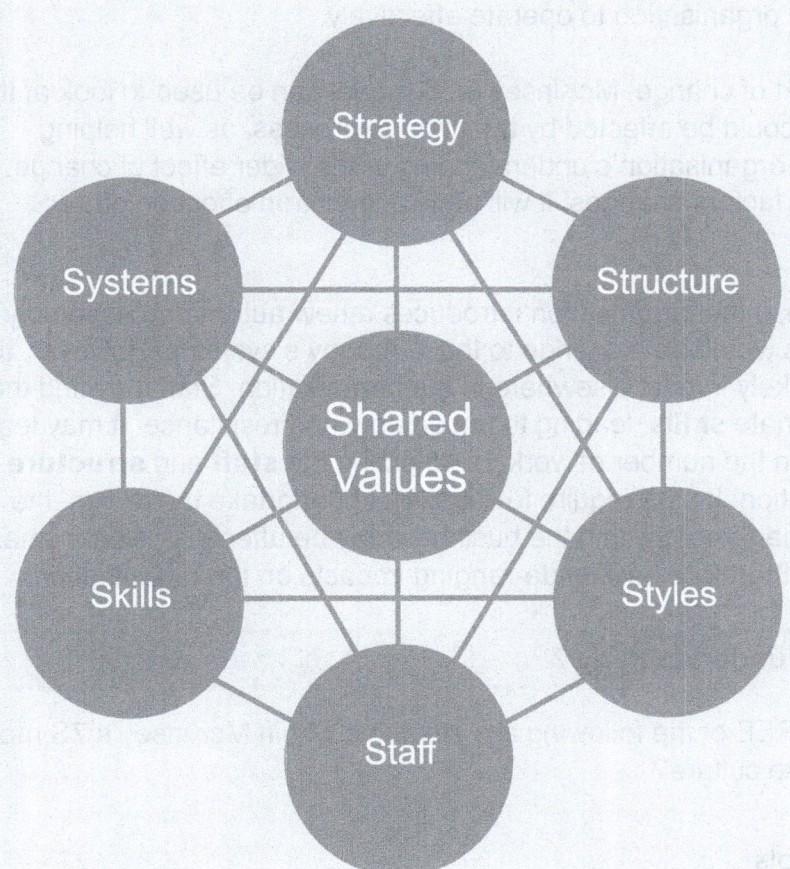

Three of these factors are referred to as 'hard' (tangible and easy to quantify):

- **Structure** – this looks at the way the organisation is structured and who reports to whom.

- **Strategy** – relates to the ways in which the organisation plans to gain a competitive advantage or achieve other objectives.
- **Systems** – these are the daily activities and procedures followed by staff.

The remaining four factors are 'soft' (less easily quantified and more subjective):

- **Skills** – the skills, abilities and competences of the organisation's employees.
- **Style** – the style of leadership adopted within the organisation
- **Staff** – the people that make up the organisation
- **Shared values** – the core values of the organisation (i.e. the paradigm)

The model suggests that all seven elements have to be aligned with each in order for the organisation to operate effectively.

In the context of change, McKinsey's 7S model can be used to look at the factors that could be affected by the change process, as well helping improve the organisation's understanding of the wider effect of change. If one of the S factors changes, it will have a knock-on effect on other S factors.

For instance, if the organisation introduces a new automated assembly process, this would be a change to the company's systems. However, this would also likely impact elsewhere in the organisation. Staff may find they lack appropriate **skills**, leading to uncertainty and resistance. It may lead to a reduction in the number of workers, affecting the **staff** and **structure** of the organisation. If staff require fewer skills to undertake their roles, the **style** of management within the business may be affected. Even a small change can therefore have wide-ranging impacts on the organisation.

Test your understanding 7

Which THREE of the following are elements within McKinsey's 7S model of corporate culture?

A   Symbols
B   Stories and myths
C   Structure
D   Support
E   Skills
F   Styles

chapter 12

Test your understanding 8

Which ONE of the following factors of the McKinsey 7S model is classified as a 'soft' element?

A   Structure

B   Strategy

C   Staff

D   Systems

6 Resistance to change

Resistance to change is the action taken by individuals and groups when they perceive that a change that is occurring is a threat to them.

Resistance is 'any attitude or behaviour that reflects a person's unwillingness to make or support a desired change'.

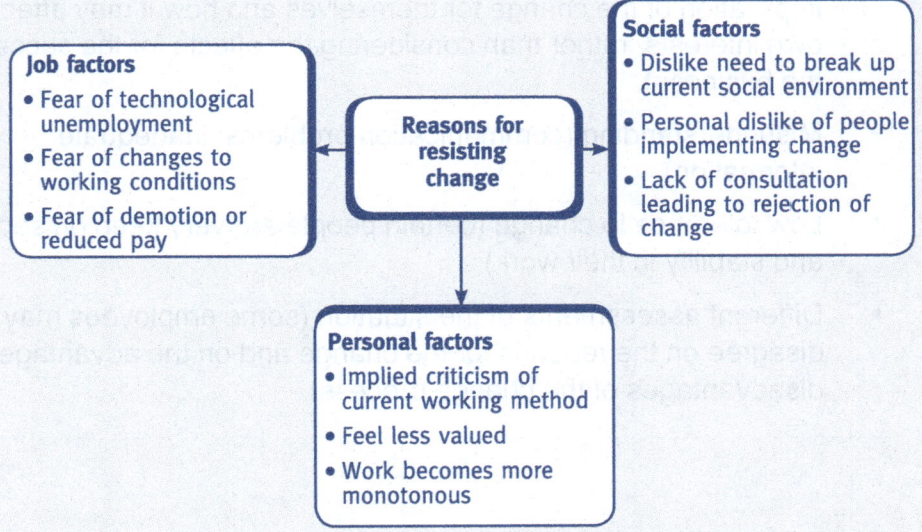

Change management – understanding the context of change

Resistance may take many forms, including active or passive, overt or covert, individual or organised, aggressive or timid. For each source of resistance, management need to provide an appropriate response, e.g.:

Source of resistance	Possible response
• The need for security and the familiar	• Provide information and encouragement, invite involvement
• Having the opinion that no change is needed	• Clarify the purpose of the change and how it will be made
• Trying to protect vested interests	• Demonstrate the problem or the opportunity that makes changes desirable

Reasons for resisting change (Kotter and Schlesinger)

According to Kotter and Schlesinger (1979) there are four reasons that explain why certain people resist change.

- Parochial self-interest (some people are concerned with the implication of the change for themselves and how it may affect their own interests, rather than considering the effects for the success of the business).

- Misunderstanding (communication problems; inadequate information).

- Low tolerance to change (certain people are very keen on security and stability in their work).

- Different assessments of the situation (some employees may disagree on the reasons for the change and on the advantages and disadvantages of the change process).

Test your understanding 9

Which THREE of the following would usually be classed as social factors leading to resistance to change?

- A Fear of unemployment
- B Dislike of person leading change
- C Lack of consultation regarding the change
- D Changes to current social environment
- E Implied criticism of current methods
- F Fear of demotion or reduced pay
- G Work becoming less interesting

Test your understanding 10

J runs a small business manufacturing personalised stationery (such as envelopes and paper). She has recently decided to automate parts of this process, meaning that all four of her current staff members will see their overtime pay reduced (though there will be no effect on their basic pay). The main activities of each staff member will not change significantly as a result of the introduction of automation.

J feels that the current overtime payments are unsupportable and that the business will be unable to grow unless the new system is introduced. Local competitors are already currently using this automated process.

Although J has communicated the situation to the staff and they are all fully aware of the problems faced by the business, they have complained bitterly to J about the proposal and have suggested that they will refuse to use the new automated system.

According to Kotter and Schlesinger, which ONE of the following is the primary reason for resistance among J's employees?

- A Differing assessments of the situation
- B Parochial self-interest
- C Misunderstanding
- D Low tolerance to change

Change management – understanding the context of change

7 Summary

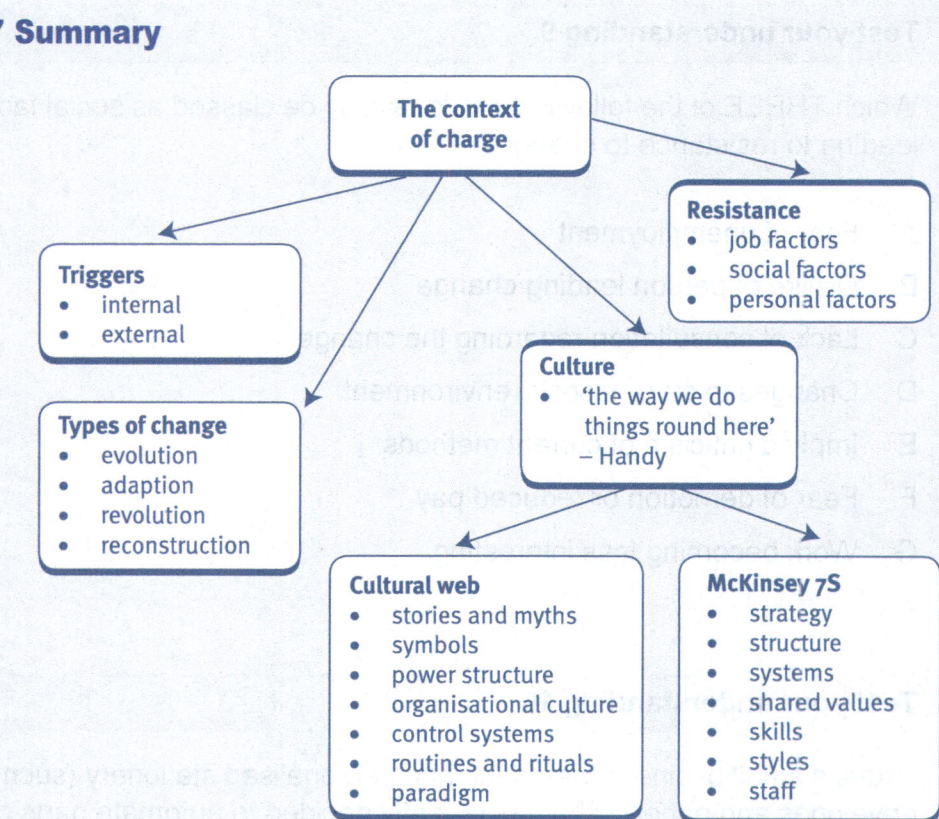

chapter 12

Test your understanding answers

Test your understanding 1

The correct answer is C

By definition.

Test your understanding 2

The correct answer is A

Change is classified with reference to two factors – extent and speed of the change.

The change in H is clearly rapid, as all the traditional products used for its chemical have been banned. It is urgently looking for alternatives to prevent a total collapse of the company.

The scope of change seems small (a realignment). H will still be producing LKL – it will simply be selling it to a different type of organisation. While this may require some changes (such as marketing and customer management), H is still fundamentally producing and selling LKL.

Test your understanding 3 – (Integration question)

Incremental change means step-by-step changes over time, in small steps. When incremental change occurs within an organisation, it is possible for the organisation to adapt to the change without having to alter its culture or structures significantly. Employees are able to adapt to the gradual changes, and are not unsettled by them.

In contrast, transformational change is a sweeping change that has immediate and widespread effects. The effect of transformational change is usually to alter the structure and culture of the organisation, often with major staff redundancies and the recruitment of new staff with new skills.

Change management – understanding the context of change

The spokesperson for the bank has argued that the change will be incremental. Since the change will take place over a long period of time, staff will have time to adapt to the new structure. There will be no compulsory redundancies and staff will be re-trained in new skills. Although some branches will close, others will remain open, and customers will be offered additional facilities through on-line banking.

The trade union leader believes that the change will be much more dramatic. He might believe that many employees will leave the bank because they are unable to adapt to the new service, or because they are unwilling to re-locate from the branches that are closed down. The bank might push through the branch closure programme more quickly than it has currently proposed, and staff redundancies could be made compulsory if there are not enough individuals willing to take voluntary redundancy.

Essentially, the two individuals take differing viewpoints because they are looking at change differently. The spokesperson for the bank wants to persuade employees to accept the change, and even welcome it. The trade union representative wants to warn employees about the potential consequences, and has therefore stressed the risks.

Test your understanding 4

The correct answer is C

The private dining room is a symbol of the authority and position of the senior managers. Trying to remove this is likely to cause resistance as senior managers will see D's suggestion as a way of reducing their status within the organisation.

The proposed change does not directly affect the senior manger's authority or position within the business, suggesting that it will not affect the power structure of B Brothers.

The removal of the private dining room is also unlikely to impact the way that the organisation controls its staff (there is no change to the way that staff are rewarded or punished) and there is no evidence that it will alter the stories and myths – i.e. what staff members believe and say about the organisation.

Test your understanding 5

The correct answer is B

The paradigm is the overall aim and purpose of the organisation. This is clearly confused at G Ltd, leading to problems with customer management.

There is no confusion over the mission itself. This has been published, meaning that staff are aware of the current mission statement. They simply do not agree that it represents the actual purpose of the organisation.

Test your understanding 6 – HBY – (Case style)

Report
To: The Board of Directors, WDG
From: A. Consultant
Date: 18/08/XX
Subject: Cultural issues and resistance at HBY

Introduction

This report will examine the impact of WDG's proposals relating to the takeover of HBY. Specifically, it will look at how these proposals will affect the culture of HBY post-acquisition.

According to Handy, culture is defined as 'the way we do things round here'.

When analysing an organisation's corporate culture, the most logical model to use is the Cultural Web. This suggests that the culture of an organisation can be broken down into six different aspects. Any attempt to significantly change the culture of the organisation, as WDG is attempting to do with HBY, is likely to lead to significant resistance.

Symbols

This looks at the symbols or symbolic actions that typify the organisation.

Within HBY, the symbols include the regular social gatherings supplied by the company. This indicates that staff wellbeing and happiness is valued by the company. Cutbacks to this area are likely to cause resistance as staff will feel that WDG is indicating that they are no longer as valued as they once were.

Power structure

This examines who is in charge (or who has the power) within the organisation.

HBY currently appears to have several levels of management, with the original founding family having ultimate control over the organisation. WDG intends to replace many of these managers with a single layer of their own management.

This is likely to upset many of HBY's employees as it will not only lead to redundancies, but it will also change the reporting system that they are currently used to.

Organisational structure

The current management structure of HBY appears to be bureaucratic, with a number of levels of management. WDG is planning to replace this with a single level of its own management, flattening the structure.

This may lead to resistance as it may reduce the chances for internal promotion for HBY's existing staff. There will be fewer management positions, many of which will be filled by WDG's staff for the foreseeable future.

Control systems

Controls appear to be few and far between under the traditional approach taken by HBY. Staff were largely expected to get on with their own jobs, with management only getting involved if there was a problem.

The new management systems proposed by WDG involve a much more hands-on approach, with employees being trained in the new systems by WDG managers. This is likely to cause resistance as staff will feel that they are no longer trusted by their management to get on with their work in an effective manner.

The shift from a bonus based on a range of indicators, which focused on quality, to pay which is piecework, and therefore only based on the level of productivity, also indicates a shift in what the business expects from its employees. This is likely to cause confusion amongst workers who are used to a quality focus.

Routines and rituals

Linked to control systems, WDG are suggesting that the existing methods used by HBY's workers for many years are inferior to the 'new, improved' WDG methods.

Employees may therefore feel that there is an implied criticism of their existing working methods by WDG, increasing resistance.

The fact that WDG has no interest in pursuing the quality accreditation that HBY have historically obtained also indicates that it places little value on the work currently being done by HBY and this, in turn, will increase resistance.

Stories and myths

The staff of HBY feels that, due to the participative style of the existing management, they have 'helped to build' the company and that they are a major reason for its historic success.

Whether this is the case or not, WDG's desire to implement the changes without any staff consultation is a departure from the management style that staff of HBY are used to and is likely to upset them.

Paradigm

Overall, HBY's approach has been a participative one, with defined roles and a strong focus on quality. WDG seems to want to shift this towards a focus on output and profitability. This fundamental move in culture is, understandably, a difficult one for the staff of HBY to accept.

Test your understanding 7

The correct answers are: C, E and F

Note that A and B are factors from the cultural web model.

Test your understanding 8

The correct answer is C

Soft factors are those that are less easy to analyse and evaluate.

Change management – understanding the context of change

Test your understanding 9

The correct answers are B, C and D

A and F are job factors, E and G are personal factors.

Test your understanding 10

The correct answer is B

J's employees are motivated by their own self-interest, rather than the ongoing success of the business.

J's staff are fully aware of the situation that the business is in – including the fact that J's rivals have adopted similar automated systems. There is no evidence that they have failed to understand how much of a threat this may be to J's operations. This suggests that options A and C are incorrect.

It is unclear whether J's staff have faced changes in their working practices in the past, so there is no evidence to support a low tolerance of change. It is therefore unlikely to be the primary reason for resistance.

Chapter 13

Change management – change leadership

Chapter learning objectives

Lead	Component
C1. Advise on the important aspects of organisational change	(b) evaluate the role of leadership in managing the change process and building and managing effective teams
C2. Evaluate tools and methods for successfully implementing a change programme	(a) Evaluate tools, techniques and strategies for managing and leading the change process
C3. Recommend change leadership processes in support of strategy implementation	(a) Evaluate the role of the change leader in supporting strategy implementation (b) Recommend appropriate leadership styles within a range of organisational change concepts

Change management – change leadership

Indicative syllabus content

- Team building, collaboration, group formation and shared knowledge and accountability
- The importance of managing critical periods of adaptive, evolutionary, reconstructive and revolutionary change
- Tools, techniques and models associated with organisational change
- Approaches, styles and strategies of change management
- Change leadership and its role in the successful implementation of strategy
- The role of the change leader in effective strategic communication
- The advantages and disadvantages of different styles of management on the successful implementation of strategy
- Executive mentoring and coaching to promote effective change leadership

chapter 13

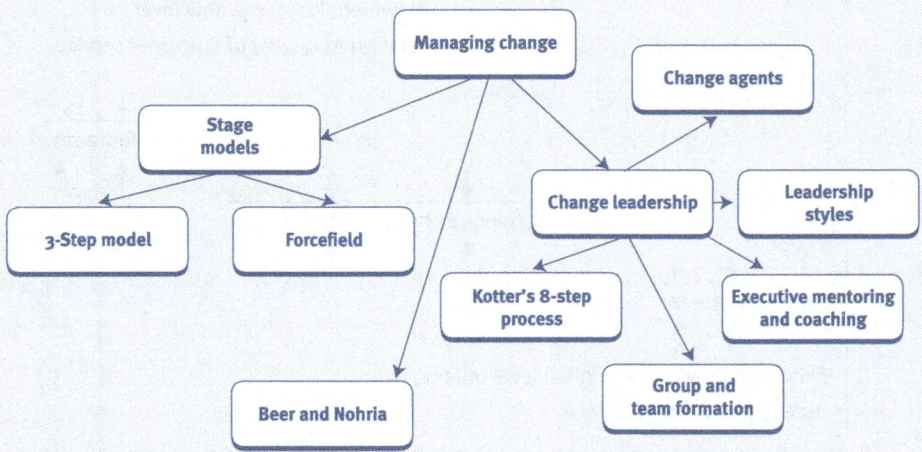

1 Introduction

As can be seen from the previous chapter, understanding the factors that impact on change management can be complex. However, even when a manager has a good understanding of the context of change within their organisation, they still need to be able to successfully implement the change itself.

Given the conflicting views of different stakeholders – such as shareholders, employees and customers – achieving change within an organisation is often difficult and prone to failure. Due to this, a number of different theorists have examined the issue and identified possible approaches to managing the change process within the organisation.

2 Stage models of the change process

Lewin's three-stage model

The three-stage model of change was proposed by Kurt Lewin in the 1950's. He argued that, in order for change to occur successfully, organisations need to progress through three stages.

This process, shown in the following diagram, includes unfreezing habits or standard operating procedures, changing to new patterns and refreezing to ensure lasting effects.

Change management – change leadership

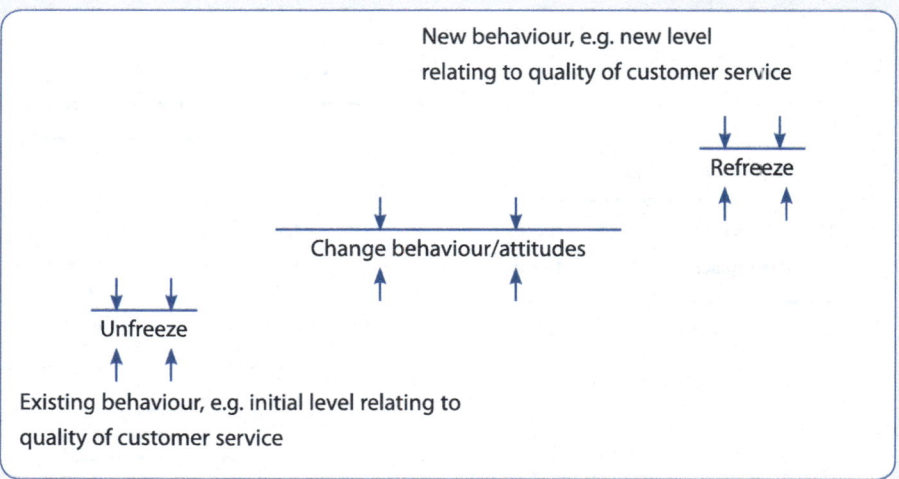

The process of change comprises three stages.

Unfreezing

In this stage, managers need to make the need for change so obvious that most people can easily understand and accept it. Unfreezing also involves creating the initial motivation to change by convincing staff of the undesirability of the present situation. Ways of destabilising the present stability could include:

- Identifying and exploiting existing areas of stress or dissatisfaction.
- Creating or introducing additional forces for change, such as tighter budgets and targets or new personnel in favour of the change.
- Increasing employee knowledge about markets, competitors and the need for change.

Essentially, effective communication and explaining the need for change is vital within the unfreeze stage.

Change

The change process itself is mainly concerned with identifying what the new behaviour or norm should be. This stage will often involve:

- Establishing new patterns of behaviour
- Setting up new reporting relationships
- Creating new reward/incentive schemes
- Introducing a new style of management

It is vital that new information is communicated concerning the new attitudes, culture and concepts that the organisation wants to be adopted, so that these are internalised by employees.

In the 'change' stage participation and involvement is often necessary so that individuals feel ownership of change.

Refreezing

Refreezing or stabilising the change involves ensuring that people do not slip back into old ways. As such it involves reinforcement of the new pattern of work or behaviour by:

- Larger rewards (salary, bonuses, promotion) for those employees who have fully embraced the new culture
- Publicity of success stories and new "heroes" – e.g. through employee of the month.

The key to this stage is therefore to ensure that change is embedded within the organisation and its culture.

Bank automation

During the recent economic problems across the world, many companies have been faced with the need to restructure their organisations in order to cut costs and improve efficiency – with many banks being particularly hard-hit.

A number of banks have been increasing the amount of automation in their branches. This involves the purchase of cash machines that are able to process deposits of cash and cheques as well as performing other basic account management functions. Many other traditional branch functions now require customers to telephone central call centres rather than going into a branch. These changes allow the bank to reduce the number of staff in their branches, saving money.

However, such an approach is likely to create significant resistance from staff – especially employees who work within the branches themselves. The bank may wish to use Lewin's three-stage model as a way of managing the change process.

Unfreezing

This involves convincing employees of the initial need for the increased automation in the branches. While this may be difficult to do, especially if employees are heavily unionised, it is a crucial step in the change management process.

Change management – change leadership

The bank may choose to explain to employees about its current position in the market and the effect that the economic downturn has had on profits. If reducing costs will help to secure the long-term survival of the entire bank, many employees may be convinced of the need to proceed with the change.

The directors of the bank may also stress any potential benefits of the proposals for the remaining branch employees. For example, a reduction in the number of basic account queries from customers may free up time for more interesting work, such as helping customers review their finances.

Change

This is the stage where the proposed change actually occurs. It will involve the reduction in the number of branch employees and the installation of new machinery into the branches.

This will require training for employees. They will need to be able to deal with customer queries and complaints about the new branch procedures as well as how to maintain the new cash machines.

Communication is vital at this stage. Employees must know what is expected of them during and after the change management process.

Refreezing

This stage tries to ensure that bank staff do not return to the old systems. In this case managers need to prevent staff from processing basic customer transactions themselves rather than convincing customers to use the new automated systems.

This may involve the creation of new reward schemes to encourage staff to adopt the new procedures. For instance, branch staff could receive an increased bonus if a high proportion of their customers start maintaining their accounts using the automated system. They may be penalised if they continue using the old systems.

Managers can also reinforce the new approach by publicising success stories of branches that have embraced the change and by promoting key members of staff who supported the automation process.

chapter 13

Criticisms of Lewin's three-stage model

Kanter et al suggest that Lewin's ice cube model is too simplistic.

They argue that the model is based on the assumptions that organisations are stable and static so change results only from concentrated effort and only in one direction.

Kanter et al argue that change is 'multi-directional and ubiquitous', that it happens in all directions simultaneously and is often a continuous process.

Test your understanding 1

According to Lewin's three-stage model, which ONE of the following activities would be part of the 'unfreezing' stage?

A   Explaining the need for change
B   Creation of new reward schemes
C   Publicity of success stories
D   Training of staff in new ways of working

Test your understanding 2 – WW – (Case style)

WW is a company specialising in industrial paint manufacturing. It has recently experienced significant growth in turnover and has opened two new factories to help it cope with the additional demand.

The managers of WW have become concerned that their current accounting software is no longer adequate for their needs. The current system is a basic one, which is mainly designed to record transactions and produce financial statements at the end of each period. Given the growth in the business, the managers of WW now need additional information, such as the production of monthly management reports and the ability to accurately cost each unit of their products.

Change management – change leadership

The current accounting system does not support these functions, meaning the accounting department is required to produce the information manually, which is both complex and time-consuming. WW's managers are concerned that this delay in obtaining management information may be putting the firm at a disadvantage in the marketplace.

The managers are therefore currently considering the purchase of a new, more complex, accounting package that will easily allow the production of the management accounting information that they need.

WW has a small accounting department with six members of staff. All of these staff members have been employees of the company for many years. The current accounting package has been in use within WW for the last seven years.

Required:

Using Lewin's three-stage model, explain how WW could manage the changeover to the new accounting package.

(15 minutes)

Force field analysis

Lewin also emphasised the importance of force field analysis. He argued that managers should consider any change situation in terms of:

- the factors encouraging and facilitating the change (the driving forces)
- the factors that hinder change (the restraining forces).

Change will only be successful if the driving forces are larger than the restraining forces.

If we want to bring about change we must change the equilibrium by:

- strengthening the driving forces
- weakening the restraining forces
- or both.

chapter 13

The model encourages us to identify the various forces impinging on the target of change, to consider the relative strengths of these forces and to explore alternative strategies for modifying the force field.

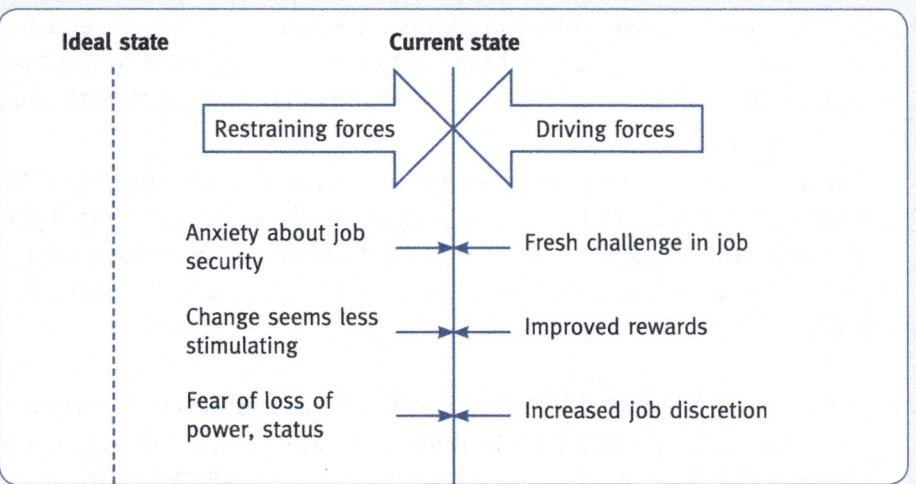

Test your understanding 3

N is the manager of a small division of NNB Ltd, which makes solar cells. N wishes to introduce a new shift system for his staff. A large number of N's staff have stated that they will not accept the new shift pattern.

N was initially uncertain of the reason for this resistance. After investigating, it was discovered that several staff members have misunderstood the proposals and spread the rumour within the division that the new shift pattern would lead to redundancies.

N plans to communicate this error to his employees and explain to them that, while the new shift pattern will improve efficiency, it will not lead to redundancies.

According to Lewin's forcefield model, N's plan to communicate with staff an example of _____ .

Which of the following phrases best fits the gap in the above sentence?

A   Reducing the restraining forces
B   Increasing the restraining forces
C   Reducing the driving forces
D   Increasing the driving forces

545

Change management – change leadership

Test your understanding 4 – GVF – (Case style)

Great Value Foods (GVF) is one of Bigland's leading supermarket chains, having traded for over fifty years. Though fierce competitive activity had reduced the major players in the industry to six large chains in the last twenty years, the competitive pressures and large-scale capital investment required had not prevented all new entrants to the market. A high proportion of all workers in the supermarket industry are unionised.

A few foreign competitors seeking new markets had managed to secure a market share by offering unbranded goods at extremely low prices. This development increased the pressure on GVF as these new entrants were attracting consumers that had been part of GVF's traditional customer base.

In the midst of these difficulties, GVF was presented with a major opportunity. One of its competitors was experiencing difficulties and offered GVF the chance to purchase 60 of their stores in the south of the country. GVF borrowed $800m and made the purchase, doubling its number of outlets.

As GVF took over management of the new stores, however, it realised that considerable time and funds would be required to convert them to its own distinctive format and to the modern standards now expected by customers. This not only delayed the expected revenue stream, but also required additional borrowing, raising GVF's gearing to uncomfortably high levels. The government of Bigland subsequently raised interest rates, increasing the financial pressure on GVF.

During all this, GVF had been seeking to catch up with its competitors in a number of ways. This had included increasing the number of own-brand products it offered, along with the development of a new central distribution system that experts agreed was one of the best in the country. However, there were delays in distribution of supplies to some stores during the run up to the country's most important festive period. This resulted in a considerable loss for the company and three of the directors considered responsible for the problems were sacked.

These problems, together with an accompanying decline in profits, resulted in a fall in GVF's share price. Investors were concerned that GVF had paid too much for its 60 southern stores and that a rights issue would be needed to reduce the company's debt burden.

GVF has recently appointed a new CEO and she has spent her first few weeks reviewing the company and its problems, She has found that the company has too many layers of management, narrow functional attitudes and a controlling, bureaucratic head office culture. She feels that the business is no longer effective or responding to customer needs.

You are currently working as a strategic management accountant for the new CEO of GVF. She has told you that she wishes to involve you in the strategic decision-making process within the company and you have just opened up the following email from her:

To: Anne Sma
From: Rebecca Smith (CEO)
Date: 12/4/20XX
Subject: Strategic change issues within GVF

Hi Anne,

As you know, I've been trying to analyse the problems within GVF and come to some sensible conclusions about our way forward as a company and I would like your help.

I know that when I was employed by GVF, several key shareholder representatives told me that they were looking forward to seeing how well I could 'turn the business around'. I have some of my own ideas about how this could be accomplished, but could you please give me a summary of the measures you think are required to turn GVF around.

I am also concerned that any proposals I make will be met with resistance by key stakeholders. Could you describe the most likely sources of resistance to change for me, please? I know several managers have mentioned a model by Lewin called 'forcefield analysis', but this isn't a model I have heard of before. I need you to explain the basics of the model to me and explain how it might be used to implement change in GVF.

I've got a meeting in an hour with the board and I need this information in time to have a look at it. If you could get it to me in 35 minutes that would be great.

Thanks

Rebecca

Required:

Reply to the email.

(35 minutes)

Beer and Nohria – Theory E & Theory O

Beer and Nohria (2000) identified that a large proportion of all business change initiatives fail. They believed that this was caused by managers becoming overwhelmed by the detail of the change management process and failing to focus on the overall goals of the change itself.

Beer and Nohria identified that every organisational change conforms to a variant of either:

- **Theory E strategies** – these are based on measures where shareholder value is the main concern. Change usually involves incentives, layoffs, downsizing and restructuring.

- **Theory O strategies** – these are 'softer' approaches to change, often involving cultural adjustment or enhancing employee capabilities through individual and organisational learning. This involves changing, obtaining feedback, reflecting and then making further changes. This requires involving employees in the change process.

Both approaches have drawbacks. A Theory E approach will tend to ignore the feelings and attitudes of their employees, which will often lead to a loss of motivation and commitment from staff members. This can damage the competitive advantage of the organisation.

Theory O organisations, on the other hand, will often fail to take the 'tough' decisions that may be needed.

To solve these problems, Beer and Nohria recommended that organisations should implement both Theory E and Theory O approaches simultaneously and try to balance the associated tensions.

Illustration 1 – Beer and Nohria

Due to the recent economic slowdown, many high-street retailers have seen a significant reduction in their profits, forcing them to consider a number of strategies to improve their results.

A **Theory E** approach means that the retailer is only concerned with the effect that falling profits has on shareholders – such as reduced dividends and share prices. The managers of the company will usually try to improve this quickly by laying off staff, reducing employee pay or closing stores that are seen as underperforming.

While this can have a positive impact on profits in the short-term, it fails to consider the needs of other stakeholders, such as employees. This can cause problems with employee motivation and commitment as staff members will not feel that the company is acting in their best interests. As such, the company may suffer from poor performance in the long-term.

A **Theory O** approach would see the retailer attempt to improve their profits by developing the organisation's capabilities and culture. For instance, a high-street retailer may train its staff to provide better customer service for shoppers. This will improve the customer experience and therefore, in the longer-term, should improve the profitability of the business. The retailer may well choose to involve staff in the decision-making process, asking for suggestions as to how customer service could be improved.

All of this is likely to make the employees feel more valued and should improve the commitment and motivation of the workforce. However, it may be insufficient in the short–term to deal with the fall in profitability and shareholders may expect more drastic, Theory E action in order to quickly improve their returns.

Beer and Nohria suggested that companies needed to be prepared to take both approaches simultaneously. This could, for example, involve some restructuring as well as a development of remaining employees. This would still need careful management as it would be easy to get the 'worst of all worlds' where staff are demotivated by the job losses while investors feel the cost cuts have not gone far enough.

Balance is needed!

Test your understanding 5

F is a clothes retailer which is struggling in the current economic downturn and is looking for ways to improve performance.

According to Beer and Nohria, which ONE of the following strategies would be consistent with a Theory O approach to change management?

A   Reduction in staff numbers

B   Store closure

C   Improved staff training

D   Reduction in product quality

Test your understanding 6 – (Integration question)

In what circumstances would Theory E be a successful approach?

3 Change leadership

In order to successfully implement change, most organisations will require someone to take overall control of the change process. This person is referred to as the **change leader**.

Who is the change leader?

The change leader is a key figure within the organisation who takes overall responsibility and control for the proposed change within the organisation.

For a major, organisation-wide change this role may well be best filled by the CEO, but it can be taken on by anyone with the appropriate power and leadership skills within the organisation.

What does the change leader do?

The change leader is responsible for articulating what change is needed and why, acting as a figurehead for the change process, as well as helping to deal with any problems or conflicts that arise during the change process.

Kotter (Leading Change, 1996) suggested that leading change is an 8-step process.

8-step process of change leadership

- **Establish a sense of urgency** – the change leader needs to help others see the need for change and convince them that it must be implemented promptly.

  Failure to create a sense of urgency leads to a lack of motivation from staff – the people who will ultimately be implementing the change you wish to create. Without motivation, they will not see the need to get involved, leading to failure. This sense of urgency is therefore vital and means that change leaders may take drastic action to create it. One company manager commissioned his organisation's first ever customer satisfaction surveys, knowing the results would be adverse and then made them public. This created a strong driving force for change within the organisation.

- **Creating the guiding coalition** – the change leader is unlikely to be able to control the entire change process by themselves. They must therefore assemble a group with enough power to lead the change process and ensure that they are able to act as a team.

  The coalition may not simply be formed from senior management, as it can include anyone with skills or knowledge which could be useful in the change process. However, they will need sufficient power – whether through job titles or reputation, to accomplish the change and (where necessary) force it through against opposition.

- **Developing a change vision** – the change leader needs to create an overall vision of the future, illustrating what the change is designed to accomplish as well as its benefits. Strategies will be developed to achieve the proposed changes.

    Failure to develop a clear, concise vision that can be communicated to stakeholders means that the project can lack focus and goal congruence. The change management process may simply collapse into a series of conflicting projects that do not move the organisation in the desired direction.

- **Communicating the vision** – the leader needs to communicate the vision and strategies identified in the previous stage to as many stakeholders as possible. This will maximise buy-in.

    Implementing major change in an organisation requires the involvement of (potentially) a large number of people at all levels. Without plenty of communication, these people will never see the importance of change and will be unwilling to make any effort towards accomplishing it.

- **Empowering broad-based action** – the change leader needs to remove obstacles to change (restraining forces) and encourage staff to get involved in generating ideas.

    Using Lewin's forcefield analysis (as discussed earlier in this chapter) can be a useful exercise here. It helps management identify what will cause resistance, so that plans can be created to deal with these issues.

- **Generating short-term wins** – plan for interim achievements that can easily be made visible, then publicise and reward staff members involved.

    Change processes can take a long time to implement – in some cases years. Most people will become demotivated if they do not see any changes within the short to mid-term. Without some short term wins, they will therefore become demotivated and cynical about the success of the change management process.

- **Never letting up** – maintain the change process, hiring, promoting and developing employees who support and implement the required changes. The use of specific change agents may be of use here (the role of change agents are explored later in this chapter).

Change management – change leadership

It is easy for an organisation to believe that its change process is complete when it has completed all relevant major projects. Unfortunately, as Lewin's three-stage model indicated earlier in the chapter, it is easy for staff to slip back into old habits and ways of working. Management will need to monitor the change process for a significant amount of time after 'completion' to ensure that the change has indeed become permanent.

- **Incorporating changes into the culture** – continually reinforce the change and communicate and reward achievement. This stage looks at ways of ensuring that the new change a standard part of everyday work and to prevent staff slipping back into their old habits.

Management need to ensure that they show staff how the changes have improved performance and how they have benefitted. It is also important to ensure that existing and future managers are supportive of the new processes. Choosing new managers who disagree with the changes that have been made could lead to staff slipping back into old habits and practises.

Test your understanding 7

X plc has been performing well for many years, with staff enjoying significant bonuses. However, recent strategic analysis by the Board of X plc has identified that there are a number of rival organisations starting to gain a share in X's traditional markets. They feel that, unless X significantly updates its working practises, it will lose its market position within three years. B was recently hired as CEO of X plc. She was selected as the company felt that she was the best candidate to lead X plc through a period of major change.

After a thorough review of X's operations, B created a powerful group of managers and directors across the organisation to help her implement her proposed, wide-ranging changes. She spent a significant amount of time explaining the process of change that was to be implemented, with a series of staff meetings under the slogan 'changing X for the new markets'. At these meeting she involved staff and tried to build their ideas into the final change strategy. The Board refused to allow B to explain the new entrants to the market, as they felt that the company would see a drop in its share price if this information was leaked to the markets.

B backed up her proposed changes with a series of interim goals. When the organisation reached these targets, she planned to widely publicise them within the organisation in order to improve motivation amongst the staff.

Unfortunately B struggled to motivate the staff and, in spite of her staff meetings, little change occurred. After six months, B had failed to reach any of her interim goals. She decided to step aside and left the company.

> Kotter suggested that there were eight steps required to successfully lead change. B's failure to achieve which of these eight steps led to the ultimate failure of the change process at X plc?
>
> A   Creation of a guiding coalition
> B   Communicating the vision
> C   Establishing a sense of urgency
> D   Generating short-term wins

Group and team formation

One key aspect of change leadership is the ability to form a group of individuals within the organisation who can help to control and implement any proposed changes (Kotter's 'guiding coalition' mentioned above). This group, as well as the other groups and teams that they form throughout the organisation, will actually implement change throughout the organisation. The change leader therefore **must** be able to manage them effectively.

A 'group' is simply a collection of individuals. The group the change leader selects may well come from various parts of the organisation, such as finance, human resources and sales – any part of the organisation that may be affected by the proposed change or have useful input into it.

There is no guarantee that this group of individuals will work well together. It is therefore very important that the change leader turns this group into a team.

A team is more than a group. It is a set of individuals who must work together in order to accomplish shared objectives.

Teams usually:

- share a common goal
- enjoy working together
- are committed to achieving certain goals.

A team will have its own culture, leader and should be geared towards achieving a certain goal – in this case, implementing the desired changes within the organisation.

A change leader needs to ensure that his change team works well together to ensure that they will effectively assist in the implementation of the change process.

Team building

Teams are not always able to achieve their goals without some outside intervention. As such, change leaders may need to create 'team-building' exercises. These are tasks that are designed to develop team members and their ability to work together.

Team building exercises tend to be based around developing the team in several areas, including:

- **improved communication**, such as through the use of problem solving exercises which force team members to discuss problems the team is facing.
- **building trust** between team members, which will help them work together effectively.
- **social interaction** between the individuals within the team can help to reduce conflict and increase their ability to work effectively.

Benefits and drawbacks of teams

The change leader needs to be aware of the potential advantages and drawbacks of using a team to help implement change within the organisation.

Benefits include:

- a mixture of skills and abilities within the team. Each member may be from a different part of the organisation and may therefore have unique skills and knowledge that can be used to help the change process
- better control, with opportunities for individual performance to be reviewed and controlled by other team members.
- improved communication – this can also lead to increased buy-in by the rest of the organisation. For example, employees within the HR department are more likely to accept change if an HR staff member is part of the change team.

However, there are problems with the use of a team, including:

- slower decision-making, as discussion is needed to come to any agreement – also potentially leading to increased conflict
- decisions may be compromises, rather than decisions that are beneficial to the business and change process as a whole
- group pressure to conform can lead to team members agreeing to decisions that they know are wrong because other team members support it

- teams may have a lack of individual responsibility, as responsibility is shared between all members. They may therefore be more willing to take riskier courses of action than individuals.

Leadership styles – Kotter and Schlesinger

Kotter and Schlesinger set out the following change approaches to deal with resistance:

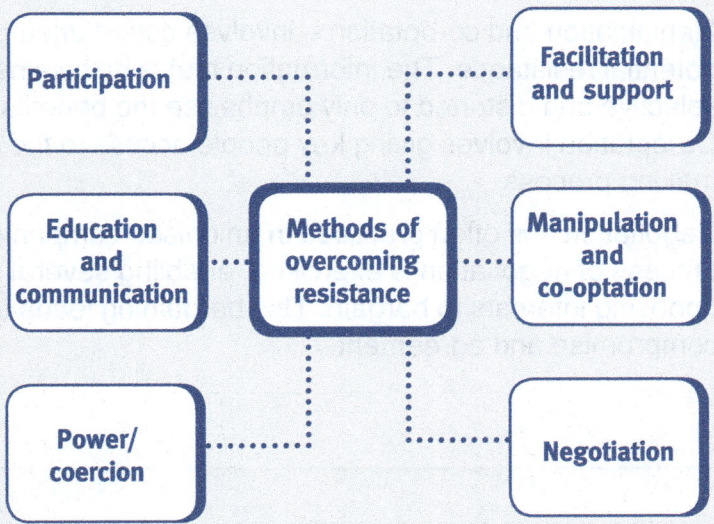

Key considerations when deciding upon a leadership style

- The speed at which change must be introduced
- The strength of the pressure for change
- The level of resistance expected
- The amount of power you hold
- How much information you need before you can implement the change and how long it will take to get that information

Explanation of the Kotter and Schlesinger styles

- Participation – aims to involve employees, usually by allowing some input into decision making. This could easily result in employees enjoying raised levels of autonomy, by allowing them to design their own jobs, pay structures, etc.

- Education and communication – used as a background factor to reinforce another approach. This strategy relies upon the hopeful belief that communication about the benefits of change to employees will result in their acceptance of the need to exercise the changes necessary.

- Power/coercion – involves the compulsory approach by management to implement change. This method finds its roots from the formal authority that management possesses, together with legislative support. This approach is often required where the speed of change needs to be rapid and where possible crises occur.

- Facilitation and support – employees may need to be counselled to help them overcome their fears and anxieties about change. Management may find it necessary to develop individual awareness of the need for change.

- Manipulation and co-optation – involves covert attempts to sidestep potential resistance. The information that is disseminated is selective and distorted to only emphasise the benefits of the change. Co-optation involves giving key people access to the decision-making process.

- Negotiation – is often practised in unionised companies. Simply, the process of negotiation is exercised, enabling several parties with opposing interests to bargain. This bargaining leads to a situation of compromise and agreement.

Illustration 2 – Kotter and Schlesinger in practice

P is an organisation which wants to undertake a significant restructuring and is concerned about staff resistance. Kotter and Schlesinger's six styles could be a useful way for the business to deal with this resistance.

Education and communication

The management of P could look at ways of helping staff see the need for (and logic of) the proposed reorganisation. This could involve, amongst other things:

- meetings with employees
- presentations
- emails.

This is useful if P's managers believe that the resistance from staff will be based on inaccurate information. For example, employees may believe that the restructuring will lead to job losses. If this is not the case, then an education programme will help put staff fears to rest. Explaining the reasoning behind the restructuring (i.e. the need to deal with new, efficient competitors) can also help improve staff support.

However, the process of communicating with all employees can be time consuming, especially in larger organisations – meaning that if P's proposed changes are urgent, this may not be the best approach. In addition, employees may simply not believe the information that P's managers are providing, meaning that the communication process will fail to be effective.

It is also worth noting that if employees do not have inaccurate information, this approach is unlikely to work. If P's plans will involve significant redundancies, then communicating this to employees will clearly not reduce resistance.

Participation and involvement

This approach requires P's managers to involve employees in the development and implementation of the reorganisation of the business. This means listening to the employees affected by the proposed changes and making use of their advice.

This approach will work well if P's employees are highly skilled and/or experienced, as they may have valuable ideas that will benefit the proposed restructuring. In addition, involving staff members in the restructuring decision-making process will significantly reduce resistance, as it increases employee buy-in.

However, if employees are less skilled or experienced, they may fail to come up with valuable input into the change process. If employees are cautious, they may fail to make the major changes that are required. For instance, if P needs to make significant job cuts in order to compete in its market, it is unlikely that staff members will make that suggestion!

Involving a large number of employees in the design and implementation of a new strategy is likely to be time consuming (as per education and communication) and is likely to therefore be inappropriate if rapid change is needed.

Facilitation and support

This involves management looking at ways of being supportive of employees who may be worried about the changes being proposed. For P this could include:

- training staff in the use of any new systems which are being introduced
- giving employees time off after the reorganisation has taken effect
- giving time off/support for any employees who are being made redundant to find another job
- listening and providing emotional support.

This is a particularly effective approach to managing a situation where resistance is caused by fear and anxiety of the proposals, such as the fear of unemployment, or the fear of not being able to do a new role adequately.

The main drawback of facilitation and support is that it, again, takes time and money – and can still ultimately be unsuccessful.

Negotiation and agreement

This would involve P negotiating with employees to find a restructuring approach which is satisfactory to both P and its staff. This could involve:

- reducing the extent of the restructuring to keep staff happy
- offering alternative benefits to employees if they support the restructuring, such as increased pay or better working conditions. Employees who are made redundant could be offered more attractive redundancy packages.

Negotiation is particularly useful when one party is clearly going to lose out under the proposed change, but still has the power to significantly resist the change process. Within P, this situation could occur if employees are heavily unionised. P may have to offer some compromises to avoid damaging strike action.

Ultimately, however, negotiation can be time consuming for the company. In addition the agreement demanded by powerful other parties may be expensive.

Manipulation and co-optation

This would occur if P's managers try to use covert attempts to influence the staff. It typically involves selective use of information.

P could consider releasing information which makes it look as if the company is in financial difficulties (even if it is not) as a way of convincing staff that the restructuring is necessary for the survival of the business. Staff may simply be scared into thinking there is a crisis coming that only the proposed restructuring can avoid.

Co-optation involves selectively promoting key staff members (or offering them incentives) if they decide to support the proposed change. This is not participation, as P's managers are not interested in these staff member's opinions – they simply want their endorsement, which may reduce resistance elsewhere in the business.

Both of these approaches have possible drawbacks. Manipulation is likely to lead to P's employees feeling that they have been lied to (if the truth ever comes out) and can therefore destroy future working relations between employees and management. Producing misleading information is also a breach of an accountant's professional code of ethics (in particular integrity and professional behaviour) and should therefore not be recommended by P's strategic management accountant.

Co-optation may lead to employees feeling that their managers are trying to 'buy their silence' and this can lead to more bad feeling and increased resistance.

However, both manipulation and co-optation are relatively cheap to undertake and can be implemented quickly. This may therefore be a consideration for P if the proposed restructuring is required urgently.

Explicit and implicit coercion

This involves P's management attempt to force the restructuring through by threatening staff (for example with the loss of their jobs, demotions, or pay cuts) or by actually dismissing them or transferring them.

Like manipulation, this is likely to cause significant bad feeling from employees and this may lead to a breakdown of future working relations.

However, it is fast, cheap and may be the most effective route to take if change is required urgently – especially if it will be unpopular, regardless of how it is introduced.

Change management – change leadership

> If P intends to fire a large proportion of its workforce as part of the restructuring process, none of the other methods discussed above are likely to lead to reduced resistance. As such, coercion may be the only possibility for the company.

Test your understanding 8

H has recently announced a series of compulsory redundancies amongst staff. It plans to offer counselling to staff members affected by this process and has offered them time off (at full pay) to allow them to look for alternative jobs.

Which ONE of Kotter and Schlesinger's leadership styles has H adopted?

A   Education and communication

B   Facilitation and support

C   Coercion

D   Participation

Test your understanding 9

U is an organisation which is currently experiencing a crisis. Due to the loss of a major customer, U feels that it has to cut a minimum of 30% of its workforce within the next month or it faces bankruptcy. U's 10,000 employees are not heavily unionised, but U expects significant resistance from staff when it announces the job losses.

Which of Kotter and Schlesinger's leadership styles would be most appropriate for U to adopt when dealing with its employees in this situation?

A   Education and communication

B   Negotiation

C   Manipulation and co-optation

D   Coercion

Test your understanding 10 – Grey – (Case style)

Grey Limited is a conglomerate organisation with two major divisions: A and B. The two divisions are run as autonomous business units as they operate in completely different markets. Both are entering a period of organisational change and the directors of Grey are considering what style of management would be the most effective for each division.

The CEO of Grey has asked you to produce a set of notes for her, suggesting which leadership style(s) would be most appropriate in each division and why. She has sent you the following background information document.

Briefing document – Divisions A and B

Division A is currently highly profitable. However, it is looking at ways of increasing its efficiency. The managers of A have decided to centralise the accounting function within the business, which will reduce overheads and allow for a reduction in the number of employees. Division A has always had an excellent relationship with its relatively small number of highly skilled staff and is concerned about how these plans may affect that.

Division B is currently loss-making. It is also planning on reducing the number of staff it employs, but wishes to do so across all departments. B has a large number of workers and initial estimates are that 18% of all staff members will be made redundant. B has undertaken similar exercises in previous years, leading to significant conflict between the relatively unskilled staff and managers. The directors of Grey have informed the managers of B that if the division does not move back into profit in the near future, the division will be closed.

Required:

Produce the notes as requested by the CEO.

(20 minutes)

> **Test your understanding 11 – (Integration question)**
>
> You are a manager who is in charge of a team that has been given the task of introducing a new management reporting system into regional offices. There is considerable resistance to the changes from the office managers, and comments that you have heard include the following.
>
> - I have more important work priorities to take up my time.
> - I'm used to the old system.
> - The new system is too complicated.
> - The new system will create more paperwork.
> - The new system will make me more accountable.
> - My job in the new system is not clear.
>
> How would you try to deal with this resistance to change?
>
> **(5 minutes)**

4 Change agents

Many organisations seek to identify and reward change agents to encourage and facilitate change. They can play a major role in helping deal with resistance to change. Usually change agents are figures who are familiar and non-threatening to other people.

The quality of the relationship between the change agent and key decision makers is very important, so the choice of change agent is critical.

Whether internal or external, the change agent is central to the process, and is useful in helping the organisation to:

- **Define the problem and its cause** – the change agent should be able to identify restraining forces or potential resistance and help management to understand the root causes behind them.

- **Diagnose solutions and select appropriate courses of action** – the change agent will be responsible for proposing ways in which these problems can be overcome and then helping management to select the most appropriate course of action.

- **Implement change** – once management have made their decision about which course of action to take, it will need to be implemented. Given that the change agent will be well informed about the proposed change and the reasons behind it, they are likely to be the best person to take the lead in implementing the change.

- **Transmit the learning process to others and the organisation overall** – the change agent should document the learning process and discussions which the company has undergone during the change process. They can then take the lead in spreading this information throughout the company.

Skills and attributes of change agents

The skills and attributes of the change agent would include:

Goals	
	• Clarity in defining the achievable
	• Sensitive to the impact of change on all stakeholders
	• Flexibility to adapt to internal and external triggers
Roles	• Team-building skills to establish work groups
	• Networking skills inside and outside the company
	• Tolerance of ambiguity and uncertainty
Communication	• Skills with colleagues and subordinates
	• Personal enthusiasm, stimulating commitment
	• Meeting management
Negotiation	• Creating vision and selling plans
	• Resolving conflict
	• Contract negotiation
Managing up	• Political awareness and influencing skills
	• Balancing goals and perceptions
	• Helicopter perspective

"Power skills" of change agents (Kanter)

Kanter identified seven 'power skills' that change agents require to enable them to overcome apathy or resistance to change, and enable them to introduce new ideas:

- ability to work independently, without the power and sanction of the senior management hierarchy behind them, providing visible support
- ability to collaborate effectively
- ability to develop relationships based on trust, with high ethical standards
- self-confidence, tempered with humility
- being respectful of the process of change, as well as the substance of the change
- ability to work across different business functions and units
- a willingness to stake personal rewards on results, and gain satisfaction from success.

Using external consultants as change agents

Advantages of using external consultants as change agents are as follows:

- They can bring a fresh perspective to the problem
- May have state-of-the-art knowledge of the required change – e.g. introducing TQM
- Being a dedicated resource they may be able to give it more time and energy
- They may have more experience and hence be better able to avoid traps and pitfalls.
- Greater objectivity as they have no personal stake in the outcomes of the change.

Test your understanding 12

M Ltd is currently considering who to choose to act as a change agent during the implementation of a new JIT system, which M currently has no experience of. M has a strong corporate culture, with excellent working relationships between managers and other employees throughout the organisation.

Which THREE of the following are advantages to M Ltd of using external consultants as change agents, rather than internal managers?

- A They can bring a new perspective to the change process
- B Improved objectivity in decision-making
- C Improved relationship and trust with employees
- D Improved ability to collaborate effectively across different functions
- E Reduced cost of the change management process
- F May have specialist knowledge of the change to be implemented

Test your understanding 13 – (Integration question)

MMM is a small company based in country A. It is currently considering the acquisition of a rival company, POR, which is based in country D. Unfortunately, the employees in country D speak a different language to staff members in country A. The directors of MMM are concerned about the effect that this could have on the viability of the acquisition.

They have decided to appoint a change agent to help control the process.

Required:

Explain how a change agent could aid in the acquisition of POR.

(10 minutes)

5 Executive mentoring and coaching

Part of managing change is helping employees to perform well after the change process is complete. For example, a manufacturing organisation that introduces a new set of targets based around production quality needs to ensure that its staff are comfortable with how best to achieve these goals.

While formal training is useful here, management may also consider initiating a process of mentoring and coaching to support staff.

Mentoring

This refers to process where a manager (or any other member of staff) offers help, guidance, advice and support to facilitate the learning and development of another.

A mentor is typically a skilled, senior member of staff who:

- offers practical advice and support
- can give technical and general guidance
- can help with the development of key work skills
- can act as a role model.

A manager could act as an ongoing mentor, giving guidance to staff about how to deal with the changes in the organisation and helping them develop the skills and abilities they need on an ongoing basis in order to be successful.

Key features of mentoring include:

- it has no specific period – mentoring is indefinite and may be ongoing until it is no longer considered necessary
- it does not have to be a formal process – mentoring does not have to have a rigid structure and can be flexible to adapt to the needs of both parties (the mentor and the mentee). The agenda is open and will change as necessary over time.
- it seeks to build wisdom – it is supposed to help the mentee apply key skills and experience to new situations.

Coaching

The CIPD defines coaching as 'developing a person's skills and knowledge so that their job performance improves, hopefully leading to the achievement of organisational objectives. It targets high performance and improvement at work. It usually lasts for a short period and focuses on specific skills and goals.'

For example, a coach may help staff improve their IT skills over a one month period, so that they are able to deal with a new computer system being installed.

Most coaching is carried out by a senior person or manager, but the most important requirement is that the coach has sufficient expertise and experience.

Key features of coaching include:

- it tends to take place on a one-to-one basis
- it has a very specific purpose and therefore tends to have a planned 'programme' that is followed over a set time period to help the individual being coached meet pre-set objectives.

Similarities between coaching and mentoring

While the approach may be different, there are similarities between coaching and mentoring.

- **Neither is about teaching, instruction or telling someone what to do.** Mentors and coaches both attempt to help members of staff to find their own solutions to problems or issues, rather than simply telling them what the best approach is.
- **Both are flexible and evolutionary approaches.** While coaching may have more pre-set objectives, these may still change over time as the needs of the member of staff being coached change.
- **They require similar skills from the individual acting as the coach or mentor.** In both cases, the coach or mentor is likely to act as a 'critical friend' who helps the staff member in their care to improve their skills and abilities.

Change management – change leadership

Generally

Note that in either case, the coach or mentor must be someone that supports the change process within the organisation. If an individual is selected that disapproves of the changes being made, their negative attitude may transfer to the employees they are trying to help, leading to increased resistance.

Mentoring and coaching are also important for **all** levels within the business. As well as workers affected by change, it will also often be useful for senior managers. They may need help to ensure they have the relevant leadership and management skills required to lead the change within the organisation.

Ultimately, coaching and mentoring is a key part of the change management process – it can help keep the change management process moving forward and help reduce the amount of resistance that the organisation faces.

Illustration 3 – Mentoring and coaching in action

Mentoring

J works within the human resources department of a large multinational organisation. He has expressed an interest to his line manager about learning more about the organisation's advertising function, with a possible long-term goal of moving departments. J's line manager arranges a secondment to the advertising department and approaches M, an advertising department manager, to act as a mentor for J during his secondment.

M's main roles as part of this mentoring process would include:

- agreeing the objectives for J's secondment – discussing what he wishes to get from the experience
- helping J understand the skills that he will need in the advertising department
- arranging relevant work experience for J during his secondment, such as attending marketing meetings and presentations
- providing relevant information to J about how the marketing department is structured and the various roles within the department
- being available to discuss questions or problems that J has during his secondment

Coaching

P works in a bank as a cashier. He needs to improve his customer management skills, as this is an area that he currently feels uncomfortable with. P's manager arranges for him to be coached by F, an experienced colleague.

F's role as coach would include:

- discuss with P what the coaching needs to achieve – what does P need/expect to get from the process? What standard of customer service should he be able to reach by the end of the coaching process?
- decide with P on the length of the coaching period and what it will entail – P may, for example, get to shadow F at work and see how she interacts with customers.
- be available for P so that he can discuss any queries or issues as they arise and help him to work towards practical solutions that he can use in his own role.
- regularly review P's progress and evaluate the overall success of the coaching process.

Test your understanding 14

Which ONE of the following statements is consistent with the concept of coaching?

A   It is typically only useful for senior management

B   It is undertaken on an on-going, long-term basis

C   It can only be carried out by senior managers

D   It is designed to help the person being coached achieve specific objectives

6 Managing decline

In reality, businesses are not always successful at expanding their business. Many managers may therefore find themselves having to manage decline rather than growth. The changes required during a period of decline pose particular dilemmas for managers as decisions often affect the organisation's workforce – its pay, conditions and job security.

When attempting to help a business recover from a period of decline, a manager's strategic priorities are likely to be:

- reducing costs to improve efficiency, and
- improving competitiveness in order to increase revenue.

Initially, when facing a downturn, the typical management response is to cut costs. While these can be cut from anywhere in the supply chain, the most obvious starting point is to reduce labour costs. At first, this may simply involve altering working patterns, such as the elimination of paid overtime or the replacement of full-time with part-time jobs. If this does not produce a sufficient cost reduction, management may move on to a program of voluntary or compulsory redundancies.

There is, however, a danger that if staff cuts are too severe then there will be reductions in the quality of the product and services provided to customers. There is also likely to be a serious impact on staff morale, potentially leading to a loss of commitment, a loss of skilled staff and an increase in conflict within the organisation.

Illustration 4 – UK public sector

It is not just businesses that have been affected by the global economic slow-down in recent years. Many governments have had to reduce their level of spending – leading to many public departments having to lay off staff.

In the UK, local and central government departments have shed hundreds of thousands of posts in an effort to cope with the tight budget restrictions that have been imposed upon them, while attempting to continue to maintain their level of service provision.

This has led to angry reactions from the heavily unionised public sector employees, with a number of strikes and protests across the country. The long-term effects of this are unknown, but the government may find it harder to attract good quality staff members in the future as public sector jobs may no longer be seen as secure.

It should be noted that many of the changes that a business may wish to make during a period of decline, such as compulsory redundancies or improving factory layout, may require some initial expenditure. The business may be unable to afford this if it is experiencing falling revenues.

In this case, managers may have to consider a fundamental change to the business strategy. This may involve:

- **Retrenchment** – this involves doing the same as before, but drastically cutting costs.
- **Turnaround** – the organisation repositions itself within the market for competitive advantage.
- **Divestment** – this involves the external sale of part of the organisation, or the internal closure of units as part of a rationalisation programme.
- **Liquidation** – the organisation is sold to one or more buyers. This is an admission of failure by the senior managers and is normally a last resort.

All four of these strategies require managers to make difficult decisions, which may have adverse effects on the organisation's stakeholders – especially employees. Whichever approach is taken, it is important that the business acts ethically towards its stakeholders when making tough decisions.

Test your understanding 15

O Ltd is experiencing a period of declining demand for its products. It has decided to look at ways of sourcing cheaper materials and reduce the number of skilled employees to enable it to maintain its profits as sales volume falls.

What approach to decline is O adopting?

A   Retrenchment
B   Turnaround
C   Liquidation
D   Divestment

Test your understanding 16 – (Integration question)

A business has found itself entering a period of decline. What measures could it consider as alternatives to reducing its labour costs?

Change management – change leadership

> **Test your understanding 17 – (Integration question)**
>
> AV Ltd is a high-quality board game manufacturer. It is part of a larger group of companies that manufacture toys and computer games. While these other businesses have prospered over the last few years, this has been at the expense of the traditional board games that AV manufactures and AV's sales have declined each year for the last several years. In addition, AV has seen increased competition from cheaper board game manufacturers, further reducing demand.
>
> The directors of AV's parent company have met to discuss their approach to AV's problems. They have all agreed that a fundamental change is needed to their strategy with regards to the company, but they are not sure what that change should be.
>
> **Required:**
>
> Discuss four possible strategies that the directors may consider, given AV's continuing decline.
>
> **(20 minutes)**

7 Ethics and change management

Most ethical issues focus on how one stakeholder group is benefited at the expense of another, so within any change process there will be a number of potential ethical dilemmas that need managing:

- Whether the change is justified – for example, boosting shareholder profits at the expense of widespread job cuts. If the change involves re-engineering and/or downsizing, then there will usually be redundancies. Ethical issues include:
    - Deciding on who to make redundant (e.g. preference to keep younger employees).
    - Fair treatment of all employees (e.g. discrimination by race, sex or age).
    - What severance package and assistance to offer.
    - Skills obsolescence.
    - Do remember that making employees redundant is not always unjustified. If it is necessary to safeguard the business in the long-term, it cannot be classed as being unethical.
- Management approach used – e.g. manipulation v participation.
- Some managers may seek to exploit change to ensure they benefit personally from new power structures and reward schemes.
- Similarly some may resist change to protect their own interests.

- The extent to which plans are made available or if a "need to know" culture is adopted.
- Whether "misinformation" is used to drive certain phases of the change process – e.g. to unfreeze the existing culture
- Accountants may be asked to manipulate figures to exaggerate the case for change

This list is not exhaustive. The CIMA E3 syllabus requires you to apply the Code of Ethics in the context of business change. This means that whenever you read through a scenario, you need to consider whether there are any business ethical issues or challenges occurring in the change process which will impact upon the ethical position of the organisation.

Illustration 5 – Chrysler

Even when tough decisions need to be made, the actions of a business do not have to be uncaring or disrespectful to the individual employees affected. As part of a US government plan to save the struggling Chrysler motor company, Chrysler's CEO was faced with having to close a number of plants.

The CEO decided to soften the blow through a series of associated plans designed to get the employees into self-employment or into other forms of work. Some employees reskilled and moved to jobs in other parts of the Chrysler group, but the majority found employment elsewhere locally.

8 The importance of adaptation and continuous change

Many authors have argued that firms need to look beyond change as an event and develop a culture where change is embraced as an ongoing process. These include:

- change-adept organisations (Kanter)
- excellent firms that seek to create a climate of change (thrive on chaos) (Peters)

Change-adept organisations – Kanter

Kanter's model focuses on two main issues. Firstly, it identifies the **three attributes of companies that manage change successfully**.

- The imagination to innovate.
- The professionalism to perform.
- The openness to collaborate.

Change management – change leadership

The model goes on to examine the **seven key skills for leaders in these change-adept organisations**.

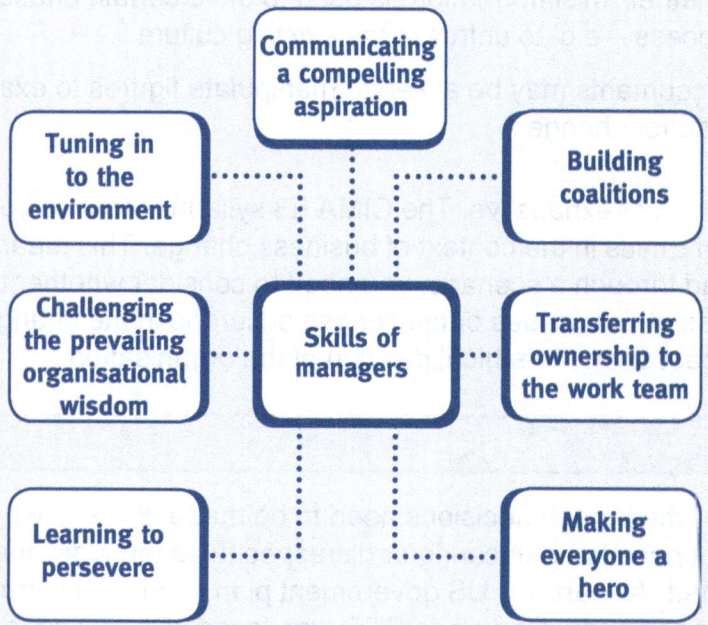

> ### Change adept organisations
>
> Rosabeth Moss Kanter looked at the characteristics of organisations that managed change successfully ('change-adept organisations'), and the qualities of their leaders and managers.
>
> **Attributes of change-adept organisations**
>
> She suggested that change-adept organisations share three key attributes:
>
> - The imagination to innovate.
>
>   Effective leaders help to develop new concepts, which are a requirement for successful change.
>
> - The professionalism to perform.
>
>   Leaders provide both personal competence and competence in the organisation as a whole, which is supported by workforce training and development. This enables the organisation to perform strongly and deliver value to ever-more-demanding customers.

- The openness to collaborate.

    Leaders in change-adept organisations make connections with 'partners' outside the organisation, who can extend the organisation's reach, enhance its products and services, and 'energise its practices'. 'Partners' will include suppliers working in close collaboration, joint venture partners, and so on.

Kanter argued that change should be accepted naturally by organisations, as a natural part of their existence. Change that is compelled by a crisis is usually seen as a threat, rather than as an opportunity for successful development. Mastering change means being the first with the best service or products, anticipating and then meeting customer requirements (which continually change) and applying new technology. This requires organisations to be 'fast, agile, intuitive and innovative'.

Skills for leaders in change-adept organisations

- Tuning in to the environment.

    A leader can actively gather information that might suggest new approaches, by tuning in to what is happening in the environment. Leaders can create a network of 'listening posts', such as satellite offices and joint ventures.

- Challenging the prevailing organisational wisdom.

    Leaders should be able to look at matters from a different perspective, and should not necessarily accept the current view of what is right or appropriate.

- Communicating a compelling aspiration.

    Leaders should have a clear vision of what they want to achieve, and should communicate it with conviction to the people they deal with. A manager cannot 'sell' change to other people without genuine conviction, because there is usually too much resistance to overcome. Without the conviction, a manager will not have the strength of leadership to persuade others.

- Building coalitions.

  Change leaders need the support and involvement of other individuals who have the resources, knowledge or 'political clout' to make things happen. There are usually individuals within the organisation who have the ability to influence others – 'opinion shapers', 'values leaders' and experts in the field. Getting the support of these individuals calls for an understanding of the politics of change in organisations.

- Transferring ownership to the work team.

  Leaders cannot introduce change on their own. At some stage, the responsibility for introducing change will be handed to others. Kanter suggested that a successful leader, having created a coalition in favour of the change, should enlist a team of other people to introduce the change.

- Learning to persevere.

  Something will probably go wrong, and there will be setbacks. Change leaders should not give up too quickly, but should persevere with the change.

- Making everyone a hero.

  A successful leader recognises, rewards and celebrates the accomplishments of others who have helped to introduce a change successfully. Making others feel appreciated for their contribution helps to sustain their motivation, and their willingness to attempt further changes in the future.

Thriving on Chaos (Tom Peters)

Tom Peters has written extensively on management theory. One of his ideas relates to 'excellent' companies that have succeeded by seeking to create a climate of continual and radical change. Peters called this 'thriving on chaos'. He suggested that:

- Incremental change is the enemy of true innovation, because it makes an organisation less willing to be truly innovative.

- Excellent firms don't believe in excellence, only in constant improvement and constant change.

- A constantly changing environment does not necessarily mean chaos: instead, it may mean that companies can handle the introduction of change successfully.

Peters suggested that the advantages of having a climate of change are as follows:

- Innovation and the introduction of new products and new methods are actively sought and welcomed.
- People who are used to change tend to accept it without resistance.
- Employees develop an external viewpoint, and are less insular and defensive in their outlook.

However, there are possible disadvantages:

- With a climate of change morale might be damaged
- Staff might become involved in office politics because of their concerns about the possible changes that might occur in the organisation.

Test your understanding 18

According to Kanter, which of the following is a required skill for leaders within change-adept organisations?

A   Tuning in to the environment
B   The imagination to innovate
C   The professionalism to perform
D   The openness to collaborate

9 Conclusion

The management of change is never an easy process and it is rare that the final outcome exactly matches the original plans. Remember that there is no recipe for success – it simply does not exist.

However, change is more likely to succeed if there is/are:

- clearly understandable goals,
- realistic time frames, rather than merely looking for a 'quick fix'
- clear guidance as to how each individual's behaviour needs to change
- clear, unified leadership with no conflict between managers
- management support for training and other necessary investment.

Change management – change leadership

Test your understanding 19 – C Co – (Case style)

C is a large multinational confectionary manufacturer which was purchased in a hostile takeover bid one year ago. The new owners, R Co, have been surprised at the number of key staff who have left over the last year. A total of 120 out of 170 managers and executives have resigned since R Co took control of the two-hundred-year-old company. The acquisition of C completed R Co's ten year geographical expansion strategy.

In particular, there have been departures among creative, design and marketing specialists. While some resignations are normal after such a bitterly fought takeover battle, industry specialists are shocked at the extent of the staff losses.

A group of remaining managers have been questioned by the board of R Co on why they think so many employees have left. The managers explained that the rate of change in C was historically slow, with a great deal of pride taken in making confectionary the old-fashioned way. C's products are considered part of the national identity of its home country and the company even has a royal license to make chocolate for the queen.

Since R Co took over, the company has changed suppliers for many of the key ingredients used in C's products, and despite pre-takeover promises to the contrary, begun devising strategies to move production overseas. Many of the managers who have left made it clear they were resisting these changes before their resignation.

R Co is a cost leader in the global confectionary market and wishes to bring C in line with the rest of the group. The board of R Co have also announced plans to remove the C name altogether and bring the newly acquired company into its own functional structure, rather than allowing it to operate as a stand-alone division.

The managers stated that in their view, the rate of change has been a problem for many employees together with what they perceive to be a 'selling out' of the C name and values.

Required:

Prepare a report for the Board of R Co, which covers the following key issues:

(a) Explain what is meant by the phrase 'resistance to change' and discuss the resistance to change at C which led to so many managers leaving

(15 minutes)

(b) Evaluate the change management process which has been undertaken at C over the last year

(15 minutes)

(c) Advise the board of R Co on an alternative strategy for C, which may avoid further loss of staff

(10 minutes)

Change management – change leadership

10 Summary

By the end of this chapter you should be able to discuss the following:

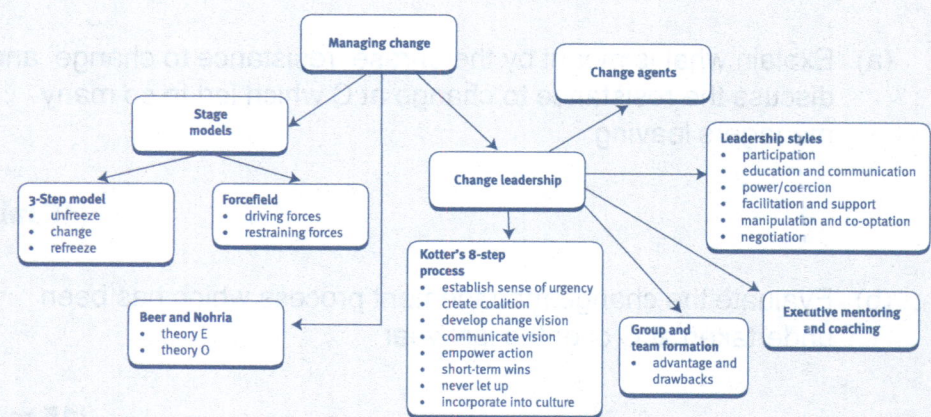

chapter 13

Test your understanding answers

Test your understanding 1

The correct answer is A

A is part of unfreezing, B and C are part of refreezing, while D is an element of change itself.

Test your understanding 2 – WW – (Case style)

Lewin's model suggests that, in order to be successful, WW will need to follow three stages in the change-over to a new accounting package.

Unfreeze

Staff need to be convinced of the need for the new accounting package. This could be difficult within WW for several reasons.

WW's six employees have used the current accounting system for many years. This may mean that they are 'stuck in their ways' and unwilling to learn the new skills required for the new system.

In addition, currently management accounting information can only be produced after a time-consuming and complex process. If a new system improves the efficiency of this process, employees may fear that they will become redundant.

To help with this, WW need to convince them of the superiority of the new system. For instance, it appears that it will make the production of management reports much faster, easing the workload for the employees.

WW also needs to communicate well with its employees. Resistance is often caused by a fear of the unknown. Managers could discuss with staff about the level of training that they will be given on the new system and attempt to allay any fears they may have about potential redundancies.

Finally, WW's managers could also stress to staff members that it will benefit the business as a whole. The current system may cause WW to be less competitive in the marketplace, which could threaten the business as a whole.

581

Change

This involves actually moving staff onto the new accounting system.

This stage will involve training all members of the accounting department on how to use the new system. Enough time must be allowed for employees to be reasonably comfortable with the new system before the change-over is made.

Communication is also vital here – employees must know when the new system will be installed and what will be expected from them. For example, what new reports will the managers expect from the system and when they will need to be prepared.

Refreeze

Finally, WW's managers must ensure that employees do not slip back into old habits and start using the old systems again.

Clearly, if the old accounting system is entirely replaced by the new one, it should be easy to ensure that staff members do not continue to use the original accounting system. However, employees may still continue preparing the management reports manually.

To avoid this, managers could refuse to accept reports in the old, manual format – instead requiring that they be produced from the new system. Staff could be rewarded for using the new system and penalised if the old methods are still used.

Test your understanding 3

The correct answer is A

The current misunderstanding is an example of a restraining force, which is holding the division back from implementing change. N's planned communication will rectify this misunderstanding, reducing the force.

chapter 13

Test your understanding 4 – GVF – (Case style)

To: Rebecca Smith
From: Anne Sma
Date: 12/4/20XX
Subject: Re: Strategic change issues within GVF

Dear Rebecca,

Thank you for your email. I have outlined the points that you requested below.

(a) **Summary of measures needed to turn around GVF**

The inefficiency of GVF management seems to be related to the structure of the company. According to the CEO, there is a need to reduce the number of layers of management, to reduce head office controls and to change attitudes from a narrow concern with departmental objectives to a broader concern for the needs of GVF as a whole.

The reduction in the layers of management will help to reduce costs and to improve communications within the business. Store managers and others may well welcome reduced interference from head office and the increased autonomy may help to motivate them.

The CEO's comment that the company was 'no longer effective or responding to customer needs' is clear from the scenario. Given its loss of customers to new entrants to the market, GVF needs to determine precisely what the needs of its customers are. This may need further investigation – although by increasing the number of own–brand products, it appears to be at least part way through this process already.

(b) (i) **Likely sources of resistance**

Resistance to change in organisations can be considered according to whether the resistance comes from individuals, groups or the organisations themselves.

Individual level

At the individual level, resistance is often caused by fear of the unknown, long-held existing habits and possible threats to position or livelihood.

In GVF, all of the above are likely to be factors. Given the present circumstances of GVF, employees are likely to fear for their job security and whether or not they will be able to continue in their current role or will have to learn a new one.

Managers will be particularly fearful, given the CEO's statement regarding the need to reduce the number of layers of management within GVF. Given that many of these managers may have much to lose and little to gain from such a restructuring, GVF could expect to see significant resistance from them.

Group level

At a group level, there will be collections of individuals who see their positions as threatened and who will join forces to resist and make mutual threats. This will particularly be the case in GVF as many of its employees are unionised, increasing the amount of co-ordinated resistance they are capable of.

Even where trade unions do not exist, it is possible for groups of employees, including managers, to collude informally to resist changes. This may be achieved by withholding information or refusing to co-operate with those seeking to implement change.

For GVF, managers and employees are unlikely to co-operate unless they can see some long-term benefits for themselves.

(ii) **Models of organisational change**

The new CEO of GVF might use the force-field theory of change proposed by Lewin. Lewin's theory suggests that there are two forces present in a change management scenario. One set he refers to as driving forces because they are forces attempting to bring about change; the other set are referred to as restraining forces as they act in the opposite direction and seek to maintain the status quo.

For GVF, the driving forces are likely to include the need for the business to be competitive. Unless GVF can improve its efficiency, its competitors will continue to take its market share. Unless GVF becomes flatter, leaner and more responsive to the market, it may ultimately collapse – especially given its high level of financial gearing.

Organisational level

At the level of the organisation, a number of factors will combine to make the change process difficult. These include the existing culture and structure of the organisation, as well as any past agreements with stakeholders.

Given that the company has traded for over fifty years, the company may be 'set in its ways', with staff unwilling to see significant changes made to longstanding arrangements or ways of working.

The proposed de-layering in GVF will threaten the jobs and status of some layers of management. This will again increase resistance.

The restraining forces will include the reasons for employee resistance mentioned above, such as loss of job security and management levels within GVF.

To be successful, the CEO will need to increase the driving forces – perhaps by improved communication with all employees, laying out the benefits of her proposed changes and the potentially dire consequences to the whole of GVF if they are not implemented.

Alternatively, the CEO may look at reducing the restraining forces. This could involve looking at ways of avoiding voluntary redundancies among managers or by supporting employees who are to be made redundant as they try to find alternative employment.

I hope this helps. If you need any more information, please don't hesitate to get in touch.

Kind regards

Anne Sma

Change management – change leadership

Test your understanding 5

The correct answer is C

Theory O looks at improving the organisation's culture and skill set- for instance through training staff.

Theory E looks at predominantly economic changes that can be made to the organisation.

Test your understanding 6 – (Integration question)

Theory E is often the approach taken in a crisis. If a business needed to make drastic or rapid cuts to its business, or undertake a major restructuring, management may have to make tough decisions in order to secure the long–term survival of the business.

In these circumstances, there may be insufficient time to involve staff in the decision–making process and doing so would likely make it harder to make the difficult choices, such as the number of job losses in the organisation.

Test your understanding 7

The correct answer is C

A assembled a large group of powerful stakeholders. This suggests that a guiding coalition was indeed formed. Her regular meetings with the staff suggested that she had no problems communicating her change vision – and her request for involvement by staff suggests that she had indeed empowered broad-based action.

However, due to the refusal of the Board to allow her to discuss the new entrants to the market, she was unable to establish a sense of urgency. This is likely compounded by the fact that staff have historically enjoyed high bonuses and that the company is seen to be doing well.

Note that A was unable to generate short term wins, but this was largely due to a lack of staff motivation. Failure was therefore caused by a lack of urgency.

chapter 13

Test your understanding 8

The correct answer is B

This is a classic example of facilitation and support.

Education and communication involve convincing staff of the benefits of the change process being undertaken. Coercion relies on the use of threats, while participation involves employees having input into the change management decision-making process. None of these other options fits this scenario.

Test your understanding 9

The correct answer is D

A is likely to take too long, given the need for rapid change and the large number of employees. B is also likely to be inappropriate due to the lack of a central union to negotiate with and the fact that it needs to lay off many of its staff in order to survive, giving little room for negotiation.

C relates to distortion of the true facts in order to convince staff of the need for change. Not only is this unethical, but it is unnecessary given the dire state of U's actual position. Untruths are not needed.

Coercion involves the use of managerial power to force change. While this is unlikely to be popular with employees, it is rapid and may be U's best option at managing the change process.

Test your understanding 10 – Grey – (Case style)

Division A

Division A appears to be making a relatively small change to its business. It is currently highly profitable – indicating that it is not currently experiencing a crisis.

As such, education and communication may be the best approach. This involves explaining the reasons behind the proposed centralisation of the accounting function and attempts to persuade the employees that this is a beneficial idea. While this is often time-consuming, A has a relatively small number of staff, which makes this approach more realistic. In addition, as the company currently has a good relationship with its workers (and likely needs to maintain this given that its staff are highly skilled and therefore very important to the company), this approach is most likely to keep the majority of staff happy.

It is possible that staff may not be convinced by the need to cut costs given that the division is highly profitable. In this case, A could choose facilitation and support – perhaps helping the staff who will be made redundant to find new jobs, such as by giving them time off for job interviews.

Finally, A could consider participation and involvement. This would see A getting its employees involved in the change process. Perhaps job losses can be avoided if employees are able to think of alternative ways of improving efficiency. This may be very time consuming, although there is no evidence of time-pressure in the scenario.

Division B

Division B is clearly in a crisis, with poor industrial relations and the potential threat of closure.

Given the serious nature of its situation, B could also adopt an education and communication style. If the alternative to job losses is a total closure of the division, this may be enough to convince employees of the need for the change. However, given the poor relations between staff and managers, as well as the tight time-constraints that B is under, this may not be realistic.

As an alternative, B could choose a manipulation and co-optation style. This involves undermining resistance in a more covert manner, perhaps by stressing the potential for the division to be closed, or down-playing the number of job losses that would be involved. It is a faster way of dealing with resistance than education and communication, but if employees feel that they are being manipulated, it may damage industrial relations further.

Finally, B could opt for coercion. This involves the managers of B forcing the staff to accept the changes. Any individuals who resist can be threatened with redundancy. Given the urgent nature of the needed change, this may be the easiest and most effective way of dealing with resistance. However, it will be likely to leave employees angry and may lead to demotivation and high employee turnover.

B may decide that its industrial relations are less important than its long-term survival, especially as employees are low skilled and will therefore be easy to replace.

Test your understanding 11 – (Integration question)

Change introduced through the use of power or manipulation is likely to add to anxiety. Education and communication will rarely succeed on their own when introducing major change. However, they are useful as a support for a negotiation or participation approach. The negotiation approach requires the existence of organised representatives and a formal procedure that is suitable for some items such as change in employment terms but would be inadvisable for other items of changing procedures, organisational changes, decentralisation, etc. In these cases, participation offers the best opportunity of allaying staff anxieties by involving them early in the change process and continuing that involvement through to completion.

Test your understanding 12

The correct answers are A, B and F

The fact that M already has a strong corporate culture with employees that work well together would suggest that C and D are all likely to be advantages of using internal change agents. There is no guarantee that the use of external consultants will be cheaper than using internal managers – in fact, the reverse may well be true.

Test your understanding 13 – (Integration question)

A change agent is a person, or group of people, who help an organisation to achieve its strategic change. If MMM appoints a change agent, he or she would carry out a number of useful functions, including:

Identify any problems and their causes

This is likely to be relatively straightforward for MMM. The biggest problem with their proposed purchase of POR is the language barrier between their staff. MMM and POR will find it almost impossible to work together as they do not understand each other's language.

This could cause the acquisition to fail.

Diagnose solutions and select appropriate courses of action

The change agent is responsible for proposing ways in which the problems that they have identified could be overcome.

For MMM, it could consider:

- sending key members of staff in both companies on external language courses, or
- hiring some additional staff members in both companies who are bilingual.

In many cases there will be a number of possible solutions. The change agent will be responsible for presenting these to management and helping them to decide which option is most appropriate for MMM.

Implement change

Once the management have selected an appropriate strategy, they will need someone to implement it. As the change agent has been part of the decision-making process, they will be the most logical choice to actually carry out the plan. In MMM, the change agent may, for example, investigate and book language courses for appropriate members of staff.

Transmit the learning process to others and the organisation overall

There may be some resistance to the proposed changes. A change agent can champion the proposals, explaining to employees why it is necessary and what the advantages will be.

The change agent will also document the decision-making process and communicate to all members of staff in both MMM and POR. This is a vital step, as employees in both businesses will need to be kept informed about the developments in the company.

Test your understanding 14

The correct answer is D

A is incorrect as coaching can be useful for all levels within the organisation. B relates to mentoring. C is inconsistent with mentoring or coaching as either can be done by any individual with the relevant skills/experience.

Test your understanding 15

The correct answer is A

By definition

Test your understanding 16 – (Integration question)

The business could attempt to:

- generate additional revenue through more effective marketing
- improve purchasing policies and procedures
- redesign the product or service offered in order to reduce production costs
- contract out services that are not considered essential to the core business (although this may result in job losses)
- consider changes to reduce duplication and improve financial control systems.

Change management – change leadership

Test your understanding 17 – (Integration question)

There are four major approaches that the directors could consider with regards to AV:

Retrenchment

This would involve AV continuing to make board games, but looking at ways to significantly cut costs. This would help increase profits and offset the decline in results that the business is experiencing.

Given that the company currently produces high-quality board games, there may be scope for the business to save money by reducing the quality of materials. This may also allow it to cut its prices and compete with the new, lower-cost market entrants.

Turnaround

For AV this would probably involve much the same approach as retrenchment. AV could attempt to reposition itself within the board games market as a low-cost manufacturer.

Liquidation

The directors could choose to sell AV to one or more investors. Given the current level of decline, they may not realise a high price for the business. This would normally be a last resort for the directors.

Divestment

As an alternative to selling the business, the directors could decide to close the business unit down. The assets could then be sold or transferred to other parts of the organisation.

Test your understanding 18

The correct answer is A

The other three are attributes of change-adept organisations themselves.

chapter 13

Test your understanding 19 – C Co – (Case style)

Report
To: The Board of R Co
From: A. Strategy
Date: 18/09/XX
Subject: Change management at C

Introduction

This report will examine a number of issues surrounding the change management process and the resistance that has been seen at C, a business recently acquired by R Co.

(a) Resistance to change

Resistance to change is the action taken by individuals and groups when they perceive that a change that is occurring is a threat to them.

Resistance is any attitude or behaviour that reflects an individual's unwillingness to make or support a desired change.

Reasons for resisting change can stem from three factors.

These are discussed below with reference to the situation at C:

Job factors

Employees may resist change because they fear changes to their working conditions, demotion or reduced pay. The managers in question at C took pride in the traditional ways of making confectionary and obviously saw these methods were under threat from R Co. In particular, the creative managers may have foreseen cuts to design and marketing budgets, since these costs are often viewed as discretionary by cost leader organisations like R.

Reduced pay, demotion and certainly inferior working conditions would all be suggested by R's aggressive strategy over the first few months of ownership.

Change management – change leadership

Personal factors

Managers may have resisted changes as they saw them as a perceived criticism of their performance in C. Changing suppliers of raw materials as well as beginning to move production overseas suggests that R Co sees C as inefficient and its cost base as too high. Altering the supply chain and sourcing overseas partners are typical strategies to reduce variable costs. It is likely that the managers felt less valued under the new management than the old.

The development of C into a cost leader would also signal more monotonous roles for many of its staff, with the emphasis on reducing costs rather than being creative with products.

Social factors

C was a well established part of the national culture in its home nation. The staff's social environment at work would have reflected this, with a great deal of pride being taken in working methods pre-takeover. For new owners to come in and disregard this heritage would lead to personal dislike of R's staff on the part of the C employees. The lack of consultation carried out by R's executives is also likely to have led to rejection of change.

(b) Evaluation of change management process carried out at C

There are some positives to the way change management has been carried out at C. Employees are in no doubt as to the intentions of R Co, and although acceptance of that may be difficult in some cases, it could be argued that, the sooner processes of change are begun, the sooner staff can get used to new methods of working.

R Co clearly has a track record of cost leadership, and to maintain a subsidiary which has a different strategy would detract from their corporate image and possibly confuse investors and customers. The sooner this mismatch is dealt with the better.

There is also a clear reason for R Co's rapid changes, in that it is possible for them to save money through moving production abroad and changing suppliers. Such rapid change will in fact increase profit margins and, arguably, benefit stakeholders in C.

C has given a clear message that it is in charge of C and again, this strategic clarity is equivalent to a 'short, sharp shock'. Once the message is communicated, there can be no doubt or confusion as to the company's intentions.

However, the results of such rapid change show that there are significant disadvantages to altering strategy upon acquisition in such a fashion. Firstly, C is a highly valued national institution, with a royal endorsement. R's actions may be seen as disrespectful and result in a consumer backlash.

Rapid transformational change only works if employees believe it is necessary to benefit the company and safeguard their jobs. In the case of C, the opposite is true, with managers feeling so strongly that the change is a mistake and that they would rather resign than see it through. The loss of so many staff, particularly in creative areas, means that new strategies will be harder to implement.

R Co is taking significant risks by adopting a cost leadership strategy for C. If in fact, it is impossible to complete the transfer of C from a differentiator to a cost leader, there will be no return to the previous strategy. C's brand names are, at best, likely to be devalued once it becomes part of the functional structure of R and at worst, completely lost.

In conclusion, the unpopularity of R's actions means they will find it harder to push continued change through and high staff turnover together with resistance to change will both remain as key obstacles to their aims.

(c) **Alternative strategy for C**

Since R Co has purchased C as part of a geographical expansion programme, the simplest alternative is to allow C to continue to operate as a division of R but to use its distribution channels to introduce some of R's products into its markets.

This parallel strategy could work well for some time and R could slowly introduce cost-cutting measures, trying to keep any promises, such as not moving production overseas for the foreseeable future.

It is likely with a slower approach that many managers could be brought on-side. The board of R Co are clearly not averse to consulting with C's staff, since they have asked for their views on the staff turnover issue. If these consultations could be extended to strategic aims and intent, the 'old' C workforce would be much happier to work under R's board, particularly if they saw the attributes of C protected rather than dismantled.

Of course, if R Co is determined to make C part of their empire and remove its identity completely, any kind of change management is likely to meet fierce resistance.

Index

A
Acquisition.....269-271
Ansoff's product/market matrix.....250-254

B
Balanced scorecard.....318-324
Balogun, Hope Hailey.....513
BCG matrix.....262-266
Beer & Nohria.....548
Benchmarking.....331-334
Big Data.....434-438
    Benefits and drawbacks.....438, 439
    Features.....436
Building block model.....328-330
Brainstorming.....212
Brand strategy.....479

C
Carroll
    CSR model.....88, 89
    CSR philosophies.....89, 90
Change
    Agents.....562-564
    Change adept organizations.....573-575
    Ethics.....572, 573
    Leadership.....550-553
    Resistance to.....527, 528
    Triggers.....510-513
    Types of change.....513-516
CIMA code of ethics.....99-103
Coaching.....567-569
Competence audit.....162
Competences.....161, 162, 167
Competitor analysis.....139, 140
Conglomerate diversification.....259
Corporate governance.....24-28
Corporate political activity.....70
Corporate social responsibility.....84-93
Cost leadership.....242, 243
Countermediation.....496
Critical success factors (CSFs).....163-167, 313
Criticality of IT.....369-372
Cross impact analysis.....214
Cultural web.....519-522
Culture.....518
Customer account profitability (CAP).....484-487
Customer acquisition.....480-482
Customer analysis.....471-475
Customer behaviour.....472-474
Customer extension.....493
Customer lifetime value (CLV).....488, 489
Customer relationship management (CRM).....484
Customer retention.....491, 492
Cyert and March.....62

D
Data mining.....431-433
Data warehousing.....430, 431
Decline.....570, 571
Delphi technique.....211
Derived demand.....212
Differentiation.....243, 244
Directors
    Role of.....22-24
Disintermediation.....495
Diversification.....252, 253, 255-261
Divestment.....275
Divisional performance.....335
Drucker mission statements.....44

E
Earl.....372
E-business.....386-389
    Benefits and drawbacks.....389-392
    Categories.....388, 389
    Stages.....387, 388
E-commerce.....386, 494
E-procurement.....467-470
Electronic data interchange (EDI).....493
Emergent approach.....12
Environmental analysis,
    Definition.....120
    Problems.....121
    Purpose.....120
Ethics
    Change management.....572, 573
    CIMA code of ethics.....99-103
    Stances.....92, 93
    Threats and safeguards.....105-107
EVA.....335, 337
Evaluating strategies.....277-283
Extranet.....391, 445, 494, 495

F
Financial performance measures.....314, 315
Fitzgerald and Moon.....328-330
Five Forces model (Porter).....125-129, 378-381
Focus.....244, 245
Force field analysis.....544, 545
Forecasting.....209-212
Foresight.....213, 214
    Five Cs model.....213
Franchising.....273, 274
Freewheeling opportunism.....14
Friedman.....86

Index

G
Game theory.....221-223
Gap analysis.....204-208
Gartner (4Vs).....436
Generic strategies.....242-247
Global competition.....140-142
Government influence.....67, 68
Group and team formation.....553-555
Groupware.....444

H
Handy.....518
Horizontal diversification.....258

I
Incrementalism.....13
Industry life cycle model.....132-136
Information strategy
    Importance.....375, 376
    IM strategy.....373, 374
    IS strategy.....373
    IT strategy.....375
    Link to business strategy.....368
Information systems.....367
Information technology.....367
International growth strategies.....276
Intranet.....391, 445, 494
Issues analysis.....214

J
Johnson, Gerry.....519
Johnson, Scholes and Whittington.....7, 92, 278
Joint methods of expansion.....271-274
Joint venture.....272

K
Kanter
    Change adept organizations.....574-576
    Power skills of change agents.....564
Kaplan and Norton.....318-320
Key performance indicators (KPIs).....163-167, 313
Knowledge management.....440-445
Kotler.....479
Kotter (change leadership).....550-552
Kotter and Schlesinger
    Reasons for resisting change.....528
    Leadership styles.....555-559

L
Learning organizations.....447
Lewin
    Three stage model.....539-543
    Force field analysis.....544, 545
Licensing.....274
Lindblom.....13
Logical incrementalism.....13
Lynch and Cross.....325

M
Management accountants
    Role of.....30-32
Market development.....251, 252
Market penetration.....250, 251
Marketing
    Audits.....490
    General.....429, 430, 477
    Push and pull.....398
McFarlan.....369
McKinsey.....525
Mendelow's power/interest matrix.....58, 59
Mentoring.....560-563
Mergers.....269
Mission
    Definition.....42
    Mission statements.....42-46
Morphological analysis.....214
M's model.....159

N
Niche.....244, 245
Neely's 4CPs.....312, 313
Networks.....444
Nolan's stage hypothesis.....383, 384
Non-market strategy.....67
Non-financial performance measures.....316

O
Objectives
    Long-term vs short term.....51
    Not for profit.....54, 55
    Primary vs secondary.....49, 50
    SMART.....49
Opportunity mapping.....214
Organic growth.....269-271
Outsourcing.....274

Index

P

Payne.....477
Performance measurement mix.....311-314
    Communication.....342, 343
    Problems.....344-347
Performance pyramid.....325, 326
PEST analysis.....122, 123
Peters, Tom.....576, 577
Porter
    Five forces.....125-129, 379-382
    Generic strategies.....242-247, 382
    Government influence.....67, 68
    IS/IT effect on competition.....387
    Porter's Diamond.....142-145
    Value chain.....169-171, 176, 384, 385
Position auditing.....200-202
Product development.....252
Product life cycle.....132-136

R

Rational model.....7-11
Real options.....224, 225
Regression analysis.....209
Reintermediation.....495, 496
Related diversification.....255
Relationship marketing.....478
Relevance trees.....214
Resistance to change
    Reasons for.....527, 528
Resource audit.....159, 160
Resources.....160
Role playing.....214

S

SAF model.....277-283
Scenario planning.....215-218
Seber.....331
Senge (Peter).....447
Service level agreements.....466
SERVQUAL.....491
Seven S model.....525, 526
Six markets model.....477
SMART.....49
Social and digital marketing.....398, 399
Social media marketing.....399, 400
Stakeholders
    Actors.....57
    Alliances.....63
    Analysis.....58, 59
    Definition.....55
    Power.....58
    Resolving conflict.....62

Strategy:
    Approaches.....7-20
    Definitions.....2, 3
    For NFPs.....17-19
    Levels.....4-6
    Non-market.....67
Strategic alliance.....272, 273
Strategic management accounting.....30-32, 52, 348
Strategic options.....241
Stretch targets.....343
Supplier relationships.....464-466
Supply chain management
    Downstream.....471-476
    General.....460, 461
    Push and pull.....462
    Upstream.....464-470
Sustainability.....94-98
SVA.....336, 337
SWOT.....200-202, 377, 378
System modelling.....210

T

Theory E & Theory O.....548, 549
Think tank.....211
Three Es.....18, 19
Three stage model of change.....539-543
Thriving on Chaos.....576, 577
Time series analysis.....209
Transaction marketing.....478
Transfer pricing.....340
Triggers for change.....510-513
Triple bottom line.....338, 339

V

Value chain.....169-171, 176, 384, 385
Value drivers.....169
Value shop.....177
Value system.....171
Vertical integration.....256-258
Virtual organisations.....397, 398
Visioning.....214
Vision statements.....47, 48

W

Web 2.0.....394-396

Index

TAG Bioleg UG
(BY1 & BY2):

Llawlyfr myfyriwr

Gareth Rowlands

Bioleg UG **CBAC** *(BY1 & BY2): Llawlyfr myfyriwr*

Cyhoeddwyd gan CBAC
245 Rhodfa'r Gorllewin, Caerdydd CF5 2YX

Cyhoeddiad cyntaf 2008
Argraffwyd gan gwmni HSW Print
Tonypandy, Rhondda, CF40 2XX   Tel: (01443) 441100

ISBN: 978 - 1 - 86085 - 649 - 5

Cyflwyniad

Yn aml, mae myfyrwyr yn ansicr beth mae angen iddynt ei wneud i baratoi ar gyfer arholiadau

Mae'r llyfryn hwn:
- ✓ yn rhoi arweiniad yn benodol ar gyfer myfyrwyr sy'n astudio Bioleg UG CBAC.
- ✓ yn ganllaw ar gyfer astudio a **dylech adeiladu ar yr wybodaeth a ddarperir trwy ddefnyddio gwerslyfr** a **nodiadau o'ch gwersi.**
- ✓ yn awgrymu rhai o'r prif bwyntiau y dylid eu nodi.
- ✓ mae'n rhoi arweiniad ynglŷn â pha ddyfnder o ymdriniaeth sydd ei hangen.

Rôl weithredol yn eich astudiaethau

- Er mwyn adolygu'n effeithiol y mae'n bwysig i chi gymryd **rôl weithredol** yn y broses. Nid oes ond ychydig werth i ddarllen drwy'ch nodiadau yn oddefol. Mae'r canllawiau'n awgrymu '**Pwyntiau gweithredu**' lle rydych yn:
- ✓ tynnu lluniau wedi eu labelu.
- ✓ llunio graffiau.
- ✓ dadansoddi tablau o ganlyniadau.
- ✓ amlygu termau allweddol a rhoi diffiniadau ohonynt.
- ✓ creu tablau cymharu.
- ✓ disgrifio prosesau trwy ddefnyddio siartiau llif a diagramau llif.
- Nid yw hyn yn golygu mai'r gweithgareddau hyn yw'r unig rai y dylech eu gwneud i baratoi ar gyfer arholiad. Awgrymiadau yn unig ydynt. Er enghraifft, fe all fod nifer o luniau eraill y dylech eu hystyried.

Awgrymiadau am adolygu

Mae arholwyr yn ymwybodol nad yw ymgeiswyr bob amser yn gallu dangos i'r arholwr yn effeithiol bob peth y maent yn ei wybod.
Er mwyn osgoi'r broblem hon mae angen:
- ✓ llunio **rhaglen adolygu** strwythuredig. Adolygwch yn rheolaidd – mae ailadrodd yn offeryn gwerthfawr wrth ddysgu ac wrth baratoi ar gyfer arholiadau. Adolygwch bob pwnc cyn gynted â'i fod wedi ei gwblhau. Ceir llwyddiant drwy weithio'n gyson yn hytrach na cheisio cofio popeth y munud olaf.
- ✓ **rhaid deall yr egwyddorion sylfaenol** e.e. trwy ddysgu diffiniadau.
- ✓ **adolygwch bob pwnc.** Bydd pob uned yn cynnwys nifer o gwestiynau strwythuredig ac un cwestiwn traethawd. Nid yw'n syniad da ceisio gweithio allan pa bynciau fydd yn 'digwydd codi'. Mae arholwyr yn cymryd gofal mawr i sicrhau bod y cwestiynau yn cwmpasu pob pwnc.
- ✓ lluniwch **ddiagramau anodedig** – mae'r rhain yn ffordd dda o adolygu!
- ✓ ceisiwch ddod yn gyfarwydd â **chwestiynau arholiadau blaenorol**.
- ✓ **mynegwch eich hun yn glir ac yn gryno** – yn aml mae myfyrwyr sy'n gwybod tipyn go lew o fioleg yn gwneud anghyfiawnder â'u hunain mewn arholiad oherwydd bod eu techneg arholiad yn wael. Mae llawer o hyn yn codi o broblemau iaith. Gall wneud y gwahaniaeth rhwng gradd dda a gradd gyffredin. Dylech allu darllen, dehongli, cofio, deall a mynegi gwybodaeth yn gryno er mwyn ateb cwestiynau arholiad yn llwyddiannus.
- ✓ rhaid i chi ddeall y **geiriau allweddol** a ddefnyddir mewn cwestiynau arholiad.

Gobeithir y bydd y canllawiau hyn yn werthfawr i'r myfyriwr.

Mae'r awdur yn brif arholwr i CBAC ac y mae wedi ysgrifennu canllawiau adolygu pellach ar gyfer y fanyleb newydd 2008 ynghyd â llyfr cwestiwn.

> Revision express "A - level study guide Biology" (Pearson Education).
> Revision express "AS Fast-track Biology" (Pearson Education)

Mae'r ddau gyhoeddiad yn ategu'r wybodaeth sydd yn y llyfryn hwn ac yn ymestyn y gweithgareddau a'r wybodaeth a amlinellir yma. Mae'r llyfryn, sy'n pwysleisio deunydd CBAC yn benodol, yn seiliedig i raddau helaeth, ond ddim yn llwyr, ar y canllawiau astudio hyn.

Gareth Rowlands Mawrth 2008

Gwefannau

www.revision-express.com

www.cbac.co.uk

1.1 Cyfansoddion Biolegol

Mae gan foleciwlau penodol eu swyddogaethau penodol mewn organebau byw. Mae'r swyddogaethau hyn yn dibynnu ar y priodweddau sydd gan foleciwl. Adeiledd (structure) y moleciwl sy'n rhoi priodweddau iddo. Dylech allu gwahaniaethu rhwng y termau: atom a moleciwl, elfen a chyfansoddyn, organig ac anorganig.

Mae dŵr yn hanfodol, fel cyfrwng ar gyfer adweithiau metabolaidd; y mae'n rhan o gyfansoddiad celloedd; mae elfennau allweddol yn bodoli mewn hydoddiant dyfrllyd; ac mae'n darparu cynefin i organebau dyfrol.

Ïonau anorganig

Mae gan ïonau anorganig swyddogaethau pwysig mewn organebau byw. Gellir eu rhannu'n ddau grŵp;
- macrofaetholynnau – sydd eu hangen mewn meintiau bychain.

magnesiwm	Ansoddyn o gloroffyl mewn dail
haearn	Ansoddyn o haemoglobin yn y gwaed
ffosffad	A geir mewn pilen blasmaidd, asidau niwclëig, ATP
calsiwm	Ansoddyn o esgyrn a dannedd

- microfaetholynnau – sy'n angenrheidiol mewn meintiau bychan iawn (mymryn), e.e. copr, sinc

Dŵr

- Mae dŵr yn foleciwl **polar** sydd heb wefr gyffredinol. Ym mhen ocsigen y moleciwl mae gwefr negyddol fechan ac ym mhen hydrogen y moleciwl mae gwefr bositif bychan. Pan fydd dau foleciwl dŵr yn agos iawn at ei gilydd bydd y gwefrau gwrthgyferbyniol yn denu ei gilydd gan ffurfio bond hydrogen. Ar eu pen eu hunain mae'r bondiau hydrogen yn wan ond gan fod cymaint ohonynt maent yn glynu gyda'i gilydd mewn fframwaith delltwaith cryf. Yr enw am y ffordd y mae moleciwlau dŵr yn glynu gyda'i gilydd yw **cydlyniad**.
Mae hyn yn golygu y gellir tynnu colofnau uchel o ddŵr i fyny tiwbiau sylem mewn coed uchel.
- Ar dymheredd arferol mae **tyniant arwyneb** dŵr **yn uwch** nag unrhyw hylif arall heblaw mercwri. Mewn pwll o ddŵr mae'r cydlyniad rhwng y moleciwlau dŵr yn creu tyniant arwyneb fel y gall y dŵr gynnal pwysau pryfyn megis sglefriwr y dŵr.
- Mae dŵr yn **hydoddydd**. Gan fod dŵr yn foleciwl polar bydd yn denu gronynnau eraill wedi'u gwefru, megis ïonau a moleciwlau polar eraill, megis glwcos. Mae hyn yn caniatáu i adweithiau cemegol ddigwydd mewn hylif a gan fod y cemegau hynny'n hydoddi mewn dŵr mae'n gweithredu fel **cyfrwng cludo** e.e. mewn anifeiliaid mae gwaed yn cludo llawer o sylweddau wedi eu hydoddi. Mewn planhigion mae dŵr yn cludo mwynau yn y sylem a swcros yn y ffloem. Ni fydd moleciwlau amholar, megis lipidau, yn hydoddi mewn dŵr.
Mae priodweddau hydroffobig lipidau yn bwysig o safbwynt cellbilenni.
- Mae **gwres sbesiffig** dŵr yn uchel. Mae angen cryn dipyn o egni gwres er mwyn codi tymheredd dŵr. Y rheswm am hynny yw bod y bondiau hydrogen rhwng moleciwlau dŵr yn cyfyngu ar eu symudiad. Mae hyn yn atal anwadaliad (newidiadau) mawr yn nhymheredd dŵr ac mae hyn yn arbennig o bwysig o ran cadw tymheredd cynefinoedd dyfrol yn sefydlog fel na fydd organebau yn gorfod dioddef tymheredd eithafol. Mae hyn hefyd yn caniatáu i ensymau yn y celloedd allu gweithio'n effeithiol.
- Mae **gwres cudd** dŵr yn uchel, h.y. mae angen egni gwres sylweddol er mwyn ei droi o fod yn hylif i fod yn anwedd. Mae hyn yn bwysig, er enghraifft i reoli tymheredd pan ddefnyddir gwres i anweddu dŵr wrth chwysu. Hynny yw, mae anweddiad dŵr oddi ar unrhyw arwyneb yn achosi oeri.
- Mae dŵr yn cyrraedd ei ddwysedd eithaf ar 4°C. Mae dŵr yn ei ffurf solet (rhew) yn llai dwys na dŵr ac felly mae'n arnofio ar yr wyneb. Mae rhew yn creu haen ynysu ac felly'n caniatáu i organebau oroesi oddi tano.
- Mae dŵr yn dryloyw fel bod goleuni yn gallu treiddio drwyddo ac felly mae'n caniatáu i blanhigion dyfrol allu ffotosyntheseiddio'n effeithiol.

Carbohydradau

Mae carbohydradau yn gyfansoddion organig sy'n cynnwys carbon, hydrogen ac ocsigen.
Mae gan garbohydradau ddwy brif **swyddogaeth**:
- gweithredu fel ffynhonnell egni i blanhigion ac anifeiliaid, e.e. siwgr, startsh, glycogen.
- Cynnal strwythur cellfuriau planhigion, e.e.cellwlos.

Mae tri phrif fath o garbohydrad - monosacarid, deusacarid a polysacarid.

Monosacaridau

Mae monosacaridau yn foleciwlau organig cymharol fychan, ac maent yn flociau adeiladu ar gyfer carbohydradau mwy. Y fformiwla gyffredinol ar gyfer monosacaridau yw CH_2O n ac mae eu henw'n adlewyrchu nifer yr atomau carbon sydd yn y moleciwl (n).
Lle bo n = 3 trios – sy'n bwysig mewn metabolaeth.
Lle bo n = 5 pentos – a ddefnyddir i ffurfio asidau niwclëig.
Lle bo n = 6 hecsos, e.e glwcos, y brif ffynhonnell egni.

Yr un fformiwla sydd ar gyfer pob siwgr, $C_6H_{12}O_6$ ond mae eu hadeiledd moleciwlaidd yn wahanol. Gan amlaf mae monosacaridau yn bodoli fel adeileddau cylchol pan maent yn hydoddi mewn dŵr. Mae glwcos yn bodoli fel dau isomer, sef ffurf α a'r ffurf β. Mae'r ddwy wahanol ffurf yn achosi gwahaniaethau biolegol sylweddol pan fyddant yn ffurfio polymerau megis startsh a cellwlos.

- ❏ *Tasg*   Lluniwch ddiagramau o gadwyn syth ac adeileddau cylchol glwcos.
  Lluniwch ddiagram ffurfiau α a β glwcos.

Deusacaridau

Mae deusacaridau wedi'u ffurfio o ddwy uned monosacarid wedi eu cysylltu gyda'i gilydd trwy ffurfio **bond glycosidaidd** *gyda dŵr yn cael ei ddileu.* Gelwir hyn yn adwaith **cyddwyso**. Gellir ffurfio deusacaridau trwy gysylltu dau fonosacarid tebyg neu drwy gyfuno dau fonosacarid gwahanol.

Monosacaridau			Deusacarid	Maent yn bodoli mewn
glwcos	+	glwcos =	maltos	siwgr brag
glwcos	+	ffrwctos =	swcros	siwgr cansen
glwcos	+	galactos =	lactos	siwgr llaeth

- ❏ *Tasg*
  1. Tynnwch lun foleciwl o maltos a ffurfir trwy gyfuno dau foleciwl o glwcos.
  2. Disgrifiwch brawf Benedict ar gyfer siwgr rhydwythol megis glwcos a phrawf wedi'i addasu ar gyfer siwgr, megis swcros, sydd ddim yn rhydwythydd.

Polysacaridau

Mae polysacaridau yn foleciwlau mawr cymhleth a elwir yn **bolymerau**. Maent yn cael eu ffurfio o nifer fawr o unedau monosacaridau wedi eu cysylltu â'i gilydd. Y ddau brif grŵp yw:

- Polysacaridau **storio** megis **startsh** (mewn planhigion) a **glycogen** (mewn anifeiliaid).
  Mae startsh yn bolymer wedi'i ffurfio o lawer o foleciwlau glwcos sy'n cael eu dal ynghyd gan fondiau glycosidaidd. Y mae'n foleciwl storio delfrydol oherwydd:
  ✓ Ei fod yn gryno.
  ✓ Ei fod yn anhydawdd ac nad yw'n cael effaith osmotig mewn celloedd.
  ✓ Ei fod yn hawdd ei dorri i lawr yn ddeusacaridau a monosacaridau.
  Mae startsh yn cael ei ffurfio o ddau bolymer, sef amylos ac amylopectin. Mae amylos yn llinol (digangen) ac yn torchi yn helics. Mae amylopectin ar y llaw arall yn canghennu ac yn ffitio i mewn yn yr amylos.
  Gelwir glycogen weithiau yn startsh anifail ac y mae'n debyg iawn i amylopectin.

- Polysacaridau **adeileddol** megis **cellwlos** mewn planhigion a **citin** mewn pryfed.
  Mae cellwlos yn cynnwys llawer o gadwyni paralel hir o foleciwlau glwcos wedi eu croes gysylltu â'i gilydd â bondiau hydrogen. Mae'r gadwyn wedi ei gwneud o unedau glwcos, ac mae ganddi foleciwlau glwcos cyfagos wedi eu cylchdroi 180°. Mae hyn yn caniatáu i fondiau hydrogen gael eu ffurfio rhwng grwpiau hydrocsyl y cadwynau paralel cyfagos ac yn helpu i roi sefydlogrwydd adeileddol i gellwlos. Mae'r cadwynau hyn wedi eu grwpio gyda'i gilydd mewn **microffibrolynnau**. Y ffibrau hyn sy'n rhoi cadernid a gwytnwch i gellfuriau planhigion.
  Mae citin yn debyg i gellwlos ond mae asidau amino wedi eu hychwanegu i ffurfio mwcopolysacarid. Mae'n gryf, yn gwrthsefyll dŵr, yn ysgafn ac yn ffurfio sgerbwd allanol pryfed.

Polysacarid	Monomer	Bond Glycosidaidd
startsh (amylos)	α glwcos	1-4
glycogen	α glwcos	1-4 ac 1-6
cellwlos	β glwcos	1-4

Tasg Lluniwch ddiagram wedi ei symleiddio o adeiledd cellwlos yn dangos y groes bontydd o fondiau H.

Disgrifiwch y prawf ïodin ar gyfer startsh.

Braster (lipidau)

Fel carbohydradau, mae lipidau hefyd yn cynnwys carbon, hydrogen ac ocsigen ond maent yn cynnwys llai o ocsigen mewn cyfrannedd â'r carbon a'r hydrogen. Maent yn gyfansoddion amholar ac felly yn anhydawdd mewn dŵr.

Mae **triglyseridau** yn cael eu ffurfio gan adweithiau cyddwyso rhwng **glyserol** ac **asidau brasterog**. Mae triglyserid yn cynnwys un moleciwl o glyserol a thri moleciwl o asid brasterog. Mae'r moleciwl glyserol mewn lipid yn wastad yr un fath ond mae'r gydran asid brasterog yn amrywio. Yn yr adwaith yma mae dŵr yn cael ei ddileu a bond ocsigen, a elwir yn **fond ester**, yn cael ei ffurfio rhwng y glyserol a'r asid brasterog.

❏ *Tasg* Lluniwch ddiagram yn cynrychioli'r canlynol:

un moleciwl o glyserol + 3 moleciwl o asidau brasterog === triglyserid + dŵr.
(fformiwla adeileddol) (fformiwla gyffredinol)

Mae sawl gwahanol asid brasterog a all adweithio gyda glyserol ond mae dau brif fath:
- Asidau brasterog **dirlawn** lle mae'r holl atomau carbon yn cael eu cysylltu gan fond **sengl**.
- Asidau brasterog **annirlawn** sy'n cynnwys un neu fwy o fondiau **dwbl** ac felly sydd â llai o atomau hydrogen nag a allai fod.
Mae bwyta gormod o fraster, yn arbennig braster dirlawn, yn ffactor sy'n cyfrannu at glefyd y galon.

Priodweddau cemegol lipidau yw:
- eu bod yn anhydawdd mewn dŵr ond yn hydoddi mewn hydoddyddion organig.
- mae braster yn solid ar dymheredd arferol ystafell ond mae olew yn hylif.

Mae **swyddogaethau** braster yn cynnwys:
- **storio egni**. Gan fod un gram o fraster yn cynhyrchu bron ddwywaith gymaint o egni ag un gram o garbohydrad mae brasterau yn ffordd effeithiol o storio egni. Mae brasterau yn cael eu defnyddio fel storfa egni mewn hadau ac anifeiliaid.
- **amddiffyn** organau mewnol bregus megis yr arennau.
- mae triglyseridau hefyd yn cynhyrchu llawer o ddŵr metabolig pan maent yn cael eu hocsidio. Mae hyn yn bwysig i anifeiliaid yr anialwch, megis y camel.
- mae triglyseridau hefyd yn cael eu storio o dan y croen lle maent yn gweithredu fel **ynysydd** gwres.

Mae *cwyrau* yn debyg i frasterau ac olewau ond maent hefyd yn cynnwys alcohol. Mae cwyr yn anhydawdd ac yn bwysig i organebau'r tir megis pryfed, lle mae'r cwtigl cwyraidd yn gostwng maint y dŵr a gollir. Mae gan ddail hefyd gwtigl cwyraidd er mwyn lleihau trydarthiad.

Ffosffolipidau

Mae ffosffolipidau yn debyg i driglyseridau ond bod grŵp ffosffad yn lle un o'r grwpiau asid brasterog.

- Mae'r rhan lipid yn amholar ac yn anhydawdd mewn dŵr (hydroffobig)
- Mae'r grŵp ffosffad yn bolar ac yn hydoddi mewn dŵr (hydroffylig).

❏ *Tasg* Lluniwch ddiagram o adeiledd ffosffolipid.

Mae ffosffolipidau yn bwysig o ran ffurfio a gweithrediad pilenni mewn celloedd.

Proteinau

- Mae proteinau yn wahanol i garbohydradau a lipidau oherwydd eu bod bob amser yn cynnwys nitrogen yn ogystal â charbon, hydrogen ac ocsigen. Mae llawer o broteinau yn cynnwys sylffwr hefyd, ac weithiau'n cynnwys ffosfforws.
- Mae proteinau yn gweithredu ystod o weithgareddau biolegol ac yn cynnwys ensymau, gwrthgyrff, hormonau, proteinau cludo yn ogystal â phroteinau adeiledd.
- Mae proteinau yn gyfansoddion mawr sydd wedi eu hadeiladu o is-unedau a elwir yn **asidau amino**. Mae oddeutu 20 o wahanol asidau amino yn cael eu defnyddio i wneud proteinau. Mae miloedd o wahanol broteinau ac mae eu siâp yn dibynnu ar drefn benodol yr asidau amino yn y gadwyn.
- Mae strwythur sylfaenol pob asid amino yr un fath, yn y ffaith bod gan bob un ohonynt **grŵp amino**, NH2-, yn un pen o'r moleciwl, a **grŵp carbocsyl**, -COOH, yn y pen arall. Y grŵp R sy'n amrywio rhwng un asid amino â'r llall.

❏ *Tasg*   Lluniwch ddiagram o fformiwla adeileddol asid amino cyffredinoledig.

Y bond peptid

Mae proteinau yn cael eu hadeiladu o gyfres linol o asidau amino. Mae grŵp amino un asid amino yn adweithio gyda grŵp carbocsyl un arall trwy ddileu dŵr. Yr enw ar y bond sy'n cael ei ffurfio yw **bond peptid** a'r cyfansoddyn sy'n deillio o hynny yw **deupeptid**. Mae nifer o asidau amino yn cael eu cysylltu â'i gilydd yn y ffordd hon yn cael eu galw'n **polypeptid**.

❏ *Tasg*   Tynnwch lun fformiwlâu adeileddol dau asid amino yn dangos dileu un moleciwl o ddŵr a ffurfio deupeptid. Labelwch y cyswllt peptid.

Adeiledd protein
Mae pedair lefel o adeiledd protein:
- **Adeiledd sylfaenol** protein yw'r gyfres o asidau amino yn ei gadwyn polypeptid. Mae'r proteinau yn wahanol i'w gilydd oherwydd amrywiaeth, nifer a threfn eu hasidau amino ansoddol a gysylltir gan **fondiau peptid** yn unig.
- Yr **adeiledd eilaidd** yw'r siâp sy'n cael ei ffurfio gan y gadwyn polypeptid o ganlyniad i fondio hydrogen. Gan amlaf dyma'r sbiral a elwir yn helics α. Dewis arall yw'r llen bletiog sy'n digwydd fel cadwyn igam-ogam wastad.
- Mae'r **adeiledd trydyddol** yn cael ei ffurfio gan blygu a throelli'r helics polypeptid i fod yn strwythur cryno. Dyma sy'n rhoi ei siâp tri dimensiwn i'r moleciwl. Mae'r siâp yn cael ei gynnal gan fondiau **deusylffid, ïonig** a **hydrogen,** e.e. proteinau crwn.
- Mae'r **adeiledd cwaternaidd** yn deillio o gyfuniad o ddau neu fwy o gadwynau polypeptid mewn ffurf trydyddol. Mae'r rhain yn gysylltiedig â grwpiau di-brotein ac maent yn ffurfio moleciwlau mawr, cymhleth, e.e. haemoglobin.

- **Tasg** Gwnewch yn siŵr eich bod yn gyfarwydd â'r gwahanol fondiau sy'n gysylltiedig â phob un o'r gwahanol lefelau o adeiledd protein. Beth sy'n digwydd i adeiledd ensymau pan maent yn cael eu dadnatureiddio?

Dosbarthu proteinau
Gellir rhannu proteinau yn ddau grŵp yn ôl eu hadeiledd:
- Mae proteinau **ffibrog** yn cyflawni swyddogaethau strwythurol. Maent yn cynnwys polypeptidau mewn cadwynau paralel neu lenni gyda chroes gysylltiadau niferus sy'n llunio ffibrau hirion e.e. ceratin (mewn gwallt). Mae proteinau ffibrog yn anhydawdd mewn dŵr, yn gryf ac yn wydn. Mae colagen yn darparu'r priodweddau gwydn sydd eu hangen mewn tendonau. Mae un ffibr yn cynnwys tair cadwyn polypeptid wedi eu troelli o amgylch ei gilydd fel rhaff.

- Mae proteinau **crwn** yn cyflawni nifer o wahanol swyddogaethau – ensymau, gwrthgyrff, proteinau plasma a hormonau. Mae'r proteinau hyn yn gryno ac yn cael eu plygu fel moleciwlau sfferig. Maent yn hydawdd mewn dŵr. Mae haemoglobin yn cynnwys pedair cadwyn polypeptid wedi eu plygu gyda'r grŵp o'r enw haem yn eu canol yn cynnwys haearn.

- *Tasg*
1. Mewn tabl neu siart llif gwnewch grynodeb o adeiledd, presenoldeb, priodweddau a swyddogaethau proteinau.
2. Lluniwch dabl yn cymharu proteinau ffibrog a chrwn.
3. Disgrifiwch y prawf biwret ar gyfer protein.

Pwyntiau gweithredu cyffredinol yn codi o'r adran hon.

1. Dylech allu defnyddio fformiwlâu adeileddol a nodir (proteinau, triglyseridau a charbohydradau) i ddangos sut mae bondiau yn cael eu ffurfio a'u torri gan gyddwysiad a hydrolysis, gan gynnwys bondiau peptid, glycosidig ac ester. Dylech allu adnabod a deall fformiwlâu adeileddol y moleciwlau hyn ond does **dim** rhaid i chi allu eu darlunio.

2. Gwnewch restr o eiriau allweddol ac ysgrifennu diffiniadau o bob un.

3. Dylech sicrhau eich bod yn gallu perthnasu adeiledd carbohydradau, brasterau a phroteinau i'w swyddogaethau.

1.2 Strwythur celloedd

Pilenni

Mae pilenni o fewn y gell:
- yn ardaloedd ar wahân i weddill y cytoplasm fel bod modd ynysu cemegau a allai fod yn niweidiol ac/neu ensymau mewn organynnau fel na fyddant yn niweidio gweddill y gell.
- darparu arwynebedd arwyneb mawr i ddal yr ensymau sy'n gysylltiedig â phrosesau metabolaidd e.e. synthesis ATP yn y pilenni mitocondriaidd.
- Darparu system gludiant o fewn y gell e.e. reticwlwm endoplasmig.

Strwythur celloedd

Mae celloedd planhigion ac anifeiliaid yn cynnwys nifer o organynnau sy'n cyflawni amrywiaeth o wahanol swyddogaethau. Yr enw ar y ffordd y mae cell wedi ei threfnu mewn manylder yw uwch strwythur y gell.

Tasg   Lluniwch ddiagram wedi ei labelu o gell planhigyn a chell anifail fel y gwelir hwy trwy ficrosgop electron.

Lluniwch ddiagram wedi ei labelu o bob un o'r organynnau.
(Mewn cwestiwn arholiad dylech allu labelu llun o gell yn ogystal â thynnu llun wedi ei labelu o organynnau unigol.)

Mae'r cytoplasm yn ddeunydd sydd wedi ei drefnu'n fanwl, mae'n cynnwys sylweddau hydawdd o'r enw cytosol lle ceir amrywiaeth o wahanol organynnau:

Cnewyllyn

Dyma'r nodwedd amlycaf yn y gell. Ei swyddogaeth yw rheoli gweithgareddau'r gell a chadw'r cromosomau. Mae'r cnewyllyn wedi ei ffinio â philen ddwbl, y **bilen gnewyllol** (neu amlen). Mae mân dyllau yn y bilen hon i ganiatáu cludo mRNA a niwcliotidau. Yr enw ar y deunydd tebyg i gytoplasm sydd yn y cnewyllyn yw **niwcleoplasm**. Mae'n cynnwys **cromatin**, sydd wedi ei ffurfio o dorchau o DNA (histonau) sydd wedi eu rhwymo i brotein. Pan fydd cellraniad mae'r cromatin yn cyddwyso i ffurfio'r cromosomau. O fewn y cnewyllyn mae corff sfferig bychan a elwir yn **gnewyllan**. Hwn sy'n gwneud RNA sy'n angenrheidiol i wneud ribosomau.

Mitocondria

Mae gan y mitocondrion bilen ddwbl sydd wedi ei gwahanu gan ofod rhyng-bilennol cul wedi ei lenwi â hylif. Mae'r bilen fewnol wedi ei phlygu at i mewn i lunio estyniadau a elwir yn **cristâu**. Mae tu mewn y mitocondrion yn cynnwys **matrics** organaidd sy'n cynnwys cyfansoddion cemegol niferus. Y mitocondria yw'r safleoedd **resbiradaeth aerobig** yn y gell. Mae rhai o'r adweithiau yn digwydd yn y matrics ac eraill yn digwydd ar y pilenni mewnol. Mae'r cristâu yn cynyddu maint yr arwyneb lle mae'r prosesau resbiradol yn digwydd. Swyddogaeth y mitocondria yw cynhyrchu egni fel ATP. Mae celloedd cyhyrau yn cynnwys niferoedd mawr o fitocondria sy'n adlewyrchu'r gweithgarwch metabolaidd uchel sy'n digwydd yno.

Reticwlwm Endoplasmig (ER)

Mae'r reticwlwm endoplasmig wedi ei ffurfio o system gymhleth o bilenni dwbl paralel sy'n ffurfio codennau gwastad. Mae'r gwaglynnau rhwng y pilenni, a elwir yn **cisternae,** yn llawn hylif. Mae'r ER wedi ei gysylltu gyda'r bilen gnewyllol ac fe all gysylltu gyda'r corff Golgi. Mae'r ceudodau wedi eu rhyng-gysylltu ac mae'r system yma'n caniatáu cludo deunyddiau i bob rhan o'r gell. Mae dau fath o ER:

- **ER garw** sydd â ribosomau ar yr arwyneb allanol. Mae gan yr ER garw swyddogaeth o gludo proteinau a wneir gan y ribosomau. Mae reticwlwm endoplasmig garw yn bresennol mewn meintiau sylweddol yn y celloedd sy'n gwneud ensymau y gellir eu secretu allan o'r gell.
- mae gan **Reticwlwm Endoplasmig llyfn** bilenni sydd heb ribosomau. Mae'r rhain yn gysylltiedig â synthesis a chludo lipidau.

Ribosomau

Mae'r rhain wedi eu gwneud o un is-uned fawr ac un is-uned fechan. Maent yn cael eu cynhyrchu yn y cnewyllan o RNA ribosom a phrotein. Maent yn bwysig ar gyfer **synthesis protein**.

Corff Golgi

Mae'r corff Golgi yn debyg i Reticwlwm Endoplasmig o ran strwythur, ond yn fwy cryno. Mae'r corff Golgi yn cael ei ffurfio wrth bod y Reticwlwm Endoplasmig wedi cael ei binsio yn y ddau ben i ffurfio fesiglau bychan. Mae nifer o'r fesiglau hyn yn cyfuno ac yn ymasio gyda'i gilydd i ffurfio'r corff Golgi. Mae proteinau yn cael eu cludo yn y fesiglau ac yn cael eu haddasu a'u pecynnu yn y corff Golgi. Er enghraifft gall proteinau gyfuno gyda charbohydradau i wneud glycoproteinau.

Ym mhen arall y corff Golgi gall fesiglau gael eu piniso i ffwrdd a gall eu cynnyrch gael eu secretu trwy ecsocytosis pan fydd y fesigl yn symud i'r gellbilen ac yn ymdoddi gyda hi.

❏ **Tasg** Lluniwch ddiagram yn dangos fesiglau yn ymasio gyda'r corff Golgi ac yn ei adael.

Mae swyddogaeth eraill y corff Golgi yn cynnwys:
- Cynhyrchu ensymau secretu.
- Secretu carbohydradau, e.e. er mwyn ffurfio waliau cellfuriau planhigion.
- Cynhyrchu glycoprotein.
- Cludo a storio lipidau.
- Ffurfio lysosomau.

Lysosomau

Mae lysosomau yn wagolynnau bychan sy'n cael eu ffurfio wrth i rannau o'r corff Golgi gael eu pinsio i ffwrdd. Maent yn cynnwys ac yn ynysu ensymau treulio oddi wrth weddill y gell.

- Maent hefyd yn gallu rhyddhau'r ensymau hyn a dinistrio organynnau sydd wedi cyrraedd pen eu hoes yn y gell. Mae'r treulio'n digwydd yn y gwagolyn sydd wedi'i leinio â philenni lle gall nifer o lysosomau ryddhau eu cynnwys.
- Maent hefyd yn gallu treulio deunydd sydd wedi cael ei gludo i mewn i'r gell, e.e. mae celloedd gwyn y gwaed yn amlyncu bacteria trwy ffagocytosis ac mae'r lysosomau'n rhyddhau eu cynnwys i'r fesiglau sy'n cael eu ffurfio ac yn treulio'r bacteriwm.

Centriolau

Fe geir centriolau ym mhob cell anifail a'r rhan fwyaf o gelloedd protoctist ond maent yn absennol yng nghelloedd planhigion uwch. Lleolir centriolau yn union du allan i'r cnewyllyn mewn rhan benodol o'r cytoplasm a elwir yn centrosom. Mae centriol yn cynnwys dau silindr gwag ar ongl sgwâr i'w gilydd. Yn ystod **cellraniad** mae'r centriolau yn rhannu ac yn symud i wahanol begynau'r gell ac yno maent yn syntheseiddio microdiwbynnau'r werthyd.

Mewn celloedd planhigion yn unig y mae'r organynnau canlynol.

Cloroplast

Mae cloroplast yn bodoli yng nghelloedd y meinwe sy'n ffotosyntheseiddio. Mae ganddynt **bilen ddwbl** a rhyngddynt y ceir yr hylif **stroma,** sy'n cynnwys ribosomau, lipid, DNA cylchol ac, o bosibl, startsh. O fewn y stroma mae nifer o godennau gwastad a elwir yn **thylacoidau.** Mae pentwr o thylacoidau yn cael ei alw'n **granwm.**
Mae pob granwm yn cynnwys rhwng dau a chant o'r codennau caeedig, paralel gwastad hyn. O fewn y thylacoidau ceir pigmentau ffotosynthetig megis cloroffyl. Mae'r drefn hon yn creu arwyneb eang er mwyn dal egni goleuni.

Gwagolyn

Mae gan gelloedd planhigion wagolyn mawr parhaol sy'n cynnwys coden llawn hylif wedi ei hamgau gan bilen sengl, y tonoplast. Mae gwagolynnau yn cynnwys cellnodd, sy'n storfa ar gyfer cemegau megis glwcos, ac sy'n darparu system osmotig sy'n gweithredu i gynnal meinweoedd ifanc.
Mae gwagolynnau mewn celloedd anifeiliaid hefyd ond mae'r rhain yn fesiglau bychan, dros dro ac fe allant fod yn niferus.

Cellfur cellwlos

Mae'r cellfur yn cynnwys microffibrolynnau cellwlos wedi eu gosod mewn matrics polysacarid. Prif swyddogaethau cellfur yw:
- darparu cryfder a chynhaliaeth.
- caniatáu dŵr i symud o gell i gell.

❏ **Tasg**   Er mwyn eich helpu i adolygu gwnewch dabl gyda'r penawdau canlynol ac yna ei lenwi:

Organynnau	Diagram syml	Swyddogaeth

Trefniadaeth Celloedd

Mae dau fath o gell: celloedd procaryotig a chelloedd ewcaryotig. Mae gan gelloedd procaryotig strwythur syml ac mae'n debyg mai'r rhain oedd y ffurfiau cyntaf o fywyd ar y Ddaear. Mae'n debyg bod celloedd ewcaryotig wedi esblygu o gelloedd ewcaryot oddeutu 1000 miliwn o flynyddoedd yn ôl.

Celloedd Procaryot ac ewcaryot

Mae bacteriwm yn enghraifft o gell **Procaryot**. Mae celloedd **Ewcaryot** yn nodweddiadol yn y rhan fwyaf o organebau gan gynnwys anifeiliaid a phlanhigion.

Celloedd Procaryotig	Celloedd Ewcaryotig
I'w cael mewn bacteria ac algâu gwyrddlas	I'w cael mewn planhigion, anifeiliaid, ffwng a phrotoctista
Nid yw'r organynnau wedi eu cau o fewn pilen	Yr organynnau wedi eu cau o fewn pilen
Mae'r DNA yn rhydd yn y cytoplasm	Mae'r DNA wedi ei leoli ar y cromosomau
Dim pilen niwclear na ER	Mae cnewyllyn penodol wedi ei gau mewn pilen
Mae'r ribosomau yn llai	Mae'r ribosomau yn fwy
Mae'r cellfur yn cynnwys mwrein	Mae'r cellfur mewn planhigion wedi ei wneud o gellwlos

❏ *Tasg*   Lluniwch ddiagram o facteriwm wedi ei labelu.
(Labeli – cellfur, pilen, plasmid, mesosom, ribosom, fflagelwm)

Firws

Mae firysau yn achosi amrywiaeth o glefydau heintus mewn pobl, anifeiliaid a phlanhigion.
Mae firysau yn eithriadol o fach a dim ond trwy ddefnyddio microsgop electron y gellir eu gweld. Gellir eu galw yn 'anghellog' gan nad oes ganddynt gytoplasm, organynnau na chromosomau. Tu allan i gell fyw mae firws yn bodoli fel 'firion' anadweithiol. Pan maent yn ymosod ar gell maent yn gallu mabwysiadau metabolaeth y gell a lluosi o fewn y gell letyol. Mae pob gronyn firws wedi ei wneud o graidd o **asid niwclëig** wedi ei amgylchynu â **chot protein**, y capsid. Mae'r rhan fwyaf o firysau yn bodoli yng nghelloedd anifeiliaid ac mae'r rheini sy'n ymosod ar facteria (bacterioffagau) yn cynnwys DNA asid niwclëig. Mae firysau anifeiliaid a phlanhigion eraill yn cynnwys RNA. Un firws sydd wedi cael ei astudio'n eang yw'r ffag T2 sef bacterioffag, sy'n heintio'r bacteriwm *Escherichia coli* (*E.coli*)

❏ *Tasg*   Tynnwch lun firws nodweddiadol, a'i labelu

Gwahaniaethau rhwng celloedd planhigion ac anifeiliaid

Mae celloedd planhigion yn cynnwys yr holl strwythurau sydd mewn celloedd anifail ynghyd â rhai nodweddion ychwanegol:

Celloedd planhigion	Celloedd anifeiliaid
cellfur	dim cellfur
cloroplastau	dim cloroplastau
gwagolyn mawr, parhaol	gwagolynnau bychan, dros dro
dim centriol	centriol
plasmodesmata	dim plasmodesmata

❏ *Tasg*   Lluniwch dabl i gymharu strwythur celloedd anifeiliaid, planhigion, procaryot a firysau.

Lefelau o drefniadaeth

Mae organebau amlgellog yn cynnwys amrywiaeth o wahanol gelloedd. Wrth iddynt ddatblygu, mae celloedd yn gwahaniaethu ac yn arbenigo er mwyn cyflawni swyddogaethau penodol e.e. mae celloedd cyhyrau yn cyfangu, celloedd nerfau yn cludo ysgogiadau. Mae rhai celloedd yn parhau mewn cyflwr anwahaniaethol ac mae ganddynt swyddogaeth fel celloedd 'pacio' e.e. parencyma mewn planhigion.
Mae **meinwe** yn cynnwys nifer o gelloedd sydd wedi gwahaniaethu yn yr un ffordd e.e. meinwe cyhyrau.
Mae gwahanol feinweoedd yn cyfuno i ffurfio **organ** e.e. y llygad.
Mae organau yn gweithio gyda'i gilydd fel **systemau** e.e. system ysgarthol.
Mae **organebau** yn cynnwys nifer o systemau sy'n gweithio gyda'i gilydd.

❏ **Tasg** gwaith microsgop

- Gwneud archwiliad histolegol o'r celloedd anifail canlynol:
✓ epitheliwm ciwboid a chiliedig.
✓ cyhyryn llyfn a rhesog.
✓ meinwe gyswllt colagen.
- Edrych ar ystod o gelloedd byw megis epidermis nionyn/ winwnsyn, celloedd alaw Canada (Canadian pondweed) (*Elodea*), celloedd cloronen tatws, *Spirogyra*.
- Astudio ystod o ficrograffau electron o gelloedd procaryot ac ewcaryot.

1.3 Cellbilen

Cellbilen

Pilen arwyneb y gell neu'r bilen blasmaidd yw'r ffin sy'n gwahanu'r gell fyw oddi wrth ei hamgylchedd anfyw. Mae'r bilen hefyd yn rheoli pa sylweddau sy'n pasio i mewn ac allan o'r gell.

Adeiledd y bilen

Mae'r gellbilen wedi cael ei ffurfio, bron yn llwyr, o **broteinau** a **ffosffolipidau**.
Mae pen ffosffad y ffosffolipid yn foleciwl polar (hydroffilig neu atynnu dŵr). Mae'n atynnu moleciwlau polar eraill megis dŵr. Mae pen asid brasterog y ffosffolipid, wedi ei ffurfio o ddwy gynffon o asid brasterog ac mae'n amholar (hydroffobig neu'n casáu dŵr) ac mae'n gwrthyrru dŵr. Mae ffosffolipidau yn gallu ffurfio haen ddeuol gydag un haen o ffosffolipid yn ffurfio dros un arall. Mae'r haen ddeuol ffosffolipid hon yn sail i adeiledd y bilen. Trwy ddefnyddio'r microsgop electron lluniodd Singer a Nicholson eu damcaniaeth o'r enw y **model Mosaig Hylifol** yn 1972. Eu cynnig oedd bod:

- haen **ffosffolipid deufoleciwlaidd**.
- yn gysylltiedig â'r haen ddeuol mae amrywiaeth o foleciwlau protein:
  ✓ mae rhai proteinau i'w cael ar neu o fewn un o'r haenau (proteinau **anghynhenid**)
  ✓ mae rhai proteinau yn ymestyn ar draws y ddwy haen (proteinau **cynhenid**)
- mae gan yr haen ffosffolipid y gallu i symud, h.y. y mae'n hylif. O edrych ar yr arwyneb mae'r proteinau wedi eu gwasgaru yma ac acw ar draws yr haen mewn trefn fosaig.
- Cyfeirir at y model fel model 'mosaig hylifol' oherwydd bod y cydrannau yn rhydd i symud ar wahân i'w gilydd.

❏ *Tasg*   Lluniwch ddiagram i ddangos adeiledd mosaig hylif y gellbilen.

Mae colesterol i'w gael mewn celloedd anifeiliaid hefyd. Mae'n ffitio rhwng y moleciwlau ffosffolipid, gan gynyddu anhyblygedd a chadernid y bilen. Mae glycolipidau (lipidau sydd wedi cyfuno gyda pholysacarid) hefyd yn bodoli yn haen allanol y bilen a chredir bod ganddynt swyddogaeth yn gysylltiedig ag adnabyddiaeth un gell o gell arall. Mae glycoproteinau hefyd yn ymwthio allan o rai pilenni.

Mae prif **swyddogaethau'r** gellbilen yn cynnwys:
- cynhaliaeth strwythurol
- secretu cemegau
- adnabyddiaeth cell i gell
- casglu maetholynnau ac anghenion eraill.

Y bilen fel rhwystr

Mae pilen arwyneb y gell yn ddetholus athraidd i ddŵr ac i rai hydoddion. Mae sylweddau sy'n hydawdd mewn lipidau yn gallu symud trwy'r gellbilen yn rhwyddach na sylweddau sy'n hydoddi mewn dŵr.

- Mae moleciwlau bychan, sydd heb eu gwefru, megis ocsigen a charbon deuocsid yn gallu pasio'n rhwydd drwy'r bilen gan eu bod yn hydawdd yn y rhan ohoni sy'n lipid.
- Mae moleciwlau sy'n hydawdd mewn lipid, e.e. glyserol, yn gallu pasio drwy'r bilen.
- Mae craidd hydroffobig y bilen yn amharu ar gludiant ïonau a moleciwlau polar.

Ni all gronynnau wedi eu gwefru (ïonau) na moleciwlau cymharol fawr megis glwcos dryledu ar draws canol amholar yr haen ddeuol ffosffolipid gan eu bod yn gymharol anhydawdd mewn lipid. Mae proteinau cynhenid yn helpu gronynnau o'r fath i basio i mewn ac allan o'r gell trwy broses odcefol a elwir yn **dryllediad cynorthwyedig**. (Mae dau fath o broteinau fel hyn: proteinau sianelu a phroteinau cludo. Yr ydym yn rhoi mwy o sylw i'r rhain yn yr adran nesaf.)

Cludiant ar draws cellbilenni

Tryllediad

Tryllediad yw symudiad moleciwlau neu ïonau o ardal lle mae crynodiad uchel ohonynt i ardal lle mae crynodiad is nes eu bod wedi cael eu dosbarthu'n gyfartal. Mae ïonau a moleciwlau bob amser mewn cyflwr o **hap symudiad** ond os oes crynodiad uchel ohonynt mewn un ardal fe fydd symudiad net oddi wrth yr ardal honno nes sefydlu ecwilibriwm neu ddosbarthiad unffurf.

Mae'r ffactorau canlynol yn effeithio ar gyfradd tryllediad:

- graddiant y crynodiad h.y. po fwyaf yw'r gwahaniaeth rhwng crynodiad moleciwlau mewn dwy ardal, yr uchaf yw'r gyfradd.
- y pellter teithio h.y. y lleiaf yw'r pellter rhwng dwy ardal y mwyaf yw'r gyfradd.
- arwynebedd y bilen – po fwyaf yw'r ardal y cyflymaf yw'r gyfradd.
- trwch y bilen – y teneuaf yw'r bilen y mwyaf yw'r gyfradd.
- ac mae cynnydd mewn tymheredd yn achosi cynnydd yn y gyfradd gan fod cynnydd yn yr egni moleciwlaidd ac felly yn symudiad y moleciwlau.

Tryllediad cynorthwyedig

Nid yw gronynnau ac ïonau wedi eu gwefru, na moleciwlau mawr megis glwcos yn gallu pasio'n rhwydd drwy'r gellbilen gan eu bod yn gymharol anhydawdd mewn lipid. Yn y gellbilen mae moleciwlau protein yn pontio'r bilen o un ochr i'r llall ac yn helpu gronynnau fel hyn i dryledu i mewn ac allan o'r gell. Mae dau fath o broteinau fel hyn:

Proteinau sianelu - mae'r rhain wedi eu gwneud o fân dyllau wedi'u leinio â grwpiau polar sy'n caniatáu i ïonau wedi eu gwefru i basio trwodd. (Gan fod y sianel yn hydroffilig, mae sylweddau sy'n hydoddi mewn dŵr yn gallu pasio trwodd). Gan fod pob protein sianelu yn benodol ar gyfer un math o ïon dim ond un ïon penodol y bydd pob protein yn caniatáu mynediad iddo. Y maent hefyd yn gallu agor a chau yn ôl anghenion y gell.

Mae **proteinau cludo** yn caniatáu tryllediad ar draws pilen y moleciwlau polar mwyaf, e.e. siwgrau ac asidau amino. Mae moleciwl penodol yn cydio yn y protein cludo yn ei safle rhwymo ac yn achosi i'r protein cludo newid ei siâp, gan ryddhau'r moleciwl drwy'r bilen.

Mae proteinau cludo a phroteinau sianelu yn cynyddu cyfradd tryllediad ar hyd y graddiant crynodiad heb orfod cael egni ar ffurf ATP trwy resbiradaeth.

❑ **Tasg** Lluniwch ddiagramau i ddangos sut mae proteinau cludo a phroteinau sianelu yn gweithredu yn y bilen.

Osmosis

Mae'r rhan fwyaf o gellbilenni yn athraidd i ddŵr a rhai hydoddion eraill yn unig. Mewn systemau biolegol mae osmosis yn fath arbennig o dryllediad sy'n ymwneud â symudiad moleciwlau **dŵr** yn unig.

Gellir diffinio osmosis fel symudiad dŵr o ardal lle mae crynodiad uchel ohono i ardal lle mae crynodiad is, trwy bilen sy'n lled-athraidd.

Mae biolegwyr yn defnyddio'r term **potensial dŵr** ψ(psi) i ddisgrifio tueddiad moleciwlau dŵr i symud o grynodiadau uchel i grynodiadau isel.

Dŵr pur sydd â'r potensial dŵr uchaf, sef sero. Y rheswm am hyn yw bod egni potensial moleciwlau dŵr yn uwch lle mae crynodiad uchel ohonynt h.y. mae'r moleciwlau dŵr yn gwbl rydd i symud o gwmpas. Pan fydd hydoddyn, e.e. siwgr yn cael ei hydoddi mewn dŵr, mae llai o foleciwlau dŵr ar gael i symud o gwmpas ac mae potensial dŵr yr hydoddiant yn cael ei leihau. Gwerth negyddol sydd gan bob potensial dŵr (ac eithrio dŵr pur). Y mwyaf crynodedig yw'r hydoddiant y mwyaf negyddol yw'r potensial dŵr; h.y. mae llai o foleciwlau dŵr rhydd. Gallwn nawr ddiffinio osmosis yn nhermau potensial dŵr.

Osmosis yw tryllediad moleciwlau dŵr o ardal lle mae potensial dŵr uchel i ardal lle mae potensial dŵr is trwy bilen lled athraidd.

Mae ψ uwch yn awgrymu bod mwy o dueddiad i ddŵr adael system. Bydd dŵr yn tryledu o ardal lle mae ψ llai negyddol (lefel uwch) i ardal lle mae ψ mwy negyddol (lefel is).

Mewn celloedd planhigion defnyddir yr hafaliad canlynol i ddisgrifio'r berthynas rhwng y grymoedd:

$$\psi = \psi_s + \psi_p$$
potensial dŵr   potensial hydoddyn   potensial gwasgedd

- Mae presenoldeb moleciwlau hydoddyn yng ngwagolyn cell planhigyn yn lleihau'r ψ.
- Yr enw ar y crynodiad sylweddau sydd wedi eu hydoddi yng ngwagolyn cell yw **potensial hydoddyn**.
- Pan fydd dŵr yn mynd i mewn i wagolyn cell planhigyn trwy osmosis bydd gwasgedd hydrostatig yn cael ei sefydlu ac yn gwthio am allan ar y cellfur. Wrth i'r gwasgedd at allan gynyddu mae'r cellfur yn datblygu grym i'r gwrthwyneb a elwir yn **botensial gwasgedd**. Gan amlaf mae'r potensial gwasgedd yn bositif.

Chwydd-dyndra a phlasmolysis

- Os yw ψ yr hydoddiant allanol yn is na'r hydoddiant sydd yn y gell dywedir ei fod yn **hypertonig** ac mae dŵr yn llifo allan o'r gell.
- Os yw ψ yr hydoddiant allanol yn uwch na'r hydoddiant sydd yn y gell dywedir ei fod yn **hypotonig** ac mae dŵr yn llifo allan o'r gell.
- Os yw crynodiad hydoddyn y gell yr un fath â chrynodiad yr hydoddiant sydd o'i amgylch, yna mae'r hydoddiant allanol a hydoddiant y gell yn **isotonig**.
- Pan roddir cell planhigyn mewn hydoddiant hypertonig y mae'n colli dŵr trwy osmosis. Mae'r gwagolyn yn crebachu a bydd y cytoplasm yn tynnu oddi wrth y cellfur. Gelwir y broses hon yn **blasmolysis** a phan mae'r broses wedi ei chwblhau dywedir bod y gell yn **llipa**.
- Gelwir y pwynt pan fydd y gellbilen yn *dechrau* symud i ffwrdd oddi wrth y cellfur yn bwynt **plasmolysis cychwynnol**.
- Bydd cell planhigyn yn ennill dŵr os bydd yn cael ei roi mewn hydoddiant hypotonig a bydd yn parhau i dynnu dŵr nes i hynny gael ei atal gan wasgedd dirgroes y cellfur. Bydd y potensial gwasgedd yn cynyddu hyd nes y bo'n gyfartal ac yn ddirgroes i'r potensial hydoddyn. Mewn theori mae'r potensial dŵr yn awr yn sero a phan na all y gell dderbyn dim mwy o ddŵr dywedir ei bod yn **chwydd-dynn**. Mae'r cyflwr o fod yn **chwydd-dynn** yn bwysig mewn planhigion, yn arbennig egin blanhigion. Mae'n cynnal ac yn cadw eu siâp a'u ffurf.
- Bydd cell anifail yn byrstio os caiff ei osod mewn hydoddiant hypotonig gan nad oes ganddo gellfur.

❏ *Tasg*

1. Lluniwch ddiagram wedi ei labelu o gell planhigyn llipa a chwydd-dynn.
2. Gwnewch restr o dermau allweddol a'u diffiniadau.
3. Byddwch yn barod i ddefnyddio'r hafaliad a roddir uchod mewn cyfrifiadau.

Endocytosis ac ecsocytosis

Prosesau yw'r rhain lle mae'r gell yn cludo deunyddiau mewn swmp.
- **Endocytosis** - mae'r gell yn amgylchynu'r bilen o amgylch y deunydd ac yn ei gymryd i mewn i'r cytoplasm o fewn gwagolyn. Mae dau fath o endocytosis:
1. **Ffagocytosis** yw'r broses lle mae cell yn gallu cael deunyddiau **solet** sy'n rhy fawr i gael eu cymryd i mewn trwy dryllediad neu gludiant actif. Mae lysosom yn ymdoddi i'r gwagolyn sy'n cael ei ffurfio, ensymau yn treulio'r deunydd solet a'r cynhyrchion yn cael eu hamsugno i'r cytoplasm. Mae ffagocytau (celloedd gwyn y gwaed) yn dinistrio bacteria ac yn gwaredu malurion cell trwy ffagocytosis.
2. Mae **Pinocytosis** yn digwydd pan fydd **hylif** yn dod i mewn trwy'r un mecanwaith â ffagocytosis, ond bod y fesiglau a gynhyrchir yn llai.

- Mae **Ecsocytosis** yn cyfeirio at sylweddau'n symud allan o gell ar ôl cael eu cludo trwy'r cytoplasm mewn fesigl. Yn aml, mae ensymau treulio yn cael eu secretu yn y ffordd hon.

Trwy ffagocytosis a secretiad, mae rhannau o'r gellbilen wastad yn cael eu colli neu eu hychwanegu.

- *Tasg*   Lluniwch ddiagram i ddangos ffagocytosis.

Cludiant actif

Yn wahanol i'r prosesau a ddisgrifiwyd hyd yma, mae cludiant gweithredol yn broses y mae'n rhaid cael **egni** ar ei chyfer gan fod **ïonau** a **moleciwlau** yn cael eu **symud** ar draws pilenni yn **erbyn graddiant crynodiad**.

Nodweddion y cludiant actif yw:
- Bod ïonau a moleciwlau yn gallu symud i gyfeiriad gwahanol i gyfeiriad tryllediad, h.y. yn erbyn graddiant crynodiad.
- Mae'r egni ar gyfer cludiant actif yn cael ei ddarparu trwy ATP, a bydd unrhyw beth sy'n effeithio ar y broses resbiradol yn effeithio ar gludiant actif.
- Ni fydd cludiant actif yn digwydd ym mhresenoldeb atalydd resbiradol, e.e. cyanid.
- Mae'r broses yn digwydd trwy'r proteinau cludo sy'n pontio'r bilen. Mae'r proteinau yn derbyn y moleciwl a'r moleciwl yn mynd i mewn i'r gell trwy newid siâp y moleciwl cludo.

Mae'r prosesau sy'n gysylltiedig â chludiant actif yn cynnwys syntheseiddio protein, cyfangiad cyhyrol, trawsyriant ysgogiad nerfol, amsugno halwynau mwynol gan wreiddiau planhigion.

- *Tasg*   Lluniwch ddiagram i ddangos sut mae proteinau cludo yn newid siâp wrth gludo moleciwlau ar draws y bilen.

1.4 Ensymau

Mewn celloedd mae adweithiau metabolaidd yn digwydd yn gyflym ac mae miloedd o adweithiau yn digwydd yr un pryd. Mae trefn a rheolaeth yn holl bwysig er mwyn cadw'r holl adweithiau hyn rhag ymyrryd â'i gilydd. Mae gweithrediad ensymau yn gwneud y nodweddion hyn o fetabolaeth yn bosibl.

Adeiledd ensymau

Mae pob ensym yn brotein crwn trydyddol lle mae'r gadwyn protein yn plygu nôl arno'i hun i siâp sffêr neu grwn. Mae gan bob ensym ei gyfres ei hun o asidau amino ac mae'n cael ei gadw yn ei ffurf drydyddol gan fondiau hydrogen, pontydd deusylffid a bondiau ïonig. Y siâp cymhleth tri dimensiwn hwn sy'n rhoi llawer o'i nodweddion i'r ensym. (Adolygwch y gwaith blaenorol ar adeiledd proteinau.)

Sut mae ensymau'n gweithio

Mae ensymau yn **gatalyddion biolegol** sy'n cyflymu cyfradd adweithiau metabolaidd.
Mae dau fath o adwaith:
1. Adwaith lle mae'r moleciwlau mwyaf yn cael eu torri i lawr yn foleciwlau llai.
2. Adwaith lle mae'r moleciwlau bychan yn cael eu hadeiladu yn foleciwlau mwy, o ran maint a chymhlethdod.

Mae ensymau yn adweithio gyda moleciwl arall a elwir yn **swbstrad**. Mae gan bob ensym ei siâp arbennig ei hun, gydag ardal, **safle actif**, lle mae moleciwlau'r swbstrad yn clymu.
Mae dehongliadau modern o'r ddamcaniaeth allwedd a chlo yn awgrymu gall y safle gweithredol newid ym mhresenoldeb y swbstrad er mwyn dethol siâp y swbstrad.
Gelwir hyn yn **ddamcaniaeth ffit anwythol**.
(Gellir dangos hyn gyda'r ensym, lysosym, ond nid oes rhaid cael manylion am yr adeiledd.)
    Ensym + swbstrad = cymhlygyn-ensym swbstrad = ensym + cynnyrch.

Priodweddau ensymau

- Mae ensymau yn **benodol**, h.y. bydd pob ensym yn catalyddu un adwaith penodol yn unig, e.e. mae swcr**as** yn gweithredu ar y siwgr, swcr**os**.
- Mae ensymau yn effeithlon iawn ac mae ganddynt **rif trosiant** uchel. Mae hyn yn golygu eu bod yn gallu trawsnewid llawer o foleciwlau'r swbstrad bob uned amser, e.e. mae gan gatalas sy'n chwalu'r cynnyrch gwastraff hydrogen perocsid yn y corff, nifer trosiant o sawl miliwn!
- Mae'n rhaid cael egni i gychwyn adweithiau cemegol a gelwir hynny yn **egni actifadu**. Mae'n rhaid cael yr egni hwn er mwyn torri'r bondiau cemegol sy'n bodoli mewn moleciwlau. Yn y corff mae ensymau yn gostwng egni actifadu'r adwaith ac felly'n lleihau'r mewnbwn o egni sydd ei angen ac yn caniatáu i adweithiau ddigwydd ar dymheredd is.

Ffactorau sy'n effeithio ar gyfradd gweithredu ensymau

Mae ensymau yn cael eu gwneud o fewn celloedd byw ond gallant weithredu o fewn y gell (mewngellol) neu'r tu allan (rhyng-gellol, allgellog) e.e. ensymau treulio yn y llwybr ymborth. Mae amgylchiadau amgylcheddol, megis tymheredd a pH, yn newid adeiledd tri dimensiwn moleciwlau ensym. Mae bondiau'n cael eu torri ac felly ffurfweddiad y safle actif yn cael ei newid.

- **Tymheredd**

Mae cynnydd yn y tymheredd yn rhoi mwy o egni cinetig i foleciwlau ac maent yn symud o gwmpas yn gyflymach gan gynyddu'r siawns y bydd moleciwlau'n gwrthdaro. Mae cynyddu tymheredd adwaith a reolir gan ensym yn cynyddu'r gyfradd adwaith. Fel rheol gyffredinol, mae'r gyfradd adweithio yn dyblu gyda phob 10°C o gynnydd mewn tymheredd hyd nes y cyrhaeddir tymheredd optimwm. Ar gyfer y rhan fwyaf o ensymau'r tymheredd optimwm yw 40°C.
Dros y tymheredd hwn mae dirgryniad cynyddol y moleciwlau yn achosi i'r bondiau hydrogen dorri gan achosi newid yn adeiledd trydyddol yr ensym. Mae hyn yn newid siâp y safle actif,

ac ni fydd y moleciwl swbstrad yn ffitio bellach. Dywedir wedyn bod yr ensym wedi cael ei **ddadnatureiddio**. Mae hyn yn newid parhaol yn yr adeiledd. Os yw'r ensymau yn dioddef tymheredd isel, megis rhewi, mae'r ensym yn anactifadu gan nad oes gan y moleciwlau egni cinetig. Ond fe all yr ensym weithio eto os bydd y tymheredd yn codi.

- **pH**

Bydd cyfradd adwaith sy'n cael ei gatalyddu gan ensym yn amrywio fel y mae'r pH yn newid. Ystod optimwm gul iawn sydd gan ensymau ac mae newid bychan mewn pH yn gallu effeithio ar y gyfradd adwaith heb effeithio ar adeiledd yr ensym. Mae newidiadau bychan yn y pH tu allan i'r optimwm yn gallu achosi newidiadau bychan cildroadwy yn adeiledd yr ensym ac mae hynny'n arwain at anactifadu. Mae eithafion pH yn gallu dadnatureiddio ensym.

Mae'r gwefrau ar gadwynau ochr asid amino yn safle actif yr ensym yn cael eu heffeithio gan yr ïonau hydrogen rhydd neu'r ïonau hydrocsyl. Wrth ffurfio cymhlygyn swbstrad ensym mae'n rhaid i'r wefr ar y safle actif gyfateb i'r rhai ar y swbstrad. Os oes gormod o ïonau $H+$(dyweder) ar y safle actif, fe all fod yr un wefr ar y safle actif a'r safle swbstrad ac felly bydd yr ensym yn gwrthyrru'r swbstrad.

Gydag eithafion pH bydd y bondiau hydrogen yn cael eu heffeithio a bydd siâp tri dimensiwn yr ensym yn newid. Bydd siâp y safle actif hefyd yn newid.

Peth arall sy'n effeithio ar ensymau yw crynodiad y swbstrad a chrynodiad yr ensym ei hun.

- **Crynodiad swbstrad**

Bydd cyfradd adwaith catalyddu ensym yn amrywio gyda newidiadau yng nghrynodiad swbstrad. Os yw maint yr ensym yn gyson bydd y gyfradd adweithio yn cynyddu wrth i'r swbstrad gynyddu ond fe ddaw pwynt lle mae holl safleoedd actif yr ensym yn gweithio i'w llawn gallu, h.y. bydd yr holl safleoedd actif yn llawn.

- **Crynodiad ensymau**

Bydd cyfradd adwaith catalyddu ensym yn amrywio yn ôl newidiadau yng nghrynodiadau ensym. Bydd cynyddu crynodiad yr ensym yn cynyddu'r gyfradd adwaith.

Tasg

1. Gwnewch restr o dermau allweddol a rhoi diffiniad o bob term.
2. Lluniwch graffiau ar wahân i ddangos effaith y ffactorau uchod ar actifedd ensym.
3. Disgrifiwch, **yn fanwl**, siâp y graff ym mhob achos.

Arbrofion gydag ensymau

Mewn arbrofion ensym mae'n hollbwysig defnyddio byfferau a rheolyddion.

- ✓ Mae **byfferau** yn cynnal pH cyson. Pan fydd byffer yn cael ei ddefnyddio mewn arbrawf ychydig iawn mae'r pH yn newid pan ychwanegir ychydig o asid neu alcali. Gellir dweud bod y byffer yn 'amsugno'r ïonau hydrogen'.
- ✓ **Rheolydd** – rheolydd yw arbrawf sy'n cael ei ddyblygu, sy'n union yr un fath â'r arbrawf o dan sylw ym mhob ffordd, heblaw am y newidyn sy'n cael ei archwilio. Cedwir y newidyn hwnnw yn gyson. Er enghraifft gellir defnyddio ensym wedi ei ferwi mewn arbrawf cymharu yn hytrach na'r ensym ei hun.

Ensymau ac atalyddion

Mae ataliad yn digwydd pan fydd actifedd ensymau yn cael ei arafu neu ei atal gan sylwedd arall. Bydd yr atalydd yn cyfuno gyda'r ensym ac yn ei atal rhag ffurfio cymhlygyn swbstrad-ensym.

Mae dau fath o atalydd:

- **Cystadleuol**, pan fydd yr atalydd yn **debyg i'r swbstrad o ran adeiledd** ac yn cystadlu gyda safle actif yr ensym, h.y. mae gan yr atalydd siâp sy'n caniatáu iddo ffitio i safle actif yr ensym yn lle'r swbstrad. Er enghraifft, mae asid malonig yn cystadlu gyda sycsinad am safleoedd actif dehydrogenas sycsinig, sy'n ensym pwysig yng nghylchred fetabolaidd Krebs mewn resbiradaeth. Os bydd y crynodiad swbstrad yn cynyddu bydd yn lleihau effaith yr atalydd. Y rheswm am hynny yw bod bodolaeth mwy o foleciwlau swbstrad yn cynyddu'r cyfle o ddod o hyd i safleoedd actif, fel bod llai ohonynt ar ôl i'r atalydd eu llenwi.

- **Anghystadleuol**, lle mae'r atalydd yn **clymu i'r ensym mewn safle sydd i ffwrdd oddi wrth y safle actif**. Mae hyn yn newid siâp cyffredinol moleciwl yr ensym, gan gynnwys y safle actif, yn y fath fodd fel na all y safle actif barhau i gynnig lle i'r swbstrad. Gan fod y swbstrad a moleciwlau'r atalydd yn clymu i wahanol rannau o'r ensym nid ydynt yn cystadlu am yr un safleoedd. Gan hynny nid yw'r gyfradd adwaith yn cael ei heffeithio gan grynodiad y swbstrad.
Er enghraifft, mae cyanid (gwenwyn resbiradol) yn cydio mewn rhan o'r ensym, cytochrom ocsidas, ac yn cyfyngu ar resbiradaeth.

❏ **Tasg** Tynnwch ddiagramau i ddangos y gwahanol fathau o ataliad.
Lluniwch graff yn dangos sut mae'r ddau fath o ataliad yn effeithio ar gyfradd adwaith ensym lle mae'r crynodiad swbstrad yn cael ei gynyddu.

1.5 Defnydd meddygol a diwydiannol o ensymau

Mae ensymau yn cael eu defnyddio'n fasnachol ar raddfa helaeth yn y diwydiannau bwyd, fferyllol ac agrocemegol

Mae **ensymau ansymudol** yn foleciwlau ensym sydd wedi eu sefydlu, eu rhwymo neu eu dal ar fatrics anadweithiol megis capsiwl gel (gleiniau alginad). Gellir pecynnu'r gleiniau hyn mewn colofnau gwydr. Gellir ychwanegu swbstrad i ben y golofn ac mae'n adweithio gyda'r ensym wrth iddo lifo'n araf i lawr y golofn. Unwaith mae'r golofn wedi cael ei sefydlu gellir ei defnyddio drosodd a throsodd. Gan fod yr ensym yn sefydlog nid yw'n cymysgu gyda'r cynnyrch ac felly mae'n rhatach i'w wahanu. Mae ensymau ansymudol yn cael eu defnyddio'n helaeth mewn prosesau diwydiannol, megis eplesiad, gan eu bod yn hawdd eu hadfer a'u hailddefnyddio.

Manteision ensymau ansymudol

Mae ansefydlogrwydd ensym yn un o'r ffactorau allweddol sy'n atal y defnydd ehangach o ensymau 'rhydd'. Gall cemegau megis hydoddyddion organig, codiad yn y tymheredd a chynnydd yn y gwerthoedd pH tu draw i'r norm, ddadnatureiddio'r ensym gan achosi gostyngiad mewn actifedd o ganlyniad i hynny. Mae atal ensymau gyda matrics polymer yn creu micro amgylchedd. Trwy ganiatáu i brosesau ddigwydd ar dymheredd uwch na'r arfer mae'r actifedd yn cynyddu a gan hynny, y cynhyrchedd. Mae'r manteision eraill yn cynnwys:

- ✓ Bod ensymau yn gallu **goddef** ystod ehangach o amodau.
- ✓ Bod yn **hawdd adfer** ensymau i'w hailddefnyddio a bod hynny'n lleihau costau cyffredinol.
- ✓ Bod modd defnyddio gyda'i gilydd **nifer o ensymau** sydd â gwahanol optima pH neu dymheredd.
- ✓ Mae'n **hawdd ychwanegu neu ddileu** ensymau gan ennill mwy o reolaeth dros yr adwaith.

Un ffordd o weithio gydag ensymau ansymudol yw defnyddio **biosynhwyryddion.** Mae'r rhain yn gweithio i egwyddor bod ensymau yn benodol a'u bod yn gallu defnyddio un math o foleciwl allan o gymysgedd hyd yn oed mewn crynodiadau isel iawn. Gellir defnyddio biosynhwyrydd i ganfod yr olion lleiaf o foleciwlau sy'n bwysig yn fiolegol mewn ffordd gyflym a chywir.

Mae potensial mawr i fiosynhwyryddion mewn meysydd diagnosis meddygol a monitro amgylcheddol. Mae'r chwiliedydd electrod yn gallu dod o hyd i newidiadau yn y swbstrad neu'r cynnyrch, mewn tymheredd neu briodweddau optegol.

Un defnydd penodol o fiosynhwyrydd yw **canfod siwgr gwaed** mewn cleifion â chlefyd y siwgr (diabetes). Yn yr achos hwn mae'r biosynhwyryddion yn defnyddio ensym, ynghyd â thrawsddygiadur, sy'n creu signal trydanol mewn ymateb i drawsffurfiad y swbstrad. Gellir mesur cryfder y signal trydanol gyda mesurydd addas.

Mae'r chwiliedydd electrod, sydd ag ensym penodol sy'n ansymudol mewn pilen, yn cael ei osod yn y sampl gwaed. Os oes glwcos yn bresennol mae'n tryledu drwy'r bilen, yn ffurfio cymhlygyn swbstrad-ensym. Mae'r adwaith yn cynhyrchu cerrynt trydanol bychan sy'n cael ei nodi gan yr electrod (y trawsddygiadur).

Mae'r cerrynt yn cael ei ddarllen gan fesurydd sy'n rhoi darlleniad ar gyfer maint y glwcos yn y gwaed. Mae lefelau normal glwcos yn y gwaed rhwng $3.89 - 5.83$ mmol dm^{-3}.

Y camau wrth ddefnyddio biosynhwyrydd.

1. Mae'r gwaed yn cynnwys cymysgedd o wahanol foleciwlau.
2. Mae'r electrod ensym yn cael ei roi mewn sampl o waed.
3. Mae glwcos yn tryledu i'r haen ensym ansymudol.
4. Ocsigen yn cael ei gymeryd i mewn.
5. Mae cyfradd mewnlifiad yr ocsigen yn gyfrannol i'r crynodiad glwcos.
6. Mae dangosydd digidol yn dangos crynodiad cywir o glwcos.

Defnyddir ensymau ansymudol hefyd mewn profion beichiogrwydd ac mewn eplesyddion er mwyn rhoi mesuriad cyflym, sensitif a phenodol o gynhyrchion.

❏ *Tasg*

1. Lluniwch ddiagram o fiosynhwyrydd a'i labelu.
2. Lluniwch dabl yn cymharu ensymau 'rhydd' ac ansymudol.

Y genom yw'r holl ddilyniannau DNA a gynhwysir yng nghromosomau organeb.

Asidau niwcleig

Mae dau fath o asid niwcleig: asid deocsiriboniwcleig (DNA) ac asid riboniwcleig (RNA).
Mae'r ddau fath wedi eu hadeiladu o unedau a elwir yn **niwcliotidau.**
Mae niwcliotidau unigol wedi cael eu ffurfio o **dair rhan** sy'n cyfuno trwy adweithiau cyddwyso. Y rhain yw:
- **asid ffosfforig** (ffosffad H_3PO_4). Mae'r un strwythur ganddo ym mhob niwcliotid.
- **siwgr pentos**, mae dau fath ohono sef:
  ✓ mewn asid riboniwcleig (RNA) ribos yw'r siwgr.
  ✓ mewn asid deocsiriboniwcleig (DNA) deocsiribos yw'r siwgr.
- **bas organig** sy'n cynnwys nitrogen.

Mae pump gwahanol fas sy'n cael eu rhannu'n ddau grŵp:
- basau **pirimidin** (adeiledd cylchol sengl) yw thymin, cytosin ac wracil.
- basau **pwrin** (adeiledd cylchol dwbl) yw adenin a gwanin.

Asid deocsiriboniwcleig (DNA)

Adeiledd DNA
- Mae DNA yn bolymer edefyn dwbl o niwcleotidau neu **polyniwcleotid**.
  (Polymer yw'r enw a roddir ar nifer fawr o unedau sy'n cael eu hailadrodd).
- Gall pob polyniwcleotid gynnwys sawl miliwn o unedau niwcleotid.
- Mae ar ffurf **helics dwbl**, siâp sy'n cael ei gynnal trwy fondiau hydrogen.
- Y siwgr pentos bob amser yw **deocsiribos.**
- Mae DNA yn cynnwys pedwar **bas organig**, sef adenin, gwanin, cytosin, a thymin.
- Mae pob edefyn yn cael ei gysylltu i'r llall gan barau o fasau organig.
- Mae cytosin bob amser yn paru gyda gwanin, adenin gyda thymin, ac mae'r basau'n cael eu cydgysylltu gan fondiau hydrogen.
- Yn syml, mae DNA yn debyg i ysgol dorchog gyda'i hochrau wedi eu gwneud o siwgrau eiledol a grwpiau ffosffad a ffyn yr ysgol wedi eu gwneud o'r basau. Mae'r basau'n cael eu cadw gyda'i gilydd gan fondiau hydrogen gwan.

❏ *Tasg*   Lluniwch ddiagram o gadwyn DNA yn dangos polyniwcleotid sy'n cynnwys tri phâr bas.

Mae gan DNA dwy brif swyddogaeth:
1. **Dyblygu** mewn celloedd sy'n rhannu.
2. Cario'r wybodaeth ar gyfer **synthesis protein**.

Asid riboniwclëig (RNA)

Adeiledd RNA.
- Mae RNA yn bolymer **un edefyn o** niwcleotid.
- Mae RNA yn cynnwys y siwgr pentos, **ribos**.
- Mae RNA yn cynnwys y **basau** organig adenin, gwanin, cytosin, ac wracil (yn lle thymin).

Mae tri math o RNA, ac mae pob un yn gysylltiedig â'r broses o synthesis protein.

- mae **RNA negeseuol (mRNA)** yn foleciwl hir un edefyn sy'n cael ei ffurfio'n helics. Mae'n cael ei gynhyrchu yn y cnewyllyn ac yn cludo'r cod genetig o'r DNA i'r ribosomau yn y cytoplasm.

- ceir **RNA ribosomaidd (rRNA)** yn y cytoplasm ac mae'n foleciwl mawr, cymhleth wedi ei ffurfio o helicsau dwbl a sengl. Mae ribosomau wedi cael eu gwneud o RNA ribosomaidd a phrotein.

- mae **RNA trosglwyddol (tRNA)** yn foleciwl bychan un edefyn. Mae'n ffurfio siâp meillionen, gydag un pen o'r gadwyn yn diweddu mewn cyfres cytosin-cytosin-adenin yn y pwynt lle mae'r asid amino y mae'n ei gario yn cydio ynddo. Ym mhen arall y gadwyn y mae cyfres o dri bas a elwir yn **wrthgodon**.
Mae moleciwlau tRNA yn dod ag asidau amino i'r ribosom fel bod modd syntheseiddio'r proteinau.

❏ *Tasg*
1. Lluniwch ddiagram o'r gwahanol fathau o RNA.
2. Lluniwch dabl yn dangos y gwahaniaethau rhwng DNA a RNA.

Mae'r broses o syntheseiddio protein yn cael ei hastudio yn A2 ond yr ydym wedi cynnwys fersiwn symlach yn yr adran hon **er gwybodaeth yn unig** fel bod gennych ddealltwriaeth o swyddogaethau'r gwahanol fathau o DNA yn y broses o syntheseiddio protein.

- Mae DNA yn cynnwys yr holl wybodaeth sydd ei hangen i wneud protein ond ni all adael y cnewyllyn.
- Mae synthesis protein yn digwydd ar y ribosomau sydd yn y cytoplasm.
- Felly mae'n rhaid cael moleciwl negeseuol i gludo'r cod gwybodaeth o'r DNA trwy'r bilen gnewyllol i'r cytoplasm. Moleciwl un edefyn yw'r **mRNA.**
- Ar ôl gadael y cnewyllyn mae'r mRNA yn cydio wrth **ribosom.**
- Yma mae'r cod yn cael ei drosi wrth i'r ribosom symud ar hyd yr mRNA a datgelu tri bas (codon) ar y tro.
- Swyddogaeth y moleciwlau tRNA yw cludo asidau amino pendol i'r ribosomau.
- Mae'r gwrthgodon ar y **tRNA** yn cyfuno gyda'r codon yn yr mRNA ac mae'r asid amino yn cydio i'r ribosom.
- Mae'r broses hon yn cael ei dyblygu wrth i'r ribosom symud ar hyd yr mRNA a phob tro yn gadael asid amino wedi ei gydio i'r asid amino blaenorol nes y bod cadwyn polypeptid yn cael ei ffurfio.

1.7 Cellraniad

Adeiledd cromosomau

Mae cromosomau wedi cael eu ffurfio o **DNA**, protein ac ychydig bach o RNA. Mae DNA yn bodoli fel un edefyn ar ffurf helics dwbl sy'n rhedeg drwy holl hyd y cromosom. Mae pob moleciwl DNA wedi ei ffurfio o lawer o ddarnau bychan a elwir yn (**g)enynnau**. Dim ond ar ddechrau cellraniad y mae'r cromosomau yn dod yn weladwy. Ychydig cyn i'r cellraniad ddigwydd bydd pob moleciwl DNA yn gwneud copi ohono'i hun. Mae edefyn o DNA yn dod yn ddau edefyn unfath. Gelwir y rhain yn **gromatidau** ac maent yn gorwedd yn gyfochrog ar hyd y rhan fwyaf o'u hyd ac yn ymuno mewn rhan arbenigol yn unig, a elwir yn **centromer**.

Mae nifer y cromosomau yng nghelloedd gwahanol rywogaethau yn amrywio. Mae gan fodau dynol 46 cromosom bob amser, mae gan bry ffrwythau 8 cromosom, a thaten 48 cromosom! Mae cromosomau yn dod mewn parau cydwedd a elwir yn barau **homologaidd**. Felly mae gan fodau dynol 23 pâr o gromosomau homologaidd.

Gelwir cyfanswm nifer y cromosomau yn nifer diploid. Mae gan gelloedd rhyw, neu gametau, hanner y nifer diploid o gromosomau, a fe'u gelwir yn **haploid**. Felly mae 23 cromosom mewn gametau dynol.

Mitosis

Mae mitosis yn cynhyrchu dwy epilgell sydd, o ran genynnau, yn unfath â'r rhiant-gell.
Wrth rannu mae celloedd yn mynd drwy batrwm cyson o ddigwyddiadau a elwir yn **gylchred celloedd**. Mae hyn yn broses barhaus ond er mwyn ei disgrifio'n fwy cyfleus mae'n cael ei hisrannu yn bedair cam ynghyd â cham 'gorffwys', a elwir yn rhyngffas, rhwng un rhaniad llawn.

Rhyngffas

Dyma'r rhan hiraf o'r gylchred. Dyma pryd mae cell sydd newydd gael ei ffurfio yn cynyddu mewn maint ac yn **cynhyrchu organynnau** a gollwyd yn ystod y rhaniad blaenorol. Mae maint y **DNA yn cael ei ddyblu** yn ystod y cyfnod hwn. Yn union cyn y cellraniad nesaf mae'r cromosomau yn dyblygu fel bod pob un yn cynnwys dau gromatid wedi eu cysylltu â'i gilydd gan y centromer. Mae gweithgaredd metabolaidd sylweddol gan fod angen egni ar ffurf ATP ar gyfer y prosesau hyn. Nid yw'r cromosomau yn weladwy yn y cyfnod rhyngffas gan fod y deunydd cromosom, sef y cromatin, wedi ei wasgaru drwy'r cnewyllyn.

Yn ystod **proffas** mae'r newidiadau canlynol yn digwydd:

1. Mae'r cromosomau'n cyddwyso (sef yn byrhau a thewychu) ac maent yn weladwy fel edau hir denau. Cyfeirir atynt yn awr fel parau o gromatidau.

2. Mewn celloedd lle mae centriolau yn bresennol, h.y. anifeiliaid a phlanhigion is, mae'r centriolau yn rhannu ac yn symud i begynau gwahanol o'r celloedd.

3. Mae microdiwbynnau protein yn ffurfio o bob centriol ac mae'r werthyd yn datblygu, gan ymestyn o begwn i begwn.

4. Tuag at ddiwedd proffas mae'r bilen gnewyllol yn ymddatod a'r cnewyllan yn diflannu.

5. Gellir gweld yn glir fod parau o gromatidau yn gorwedd yn rhydd yn y cytoplasm.

Yn ystod **Metaffas** mae'r cromosomau yn trefnu eu hunain yng nghanol neu ar gyhydedd y werthyd ac maent yn cydio mewn ffibrau gwerthyd arbennig yn y centromer. Wrth i'r ffibrau hyn gyfangu mae'r cromatidau unigol yn cael eu tynnu ychydig ar wahân.

Mae **Anaffas** yn gyfnod cyflym iawn. Mae'r centromer yn hollti a ffibrau'r werthyd yn cyfangu ac yn tynnu'r cromatidau sydd bellach wedi eu gwahanu at y pegynau, y centromer yn gyntaf.

Y **Teloffas** yw cyfnod olaf mitosis. Erbyn hyn mae'r cromosomau wedi cyrraedd pegynau'r celloedd a chyfeirir atynt fel cromosomau unwaith eto. Maent yn datod ac yn ymestyn. Mae'r werthyd yn torri i lawr, y centriolau yn dyblygu, y cnewyllan yn ailymddangos a'r bilen gnewyllol yn ailffurfio. Mewn celloedd anifeiliaid mae cytocinesis yn digwydd trwy ddarwasgiad canol y rhiant-gell o'r tu allan at i mewn. Mewn celloedd planhigion, mae cellblat yn ffurfio ar draws cyhydedd y rhiant-gell o'r canol tuag allan ac mae cellfur newydd yn cael ei gosod.

❏ *Tasg*
1. Gwnewch restr o'r geiriau allweddol a'u diffiniadau, e.e. mae **homologaidd** yn golygu bod gan gell ddiploid bob cromosom bartner sy'n union yr un hyd gydag union yr un genynnau.
2. Lluniwch dabl yn crynhoi'r newidiadau sy'n digwydd ym mhob un o bedwar cam mitosis.
3. Lluniwch siart cylch yn dangos yr amser cymharol a gymer pob cyfnod o'r cylchred celloedd.
4. Lluniwch ddiagram wedi ei labelu yn dangos cyfnodau mitosis.

Pwysigrwydd mitosis

- Mae mitosis yn cynhyrchu dwy gell sydd â'r un nifer o gromosomau â'r rhiant-gell ac mae pob **cromosom yn gopi manwl** o'r rhai gwreiddiol. Mae'r rhaniad yn caniatáu cynhyrchu celloedd sydd, o ran **genynnau, yn union yr un fath â'r rhiant** ac mae hynny'n rhoi sefydlogrwydd genetig.
- Trwy gynhyrchu celloedd newydd, mae mitosis yn arwain at **dwf** organeb ac yn caniatáu **atgyweirio** meinweoedd ac amnewid celloedd marw. Un enghraifft o fitosis mewn planhigion yw blaen y gwreiddyn. Mewn croen dynol, mae celloedd marw ar arwyneb y croen yn cael eu disodli gan gelloedd unfath oddi tanynt.
- Canlyniad **atgynhyrchu anrhywiol** yw epil cyfan sy'n unfath â'r rhiant.
Mae hyn yn digwydd mewn organebau ungellog megis burum a bacteria. Y mae hefyd yn digwydd mewn rhai planhigion sy'n blodeuo lle mae organau megis bylbiau, cloron ac ymledyddion yn cynhyrchu niferoedd mawr o epil unfath mewn cyfnod cymharol fyr. Nid oes amrywiaeth rhwng pob unigolyn. Ond mae'r rhan fwyaf o'r planhigion hyn yn atgenhedlu'n rhywiol hefyd.

Meiosis

- Mae'n bwysig bod gametau yn haploid gan fod hanner y cromosomau, yn ystod ffrwythloniad, yn dod oddi wrth y gwryw a hanner oddi wrth y fenyw er mwyn cynhyrchu sygot diploid.
- Mae meiosis yn cynhyrchu pedair gwahanol gell haploid yn ystod atgenhedlu rhywiol ac mae dau raniad olynol.

Meiosis I – lle mae nifer y cromosomau yn lleihau a chroesi drosodd yn digwydd.
Meiosis II - lle mae'r ddau gnewyllyn haploid newydd yn rhannu eto mewn rhaniad sy'n unfath â rhaniad mitosis.

Fel mitosis, mae meiosis yn broses raddol ond er hwylustod mae'n cael ei rhannu'n bedwar cyfnod sef cyfnod proffas, metaffas, anaffas a theloffas. Mae'r cyfnodau hyn yn digwydd unwaith ym mhob un o'r ddau raniad.

Nid *oes rhaid i chi ddisgrifio proses meiosis yn ei chyfanrwydd ond dylech allu disgrifio pwysigrwydd y gwahaniaethau rhwng mitosis a meiosis.*

Mae'r cyfnod cyntaf mewn meiosis, sef **proffas,** yn debyg i'r proffas mewn mitosis oherwydd bod y cromosomau yn lleihau ac yn tewychu ac yn dod yn weladwy, ond mewn meiosis maent yn **gysylltiol yn eu parau homologaidd**. Yr enw am baru'r cromosomau yw **synapsis**. Mae pob pâr o gromosomau, un oddi wrth y fam ac un oddi wrth y tad yn cael eu galw'n **ddeufalent**. Mae pob deufalent yn cynnwys pedwar edefyn wedi eu gwneud o bedwar cromosom yr un wedi eu rhannu'n ddau gromatid. Mae'r cromatidau yn lapio o amgylch ei gilydd ac wedyn yn gwrthyrru ei gilydd yn rhannol ond maent yn dal i fod wedi eu cysylltu ar bwyntiau arbennig a elwir yn **ciasmata**. Yn y pwyntiau hyn gall cromatidau dorri ac ail-gyfuno gyda chromatid gwahanol ond cyfatebol. Yr enw am gyfnewid darnau o gromosomau fel hyn yw **croesi drosodd** ac mae'n ffynhonnell amrywiaeth genetig.

Yn ystod cyfnod cyntaf o feiosis, sef **metaffas**, mae'r parau o gromosomau homologaidd yn trefnu eu hunain ar hap ar gyhydedd y werthyd. Ar hap y penderfynir sut y bydd y cromosomau homologaidd yn cael eu trefnu ar y cyhydedd a phan maent yn gwahanu fe geir gwahanol gyfuniadau. Mae'r **dosraniad ar hap** a'r **amrywiaeth annibynnol** o gromosomau sy'n deillio o hynny yn cynhyrchu cyfuniadau genetig newydd.

Tabl yn cymharu mitosis a meiosis.

Mitosis	Meiosis
Un rhaniad yn arwain at ddwy epilgell	Mae dau raniad yn arwain at bedair epilgell
Nid oes newid yn nifer y cromosomau	Hanerir nifer y cromosomau
Nid yw cromosomau homologaidd yn cydgysylltu mewn parau	Mae cromosomau homologaidd yn cysylltu mewn parau
Nid yw croesi drosodd yn digwydd	Mae croesi drosodd yn digwydd a chiasmata yn ymffurfio
Mae'r epilgelloedd yn unfath yn enetig	Mae'r epilgelloedd yn wahanol yn enetig

Meiosis ac amrywiaeth

Yn yr hirdymor, os yw rhywogaeth am oroesi mewn amgylchedd sy'n newid yn barhaus ac am barhau i gytrefu amgylcheddau newydd, yna mae'n rhaid cael ffynonellau amrywiaeth. Mae tair ffordd o greu amrywiaeth:

- Mae pob un o'r cromosomau sy'n ffurfio pâr homologaidd yn cynnwys deunyddiau genetig gwahanol. Yn ystod atgenhedlu rywiol mae **genoteip un rhiant yn cael ei gymysgu gyda genoteip y llall** pan fydd gametau haploid yn ymasio.
- Mae'r parau o **gromosomau homologaidd** yn trefnu eu hunain ar hap ar y werthyd yn ystod metaffas 1 meiosis. Pan fyddant wedyn yn **gwahanu** maent yn gwneud hynny'n gwbl **annibynnol** o'i gilydd, fel bod yr epilgelloedd neu'r gametau yn cynnwys gwahanol gyfuniadau o gromosomau.
- **Croesi drosodd** pan ffurfir ciasmata yn ystod proffas 1 meiosis. Gall rhannau cyfatebol o gromosomau homologaidd gael eu cyfnewid gan gynhyrchu cyfuniadau newydd a gwahanu genynnau cysylltiedig.

2.1 Bioamrywiaeth ac Esblygiad

Mae bioamrywiaeth yn ffordd o fesur nifer y rhywogaethau sydd ar y blaned; difodiant yw'r enw ar golli'r rhywogaethau. Dros y 200 mlynedd diwethaf mae rhai o weithgareddau dynol wedi cael effaith negyddol ar yr amgylchedd ac mae hynny yn ei dro wedi effeithio ar oroesiad planhigion ac anifeiliaid. Erbyn hyn mae gwyddonwyr wedi dod i ddeall fod argyfwng yn bodoli mewn bioamrywiaeth, gyda gostyngiad cyflym yn amrywiaeth bywyd ar y Ddaear. Mae coedwigoedd glaw trofannol a'r riffiau cwrel ymhlith yr ecosystemau mwyaf amrywiol ar y blaned ac mewn cymhariaeth ag ecosystemau eraill mae crynodiad llawer mwy o rywogaethau i'r cilometr sgwâr. Serch hynny, mae coedwigoedd glaw trofannol yn cael eu dinistrio ar raddfa ddychrynllyd i wneud lle i ymdopi â chynnydd yn y boblogaeth ddynol ac i gynnal y boblogaeth honno. Yr un perygl mwyaf i fioamrywiaeth ar y blaned yw'r newidiadau a achosir i gynefinoedd gan fodau dynol.

Bioamrywiaeth a difodiant

Mae gweithgareddau dynol yn newid yr ecosystemau y mae dyn a rhywogaethau eraill yn dibynnu arnynt. Yn y moroedd mae'r stoc o sawl rhywogaeth o bysgod yn cael eu peryglu trwy orbysgota, ac mae rhai o'r ardaloedd mwyaf cynhyrchiol ac amrywiol, megis y riffiau cwrel a'r morydau yn dod o dan bwysau difrifol. Yn fyd-eang mae'n bosibl bod cyfradd difodiant rhywogaethau hyd at 50 gwaith yn uwch nag unrhyw adeg arall yn ystod y 100,000 blwyddyn ddiwethaf.

Mae difodiant yn broses naturiol sydd wedi bod yn digwydd ers i fywyd esblygu gyntaf. Yr hyn sydd wrth wraidd yr argyfwng presennol mewn bioamrywiaeth yw *cyfradd* gyfredol difodiant. Mae gwyddonwyr erbyn hyn yn credu bod cyfradd 'gefndirol' arferol difodiant yn un rhywogaeth y flwyddyn allan o bob miliwn. Amcangyfrifir yn awr bod gweithgarwch dynion mewn ardaloedd trofannol yn unig wedi achosi cynnydd o rwng 1000 a 10,000 yng nghyfradd difodiant! Drwy'r byd i gyd mae dinistr anferthol wedi cael ei achosi i gynefinoedd trwy amaethyddiaeth, datblygu trefol, coedwigaeth, mwyngloddio a llygredd amgylcheddol. Effeithiwyd ar fywyd y môr hefyd. Mae oddeutu un rhan o dair o rywogaethau pysgod môr y blaned yn dibynnu ar riffiau cwrel. Os yw'r dinistr yn parhau ar y gyfradd bresennol gallai tua hanner y riffiau fod wedi diflannu yn ystod yr 20 mlynedd nesaf.

Rhywogaethau mewn perygl

Mae'r mwyafrif helaeth o drigolion blaenorol y Ddaear, gan gynnwys y dinosoriaid anferthol a oedd unwaith yn tra-arglwyddiaethu a'r rhedyn coed wedi mynd i ddifodiant. Mae hyn yn bennaf oherwydd newidiadau yn yr hinsawdd, newidiadau daearegol a newidiadau biotig. Erbyn hyn mae gweithgarwch dynol wedi cymryd drosodd fel prif achos esblygiad rhywogaethau. Mae llawer o'r mamolion mwyaf, e.e. gorilaod y mynydd-dir, y panda mawr, teigrod ac eirth gwyn o dan fygythiad.

Mae tri phrif reswm dros y gostyngiad yn eu niferoedd:

- colli cynefinoedd
- gor-hela gan ddynion
- cystadleuaeth oddi wrth rywogaethau sydd wedi cael eu cyflwyno i'w cynefin.

Mae rhywogaethau eraill dan fygythiad oherwydd rhesymau ychwanegol megis:
- datgoedwigo
- llygredd
- draenio gwlypdiroedd.

Cydnabyddir erbyn hyn y gall pob rhywogaeth fod yn ased pwysig i'r ddynoliaeth, yn ffynhonnell bosibl o fwyd, cemegau gwerthfawr neu enynnau gwrth-glefyd. Er enghraifft, ymhlith y planhigion niferus sy'n tyfu yn y coedwigoedd glaw trofannol fe all fod rhai sydd â phriodweddau meddygol. Wrth i unrhyw rywogaeth o blanhigion gael ei difodi cyn archwilio eu priodweddau cemegol fe allai'r golled fod yn amhosibl ei hamgyffred. Gan hynny mae angen **cadwraeth rhywogaethau**, sef cynllunio cadwraeth bywyd gwyllt.

Esblygiad

Beth sydd wedi achosi bodolaeth cymaint o wahanol fathau o ffurfiau o fywyd ar y Ddaear?
Esblygiad yw'r broses dros gyfnodau maith iawn lle mae rhywogaethau newydd yn cael eu ffurfio o rywogaethau oedd yn bodoli'n barod. Mewn bioleg defnyddir y term yn benodol ar gyfer y prosesau sydd wedi trawsnewid bywyd ar y Ddaear o'i gychwyn cynnar hyd at yr amrywiaeth enfawr o ffurfiau ffosiledig a byw y gwyddom amdanynt heddiw.

Rhoddwyd damcaniaeth esblygiad gerbron am y tro cyntaf gan Charles Darwin. Yn ystod ei ymweliad ag Ynysoedd y Galapagos casglodd Darwin dystiolaeth ddaearegol a thystiolaeth ffosil a oedd yn cefnogi'r syniad bod bywyd yn newid gydag amser. Yn 1859 cynigiodd mai dethol naturiol oedd y grym a oedd yn achosi newid mewn poblogaethau.

Pelydriad addasol mewn pincod ar Ynysoedd y Galapagos

Yn 1832, pan oedd Darwin yn 22 oed, fe deithiodd i Dde America i wneud arolwg gwyddonol. Bu'n astudio fflora a ffawna'r tir mawr yn Ne America a rhai o'r ynysoedd o'i amgylch, gan gynnwys Ynysoedd y Galapagos. Ffurfiwyd yr ynysoedd hyn yn gymharol ddiweddar o ran amser daearegol, o ganlyniad i weithgarwch folcanig. Ei dasg oedd arsylwi, disgrifio a dosbarthu'r planhigion a'r anifeiliaid a welai yno. Hefyd fe gasglodd ffosiliau yn y creigiau ac roedd y rhain yn dangos iddo fod gwahanol ffurfiau o fywyd wedi mynd trwy lawer o newidiadau yn y gorffennol.

Ymhlith yr anifeiliaid niferus a astudiwyd gan Darwin ar Ynysoedd y Galapagos oedd y pincod. Gwelodd fod undeg pedwar gwahanol rywogaeth ohonynt. O safbwynt daearegol, cafodd yr ynysoedd eu ffurfio yn gymharol ddiweddar ac mae'n rhaid bod unrhyw anifeiliaid oedd yno wedi cyrraedd yr ynysoedd o'r tir mawr, oddeutu 600 milltir i ffwrdd. Nid yw pincod yn gallu hedfan yn bell iawn, ac awgrymodd Darwin bod un rhywogaeth hynafiadol o bincod wedi cyrraedd yr ynysoedd gyda chymorth y prifwynt. Gan nad oedd unrhyw rywogaethau eraill o adar ar yr ynysoedd roedd amrywiaeth o fwyd ar gael i'r pincod a fu'n cytrefu'r ynysoedd. Gwelodd sut yr oedd y pincod unigol yn wahanol rhwng un ynys â'r llall. Y prif wahaniaethau oedd maint a siâp y pig ac yr oedd hyn yn gysylltiedig â'r gwahanol fathau o fwyd yr oeddynt yn ei fwyta e.e. pryfed, hadau, ffrwythau.

❏ **Tasg** Tynnwch lun y gwahanol fathau o bigau pincod a disgrifiwch sut y mae'r pigau wedi eu haddasu ar gyfer gwahanol fwydydd.

Ar bob ynys roedd yn ymddangos bod epil y pincod wedi etifeddu'r nodweddion oedd yn gwneud i'r aderyn weddu orau i'r ynys benodol honno. Awgrymodd Darwin bod y pincod wedi datblygu o hynafiad cyffredin a bod y gwahanol fathau o bigau wedi datblygu dros amser maith ac wedi arbenigo er mwyn bwydo ar ffynhonnell benodol o fwyd. Mae hyn yn enghraifft o **belydriad addasol**.

Dethol naturiol

Trwy arsylwi ar amrywiaeth o fewn poblogaeth a'r tueddiad i'r boblogaeth o oedolion fod yn sefydlog o safbwynt niferoedd, cynigiodd Darwin y syniad o ddethol naturiol.
Mae'r ddamcaniaeth yn seiliedig ar yr arsylwadau canlynol:
- Mewn unrhyw boblogaeth mae yna **amrywiad**.
- Mae gan unigolion o fewn poblogaeth y potensial i gynhyrchu nifer fawr o epil er bod nifer yr oedolion yn tueddu i aros yr un fath o un genhedlaeth i'r llall.

Ar sail yr arsylwadau hyn daeth Darwin i'r casgliadau canlynol:
✓ Mae brwydr (**cystadleuaeth**) i oroesi a dim ond y mwyaf cymwys sy'n goroesi
✓ Mae'r unigolion sy'n **goroesi ac yn atgenhedlu** yn trosglwyddo eu nodweddion mwyaf ffafriol i'w hepil.
✓ Dros gyfnod, mae grŵp o unigolion a oedd gynt yn perthyn i'r un rhywogaeth yn gallu hollti i ddau grŵp gwahanol sy'n ddigon gwahanol i'w gilydd i fod yn ddwy rywogaeth ar wahân.

(Gellir diffinio rhywogaeth fel grŵp o organebau sy'n rhannu nifer helaeth o nodweddion cyffredin ac sy'n gallu bridio gyda'i gilydd i gynhyrchu epil ffrwythlon. Os yw'r grŵp o organebau wedi datblygu i fod mor wahanol fel nad ydynt yn gallu bridio gyda'i gilydd yna maent wedi dod yn ddwy wahanol rywogaeth.)

Newid graddol dros gyfnodau maith ynteu lamu sydyn?

Mae tystiolaeth sylweddol iawn i awgrymu bod hinsawdd y Ddaear wedi newid yn y gorffennol. Oddeutu tair miliwn o flynyddoedd yn ôl yr oedd hinsawdd y Ddaear yn llawer cynhesach nag ydyw ar hyn o bryd. Yr adeg honno yr oedd coedwigoedd yn tyfu cyn belled i'r gogledd ag arfordir yr Ynys Las â'r Arctig. Yr oedd y capiau iâ dros y ddau begwn yn deneuach, a lefelau'r môr tua 35 metr yn uwch nag ydynt heddiw. Dechreuodd oes yr iâ cyntaf oddeutu 2.3 miliwn o flynyddoedd yn ôl. Sut mae gwyddonwyr yn gwybod am y newidiadau hyn a'r ffordd y mae'r newidiadau wedi effeithio ar fywyd ar y blaned?

Palaeontoleg yw'r astudiaeth o blanhigion ac anifeiliaid y gorffennol daearegol, fel y cynrychiolir hwy gan eu holion ffosil. Trwy ddosbarthu anifeiliaid a phlanhigion sydd wedi eu difodi mewn dilyniant daearegol, mae'n bosibl awgrymu sut y gallai un grŵp fod wedi esblygu i grŵp arall. Mae'r ffaith bod ffosiliau yn cael eu ffurfio mewn creigiau gwaddod yn helpu palaeontolegwyr i wneud hynny. Wrth ffurfio creigiau gwaddod mae haenau o silt yn caledu, ac mae haenau yn ffurfio un ar ben y llall. Mae'r graig sy'n deillio o hynny yn cynnwys cyfres o haenau (strata) llorweddol gyda phob haen yn cynnwys ffosiliau sy'n nodweddiadol o'r amser y gosodwyd yr haen. Mae'r creigiau hynaf, ac felly'r ffosiliau cynharaf wedi eu cynnwys yn yr haenau isaf; mae'r creigiau a'r ffosiliau mwyaf diweddar yn yr haenau uchaf. Yn aml gellir dweud yn union beth yw oedran creigiau trwy dechnegau dyddio radiometrig. Mae ffosiliau yn cael eu dyddio trwy'r dull radiocarbon. Trwy wybod beth yw oed y creigiau ac astudio'r cofnod ffosiliau mae gwyddonwyr yn gwybod y drefn ddilyniant a'r amser yr ymddangosodd y prif grwpiau o organebau byw.

Mae damcaniaeth Darwin yn seiliedig ar y syniad bod rhywogaethau yn newid yn raddol o un ffurf i ffurf arall dros gyfnodau maith. Hyd yn ddiweddar roedd bron pob biolegydd yn cymryd safbwynt tebyg. Os yw'r syniad yma'n gywir, gellir disgwyl y byddai ffurfiau canolradd, neu 'ddolenni coll', yn bodoli mewn haenau dilynol o graig rhwng un rhywogaeth o ffosiliau a'r nesaf. Ond mae ffurfiau canolradd yn syndod o brin yn y cofnod ffosiliau.

- Mae creadaethwyr yn mynnu bod prinder ffurfiau canolradd yn dystiolaeth o 'greadaeth arbennig' yn hytrach nag esblygiad rhywogaethau.
- Mae dau wyddonydd Americanaidd, Eldridge a Gould wedi cynnig dehongliad gwahanol. Maent yn awgrymu y gall rhywogaethau newydd ddod i fodolaeth yn gyflym, efallai o fewn ychydig filoedd o flynyddoedd, gan aros yn ddigyfnewid wedyn am filiynau o flynyddoedd cyn newid eto. Mae'n bosibl bod esblygiad sydyn rhywogaethau newydd yn digwydd ar ymylon yr ardal lle mae'r boblogaeth yn byw ac mae *ychydig* yn unig o unigolion sy'n gysylltiedig â'r broses. O dan yr amgylchiadau hyn, byddai'n anarferol gweld newidiadau graddol rhwng rhywogaethau dilynol yn y cofnod ffosiliau. Pan fydd newid anffafriol yn yr amgylchedd gorfodir rhywogaethau i symud i amgylchiadau gwell. Felly mae organebau yn mudo yn ogystal ag esblygu! Mae'n bosibl bod y rhywogaethau sy'n methu symud i gynefin ffafriol yn darfod yn y cyfnod hwn. Mae'r cynhesu byd-eang presennol yn gwneud i'r capiau iâ pegynol ddadmer ac mae hynny'n effeithio ar yr organebau sydd yn byw yn yr ardal honno. Mae eirth gwyn mewn perygl o ddifodiant.

Pan fydd y newidiadau yn eithafol mae difodiant mas yn digwydd.

Mas-ddifodiant

Mae gwyddonwyr o'r farn bod mas-ddifodiant wedi digwydd nifer o weithiau gan awgrymu na fu 'newid graddol' yn y ffordd a awgrymir gan ddamcaniaeth dethol naturiol. Er enghraifft roedd mas-ddifodiant 250 miliwn o flynyddoedd yn ôl pan ddilëwyd dros 80% o grwpiau infertebrat y môr!
Digwyddodd mas-ddifodiant arall 65 miliwn o flynyddoedd yn ôl pan ddifodwyd y dinosoriaid. Yn y don enfawr o belydriad addasol a ddigwyddodd dros gyfnod o 100 miliwn o flynyddoedd yr oedd y dinosoriaid wedi datblygu i fod yn grŵp trechol o fertebratau ar y Ddaear. Yr oeddent yn grŵp hynod o amrywiol o ran siâp, maint y corff ac o ran cynefin, ac maent yn cynnwys yr anifeiliaid mwyaf a fu'n byw ar dir erioed. Roedd hinsawdd y Ddaear yn gynnes ac yn gyson, yn debyg iawn i'r sefyllfa bresennol yn y trofannau. Daeth Oes y Dinosoriaid i ben pan achosodd rhyw ddigwyddiad cataclysmig mas-ddifodiant o fywyd ar y ddaear.

Cynigiwyd nifer o wahanol ddamcaniaethau i egluro difodiant y dinosoriaid:
- ✓ Mae tystiolaeth dda y bu newid amlwg yn yr hinsawdd ac yn lefelau'r tir ac mae'n bosibl y bu gostyngiad amlwg mewn tymheredd dros lawer o'r Ddaear. Mae'n bosibl bod dinosoriaid yn arbennig o sensitif i newidiadau o'r fath yn yr hinsawdd yn rhannol oherwydd eu bod yn gorfod bwyta cymaint o fwyd er mwyn cadw'n fyw.
- ✓ Mae damcaniaeth arall yn awgrymu bod asteroid, 10 cilometr mewn diamedr wedi taro'r Ddaear 65 miliwn o flynyddoedd yn ôl. Gallai'r ergyd fod wedi achosi ffrwydradau folcanig a fyddai'n rhyddhau cymylau enfawr o lwch a allai fod wedi tywyllu'r haul am rai blynyddoedd gan atal planhigion rhag ffotosyntheseiddio, byddai hynny wedi achosi newyn eithriadol, yn arbennig ymhlith yr anifeiliaid mwyaf. Y mae hefyd yn llai hysbys bod bron i hanner y rhywogaethau o infertebratau'r môr wedi mynd i ddifodiant yn ystod y cyfnod hwn.

Egwyddorion Tacsonomeg

Credir bod rhwng 3 miliwn a 30 miliwn rhywogaeth o organebau byw ar y Ddaear ond hyd yma, dim ond oddeutu dwy filiwn o wahanol fathau o organebau sydd wedi cael eu disgrifio a'u dynodi. Tacsonomeg (neu ddosbarthiad) yw'r term am ddosbarthu organebau byw mewn grwpiau o faint sy'n haws eu trin. Dylech wybod am egwyddorion dosbarthu modern sy'n dangos sut y gall organebau fod yn perthyn i'w gilydd trwy esblygiad, ar sail y nifer o nodweddion sy'n gyffredin iddynt.

Mae organebau yn cael eu grwpio mewn cynllun hierarchaidd

Tacsonomeg yw'r astudiaeth wyddonol o amrywiaeth organebau byw.
Mae cyfundrefn ddosbarthu yn gosod trefn a chynllun cyffredinol i amrywiaeth enfawr bywyd.
Wrth ddisgrifio organebau byw bydd tacsonomegwyr yn chwilio am yr hyn sy'n debyg ac yn wahanol rhyngddynt.

- ✓ Os yw organebau wedi esblygu ar hyd yr un llinellau fe ellir gweld tebygrwydd rhyngddynt. Er enghraifft, y gwahanol rannau sydd mewn genau pryfed. Mae rhai rhannau o'r genau yn cael eu defnyddio i roi pigiad, e.e. mosgito benywaidd; eraill er mwyn cnoi llystyfiant e.e. locustiaid; ac eraill er mwyn sugno bwyd hylifol e.e. glöyn byw. Mae'r gwahanol fathau o enau yn dilyn patrwm sylfaenol digon tebyg i'w gilydd. Mae astudio ymddangosiad corfforol organebau yn caniatáu i fiolegwyr ddosbarthu organebau gyda'i gilydd yn ôl y graddau o debygrwydd rhyngddynt.
- ✓ Y mae hefyd yn bosibl astudio i ba raddau y mae organebau yn perthyn i'w gilydd. Mae organebau sydd â hynafiaid cyffredin yn cael eu dosbarthu'n agos at ei gilydd a rhai sydd â pherthnasau pellach yn cael eu dosbarthu ymhellach oddi wrth ei gilydd. Yn yr achosion hynny, mae nodweddion biocemegol protein a chyfansoddiad DNA yn bwysicach na thebygrwydd corfforol.

Mewn cyfundrefn ddosbarthu, mae gwyddonwyr yn gosod organebau tebyg yn agos at ei gilydd ac yn dosbarthu'r rhai annhebyg yn bellach oddi wrth ei gilydd. System hierarchaidd yw cyfundrefn ddosbarthu sy'n seiliedig ar grwpiau mawr yn cael eu rhannu'n barhaus i grwpiau llai.
Cafodd y drefn ddosbarthu naturiol a ddefnyddir heddiw ei dyfeisio gan y gwyddonydd o Sweden, Linnaeus, yn y 18fed ganrif. O dan y cynllun hwn mae organebau yn cael eu grwpio gyda'i gilydd yn ôl eu tebygrwydd sylfaenol. Dyfeisiwyd cyfundrefn hierarchaidd er mwyn gwahaniaethu rhwng grwpiau mawr o organebau gan roi cyfres o enwau gradd i ddynodi gwahanol lefelau o fewn yr hierarchaeth.
Tacson yw'r enw ar lefel yn yr hierarchaeth ddosbarthu ac mae'n gasgliad o organebau sy'n rhannu rhai nodweddion sylfaenol.
Gan ddechrau gyda'r grŵp lleiaf:

- **rhywogaeth** – grŵp o organebau sy'n rhannu nifer fawr o nodweddion cyffredin ac sy'n gallu bridio gyda'i gilydd i gynhyrchu epil ffrwythlon. (Yr unig adeg y gellir cynhyrchu epil ffrwythlon yw pan fydd cromosomau homologaidd yn gallu paru adeg meiosis.) Enghreifftiau yw *Locusta* (Locust), *Rosa* (Rhosyn).
- **genws** – grŵp o fewn rhywogaeth sy'n perthyn yn agos i'w gilydd. *Locusta migratoria* (locust mudol), *Rosa canina* (Rhosyn y cŵn).
- **teulu** - grŵp o genera (lluosog genws), e.e. Rosaceae (Rhosod)
- **urdd** – grŵp o deuluoedd sy'n perthyn i'w gilydd, e.e. Orthoptera (sy'n cynnwys locustiaid, sioncod y gwair a chricyllod).
- **dosbarth** – grŵp o raddau tebyg, e.e. Insecta (Pryfed).
- **ffylwm** – grŵp mawr o'r holl ddosbarthiadau sy'n rhannu rhai nodweddion cyffredin, e.e. Arthropodau (sy'n cynnwys pryfed, corynnod, nadroedd cantroed a nadroedd miltroed, cramenogion).
- **teyrnas** – y grŵp tacsonomaidd mwyaf, e.e. anifeiliaid, planhigion
- ✓ Wrth symud i fyny'r hierarchaeth o rywogaeth i deyrnas mae'r berthynas rhwng yr organebau yn y grwpiau yn pellhau.
- ✓ Wrth symud i lawr yr hierarchaeth o deyrnas i rywogaeth mae perthynas agosach rhwng yr organebau â'i gilydd.

Y Gyfundrefn Finomaidd

Mae gan lawer o organebau byw enwau cyffredin, a all amrywio o un rhan o'r wlad i ran arall. Gall hyn fod yn ddryslyd a hyd yn oed yn fwy dryslyd os oes rhaid enwi a disgrifio rhywogaeth benodol mewn papur ymchwil gwyddonol, a fydd o bosibl yn cael ei ddarllen gan wyddonydd mewn gwlad arall.
Er mwyn goresgyn y broblem hon, mae organebau yn cael eu henwi yn ôl y **gyfundrefn finomaidd.** Cyflwynwyd y gyfundrefn hon gan Linnaeus yn 1753 ac mae'n seiliedig ar ddefnyddio Lladin fel iaith ryngwladol. Rhoddir dau enw i bob organeb, enw ei genws ac enw ei rywogaeth. Mae'r gyfundrefn yn golygu bod organeb yn cael dynodiad manwl ar sail fyd-eang, yn wahanol iawn i'r enw cyffredin arno. Mae'r gyfundrefn binomial yn dal i gael ei defnyddio'n llwyddiannus heddiw, nid yn unig oherwydd bod gan bob organeb benodol ei henw gwyddonol unigryw ei hun ond am ei bod yn caniatáu i fiolegwyr gydnabod bod perthynas agos iawn rhwng dwy rywogaeth e.e. *Panthera leo* (llew) a *Panthera tigris* (teigr).

Wrth ddefnyddio'r gyfundrefn finomaidd mae'n rhaid dilyn rhai rheolau penodol:
- ✓ Enw'r genws sy'n dod gyntaf ac mae bob amser yn dechrau gyda phrif lythyren.
- ✓ Enw'r rhywogaeth sy'n dod yn ail ac mae'n dechrau gyda llythyren fach.
- ✓ Y tro cyntaf y defnyddir yr enw gwyddonol mewn testun mae'n rhaid cynnwys yr enw llawn e.e. *Panthera tigris*
- ✓ Gellir wedyn talfyrru enw'r genws, *P.tigris.*
- ✓ Dylai'r ddau enw gael eu hysgrifennu mewn llythrennau italig.

Y Dosbarthiad pum teyrnas

Hyd yn ddiweddar, peth cyffredin oedd rhannu pob organeb byw yn ddwy deyrnas, planhigion ac anifeiliaid. Gan fod rhai organebau y gellir eu dosbarthu i'r ddwy deyrnas a rhai nad ydynt yn gweddu i'r naill na'r llall, cynigiwyd y dosbarthiad pum teyrnas.

Teyrnas Prokaryotae   Teyrnas Protoctista   Teyrnas Anifeiliaid   Teyrnas Ffyngau   Teyrnas Planhigion

Prokaryotae

Mae prokaryotae yn organebau ungellog, ac maent yn cynnwys bacteria ac algâu glaswyrdd (Cyanobacteria).
Nid oes ganddynt gellbilenni mewnol; dim pilen gnewyllol; dim reticwlwm endoplasmig, dim mitocondria a dim corff Golgi. Mae ganddynt gellfur ond nid yw wedi ei wneud o gellwlos.

Protoctista

Organebau ewcaryotig bychan yw'r rhan fwyaf o aelodau'r deyrnas yma, ac mae ganddynt organynnau wedi eu rhwymo â philen a chnewyllyn gyda philen gnewyllol. Yn y deyrnas hon y mae organebau nad ydynt yn blanhigion, anifeiliaid na ffyngau. Mae'r deyrnas yn cynnwys algâu, llwydni dŵr, llwydni llysnafedd a'r protosoa.

Ffyngau

Mae aelodau'r deyrnas hon yn ewcaryotig, gyda'r corff wedi ei wneud o rwydwaith o edafedd a elwir yn hyffae, sy'n ffurfio myceliwm. Mae ganddynt gellfur anhyblyg wedi ei wneud o gitin. Nid oes ganddynt bigmentau ffotosynthetig ac y maent yn bwydo mewn dull heterotroffig. Mae pob aelod o'r grŵp naill ai yn saproffytig neu'n barasitig. Mewn rhai is-grwpiau nid oes gan yr hyffae groesfuriau, ond mewn rhai eraill mae croesfuriau, neu septa, yn bodoli. Maent yn atgenhedlu drwy sborau sydd heb fflagela. Enghreifftiau ohonynt yw: *Penicillium,* burum, madarch.

Plantae

Mae aelodau'r deyrnas hon yn amlgellog ac yn cyflawni ffotosynthesis. Mae'r celloedd yn ewcaryotig, gyda muriau cellwlos, gwagolynnau yn cynnwys cellnodd, a chloroplastau yn cynnwys pigmentau ffotosynthetig.
Mae'r prif ffyla planhigion yn cynnwys:
- ✓ planhigion anflodeuol
- ✓ mwsogl a llys yr afu
- ✓ rhedyn
- ✓ conwydd
- ✓ planhigion blodeuol

Y planhigion blodeuol (Angiospermau) yw'r grŵp mwyaf trechol o blanhigion ar y Ddaear. Maent yn cynnwys pob un o'n prif gnydau ac maent felly yn ffynhonnell bwysig o fwyd. Mae gan y blodau hadau sydd wedi eu cau o fewn ffrwyth sy'n cael eu ffurfio o fur yr ofari.

Animalia

Mae aelodau o deyrnas anifeiliaid yn ewcaryotau amlgellog, heterotroffig. Nid oes gan eu celloedd gellfur, ac maent yn dangos cydsymud nerfol.

- Mae pob ffylwm yn cynnwys organebau sy'n cael eu grwpio gyda'i gilydd yn ôl glasbrint sylfaenol.
- Mae rhai ffyla yn cynnwys mwy o rywogaethau nag eraill.
- Mae'r deyrnas anifeiliaid yn cael ei rhannu'n ddau brif grŵp:
✓ Anghortadau, sy'n aml yn cael eu galw'n infertebratau
✓ Cordatau – mae gan bob un ond y symlaf o'r cordatau asgwrn cefn ac felly cyfeirir atynt fel fertebratau.
Mae 95% o bob anifail yn infertebratau a dim ond 5% yn fertebratau.

Mae'r deyrnas anifeiliaid yn cael ei rhannu'n 20 prif ffyla a nifer o rai llai. Maent yn cynnwys:
- Infertebratau
✓ sglefren fôr
✓ llyngyren ledog
✓ llyngyr
✓ llyngyr segmentiedig
✓ molwsgiaid
✓ arthropodau
✓ sêr môr
- Fertebratau (pysgod, amffibiaid, ymlusgiaid, adar a mamolion)

Ar y lefel yma nid oes rhaid astudio prif nodweddion pob un o'r ffyla hyn.
Byddwn yn astudio'r tri ffyla anifeiliaid canlynol, anelidau, arthropodau a fertebratau wrth iddynt godi mewn adrannau eraill o'r uned hon h.y. cyfnewid nwyon, system cylchrediad ac atgenhedlu.

Detholiad o ffyla anifeiliaid

Anelidau

Mae 8,000 o rywogaethau o anelidau wedi eu henwi. Maent yn cynnwys mwydod, gelod a lygwn. Mae'r nodweddion canlynol yn gyffredin i bob aelod o'r fflylwm:

- ✓ corff hir, tenau mewn segmentau, gallwch weld y segmentau ar ffurf cylchoedd ar y tu allan
- ✓ corff wedi ei rannu'n fewnol gan raniadau (septa)
- ✓ ceudod y corff wedi ei lenwi â hylif (ceudod gwaed)
- ✓ sgerbwd hydrostatig
- ✓ un pen gellir ei ddynodi'n 'ben' gydag ymennydd cyntefig a system nerfol yn rhedeg drwy'r corff i gyd
- ✓ segmentau arbenigol sy'n gyfrifol am wahanol swyddogaethau, e.e. atgenhedliad, ysgarthiad
- ✓ croen athraidd, tenau y gellir cyfnewid nwyon drwyddo
- ✓ system cylchrediad gwaed caeedig yn cynnwys pigment sy'n cludo ocsigen.

Arthropodau

Yr arthropodau yw'r ffyla mwyaf niferus a llwyddiannus o blith yr holl anifeiliaid. Maent yn cynnwys nadroedd miltroed a nadroedd cantroed, cramenogion, corynnod a phryfed. Pryfed yw'r dosbarth mwyaf llwyddiannus o lawer o fewn y ffylwm gyda dros filiwn o rywogaethau.

Mae'r nodweddion canlynol yn gyffredin i arthropodau:
- ✓ corff wedi ei rannu'n segmentau
- ✓ corff wedi ei rannu ymhellach yn ben, thoracs ac abdomen
- ✓ ymennydd wedi ei ddatblygu'n dda
- ✓ sgerbwd allanol caled wedi ei wneud o gitin
- ✓ coesau cymalog mewn pâr
- ✓ system cylchrediad gwaed agored
- ✓ ceudod sy'n amgylchynu organau'r corff.

Dau ddatblygiad esblygiadol pwysig yw:
- **coesau cymalog** wedi eu haddasu i gyflawni amrywiaeth o swyddogaethau, gan gynnwys cerdded, nofio, neidio, bwyta, atgenhedlu awyru tagellau, os yn bresennol.
- **sgerbwd allanol** – mae haen allanol o gelloedd y corff yn secretu cwtigl trwchus, sy'n cynnwys citin yn bennaf. Mae hwn yn cyflawni sawl swyddogaeth:
- ✓ amddiffyn yr organau mewnol
- ✓ amddiffyn oddi wrth ysglyfaethwyr
- ✓ darparu pwynt cyswllt ar gyfer y cyhyrau
- ✓ cynhaliaeth – mewn anifeiliaid bychan mae adeiledd tiwbaidd gwag o amgylch y corff yn rhoi mwy o gynhaliaeth na rhoden silindrog solid oddi mewn iddo (sgerbwd mewnol fel sydd gan fertebratau) wedi ei wneud o'r un faint o ddeunydd.
- ✓ yn y rhan fwyaf o arthropodau daearol mae'r sgerbwd allanol wedi ei orchuddio â haen o gwyr er mwyn colli llai o ddŵr.

Yr un prif anfantais sydd gan sgerbwd allanol yw ei fod o faint sefydlog ac nad yw'n tyfu gyda'r anifail. Mae hyn yn wahanol i sgerbwd fertebrat mewnol sy'n cynyddu yn ei faint wrth i'r corff dyfu. Er mwyn tyfu mae'n rhaid i'r arthropod ddiosg ei sgerbwd allanol o bryd i'w gilydd (ecdysis). Mae hyn yn gadael yr anifail yn arbennig o agored i niwed wrth i'r sgerbwd allanol newydd galedu.

Mae pob arthropod yn rhannu'r un nodweddion sylfaenol a restrir uchod ond maent yn cael eu hisrannu'n bedwar dosbarth yn ôl y gwahaniaethau rhwng yr anifeiliaid sydd ym mhob dosbarth. Mae'r prif wahaniaeth yn ymwneud â nifer y coesau sydd gan yr anifail:

- Nadroedd miltroed a nadroedd cantroed – mae ganddynt sawl pâr o goesau, un neu ddau ym mhob segment
(mae gan nadroedd cantroed un pâr o goesau ym mhob segment a nadroedd miltroed ddau bâr o goesau ym mhob segment).
- Cramenogion – mae ganddynt rhwng 10 a 20 pâr o goesau.
- Corynnod – mae ganddynt bedwar pâr o goesau.
- Pryfed – mae ganddynt dri phâr o goesau.

Y dosbarth pryfed

Mae'n ffaith anhygoel fod 75% o bob anifail yn bryfed! Dyma'r grŵp mwyaf llwyddiannus, o lawer ymysg anifeiliaid y Ddaear. Maent yn fwy llwyddiannus na bodau dynol mewn llawer i ffyrdd.
Mae pryfed ar gael yn y rhan fwyaf o gynefinoedd ac maent hefyd yn gallu hedfan.
Mae pryfed yn perthyn i'r ffylwm arthropod ond maent yn cael eu hisrannu'n bryfed gan fod ganddynt y nodweddion penodol canlynol nad ydynt ar gael mewn arthropodau eraill:

- ✓ Mae ganddynt dri phâr o goesau, un pâr ar gyfer pob un o segmentau'r thoracs.
- ✓ Ar eu pen mae ganddynt bâr o deimlyddion a llygaid cyfansawdd.
- ✓ Cyfnewidir nwyon drwy'r tagellau mewn pryfed dyfrol a thrwy'r traceau ym mhryfed daearol.
- ✓ Mae sawl rhywogaeth o bryfed wedi esblygu adenydd, a dyma'r infertebratau sy'n gallu hedfan. Maent yn beiriannau hedfan pwerus ac mae'r gallu yma i hedfan wedi chwarae rhan bwysig yn eu llwyddiant.

Mae bodolaeth dau bâr o adenydd a chwe choes yn yr oedolyn yn nodwedd ddiagnostig mewn pryfed. Wrth i rai grwpiau o bryfed esblygu mae'n bosibl bod rhai o'r nodweddion hyn wedi cael eu colli yn eilaidd. Mae hynny wedi digwydd yn esblygiad chwain a llau.

Fertebratau

Mae 60,000 rhywogaeth o'r Cordatau wedi cael eu henwi. Yn eu plith mae llyffantod, nadroedd, eryrod a bodau dynol.
Mae gan fertebratau:
- ✓ asgwrn cefn.
- ✓ ymennydd datblygedig wedi ei gau mewn creuan (craniwm).

Mae'r fertebratau yn cael eu hisrannu'n bum dosbarth:
- ✓ pysgod – ffurfiau dyfrol sydd â chen, esgyll a thagellau.
- ✓ amffibiaid - dyma oedd y fertebratau cyntaf ar y tir, maent yn byw yn rhannol ar y tir ac yn rhannol yn y dŵr. Mae ganddynt groen meddal, llaith. Mae'r wyau'n cael eu ffrwythloni'n allanol mewn dŵr lle maent hefyd yn datblygu. Mae eu hepil (larfau) yn ddyfrol ac mae ganddynt dagellau, mae'r oedolion gan amlaf yn ddaearol ac mae ganddynt ysgyfaint syml.
- ✓ ymlusgiaid – mae'r rhain yn ddaearol yn bennaf ac mae ganddynt groen sych gyda chen. Mae ganddynt ysgyfaint. Mae'r wyau yn cael eu ffrwythloni'n fewnol, yn cael eu gorchuddio gyda phlisgyn ac yn cael eu dodwy ar y tir.
- ✓ adar – maent yn debyg i ymlusgiaid mewn sawl ffordd. Mae'r gwahaniaethau yn ymwneud yn bennaf â'r gallu i hedfan a datblygiad plu, gyda'r coesau blaen wedi datblygu i fod yn adenydd. Mae ganddynt ysgyfaint ac mae gan yr wyau blisgyn caled.
- ✓ mamolion – croen gyda blew. Mae mamolion ifanc yn cael eu geni'n fyw ac yn cael eu bwydo ar laeth. Mae ganddynt ysgyfaint. Maent yn cael eu hisrannu'n ymhellach yn ddau grŵp:
  - bolgodog e.e. cangarŵ – bydd eu hepil yn cael eu geni mewn cyflwr anaeddfed iawn ac yn datblygu yng nghod y fenyw.
  - brych – mae'r epil yn datblygu'n sylweddol yng nghroth y fam, ac yn derbyn maeth drwy'r brych cyn iddynt gael eu geni.

Tystiolaeth o linach gyffredin

I grynhoi, tacsonomeg yw astudio grwpiau neu ddosbarth organebau. Mae'n ymwneud â:
- ✓ darganfod a disgrifio amrywiaeth fiolegol
- ✓ ymchwilio i'r gydberthynas esblygiadol rhwng organebau
- ✓ dosbarthu'r organebau hyn er mwyn adlewyrchu'r berthynas rhyngddynt.

Mae damcaniaeth esblygiad yn awgrymu bod grwpiau o organebau sydd wedi eu gwahanu'n hollol oddi wrth ei gilydd yn rhannu llinach gyffredin.
Gan hynny gellid disgwyl eu bod yn rhannu rhai nodweddion cyffredin yn adeileddol. Y tebycaf yr ydynt i'w gilydd yr agosaf y maent yn perthyn o safbwynt esblygiad. Tybir bod grwpiau sydd ag ychydig yn gyffredin wedi canghennu oddi wrth hynafiaid cyffredin yn llawer cynharach, o ran hanes daearegol, na grwpiau sydd â llawer o nodweddion cyffredin.

Aelod pentadactyl

I benderfynu pa mor agos i'w gilydd y mae dwy organeb yn perthyn mae'n rhaid i fiolegydd chwilio am adeiladwaith tebyg, er y gallent fod â swyddogaethau cwbl wahanol. Gallai hynny awgrymu tarddiad cyffredin. Dywedir bod strwythurau o'r fath yn **homologaidd**. Enghraifft dda o hyn yw **aelod pentadactyl** fertebratau.

Mae gan aelod pentadactyl bum digid (neu fys). Gellir ei weld yn y pedwar dosbarth o fertebratau daearol, sef amffibiaid, ymlusgiaid, adar a mamolion. Mae adeiledd yr aelod yr un fath yn sylfaenol ym mhob dosbarth. Ond mae aelodau'r gwahanol fertebratau wedi addasu ar gyfer gwahanol swyddogaethau, megis gafael, cerdded, nofio a hedfan, mewn detholiad o fertebratau. Enghreifftiau o addasiadau i'r aelod pentadactyl ar gyfer gwahanol swyddogaethau yw'r fraich ddynol, adain ystlum, asgell morfil, adain aderyn a choes ceffyl.

Trwy ddefnyddio gwybodaeth o'r fath mae'n bosibl llunio cart esblygol lle mae gan gynhyrchion terfynol esblygiad rai nodweddion adeileddol cyffredin rhyngddynt â'i gilydd a rhyngddynt â'r llinach hynafiadol y maent wedi deillio ohoni. Y tebycaf yw dwy organeb i'w gilydd y mwyaf diweddar y tybir eu bod wedi dargyfeirio.

Ond fe all fod perygl i dybio fod dau anifail yn perthyn i'w gilydd dim ond am eu bod yn edrych yn debyg. Ystyriwch siarc, llamhidydd a phengwin. Mae un yn bysgodyn, un yn aderyn a'r llall yn famolyn. Wrth astudio sgerbwd yr aelodau blaen mae'n bosibl dod i'r casgliad bod gan y dolffin a'r pengwin aelodau pentadactyl wedi'u haddasu, ond nad oes gan y pysgodyn hynny. Mae'r siarc a'r dolffin yn anifeiliaid sydd ag aelodau blaen tebyg i'w gilydd gan eu bod yn byw mewn amgylcheddau tebyg a'u bod wedi ymaddasu ar gyfer yr amgylchedd hwnnw, nid oherwydd bod ganddynt hynafiad cyffredin. Hynny yw, mae'r strwythurau, yr aelodau, yn perfformio'r un swyddogaeth. Disgrifir strwythurau o'r fath fel rhai **cydweddol**. Enghraifft debyg yw adenydd adar a phryfed.

Technegau biocemegol

Yn ystod y blynyddoedd diwethaf mae dadansoddi protein a DNA wedi cael ei ddefnyddio i gadarnhau cydberthynas esblygol.
- ✓ Mae'r dilyniant o asidau amino wedi cael ei ddadansoddi mewn rhan o foleciwl ffibrinogen gwahanol famolion. Gwelwyd bod y dilyniant yn amrywio i wahanol raddau rhwng un rhywogaeth a'r llall ac mae hynny wedi galluogi gwyddonwyr i lunio cart esblygol bosibl ar gyfer mamolion.
- ✓ Ar brydiau fe all fod yn ddigonol defnyddio technegau megis cromatograffaeth ac electrofforesis, i wahanu a chymharu sylweddau cemegol penodol sy'n bresennol mewn gwahanol rywogaethau. Gall hynny ddangos nodweddion sy'n debyg neu'n wahanol sy'n dangos pa mor agos y mae'r rhywogaethau yn perthyn i'w gilydd.
- ✓ Mae'n bosibl cymharu'r dilyniant o fasau mewn gwahanol organebau. Y mwyaf tebyg yw'r dilyniannau, yr agosaf y tybir y mae'r organebau yn perthyn i'w gilydd o safbwynt esblygiad. Gelwir y dechneg hon yn groesrywedd DNA.

Trwy gymharu DNA o amrywiaeth o rywogaethau byw gellir cael awgrym meintiol o ba mor agos y mae'r genynnau yn perthyn i'w gilydd. I ddarganfod pa mor agos y mae dwy rywogaeth o brimatiaid yn perthyn i'w gilydd, e.e. bodau dynol a tsimpansïaid, echdynnir haenau DNA o'r ddwy rywogaeth, eu gwahanu a'u torri'n ddarnau. Wedyn mae'r darnau o'r ddwy rywogaeth yn cael eu cymysgu a'u dadansoddi. Mae'r dechneg yn rhoi canlyniadau sy'n dangos bod 97.6% o DNA tsimpansïaid a bodau dynol yn gyffredin, tra bo 91.1% o DNA bodau dynol a mwncïod rhesws yn gyffredin. Mae astudiaethau diweddar sy'n defnyddio'r dechneg hon wedi dangos hefyd bod perthynas agos rhwng y hipopotamws a'r morfil.

2.2 Addasiadau ar gyfer cyfnewid nwyon

Mae pob organeb byw yn cyfnewid nwyon gyda'r amgylchedd. Mae'n rhaid iddynt gael ocsigen er mwyn troi moleciwlau organig, megis glwcos, yn egni trwy'r broses resbiradaeth. Yn eu tro, mae'n rhaid cael gwared â nwyon gwastraff. Mae organebau yn byw mewn gwahanol amgylcheddau; rhai mewn dŵr ac eraill ar dir. Mae amgylchedd dyfrol yn weddol sefydlog ond gall bywyd ar dir fod yn fwy eithafol, gan amrywio o atmosffer tenau copa mynydd, i wres tanbaid yr anialwch cras. Er mwyn goroesi mae organebau byw wedi addasu mewn gwahanol ffyrdd.

Goresgyn problemau sy'n gysylltiedig â chynyddu maint

Cyfnewid nwyon yw'r broses lle mae ocsigen yn cyrraedd celloedd a charbon deuocsid yn cael ei dynnu ohonynt. Ni ddylid cymysgu rhwng hynny â resbiradaeth.

Mae anifeiliaid a phlanhigion wedi esblygu arwynebau arbennig ar gyfer cyfnewid nwyon fel bod tryleadiad nwyon i mewn ac allan o gelloedd yn gallu digwydd yn gyflym ac yn effeithlon. Mae arwynebau ar gyfer cyfnewid nwyon megis tagellau pysgod, alfeoli mewn ysgyfaint mamolyn, y tracea mewn pryfed a'r celloedd mesoffyl sbwngaidd mewn dail planhigyn, i gyd yn arwynebau ardderchog ar gyfer cyfnewid nwyon.

Er mwyn cael tryleadiad ar y gyfradd uchaf bosibl mae'n rhaid i arwyneb resbiradol fod â'r nodweddion canlynol:

✓ bod ag **arwyneb digon mawr** mewn cymhariaeth â maint yr organeb er mwyn diwallu anghenion yr organeb
✓ bod yn **denau**, fel bod y llwybrau tryleadiad yn fyr
✓ bod yn **athraidd** er mwyn gadael i'r nwyon resbiradol basio drwodd
✓ bod yn **llaith** fel bod cyfrwng ar gael i'r nwyon hydoddi ynddo cyn tryleadiad
✓ cynnal graddiant crynodiad.

- Mewn organebau **ungellog syml** megis yr *Amoeba*, y gellbilen yw'r arwyneb cyfnewid nwyon. Mae'r organeb yn byw mewn dŵr ac mae tryleadiad nwyon yn digwydd dros holl arwyneb y corff cyfan. Mae gan gell unigol arwyneb mawr o gymharu â'i maint. Dywedir felly bod ei chymhareb arwyneb i gyfaint yn uchel. Mae effeithlonrwydd tryleadiad nwyon yn diwallu anghenion yr organeb. Mae'r bilen yn denau ac yn llaith, ac mae'r llwybrau tryleadiad yn fyr.

- Mae'n rhaid bod pendraw ar faint celloedd ac mae pwynt lle mae'r llwybr tryleadiad mor hir fel bod y broses o dryleadiad yn dod yn aneffeithlon. O safbwynt esblygiad, yr unig ffordd y gall organebau barhau i dyfu o ran maint oedd casglu'r celloedd gyda'i gilydd, hynny yw, dod yn **amlgellog**. Ond, y mwyaf yw'r organeb y lleiaf yw'r gymhareb arwyneb i gyfaint. Hefyd, mae'n rhaid cyfnewid deunyddiau rhwng gwahanol organau yn ogystal â rhwng organau a'r amgylchedd. Mae hynny'n golygu bod y ddarpariaeth ar gyfer nwyon, a ddarperir gan dryleadiad trwy arwyneb y gell, yn annigonol i ddiwallu anghenion yr organeb. Canlyniad hynny yw bod y broses o dryleadiad yn rhy araf.

- Mewn **anifeiliaid amlgellog syml**, megis mwydod, nid oes angen llawer o ocsigen gan eu bod yn symud yn araf a bod eu cyfradd fetabolaidd yn isel iawn. Mae ocsigen a charbon deuocsid yn tryledu ar draws arwyneb y croen ac nid oes ganddynt organau arbennig ar gyfer cyfnewid nwyon.
✓ Mae **llyngyr lledog** yn anifeiliaid dyfrol sydd wedi esblygu siâp gwastad. Mae hyn yn cynyddu'r gymhareb arwyneb i gyfaint yn sylweddol ac yn sicrhau nad oes unrhyw ran o'r corff yn bell o'r arwyneb, h.y. mae llwybrau tryleadiad yn fyr.
✓ Mae **mwydod** yn organebau daearol sydd wedi datblygu siâp tiwbaidd ac maent wedi eu cyfyngu i amgylchedd llaith y pridd. Mae ei siâp hir estynedig yn golygu bod ganddo gymhareb arwyneb i gyfaint uchel, o gymharu ag organeb fwy cywasgedig o'r un cyfaint. Er nad oes rhaid iddo gael arwyneb arbennig ar gyfer cyfnewid nwyon, mae'n rhaid iddo gadw ei groen yn llaith trwy secretu mwcws ar yr arwyneb.

Ond, unwaith bod yr ocsigen i mewn yn y corff mae'n rhaid ei gludo dros bellter i'r celloedd mewnol niferus. Mae gan y mwydyn system waed caeedig, gyda'r gwaed yn cael ei gludo mewn pibellau. Mae'r gwaed hefyd yn cynnwys pigment resbiradol ar gyfer cludo ocsigen.

Mae ocsigen yn tryledu i'r capilarïau gwaed o dan arwyneb y croen ac yn cael ei gludo mewn pibellau i'r celloedd, gyda charbon deuocsid yn cael ei gludo i'r cyfeiriad dirgroes. Yn y ffordd hon y mae'r system waed yn cynnal graddiant tryediad yn yr arwyneb resbiradol.

- Mae gan **anifeiliaid amlgellog sy'n fwy o faint a mwy datblygedig,** megis pryfed, pysgod, ymlusgiaid a mamolion, gyfradd fetabolaidd uchel. Mae hynny'n golygu bod rhaid iddynt gael mwy o egni a bod angen llawer o ocsigen arnynt. Hefyd, po fwyaf yw'r organeb, y lleiaf yw'r gymhareb arwyneb i gyfaint. Gyda chynnydd mewn maint ac arbenigedd, mae meinweoedd ac organau yn dod yn fwy dibynnol ar ei gilydd. Er mwyn cyfnewid nwyon yn fwy effeithlon mae'r organebau hyn wedi datblygu **arwyneb cyfnewid arbenigol** er mwyn gwrthbwyso'r galw am ocsigen ychwanegol.

✓ Mae gan **bryfed** daearol diwbiau o elwir yn draceau, sy'n llawn o aer.
✓ Mewn pryfed dyfrol a **physgod** gwelir bod yr arwynebau cyfnewid resbiradol i gael ar ffurf **tagellau**.
✓ Mae grwpiau o anifeiliaid daearol megis **adar, ymlusgiaid a mamolion** wedi datblygu **ysgyfaint**.

Mae'n rhaid i bob un o'r gwahanol fecanweithiau hyn gael dull o **awyru** fel bod yr arwynebau resbiradol yn cael cyflenwad ffres o ocsigen er mwyn cynnal y graddiant tryediad. Felly, swyddogaeth y mecanwaith awyru yw symud y cyfrwng resbiradu, sef aer neu ddŵr, dros yr arwyneb resbiradol.

Y mae'r gwahanol grwpiau hyn o anifeiliaid hefyd wedi datblygu:
✓ **system gludo fewnol** - a ddarperir gan system cylchrediad gwaed er mwyn symud nwyon rhwng y celloedd sy'n resbiradu a'r arwyneb resbiradol.
✓ **pigment resbiradol** yn y gwaed – er mwyn cynyddu ei allu i gludo ocsigen.

Cyfnewid nwyon yn y pysgodyn

Mae gan organebau dyfrol broblem o ran cyfnewid nwyon gan fod dŵr yn cynnwys llawer llai o ocsigen nag y mae aer yn ei gynnwys ac oherwydd bod cyfradd tryediad mewn dŵr yn arafach. Hefyd mae dŵr yn gyfrwng mwy dwys nag aer ac nid yw'n llifo mor rhwydd. Gan fod pysgod yn actif iawn mae'n rhaid iddynt gael cyflenwad da o ocsigen. Mewn pysgod mae cyfnewid nwyon yn digwydd ar draws arwyneb arbennig, y **dagell** a chedwir llif unffordd o ddŵr i lifo gan fecanwaith arbennig ar gyfer pwmpio. Mae dwysedd y dŵr yn atal y tagellau rhag cwympo a gorwedd un ar ben y llall, a fyddai'n lleihau'r arwynebedd arwyneb. Mae tagellau wedi cael eu gwneud o blygion niferus, gan ddarparu arwynebedd arwyneb mawr y gall dŵr lifo drosto, gan gyfnewid nwyon.

Mae pysgod yn cael eu rhannu yn ddau brif grŵp yn ôl y deunydd sy'n ffurfio eu sgerbwd.
- Mae gan **bysgod cartilagaidd** e.e. siarcod, sgerbwd sydd wedi ei wneud o gartilag yn gyfan gwbl. Mae bron bob un yn byw yn y môr. Yn union du ôl i'r pen ar y ddwy ochr mae pum hollt tagell sy'n agor i agen y dagell (*gill slit*). Mae dŵr yn mynd i mewn drwy'r geg ac yn cael ei orfodi drwy agennau'r tagellau pan fydd llawr y geg yn cael ei godi. Bydd gwaed yn teithio drwy gapilarïau'r dagell i'r un cyfeiriad â dŵr y môr. Mewn **llif cyfochrog** o'r fath mae'r cyfnewid nwyon yn gymharol aneffeithlon.
- Mae gan **bysgod esgyrnog** sgerbwd mewnol wedi ei wneud o esgyrn ac mae'r tagellau wedi eu gorchuddio â fflap a elwir yn opercwlwm. Ceir pysgod esgyrnog mewn dŵr croyw a dŵr y môr a hwy yw'r mwyaf niferus o lawer o fertebratau dyfrol. Mae oddeutu saith gwaith mwy o rywogaethau o bysgod esgyrnog nag sydd o rywogaethau cartilagaidd. Mae trefniant o **lif gwrth gerrynt** ar gyfer cyfnewid nwyon lle mae gwaed yng nghapilarïau'r dagell yn llifo i gyfeiriad gwahanol i'r dŵr sy'n llifo dros arwyneb y dagell (gweler y dudalen nesaf).

Mewn pysgod esgyrnog mae pedwar pâr o dagellau yn y ffaryncs (gwddf) ac mae pob tagell yn cael ei chynnal gan fwa tagell. Ar hyd pob bwa tagell mae llawer o blatiau tenau a elwir yn lamelâu tagell ac ar y rhain y mae'r arwynebau cyfnewid nwyon, sef y platiau tagell. Tu allan i'r dŵr mae'r tagellau yn cwympo gan fod y lamelâu tagell yn gorwedd un ar ben y llall ac yn glynu gyda'i gilydd. Ond yn y dŵr maent yn cael eu cynnal ac yn darparu arwynebedd arwyneb helaeth. Mae'r platiau tagell yn cynnwys capilarïau gwaed ac mae'r ocsigen yn pasio drwy'r platiau tagell i'r capilarïau a charbon deuocsid yn pasio allan i'r dŵr.

❑ **Tasg** 1. Lluniwch ddiagram toriad llorweddol drwy'r ffaryncs a'r tagellau
2. Lluniwch ddiagram wedi ei labelu o adeiledd manwl y tagellau mewn pysgodyn <u>esgyrnog</u>.

I grynhoi: Mae tagellau yn darparu
- arwyneb arbenigol yn hytrach na defnyddio holl arwyneb y corff
- arwyneb mawr sy'n cael ei ymestyn ymhellach gan ffilamentau tagell
- rhwydwaith helaeth o gapilarïau gwaed sy'n caniatáu tryleidiad effeithlon a haemoglobin ar gyfer cludi ocsigen.

Er mwyn cynyddu effeithlonrwydd mae'n rhaid i ddŵr gael ei yrru dros y ffilamentau tagell gan wahaniaethau yn y gwasgedd fel bod llif parhaus, anghyfeiriadol o ddŵr yn cael ei gynnal. Cynhelir pwysedd is yn y ceudod opercwlwm nag yn y ffaryncs bochaidd. Mae'r opercwlwm yn gweithredu fel falf, sy'n gadael dŵr allan, ac fel pwmp sy'n tynnu dŵr heibio'r ffilamentau tagell. Mae'r geg hefyd yn gweithredu fel pwmp.

Mae'r **mecanwaith awyru** sy'n gorfodi dŵr dros ffilamentau tagell yn gweithredu fel a ganlyn:-

ceg	agor
opercwlwm	cau
llawr y ceudod bochaidd	gostwng
maint	cynyddu
gwasgedd	lleihau

dŵr yn llifo i mewn

Llif gwrth gerrynt

Mae'r arwynebau cyfnewid nwyon wedi eu gosod yn y fath fodd fel bod dŵr sy'n pasio o'r ffaryncs i'r siambr opercwlwm, yn llifo rhwng y platiau tagell mewn cyfeiriad gwahanol i lif y gwaed. Mae hynny'n cynyddu effeithlonrwydd gan fod y graddiant tryleidiad rhwng y llifoedd cyfagos yn cael ei gynnal am hyd gyfan y ffilament tagell. Hynny yw, mae'r gwaed wastad yn cwrdd â dŵr sydd â lefel gymharol uwch o ocsigen. Mae'r system hon yn caniatáu i dagellau pysgodyn esgyrnog dynnu 80% o'r ocsigen allan o'r dŵr. Mae hynny dair gwaith yn uwch na'r gyfradd echdynnu ocsigen o aer mewn ysgyfaint dynol. Mae'r lefel uchel hon o echdynnu yn holl bwysig i bysgod gan fod oddeutu 25 gwaith llai o ocsigen mewn dŵr nag mewn aer.

Y ffordd y mae grwpiau fertebrat wedi addasu i gyfnewid nwyon ar dir

Mae fertebratau yn cynnwys y pum dosbarth, pysgod, amffibiaid, ymlusgiaid, adar a mamolion. Credir bod bywyd wedi esblygu mewn dŵr gydag anifeiliaid yn esblygu er mwyn cytrefu'r tir a rhai yn ymaddasu ar gyfer hedfan. Nid yw tagellau yn gweithio tu allan i ddŵr ac felly roedd angen i anifeiliaid esblygu ffurf arall o arwyneb cyfnewid nwyon, sef yr ysgyfaint. Mae adar a mamolion yn arbennig o actif ac wedi addasu ar gyfer cyfnewid gydag aer sy'n gyfrwng llai dwys na dŵr. Gan hynny mae ganddynt ysgyfaint mewnol er mwyn colli cyn lleied ag y bo modd o ddŵr a gwres. Byddwn yn delio'n fanwl gydag awyriad ac adeiledd yr ysgyfaint dynol maes o law.

Amffibiaid

Mae'r amffibiaid yn cynnwys llyffantod, brogaod a madfall y dŵr. Mae'n debyg mai dyma oedd y grŵp cyntaf o fertebratau i gytrefu'r tir. Mae llyffantod yn nodweddiadol o amffibiaid gan eu bod yn byw mewn cynefinoedd llaith a bod rhaid iddynt gael dŵr ar gyfer ffrwythloniad (mae'r ffrwythloniad yn allanol ac mae'r gametau yn nofio mewn dŵr - gweler adran 2.4). Mae'r larfau (penbyliaid) hefyd yn byw mewn dŵr ac mae ganddynt dagellau. Mae'r trawsnewidiad o fod yn larfa i fod yn oedolyn sy'n byw ar y tir yn golygu newidiadau mawr yn ffurf y corff. Gelwir hyn yn fetamorffosis. Mae'r oedolyn anactif yn defnyddio'r croen llaith fel arwyneb resbiradol ac mae hynny'n rhoi digon o ocsigen ar gyfer ei anghenion. Ond pan fydd yn actif, e.e. wrth baru, bydd y llyffant yn defnyddio ei ysgyfaint fel arwyneb resbiradol.

Ymlusgiaid

Mae ymlusgiaid yn cynnwys crocodeilod, madfall a nadroedd. Mae'r ychydig ymlusgiaid sydd ar ôl heddiw yn ddisgynyddion i grŵp o anifeiliaid a oedd yn llwyddiannus iawn ar un adeg, gan gynnwys dinosoriaid, a oedd yn tra-arglwyddiaethu ar y Ddaear tua 200 miliwn o flynyddoedd yn ôl. Y maent wedi eu haddasu'n llawer gwell nag amffibiaid ar gyfer byw ar y ddaear. Mae ymlusgiaid yn gallu symud ar bob un o'u pedwar aelod heb i'r bongorff ei hun gyffwrdd â'r ddaear. Mae parau o asennau yn ymestyn allan o'r asgwrn cefn gan roi cynhaliaeth i'r corff ac amddiffyn yr organau sydd yng ngheudod y corff. Mae'r asennau hefyd yn gysylltiedig ag awyru'r ysgyfaint. Mae gan yr ysgyfaint adeiledd mewnol mwy cymhleth nag sydd mewn amffibiaid, gyda mewn-dwf y meinweoedd yn cynyddu'r arwynebedd arwyneb ar gyfer cyfnewid nwyon.

Adar

Mae adeiledd mewnol ysgyfaint adar yn debyg i'r hyn sydd mewn mamolion. Ond mae'n rhaid cael llawer iawn o ocsigen er mwyn darparu'r egni ar gyfer hedfan. Mae awyru'r ysgyfaint yn llawer mwy effeithlon mewn adar nac mewn fertebratau eraill. Mae'n cael ei gynorthwyo gan system o godennau aer sydd wedi eu cysylltu â'r ysgyfaint. Mae'r codennau aer yn gweithredu fel meginau. Pan fydd yr aderyn yn anadlu i mewn, bydd unrhyw aer sydd ar ôl yn yr ysgyfaint o awyriad blaenorol, yn cael ei sugno i'r codennau. Bydd yr ysgyfaint yn cael ei lenwi gydag awyr iach, gan osgoi'r lle gwag sydd yn ysgyfaint fertebratau eraill, megis mamolion. Achosir awyriad yr ysgyfaint gan symudiad yr asennau, nid oes llengig fel sydd yn y corff dynol. Wrth hedfan bydd symudiad y cyhyrau hedfan yn awyru'r ysgyfaint. Mae'r cyfnewid nwyon yn effeithlon iawn ac nid oes bron ddim nwyon gweddilliol yn aros ar ôl ym mhibellau'r ysgyfaint.

Mae pryfed wedi esblygu mecanwaith gwahanol ar gyfer cyfnewid nwyon

Mae gan y rhan fwyaf o bryfed adenydd ac maent yn eithriadol o effeithiol yn yr awyr. Mae hedfan yn golygu gwario llawer o egni ac felly mae'n rhaid i bryfed gael cyflenwad da o ocsigen. Maent wedi esblygu system o gyfnewid nwyon sy'n wahanol i system anifeiliaid eraill y tir. Mae cyfnewid nwyon yn digwydd trwy barau o dyllau a elwir yn sbiraglau, sy'n rhedeg ar hyd ochr y corff. Mae'r sbiraglau'n arwain at system o diwbiau aer canghennog wedi eu leinio â chitin, a elwir yn tracea. Gall y sbiraglau agor a chau fel falfiau. Mae hynny'n caniatáu cyfnewid nwyon ac yn lleihau colli dŵr.

Mae pryfed sy'n gorffwys yn dibynnu ar drylediad i dderbyn ocsigen a chael gwared â charbon deuocsid. Yn ystod cyfnodau o weithgarwch, megis wrth hedfan, mae symudiadau'r abdomen yn awyru'r tracea. Gelwir pennau pellaf y canghennau traceol yn traceolau; yma mae nwyon yn cael eu cyfnewid sy'n golygu bod ocsigen yn pasio'n uniongyrchol i'r celloedd.

- **Tasg**   Lluniwch ddiagram syml i ddangos canghennau tracea.

Er mwyn goroesi ar dir mae'n rhaid i organebau daearol gadw dŵr. Ond ar yr un pryd mae'n rhaid i'r arwynebau cyfnewid nwyon fod yn llaith er mwyn gallu tryledu'n effeithlon. Gan hynny mae'n rhaid i'r organau ar gyfer cyfnewid nwyon fod y tu mewn i'r corff. Wrth i chi adolygu'r adran hon dylech ystyried beth yw manteision ysgyfaint mewnol o'i gymharu â thagell allanol o safbwynt addasu ar gyfer bywyd ar y tir.

System resbiradol dynol

Adeiledd y system resbiradol dynol

Mae'r ysgyfaint wedi eu hamgáu mewn adran aerglos, sef y **thoracs**, ac ar ei waelod mae llen o gyhyryn siâp cromen a elwir yn **llengig**. Mae aer yn cael ei dynnu i'r ysgyfaint trwy'r tracea. Mae'r ysgyfaint yn cynnwys rhwydwaith canghennog o diwbiau a elwir yn **bronciolynnau** sy'n canghennu allan o bâr o **fronci**.

❏ *Tasg* Lluniwch ddiagram wedi ei labelu o'r system resbiradol.
(dylid cynnwys y rhannau canlynol wedi eu labelu: epiglotis, tracea, bronci, bronciolynnau, alfeoli, pilen eisbilennol yr ysgyfaint, asennau, cyhyrau rhyngasennol, llengig.)

Cyfnewid nwyon yn yr alfeolws

Yr arwynebau ar gyfer cyfnewid nwyon yw'r alfeoli (codennau aer) sy'n darparu arwynebedd arwyneb helaeth iawn mewn cymhariaeth â maint y corff. Maent yn gweddu'n dda fel arwyneb cyfnewid nwyon oherwydd:
✓ Bod eu harwyneb yn llaith fel y gall nwyon hydoddi
✓ Bod y waliau'n denau gan hybu tryediad trwy ddarparu llwybr tryediad byr
✓ Mae pob alfeoli wedi ei orchuddio gan rwydwaith helaeth o gapilarïau er mwyn cynnal graddiant tryediad, gan fod gwaed bob amser yn cludo ocsigen i ffwrdd o'r alfeolws ac yn dod yn ôl wedi ei lwytho gyda charbon deuocsid.

❏ *Tasg* Lluniwch ddiagram wedi ei labelu o un alfeolws sengl

Tabl yn dangos % cyfansoddiad aer yn yr ysgyfaint.

Nwy	Aer mewnanadledig	Aer alfeolaidd	Aer allananadledig
Ocsigen	20.95	13.80	16.40
Carbon deuocsid	0.04	5.50	4.00
Nitrogen	79.01	80.70	79.60
Dŵr	newidiol	dirlawn	dirlawn

Mae canran yr ocsigen yn yr alfeolws yn is nac mewn aer a anadlir i mewn gan fod yr aer hwnnw yn cymysgu gyda'r aer sydd eisoes yn yr ysgyfaint ac sydd â chanran is o ocsigen.

Awyriad yr ysgyfaint

Mae mamolion yn awyru eu hysgyfaint trwy anadliad gwasgedd negyddol, sy'n gorfodi aer i lawr i'r ysgyfaint. Hynny yw, er mwyn i aer fynd i mewn i'r ysgyfaint mae'n rhaid i'r gwasgedd yn yr ysgyfaint fod yn is na gwasgedd atmosfferig.

	Mewnanadliad (anadlu i mewn)	Allanadliad (anadlu allan)
Cyhyryn rhyngasennol allanol	cyfangu	llaesu
asennau	i fyny ac allan	i lawr ac i mewn
llengig	Cyfangu a gwastatáu	llaesu
Cyfaint y thoracs	cynyddu	lleihau
Gwasgedd yn y thoracs	lleihau	cynyddu
Gwasgedd aer allanol (atmosfferig)	Yn uwch felly aer yn symud i mewn	Yn is felly aer yn symud allan

Mae pilenni eisbilennol yr ysgyfaint yn amgylchynu pob ysgyfaint ac yn leinio'r thoracs, a rhyngddynt mae ceudod yn cynnwys hylif eisbilennol. Wrth anadlu mae'r hylif hwn yn gweithredu fel iraid sy'n caniatáu symudiad di-ffrithiant yn erbyn mur mewnol y thoracs. Er mwyn atal yr alfeoli rhag cwympo wrth anadlu allan y mae cemegyn atal gludo a elwir yn arwynebydd (syrffactydd) yn gorchuddio eu harwyneb ac yn lleihau'r tyniant arwyneb.

Cyfnewid nwyon mewn planhigion

Fel y mae'n rhaid i anifeiliaid resbiradu drwy'r amser, felly hefyd mae'n rhaid i blanhigion! Ond mae celloedd planhigion sy'n cynnwys cloroplastau hefyd yn gallu gweithredu'r broses o ffotosynthesis. Yn ystod y dydd bydd planhigion yn ffotosyntheseiddio yn ogystal â resbiradu. Mae'r rhan fwyaf o'r carbon deuocsid y maent eu hangen ar gyfer ffotosynthesis yn tryledu i'r dail o'r amgylchedd. Ond, mae rhywfaint o'r carbon deuocsid yn cael ei ddarparu trwy resbiradu. Mae'r rhan fwyaf o'r ocsigen a gynhyrchir trwy ffotosynthesis yn tryledu allan o'r dail. Yn ystod y nos, resbiradu yn unig y mae'r dail ac y maent angen cyflenwad o ocsigen o'r amgylchedd. Er bod rhywfaint o ocsigen yn mynd i mewn i'r gwreiddyn trwy dryediad mae'r rhan fwyaf o gyfnewid nwyon yn digwydd yn y dail.

Y ddeilen fel organ cyfnewid nwyon

Mae adeiledd dail planhigion sy'n blodeuo yn gysylltiedig â'u swyddogaeth o gyfnewid nwyon.
Er mwyn ei gwneud yn bosibl i gyfnewid nwyon yn effeithlon:
- mae llafn y ddeilen yn denau ac yn wastad gydag arwynebedd arwyneb eang
- mae'r meinwe mesoffyl sbwngaidd yn caniatáu i nwyon gylchredeg
- mae meinweoedd y planhigyn wedi eu treiddio gyda gofodau o aer
- mae'r mandyllau stomataidd yn caniatáu cyfnewid nwyon.

❏ **Tasg** Lluniwch ddiagram T.A.(toriad ardraws) wedi ei labelu o ddeilen angiosberm.
(dylid cynnwys y labeli canlynol: cwtigl, epidermis, mesoffyl palisâd, mesoffyl sbwngaidd, sypyn fasgwlar, gwagle aer, stomata, celloedd gwarchod.)

Bydd nwyon yn tryledu drwy'r stomata ar hyd graddiant crynodiad. Unwaith y maent yn y ddeilen bydd y nwyon yn y siambrau aer is-stomataidd yn tryledu drwy'r gwagleoedd rhyng-gellol sydd rhwng y celloedd mesoffyl ac i mewn i'r celloedd. Bydd cyfeiriad y tryediad yn dibynnu ar amodau amgylcheddol ac ar anghenion y planhigyn. Yr hyn sy'n bwysig yw'r cyfnewid net o garbon deuocsid ac ocsigen mewn perthynas â resbiradu a ffotosynthesis.

Addasiadau'r ddeilen ar gyfer ffotosynthesis

Er mwyn sicrhau eu bod yn gallu amsugno goleuni yn effeithlon, mae'r ddeilen wedi addasu fel a ganlyn:
- Mae gan y dail arwynebedd arwyneb mawr er mwyn dal cymaint o heulwen â phosibl.
- Mae'r dail yn gallu troi fel eu bod ar ongl sy'n berpendicwlar i'r haul yn ystod y dydd fel bod yr arwynebedd mwyaf posibl yng ngolwg yr haul.
- Mae'r dail yn denau fel bod goleuni yn gallu treiddio haenau isaf y celloedd.
- Mae'r cwtigl a'r epidermis yn dryloyw fel bod goleuni'n gallu treiddio i'r mesoffyl.
- Mae'r celloedd palis yn hir ac wedi eu trefnu'n drwchus mewn haen, neu haenau.
- Mae'r celloedd palis wedi'u llenwi â chloroplastau a'u trefnu fel bod yr acsis hir yn berpendicwlar i'r arwyneb.
- Gall y cloroplastau droi a symud gyda'r celloedd mesoffyl. Mae hynny'n galluogi iddynt drefnu eu hunain fel eu bod yn y sefyllfa orau i amsugno goleuni'n effeithlon.
- Mae'r gwagleoedd aer rhyng-gellol yn y mesoffyl sbwngaidd yn caniatáu i garbon deuocsid dryledu i'r celloedd ac i ocsigen dryledu allan.

Stomata

Stomata yw'r mandyllau bychan a geir ar arwyneb isaf y ddeilen. O amgylch pob mandwll mae dwy gell warchod. Mae celloedd gwarchod yn anghyffredin oherwydd bod ganddynt gloroplastau a muriau sydd wedi eu tewychu'n anwastad, gyda'r mur mewnol yn drwchus a'r un allanol yn denau. Mae'r stomata yn caniatáu cyfnewid nwyon rhwng yr amgylchedd a meinweoedd mewnol y ddeilen. Ond mae dŵr hefyd yn anweddu o blanhigyn drwy'r stomata. Bydd planhigion yn gwywo os byddant yn colli gormod o ddŵr. Gan fod goleuni'n taro ar wyneb uchaf y ddeilen, mae cyfyngu stomata i'r arwyneb isaf yn sicrhau bod llai o ddŵr yn cael ei golli. Mae presenoldeb cwtigl cwyraidd ar yr arwyneb uchaf hefyd yn lleihau'n sylweddol y dŵr sy'n cael ei golli. Yn y rhan fwyaf o blanhigion mae'r stomata yn cau yn y nos.

- **Tasg**   Lluniwch ddiagram TA ag uwcholwg o stomata.

Mecanwaith agor a chau y stomata

- Mae stomata yn fandyllau yn yr epidermis, gyda dwy gell warchod o boptu bob un. Mae'r celloedd gwarchod yn wahanol i gelloedd epidermaidd eraill gan eu bod yn cynnwys cloroplastau. Mae mur mewnol pob cell warchod yn fwy trwchus na'r mur allanol.
- Gall celloedd gwarchod o amgylch y stomata newid eu siâp er mwyn agor a chau'r stomata gan helpu i reoli cyfnewid nwyon ac i reoli faint o ddŵr sy'n cael ei golli.
- Canlyniad anochel o'r angen i du mewn y ddeilen fod yn agored i'r amgylchedd er mwyn cyfnewid nwyon yw bod dŵr yn cael ei golli o'r dail trwy broses trydarthiad. Yn gyffredinol, mae stomata yn agored yn ystod y dydd ac wedi cau yn y nos. Mae hynny'n atal y planhigyn rhag colli dŵr yn ddiangen pan na fydd y goleuni â digon o danbeidrwydd golau i alluogi ffotosynthesis i ddigwydd.

Bydd celloedd gwarchod yn newid siâp oherwydd newidiadau mewn chwydd-dyndra.
Os bydd dŵr yn mynd i mewn i'r celloedd gwarchod maent yn mynd yn chwydd-dynn a'r mandyllau'n agor
Os bydd dŵr yn ymadael â'r celloedd gwarchod maent yn mynd yn llipa a'r mandwll yn cau

- **Tasg**   Lluniwch ddiagram wedi ei labelu o stomata wedi agor ac wedi cau.

Cynigiwyd nifer o ddamcaniaethau i egluro sut mae hyn yn digwydd. Dyma un ddamcaniaeth.

Yn ystod y dydd mae'r mecanwaith ar gyfer agor y stomata yn digwydd fel a ganlyn:

- mae pympiau ïon potasiwm (K^+) yng nghellbilenni y celloedd epidermaidd amgylchynol yn cludo ïonau K^+ yn weithredol i'r celloedd gwarchod
- mae startsh wedi ei storio yn cael ei droi'n malad
- mae potensial dŵr y celloedd gwarchod yn gostwng (yn dod yn fwy negyddol) a dŵr yn mynd i mewn trwy osmosis
- mae'r celloedd gwarchod yn mynd yn chwydd-dynn ac yn gwyro oddi wrth ei gilydd gan fod eu muriau allanol yn deneuach na'r muriau mewnol, felly mae'r mandwll yn lledu.

Bydd y broses yn digwydd i'r gwrthwyneb gyda'r nos a'r mandwll yn cau.

- **Tasg**   Disgrifiwch y mecanwaith ar gyfer cau'r stomata.

Seroffytau

Mae seroffytau yn blanhigion sydd wedi eu haddasu ar gyfer byw dan amodau lle mae dŵr yn brin iawn. Mae ganddynt adeiledd sydd wedi ei addasu er mwyn atal colli dŵr yn ormodol. Fe all seroffytau gau'r stomata yn ystod y dydd a'u hagor yn ystod y nos er mwyn cadw dŵr. Yn ystod cyfnodau o brinder dŵr (sychder) fe all stomata'r mesoffytau gau yn ystod y dydd hefyd.

2.3 Addasiadau ar gyfer cludo

Mae ocsigen yn mynd i'r gwaed wrth dryledu drwy'r arwynebau resbiradol, megis alfeoli'r ysgyfaint. Ond byddai symud ocsigen o amgylch y corff drwy drylediad yn unig yn broses araf iawn. Ni allai mwydyn anactif hyd yn oed ennill mwy na tua 10% o'r ocsigen y mae ei angen pe bae'n gorfod dibynnu ar drylediad i ddosbarthu'r nwy trwy ei gorff cyfan. Mae'n rhaid i bob organeb amlgellog bron gael dull cyflym o gludo nwyon trwy system gludo fewnol. Mae'n rhaid iddynt gael system gludo er mwyn cludo ocsigen, maetholion, carbon deuocsid a chynhyrchion gwastraff yn ôl ac ymlaen o'r arwynebau cyfnewid.

Mae gan famolion, megis bodau dynol, system gylchrediad sy'n cynnwys:
✓ gwaed sy'n cael ei gludo drwy'r system
✓ pibellau gwaed sy'n diwbiau ar gyfer cludo'r gwaed
✓ calon i bwmpio'r gwaed drwy'r pibellau gwaed.
✓ Yn nodweddiadol mae gwaed yn cynnwys pigment resbiradol (nad yw ar gael mewn pryfed) sy'n cynyddu maint yr ocsigen y gellir ei gludo.

System agored neu gaeedig

Mae gan bryfed system waed agored.

Mewn system waed agored mae'r gwaed yn cael ei bwmpio ar bwysedd cymharol isel o un prif galon hir ddorsal (top) siâp tiwb sy'n rhedeg drwy holl hyd y corff. Mae'r gwaed yn cael ei bwmpio allan o'r galon hon i waglynnau, a elwir yn gyfunol yn geudod gwaed (hemosel), o fewn ceudod y corff. Mae'r gwaed yn trochi'r meinweoedd yn uniongyrchol a deunyddiau yn cael eu cyfnewid. Nid oes llawer o reolaeth dros gyfeiriad y cylchrediad. Bydd y gwaed yn dychwelyd yn raddol i'r galon. Yno bydd falfiau a thonnau cyfangiad mur y cyhyrau yn symud y gwaed ymlaen i gyfeiriad y pen lle mae'r cylchrediad agored yn cychwyn eto. Nid oes pigment resbiradol mewn pryfed gan <u>nad</u> yw gwaed pryfyn yn cludo ocsigen. Bydd ocsigen yn cael ei gludo'n uniongyrchol i'r meinweoedd trwy'r traceau.

Mewn system cylchrediad caeedig bydd y gwaed yn cylchredeg mewn system barhaus o diwbiau, sef y pibellau gwaed. Bydd gwaed yn cael ei bwmpio gan galon gyhyrog ar bwysedd uchel sy'n achosi cyfradd llif cyflym. Nid yw organau mewn cysylltiad uniongyrchol â'r gwaed ond maent yn cael eu trochi gan hylif meinweol sy'n llifo allan o gapilarïau sydd â muriau tenau. Mae'r gwaed yn cynnwys pigment gwaed sy'n cludo ocsigen.

Mae'r mwydyn yn enghraifft o anifail sydd â system cylchrediad caeedig. Mae ganddo bibellau dorsal a fentrol sy'n rhedeg drwy holl hyd y corff ac mae'r rhain yn cael eu cysylltu gan bum 'ffug galon'. Bydd gwaed yn symud trwy'r pibellau trwy gael ei bwmpio gan y 'ffug galonnau' hyn.

Cylchrediad sengl a chylchrediad dwbl

Mae dau fath o system gylchrediad caeedig, gan ddibynnu a yw'r gwaed yn pasio drwy'r galon unwaith ynteu dwywaith bob tro y mae'n cylchredeg drwy'r corff.

- Cylchrediad sengl sydd gan bysgod. Mae'r galon yn pwmpio gwaed deocsigenedig i'r tagellau, bydd gwaed ocsigenedig wedyn yn cael ei gario i'r meinweoedd, ac oddi yno bydd gwaed deocsigenedig yn dychwelyd i'r galon. Bydd y gwaed yn mynd drwy'r galon unwaith yn ystod pob cylchrediad o'r corff.
- Mae gan famolion gylchrediad dwbl.
✓ Y cylchrediad ysgyfeiniol - mae ochr dde'r galon yn pwmpio gwaed deocsigenedig i'r ysgyfaint. Yna bydd gwaed ocsigenedig yn dychwelyd i ochr chwith y galon.
✓ Cylchrediad hollgorffol - mae ochr chwith y galon yn pwmpio'r gwaed ocsigenedig i'r meinweoedd. Wedyn bydd gwaed deocsigenedig yn dychwelyd i ochr dde'r galon. Yn ystod pob cylchrediad bydd y gwaed yn pasio drwy'r galon dwywaith, unwaith trwy'r ochr dde ac unwaith trwy'r ochr chwith.
  ❏ **Tasg** Lluniwch ddiagramau wedi eu labelu i ddangos cylchrediad y gwaed mewn pysgodyn ac mewn corff dynol.
  Nodwch enwau'r prif bibellau gwaed sy'n gysylltiedig â'r galon ddynol – fena cafa, rhydweli ysgyfeiniol, gwythïen ysgyfeiniol, aorta ddorsal.

Y system gylchrediad ddynol a phibellau gwaed cysylltiedig

Mae'r system gylchrediad ddynol yn cynnwys cylchrediad gaeedig ddwbl gyda chalon sydd â dwy atriwm a dau fentrigl. Mae'r system gludo yn ymgorffori **pwmp** (y galon) i gynnal gwasgedd uchel, **falfiau** i reoli'r llif a **phibellau** i ddosbarthu'r gwaed.

Mae tri prif fath o bibellau gwaed: rhydwelïau, gwythiennau a chapilarïau.

Mae **rhydwelïau** yn cludo gwaed oddi wrth y galon. Mae gan rydwelïau furiau trwchus, cyhyrog i wrthsefyll gwasgedd uchel y gwaed a dderbynnir o'r galon. Mae cyfangiad y cyhyrau rhydwelïol hefyd yn helpu i gynnal gwasgedd wrth i'r gwaed gael ei gludo ymhellach oddi wrth y galon.

Mae'r rhydwelïau yn canghennu'n bibellau llai a elwir yn rhydwelïynnau sy'n is-rannu ymhellach yn **gapilarïau** sydd â muriau tenau. Mae'r capilarïau yn ffurfio rhwydwaith enfawr sy'n treiddio holl feinweoedd ac organau'r corff. Bydd gwaed o'r capilarïau yn casglu mewn gwythienigau, sydd yn eu tro yn gwagio gwaed i **wythiennau**, sy'n ei ddychwelyd i'r galon.

❏ *Tasg*   Lluniwch ddiagram wedi ei labelu a chynllun cyffredinol o'r system gylchrediad gwaed yn y corff dynol.
(Enwch y prif bibellau gwaed sy'n gysylltiedig â'r galon yn unig.)

Adeiledd a swyddogaeth pibellau gwaed

Yr un adeiledd o dair haen sydd gan **rydwelïau a gwythiennau** ond mae cyfrannau y gwahanol haenau yn wahanol.

Mewn rhydwelïau a gwythiennau:

- yr **endotheliwm** yw'r haen fewnol, y mae'n un gell o drwch ac mae'n darparu leinin esmwyth i leihau ffrithiant ac i sicrhau ei fod yn amharu cyn lleied â phosibl ar lif y gwaed.
- mae'r haen ganol wedi ei wneud o **ffibrau elastig** a **chyhyryn llyfn**. Mae'r haen hon yn fwy trwchus yn y rhydwelïau nag yn y gwythiennau er mwyn dygymod â newidiadau yn llif a phwysedd y gwaed wrth i'r gwaed gael ei bwmpio o'r galon.
- mae'r haen allanol wedi cael ei gwneud o **ffibrau colagen** sy'n gallu gwrthsefyll gorestyniad.

Mae gan **wythiennau** ddiamedr mwy a muriau teneuach na rhydwelïau gan fod pwysedd a llif y gwaed yn llai.

Mae gan wythiennau **falfiau cilgant** (siâp hanner lleuad) ar eu hyd er mwyn sicrhau bod y gwaed yn llifo i un cyfeiriad yn unig (atal ôl-lifiad). Nid yw'r rhain ar gael mewn rhydwelïau, ac eithrio'r falfiau aortig.

Muriau tenau sydd gan y **capilarïau** wedi eu gwneud o haen o endotheliwm fel eu bod yn athraidd i ddŵr a sylweddau sydd wedi hydoddi, fel glwcos. Yn y capilarïau mae defnyddiau'n cael eu cyfnewid rhwng y gwaed a'r meinweoedd.

Diamedr bychan sydd gan y capilarïau ac mae ffrithiant gyda'r muriau yn arafu llif y gwaed. Er bod y diamedr yn fychan mae llawer o gapilarïau yn y gwely capilarïau ac mae hynny'n golygu bod cyfanswm croesdoriad yr ardal yn lleihau llif y gwaed ymhellach. Mae'r cyflymder isel hwn mewn pibellau sydd a muriau tenau iawn yn hybu eu gallu i gyfnewid deunyddiau gyda'r hylif meinweol sydd o'u hamgylch. (Gallech feddwl y dylai'r gwaed deithio'n gyflymach drwy'r capilarïau na thrwy'r rhydwelïau, gan fod diamedr y capilarïau yn llai. Ond cyfanswm croes toriad yr ardal sy'n cludo'r gwaed sy'n penderfynu ar gyfradd y llif.)

❏ *Tasg*   1. Lluniwch ddiagram wedi ei labelu o rydweli, gwythïen a chapilari.
                 2. Lluniwch dabl manwl yn cymharu rhydwelïau a gwythiennau.

Y galon

Mae'n rhaid cael pwmp i gylchredeg gwaed mewn system gylchrediad gwaed. Mae'r galon wedi ei gwneud o siambr casglu sydd â muriau cymharol denau a siambr pwmpio sydd â muriau trwchus. Mae'r ddwy siambr wedi eu rhannu'n ddwy, fel bod modd gwahanu'r gwaed ocsigenedig yn llwyr oddi wrth y gwaed deocsigenedig. Mae'r galon felly, i bob pwrpas, yn ddau bwmp ochr yn ochr.

Y galon

Mae'r galon a'i phedair siambr wedi ei lleoli yn y thoracs rhwng y ddau ysgyfaint. Mae wedi ei gwneud yn bennaf o gyhyryn **cardiaidd**, sy'n feinwe arbenigol a all gyfangu ac ymlacio (llaesu) yn rhythmig, ohono'i hun, trwy gydol oes yr unigolyn. Dywedir bod cyhyryn y galon yn 'myogenig'.

❑ *Tasg* Lluniwch ddiagram wedi ei labelu o groesdoriad fertigol calon mamolyn.

Y gylchred gardiaidd

Mae'r gylchred gardiaidd yn disgrifio'r gyfres o ddigwyddiadau sy'n gysylltiedig ag un curiad calon. Wrth i'r galon bwmpio ceir cyfangiadau (**systole**) ac ymlaciadau (**diastole**) bob yn ail.
Mae tri cham yn y gylchred gardiaidd:
- Cam 1 – Mae'r fentrigl chwith a'r dde yn ymlacio, mae'r falfiau teirlen a dwylen yn agor wrth i'r atria gyfangu ac mae gwaed yn llifo i'r fentriglau.
- Cam 2 – Mae'r atria yn ymlacio ac mae'r fentriglau de a chwith yn cyfangu gyda'i gilydd gan wasgu gwaed allan o'r galon i'r rhydweli ysgyfeiniol a'r aorta wrth i'r falfiau cilgant gael eu hagor. Mae'r falfiau teirlen a dwylen yn cau oherwydd y cynnydd mewn pwysedd yn y fentrigl. Mae'r rhydweli ysgyfeiniol yn cludo gwaed deocsigenedig i'r ysgyfaint ac mae'r aorta yn cludo gwaed ocsigenedig i wahanol rannau o'r corff.
- Cam 3 – Mae'r fentriglau'n ymlacio ac mae'r pwysedd yn y fentriglau yn disgyn. Mae gwaed dan bwysedd uchel yn y rhydweliau yn gwneud i'r falfiau cilgant gau, gan atal gwaed rhag mynd yn ôl i'r fentriglau. Bydd gwaed o'r fena cafa a'r gwythiennau ysgyfeiniol yn mynd i mewn i'r atria a bydd y gylchred yn ailgychwyn.

Dyma'r ffordd y mae gwaed yn llifo drwy ochr chwith y galon.
- Mae'r atriwm chwith yn ymlacio ac yn derbyn gwaed ocsigenedig o'r wythïen ysgyfeiniol.
- Pan fydd yn llawn bydd y pwysedd yn gorfodi'r falf dwylen, sydd rhwng yr atriwm a'r fentrigl, i agor.
- Bydd y fentrigl chwith yn ymlacio ac yn tynnu gwaed o'r atriwm chwith.
- Bydd yr atriwm chwith yn cyfangu gan wthio gweddill y gwaed i'r fentrigl de drwy'r falf.
- Bydd yr atriwm chwith wedi ymlacio a'r falf dwylen wedi ei chau, bydd y fentrigl chwith yn cyfangu.
- Mae'r muriau cyhyrog cryf yn gwasgu'n galed ac yn gwthio gwaed o'r galon trwy'r falfiau cilgant a thrwy'r rhydweliau ysgyfeiniol a'r aorta.

❑ **Tasg** Disgrifiwch lif y gwaed drwy ochr dde'r galon.

- Mae dwy ochr y galon yn gweithio gyda'i gilydd, h.y. mae'r ddau fentrigl yn cyfangu ar yr un pryd, a'r ddau atriwm yn cyfangu ar yr un pryd. Gelwir un cyfangiad ac ymlaciad llawn yn guriad calon.
- Ar ôl cyfangu, ac wedi gwagio'r holl waed o'r adran, mae'r fentrigl yn ymlacio i gael ei lenwi gyda gwaed unwaith eto.
- Mae mwy o gyhyrau yn y fentriglau nag yn yr atria felly maent yn cynhyrchu mwy o wasgedd i wthio'r gwaed ymhellach.
- Mae mur cyhyrog y fentrigl chwith yn fwy trwchus nag yn y fentrigl de gan fod yn rhaid iddo bwmpio'r gwaed yr holl ffordd o amgylch y corff, mae'r fentrigl de yn pwmpio'r gwaed i'r ysgyfaint yn unig, sy'n llai o ffordd.

Newidiadau gwasgedd yn y galon

- Mae'r gwasgedd uchaf yn digwydd yn yr aorta/rhydwelïau ac mae eu rhythm yn codi a disgyn mewn ymateb i gyfangiad fentriglaidd.
- Mae ffrithiant gyda muriau'r pibellau yn achosi'r gwasgedd i ostwng yn raddol. Mae gan rydwelïynnau arwyneb helaeth rhyngddynt i gyd a thyllfedd (bore) gymharol gul fel bod lleihad sylweddol yng ngwasgedd yr aorta. Y mae'r gwasgedd yn dibynnu a ydynt wedi ymagor neu gyfangu.
- Mae gan y gwelyau capilarïau helaeth arwyneb mawr mewn croestoriad. Mae'r gwelyau hyn yn creu mwy byth o ymwrthedd i lif y gwaed.
- Mae yna berthynas rhwng gwasgedd a chyflymder ac mae'r gwasgedd yn gostwng rhagor fyth oherwydd gollyngiad gwaed o'r capilarïau i'r meinweoedd.
- Nid oes rhythm yn y gwaed sy'n llifo'n ôl i'r galon ac mae'r gwasgedd yn y gwythiennau yn isel a gellir ei gynyddu gan effaith tylino'r cyhyrau.

❑ *Tasg*   1. Lluniwch ddiagramau wedi eu labelu yn dangos y gylchred gardiaidd.
2. Astudiwch graffiau yn dangos newidiadau mewn cyfaint a gwasgedd yn y gylchred gardiaidd.

Rheoli curiad y galon

Mae cyhyryn y galon yn **fyogenig h.y.** mae'r curiad yn cael ei ysgogi o fewn y cyhyryn ei hun ac nid oherwydd ysgogiad nerfol.

- Ym mur yr atriwm ar y dde mae ardal o ffibrau cardiaidd arbenigol a elwir yn **nod sinoatraidd** (SAN) sy'n gweithio fel **rheoliadur**.
- Mae ton o ysgogiad trydanol yn codi yn y pwynt yma ac yn ymledu dros y ddau atriwm yn gwneud iddynt gyfangu fwy neu lai ar yr un pryd.
- Atelir yr ysgogiad trydanol rhag ymledu i'r fentriglau gan haen denau o feinwe gysylltiol. Mae'r haen yn gweithredu fel ynysydd (mae'n bwysig nad yw cyhyrau'r fentriglau yn dechrau cyfangu nes bod cyhyrau'r atria wedi gorffen cyfangu).
- Mae'r ysgogiad yn cyrraedd ardal arbenigol arall o ffibrau cardiaidd, y **nod atrio-fentriglaidd** (AVN), sy'n gorwedd rhwng y ddau atriwm ac sy'n trosglwyddo'r cynhyrfiad i feinweoedd arbenigol yn y fentriglau.
- O'r AVN mae'r cynhyrfiad yn pasio i lawr y **Sypyn His** i'r apecs. Mae'r Sypyn yn canghennu yn **ffibrau Purkinje** ym muriau'r fentrigl sy'n cario'r don o gynhyrfiad i fyny drwy gyhyryn y fentrigl.
- Mae'r ysgogiadau yn gwneud i'r cyhyryn cardiaidd ym mhob fentrigl gyfangu ar yr un pryd o'r apecs i fyny.

Tasg   Lluniwch ddiagram wedi ei labelu o groestoriad fertigol drwy'r galon yn dangos lleoliad y nod sino- atraidd, y nod atrio-fentriglaidd a'r Sypyn His.

Gwaed a chludo deunyddiau

Mewn mamolion mae system gludo yn darparu cyswllt rhwng ardaloedd arbenigol ar gyfer cyfnewid nwyon a'r celloedd sydd angen ocsigen a maetholion. Gan fod yr holl gelloedd yn cael eu trochi mewn cyfrwng dyfrllyd, mae deunyddiau'n cael eu cludo yn ôl ac ymlaen o'r celloedd hyn mewn hydoddiant yn bennaf. Yr hylif lle mae'r deunyddiau'n cael eu hydoddi neu eu dal yw gwaed. Mae ocsigen yn cael ei gludo ar ffurf ocsihaemoglobin yng nghelloedd coch y gwaed. Er mwyn rhyddhau'r ocsigen gweithredir yr effaith Bohr lle mae'r pH is a achosir gan garbon deuocsid wedi ei hydoddi yn lleihau affinedd ocsigen â'r haemoglobin fel bod ocsigen yn cael ei ryddhau lle mae'r angen mwyaf.

Cyfansoddiad gwaed

Mae gwaed yn feinwe wedi ei wneud o **gelloedd** (45%) mewn **plasma** hylifol (55%).
- Mae **plasma** wedi ei wneud o ddŵr yn bennaf (90%), gyda moleciwlau hydawdd o fwyd, cynhyrchion gwastraff, hormonau, proteinau plasma, ionau mwynol a fitaminau wedi hydoddi ynddo.
- Mae dau fath o **gelloedd gwaed**:
✓ erythrocytau neu gelloedd coch y gwaed (corffilod coch)
✓ lewcocytau neu gelloedd gwyn y gwaed (corffilod gwyn)

Swyddogaethau gwaed

- Mae plasma – yn **cludo** carbon deuocsid, cynhyrchion bwyd wedi ei dreulio, hormonau, proteinau plasma, ffibrinogen, gwrthgyrff ac yn y blaen a hefyd yn dosbarthu gwres.
- Mae celloedd coch y gwaed wedi eu llenwi gyda'r pigment **haemoglobin**. O ran siâp maent yn ddeugeugrwm ac nid ydynt yn cynnwys cnewyllyn. Eu swyddogaeth yw **cludo ocsigen.**
- Celloedd gwyn y gwaed – mae dau grŵp ohonynt:
✓ granwlocytau, mae'r rhain yn **ffagocytig**, mae ganddynt gytoplasm gronynnog, cnewyllyn llabedog ac maent yn **amlyncu** bacteria.
✓ agranwlocytau, sy'n cynhyrchu **gwrthgyrff a gwrthdocsinau**, mae ganddynt gytoplasm clir a chnewyllyn sfferig.

Cludo ocsigen

Mae gwasgedd rhannol ocsigen (pO_2) yn fesur o grynodiad ocsigen. Y mwyaf yw crynodiad yr ocsigen sydd wedi hydoddi'r uchaf yw ei wasgedd rhannol.
✓ Gwasgedd atmosfferig normal = 100 kiloPascal.
✓ Gwasgedd rhannol ocsigen = 21 kiloPascal.
  (gan fod oddeutu 21% o'r atmosffer yn ocsigen).
Mae celloedd coch y gwaed yn llwytho (codi) ocsigen yn yr ysgyfaint lle mae'r gwasgedd rhannol yn uchel ac mae'r haemoglobin yn ddirlawn gydag ocsigen. Mae'r celloedd yn cludo'r ocsigen i'r meinweoedd resbiradu, e.e. i'r cyhyrau, ar ffurf ocsihaemoglobin. Mae'r gwasgedd rhannol yn isel yno (gan fod ocsigen yn cael ei ddefnyddio wrth resbiradu er mwyn creu egni). Yna mae ocsihaemoglobin yn dadlwytho ei ocsigen, h.y. y mae'n **daduno**.
Byddech yn disgwyl i graff dirlawn haemoglobin (sydd â gwasgedd rhannol cynyddol o ocsigen) ddangos llinell syth yn haneru'r ddwy echelin. Ond mewn gwirionedd mae samplau o haemoglobin sy'n agored i gynnydd yng ngwasgedd rhannol ocsigen yn dangos **cromlin ddaduniad ocsigen**.
❏ **Tasg** Tynnwch lun cromlin daduniad ocsigen ar gyfer oedolyn dynol.
Mae pigment resbiradol effeithlon yn codi ocsigen yn rhwydd ar arwyneb resbiradol ac yn ei ollwng wrth gyrraedd y meinweoedd. Mae gan bigmentau resbiradol affinedd uchel tuag at ocsigen pan fydd y crynodiad yn uchel ond mae hynny'n lleihau pan fydd y crynodiad yn isel. Mae nodweddion arbennig haemoglobin yn sicrhau ei fod, pan fo'r gwasgedd rhannol ocsigen yn uchel, megis yn yr ysgyfaint, yn cyfuno'n rhwydd gyda meintiau mawr o nwy, h.y. bydd yr haemoglobin bron yn hollol ddirlawn gydag ocsigen. Mae maint yr ocsigen sy'n cael ei gludo gan haemoglobin yn dibynnu nid yn unig ar wasgedd rhannol yr ocsigen ond hefyd ar wasgedd rhannol carbon deuocsid.

Pan fydd gwasgedd rhannol carbon deuocsid yn uwch bydd y gromlin daduniad ocsigen yn symud i'r dde. Gelwir y ffenomen hon yn **effaith Bohr**. Pan fydd ocsigen yn cyrraedd meinweoedd resbiradu, megis cyhyryn, bydd gwasgedd rhannol uchel o garbon deuocsid yno yn galluogi'r haemoglobin i ddadlwytho ei ocsigen yn fwy parod.

I grynhoi:
- Pan fydd y pigment resbiradol **haemoglobin** yn agored i gynnydd graddol mewn crynodiad ocsigen bydd yn amsugno ocsigen yn gyflym i ddechrau ond yn arafach wrth i'r crynodiad barhau i godi. Gelwir y gydberthynas hon yn **gromlin daduniad ocsigen**.
- Y mwyaf y mae cromlin ddaduniad haemoglobin yn symud i'r dde, y lleiaf parod fydd yr haemoglobin i godi ocsigen, a'r mwyaf parod fydd y gollyngiad ocsigen yn digwydd.
- Y mwyaf y mae'r gromlin daduniad haemoglobin yn symud tua'r chwith, y mwyaf parod fydd yr haemoglobin i godi ocsigen, ond y lleiaf parod fydd y pigment i'w ryddhau.
- Mae rhyddhau ocsigen o haemoglobin yn cael ei hwyluso gan bresenoldeb carbon deuocsid, pan fydd gwasgedd rhannol ocsigen yn uchel, megis yng nghapilarïau'r ysgyfaint, bydd ocsigen yn cyfuno gyda'r haemoglobin i ffurfio ocsihaemoglobin.
- Pan fydd gwasgedd rhannol ocsigen yn isel, megis yn y meinweoedd resbiradol, bydd yr ocsigen yn daduno oddi wrth yr haemoglobin.
- Pan fydd gwasgedd rhannol carbon deuocsid yn uchel, mae haemoglobin yn codi ocsigen yn llai effeithlon ac yn ei ryddhau yn fwy effeithlon.

Cromlin ddaduniad haemoglobin y ffoetws

Mae gwaed y ffoetws a'r fam yn llifo'n agos at ei gilydd yn y brych ond yn anaml y maent yn cymysgu. Er mwyn galluogi haemoglobin y ffoetws i amsugno ocsigen o haemoglobin y fam yn y brych mae gan y ffoetws haemoglobin sy'n wahanol (mewn dwy o'r pedair cadwyn polypeptid) i haemoglobin yr oedlyn. Mae'r gwahaniaeth adeileddol hwn yn gwneud i gromlin ddaduniad haemoglobin y ffoetws symud i'r chwith mewn cymhariaeth â'r oedolyn. Mae haemoglobin y ffoetws yn cyfuno gydag ocsigen yn rhwyddach nag y gwna haemoglobin y fam. Hynny yw, mae gan haemoglobin y ffoetws mwy o affinedd tuag at ocsigen.

❑ *Tasg*   Lluniwch gromlin o ddaduniad ocsigen ar gyfer haemoglobin y ffoetws.

Cludiant ocsigen mewn anifeiliaid eraill

Nid yw cyfansoddiad cemegol haemoglobin yr un fath ym mhob anifail. Mae rhai anifeiliaid wedi eu haddasu ar gyfer byw mewn cynefinoedd lle mae lefelau isel o ocsigen.
- Mae cyfradd fetabolaidd y lygwn yn isel ac mae'n byw yn y tywod ar lan y môr (gelir gweld castau'r lygwn pan mae'r llanw allan). Mae'r lygwn yn pwmpio dŵr y môr trwy'r twnnel lle mae'n byw, gan ei alluogi i fanteisio ar yr ychydig ocsigen hydoddedig sydd ar gael. Er mwyn gallu llwytho'r ocsigen yn haws mae ganddo haemoglobin sydd â chromlin daduniad ymhell i'r chwith o'i gymharu â chromlin ddaduniad haemoglobin corff dynol.
- Wrth i'r uchder gynyddu mae gostyngiad yn y gwasgedd atmosfferig. Mae hyn yn bwysig i anifeiliaid, megis y lama, gan fod gwasgedd rhannol ocsigen ar yr atmosffer yn is mewn llefydd uchel.
  I wneud iawn am hyn:
✓ Mae gan y lama haemoglobin sy'n fwy parod i lwytho ocsigen yn yr ysgyfaint. Mae gan haemoglobin o'r math yma gromlin daduniad sydd i'r chwith o haemoglobin arferol.
✓ Mewn mannau uchel mae nifer y celloedd coch yng ngwaed mamolion yn cynyddu.

Myoglobin

Mae myoglobin yn llawer mwy sefydlog na haemoglobin ac mae ei gromlin daduniad ymhell i'r chwith o haemoglobin. Mae gan fyoglobin ganran uwch o ddirlawnder ocsigen nag sydd gan haemoglobin beth bynnag yw gwasgedd rhannol ocsigen. Yn arferol, mae'r cyhyryn resbiradu yn cael ei ocsigen o haemoglobin. Ond os bydd gwasgedd rhannol ocsigen yn mynd yn isel iawn, e.e. wrth ymarfer corff, bydd yr ocsimyoglobin yn dadlwytho ei ocsigen. Mae myoglobin felly yn gweithredu fel storfa egni mewn cyhyrau.

Bydd rhywfaint o garbon deuocsid yn cael ei gludo yng nghelloedd coch y gwaed ond mae'r rhan fwyaf ohono yn cael ei droi'n ddeucarbonad yng nghelloedd coch y gwaed, yna'n cael ei hydoddi yn y plasma. Mae'r symudiad clorid yn cyfeirio at fewnlif o ionau clorid i gelloedd coch y gwaed er mwyn cadw niwtraliaeth drydanol.

Cludiad carbon deuocsid - y syfliad clorid

Mae haemoglobin yn gweithredu fel byffer sy'n helpu i gynnal pH y gwaed drwy dynnu ionau hydrogen o'r hydoddiant.

Mae carbon deuocsid yn cael ei gludo yng nghelloedd y gwaed a phlasma mewn 3 ffordd:
- 5% mewn hydoddiant yn y plasma.(Nid yw hyn yn ddigon i ddiwallu anghenion y rhan fwyaf o organebau.)
- 85% fel hydrogencarbonad
- 10% mewn cyfuniad gyda haemoglobin i ffurfio carbamino-haemoglobin.

Mae'r canlynol yn disgrifio cyfres o adweithiau a elwir yn **syfliad clorid**:
- ✓ Mae carbon deuocsid yn tryledu i gelloedd coch y gwaed ac yn cyfuno gyda dŵr i ffurfio **asid carbonig**.
- ✓ Mae asid carbonig yn daduno yn ïonau H^+ a HCO^{3-}, ac mae'r adwaith yn cael ei gatalyddu gan **anhydras carbonig**.
- ✓ Mae ïonau HCO^{3-} yn tryledu allan o gelloedd coch y gwaed i'r plasma lle maent yn cyfuno gydag ïonau Na^+ o ddaduniad sodiwm clorid i ffurfio sodiwm hydrogen carbonad.
- ✓ Mae ïonau H^+ yn darparu'r amodau lle gall **ocsihaemoglobin** ddaduno yn ocsigen a haemoglobin.
- ✓ Mae ïonau H^+ yn cael eu byffro gan eu cyfuniad gyda haemoglobin ac oherwydd bod **asid haemoglobinig** (HHb) yn cael ei ffurfio.
- ✓ Mae'r ocsigen yn tryledu allan o gelloedd coch y gwaed i'r meinweoedd.
- ✓ Er mwyn cydbwyso symudiad yr ïonau â gwefr negatif am allan, mae **ïonau clorid** yn tryledu i mewn.
- ✓ Gelwir hynny yn **syfliad clorid** a dyma sut y cynhelir **niwtraliaeth electrocemegol** celloedd coch y gwaed.

Tasg Gan ddefnyddio diagram neu siart llif rhowch grynodeb o'r prif ddigwyddiadau cemegol sy'n digwydd mewn cell coch y gwaed pan fydd yn cyrraedd y meinweoedd.

Hylif rhyng-gellol

Y **capilarïau** yw'r safle lle mae'r cyfnewid yn digwydd rhwng gwaed a chelloedd y corff. Maent wedi addasu'n dda er mwyn caniatáu i ddeunyddiau gael eu cyfnewid rhwng y gwaed a'r celloedd.
- ✓ mae ganddynt furiau tenau, athraidd
- ✓ maent yn darparu arwynebedd arwyneb eang ar gyfer cyfnewid deunyddiau
- ✓ mae gwaed yn llifo'n araf iawn drwy'r capilarïau fel bod digon o amser i gyfnewid deunyddiau.

❏ **Tasg** Lluniwch ddiagram wedi ei labelu i ddangos rhwydwaith capilarïau.

Mae gwaed yn cynnwys plasma hylifol sy'n cludo celloedd y gwaed, deunyddiau wedi eu hydoddi a moleciwlau mawr, a elwir yn broteinau plasma. Mae'r gwaed wedi ei gynnwys mewn system gaeedig ond bydd hylif o'r plasma yn dianc trwy furiau'r capilarïau. Gelwir yr hylif hwn yn **hylif meinweol** ac mae'n trochi'r celloedd, ac yn eu cyflenwi gyda glwcos, asidau amino, asidau brasterog, halwynau ac ocsigen. Mae'r hylif meinweol hefyd yn tynnu deunyddiau gwastraff o'r celloedd.

Hylif meinweol = plasma heb broteinau plasma.

- Y ffactorau sy'n gyfrifol am symudiadau hydoddion a dŵr i mewn ac allan o'r capilarïau yw pwysedd gwaed a thryllediad.
- Pan fydd gwaed yn cyrraedd pen rhedwelïol capilari y mae dan wasgedd oherwydd bod y galon yn pwmpio ac oherwydd gwrthwynebedd i lif gwaed yn y capilarïau. Mae'r **gwasgedd hydrostatig** hwn yn gorfodi'r hylif sydd yn y gwaed trwy furiau'r capilari i'r gwaglynnau sydd rhwng y celloedd.
- Gwrthwynebir y llif yma tuag allan gan y gostyngiad ym **mhotensial dŵr** y gwaed, sy'n cael ei greu gan bresenoldeb proteinau plasma.
- Mae gwasgedd hydrostatig y gwaed yn fwy na'r grymoedd osmotig felly mae llif net o ddŵr allan o'r gwaed. (Wrth i'r dŵr basio drwy fur y capilarïau mae'n cludo hydoddion gydag ef.)
- Ym mhen rhedwelïol y gwely capilari mae'r graddiant tryllediad ar gyfer hydoddion megis glwcos, ocsigen ac ïonau yn ffafrio symudiad o'r capilarïau i'r hylif meinweol. Y rheswm am hynny yw bod y sylweddau hyn yn cael eu defnyddio yn ystod metabolaeth celloedd.
- Ym mhen gwythiennol y gwely capilari mae'r pwysedd gwaed yn is ac mae dŵr yn pasio i'r capilarïau drwy osmosis. Mae presenoldeb y proteinau plasma yn lleihau potensial dŵr y gwaed ac mae hynny'n achosi mewnlifiad net o ddŵr.
- Yn y pen gwythiennol mae hylif meinweol yn codi CO_2 a sylweddau ysgarthiol eraill. Mae rhywfaint o'r hylif yma yn pasio nôl i'r capilarïau, ond mae rhywfaint yn draenio i'r system lymffatig ac yn dychwelyd yn y man i'r system wythiennol drwy'r ddwythell thorasig, sy'n gwagio i wythïen ger y galon.

(Byddwch yn astudio swyddogaethau eraill y system lymffatig yn U2 ac er gwybodaeth yn unig y nodir y canlynol.)
Lymff yw'r hylif meinweol sy'n draenio i gapilarïau lymffatig pengaead (*blind-ending*) ymhlith y meinweoedd. Mae'r lymff yn symud drwy bibellau oherwydd cyfangiad y cyhyrau y mae'r pibellau'n pasio drwyddynt. Mae chwarennau lymff a nodau lymff sy'n gysylltiedig â'r pibellau lymff yn chwarae rôl bwysig o ran ffurfio lymffocytau ac atal heintiad.

Cludiant mewn planhigion

Mae'r gwreiddiau yn amsugno dŵr o'r pridd ac mae'n rhaid i'r dŵr hwn gael ei gludo gryn bellter i'r dail lle mae'n cael ei ddefnyddio yn y broses o ffotosynthesis. Yn ei dro, mae'n rhaid i'r siwgr a gynhyrchir gael ei gludo i ble mae ei angen. Mae planhigion wedi esblygu dwy system wahanol o diwbiau, y sylem i gludo dŵr a'r ffloem i gludo siwgr.

Meinweoedd fasgwlar

Mae'r meinweoedd fasgwlar wedi cael eu gwneud o:
- feinwe **sylem**, sy'n cludo dŵr a halwynau mwynol o'r gwreiddiau i'r dail.
- feinwe **ffloem,** sy'n cludo cynhyrchion hydawdd ffotosynthesis (swcros ac asidau amino) o'r dail i rannau eraill o'r planhigyn.

Adeiledd y sylem

Mae sylem wedi ei ffurfio o bedwar gwahanol math o gelloedd:
- **llestrau** – y prif gelloedd dargludol
- **traceidiau-** sydd hefyd yn cludo dŵr ond sydd heb gael eu haddasu cystal â'r llestrau ar gyfer y swyddogaeth hon
- **ffibrau** – nid oes ganddynt swyddogaeth cludo dŵr ond maent yn rhoi cynhaliaeth
- **parencyma sylem** – mae hwn yn gweithredu fel meinwe pacio.

Mae'r llestrau a'r traceidiau yn gelloedd marw ac maent yn ffurfio systemau o diwbiau y gall dŵr deithio drwyddynt. Mae'r celloedd yn farw oherwydd bod **lignin** wedi cael ei ddyddodi ar gellfuriau cellwlos fel eu bod yn anathraidd i ddŵr a hydoddion. Mae'r celloedd yma hefyd yn rhoi cynhaliaeth a chryfder mecanyddol i'r planhigyn.

Dosbarthiad sylem

Mae dosbarthiad meinwe sylem yn wahanol yn y prif goesyn, y dail a'r gwreiddiau.
- Yn y **coesyn** mae'n digwydd fel rhan o'r sypynnau fasgwlar perifferol. Mae'r drefn honno'n rhoi cynhaliaeth hyblyg ond hefyd yn gallu gwrthsefyll y straen o blygu.
- Yn y **dail** mae'r trefniant o feinweoedd fasgwlar yn yr wythïen ganol a'r rhwydwaith o wythiennau hefyd yn rhoi nerth hyblyg ac yn gwrthsefyll straen rhwygo.
- Yn y **gwreiddiau**, mae'r trefniant canolog yn ddelfrydol ar gyfer gwrthsefyll straen fertigol (tynnu) ac felly'n helpu i angori'r planhigyn.

❑ *Tasg*
1. Lluniwch ddiagramau o doriad ardraws a thoriad hydredol o ffloem sylfaenol.
2. Lluniwch ddiagram wedi ei labelu o doriad ar draws prif goesyn deugotyledon.
3. Lluniwch ddiagram wedi eu labelu o wreiddyn sylfaenol deugotyledon.

Codi dŵr i'r gwreiddiau

Mae llawer iawn o ddŵr yn cael ei golli drwy stomata'r dail drwy'r broses drydarthiad ac mae'n rhaid cael dŵr o'r pridd yn ei le. Yr ardal sy'n codi'r mwyaf o ddŵr yw parth y gwreiddflewyn lle mae arwynebedd arwyneb y gwreiddyn yn cael ei gynyddu'n aruthrol oherwydd presenoldeb gwreiddflew.

Mae dŵr o'r pridd yn cynnwys hydoddiant gwan o halwynau mwynol felly mae ei botensial dŵr yn uchel. Mae gwagolyn y gell wreiddflew yn cynnwys hydoddiant cryf o sylweddau wedi eu hydoddi ac mae ganddo botensial dŵr isel. Mae dŵr yn symud i'r gell wreiddflew i lawr graddiant potensial dŵr o botensial dŵr uchel i botensial dŵr isel trwy osmosis. Mae dŵr yn gallu symud ar draws celloedd cortecs y gwreiddyn ar hyd tri llwybr:
- yr **apoplast** – trwy'r cellfur
- y **symplast** – trwy'r cytoplasm a'r plasmodesmata
- a'r **llwybr gwagolynnol** – o wagolyn i wagolyn.

Ond ystyrir mae'r ddau brif lwybr yw'r llwybrau symplast ac apoplast. Mae'n debygol bod y rhan fwyaf o'r dŵr yn dilyn y llwybr apoplast gan mai dyma'r cyflymaf o'r ddau.

Mae'r meinwe sylem ynghanol y gwreiddyn ac mae wedi ei amgylchynu gan haen sengl o gelloedd a elwir yn **endodermis**. Mae cellfuriau'r endodermis wedi eu trwytho gyda deunydd cwyraidd a elwir yn swberin. Mae hyn yn ffurfio band amlwg a elwir yn **stribed Casparaidd**. Mae'r swberin yn wrth-ddŵr ac mae'r stribed Casparaidd yn atal defnyddio'r llwybr apoplast. Yr unig ffordd y gall dŵr basio ar draws yr endodermis i'r sylem yw ar hyd y llwybr symplast. Mae peth tystiolaeth y gall halwynau wedyn fod yn cael eu secretu'n weithredol i'r meinwe fasgwlar o'r celloedd endodermaidd. Mae hyn yn gwneud y potensial dŵr yn y sylem yn fwy negyddol, fel bod dŵr yn cael ei dynnu i mewn o'r endodermis. Mae hynny'n hybu symudiad dŵr i mewn i'r sylem o'r cortecs. Mae'r graddiant potensial dŵr a gynhyrchir yn creu grym a elwir yn **wreiddwasgedd**.

❑ **Tasg**   Lluniwch ddiagram o gell endodermaidd yn dangos y stribed Casparaidd.

Mewnlifiad mwynau

Yn gyffredinol, mae'r mwynau yn cael eu dwyn i mewn gan y gwreiddflew trwy **gludiant actif** o'r hydoddiant pridd.

Unwaith eu bod wedi cael eu hamsugno gall yr ïonau mwynol symud ar hyd y llwybr apoplast gan gael eu cludo mewn hydoddiant wrth i'r dŵr gael ei dynnu i fyny'r planhigyn yn y llif trydarthiad. Pan fydd y mwynau'n cyrraedd yr endodermis mae'r stribed Casparaidd yn atal symudiad pellach ar hyd cellfuriau. Mae'r ïonau yn mynd i mewn i gytoplasm y gell ac yn tryledu oddi yno neu'n cael eu cludo'n weithredol i'r sylem. Er enghraifft, mae nitrogen yn arferol yn dod i mewn i'r planhigyn ar ffurf ïonau nitrad neu ïonau amoniwm sy'n tryledu ar hyd y graddiant crynodiad i mewn i'r llif apoplast ond maent yn mynd i mewn i'r symplast trwy gludiant actif yn erbyn y graddiant crynodiad ac yna'n llifo trwy'r plasmodesmata yn y llif cytoplasmig.

Yn yr endodermis, mae'n rhaid i'r ïonau gael eu codi'n weithredol er mwyn osgoi'r stribed Casparaidd sy'n caniatáu i'r planhigyn godi'r ïonau yn ddetholus yn y pwynt yma.

Symudiad dŵr o'r gwreiddyn i'r dail

- Mae dŵr yn teithio yn y sylem i fyny drwy'r coesyn i'r dail, lle mae'r rhan fwyaf ohono yn anweddu oddi ar arwyneb mewnol y dail ac yn gadael, ar ffurf anwedd dŵr, i'r atmosffer.
- Mae trydarthiad dŵr o'r dail yn tynnu dŵr ar draws y ddeilen o'r meinwe sylem ar hyd yr un tri llwybr ag sydd yn y gwreiddyn.
- Wrth i foleciwlau dŵr adael celloedd sylem yn y dail, maent yn tynnu moleciwlau dŵr eraill i fyny. Gelwir yr effaith hwn o dynnu yn **dyniant trydarthol** ac mae'n bosibl oherwydd y grymoedd **cydlynol** mawr sydd rhwng y moleciwlau dŵr a'r grymoedd **adlyniad** sy'n bodoli rhwng y moleciwlau dŵr a leinin hydroffilig y llestrau. Mae'r ddau rym yma yn cyfuno er mwyn cynnal y golofn o ddŵr yn y sylem.
- Gelwir y ddamcaniaeth ynglŷn â'r mecanwaith sy'n symud dŵr i fyny'r sylem yn ddamcaniaeth **cydlyniad-tyniant.**
- Mae grym **capilaredd** yn rym arall a all gyfrannu at godiad y dŵr yn y sylem. Mae dŵr yn codi i fyny tiwbiau cul trwy weithred capilari ond mae'n debygol bod y grym hwn yn fwy perthnasol mewn planhigion bychan nag mewn coed mawr.

❑ **Tasg**   Rhestrwch y grymoedd sy'n gysylltiedig â chludiant dŵr o'r gwreiddyn i'r ddeilen.

Trydarthiad

Problem fawr sy'n wynebu pob organeb daearol yw sut i osgoi sychiad. Mae planhigion tir gan amlaf yn colli anwedd dŵr i'r atmosffer yn barhaus. Yn wir, gall planhigyn golli 99% o'r dŵr y mae'n ei amsugno wrth iddo anweddu drwy'r dail. Gelwir anweddiad dŵr o du mewn i'r dail trwy'r stomata i'r atmosffer yn **drydarthiad** ac mae'n achosi'r **llif trydarthol.** Mae pob planhigyn yn gorfod cydbwyso codi dŵr a cholli dŵr. Os yw planhigyn yn colli mwy o ddŵr nag y mae'n ei amsugno yna mae'n gwywo. Os yw planhigyn yn colli gormod o ddŵr y mae'n cyrraedd pwynt lle na all adfer ei chwydd-dyndra ac mae'n marw.

Mae planhigion yn wynebu cyfyng-gyngor. Mae'n rhaid i'r stomata fod yn agored yn ystod y dydd er mwyn caniatáu cyfnewid nwyon rhwng meinweoedd y ddeilen a'r atmosffer. Ond mae bodolaeth mandyllau yn y dail yn golygu bod dŵr gwerthfawr yn cael ei golli o'r planhigyn. Mae rhan fwyaf o'r dŵr yn cael ei golli drwy'r stomata er bod oddeutu 5% o gyfanswm yr anwedd dŵr a gollir yn gallu digwydd trwy epidermis y ddeilen. Yn arferol mae'r golled hon yn cael ei lleihau oherwydd bodolaeth y cwtigl cwyraidd ar arwyneb y dail.

Gelwir cyfradd colli dŵr o blanhigion yn **gyfradd trydarthu** ac mae'n ddibynnol ar ffactorau allanol megis **tymheredd, lleithder** a **symudiad yr aer**. Gan hynny mae unrhyw ffactor sy'n cynyddu'r graddiant potensial dŵr rhwng yr anwedd dŵr yn y ddeilen a'r atmosffer o'i hamgylch yn cynyddu'r gyfradd trydarthu.

- **Tymheredd** – mae codiad yn y tymheredd yn darparu egni cinetig ychwanegol ar gyfer symud moleciwlau dŵr. Mae'r egni ychwanegol hwn yn cyflymu cyfradd anweddu dŵr o furiau'r celloedd mesoffyl, ac os yw'r stomata yn agored, yn cyflymu cyfradd tryleidiad yr anwedd dŵr i'r atmosffer amgylchol. Mae potensial dŵr yr atmosffer yn lleihau wrth i'r tymheredd godi ac mae'n gallu dal mwy o leithder.
- **Lleithder** – mae'r aer tu mewn i'r ddeilen yn ddirlawn gydag anwedd dŵr ond mae lleithder yr atmosffer o amgylch y ddeilen yn amrywio, gyda gwerthoedd dros 70% yn brin ym Mhrydain. Gan hynny mae'r graddiant potensial dŵr rhwng y ddeilen a'r atmosffer bob amser yn fawr a phan fydd y stomata yn agored bydd anwedd dŵr yn tryledu'n gyflym o'r ddeilen.
- **Symudiad aer** – mae trydarthiad yn yr aer llonydd yn arwain at gasglu haen o aer dirlawn ar arwyneb y dail. Mae hyn yn creu rhwystr sylweddol i dryledu anwedd dŵr trwy'r stomata ac felly yn lleihau cyfradd trydarthu. Mae symudiad yr aer oddi amgylch yn lleihau trwch yr haen o aer dirlawn ac yn achosi cynnydd yn y trydarthu.
- Mae **tanbeidrwydd golau** hefyd yn effeithio ar drydarthiad trwy reoli graddfa agoriad y stomata.

Mewn gwirionedd, nid yw'r **ffactorau** hyn yn gweithredu'n annibynnol ond yn hytrach yn **rhyngweithio** e.e. mae mwy o ddŵr yn cael ei golli ar ddiwrnod gwyntog, sych nag ar ddiwrnod llaith, llonydd. Y rheswm am hyn yw bod gan siambr is-stomataidd botensial dŵr uchel gan fod muriau'r celloedd mesoffyl sbwngaidd yn ddirlawn o ddŵr. Mae'r dŵr yn anweddu o'r muriau ac yn symud i lawr graddiant o botensial dŵr o'r planhigyn i'r atmosffer sydd â chanran isel o leithder cymharol; gan fod y gwynt wedi lleihau trwch yr haen o aer dirlawn ar arwyneb y ddeilen.

Mae'r gyfradd trydarthu yn cael ei mesur trwy ddefnyddio **potomedr.**
Mewn gwirionedd mae'n mesur graddfa amsugno dŵr ond os yw celloedd y planhigyn yn hollol chwydd-dynn mae'r gyfradd amsugno a'r gyfradd trydarthu yn union yr un fath.

❑ *Tasg* Lluniwch graffiau yn dangos sut mae ffactorau amgylcheddol yn effeithio ar y gyfradd trydarthu.

Mesoffytau, seroffytau a hydroffytau

Mae'n bosibl dosbarthu planhigion yn dri grŵp ar sail eu hadeiledd, mewn perthynas â'r prif gyflenwad dŵr. Hydroffytau (planhigion dŵr), seroffytau (planhigion sy'n byw mewn amgylchiadau lle mae dŵr yn brin) a mesoffytau (planhigion sy'n byw mewn amodau lle mae cyflenwadau digonol o ddŵr). Mae'r rhan fwyaf o blanhigion tir sy'n tyfu mewn ardaloedd tymherus yn perthyn i'r olaf o'r categorïau hyn. Gan amlaf mae'r dŵr y maent yn ei golli trwy drydarthiad yn cael ei amnewid yn rhwydd trwy godi dŵr o'r pridd, felly nid oes angen dulliau arbennig o gadwraeth dŵr. Os bydd planhigyn o'r fath yn colli gormod o ddŵr bydd y planhigyn yn gwywo a'r dail yn mynd yn llipa. Mae arwyneb y ddeilen yn cael ei leihau a ffotosynthesis yn mynd yn llai effeithlon.

- Mae **hydroffytau** yn tyfu o dan y dŵr neu'n rhannol o dan y dŵr. Un enghraifft yw lili'r dŵr, sydd wedi ei gwreiddio yn y mwd ar waelod llyn ac sydd â dail yn arnofio ar wyneb y dŵr. Mae hydroffytau wedi eu haddasu fel a ganlyn:
✓ Gan fod dŵr yn gyfrwng cynhaliol nid oes ganddynt ddim neu fawr ddim o feinweoedd cynnal lignedig.
✓ Gan eu bod wedi eu hamgylchynu â dŵr nid oes rhaid cael meinwe cludiant, felly nid yw'r sylem wedi ei ddatblygu'n dda.
✓ Nid oes gan y dail ddim neu fawr ddim cwtigl.
✓ Mae stomata ar gael ar arwyneb ochr uchaf y dail.
✓ Mae gan y coesyn a'r dail wagolynnau mawr ar gyfer aer, sy'n ffurfio cronfa o ocsigen a charbon deuocsid. Mae'r nwyon hyn hefyd yn galluogi hynofedd (buoyancy) meinweoedd y planhigyn i arnofio pan fyddant o dan ddŵr.

❏ *Tasg*   Lluniwch ddiagram cynllun o doriad ardraws ddeilen Lili'r Dŵr

- Mae **seroffytau** yn blanhigion sy'n dangos addasiadau seromorffig. Mae'r planhigion hyn wedi eu haddasu ar gyfer byw dan amodau o brinder dŵr ac wedi datblygu adeiledd addasedig er mwyn atal colli gormod o ddŵr. Fe allant fod yn byw yn ardaloedd poeth, sych yr anialwch; mewn ardaloedd oer lle mae dŵr yn y pridd wedi rhewi dros gyfnod hir o'r flwyddyn, neu mewn lleoliadau agored, gwyntog. Mae *Ammophila arenaria* (**moresg**) yn enghraifft o seroffyt sy'n cytrefu twyni tywod o amgylch yr arfordir. Mae twyni tywod yn gynefin sy'n ei gwneud yn anodd i mesoffyt oroesi yno am nad oes dim pridd, gan fod dŵr glaw yn draenio allan yn gyflym, a gan fod gwyntoedd cyflym, ewyn hallt a diffyg cysgod rhag yr haul.

❏ *Tasg*   Lluniwch ddiagram wedi ei labelu a'i anodi o o doriad ar draws o ddeilen moresg.

Mae moresg yn dangos yr addasiadau canlynol:
✓ **Dail rholiedig** – mae celloedd epidermaidd mawr gyda muriau tenau sydd wrth fôn y rhigolau yn crebachu pan maent yn colli dŵr oherwydd trydarthu gormodol, gan wneud i'r ddeilen rolio i mewn ar ei hunan. Effaith hynny yw lleihau arwyneb y ddeilen lle gall trydarthu ddigwydd.
✓ **Stomata suddedig** – mae stomata mewn rhigolau ar ochr fewnol y ddeilen. Maent wedi eu lleoli mewn pyllau neu bantiau fel bod aer llaith yn cael ei ddal tu allan i'r stomata. Mae hyn yn lleihau graddiant potensial dŵr rhwng y ddeilen a'r atmosffer ac felly'n lleihau cyfradd tryediad dŵr.
✓ **Blew** – mae blew anystwyth, sy'n cloi i'w gilydd yn dal anwedd dŵr ac yn lleihau'r graddiant potensial dŵr.
✓ **Cwtigl trwchus** – mae'r cwtigl yn haen cwyraidd dros arwyneb y ddeilen sy'n lleihau maint y dŵr a gollir. Y mwyaf trwchus yw'r cwtigl y lleiaf yw cyfradd trydarthu y cwtigl.

Addasiadau seroffytig ychwanegol
✓ Mae deilen yr Hacea wedi datblygu meinwe sglerencyma gyda muriau trwchus yn y ddeilen ac mae hynny'n ei hatal rhag cwympo mewn cyfnodau o sychder ac felly'n cynnal yr arwyneb sydd ar gael ar gyfer ffotosynthesis.
✓ Mae gan gacti goes suddlon ar gyfer storio dŵr ac mae'r dail wedi cael eu lleihau i fod yn bigau. Mae gan lawer o gacti y gallu i gau eu stomata yn ystod golau dydd.
✓ Mae gan binwydd ddail fel nodwyddau. Mae hynny'n lleihau'r arwyneb sy'n gallu colli dŵr.
- Mae **mesoffytau** yn ffynnu mewn cynefinoedd sydd â chyflenwad digonol o ddŵr. Mae'r rhan fwyaf o blanhigion ardaloedd tymherus yn fesoffytau ac, yn bwysig iawn, mae'r rhan fwyaf o'n planhigion a ddefnyddir fel cnydau yn fesoffytau. Maent wedi eu haddasu i dyfu orau mewn priddoedd sydd wedi eu draenio'n dda mewn aer cymharol sych. Mae mesoffytau yn colli llawer o ddŵr ond atelir colledion gormodol trwy gau'r stomata. Mae'r dŵr sy'n cael ei godi yn ystod y nos yn gwneud iawn am y dŵr a gollir yn ystod y dydd.
Mae'n rhaid i fesoffytau oroesi adegau anffafriol o'r flwyddyn, yn arbennig pan fydd y tir wedi rhewi.
✓ Mae llawer o goed a llwyni yn colli eu dail cyn y gaeaf.
✓ Mae rhannau awyrol llawer o blanhigion amhrennaidd yn crino a marw o ganlyniad i rew (iâ) neu wyntoedd oer ond mae eu horganau tanddaearol yn goroesi e.e. bylbiau, cormau (corms).
✓ Mae'r rhan fwyaf o fesoffytau unflwydd (planhigion sy'n blodeuo, yn cynhyrchu hadau a marw yn yr un flwyddyn) yn goroesi'r gaeaf ar ffurf hadau cwsg.

Trawsleoliad

Mae cynhyrchion ffotosynthesis yn cael eu cludo yn y ffloem, i ffwrdd oddi wrth safle synthesis yn y dail (y 'tarddiad'), i bob rhan arall o'r planhigyn lle maent yn cael eu defnyddio ar gyfer twf neu storio (y 'suddfan'). Mewn planhigion gelwir cludiant y deunyddiau organig hydawdd, swcros ac asidau amino yn drawsleoliad.

Adeiledd ffloem

Mae ffloem yn feinwe byw sy'n cynnwys pedwar math o gell:
- **tiwbiau hidlo**
- **cymargelloedd**
- **ffibrau ffloem**
- **parencyma ffloem.**

Y tiwbiau hidlo yw'r unig gyfansoddion o'r ffloem sy'n amlwg wedi addasu ar gyfer llif hydredol deunyddiau. Maent wedi eu ffurfio o gelloedd a elwir yn elfennau hidlo wedi eu gosod ben i ben. Nid yw'r muriau pen yn chwalu ond maent wedi eu tyllu â mandyllau. Gelwir yr ardaloedd hyn yn **blatiau hidlo**. Mae ffilamentau cytoplasmig sy'n cynnwys protein ffloem yn ymestyn o un gell hidlo i'r llall drwy'r mandyllau sydd yn y plât hidlo. Nid oes gan y tiwbiau hidlo gnewyllyn ac yn ystod eu datblygiad mae'r rhan fwyaf o'r organynnau cell arferol yn diflannu. Mae pob elfen o'r tiwb hidlo wedi ei gysylltu'n agos gydag o leiaf un gymargell, sydd â chytoplasm dwys, cnewyll sydd wedi eu lleoli'n ganolog, llawer o fitocondria, ac maent wedi eu cysylltu i'r elfen tiwb hidlo gan **blasmodesmata**.

☐ *Tasg* 1. Lluniwch ddiagram toriad ardraws a thoriad hydredol o ffloem sylfaenol.
2. Arsylwch adeiledd ffloem fel y'i gwelir o dan ficrosgop electron.

Cludiant yn y ffloem

Mae llawer o dystiolaeth arbrofol yn awgrymu mai y ffloem yw'r meinwe sy'n ymwneud â thrawsleoliad sylweddau organig megis swcros ac asidau amino. Cafwyd tystiolaeth gynnar o **arbrofion cylchu** lle tynnwyd silindrau o feinwe rhisgl allanol (tynnu'r ffloem) o goesynnau prennaidd ac wedyn dadansoddi cynnwys y ffloem uwchben ac o dan y silindr. Yn fwy diweddar, defnyddiwyd y dechneg o olrhain ymbelydrol gyda metabolynnau wedi eu labelu a samplu uniongyrchol o gynnwys tiwbiau hidlo unigol, gan ddefnyddio gên-rannau llyslau (aphid) fel micro-pipedau. Mae gan y llyslau gên-rannau (stylet) debyg i nodwyddau gwag, sy'n cael eu gwthio ganddynt i mewn i'r tiwbiau hidlo i fwydo ar y sudd. Er mwyn samplu'r sudd ffloem mae'r llyslau yn cael ei roi o dan anaesthetig a thorrir y stylet i ffwrdd, gan ei adael ynghlwm i'r planhigyn. Gan fod y sudd o dan wasgedd, y mae'n llifo allan o'r tiwb mân iawn a gellir ei gasglu a'i ddadansoddi. Mae'r arbrofion hyn hefyd wedi galluogi gwyddonwyr i ddangos bod trawsleoli yn broses gyflym, llawer rhy gyflym iddi gael ei hegluro fel trylediad.

Mae **labelu radioisotop** yn dechneg lle mae carbon deuocsid yn cael ei labelu gyda charbon ymbelydrol ac yn cael ei gyflenwi i ddeilen planhigyn mewn goleuni. Mae'r carbon ymbelydrol yn cael ei osod yn y siwgr a gynhyrchir trwy ffotosynthesis a gellir olrhain ei drawsleoliad i rannau eraill o'r planhigyn trwy ddefnyddio awtoradiograffeg. Rhoddir y ddeilen 'ffynhonnell' a'r meinweoedd 'suddfan' yn gadarn ar ffilm ffotograffig yn y tywyllwch am 24 awr. Pan ddatblygir y ffilm, mae presenoldeb ymbelydredd ar rannau o'r meinwe yn dangos ar ffurf 'niwl' ar y negatifau. Mae'r dechneg yn dangos bod y siwgr yn cael ei gludo i fyny ac i lawr gan fod yr ymbelydredd i'w weld yn rhannau awyrol y planhigyn yn ogystal ag yn y gwreiddiau. Mae awtoradiograff o doriad ardraws coesyn planhigyn sydd wedi ei drin yn dangos niwl lle bu'r ffloem mewn cysylltiad â'r ffilm yn unig.

Damcaniaethau ynglŷn â thrawsleoli

Mae cyfradd y llif a arsylwir yn llawer rhy gyflym i fod wedi cael ei achosi gan dryllediad. Arsylwyd bod swcros yn cael ei drawsleoli mewn tiwbiau hidlo ar gyfradd o 25 – 100 cm yr awr o'i gymharu â dim ond y 0.2 mm y dydd sy'n bosibl trwy drylediad.

Y brif ddamcaniaeth a roddir gerbron i egluro cludiant hydoddion organaidd yw **rhagdybiaeth llif-más** (1937). Mae'r rhagdybiaeth yma yn awgrymu bod llif-más goddefol o siwgrau o ffloem y ddeilen lle mae'r crynodiad uchaf (y ffynhonnell) i ardaloedd eraill, megis meinweoedd sy'n tyfu, lle mae crynodiad is (y suddfan).
(Nid oes rhaid i chi gael manylion am fecanwaith y rhagdybiaeth hon.)

Mae'r dadleuon yn erbyn y ddamcaniaeth yn cynnwys:
- ✓ Y ffaith nad yw'n egluro bodolaeth y platiau hidlo sydd, mae'n ymddangos, yn gweithredu fel cyfres o rwystrau i'r llif.
- ✓ Arsylwyd bod swcros ac asidau amino yn symud ar gyfraddau gwahanol ac mewn gwahanol gyfeiriadau yn yr un meinwe.
- ✓ Mae cyfradd dreulio ocsigen meinwe ffloem yn gymharol uchel ac mae trawsleoli yn cael ei arafu neu ei atal yn gyfan gwbl os bydd gwenwynau resbiradol megis potasiwm cyanid yn mynd i mewn i'r ffloem.
- ✓ Mae'r cymargelloedd yn cynnwys mitocondria niferus ac yn cynhyrchu egni ond nid yw'r rhagdybiaeth llif-más yn awgrymu swyddogaeth i'r cymargelloedd.

Mae damcaniaethau diweddar a roddwyd ger bron yn awgrymu:
- ✓ Y gallai proses weithredol fod yn gysylltiedig â hyn.
- ✓ Arsylwyd y gallai ffrydio yn y cytoplasm mewn tiwbiau hidlo unigol fod yn gyfrifol am symudiadau dau gyfeiriadol ar hyd tiwbiau hidlo unigol, cyn belled â bod rhyw fecanwaith i gludo hydoddion ar draws y platiau hidlo.
- ✓ Mae rhai gwyddonwyr wedi arsylwi bod ffilamentau protein yn pasio drwy'r mandyllau hidlo ac yn awgrymu bod gwahanol hydoddion yn cael eu trawsgludo ar hyd gwahanol ffilamentau.

Ar hyn o bryd nid oes gan wyddonwyr ddealltwriaeth lawn o fecanwaith trawsleoli ac mae llawer o ddadlau yn parhau.

(Nid yw'n ofynnol i chi roi manylion am unrhyw un o'r damcaniaethau hyn.)

2.4 Strategaethau atgenhedlu

Gellir diffinio cylchred bywyd organeb fel y gyfres o newidiadau y mae'n mynd drwyddo yn ystod ei oes, o'i darddiad trwy atgenhedliad hyd at ei farwolaeth. Er mwyn i rywogaeth oroesi, mae'n rhaid iddo gynhyrchu unigolion newydd. Atgenhedlu yw'r gallu i gynhyrchu unigolion eraill o'r un rhywogaeth ac mae'n nodwedd sylfaenol o bethau byw. Gellir cynhyrchu unigolion newydd trwy atgenhedlu rhywiol neu atgynhyrchu anrhywiol, neu mewn rhai rhywogaethau, trwy'r ddau ddull. Mewn anifeiliaid mae atgynhyrchu anrhywiol yn llawer llai cyffredin nag ydyw mewn planhigion, protoctistau a phrocaryotau.

Atgenhedlu rhywiol ac anrhywiol

Mewn planhigion ac anifeiliaid cyflawnir atgenhedlu mewn dwy ffordd.
Atgynhyrchu anrhywiol – mae'r dull hwn yn cynhyrchu nifer fawr o unigolyn yn gyflym, pob un gyda chyfansoddiad genetig unfath. **Clôn** yw'r enw ar grŵp o epil unfath yn enetig a gynhyrchir drwy'r dull hwn. Enghreifftiau o ddulliau anrhywiol mewn anifeiliaid yw ymholltiad deuaidd ac ymflagurol. Enghreifftiau mewn planhigion yw bylbiau e.e. Cennin Pedr, ymledyddion e.e. mefus, cloron e.e. tatws.
Atgenhedlu rhywiol – gyda'r dull hwn mae dau riant gan amlaf, mae'n llai cyflym nag atgynhyrchu anrhywiol ac mae'n cynhyrchu epil sy'n wahanol yn y genynnau. Mae ymasiad gametau haploid bob amser yn gysylltiedig â'r dull hwn o atgenhedlu.

Manteision ac anfanteision

Gydag atgynhyrchu anrhywiol mae diffyg amrywiaeth yn anfantais o ran addasu ar gyfer newid amgylcheddol ond y brif fantais yw bod gwneuthuriad genetig sy'n addas ar gyfer set penodol o amodau, yn gallu cael ei atgynhyrchu gan greu nifer fawr o unigolion o'r math llwyddiannus hwn.
Manteision atgenhedliad rhywiol:
- ✓ Mae cynnydd mewn amrywiaeth genetig fel bod y rhywogaeth yn gallu addasu i newidiadau amgylcheddol.
- ✓ Mae'n caniatáu datblygiad cyfnod gwrthiannol yn y cylchred bywyd gan alluogi'r rhywogaeth i wrthsefyll amodau anffafriol.
- ✓ Mae ffurfio sborau, hadau a larfau yn galluogi'r epil i wasgaru. Mae hynny'n lleihau cystadleuaeth mewnrhywogaethol ac yn galluogi amrywiaeth genetig i ddatblygu yn ôl yr angen.

Er bod mwtaniadau yn brin, maent yn helpu i greu ychydig o amrywiaeth mewn atgynhyrchu anrhywiol. Mae mwtaniadau yn digwydd yn fwy aml (ond yn dal i fod yn brin) yn ystod atgenhedlu rhywiol oherwydd bod y broses yn un fwy cymhleth.

Cynhyrchu gametau

Mae gan organebau byw corffgelloedd **diploid** a chelloedd rhyw (**gametau**) **haploid**.
Mae corffgelloedd gyda'r nifer llawn o gromosomau yn cael eu gwneud trwy **mitosis**.
Mae celloedd haploid gyda hanner y nifer o gromosomau yn cael eu cynhyrchu trwy **meiosis**.
Adeg ffrwythloni mae'r sberm haploid yn ymasio gydag ŵy haploid gan gynhyrchu ŵy ffrwythlon diploid. Yna mae'r sygot a ffurfir yn rhannu llawer gwaith trwy fitosis i dyfu yn unigolyn newydd.
Yn arferol mae'r gwryw a'r fenyw yn cynhyrchu gametau o wahanol faint. Mae'r gamet **gwryw** yn fychan ac yn hynod **symudol** ac mae'r gamet **benywaidd** yn fawr ac yn ddisymud, gan amlaf oherwydd presenoldeb **bwyd wedi ei storio**.
Mae wyau mamolion yn wahanol yn y ffaith nad ydynt yn cynnwys llawer o fwyd wedi ei storio ac yn hytrach mae'r deunyddiau ar gyfer datblygu ar gael o gyflenwad gwaed y fam drwy'r brych.

Ffrwythloni allanol a mewnol

- Mae llawer o organebau dyfrol yn gollwng eu gametau yn uniongyrchol i'r môr neu i ddŵr croyw. Gan fod y gametau yn cael eu gwasgaru'n gyflym gan y dŵr, mae posibilrwydd cryf na fydd llawer o'r wyau yn dod ar draws sberm. Mewn anifeiliaid gelwir y math yma o ffrwythloni yn ffrwythloni **allanol**. Mae gwastraff sylweddol felly ac mae'n rhaid cynhyrchu nifer fawr o gametau o'r ddau ryw. Yn y llyffant mae paru rhywiol yn hwyluso'r broses o ddod â'r sberm a'r ŵy at ei gilydd. Pan fydd y fenyw wedi dodwy'r wyau bydd y gwryw yn gollwng hylif semenol drostynt ar unwaith. Er bod amffibiaid yn gyffredinol yn gallu symud yn effeithlon ar dir, mae llawer ohonynt yn gorfod mynd yn ôl i'r dŵr i fridio ac mae'r ffrwythloni yn allanol.

- Yn y rhan fwyaf o anifeiliaid daearol serch hynny, mae ffrwythloni yn digwydd tu mewn i gorff y fenyw a gelwir hynny yn ffrwythloni **mewnol**. Yn gyffredinol, mae'n rhaid defnyddio rhyw fath o organ fewnysbeidiol i gyflwyno'r sberm i gorff y fenyw.

Mae nifer o fanteision i ffrwythloni mewnol;
1. Mae llai o berygl y bydd gametau yn cael eu gwastraffu.
2. Mae'n caniatáu i'r gamet gwryw fod yn annibynnol o'r angen am ddŵr er mwyn symud.
3. Gellir amgáu ŵy sydd wedi ei ffrwythloni o fewn haen amddiffynnol cyn iddo adael corff y fenyw. Dyna beth sy'n digwydd mewn anifeiliaid sy'n dodwy wyau. Mae rhai anifeiliaid yn mynd â'r syniad yma ymhellach gyda'r embryonau yn datblygu o fewn y rhiant benywaidd ac yn cael maeth ganddi. Mae hyn yn cyrraedd penllanw datblygiad yn y mamolion sy'n maethu'r epil sy'n datblygu cyn iddynt gael eu geni trwy gyfrwng brych.

Datblygiad y sygot

Mewn llawer o anifeiliaid mae'r ŵy ffrwythlonedig neu'r sygot yn datblygu tu allan i gorff y rhiant. Mae'r epil sy'n datblygu yn ysglyfaeth hawdd i ysglyfaethwyr eu dal ac maent yn darparu bwyd i rywogaethau eraill. Mae llawer o wyau yn cael eu cynhyrchu er mwyn sicrhau bod ychydig, o leiaf, yn goroesi. Gyda phryfed, er bod y ffrwythloni'n fewnol, mae'r wyau ffrwythlonedig yn arferol yn cael eu dodwy ar ffynhonnell addas o fwyd a bydd yr embryo yn datblygu y tu allan i'r corff. Mae ffrwythloni mewnol yn sicrhau bod yr holl sberm yn cyrraedd system genhedlu'r fenyw.

Wrth ddatblygu'n raddol ar gyfer bywyd ar y ddaear esblygodd ŵy amniot mewn ymlusgiaid ac adar. Mae gan yr ŵy geudod wedi ei lenwi â hylif a'i amgylchynu gan bilen gyda phlisgyn amddiffynnol tu allan iddo, a'r cyfan yn amgáu'r embryo yn y cwd melynwy. Mae adar yn gori ar wyau a'r embryo yn cwblhau ei ddatblygiad tu allan i gorff y fam.

Mewn mamolion mae'r epil yn aros yng nghroth y fam am gyfnod sylweddol iawn ond does dim plisgyn (cragen). Mae'r embryo yn cael ei faethu yno gyda chyflenwad gwaed y fam trwy'r brych. Bydd yr epil yn cael eu geni mewn cyflwr cymharol uchel o ddatblygiad.

Gofal rhieni

Fel y dywedwyd cynt, mae llawer o rywogaethau anifeiliaid yn atgenhedlu drwy ffurfio a dodwy wyau sydd wedi eu ffrwythloni sy'n cael eu gadael i ddatblygu ar eu pen eu hunain. Nid oes dim neu fawr ddim gofal gan y rhieni. Mae rhywogaethau eraill yn darparu rhyw fath o ofal rhieni, e.e. mae'r grothell (stickleback) gwryw yn gofalu am yr wyau ffrwythlon mewn tiriogaeth a amddiffynnir ganddo ac mae'n eu gwyntyllu i ddarparu ocsigen nes iddynt ddeor a nofio i ffwrdd. Mae gofal amlwg gan y rhieni yn nodweddiadol yn y rhan fwyaf o rywogaethau o adar a mamolion. Mae'n cynnwys darparu lloches rhag amodau amgylcheddol anffafriol, bwydo, gwarchod oddi wrth ysglyfaethwyr, ac mewn rhai rhywogaethau hyfforddi'r ifanc wrth iddynt baratoi ar gyfer bywyd fel oedolion. Yn gyffredinol, y mwyaf o ofal a ddarperir gan y rhieni y lleiaf yw'r nifer o epil a gynhyrchir. Mae rhai mathau o bysgod yn cynhyrchu dros 100 miliwn o wyau wrth silio (spawn). Yn y pegwn arall mae rhai mamolion, gan gynnwys bodau dynol, yn cynhyrchu un epil yn unig ar y tro gan amlaf.

Unrhywiol a deurywiad

Gyda'r rhan fwyaf o anifeiliaid mae organau rhywiol gwryw a benyw yn perthyn i wahanol unigolion, hynny yw mae'r unigolion yn unrhywiol. Gyda'r rhan fwyaf o blanhigion blodeuol, cynhyrchir gametau gwryw a benyw ym mhob unigolyn, hynny yw mae'r unigolion yn ddeurywiol. Mae gan hynny fantais biolegol oherwydd bod pob unigolyn yn gallu ffurfio wyau wedi eu ffrwythloni. Yr anfantais yw'r posibilrwydd bod hunan-ffrwythloni yn arwain at fewnfridio, hynny yw cynhyrchu epil sydd â llai o amrywiaeth genetig. Efallai nad oes gan blanhigion organau mewnysbeidiol fel y cyfryw ond mae technegau arbennig wedi esblygu i drosglwyddo'r gametau gwryw i gelloedd yr wy ac yna bydd yr embryo yn datblygu o fewn corff y rhiant-blanhigyn

(Nid oes rhaid cael manylion am adeiledd blodyn na gwahanol ddulliau o beillio.)

Llwyddiant pryfed

Mae pryfed yn grŵp llwyddiannus iawn o anifeiliaid sy'n ddaearol yn bennaf (er bod larfau nifer o rywogaethau yn ddyfrol). Mae llawer mwy o rywogaethau o bryfed nag sydd gan y ffurfiau eraill o fywyd gyda'i gilydd, sef dros 1 miliwn o wahanol rywogaethau. Gan eu bod mor niferus, amrywiol a gwasgaredig, maent yn effeithio ar fywydau pob organeb daearol eraill yn arbennig bodau dynol. Mae pobl yn dibynnu ar bryfed fel gwenyn i beillio cnydau ond mae pryfed hefyd yn cludo heintiau gan gynnwys malaria a salwch hunglwyf (sleeping sickness) Affrica. Mae pryfed hefyd yn cystadlu gyda phobl am fwyd a bydd biliynau o bunnoedd yn cael eu gwario bob blwyddyn ar bryfleiddiaid.

Mewn pryfed, yn ystod datblygiad y sygot, mae'r ffurf rhyngolyn (intermediate), y cyfeirir ato naill fel **nymff** neu **larfa,** yn cael ei ffurfio. Mae'r rhain yn ffurfiau ifanc sy'n datblygu o gyfnod yr ŵy yn y cylchred bywyd. Mae gan bryfed sgerbwd allanol caled (sgerbwd allanol) ac er mwyn tyfu mae'n rhaid iddynt ddiosg neu fwrw eu croen. Maent yn gwneud hynny nifer o weithiau yn ystod eu datblygiad. Mae sioncyn y gwair a locustiaid yn enghreifftiau o bryfed sy'n datblygu o'r nymffod. Dywedir eu bod yn mynd trwy **fetamorffosis anghyflawn** lle mae'r nymff ifanc, sy'n debyg i'r oedolyn, yn deor o'r ŵy ffrwythlonedig ac yn bwrw ei groen nifer o weithiau nes cyrraedd ei faint llawn.

Ond mae'r rhan fwyaf o rywogaethau o bryfed yn datblygu o gyfnod larfal sy'n hollol wahanol i'r oedolyn. Mae'r broses yn golygu nifer sylweddol o newidiadau ac fe'i gelwir yn **fetamorffosis cyflawn**. Mae gan y pryfed hyn, megis glöynnod byw a phryfaid tŷ, gyfnod ychwanegol hefyd a elwir yn **bwpa** neu crysalis. Mae'r larfa yn deor o'r ŵy wedi eu harbenigo i fwyta a thyfu. Yn y pwpa mae'r larfa yn mynd trwy gyfnod o newid ac yn dod allan fel oedolyn sy'n arbenigo mewn gwasgariad ac atgenhedlu.

Planhigion

Mae ffurfiau syml o blanhigion megis algâu, e.e. gwymon, wedi eu cyfyngu i amgylchedd dyfrol am o leiaf ran os nad y cyfan o'u bywydau. Mae grwpiau eraill o blanhigion megis mwsogl a rhedyn wedi eu cyfyngu i ardaloedd llaith gan fod rhaid i'r gametau gwryw gael haen denau o ddŵr er mwyn nofio at yr ŵy. Ydych chi'n synnu fod gan ffurfiau llai datblygedig o blanhigion gametau mudol fel sydd gan anifeiliaid? Fel yr anifeiliaid tir llwyddiannus, fe ddaeth y conwydd a phlanhigion blodeuol yn annibynnol o ddŵr ar gyfer atgynhyrchu ac yr oeddent felly yn gallu cytrefu'r tir.

Mae planhigion blodeuol wedi eu haddasu'n dda ar gyfer bywyd ar dir o safbwynt eu morffoleg, e.e. llestrau sylem sy'n cludo dŵr yn effeithlon, a'u system atgynhyrchu. Maent wedi datblygu gronynnau paill gwrywaidd gyda chroen caled sy'n gallu gwrthsefyll sychu. Roedd hyn yn ei gwneud yn bosibl iddynt gael eu trosglwyddo i'r stigma yn rhan benywaidd y planhigyn heb i amodau amgylcheddol effeithio arnynt. Mae gan blanhigion megis gweiriau flodau bychan, gwyrdd anamlwg ac mae'r paill yn cael ei gario gan y gwynt. Mewn planhigion sydd â blodau lliwgar iawn a phersawr i'w gwneud yn ddeniadol, bydd y paill yn cael ei gludo i'r stigma gan y pryfed. Mae'r gametau gwryw yn teithio drwy feinwe'r rhan benywaidd i'r ŵy trwy diwb paill. Mae hynny'n golygu nad yw atgenhedlu rhywiol yn dal i ddibynnu bellach ar i'r gametau orfod teithio drwy haen o ddŵr er mwyn cyrraedd cell yr ŵy. Yn dilyn ffrwythloniad, bydd yr ŵy ffrwythlonedig yn datblygu'n hedyn sy'n cynnwys storfa fwyd.

Planhigion blodeuol yw'r mwyaf llwyddiannus o bob planhigyn daearol. Mae dros 300,000 o rywogaethau ac fe'u ceir ym mhob math o gynefin. Un nodwedd allweddol o'u llwyddiant yw'r berthynas rhyngddynt ag anifeiliaid, e.e. mae planhigion yn denu anifeiliaid, yn arbennig pryfed, at eu blodau er mwyn bwydo ac maent yn manteisio ar eu symudedd er mwyn peillio a gwasgaru hadau. Datblygiad pwysig arall oedd amgáu'r wyau mewn **ofari** ac esblygiad yr **hedyn**. Mae'r hadau sy'n deillio o ffrwythloniad yn cynnwys cronfa fwyd ac mae ganddynt groen sy'n gallu gwrthsefyll amodau anffafriol.

Paham y mae planhigion blodeuol mor llwyddiannus?

1. Gan amlaf mae'r cyfnod rhwng cynhyrchu blodau a gosod yr hadau yn ychydig wythnosau.
2. Mae cynhyrchu'r hedyn gyda storfa fwyd yn galluogi'r embryo i ddatblygu nes bod dail wedi cael eu ffurfio uwch y ddaear a'u bod yn gallu ffotosyntheseiddio. Mae'r hedyn hefyd yn amddiffyn yr embryo rhag sychu a pheryglon eraill.
3. Yn gyffredinol mae dail yn golldail, yn suddlon ac yn pydru'n gyflym wrth syrthio ar y ddaear. Mae hynny'n cynhyrchu hwmws (deilbridd) ac o ganlyniad mae ionau'n cael eu hailgylchu'n gyflym i'w hailddefnyddio gan y planhigion.

2.5 Addasiadau ar gyfer maethiad

Mathau o faethiad

Trwy'r broses maethiad mae organebau yn cael yr **egni** i gynnal prosesau bywyd ac yn cael y **mater** i greu a chynnal eu strwythur. Mae'r rhain i'w cael o faetholion.
Mae organebau **awtotroffig** megis planhigion gwyrdd yn defnyddio'r deunyddiau organig syml carbon deuocsid a dŵr er mwyn cynhyrchu egni – gan gynnwys cynhyrchu cyfansoddion organig cymhleth. Mae organebau **heterotroffig** yn defnyddio deunydd bwyd organig cymhleth.

Maethiad Awtotroffig

Gelwir organebau sy'n gallu gwneud eu bwyd eu hunain yn organebau awtotroffig.
Maent yn darparu bwyd ar gyfer pob ffurfiau eraill o fywyd ac felly fe'u gelwir hefyd yn gynhyrchwyr.
Mae dau fath o faeth hunanborthi:
- **Ffotosynthesis** yw'r broses a ddefnyddir gan blanhigion gwyrdd i adeiladu moleciwlau organig cymhleth megis siwgrau, o garbon deuocsid a dŵr. Mae'r ffynhonnell egni ar gyfer y broses hon yn dod o oleuni'r haul sy'n cael ei amsugno gan gloroffyl a phigmentau cysylltiedig. Mae algâu a rhai mathau o facteria hefyd yn gallu gwneud ffotosynthesis trwy ddefnyddio egni o'r haul.
- **Cemosynthesis** yw'r broses a gyflawnir gan facteria awtotroffig. Maent yn defnyddio'r egni sy'n deillio o ddulliau resbiradu er mwyn syntheseiddio bwyd organig.

Maeth heterotroffig

Nid yw heterotroffau yn gallu gwneud eu bwyd organig eu hun. Mae'n rhaid iddynt ddefnyddio deunydd bwyd organig cymhleth a gynhyrchir gan organebau awtotroffig. Gan eu bod yn bwyta neu'n defnyddio bwyd sydd wedi ei wneud yn barod fe'u gelwir yn ddefnyddwyr. Mae pob anifail yn ddefnyddiwr ac yn dibynnu ar gynhyrchwyr i gael eu bwyd. Mae heterotroffau yn cynnwys anifeiliaid, ffwng, rhai mathau o brotoctistau a bacteria.

Mae nifer o wahanol fathau o faeth heterotroffig.

- **Bwydwyr Holosoig**

Mae hyn yn cynnwys bron pob anifail. Maent yn cymryd y bwyd i mewn i'w cyrff ac yn ei dorri i lawr drwy'r broses o dreuliad. Mae'r rhan fwyaf yn cyflawni'r broses hon tu mewn i'r corff trwy system dreulio arbenigol. Yna bydd y deunydd a dreuliwyd yn cael ei amsugno i feinweoedd y corff ac yn cael ei ddefnyddio gan gelloedd y corff. Gelwir anifeiliaid sy'n bwydo ar blanhigion yn unig yn llysysyddion, mae'r rhai sy'n bwyta anifeiliaid eraill yn gigysyddion, a gelwir anifeiliaid sy'n byw ar ddeunyddiau marw neu sy'n pydru yn **detritysyddion.**

- **Saproffytau**

Enw arall ar y grŵp yma yw saprobiontau, ac maent yn cynnwys pob ffwng a rhai bacteria. Maent yn bwydo ar ddeunydd sy'n farw neu sy'n pydru ac nid oes ganddynt system dreulio arbenigol. Maent yn bwydo trwy secretu ensymau megis proteas, amylas, lipas a chellwlas ar y deunydd bwyd **tu allan** i'r corff ac yna'n amsugno'r cynhyrchion hydawdd ar draws y gellbilen trwy drylediad. Gelwir hynny yn **dreuliad allgellog**. Gelwir saproffytau yn **ddadelfenyddion** ac mae eu gweithgareddau yn bwysig er mwyn dadelfennu sbwriel dail ac ailgylchu maetholion gwerthfawr, megis nitrogen.

- **Parasitiaid**

Mae parasit yn organeb sy'n bwydo ar organeb byw arall, a elwir yn organeb letyol. Mae rhai parasitiaid yn byw yng nghorff yr organeb letyol ac eraill yn byw ar yr arwyneb. Mae'r organeb letyol bob amser yn dioddef rhyw gymaint o niwed ac weithiau'n marw. Ystyrir bod parasitiaid yn organebau datblygedig iawn ac maent yn arddangos addasiadau sylweddol ar gyfer eu ffordd benodol o fyw. Enghreifftiau o barasitiaid yw'r llyngyr, malltod (blight) tatws, a achosir gan ffwng, a *Plasmodium*, parasit sy'n achosi malaria.

- **Cydymddibyniaeth**

Gelwir hyn hefyd yn symbiosis ac mae'n golygu cydgysylltiad agos rhwng aelodau o ddwy rywogaeth wahanol, ond yn yr achos hwn mae'r ddwy organeb yn cael rhyw fudd o'r berthynas, e.e. micro-organebau yn treulio cellwlos yng ngholudd llysysydd. Mae gwartheg a defaid yn bwydo ar wair yn bennaf, ac mae cyfran helaeth o'r gwair wedi ei wneud o gellfuriau cellwlos. Fel llysysyddion eraill nid yw gwartheg a defaid yn secretu'r ensym cellwlas ac felly nid ydynt yn gallu treulio cellwlos. Yn lle hynny mae ganddynt bacteria cydymddibynol sy'n byw mewn rhan benodol o stumog arbenigol yr anifail (y rwmen). Bydd y bacteria hyn yn cynhyrchu'r ensymau ar eu cyfer a'r fantais i'r bacteria yw eu bod yn cael cynhyrchion treuliad eraill ac amodau addas iddynt dyfu.

Adeiledd y coludd

Nid yw heterotroffau yn gallu synthesieiddo y rhan fwyaf o'r bwyd y maent ei angen felly maent yn dibynnu ar ffynhonnell o fwyd wedi ei baratoi'n barod. Mae'n rhaid cael y bwyd hwn fel ffynhonnell egni ar gyfer gweithgareddau fel symud ac er mwyn syntheseiddio meinweoedd y corff. Mae'n rhaid i'r moleciwlau organig gael eu torri lawr drwy dreuliad a chael eu hamsugno i feinweoedd y corff o'r system dreulio cyn cael eu defnyddio yng nghelloedd y corff. Mae treuliad ac amsugniad yn digwydd yn y coludd, sy'n diwb hir, gwag a chyhyrog. Mae'r coludd wedi ei drefnu fel bod ei gynnwys yn gallu symud i un cyfeiriad yn unig. Mewn organebau syml sy'n byw ar un math o fwyd yn unig nid yw'r coludd wedi ei wahaniaethau. Ond mewn organebau mwy datblygedig sydd â diet amrywiol mae'r coludd wedi ei rannu'n wahanol rannau ar ei hyd gyda phob rhan yn arbenigo ar gyflawni rhai camau penodol yn y broses o dreuliad mecanyddol a chemegol yn ogystal ag amsugniad.

Swyddogaethau'r system dreulio

Yn y corff dynol prif rannau'r coludd yw'r geg, yr oesoffagws (llwnc), y stumog, y coluddyn bach (dwodenwm, ilewm), y coluddyn mawr a'r anws. Mae'r bwyd yn cael ei brosesu wrth iddo basio ar hyd gwahanol rannau o'r coludd. Mae'n cael ei yrru ar hyd y coludd gan broses peristalsis.

- **Amlynciad** yw'r broses o gymeryd bwyd i mewn i'r corff drwy'r geg.
- **Treuliad** yw torri'r moleciwlau mawr, anhydawdd o fwyd yn foleciwlau syml, hydawdd trwy ddefnyddio ensymau. Mae treuliad **mecanyddol** yn y corff dynol yn digwydd trwy weithred y dannedd o dorri a malu'r bwyd ac yna gan gyfangiadau rhythmig y coludd. Mae gan fur y coludd, yn arbennig y stumog, haenau o gyhyrau ar gyfer y swyddogaeth hon. Mae'r rhain yn gyfrifol am gymysgu'r bwyd a'i wthio ar hyd y coludd. Mae gan y weithred gorfforol hon swyddogaeth bwysig gan ei bod yn cynyddu'r arwyneb y mae ensymau yn gallu gweithredu arno. Cyflawnir y weithred **gemegol** o dreulio trwy secretu ensymau treuliad. Mae'r ensymau yn cael eu secretu naill ai gan:
  - ✓ chwarennau a leolir tu allan i'r coludd, e.e. chwarennau poer a'r pancreas
  - ✓ chwarennau a leolir ym mur y coludd ei hun
- **Amsugniad** yw llwybr y bwyd treuliedig trwy fur y coludd i mewn i'r gwaed.
- **Carthiad** yw gwagio allan o'r corff unrhyw fwyd na ellir ei dreulio e.e. cellfuriau cellwlos planhigion.
- ❏ **Tasg** Lluniwch ddiagram wedi ei labelu o'r llwybr ymborth dynol a'r organau cysylltiedig.
      (Dylech labelu'r canlynol - ceudod bochaidd, tafod, chwarennau poer, oesoffagws, stumog, dwodenwm, ilewm, coluddyn, rectwm, anws a'r organau cysylltiedig; yr iau/ afu a'r pancreas.)

Adeiledd coludd mewn mamol

Ar ei hyd o'r geg i'r anws, mae mur y coludd yn cynnwys pedair haen o feinwe yn amgylchynu ceudod (lwmen) y coludd.
- Mae'r **serosa** allanol wedi ei lunio o haen o feinwe cysylltiol gwydn sy'n amddiffyn mur y coludd ac yn lleihau ffrithiant oddi wrth organau eraill yn yr abdomen wrth i'r coludd symud yn ystod y broses o dreulio bwyd.

- Mae'r haen o **gyhyrau** wedi ei lunio o ddwy haen o gyhyrau sy'n rhedeg i wahanol gyfeiriadau:
  - ✓ y cyhyryn crwn mewnol
  - ✓ y cyhyryn hydredol allanol.

Rhyngddynt, mae'r cyhyrau hyn yn achosi tonnau o gyfangiadau cyhyrol, **peristalsis**, sy'n gyrru'r bwyd ar hyd y coludd. Tu ôl i'r bêl o fwyd mae'r cyhyrau crwn yn cyfangu a'r cyhyrau hydredol yn ymlacio, gan helpu i symud y bwyd yn ei flaen.

❏ **Tasg** Lluniwch ddiagram wedi ei labelu i ddangos peristalsis.

- Mae'r **is-mwcosa** wedi ei lunio o feinwe cysylltiol sy'n cynnwys gwaed a phibellau lymff i gario ymaith y cynhyrchion bwyd sydd wedi eu hamsugno yn ogystal â nerfau sy'n cydgysylltu'r cyfangiadau cyhyrol sy'n cyfrannu at broses peristalsis.

- Y **mwcosa** yw'r haen fewnol ac mae'n leinio mur y coludd. Mae'n secretu mwcws sy'n iro ac amddiffyn y mwcosa. Mewn rhai rhannau o'r coludd mae'r haen hon yn secretu suddion treulio, mewn rhai eraill mae'n amsugno bwyd sydd wedi ei dreulio.

- **Tasg** Adeiledd histolegol yr ilewm.
    (Tynnwch lun o'r ilewm gan labelu'r canlynol - serosa, haen cyhyryn hydredol, haen cyhyryn crwn, ismwcosa, mwcosa mwscwlaris, pilen fwcaidd, celloedd gobled, lacteal, fili a chyhyryn.)

Chwarennau yn y coludd

Mae chwarennau yn cynhyrchu llawer iawn o secretiadau, rhai ohonynt yn cynnwys ensymau treulio. Mae tri math o chwarennau yn y coludd:
- chwarennau mawr a geir tu allan i'r coludd sydd â secretiadau yn pasio drwy bibellau neu ddwythellau i geudod y coludd
- ✓ chwarren boer sy'n secretu poer i'r geg
- ✓ yr iau/afu sy'n secretu bustl i'r dwodenwm
- ✓ y pancreas sy'n secretu sudd pancreatig i'r dwodenwm
- chwarennau ar ffurf celloedd yn yr ismwcosa
- ✓ chwarennau sy'n secretu mwcws i'r dwodenwm
- chwarennau ar ffurf celloedd yn y mwcosa
- ✓ chwarennau gastrig ym mur y stumog sy'n secretu sudd gastrig i'r stumog
- ✓ chwarennau a geir wrth fôn filws yn y coluddyn bach sy'n secretu ensymau i'r coluddyn bach.

Treuliad

Mae gan fodau dynol ddiet amrywiol felly mae'r coludd wedi ei rannu'n wahanol rannau ar ei hyd. Mae pob rhan yn arbenigo ar gyflawni camau penodol yn y broses o dreuliad mecanyddol a chemegol yn ogystal ag amsugniad. Yn y fan hon dylech adolygu'r gwaith ar 'Gyfansoddion biolegol ac ensymau' o Uned BY1.

Treuliad

Nid yw'n bosibl i gelloedd epithelaidd y coludd amsugno maetholynnau oni bai bod y moleciwlau mawr o garbohydradau, brasterau a phroteinau yn cael eu torri lawr yn gyntaf neu eu treulio yn gynhyrchion llai gan ensymau. Gelwir yr ensymau treulio hyn yn **hydrolasau** ac maent yn catalyddu hydrolysis y swbstrad trwy ychwanegu moleciwl o ddŵr. Mae angen gwahanol ensymau er mwyn treulio gwahanol swbstradau bwyd a gan amlaf mae angen mwy nag un math o ensym er mwyn treulio unrhyw fwyd penodol yn llwyr.

Yn ystod treuliad bydd:

- **Carbohydradau** (polysacaridau) yn cael eu torri i lawr yn ddeusacaridau yn gyntaf ac wedyn yn fonosacaridau. Mae'r ensym **amylas** yn hydrolysu starts i'r deusacarid maltos ond mae'n rhaid cael ensym arall **maltas** er mwyn torri'r maltos i lawr i'r monosacarid, **glwcos**.
- Bydd **proteinau** yn cael eu torri i lawr yn polypeptidau, yna yn ddeupeptidau, ac yn olaf yn **asidau amino**.
  Yr enw cyffredinol a roddir i ensym sy'n treulio protein yw **peptidas**.
  Mae proteinau yn foleciwlau eithriadol o fawr felly bydd **endopeptidasau** yn hydrolysu bondiau peptid o fewn y moleciwl protein a bydd **ecsopeptidasau** yn hydrolysu bondiau peptid ym mhennau y polypeptidau byrrach hyn.
- Bydd **braster** yn cael eu torri i lawr yn **asidau brasterog a glyserol** gan un ensym yn unig, sef **lipas**.

Mae gwahanol ensymau yn hoffi gwahanol lefelau o pH felly bydd y gwahanol ensymau yn gweithredu mewn rhannau penodol o'r coludd. Mae'r adran ganlynol gyda gwahanol arbenigeddau'r rhannau hyn.

Rhannau arbenigol

Y geg

Mae treuliad mecanyddol yn cychwyn yn y geg lle bydd bwyd yn cael ei gnoi gan y dannedd. Bydd y bwyd hefyd yn cael ei gymysgu gyda phoer o'r chwarennau poer. Mae poer yn secretiad dyfrllyd, sy'n cynnwys mwcws ac amylas poerol, ynghyd â rhywfaint o ïonau mwynol sy'n helpu i gadw pH y geg ychydig yn alcalïaidd, sef y pH optimaidd ar gyfer amylas. Mae poer yn bwysig er mwyn iro'r bwyd cyn iddo gael ei lyncu. Mae **amylas** yn chwalu'r **starts** gan adael **maltos**. Ar ôl cnoi bydd y bêl o fwyd yn cael ei llyncu ac mae mwcws yn iro taith y bwyd i lawr yr oesoffagws.

Y stumog

Bydd bwyd yn mynd i mewn i'r stumog ac yn cael ei gadw yno gan gywasgiad dau gylch o gyhyrau, un wrth y fynediad i mewn i'r stumog ac un lle mae'r stumog yn cysylltu â'r dwodenwm. Gall bwyd aros yn y stumog am hyd at bedair awr ac yn ystod y cyfnod hwn bydd cyhyrau mur y stumog yn cyfangu'n rhythmig ac yn cymysgu bwyd gyda sudd gastrig sy'n cael ei secretu gan chwarennau ym mur y stumog. Mae sudd gastrig yn cynnwys asid sy'n rhoi pH of 2.0 i gynnwys y stumog. Mae hwn hefyd yn darparu'r pH optimaidd ar gyfer yr ensymau, ac mae'r asid yn lladd y rhan fwyaf o'r bacteria sydd yn y bwyd. Mae sudd gastrig hefyd yn cynnwys ensymau **peptidas** sy'n hydrolysu'r **protein** a'i droi'n **polypeptidau**. Mae mwcws yn bwysig er mwyn ffurfio leinin sy'n amddiffyn mur y stumog rhag yr ensymau a'r asid yn ogystal â helpu i symud y bwyd yn y stumog.

Y coluddyn bach

Mae'r coluddyn bach wedi ei rannu'n ddwy ran, y dwodenwm a'r ilewm.

Mae ymlacio'r cyhyryn wrth fôn y stumog yn caniatáu i feintiau bychan o'r bwyd sydd wedi ei dreulio'n rhannol fynd i mewn i'r dwodenwm ychydig ar y tro. Y dwodenwm yw'r 20cm cyntaf o'r coluddyn bach ac mae'n derbyn secretiadau o'r iau/ afu ac o'r pancreas.

- Mae **bustl** yn cael ei gynhyrchu yn yr iau/ afu a'i storio yng nghoden y bustl lle mae'n pasio i'r dwodenwm trwy ddwythell y bustl. Nid yw'n cynnwys unrhyw ensymau ond mae'r halwynau bustl yn bwysig i **emwlsio'r lipidau** sy'n bresennol yn y bwyd. Cyflawnir yr emwlsio drwy leihau tyndra arwyneb y lipidau, fel bod globylau mawr yn chwalu yn ddefnynnau bychan iawn. Mae hynny'n sicrhau bod gweithred yr ensym **lipas** yn fwy effeithlon gan fod gan y defnynnau lipid arwynebedd llawer iawn mwy nawr. Mae bustl hefyd yn helpu i niwtralu asidedd y bwyd wrth iddo ddod o'r stumog.
- Mae'r **sudd pancreatig** yn cael ei secretu o'r chwarennau ecsocrin yn y pancreas ac yn mynd i mewn i'r dwodenwm drwy'r ddwythell bancreatig. Mae'n cynnwys nifer o wahanol ensymau:
- ✓ **endopeptidasau** sy'n hydrolysu **protein** a'u troi'n **peptidau**.
- ✓ **amylas**, sy'n chwalu unrhyw **starts** sydd ar ôl a'i droi'n **maltos**.
- ✓ **lipas**, sy'n hydrolysu **lipidau** a'u troi'n **asidau brasterog a glyserol**.

Mae muriau'r dwodenwm yn cynnwys chwarennau sy'n secretu sudd alcalïaidd a mwcws. Mae'r sudd alcalïaidd yn helpu i gadw cynnwys y coluddyn bach ar y pH priodol ar gyfer gweithrediad ensymau, ac mae'r mwcws ar gyfer iro ac amddiffyn.

Bydd yr ensymau sy'n cael eu secretu gan gelloedd ar flaenau'r fili yn cwblhau treuliad.
- ✓ Mae **maltas** yn hydrolysu **maltos** yn ddau foleciwl **glwcos**.
- ✓ Mae **endopeptidasau** ac **ecsopeptidasau** yn cwblhau treuliad polypeptidau sy'n eu troi'n asidau amino.

Monosacaridau yw cynhyrchion terfynol treuliad carbohydrad. Mae'r cam olaf o dreuliad carbohydradau yn fewngellol, wrth i ddeusacaridau gael eu hamsugno gan bilen blasmaidd celloedd yr epitheliwm cyn cael eu torri i lawr yn fonosacaridau.

Amsugniad

Mae'r ilewm wedi addasu'n dda ar gyfer amsugniad:
- Yn y corff dynol mae'r ilewm yn hir iawn.
- Mae'r leinin wedi plygu er mwyn rhoi arwyneb mawr mewn cymhariaeth â thiwb llyfn.
- Ar y plygion mae nifer o ymestyniadau niferus fel bysedd a elwir yn fili.
- Ar arwyneb y fili mae celloedd epithelaidd sydd ag ymestyniadau microsgopig a elwir yn microfili. Mae'r rhain yn cynyddu arwyneb cellbilen y celloedd epithelaidd ar gyfer amsugniad.

Mae amsugniad yn digwydd ar ôl treuliad, yn y coluddyn bach yn bennaf. Gan fod angen egni ar gyfer amsugniad actif, mae'r celloedd epithelaidd hefyd yn cynnwys niferoedd mawr o fitocondria.

Tasg Lluniwch ddiagram o groesdoriad manwl trwy filws gan ddangos yr ardaloedd lle mae gwahanol gynhyrchion treuliad yn cael eu hamsugno.

- Mae **glwcos ac asidau amino** yn cael eu hamsugno ar draws epitheliwm y fili trwy gyfuniad o dryllediad a chludiant actif. Maent yn pasio i mewn i'r rhwyllen capilarïau sy'n cyflenwi pob filws. Mae'r gwaed o'r gwythienigau, sy'n cynnwys y bwyd sydd wedi ei dreulio, yn cyrraedd yr wythïen bortal hepatig yn y man ac yn cael ei gludo i'r iau/ afu.
- Mae **asidau brasterog a glyserol** yn cael eu pasio i'r lacteal. Mae'r lacteal yn lymff capilari pengaead sydd yng nghanol pob filws. Bydd asidau brasterog a glyserol yn cael eu cludo i'r system lymffatig sydd yn y man yn agor allan i lif y gwaed yn y ddwythell thorasig.

I grynhoi, mae'r dulliau canlynol o gludiant yn digwydd:
Bydd asidau brasterog, glyserol a'r rhan fwyaf o fitaminau yn pasio drwy bilen y celloedd epithelaidd drwy dryllediad. Ond mae'n rhaid i'r glwcos, yr asidau amino a'r deupeptidau gael egni ar ffurf ATP i gael eu hamsugno'n actif. Mae deupeptidau wedyn yn cael eu treulio'n fewngellol a'u troi'n asidau amino syml. Mae glwcos ac asidau amino wedyn yn tryledu o'r gell epithelaidd i'r gwaed.

Y coluddyn mawr

Mae'r coluddyn mawr tua 1.5 metr o hyd yn cael ei rannu'n caecwm, y pendics, y colon a'r rectwm. Bydd dŵr a halwynau mwynol yn cael eu hamsugno o'r colon ynghyd â fitaminau sy'n cael eu secretu gan ficro-organebau sy'n byw yn y colon. Y bacteria hyn sy'n gyfrifol am wneud fitamin K ac asid ffolig. Erbyn iddo gyrraedd y rectwm, bydd bwyd anhydraul mewn cyflwr lled solid. Mae'n cynnwys gweddillion o gellwlos heb ei dreulio, bacteria a chelloedd marw ac mae hyn yn pasio ar hyd y colon i gael ei garthu yn ymgarthion. Gelwir y broses hon yn ymgarthu.

Defnydd o gynhyrchion treuliad

Wrth i brosesau treuliad ac amsugniad ddod i ben mae'r cynhyrchion bwyd hydawdd yn cael eu cludo yn llif y gwaed i'r meinweoedd i gael eu **cymathu** neu i ddarparu **egni.**
- Bydd glwcos yn cael ei amsugno o'r gwaed gan gelloedd i'w ryddhau fel egni wrth resbiradu, a bydd unrhyw glwcos sydd dros ben yn cael ei storio mewn celloedd braster.
- Bydd asidau amino yn cael eu hamsugno ar gyfer syntheseiddio protein, nid oes modd storio unrhyw asidau amino sydd dros ben felly maent yn cael eu dadamineiddio. Mae'r grwpiau amino sydd dros ben yn cael eu troi'n wrea a'r gweddill yn garbohydrad i'w storio.
- Mae lipidau yn cael eu defnyddio ar gyfer pilenni a hormonau, a'r gweddill yn cael ei storio fel braster.

Addasiadau ar gyfer gwahanol ddietau

Mae ymlusgiaid ac amffibiaid yn llyncu bwyd yn gyfan ar unwaith pan fydd yn cael ei ddal, ond mewn mamolion mae bwyd yn cael ei gadw yn y geg i gael ei dorri a'i gnoi. Mae gan famolion daflod (palate) sy'n gwahanu'r llwybr aer (ceudod trwynol) oddi wrth y geg. Mae hyn yn golygu y gellir cadw bwyd yn y geg yn hytrach na'i lyncu'n gyfan rhwng anadlu. Mae coludd cigysydd yn fyr, sy'n adlewyrchu mor hawdd y mae protein yn cael ei dreulio. Ond, mae coludd llysysydd yn hir gan fod treulio deunydd planhigion yn anodd. Gan fod bwyd yn cael ei gadw yn y geg i'w dorri, ei wasgu, ei falu neu ei lafnu yn ôl y diet, mae mamolion wedi esblygu gwahanol fathau o ddannedd gyda phob math yn arbenigo ar swyddogaeth wahanol.

Mae gan llysysyddion a chigysyddion ddannedd sydd wedi addasu'n arbennig ar gyfer eu diet.

Dannedd

Mae dannedd yn bwysig yn y broses o dreuliad mecanyddol bwyd. Mae cnoi bwyd yn bwysig gan ei fod yn ei wneud yn haws i'w lyncu, ac hefyd yn cynyddu'r arwynebedd arwyneb ar gyfer gweithrediad ensymau. Mae bodau dynol yn hollysyddion, mae hynny'n golygu eu bod yn bwyta deunydd planhigion ac anifeiliaid. Nid yw'r dannedd wedi addasu'n hynod ond mae pedwar gwahanol fath o ddannedd gyda gwahanol swyddogaethau, ac mae hynny'n adlewyrchu'r diet cymysg. Mae gan fodau dynol gyfanswm o 32 o ddannedd ac mae'r rhain yn cynnwys:

- Wyth **blaenddant** siâp cŷn ym mlaen y geg er mwyn brathu a thorri.
- Pedwar dant **llygad** pigfain sy'n gweithredu fel blaenddannedd.
- Deg dant mawr, gwastad, ar y naill ochr a'r llall sy'n cael eu defnyddio ar gyfer cnoi. Y rhain yw'r **gogilddannedd** a'r **cilddannedd**.

Dannedd llysysyddion

Mae rhan fwyaf o'r cig a'r llaeth sy'n cael ei fwyta gan bobl yn dod oddi wrth wartheg a defaid. Mae'n bwysig felly i ni wybod sut y maent yn bwyta.

Mae bwyd planhigol yn ddeunydd gwydn ac mae dannedd llysysyddion wedi addasu i sicrhau ei fod yn cael ei falu'n drylwyr cyn cael ei lyncu. Mae gan lysysydd sy'n pori, megis buwch neu ddafad, blaenddannedd ar y genau gwaelod yn unig ac maent yn torri'r bwyd yn erbyn pad cornaidd ar y genau uchaf. Nid oes gwahaniaeth rhwng y dannedd llygad a'r blaenddannedd. Mae bwlch a elwir yn ddiastema yn gwahanu'r dannedd blaen oddi wrth y dannedd ochr neu'r gogilddannedd. Mae'r dafod yn gweithio yn y bwlch yma gan symud y glaswellt sydd newydd ei dorri i'r arwynebau malu helaeth ar ddannedd y bochau. Mae'r gên yn troi mewn cylch llorweddol i falu'r bwyd. Mae'r dannedd boch yn cloi i mewn i'w gilydd fel y llythyren W yn ffitio i mewn i lythyren M. Dros amser mae'r arwynebau malu yn gwisgo, a'r ymylon miniog o enamel yn dod i'r golwg sy'n cynyddu effeithlonrwydd y broses o falu. Mae gan y dannedd wreiddiau agored, digyfyngiad fel eu bod yn gallu parhau i dyfu drwy gydol oes yr anifail.

Dannedd cigysyddion

Mae gan famolion cigysyddol fel y teigr, ddannedd sydd wedi eu haddasu ar gyfer dal a lladd eu hysglyfaeth, torri neu falu esgyrn a rhwygo cig. Mae'r blaenddannedd miniog yn gafael yn y cnawd a'i rwygo oddi wrth yr esgyrn. Mae'r dannedd llygad yn fawr, yn grwm ac yn bigfain er mwyn gafael yn yr ysglyfaeth, ei ladd a rhwygo'r cnawd. Diben y gogilddannedd a'r cilddannedd yw torri a gwasgu. Mae gan gigysyddion bâr o ddannedd boch arbenigol, a elwir yn ysgithrog, sy'n llithro heibio ei gilydd fel llafnau siswrn garddio. Mae cyhyrau'r genau wedi datblygu'n gryf er mwyn galluogi'r cigysydd i afael yn dynn yn ei ysglyfaeth ac i helpu i wasgu'r esgyrn. Nid yw'r genau yn symud o ochr i ochr o gwbl, dim ond mewn llysysyddion y ceir hynny, gan y byddai'n arwain at daflu'r genau o'i le wrth drin yr ysglyfaeth. Mae mwy o symudiad i fyny ac i lawr nag sydd mewn llysysyddion fel bod y genau'n gallu agor yn llydan i ddal a lladd yr ysglyfaeth.

❏ **Tasg** Lluniwch ddiagramau wedi eu labelu yn dangos dannedd dafad a chath.

Anifeiliaid cnoi cil

Mae anifeiliaid yn cynhyrchu 35% o'r holl brotein sy'n cael ei fwyta gan fodau dynol. Mae bron i hanner hwnnw yn dod oddi wrth **anifeiliaid cnoi cil**, megis gwartheg a defaid, sy'n bwyta gwair a phorthiant (forage) yn bennaf. Mae cyfran fawr o fwyd yr anifeiliaid hyn yn gellfuriau cellwlos. Mae gan anifeiliaid cnoi cil stumog arbenigol neu rwmen lle mae'r bacteria cydymddibynol yn byw.

Mae cydymddibyniaeth neu symbiosis yn golygu cydberthynas agos rhwng aelodau o ddwy rywogaeth wahanol lle mae'r ddwy organeb yn cael rhyw fudd o'r berthynas. Nid oes gan anifeiliaid llysysol megis gwartheg a defaid y gallu i gynhyrchu ensymau cellwlas ac felly nid ydynt yn gallu treulio cellwlos. Mae cellfuriau cellwlos yn gyfran uchel o ddeunydd planhigion. Mae rhai llysysyddion penodol, er enghraifft gwartheg wedi ffurfio perthynas gyda bacteria sy'n treulio cellwlos ac sy'n byw yng ngholudd y fuwch. Yn y berthynas hon mae'r mamolyn yn cael cynhyrchion treuliad cellwlos ac mae'r bacteria yn cael cyflenwad parhaus o fwyd ac yn gallu tyfu mewn amgylchedd gwarchodol, addas.

Mae'r fuwch yn neilltuo rhan o'i choludd lle gall y bacteria fyw a threulio'r cellwlos ar gyfer y fuwch. Ond mae'n rhaid i'r rhan yma o'r coludd gael ei chadw ar wahân, oddi wrth y prif ardal treulio fel bod:
- ✓ bwyd yn gallu cael ei gadw yno'n ddigon hir i'r bacteria dreulio'r cellwlos.
- ✓ ac fel bod y bacteria wedi eu hynysu oddi wrth sudd treulio y mamolyn ei hun fel eu bod yn y pH optimaidd ar gyfer eu gweithgareddau, heb gael eu lladd gan pH eithafol.

Mae gan anifeiliaid cnoi cil 'stumog' sydd wedi ei ffurfio o bedair siambr. Mae tair o'r siambrau hyn wedi deillio o ran isaf yr oesoffagws ac mae un ohonynt yn stumog wirioneddol.

Mae treuliad cellwlos yn digwydd fel a ganlyn:
- Mae'r glaswellt yn cael ei dorri gan y dannedd, ei gymysgu gyda phoer, ac mae'r cil (cud) sy'n cael ei ffurfio yn cael ei lyncu.
- Yn y rwmen, y 'stumog' cyntaf, mae'r cil yn cael ei gymysgu gyda bacteria treulio cellwlos i gynhyrchu glwcos. Mae hwn yn cael ei eplesu i ffurfio asidau organig, sy'n cael eu hamsugno i'r gwaed ac yn rhoi egni i'r fuwch. Y cynhyrchion gwastraff yw carbon deuocsid a methan sy'n cael eu pasio allan.
- Mae'r cil yn cael ei basio i'r rhan nesaf cyn cael ei daflu i fyny i'r geg a'i gnoi eto.
- Mae'r cil yn pasio'n uniongyrchol i'r trydydd 'stumog' lle mae dŵr yn cael ei ailamsugno.
- Mae'r pedwerydd 'stumog' sef yr olaf yn gweithredu fel stumog arferol, gyda phrotein yn cael ei dreulio.
- Mae'r bwyd a dreuliwyd yn pasio i'r rhan nesaf, y coluddyn bach, lle mae cynhyrchion y treuliad yn cael eu hamsugno.

Mae'r anifeiliaid cnoi cil yn fwy effeithlon na llysysyddion eraill o ran echdynnu'r maetholion allan o gellwlos. Mae'r rwmen yn cynnwys amrywiaeth ehangach o organebau cydymddibynol na'r caecwm ac maent yn gallu torri'r cellwlos i lawr yn fwy effeithlon. Mantais arall mewn anifeiliaid cnoi cil yw mai'r rwmen yw'r 'stumog' cyntaf sydd wedi ei leoli cyn y prif ardal cynhyrchu ensymau, fel bod y bacteria sy'n marw yn pasio drwy'r rhan yma gyda'r bwyd gan ddarparu ffynhonnell bwysig o brotein.

❑ **Tasg** Cymharwch wahanol rannau coludd llysysydd gyda choludd anifail cnoi cil.

Maethiad Parasitig

Mae parasitiaid yn organebau sy'n byw ar neu mewn organeb arall a elwir yn organeb letyol, ac maent yn cael eu maeth ar draul yr organeb letyol. Gan hynny mae parasitiaid yn achosi niwed i ryw raddau ac weithiau'n lladd yr organeb letyol. Mae llawer o organebau yn dioddef o barasitiaid am o leiaf rhan o'u bywydau. Y parasitiaid sy'n effeithio ar blanhigion yw bacteria, ffyngau, firysau, nematodau a phryfed; ac effeithir ar anifeiliaid gan facteria, ffyngau, firysau, proctista, llyngyr, nematodau, pryfed a gwiddon (mites). Mae gan facteria, hyd yn oed, eu parasitiaid eu hunain sef firysau a elwir yn bacterioffagau! Mae astudio parasitiaid yn bwysig yn economaidd gan eu bod yn achosi clefydau mewn bodau dynol, cnydau ac anifeiliaid dof.

Llyngyr porc – parasit yn y coludd

Mae bywyd yn frwydr i bob anifail, gan fod rhaid iddynt osgoi cystadleuaeth gydag anifeiliaid eraill ac osgoi bod yn ysglyfaeth iddynt. Mae parasitiaid wedi arbenigo ac wedi mynd trwy newidiadau esblygiadol sylweddol er mwyn goroesi yn yr organeb letyol. Mae'r parasit y coludd (*Taenia solium*) yn enghraifft arbennig o dda.

Meddyliwch fyw yng ngholudd anifail arall! Mae'r llyngyr ar ffurf rhuban a gall fod hyd at 10 metr o hyd! Mae ganddo 'ben' wedi ei wneud o gyhyrau sydd â sugnolynau a bachau. Mae ei gorff yn cynnwys cyfres o segmentau tenau. Mae gan y llyngyr porc ddwy organeb letyol. Y prif organeb letyol yw'r corff dynol a'r organeb letyol eilaidd yw'r mochyn. Mae'r mochyn yn cael ei heintio os yw'n bwydo mewn sianeli draenio sydd wedi eu halogi gan garthion dynol. Mae pobl yn cael eu heintio drwy fwyta porc heintus heb ei goginio'n ddigonol.
(Nid oes rhaid gwybod am y gylchred bywyd.)

Er bod y llyngyr yn byw mewn ffynhonnell uniongyrchol o fwyd mae'n gorfod goroesi yn yr amodau ymosodol sy'n bodoli yn y coludd.
Dyma'r problemau y mae'n rhaid i barasit y coludd eu goresgyn er mwyn goroesi:
- Mae'n byw wedi ei amgylchynu gan suddion treulio a mwcws.
- Mae bwyd, wedi ei gymysgu gyda suddion treulio, yn symud yn barhaus ac yn cael ei gorddi yn ogystal â'i wthio ar hyd y coludd gan gyfangiadau peristaltig y mur cyhyrol.
- Mae'n byw mewn amodau eithafol o pH ar hyd y coludd cyfan.
- System imiwnedd yr organeb letyol.
- Os bydd yr organeb letyol yn marw bydd y parasit hefyd yn marw.

Addasiadau ar gyfer goroesi

Er mwyn goroesi mae'n rhaid i'r llyngyr:

- Fod â dull o dreiddio i'r organeb letyol
- bod â dull o gydio yn yr organeb letyol
- Amddiffyn ei hun rhag ymatebion imiwnedd yr organeb letyol
- Datblygu dim ond yr organau sy'n hanfodol er mwyn goroesi
- Cynhyrchu llawer o wyau
- Bod ag organeb rhyngol
- Bod â chyfnodau gwrthiannol yn eu cylchred bywyd er mwyn gallu byw am gyfnod oddi wrth yr organeb letyol

Maent wedi esblygu'r addasiadau adeileddol canlynol ar gyfer eu dull parasitig o fyw:

- Sugnolynau a rhes ddwbl o fachau crymanog i gydio ym mur y coludd.
- Gorchudd i'r corff sy'n eu hamddiffyn rhag ymatebion imiwnedd yr organeb letyol.
- Cwtigl trwchus a chynhyrchu sylweddau ataliol ar arwyneb y segmentau i atal cael eu treulio gan ensymau'r organeb letyol.
- Gan eu bod yn byw mewn amgylchedd sefydlog nid oes rhaid iddynt symud o gwmpas ac nid oes rhaid cael system synhwyraidd. Mae hynny wedi arwain at ddirywiad organau diangen. Mae ganddynt system ysgarthol a system nerfol syml ond mae'r rhan fwyaf o'r corff yn ymwneud ag atgenhedlu.
- Mae'r llyngyr yn denau iawn ac mae ganddynt gymhareb uchel o arwynebedd arwyneb i gyfaint. Mae wedi ei amgylchynu gan fwyd wedi ei dreulio felly mae ei system dreulio yn syml iawn a gellir amsugno bwyd sydd wedi ei dreulio yn barod dros holl arwyneb ei gorff.
Gan na allai'r coludd ddygymod â dau llyngyr mae pob segment yn cynnwys organau atgenhedlu gwrywaidd a benywaidd. Mae nifer fawr iawn o wyau yn cael eu cynhyrchu, gyda phob segment aeddfed yn cynnwys hyd at 40,000 o wyau. Mae segmentau aeddfed yn pasio allan o gorff yr organeb letyol gyda'i garthion. Mae gan yr wyau blisgyn gwydn a gallant oroesi nes cael eu bwyta gan yr organeb letyol eilaidd. Maent wedyn yn gallu datblygu ymhellach a bydd yr embryonau sy'n deor o'r wyau yn symud i gyhyrau'r mochyn ac yn aros yng nghwsg yno nes i gig y mochyn gael ei fwyta gan fod dynol.

Effeithiau niweidiol y llyngyr porc.
Pan maent yn oedolion nid yw'r llyngyr yn achosi llawer o anghysur ond pan fydd yr wyau'n cael eu bwyta gan fodau dynol, mae'r embryonau cwsg yn ffurfio codennau mewn gwahanol organau ac yn difrodi'r meinwe oddi amgylch. Gellir trin oedolion gyda chyffuriau priodol. Mae mesurau iechyd cyhoeddus ac archwilio cig yn aml yn fesurau hanfodol.

❏ **Tasg**   Lluniwch ddiagram wedi ei labelu o 'ben' llyngyr yn dangos y segmentau sydd ynghlwm ag ef.